# The Genius of Invective

## Ibn Zaydūn's Letter Explained

# Letter from the General Editor

The Library of Arabic Literature makes available Arabic editions and English translations of significant works of Arabic literature, with an emphasis on the seventh to nineteenth centuries. The Library of Arabic Literature thus includes texts from the pre-Islamic era to the cusp of the modern period, and encompasses a wide range of genres, including poetry, poetics, fiction, religion, philosophy, law, science, travel writing, history, and historiography.

Books in the series are edited and translated by internationally recognized scholars. They are published as hardcovers in parallel-text format with Arabic and English on facing pages, as English-only paperbacks, and as downloadable Arabic editions. For some texts, the series also publishes separate scholarly editions with full critical apparatus.

The Library encourages scholars to produce authoritative Arabic editions, accompanied by modern, lucid English translations, with the ultimate goal of introducing Arabic's rich literary heritage to a general audience of readers as well as to scholars and students.

The publications of the Library of Arabic Literature are generously supported by Tamkeen under the NYU Abu Dhabi Research Institute Award G1003 and are published by NYU Press.

Philip F. Kennedy
*General Editor, Library of Arabic Literature*

# سرح العيون في شرح رسالة ابن زيدون

ابن نباتة

# The Genius of Invective

## Ibn Zaydūn's Letter Explained

Ibn Nubātah

Edited and translated by

Peter Webb

Volume editor

Maurice Pomerantz

NEW YORK UNIVERSITY PRESS

*New York*

NEW YORK UNIVERSITY PRESS
*New York*



Library of Congress Cataloging-in-Publication Data

Names: Ibn Nubātah, Muḥammad ibn Muḥammad, 1287-1366, author. | Ibn Nubātah, Muḥammad ibn Muḥammad, 1287-1366. Sarḥ al-ʻuyūn. | Ibn Nubātah, Muḥammad ibn Muḥammad, 1287-1366. Sarḥ al-ʻuyūn. English. | Webb, Peter, 1978- editor, translator.
Title: The genius of invective : Ibn Zaydun's letter explained : an edition and translation with commentary / edited and translated by Peter Webb.
Description: New York : New York University Press, 2025. | Includes bibliographical references and index. | Summary: "In eleventh-century Cordoba, the celebrated poet Ibn Zaydun found himself jockeying for the affections of Walladah, accomplished poet and free-spirited daughter of an Umayyad caliph. Looking to embarrass a rival suitor, Ibn Zaydun mischievously wrote and publicized an eloquent, erudite, and searing rejection letter in Walladah's name, which went on to become one of the most widely read works of Arabic literature. His letter was so rich with historical references and sophisticated metaphors that it became a cultural touchstone among the literary elite. One could not belong in refined circles if one did not understand Ibn Zaydun's letter. Three centuries later, the Egyptian litterateur Ibn Nubatah wrote a guide to this widely-admired text. In The Genius of Invective, a brilliant work of explication, Ibn Nubatah supplements Ibn Zaydun's complete letter with concise biographies of every figure referenced in it and glosses arcane Arabic terms. This wide-ranging volume offered readers a veritable encyclopedia of the key cultural and literary references that peppered Ibn Zaydun's famous letter. As impressive in its own right as the remarkable letter that inspired it, The Genius of Invective is a peerless example of the breadth, depth, and complexity of the Arabic classical literary tradition"-- Provided by publisher.
Identifiers: LCCN 2024025834 | ISBN 9781479835874 (hardback) | ISBN 9781479835898 (ebook)
Subjects: LCSH: Ibn Zaydūn, Aḥmad ibn ʻAbd Allāh, 1003 or 1004-1071. Risālah al-hazalīyah. | LCGFT: Literary criticism.
Classification: LCC PJ7750.I28 R5435313 2025 | DDC 892.7/134--dc23/eng/20241029

LC record available at https://lccn.loc.gov/2024025834

New York University Press books are printed on acid-free paper, and their binding materials are chosen for strength and durability.

The manufacturer's authorized representative in the EU for product safety is Mare Nostrum Group B.V., Mauritskade 21D, 1091 GC Amsterdam, The Netherlands. Email: gpsr@mare-nostrum.co.uk.

Series design by Titus Nemeth and Stuart Brown.

Typeset in Sakkal Kitab Medium.

Typesetting and digitization by Stuart Brown.

Manufactured in the United States of America
c10 9 8 7 6 5 4 3 2 1

# Table of Contents

# Acknowledgments

I chose to translate Ibn Nubātah's *Sarḥ al-ʿuyūn* from a desire to transmit a digestible and approachable text containing a good cross section of Muslim-era Arabic stories about the pre-Islamic past. At the outset, Ibn Nubātah's book was one of several possibilities I was considering, and quite how it muscled its way into being selected is not something I can precisely remember now. Having chosen Ibn Nubātah, a quick search of extant manuscripts revealed that two copies were housed in the Leiden University Libraries, only a few dozen yards from my office, and so these beckoned as the first point of call. My first order of thanks is therefore due to the then keeper of oriental manuscripts, Arnoud Vrolijk, who generously made the two copies available and commissioned excellent digital images. Thanks to a small grant from Leiden University, I engaged two students, Rebecca Ruf and Ralph Vlaeminck, to assist with an initial study and transcription of the Leiden material.

The findings were surprising. It soon became apparent that I was not the first person to have considered *Sarḥ al-ʿuyūn* a handy reference work to the Arabic classics—many generations ago, Arabic readers in diverse locales had been demanding copies too. I had clearly alighted on a cultural phenomenon of unrealized magnitude, and the journey of producing this volume rapidly left the confines of Leiden University. Within a few months, Rebecca, Ralph, and I were working through some ten manuscripts from European and Egyptian collections (I am grateful to the Library of Arabic Literature (LAL) for procuring images of one of the Cairo manuscripts). At this stage, we discovered that *Sarḥ al-ʿuyūn* was not one book but two—a Short and a Long version—and that all previous printings of the text had only considered the Long version. By this time too, it was clear that the Leiden copy we were transcribing was a rather shoddy example, the work of a poor or perhaps rushed copyist, and that better manuscripts were needed. At this juncture, the contracts of Rebecca and Ralph had run their course, and I was left to search on my own. A dozen further manuscripts turned into fifty more, and within a year, the count was over a hundred, hailing from Morocco to Iran. Now it was clear that *Sarḥ al-ʿuyūn* was in fact a global phenomenon of the premodern Afro-Euro-Asiatic world.

The burgeoning host of manuscripts forced a decision: All were reporting either the Long or Short version of the text with virtually no variation, and one would need to be nominated as the exemplar for this project. I chose a copy of the Short version from Istanbul. It was a good manuscript, well copied, with few oversights, and it had something potent in its favor. In its colophon, the copyist states that he mixed his ink with water of Mecca's Zamzam Well, and given the sanctity of the site and the fact that the same water had been used by angels to purify Muḥammad, the copyist asks readers of the manuscript to treat it with due respect. Since perhaps nothing demonstrates respect for a text more than critically editing it, I hope my efforts please that anonymous copyist.

Once transcribed, the text was translated and presented to LAL to commence the editing process. Initially, Everett Rowson was chosen as the volume editor, and the first round of fruitful discussions over the obstinate parts of Ibn Nubātah's text were happily undertaken with Everett's comments. Unfortunately, for reasons altogether apart from Ibn Nubātah, Everett's oversight extended only to the first part of the translation, and the job of volume editor then became the commission of Maurice Pomerantz. I thank Maurice for the lively and jovial discussions that took us through the entire text. Incidentally, the sustained pleasure I had during the long review process would seem proof that Ibn Nubātah created a friendly and distinctly fun survey of the Arabic classics.

More thanks are due to the LAL Executive Board and the anonymous reviewer who undertook the final review of what had by then become a hefty tome presenting Arabic and English conundrums in need of close consideration and deft mending. I am grateful for their comments, suggestions, and solutions. I am most grateful for Shawkat Toorawa's involvement at some particularly important moments of this book's genesis, and while I was not in direct contact with the other LAL editors, their diligent attention in the background to solve key issues was apparent through the whole process, and I express my gratitude to them now.

Given that we are told that "the last is better for you than the first" (Q Ḍuḥā 93:4), my last expression of thanks must be reserved for my mother, who read more drafts of the translation than anyone else. Much of this volume's evolution into what is hoped to be a fine representative of Ibn Nubātah in English was undertaken via the suggestions of my mother's reading and rereading of the progressing drafts, starting from the first rough conversions of the Arabic into English, down to the proofs.

This book has accordingly incurred many debts of gratitude to the many pairs of eyes that participated in what seemed nearly countless cycles of review, amendment, and revision, and that only reluctantly drew to a close in the form the book takes here. After so many expert and wise minds have tried to distill and correct the original draft of mine, may any errors that remain stand as testament to the adage *al-kamāl li-llāh*—"Perfection is for God."

# Introduction

However you define the word "classic," *The Genius of Invective* (*Sarḥ al-ʿuyūn*) almost certainly qualifies. For a start, it enjoyed tremendous popularity over a vast area for a long period and was translated several times before 1800. The book results from the creativity of two classical literary figures: it was written by Ibn Nubātah, one of the most celebrated writers from medieval Egypt, and it explains the meanings of a letter written by Ibn Zaydūn, a preeminent literary figure of Muslim Spain.[1] That letter by Ibn Zaydūn was cherished across centuries of Arabic readership as a paragon of literary high style, and *The Genius of Invective* draws from a deep well of time-honored stories about famous historical figures that been constantly told across many layers of Arabic writing. This is perhaps the most classic aspect of the book—it narrates the enduring, timeless, archetypal stories through which Muslim-era readers understood the core of Arab, Persian, and Greek culture and identity. For the past millennium, educated people across the Middle East have appreciated these stories as the pinnacle of culture and knowledge, and *The Genius of Invective* offered them a handy one-volume explanation of these classics. It was a one-stop shop for knowledge that anyone who aspired to become a someone in the Muslim world would want to learn.

*The Genius of Invective*'s popularity was remarkable. I have identified nearly two hundred manuscript copies written between 1500 and 1900, an outstanding number for an Arabic literary work, and copies were produced and consumed across wide horizons. The major centers of Arabic learning in Morocco, Tunis, Cairo, Istanbul, and Baghdad each possessed multiple copies, as might be expected, but the book also made its way into unexpected places. Two copies were housed in the library of the nineteenth-century Tukulor Jihad caliphate along the banks of the Niger River in Mali, while, around the same time, in India's middle Ganges Plain, another copy entered the collection of a prominent Sufi center in Gorakhpur.[2] For *The Genius of Invective* to meet such reception far from the core Arabic-speaking lands in libraries of predominantly Islamic legal and devotional texts, it must have offered something special. Around the same period, when Omanis began settling in Zanzibar, they brought *The Genius of Invective* with them too, and it is one of the sole Arabic literary texts that survives on the archipelago.[3] In Turkey, an eighteenth-century Ottoman translation was popular,[4] and fascination with *The Genius of Invective* also entered Europe—most European universities engaged in Arabic studies during the seventeenth and eighteenth centuries acquired copies.[5] Early European Arabists also copied the text themselves,[6] and several translated it into Latin.[7] It appears that one could have found a copy of *The Genius of Invective* anywhere Arabic was studied: by the numbers and geographical circulation, it was one of the most popular Arabic literary works ever composed.[8]

At the dawn of the twentieth century, *The Genius of Invective* was still going strong. The advent of the printing press in the Middle East saw multiple print runs between 1841 and 1905,[9] and the principal university in the Middle East, al-Azhar in Cairo, possessed eighteen copies alongside three manuscripts.[10] Yet, despite the sustained success as a mainstay in the Arabic library across thousands of miles and hundreds of years of readers, the popularity of *The Genius of Invective* suffered a precipitous decline in the early 1900s, and it languishes today in comparative obscurity. The cause can be linked to changing intellectual tastes in the late nineteenth century, when scholars became increasingly concerned with authenticity, a return to original sources, and the Abbasid "Golden Age." *The Genius of Invective*, a medieval text from the Mamluk era, fell into a category of "late," "post-classical," and "decline-period" literature,[11] and with surprising unanimity, and in contrast to centuries of readers before, twentieth-century readership forgot about *The Genius of Invective*.

The century of inattention has distanced us from grasping the book's value and understanding the culture of those centuries of readers who avidly consumed it. This new edition of the Arabic text and English translation is intended to return *The Genius of Invective* to readerly consciousness, both Arabic and non-Arabic, and awaken our senses to the generations of readers who preceded us, stimulating curiosity to understand those manifold peoples who cherished Arabic culture across the many geographic, ethnic, and linguistic zones of the early-modern world.

## Origins

It is a little ironic that a book of such serious scholarly import owes its origins to a frivolous letter written amid a curious three-way love tryst. The story begins in Cordoba sometime during the 420s/1030s. The Umayyad dynasty, which had ruled Spain for several centuries, collapsed in stages between 407/1016 and 422/1031, and its former territories were parceled among competing city states. However, in the new emirate of Cordoba, a daughter of one of the last Umayyad caliphs was able not only to survive her family's downfall, but to thrive in the upper echelons of cultured society. Her name was Wallādah. She was admired for her erudition and desired for her wit and coquettishness (which included discarding her hijab). She held salons for poets, scholars, and courtiers; she was an esteemed poet herself; and her admirers included Ibn ʿAbdūs, chief vizier of Cordoba, and Ibn Zaydūn, the celebrated litterateur, who at the time had a lesser rank than his rival.[12]

According to the story, Ibn ʿAbdūs ventured the bold step of proposing to Wallādah, and sent the message via a servant girl, but Ibn Zaydūn got wind of the matter, and before Wallādah had a chance to send her own response, Ibn Zaydūn took the liberty of replying on her behalf. Pretending to be Wallādah, Ibn Zaydūn wrote, in her name, an incredibly eloquent and erudite letter setting out a comprehensive, unequivocal, and absolutely searing rejection of Ibn ʿAbdūs's proposal. The salacious details of the *Letter*'s origins and Ibn Zaydūn's gender-reversing maneuver to save his relationship with Wallādah may simply be embellishments that emerged over some centuries of retelling as the tale became an Arabic literary legend, but the *Letter* is nonetheless a remarkable piece of Arabic writing. As we shall detail below, the *Letter* was probably a literary exercise undertaken in jest; regardless, Ibn Zaydūn's fantastic eloquence was much admired, and his marshaling of so many learned and cultural references and metaphors in the *Letter* ensured it would become an exemplar of the best that Arabic writing can achieve. Once it was anthologized and spread across Arabic-speaking lands, it earned praise for being "crammed full of all kinds of cultured style,"[13] and it became a classic, continuously recopied between 1400 and 1900. A remark appended to the end of an eighteenth-century copy of the *Letter* articulates readers' enduring admiration some seven hundred years after Ibn Zaydūn's death: "And so ends the Letter, the equal of which has never been seen or heard since."[14]

## Ibn Zaydūn

The writer of the *Letter* was a remarkable man. Ibn Zaydūn was born in 394/1003 into an educated family of jurists and court officials during the waning years of the Umayyad caliphate in Cordoba. Combining a mastery of contemporary cultural repertoire with his own creative flair, Ibn Zaydūn shone in the field of erudite Arabic literary expression, and in a context where knowledge of such literary culture constituted a core aspect of social worth, he mightily impressed his peers and rose through the ranks of society.

By the time Ibn Zaydūn was in his thirties, the Umayyad caliphate had collapsed and Cordoba had a new ruling clan, the Jahwarids, to whom Ibn Zaydūn offered his services as a courtier and official. What then transpired is a little unclear: the sources offer only glimpses into the politicking of the Jahwarid court, but it is certain that Ibn Zaydūn's eloquence and intelligence helped his rapid promotion to high status, and he enjoyed a decade of success. However, such traits also breed jealousy, and he was not for want of enemies. Around 432/1041, their plotting succeeded in arranging his arrest on charges of misappropriating property, and Ibn Zaydūn spent almost two years in prison. One of his most famous prose works, *The Serious Letter* (*al-Risālah al-jiddiyyah*), was written during this incarceration, a plea for clemency addressed to the Jahwarid ruler. Whether or not the letter succeeded is unclear, but Ibn Zaydūn did escape prison and was then pardoned by the Jahwarid ruler. Having returned to court favor by 435/1044, he served as an important court ambassador. But Ibn Zaydūn's enemies plotted against him afresh, and he permanently quit Cordoba for the court of the rival regime in Seville, where he acquired a high-ranking post in 441/1049, and he maintained his status there until his death in 484/1091.

Such is the outline, but the details of Ibn Zaydūn's life are otherwise obscure. Most information is gleaned from sources written long after his death, there are various complications and some contradictions, and we have nothing approaching a detailed biography of the man. Ibn Zaydūn is instead famed for his rhetorical brilliance and literary achievements, and the writers of the biographies—all of them literary figures themselves—idolized Ibn Zaydūn as a writer and, especially, as a poet. Their esteem for him was expressed through glowing reports about his literary talent and examples of his work. The minutiae of his life seem to have concerned them much less.

Thanks to his talent, Ibn Zaydūn thereby emerges from history achieving the very goal to which the medieval Persian poet Saʿdī aspired when he composed the lines:

May these well-set verses endure the years
    After our atoms are but specks of dust.
My goal was for them to survive us,
    As I see no permanence for this life of mine.[15]

The corporeal Ibn Zaydūn undoubtedly had an interesting life in eleventh-century Andalusia, but its particulars are lost to the past, and what is remembered is the literature he composed. His poetry attained the touchstone of what all Arabic poets from the eighth century to the nineteenth felt was ideal, and his prose writings, at the forefront the *Serious Letter* Ibn Zaydūn wrote in prison and the *Frivolous Letter* he wrote impersonating Wallādah, likewise became the model for what was considered clever, stylistic, and elegant in the classical Arabic tradition. His prose style challenges the reader through difficult vocabulary, but also charms, through the rhymes and rhythms that run through its phrases, and by including incisive lines of poetry selected from works of earlier poets to emphasize key points. The cleverness and erudition of the *Frivolous Letter*—the *Letter* as discussed here—merit special attention.

## The *Letter*

Despite the *Letter*'s indisputable fame across a millennium of readership, readers today will likely find it both difficult to understand and quite evidently absurd. The difficulty is apparent: even a seasoned Arabic reader will puzzle over the rare words and unfamiliar names that form the majority of text, and upon a first reading, merely reaching the end of the *Letter* constitutes a worthy act of perseverance; full comprehension is another matter altogether. The absurdity manifests in several facets: Ibn Zaydūn's attempt to write as if he were Wallādah is audacious, and the extent to which he attacks Ibn ʿAbdūs's character transcends all boundaries. We shall discuss the absurdity first.

Close reading through the absurdity reveals that the *Letter* is decidedly clever and hides a deft twist. It is structured as a layer of nested arguments that resemble the ways in which lawyers are taught to argue cases today. As opposed to putting all the argument's eggs in one basket, cleverly constructed cases present a succession of independent arguments, such that if one or more fails to convince, the others can still be upheld and the case won.

In the *Letter*, the opening submission begins with a long list of statements detailing how implausibly talented, strong, brave, and brilliant Ibn ʿAbdūs boasted he was, and sums up with a categorical rebuttal expressing the verdict that Ibn ʿAbdūs is, on the contrary, completely worthless, he has badly overreached himself, and Wallādah is now angry. The *Letter* then proceeds to Submission 2: Even if it is found that Ibn ʿAbdūs is as mentally gifted and bodily strong as he alleged, he is nonetheless physically ugly, and therefore Wallādah still cannot reasonably be expected to accept his proposal. Submission 3 is that even if it is found that Ibn ʿAbdūs is not as ugly as supposed, he was nevertheless wrong to presume that he is as great a man as Ibn Zaydūn, and the accompanying verdict here is that Wallādah can never reasonably accept Ibn ʿAbdūs given that Ibn Zaydūn is available to her. Submission 4 is the *Letter*'s last: If all the foregoing submissions fail, and if Ibn ʿAbdūs is truly as clever, handsome, and accomplished as he claimed, the final point is that he is impotent, and the final verdict is that Wallādah has no use for an impotent man. With this, it seems the *Letter* decided it had exhausted all possible arguments to marshal against Ibn ʿAbdūs, but it closes with a twist: a conditional pardon with vague consequences. The *Letter* explains that Wallādah will let Ibn ʿAbdūs off with a warning, but if he ventures a second time, he will be sent into the countryside, where peasants will slap him about and violate his anus with vegetables.

The patent absurdity of the ending suggests that the truth behind the *Letter*'s composition is different from the daring, gender-reversing story of rival lovers. Thinking realistically, Ibn Zaydūn's bold move to impersonate the former caliph's daughter and write a scathing letter against the current highest-ranking minister of the realm was perilous. Eleventh-century texts from Europe, the Middle East, and beyond are replete with gruesome tales of the terrifying punishments applied to those who offended people in power, and if Ibn Zaydūn was at all serious, it is incredible that no grievous punishment followed. It is equally curious that the *Letter*, after fulminating so venomously against Ibn ʿAbdūs, would conclude with such a simple pardon and facetious, bawdy threat. Because Wallādah's anger dissipates so abruptly, Ibn ʿAbdūs escapes any actual consequences for his vaunting transgression, and the *Letter*'s vitriolic tone descends so quickly into a carnivalesque denouement, a perceptive reading will discern an ulterior message afoot. All is not as it seems, and herein

I sense a palpable restraint at play, which ultimately explains the *Letter*'s real genesis and purpose.

The flow and outcome of the *Letter* strike a chord akin to the Shakespearean treatment of the farcical nobleman Falstaff, specifically that character's travails in *The Merry Wives of Windsor*. In the English context ca. 1600, Shakespeare, as a commoner, was not really in a position to ridicule the nobility outright, and his deft critique of wayward noblemen took the form of the Falstaff character, whose vainglorious amorous misadventures in *Merry Wives* result in the frivolous and bawdy punishment of being stuffed into a basket of dirty laundry and culminate in his ridicule at the hands of children by night in the forest. The punishment's lack of severity reveals the joke: there are no terminal consequences—Falstaff is not dispossessed, nor do his nemeses emerge materially better. The ribald, depoliticized nature of Falstaff's "punishment" enables the audience's experience to remain at the level of aesthetic response and mirth with a touch of schadenfreude, but without invoking serious political intent. Just as the character Falstaff is basically let off the hook despite his transgressions, so too is the audience permitted to get away with its laughter. As for Ibn ʿAbdūs's attempted assignation with Wallādah, its purported irony, absurdity, and failure mirror the core of Falstaff's misadventures in the direction of mistresses Ford and Page. By analogy, and contrary to the reported tale, it would seem likely that Ibn Zaydūn did not surreptitiously write the *Letter* to embarrass the vizier; nor did he send it under Wallādah's name; nor, in all likelihood, did he send a physical letter to Ibn ʿAbdūs at all. Rather, the tenor and content of the *Letter* correspond to the anecdotes and bawdy poems recorded elsewhere about Ibn Zaydūn's and Ibn ʿAbdūs's dalliances with Wallādah. Precisely who made the first advances on Wallādah, how she responded to any of them, and whether or not either man ever proposed to her is lost in the lore about the *Letter*, which took several paths over varied retellings.[16] There is little reason to doubt Ibn Zaydūn's authorship of the *Letter*, but the intrigue and secrecy inherent in the reported backstory are probably overdramatizations: Ibn Zaydūn had a reputation among his contemporaries as a risqué satirist,[17] and the *Letter* is likely a crowning piece. It would seem that he arranged for the *Letter* to be made public in the social circle of Wallādah, Ibn ʿAbdūs, and others with the intention that all would appreciate it as a piece of humorous literature, and appreciate its author's considerable talent for his ability to compose it. The nature of their appreciation brings us to the equally important issue of the *Letter*'s patent erudition.

As noted, readers will find the *Letter* difficult to understand at first. The insults are couched in a thicket of metaphorical allusions to the names of historical characters, conveyed with arcane vocabulary and aphorisms from ancient Arabic. Native Arabic speakers and even those who are well educated do not employ this wide an array of vocabulary in everyday life, and while all the words written by Ibn Zaydūn can be found in Arabic dictionaries, there is a deliberate choice toward arcane and obscure vocabulary. Despite this, the *Letter*'s style skips along briskly, dropping the names and nouns in the most effortless, fluent, and offhand fashion, as if they are quotidian expressions of casual parlance, but a reader cannot comprehend the *Letter* or appreciate its eloquence unless he can handle all of the allusions and vocabulary, which means one must be steeped in classical Arabic language and culture.

The second level of enjoying the *Letter* is therefore readers' own self-satisfaction in knowing that their knowledge of Arabic literature and culture is good enough to grasp the allusions. Wallādah, her learned compatriots, and (presumably) Ibn ʿAbdūs were people who cultivated such aptitude: they were denizens of a cultural milieu in which mastery of Arabic in all its peculiarities was a mark of social belonging and individual worth. Thus Ibn Zaydūn, in creating such a masterpiece of obscurity, claimed a spot at the pinnacle of the cultural ladder, while all those who could make sense of his work gained satisfaction in the knowledge that they were making progress up the rungs of that same ladder.

## Ibn Zaydūn's *Letter* and the Arabic "Classics"

The fact that knowledge of seemingly arcane Arabisms would constitute such a concrete marker of status in Ibn Zaydūn's fifth-/eleventh-century Cordoba is central to understanding the *Letter*'s purpose and the subsequent popularity of its commentary, *The Genius of Invective*. The *Letter* refers to ninety-eight historical persons by name, with a brief one- or two-word allusion to a characteristic or event associated with each. The purpose of most of these allusions is to describe a character in the form of idealized, hyperbolic extremes to highlight the absurdity of Ibn ʿAbdūs's claims about himself. As examples, the letter ridicules Ibn ʿAbdūs for daring to present himself as more generous than Ḥātim al-Ṭāʾī, faster than al-Sulayk ibn al-Sulakah, and more eloquent than Saḥbān. In order for the insults to make sense, a reader first needs to know who these people are, and then have a grasp of those historical characters' signature features. The names and allusions might appear impenetrable to readers today, such that the knowledge required to unlock their connotations might be derided as trivia, but this was not the case in Ibn Zaydūn's time, or for several generations before and many generations after him. The names were certainly knowable, and fully educated and well-read savants of Arabic culture and literature would have aspired to be conversant with most of them. There is, accordingly, a great deal of cultural knowledge embedded in the insults, and a core achievement of the *Letter* is the number, breadth, complexity, and importance of such cultural references packed within.

The names are nearly all cited in positive contexts: they represent persons synonymous with kingship, nobility, generosity, bravery, perspicacity, horsemanship, poetic expression, learning, eloquence, and virtue—in essence, they constitute the traits that combine into the idealized noble character. A few others are famous examples of bad luck or ill omen, and some are more lighthearted figures, but what all share is a demonstrable cultural ubiquity: Ibn Zaydūn did not pluck random names from history, there are no figures mentioned whom history had forgotten, and he did not select the most abstruse figures possible. On the contrary, with only a few exceptions, all can be found in the standard reference works of Arabic literature circulating in Ibn Zaydūn's day. Over the succeeding centuries, references to the same characters and stories would recur across a wide cross section of Arabic writing: the individuals constitute what scholars would identify as a core, stable cultural repertoire.

The names include Greeks, Romans, Persians, Arabs, and some early-Muslim-era Iraqis. Chronologically, the majority lived in the pre-Islamic era (seventy of the ninety-eight), and ethnically, Arabians predominate (sixty-five, two-thirds of the total). Analyzing the groups further, the named Persians are all fabled kings and queens of pre-Islamic Iran; the Greeks and Romans are primarily philosophers and physicians. While there are twelve names of cultural producers from early Islamic times, they are predominantly Iraqi-domiciled philosophers, writers, and poets of the early Abbasid era—only two date from later than the ninth century (the fourth-/tenth-century poet al-Mutanabbī and the astrologer Abū Maʿshar). Thus, everyone whom Ibn Zaydūn named in his *Letter* died more than a century before his time, and the clear majority predate him by almost half a millennium or more. Taking stock, Ibn Zaydūn avoids all mention of contemporaries and even near contemporaries, and there are no Andalusians: the names are exclusively from the Arabic literature of Iraq, referencing peoples from a past world, emphatically removed in time and space from Ibn Zaydūn's contemporary Andalusia.

Noteworthy also is the preponderance of pre-Islamic Arabian figures, and an essentially complete absence of any characters whose biographies have importance for the history of Islam. Several individuals named in the *Letter* had interactions with the Prophet and the early caliphs, but there are none of the warrior heroes, pious figures, Prophetic Companions, or Hadith narrators whose memories constitute the core of Muslim religious identity.[18] Instead, the figures are those whose memory is associated with the values and ethics of Arabness—the stereotyped noble Arab character. This is a central cultural feature of the *Letter*: for Ibn Zaydūn and his contemporaries, the core of archetypal Arabness was a historic identity that began in pre-Islam and continued up to the early Islamic period, and the *Letter*'s repertoire reflects this. Its material is the true core of "classical Arabic"—"classical" in the way Ibn Zaydūn and friends would have conceptualized it—the Arabic language and historical persons associated with Arabia in the period spanning from the century or so before Muḥammad to, at the latest, the early Abbasid era (approximately AD 500 to approximately 184/800). This was the period of "high Arabness," an epoch Muslims viewed with acute nostalgia as the time when the Arabic language was purest and Arabs most purely embodied the ideal Arab spirit. Manifold authors articulated that notion already in the third/ninth century in comments about the purity of Arab culture being terminally diluted,[19] and Ibn Zaydūn, in largely eschewing Arabic cultural figures who lived after the eighth century, conforms to this worldview. The *Letter*'s repertoire is of a past, lost, idealized Arab Arabia, and is intriguingly detached from the religious history of Islam.

On one level, the *Letter*'s selection of characters reflects a lighthearted literary experiment on a frivolous subject matter, and hence it may have seemed sacrilegious to invoke the memory of pious ancestors. To this point, Ibn Zaydūn's other celebrated letter, the *Serious Letter* written in his attempt to be pardoned from an imprisonment, is replete with allegorical references like the present *Letter*, but most are to events of significance in the history of Islam.[20] In patently serious matters, therefore, Ibn Zaydūn called upon icons of Islamic history to elicit clemency. On a deeper level, however, the pre-Islamic, nonreligious figures in the present *Letter* are far from paragons of foolishness: they constitute an ethical and cultural worldview that extols philosophy, virtue, the nature of kingship, and the beauty of the Arabic language, and the characters reflect this in the way Ibn Zaydūn summons their names. The Persians taught justice and kingship, the Greeks and Romans taught philosophy, and the Arabs of the Arabian past showed the hallmarks of individual virtue, heroism, and linguistic virtuosity. A few Abbasid-era literary and scientific emulators were deemed worthy enough to earn a seat in this pantheon of the great and good of the past, but in the mind of Ibn Zaydūn, his near contemporaries had no discernible place in the halls of quotable worthiness.

The archetypes of humanity's best were locked in the safety of a distant past. And knowledge of that past, essentially the entirety of the material in the *Letter*, was codified in a process of Iraqi cultural production between the second/eighth and fourth/tenth centuries. The distillation of this cultural knowledge in fourth-/tenth-century Iraqi literature reached the Andalusia of Ibn Zaydūn's early life, and Andalusians embraced the knowledge, esteeming their acquired mastery of it as a hallmark of their own culture.[21] Knowing the past of Arabia and the Middle East gave the Andalusians security in their contemporary desires to express Arab identity, and that corpus of knowledge became their treasured cultural capital.

A further testament to the profound importance attached to these figures is revealed in how little the stories and cast of characters changed in the centuries that followed Ibn Zaydūn. The figures he cited would never fall out of fashion, their numbers would never be materially augmented, and their stories would not change substantially. A steady line of learned Arabic literature preserved the memories intact despite myriad repetitions in manifold places. What counted as essential cultural knowledge in fifth-/eleventh-century Andalusia also mattered in fourth-/tenth-century Iraq, as it retained its value in sixth-/twelfth-century Egypt and tenth-/sixteenth-century Turkey. These places did not all have the same relationships with Arab identity, but they shared a deep fascination with the particular vision of the past and they maintained it in a remarkably stable state. Pious ancestors, Sufis, and principled leaders of Islamic learning would naturally play a major role in shaping Muslim self-perception, but the role of the profane figures in constituting a sense of human worth should not be overlooked. Via the characters named in the *Letter*, we behold the cusp of an Arabic classical tradition: an established repertoire of pre-Islamic memories that retained value for Muslims across time and space, a textual analogue to the classics of Greece and Rome for Christian Europeans epitomized in the *all'antica* style of the ancient past, which was beloved and replicated in Europe from the Renaissance (and before) into the present.

The *Letter*'s employment of this classical repertoire to create meaning via historical allusions relies on its audience's keen interest in learning that particular history to appreciate the literary accomplishment.[22] The *Letter*'s style of rattling off a brisk barrage of names and old Arabic expressions comes across so effortlessly because Ibn Zaydūn treats these ancient names as simple historical facts, which indeed they are. Ibn Zaydūn did not need to invent anything, and he does not labor any point or contort his writing—the meanings he intended were there and waiting to be used. The *Letter* is a display of cultural mastery cleverly employed to construct an "in joke" for those educated enough to be in the know. The importance of being in the know by possessing the knowledge would remain a touchstone of social worth for centuries, and this brings us to Ibn Nubātah, author of *The Genius of Invective* commentary edited and translated in this book.

## Ibn Nubātah and the Commentary on Ibn Zaydūn's *Letter*

Ibn Nubātah resembled something of an Ibn Zaydūn of his own time and place. He was a renowned poet and letter writer, esteemed by his contemporaries as one of the most accomplished litterateurs of eighth-/fourteenth-century Egypt and Syria—though his career arc did not rise quite so high as that of Ibn Zaydūn. Born in Egypt in 686/1287 into an educated but not politically prominent family, Ibn Nubātah emerged on the literary scene around the age of thirty with the presentation of a literary anthology designed to show his mastery of the classical Arabic repertoire. The work engages essentially the same styles and repertoire mastered by Ibn Zaydūn three centuries earlier in Andalusia. Following the circulation of his anthology, Ibn Nubātah moved to Syria in 716/1316 in search of literary men and patrons who could appreciate and remunerate his talent. He settled in Damascus but regularly traveled through the important regional urban and cultural centers. He earned his living by composing praise poetry and eulogies to cultivate a social circle of wealthy and powerful patrons, and met a particularly warm reception at the court of Abū l-Fidā' (672–732/1273–1331), the ruler of Hama and a learned scholar and writer in his own right. For forty-five years, Ibn Nubātah remained in Syria, at times enjoying good stipends from wealthy patrons, while at a few junctures he needed recourse to government jobs as a writer and functionary in the chancery to provide for his daily bread. Despite evident fluctuations in his income, his fame as a literary scholar was nonetheless secure, though he never rose to any high political positions; Ibn Nubātah may have preferred to eschew the fraught world of power in favor of belles lettres. In 761/1360, when Ibn Nubātah was seventy-five, the sultan al-Nāṣir Ḥasan invited him back to his native Egypt, where he was provided with a pension and an official chancery title, and there he died in 768/1366.[23]

Ibn Nubātah's literary activity focused primarily on crafting his own poetic and prose compositions,[24] though he demonstrated mastery of the classics of Arabic literature and culture in making anthologies of earlier poets and some compendiums of prose selections. *The Genius of Invective* is one of the few works in which Ibn Nubātah's own voice is largely absent—here, his intention was to explain the cultural references made by Ibn Zaydūn via quotation from the most famous and authoritative early sources.

## *The Genius of Invective*: Structure and Contents

The impetus behind the writing of *The Genius of Invective* stemmed from the early years of Ibn Nubātah's sojourn in Syria, ca. 720–32/1320–31, when he enjoyed a close relationship with Abū al-Fidā' in Hama.[25] By this period, Ibn Zaydūn's *Letter* had already been established in the Muslim East. Whether it had arrived soon after its original composition or in the later thirteenth century, when Andalusian settlers in Egypt brought anthologies of their literature with them, is unclear,[26] but the text of the *Letter* is recorded in full by the Egyptian al-Nuwayrī (d. 724/1324),[27] and Ibn Nubātah alludes to slight variations between different versions, meaning multiple manuscripts were circulating in early eighth-/fourteenth-century Syria.[28] The popularity of the *Letter* is easily understood: the Egyptian and Syrian literary savants were interested in the same classical stories as Ibn Zaydūn's Andalusian contemporaries, and Abū l-Fidā' was one such enthusiast for the culture. According to Ibn Nubātah's Preface to *The Genius of Invective*, his learned courtly circle requested a commentary on the *Letter*, which Ibn Nubātah dedicated to the ruler.

*The Genius of Invective* reproduces Ibn Zaydūn's *Letter* in full, and at each instance where a historical person is mentioned, Ibn Nubātah inserts a biography explaining that character's identity. Ibn Nubātah found the requisite biographical information by combing a corpus of established literary and historical texts—in the main, a corpus of well-known writings composed between the ninth and eleventh centuries. At the forefront are Abū Tammām's *al-Ḥamāsah* for a number of poems, al-Iṣbahānī's *Kitāb al-Aghānī* for much of the material, and several works by al-Tawḥīdī (310–414/922–1023), alongside various quotations from Ibn Ḥamdūn's (495–562/1102–67) *al-Tadhkirah* and the *Amālī* of al-Sharīf al-Murtaḍā (355–436/965–1044).[29] Ibn Nubātah restricted his own literary flourish to the short preface, and, akin to his patron Abū al-Fidā''s method of writing history, Ibn Nubātah wrote *The Genius of Invective* as a condensed compilation. He copied selections from the above sources, either verbatim or abbreviated to impart the key information more economically. Ibn Nubātah so refrained from entering into the narratives that even when the sources were contradictory, he rarely voiced his own opinion, restricting his interventions to periodic grammatical commentary.

The transmission of the fourth-/tenth-century material intact through the eighth-/fourteenth-century *The Genius of Invective* is yet another aspect of the stable maintenance of the "classic" tradition discussed in the previous section. Ibn Nubātah positions himself as a messenger: he is a conveyer of knowledge already codified by Iraqis three to four hundred years earlier. While Ibn Nubātah was in charge of the selections and could control the narrative by his organization of the material, his sources are all still extant, and readers familiar with them will not find anything particularly new in *The Genius of Invective*. However, that cultural conservatism was likely one of the book's core strengths. Ibn Nubātah demonstrated his erudition via replicating what was known in his day about the figures of the *Letter*, and the book was therefore a trusted reference work since it made no material additions to what was then the received narrative of the past. Those interested in the knowledge wanted to receive it unaltered, and Ibn Nubātah provided that service.

Ibn Nubātah's format in *The Genius of Invective* is consistent and concise in conveying key data. For each historical figure, the biography sets out the person's various names and nicknames, lineage (underlining the tribal lens through which Arabian peoples were memorialized in Arabic literature), and main claim to fame. Ibn Nubātah then narrates anecdotes about the life of the character. There is neither intention for completeness nor strict chronological order; Ibn Nubātah offers a digest that conveys the flavor of the character's identity via a selection of the more famous or interesting stories of the characters' biographies culled from the older sources. The anecdotes usually close with discussion of the character's death, but this is not the end of the biography. Ibn Nubātah concludes most entries with selections of poetry or wise sayings attributed to the characters, which underscores how cultural production (and for Arabs, poetry in particular) was perceived as a core component of the identity of the worthy exemplars from the past.

From the information Ibn Nubātah provides, a reader of *The Genius of Invective* will be able to understand the *Letter* and will become acquainted with a manageable cache of knowledge about each character. The information is less than the sum of all that could be known from more comprehensive reading of the wider sources; thus, it does not make anyone an expert in the cultural heritage, but it certainly makes readers conversant, providing them with material we can imagine they memorized and reproduced in apt moments during their everyday encounters in learned assembly. Herein is the kernel of *The Genius of Invective*'s popularity. Ibn Zaydūn's *Letter* mentions many historical figures of the classic repertoire, and since *The Genius of Invective* comments on each of them, the book is a synopsis of a broad spectrum of the hallowed memories of the pre-Islamic past. There are indeed more figures in the classical pantheon about whom one could learn, but the cast of ninety-eight from Ibn Zaydūn's *Letter* is sufficiently ample: if one knows about them, one has command of a fair sample of the Arabic classics and can present oneself in society with a legitimate air of learnedness.

*The Genius of Invective* is thus quintessentially a popular book—a digest for the general literate public that enables nonspecialist readers to obtain sufficient information about classic characters without the trouble of plowing through the more detailed sources. The key sources are gigantic—consider the size of the classic compendiums written in the fourth/tenth century: al-Iṣbahānī's *al-Aghānī* runs to twenty-five volumes in the modern edition, and Ibn ʿAbd Rabbihi's *al-ʿIqd al-farīd* is seven. Further important collections of Arabian anecdotes appeared in the fourth/tenth and sixth/twelfth centuries, such as al-Zamakhsharī's *Rabīʿ al-abrār wa-nuṣūṣ al-akhbār* and Ibn Ḥamdūn's *al-Tadhkirah*, but these are likewise multivolume affairs. In short, the time that the single-volume *Genius of Invective* saves readers is a significant consideration.

It should be clear now why *The Genius of Invective* found its way into so many libraries, from Mali to India, from England to Zanzibar. Most students in the madrasas of the late medieval and early-modern Middle East were attending in order to study Islamic law, not Arabic literature, but they evidently appreciated the cultural value of the profane stories, and a handy resource would suit them well. Furthermore, most readers across the early-modern Muslim world were not necessarily expert in tackling Arabic literary texts, and while many would appreciate the cultural importance of the material, the level of mastery displayed by the likes of Ibn Zaydūn and Ibn Nubātah was not attainable for all. For the bulk of readers, Arabic was a shoreless sea of allusions and history, which they deeply respected without necessarily knowing, and for these readers a simplified text like *The Genius of Invective*, which makes the classical stories more accessible, would be especially valuable.[30]

The spike in manuscript production from the sixteenth century, and the very considerable concentration in Ottoman libraries, bolsters our impressions. The Ottomans were outsiders to the core Arabic lands, but in the early tenth/sixteenth century they came to control almost the entire Arabic-speaking Middle East. *The Genius of Invective* needs also to be seen as a cultural tool for educated Ottoman readers who wanted to get up to speed on the classics of Arabic literature[31] but who did not have the time to pore over the massive compendiums of the classical stories. Consider that manuscript collections in Turkey today contain nineteen copies of *The Genius of Invective* in Arabic, alongside eighteen manuscripts of the Turkish translation, whereas those same Ottoman libraries house only sixteen copies of al-Iṣbahānī's *al-Aghānī*, most of which are incomplete. The role of *The Genius of Invective* in instructing the core of Arabic culture for non-native speakers is likely also the reason for the extensive cache of manuscripts produced in Qajar-era Iran, the two from the Tukulor caliphate in Mali, and the one from Gorakhpur in India, as well as the thirty-odd copies held in European collections. Early Orientalists were also outsiders to Arabic traditions, but were keen to learn, and *The Genius of Invective* would have been an easy way in.

After six hundred years of brisk circulation, and after multiple editions in early print runs, the sudden disinterest in *The Genius of Invective* as the twentieth century unfolded is stark. The change underlines the powerful forces wielded by colonial politics and European academic paradigms, which combined to promote the earlier writings of the Abbasid "Golden Age," and *The Genius of Invective* was ill equipped to impress the new tastes. It is a derivative book—after study of the manuscripts and comparison with its sources, the text is hardly revolutionary in a meaningful sense. It conveys knowledge, but as facts more than stories. To lean on a classical Greco-Roman analogy regarding sources for Greek mythology, *The Genius of Invective* is more like the laconic, workmanlike *Library* of Apollodorus than the elegant and engaging *Metamorphoses* of Ovid. *The Genius of Invective* packages cultural repertoire in a handy fashion and brings together anecdotes from multiple sources, but a well-read literary savant will not find many surprises.

Thus, the text did not meet the twentieth century's budding standards of literary originality, and Ibn Nubātah's star and those of his writerly cohort rapidly waned as their books were sidelined in favor of the writings of their Abbasid predecessors. However, while moderns entertain desires to tackle the original sources and find the authentic origins of history, the reality is that the Abbasid-era originals, such as *al-Aghānī*, are dauntingly voluminous. Today, therefore, if we are to realistically propagate the spirit of Arabic culture and its classical literature, we need handier books. It is hoped that with this new edition and translation, *The Genius of Invective* can make itself available once again to serve its long-standing yeoman's work as a general educator.

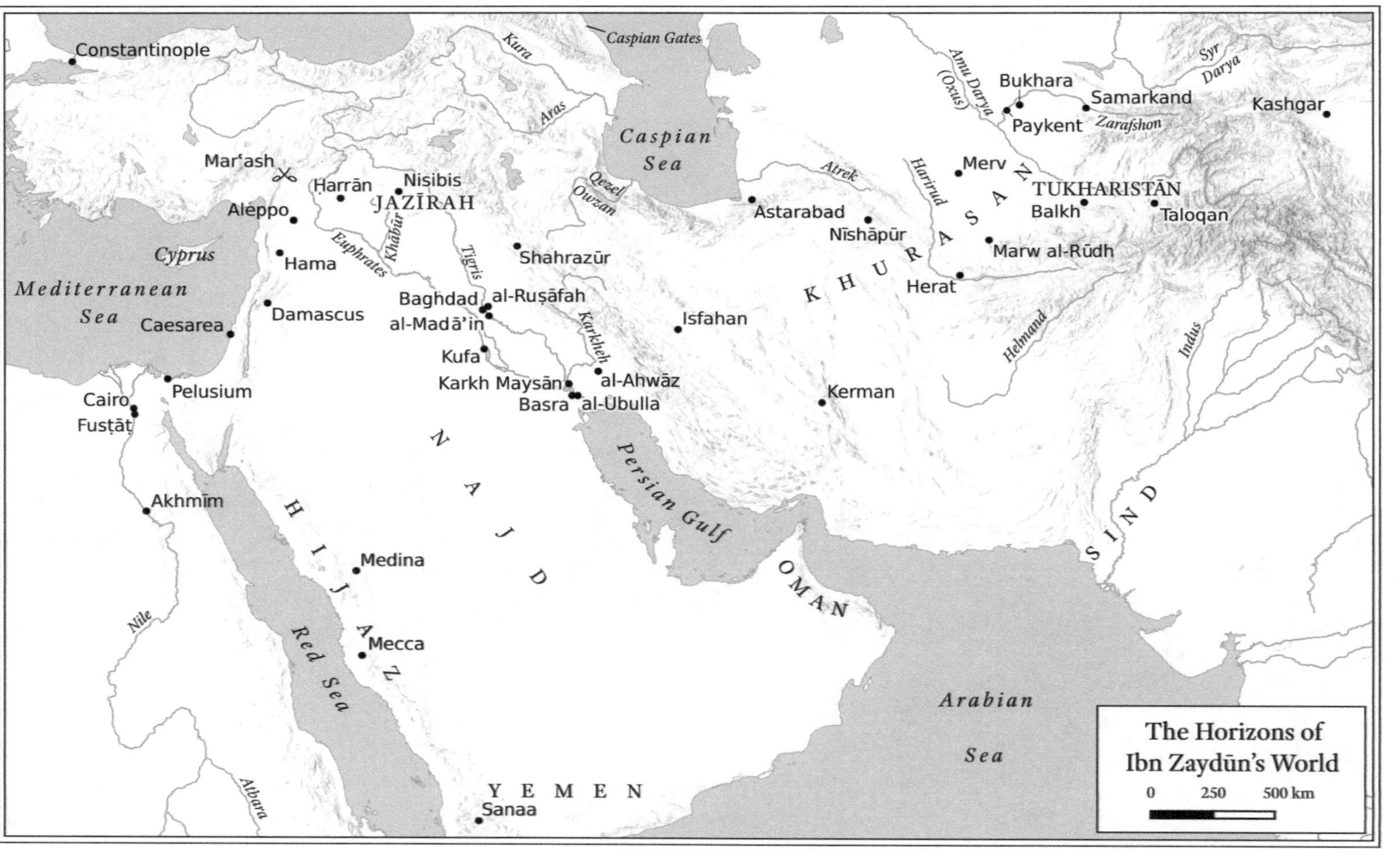
The Horizons of Ibn Zaydūn's World
0
250
500 km
Constantinople
Caspian Gates
Kura
Aras
Caspian Sea
Amu Darya (Oxus)
Bukhara
Paykent
Samarkand
Zarafshon
Syr Darya
Kashgar
Mar'ash
Ḥarrān
Nisibis
JAZĪRAH
Aleppo
Cyprus
Hama
Euphrates
Khābūr
Tigris
Qezel Owzan
Shahrazūr
Atrek
Astarabad
Nīshāpūr
Harirud
Merv
TUKHARISTĀN
Balkh
Taloqan
Marw al-Rūdh
KHURASAN
Herat
Mediterranean Sea
Damascus
Caesarea
Baghdad
al-Ruṣāfah
al-Madā'in
Karkheh
Isfahan
Kufa
Karkh Maysān
al-Ahwāz
Basra
al-Ubulla
Kerman
Helmand
Indus
Pelusium
Cairo
Fusṭāṭ
NAJD
Persian Gulf
Akhmīm
HIJAZ
Medina
SIND
OMAN
Nile
Red Sea
Mecca
Arabian Sea
YEMEN
Sanaa
Atbara

Arabia, Syria, and Iraq
500–650 AD
Cities founded in the Muslim era appear in parentheses
Tribal territories are approximate
0
250
500 km
Ceyhan
Harran
Khābūr
Ṣiffīn
Circesium
Palmyra
Euphrates
Tigris
(Baghdad)
al-Anbār
al-Madā'in
Karkheh
Yarmūk
Jordan
al-Ḥīrah (Kufa)
(al-Wāsiṭ)
al-Qādisiyyah
(Basra)
GHASSĀN
NAJD
ṬAYYI'
Tabūk
Taymā'
Persian Gulf
TAMĪM
AL-BAḤRAYN
HIJAZ
YARBŪ'
Fadak
GHAṬAFĀN
'ABS
Yathrib
(Medina)
BAKR
TAGHLIB
AL-YAMĀMAH
Ma'ūnah Well
DHUBYĀN
'ĀMIR
al-Kurā'
Mecca
'Ukāẓ
al-Ṭā'if
OMAN
(400 KM)
KINĀNAH
Tabālah
KHATH'AM
AZD
KINDAH
Red Sea
Atbara
Sanaa
YEMEN
ḤIMYAR
Gulf of Aden

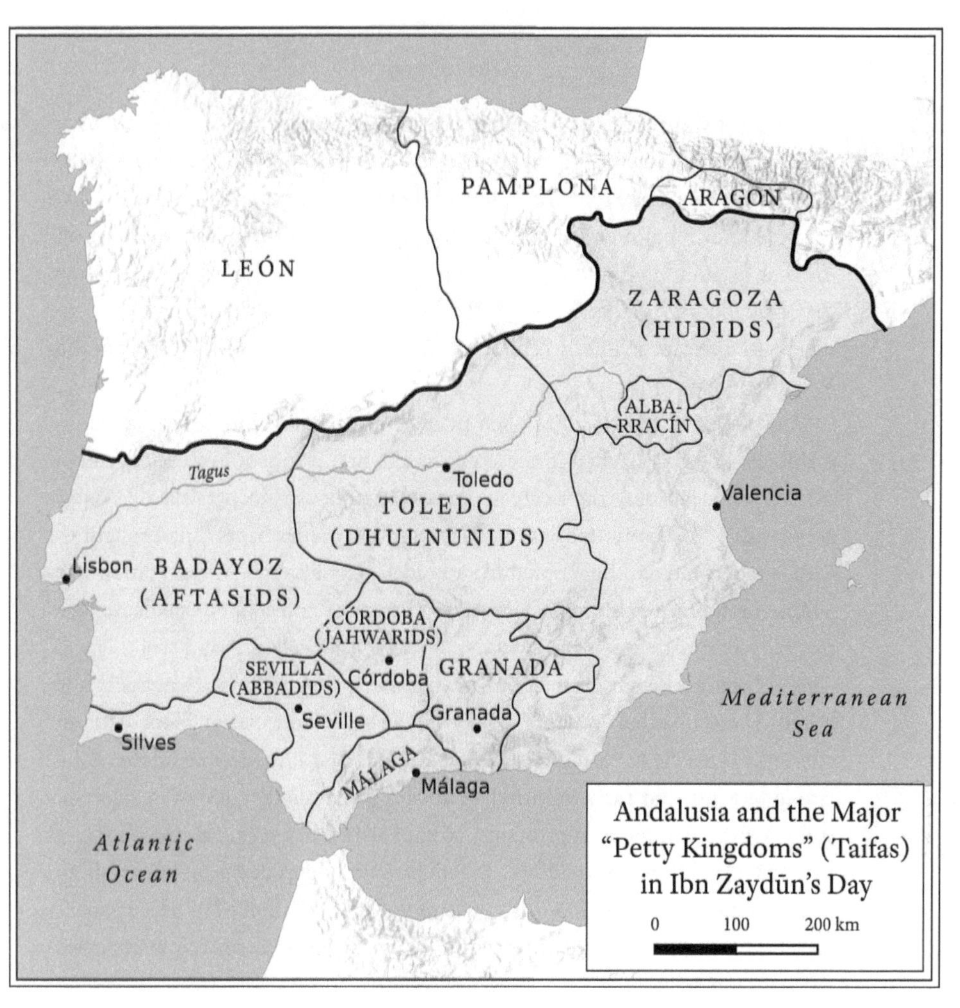


Andalusia and the Major "Petty Kingdoms" (Taifas) in Ibn Zaydūn's Day

# Note on the Text

## The Edition

This edition was produced from study of over 50 manuscripts of *The Genius of Invective*. As my research into *The Genius of Invective* continues, many more manuscripts continue to emerge, but while I have identified some 190 at present, the additional manuscripts do not appear to alter the essential form of the text as embodied in the 50 consulted. The 50 yielded consistent patterns that provide a grounded grasp of the book's transmission and enable us to offer here the first scholarly edition of *The Genius of Invective* reflective of the breadth of its manuscripts.

*The Genius of Invective* has been printed eight times, but very few manuscripts had been consulted in the process. The first printing, in Copenhagen in 1821, reproduced only the Arabic-text sections relevant to pre-Islamic Arabs, accompanied by Latin translation, based on two manuscripts, one brought to Copenhagen and another copied from Leiden. The first full Arabic edition was a lithograph printing in Cairo (1278/1862). Its editor notes that he made numerous corrections to the manuscripts upon which he relied,[32] and while it was clearly produced from more than one manuscript (variations are occasionally noted in the margins), there are only fifteen such notes throughout without citation to specific manuscripts. The subsequent four lithograph editions of the late nineteenth and early twentieth centuries give no indication of manuscript study. Of the two modern printings, al-Bābī al-Ḥalabī's seems a direct copy of the 1278/1862 lithograph, and Abū al-Faḍl Ibrāhīm's reproduces the Alexandrian printed edition of 1290/1874: his notes refer to consultation of two Cairo manuscripts, though cross-reference of the text with those manuscripts uncovers some discrepancy.

The manuscripts consulted in producing the present edition divide into two families, which can be labeled "Long" and "Short." The Long family comments on every aspect of Ibn Zaydūn's letter, including grammatical discussions of Ibn Zaydūn's language and biographies for the historical persons mentioned in the *Letter* by name as well as persons whose names arise incidentally from Ibn Nubātah's own commentary.[33] The Short family only elaborates upon persons expressly named in the *Letter* itself, some biographies are lightly abridged compared to the Long version, and there is limited grammatical discussion. None of the Short family contains indications that they were later abridgments of Ibn Nubātah's Long version. I have found no indication in contemporary sources of any writers credited with abridging the text, and since the Short versions follow each other very closely, it is unlikely that they represent discrete efforts of different copyists to epitomize the Long version.[34] Although the three oldest extant copies of *The Genius of Invective* are from the Long family,[35] the abiding consistencies within the Short family manuscripts indicate that they stem from an early exemplar too. While it is possible that Ibn Nubātah himself authored the Short version, there are nonetheless slight discrepancies between Short family manuscripts, so the story likely holds as-yet-undiscovered complexities, which will need further study beyond the scope of this volume. A little over half of the total number of extant manuscripts are Long versions, though the Short version was the more widely circulated: for instance, the copies in Mali, Zanzibar, India, and all the manuscripts collected in Europe between the seventeenth and mid-nineteenth centuries are Short.

Given that the Long version's Arabic grammatical discussions are not germane to English-language audiences, and since the Short version has never been printed before, it was decided to produce the Short version here. Of the fifty consulted manuscripts, twenty-three were Short, and since the variations were minuscule, they evidence a stable manuscript tradition, though each manuscript has its own shortcomings. *The Genius of Invective*'s popularity meant that demand for copies was high, and most manuscripts were written by professional copyists, members of what Julia Bray aptly dubs the "artisan knowledge economy" of the early-modern period,[36] a number of whom produced copies hastily and with evident bafflement at the more challenging aspects of the text. Names of some of the more obscure historical personalities were miswritten, lines of difficult poetry were corrupted, phrases were incorrectly rendered, and these scribes lacked the time or inclination to find solutions, so the task of resolving the issues through cross-referencing and correction falls to modern editors.

The first editor of a printed *Genius of Invective*, Muḥammad ibn ʿAbd al-Raḥmān al-ʿAdawī, epitomized the travails of a would-be editor in a poem he appended to the colophon of the 1278/1862 printing:

The *Letter* contains learning and meaning:
Clear perfection: none compare.
And *Genius of Invective* added lucidity,
Shining vivid light on the beauty.
...
But the manuscripts—before this printing—
Their errors warped the whole thing.
The book, stricken by gross mistakes,
Was nursed to health by editing.[37]

The Short version's convalescence can be attained via MS Istanbul Süleymaniye Aşir Efendi 298 (I1). Its copyist evidences considerable care in checking his work, and he commits, on the whole, fewer errors than other Short versions consulted. Incidentally, I1's copyist also informs us that he mixed his ink with the water of Mecca's Zamzam well, and so implores us to treat the text reverently (§86.2). All in all, it seems reasonable to follow his word: I1 allows us to produce an edition with relatively limited corrections and footnotes, and we used it as the basis for the Arabic text.

Despite the overall high quality of I1 and its reliability, the copyist did nonetheless make several hundred errors over the fifty-one thousand words of the text, though almost all of them are omissions of single words or letters and the common *taṣḥīf* and *taḥrīf* mistakes of mis-pointing Arabic letters, writing letters in the wrong order, or confusing letters of similar shape. In some further cases, I1 presents more vexing corruptions and has larger lacunae of missing phrases. To produce the Arabic text of this edition, the following editorial principles were applied:

1. Where corrections to I1 are obvious slips, our Arabic text is corrected without footnotes indicating the error (this is predominantly in the case of *taṣḥīf* and *taḥrīf*, patent misreadings of the Arabic stem, a missing letter within a word, or mistakes in gender and number agreements between nouns and adjectives or verbs and nouns).
2. Where the errors are more significant, or where I1 produces readable Arabic, though likely in error, first recourse for correction was to the other Short version manuscripts, particularly Berlin Wetzstein I 48 (B1), Istanbul Süleymaniye Laleli 1826 (I6), and Paris Arabe 5358 (Ba1), as they are good-quality manuscripts, and, being written in Egypt, Turkey, and Mali, respectively, they offer a representative sample that spans the

geographical spread of the Short version. In these cases, the corrected word is inserted in the body text, and the word's form in I1 is noted in the Arabic critical apparatus.

3. Where all the Short version manuscripts seem to be erroneous, recourse was taken to the Long version manuscript Istanbul Süleymaniye Râgıb Paşa 1136 (I3), since it was very carefully prepared, vocalized, and checked. I3 was usually the final arbiter, but in some places I3 needed correction from a wider search of other Long versions; additionally, a handful of Persian words were corrected via recourse to the marginal notes made by the Persian-speaking reader of Tehran Majlis-i Shūra 164 (T1).
4. In a small number of places, both the Short and Long version manuscripts are erroneous; this suggests mistakes entered the early exemplars or even Ibn Nubātah's original. These are noted and corrections discussed in the English endnotes.
5. As noted above, in a small number of cases, whole stories or sentence-long chunks of text are omitted from some Short version manuscripts, but appear in others. The basis manuscript I1 is overall one of the most complete, and only rarely lacks text that can be found in other Short version manuscripts. These few cases of significant texts missing from I1 but present in other Short manuscripts are included in the Appendix at the end of this volume.

*Other Editing Principles*

1. I1's copyist checked the text and made some marginal corrections; these corrections are reflected in the Arabic, and no note is made in the interests of reducing the critical apparatus.
2. In accordance with the Library of Arabic Literature style, no short vowels are marked except to indicate passive verbs and rare cases where a word could be misread. However, poetry is fully vocalized, and in prose both the *shaddah* consonant-doubler marks and indefinite masculine accusative endings are added.
3. I1 is written in a clear and mostly careful hand, but not all letters are dotted: where dots were added, we make no notes. Where words were incorrectly dotted by the copyist, they are corrected in the text and are only noted if the variant pointing might suggest an alternative and legitimate reading.

4. I1 bears some cosmetic orthographic irregularities, particularly in rendering final *alif* as *ṭawīlah* or *maqṣūrah* or as a *yāʾ*: all are regularized to modern standard and no note is made.
5. All cases where I1's copyist rendered the long *alif* in some personal names with the "dagger *alif*" (e.g., al-Ḥārith: الحٰرث) are converted into the long *alifs*.
6. The names of pre-Islamic Persian rulers exhibit a particular orthography across almost all manuscripts: names ending in "d" in Persian are written with a "dh" in Arabic (for example, Jamshīd is written Jamshīdh (§10.3), Qubād becomes Qubādh (§6.4)), the letter "r" in some names is consistently transformed into "z" (for example Ardashīr is written Azdashīr §9.1), and the final "th" in Gayomarth is written with a "t" (§6.4). These transformations are revealing for the history and mechanics of rendering old Persian words into premodern Arabic, but they are no longer the current spellings of the Persian names in Arabic, and in the edition, they have been rendered in their now-common forms.
6. I1's copyist abbreviated the invocation تعالى (Exalted) after God's name. We render it in full.
7. I1 passed through several hands—five different individuals marked their ownership on its title page—and at least one subsequent owner made (quite accurate) vocalization additions to parts of the text; these vocalizations and other annotations are omitted.
8. The *hamzat al-qaṭʿ* is rendered according to modern conventions.

*Sigla*

The following lists the manuscripts cited in the critical apparatus.

Short Version Manuscripts

| | |
|---|---|
| إ١ (I1) | Istanbul Süleymaniye Asirefendi 298 |
| إ٥ (I5) | Istanbul Süleymaniye Giresun 164 |
| إ٦ (I6) | Istanbul Süleymaniye Laleli 1826 |
| أز١ (Az1) | Cairo al-Azhar 53532 |
| ب (B) | British Library OR 20 |
| با١ (Ba1) | Paris Arabe 5358 |
| بر١ (Br1) | Berlin Wetzstein I 48 |
| بر٢ (Br2) | Berlin Glasser 37 |
| ر٢ (R2) | Riyadh University 2215 |

| | |
|---|---|
| غ (G) | Granada Biblioteca de la Escuela de Estudios Arabes 12 |
| ق١ (Q1) | Cairo Dār al-Kutub 5127 |
| ل١ (L1) | Leiden OR 705-1 |
| ل٢ (L2) | Leiden OR 817 |
| ل٣ (L3) | Leiden OR 1605 |

Long Version Manuscripts

| | |
|---|---|
| إ٢ (I2) | Istanbul Köprülü Fazıl Ahmed Paşa 1320 |
| إ٣ (I3) | Istanbul Süleymaniye Râgıb Paşa 1136 |
| إ٤ (I4) | Istanbul Süleymaniye Esad Efendi i 2788 |
| إ٧ (I7) | Istanbul Süleymaniye Reisulküttab 830 |
| إ٨ (I8) | Istanbul Hamidiye 1136 |
| أز٢ (Az2) | Cairo al-Azhar 16011 |
| ت١ (T1) | Tehran Majlis-i Shūra 164 |
| با٢ (Ba2) | Paris Arabe 3315 |
| ر١ (R1) | Riyadh University 4100 F |
| ق٢ (Q2) | Cairo Dār al-Kutub 706 *Adab Taymūr* |
| ق٣ (Q3) | Cairo Dār al-Kutub 52 *Adab m* |
| م (M) | Mashhad al-Hayāt 286 |

Additional Manuscripts of Ibn Zaydūn's *Letter*

| | |
|---|---|
| ق٤ (Q4) | Cairo Dār al-Kutub 7 |
| ر٣ (R3) | Riyadh University 1245 |

## The Translation

*The Genius of Invective* was intended as a didactic text that explains the core and interesting elements an educated reader needed to know about major figures in the Arabic historical imaginary. It was written as a handy educational text on Arabic literature and history, and the present translation intends to replicate the book's edifying essence such that English readers can likewise use it to work their way into and around the classics of Arabic history. Accordingly, in addition to the Glossary, a system of cross-referencing is included in the endnotes: where a historical person who is the subject of a biography in the book is mentioned in passing, we note the paragraph number where the fuller biography can be found. Ibn Nubātah also employed such internal cross-referencing, and these too are rendered via the endnotes. Since Ibn Nubātah's intention was to make the historical material clear to readers, we have also added further details in endnotes for English readers. Ibn Nubātah could assume his readers had a certain degree of background knowledge that is not necessarily the case for a non-Arabic, non-Muslim readership: the endnotes are designed to briefly supply the cultural-specific background. Also, with the benefit of several centuries' worth of scholarship, we can correct cases where Ibn Nubātah makes statements that appear factually incorrect; these are also set out in endnotes.

In accordance with *The Genius of Invective* commentary approach, Ibn Nubātah interjects material in the midst of poems and prose to comment on unusual Arabic linguistic features or to gloss the meanings of particularly difficult lines of Arabic poetry. Commentary interjections are set in parentheses in the translation.

The Qur'an is regularly cited throughout the text, and, pursuant to LAL style, the translations of the Qur'anic passages are quoted from the published translationsof Maulana Wahiduddin Khan, except in a very small number of instances where the precise wording of Wahiduddin's translation needed slight amendments in order to illustrate to English readers the point being made in *The Genius of Invective*. These exceptions are stated in the endnotes.

The body text of *The Genius of Invective* employs three distinct Arabic literary registers. Some tracts use elaborate belles lettres style, others are straightforward storytelling prose, and there is much poetry. This translation tailors the English to reflect these different registers.

*Elaborate Belles Lettres*

Ibn Zaydūn's *Letter*, Ibn Nubātah's preface, and several excerpts of high-style epistolography quoted by Ibn Nubātah in the commentary are written in embellished Arabic that uses a vast vocabulary and complex clause structures to cleverly unfurl messages. There are also passages of rhyming prose (*saj*ʿ), where the construction of rhythm is central to the aesthetic. I endeavored to reflect the florid Arabic of these passages with suitably ornate English, and where the rhyme and alliteration are centerpieces of the Arabic, I mimicked them in English as far as was practicable.

*Storytelling Prose (*Akhbār*)*

The bulk of *The Genius of Invective* consists of prose narratives that Ibn Nubātah copied verbatim or abridged from earlier biographical and historiographical sources. In these passages, the original narrators' intention was to impart a story in a realistic fashion: action is described dispassionately, and the narrative develops via the direct speech of the characters and not through the indirect speech of an omniscient narrator. The Arabic is tight and economical, nouns and clarifications required in English are often absent, and direct speech is almost invariably introduced by *qāla* ("he said"). This is the standard, workmanlike style of Arabic storytelling prose, and the manner in which it conveys facts in a readily consumable form was likely a key factor in *The Genius of Invective*'s popularity and wide diffusion.

To replicate this register in English, I keep the translation unadorned and quick-flowing, and I retain all the direct quotations. In order for the English to run as smoothly as the Arabic, some interventions were necessary, such as the reorganization of clauses, the repetition of names where the Arabic only offers pronouns, and the addition of words to express causal connectives between actions where the Arabic suffices with the particles *wa-* and *fa-* ("and," "so"). The Arabic's endless repetitions of the verb *qāla* to introduce each quotation also detract from the narrative's meaning in English, and I therefore replace some of those "he saids" with other verbs to suit the tenor of the speech: readers will find, for example, "replied," "responded," "remarked," "cried," "called," "questioned," and "told" where the Arabic has *qāla*.

Ibn Nubātah's economical style is also devoid of contextualization, and the historical figures to which he alludes were often well known, so he could jump into the action in medias res in ways that will, in some places, stump his modern English readers. To ease the abruptness, I add titles of historical characters who are mentioned only by name (such as caliphs and famous viziers), and add some references to places and context, and, in a few cases, a phrase to aid comprehension where the text would be otherwise obscure. Readers' attention is also drawn to the Glossary, where all people and places mentioned in *The Genius of Invective* are briefly defined.

Another amendment concerns the treatment of Arabic names. In Arabic, individuals often have multiple names. For instance, the author of this book could be known as (a) Jamāl al-Dīn, his nickname; (b) Muḥammad, his given name; (c) Ibn Muḥammad, a patronymic invoking the name of his father; (d) Abū Bakr, a teknonym invoking the name of his son; or (e) Ibn Nubātah, another nickname taken from the name of one of his great-grandfathers. As convention has it, the author is almost always identified as Ibn Nubātah, but many figures in Arabic literature, including those who feature in *The Genius of Invective,* used multiple names. Since Arabic names are already unfamiliar enough to non-Arabist audiences, the proliferation of different names for the same person is potentially bewildering. For each character in the text, I picked one name, and applied it everywhere the character is mentioned. For example, the pre-Islamic tribal leader ʿĀmir ibn Mālik is known by mixtures of his given name, "ʿĀmir"; his teknonym, "Abū Barāʾ"; and the nickname *Mulāʿib al-Asinnah* ("Spear Brandisher"). In my translation, he only appears as "Spear Brandisher."

*Poetry*

There are more than one thousand lines of poetry in *The Genius of Invective,* ranging from pre-Islamic poems with their vast range of arcane vocabulary that Muslim-era scholars needed specialized study to comprehend, to the rhetorically verdant poetry with learned embellishments that established itself from the early Abbasid period.

Given that much of this poetry is counted among the classics of Arabic literature, and since Ibn Nubātah included it to evidence the poets' skills of composition, it is desirable to preserve a poetic register in English. Moreover, Ibn Nubātah embraced the typical Arabic literary style, including poetry in order to enliven the lengthy passages of straightforward storytelling prose: it would therefore be a disservice to English readers to compel them to march through the prose without providing them with some enjoyment of the poetry. In order to achieve this, the translations of poetry are motivated by an intention to retain the poetry's aesthetic purpose and literary flourish.

My approach was to start from the principle that the precise expressions and vocabulary of the original Arabic should be maintained as the priority, while avoiding the pitfalls of overly literal translation. Word-for-word translation is impossible for many Arabic poetic lexemes, since the poets summoned rare words with specific meanings that can take a phrase or more to render in English. The intense specificity of Arabic poetic vocabulary was an important part of the original readers' enjoyment (and satisfaction for the learned reader, who could engage in a little intellectual back-patting for knowing the hard words!). The English language, however, does not revere arcana with the same zeal as Arabic, and so the Arabic does not map at all aesthetically onto an English grid. Wholly literal translations therefore do not produce poetry in English, and this hinders English readers' enjoyment, and, indeed, the purpose of the poem's inclusion in the original. To convey the sense and function of the Arabic poetry in English, I substituted some of the more prolix or convoluted Arabic passages with more fluent English equivalents, and I aimed to be as concise in the English as possible, in part because the Arabic itself is usually concise, and, moreover, because this is the style of modern English-language poetry that traces into the nineteenth century and matured in the twentieth. In some cases, therefore, readers comparing the Arabic with the English will notice that not every word of the Arabic is translated, and phrases are retooled as concisely as possible; I hope readers agree that this was a small price to pay.

The meter of Arabic poetry required each verse to conform to a pattern of two halves (hemistichs), with the rhyming consonant and vowel occurring at the end of the second hemistich. Because the meaning of the Arabic verse usually flows over both halves of the line, and because the meter is not replicable in English, this translation opts for some poetic freedom in the formatting of the verses in English. We have retained the traditional scholarly format of rendering each hemistich as a separate line in English, but instead of formatting them as the pairs in which they appear in Arabic, indentation follows the now common practice in English poetry of indenting lines according to the flow of their meaning. If sentiments are expressed over a series of lines, they are accordingly formatted via indenting to constitute a visually recognizable chunk of text that flows down from the opening sentiment, and when the poet introduces a new thought, the first line is formatted with no indentation.

### *A Quirk in Ibn Zaydūn's* Letter

The largest section of Ibn Zaydūn's *Letter* (§§0.2–5) is the tract containing the host of pre-Islamic and other classical characters named in the extensive list that ridicules the traits of Ibn ʿAbdūs. This list is inaugurated by a verb ambiguously rendered in the manuscripts and printed editions of the text. At least three forms are attested, each based on the root *kh-y-l*, permitting multiple interpretations of the verb's subject and meaning. Manuscripts R, C1, C2, C3, and I2, and Abū l-Faḍl Ibrāhīm's 1964 printed edition have *khilta*, meaning that the letter's addressee, Ibn ʿAbdūs, imagines the following traits about himself. Manuscript B and the 1957 al-Bābī al-Ḥalabī edition, on the other hand, expressly mark the verb as feminine, *khayyalat*, meaning the messenger woman's praise was so effusive that the writer facetiously intones that she was led to believe that Ibn ʿAbdūs must embody the following traits. Outside of the *Genius of*

*Invective* manuscript traditions, the letter was included in al-Nuwayrī's *Nihāyat al-arab fī funūn al-adab* (7:208) and al-Qalqashandī's *Ṣubḥ al-aʿshā* (1:460), and both render the phrase in the feminine active form, *khayyalat*. ʿAlī ʿAbd al-ʿAẓīm's 1957 edition of Ibn Zaydūn's poetry and letters has the second-person masculine passive *khuyyilta* (637), which has a similar meaning to *khilta*. ʿAbd al-ʿAẓīm produced his version from the *Nihāyat al-arab*, *Sarḥ al-ʿuyūn*, and a collection of texts preserved in Cairo (MS Dār al-Kutub *Adab* 7). Four manuscripts of *The Genius of Invective* (L1, L2, I4, G), the 1863 printed edition, and the version of the letter in C4 leave the verb unvoweled, permitting either the feminine *khayyalat* or masculine *khuyyilta*. In the context of the letter, the feminine reading perhaps makes the most sense: the list of traits following this verb constitutes an exercise in which Ibn Zaydūn shows off his mastery of Arabic culture, and is intended to baffle both Ibn ʿAbdūs and all subsequent readers. Thus, its rhetorical effect is to express both Wallādah's erudition and her exasperation at Ibn ʿAbdūs's attempt to woo her, and it is not meant to record either the actual fancies of Ibn ʿAbdūs or the words of his messenger. Accordingly, the verb is treated in our edition of the *Letter* as *khayyalat*, expressing that the woman's exaggerated praise engendered the lofty and ludicrous conception of Ibn ʿAbdūs's worth.

# Notes to the Introduction

1 High praise of Ibn Nubātah's writerly skill is widely attested (Ibn Ḥajar, *al-Durar al-kāminah fī aʿyān al-miʾah al-thāminah*, 4:339; al-Maqrīzī, *al-Muqaffā l-kabīr*, 7:58; Ibn Īyās, *Badāʾiʿ al-zuhūr fī waqāʾiʿ al-duhūr*, 1.2:62). Al-Shawkānī (d. 1250/1834) states: "In my opinion, he was unequivocally the most accomplished of the post-classical poets (*ashʿar al-mutaʾakhkhirīn*)" (*al-Badr al-ṭāliʿ bi-maḥāsin man baʿd al-qarn al-sābiʿ*, 2:252). Ibn Zaydūn was acclaimed by his contemporaries (al-Ḥumaydī, *Jadhwat al-muqtabas fī tārīkh ʿulamāʾ al-andalus*, 188), and admiration increased over the centuries, both in the Muslim West (Ibn Bassām, *al-Dhakhīrah fī maḥāsin ahl al-jazīrah*, 1:260–61; Ibn Khāqān, *Qalāʾid al-ʿUqyān*, 175; al-Marrākushī, *al-Muʿjib fī talkhīṣ akhbār al-Maghrib*, 75–76) and the East (Ibn Khallikān, *Wafayāt al-aʿyān*, 1:139–41; al-Ṣafadī, *al-Wāfī bi-l-wafayāt*, 7:87–94).

2 The Mali manuscripts: MSS Paris Bibliothèque Nationale Arabe 5358, 5488. Their provenance and connection to the Tukulor caliphate are discussed in Blochet, *Catalogue des manuscrits arabes des nouvelles acquisitions (1884–1924)*, 97; India: MS Aligarh Muslim University Subhanallah Collection SC 892.725/7.

3 MS Zanzibar Archive 4/20.

4 At least twenty-five manuscripts of the Turkish translation survive, most in Istanbul, but copies spread farther afield to Erzerum (MS 2289) and Cairo (MS Adab Talat 142).

5 By 1700, Oxford had acquired four copies, Leiden and Gotha two each, and Copenhagen, Tübingen, and Vienna one each. By the end of the eighteenth century, Leiden had acquired another copy and Heidelberg one copy.

6 Copenhagen National Library Cod.Arab. 230, Leiden Or. 1605, and Granada Biblioteca de la Escuela de Estudios Arabes 12 were copied in Europe.

7 Leiden Or. 1104a is a partial translation written c. 1650; in 1755, Reiske published a translation of Ibn Zaydūn's *Letter* based on another Leiden *Genius of Invective* manuscript, Hirt republished the *Letter* and a chapter of *The Genius of Invective* in 1770, and the Danish Orientalist Rasmusen produced a bilingual Latin-Arabic edition in 1821.

8 Without comprehensive manuscript catalogues, enumerating copies of Arabic texts is difficult, but while the myriad surviving manuscripts of the most famous texts on Islamic law, devotional literature, and grammar dwarf the *Genius of Invective* copies,

like-for-like comparison with manuscripts of literary texts reveals the book's popularity. I am aware of only four literary texts with manifestly larger numbers of extant manuscripts: al-Ḥarīrī's *Maqāmāt*, *Kalīlah wa-Dimnah*, al-Damīrī's *al-Ḥayawān*, and collections of and commentaries upon al-Mutanabbī's poetry, and even these texts did not all enjoy as wide a geographical spread as *The Genius of Invective*. Most of the most famous premodern Arabic literary texts today, such as the works of al-Jāḥiẓ, the *Muʿallaqāt* poems, and al-Iṣbahānī's *al-Aghānī*, survive in far fewer copies than *The Genius of Invective*.

9 The Ottoman translation was published in vast quantities in 1841, and there were five Arabic editions printed in Egypt between 1862 and 1905.

10 Maktabat al-Azhar, *Fahris al-kutub al-mawjūdah bi-l-maktabat al-azhariyyah 1368/1949*, 5:140–41, 8:107.

11 For discussion of the effects of the new paradigms on medieval Arabic literature, see Bauer, "In Search of 'Post-Classical' Literature," 138–44.

12 For Wallādah's biography, see Ibn Bashkuwāl, *al-Ṣilah fī tārīkh aʾimmat al-Andalus*, 2:347; Ibn Diḥyah, *al-Muṭrib min ashʿār ahl al-Maghrib*, 7–10; and al-Kutubī, *Fawāt al-wafayāt*, 4:252–53. The biography is fragmentary, and Wallādah became something of a literary legend; for close critical analysis of what can be reconstructed, see Garulo, "La biografía de Wallada." The biography of Ibn Zaydūn himself and the circumstances of the *Letter* are likewise obscure: the testimony of all the extant sources is evaluated in Webb, "Andalusian Literature on a Global Stage."

13 Al-Ṣafadī, *al-Wāfī*, 7:90; Ḥajjī Khalīfah, *Kashf al-ẓunūn ʿan asāmī l-kutub wa-l-funūn*, 1:841. For details on the *Letter* and its reception in the centuries after Ibn Zaydūn, see Webb, "Andalusian Literature on a Global Stage."

14 Munich BSB Cod.arab. 574 f.8a.

15 Saʿdī, *Gulistān*, 5–7.

16 Ibn Bassām, *al-Dhakhīrah*, 1:332–35; Ibn Diḥyah, *al-Muṭrib*, 7–10. For full references to the sources and their intriguing silence regarding the actual circumstances of the *Letter*, see Webb, "Andalusian Literature on a Global Stage."

17 Al-Ḥumaydī refers to Ibn Zaydūn's ribald invective as "filthily rude" (*khabīth al-hijāʾ*) (*Jadhwat al-muqtabas*, 188).

18 The lone figure with Islamic connection is the jurist Mālik ibn Anas, though he is one of the early Abbasid-era figures and is mentioned in the context of the great thinkers of the early Abbasid times, alongside philosophers and writers such as al-Jāḥiẓ, al-Naẓẓām, and Sahl ibn Hārūn. There are no representatives of the early Islamic movement in Arabia, and no sections of the *Letter* appeal to manifestly Islamic sentiments.

19 For discussion of this trend in conceptualizing Arabness in third-/ninth- and fourth-/tenth-century Arabic writing, see Webb, *Imagining the Arabs: Arab Identity and the Rise of Islam*, 297–319.

20 The *Serious Letter* (*al-Risālah al-Jiddiyyah*) received a commentary by Ibn Nubātah's contemporary, al-Ṣafadī; see al-Ṣafadī, *Tamām al-mutūn fī sharḥ Risālat Ibn Zaydūn*.

21 Aspects of the adoption of Arab identity in Andalusia are detailed in Fierro, "Genealogies of Power in al-Andalus," 42–44; the *Arabica*-citing escapades of Ibn Zaydūn's *Letter* add a further contour to this important exercise in identity making.

22 Express praise of the *Letter* for its expert marshaling of history is detailed in al-Qalqashandī, *Subḥ al-aʿshā*, 1:460.

23 For a detailed year-by-year account of Ibn Nubātah's life, see Bauer, "Ibn Nubātah al-Miṣrī (686–768/1287–1366)," 10–36, and Bauer, "Jamāl al-Dīn Ibn Nubātah."

24 For overviews of Ibn Nubātah's many writings, see Bauer, "Jamāl al-Dīn Ibn Nubātah"; an important collection of Ibn Nubātah's prose, *al-Zahr al-manthūr*, and his epistles are edited and analyzed in Herdt's edition of Ibn Nubātah, *Kitāb Zahr al-manthūr*.

25 *The Genius of Invective* is not dated, but Ibn Nubātah explains that he wrote it during his "northern sojourn"—that is, after his move to Syria in 716/1316—and since its dedication to Abū l-Fidā' refers to the ruler by his title *al-Malik al-Mu'ayyad*, it must have been written after Abū l-Fidā' received this title in 720/1320.

26 No early manuscripts of the *Letter* survive and it was not incorporated into early anthologies of Andalusian literature. Ibn Zaydūn was known to Eastern scholars ca. AD 1200, but primarily as a poet (the Ashrafiyya Library in Damascus held a copy of his *Dīwān* (Hirschler, *Medieval Damascus*, #665), and much poetry is preserved in al-ʿImād al-Iṣbahānī's *Kharīdat al-Qasr wa-jarīdat al-ʿaṣr*, 2:48–71); however, Ibn Zaydūn is not mentioned in Yāqūt's (d. 626/1229) *Irshād al-arīb bi-maʿrifat al-adīb*. His fame in the East grew through the 1200s (Ibn Khallikān, *Wafayāt al-aʿyān*, 1:139–41; al-Andalusī, *al-Mughrib fī ḥulā l-Maghrib*, 1:30–36), and the *Letter* and Ibn Zaydūn's relationship with Wallādah were known by AD 1300 (al-Kutubī, *Fawāt al-wafayāt*, 4:252–53; al-Ṣafadī, *al-Wāfī*, 7:90). The text of the *Letter* may first have been copied in the East by Jamāl al-Dīn ʿAlī ibn Ẓāfir (d. 613/1216), an Egyptian historian and litterateur who authored *Nafā'is al-dhakhīrah*, a summary of Ibn Bassām's anthology of Andalusian literature with "additions, such as more verses of poetry, epistles, and prose selections" (al-Ṣafadī, *al-Wāfī*, 20:450–51). Al-Ṣafadī relied on Ibn Ẓāfir's expanded text of another of Ibn Zaydūn's epistles (*al-Wāfī*, 7:88–90; selections from that epistle are in Ibn Bassām, *al-Dhakhīrah*, 1:262–65), so Ibn Ẓāfir may also have included our *Letter*. Because Ibn Ẓafir's work was not immediately famous (no manuscripts appear to survive), the *Letter*

probably spread gradually at first (see further discussion in Webb, "Andalusian Literature on a Global Stage").

27 Al-Nuwayrī, *Nihāyat*, 7:207–13.

28 Ibn Nubātah, *Sarḥ al-ʿuyūn* (1964 edition), 35.

29 Ibn Nubātah also frequently consulted the seventh-/thirteenth-century Ibn ʿAsākir's *Tārīkh Madīnat Dimashq*, though that text is itself a verbatim compilation of earlier sources.

30 The poetry selections are of course difficult and demand educated readers since Ibn Nubātah does not gloss them, but the hard texts are conveniently placed toward the end of the biographies. Therefore, less-specialized readers could glean what they needed and move on, while *The Genius of Invective* also provides for more eager savants with the poetic selections.

31 For other aspects of Ottoman-era acculturation into Arabic writings, see Pfeifer, "Encounter after the Conquest."

32 Ibn Nubātah, *Sarḥ al-ʿuyūn* (1862), 260–61.

33 Ibn Nubātah explains his rationale for elaborating upon such incidental references (Ibn Nubātah, *Sarḥ al-ʿuyūn* (1964 printing), 267).

34 An exception illustrating the general rule is a manuscript in the King Saʿūd University in Riyadh (MS 6254 Q 1253/2) transcribed by ʿUmar al-Ṭarābīshī in 1276/1862. It is entitled a commentary on "Ibn Zaydūn's letter to Wallādah," and while it does not mention Ibn Nubātah's authorship and it elides the personal remarks of Ibn Nubātah in the introductory and concluding sections, it is clearly a cribbed copy of *Sarḥ al-ʿuyūn* with little addition from al-Ṭarābīshī himself. The Short copies of *Sarḥ al-ʿuyūn*, on the other hand, are so internally consistent that it appears impossible for them to have had individual geneses.

35 Damascus MS Maktabat al-Asad 3223 Adab 52; Istanbul MS Köprülü Fazıl Ahmed Paşa 1320; Tehran MS Majlis-i Shūra 16.

36 See Julia Bray's Introduction to al-Tanūkhī, *Stories of Piety and Prayer*, xxvii.

37 Ibn Nubātah, *Sarḥ al-ʿuyūn* (1862 edition), 261, my translation.

# رسالة ابن زيدون الهزليّة

# The Frivolous Letter

١،٠ أمّا بعد أيّها المصاب بعقله المورّط بجهله البيّن سقطه الفاحش غلطه العاثر في ذيل اغتراره الأعمى عن شمس نهاره الساقط سقوط الذباب على الشراب المتهافت تهافت الفراش في الشهاب فإنّ العجب أكذب ومعرفة المرء نفسه أصوب

٢،٠ إنّك راسلتني مستهديًا من صلتي ما صفرت منه أيدي أمثالك متصدّيًا من خلّتي لما قرعت دونه أنوف أشكالك مرسلاً خليلتك مرتادة مستعملاً عشيقتك قوّادة كاذبًا نفسك أنّك ستنزل عنها إليّ وتخلف بعدها عليّ

وَلَسْتَ بِأَوَّلِ ذِي هِمَّةٍ     دَعَتْهُ لِمَا لَيْسَ بِٱلنَّائِلِ

ولا شكّ أنّها قلتك إذ لم تضنّ بك وملّتك إذ لم تغر عليك فإنّها أعذرت في السفارة لك وما قصّرت في النيابة عنك زاعمة أنّ المروءة لفظ أنت معناه والإنسانية اسم أنت جسمه وهيولاه قاطعة أنّك انفردت بالجمال واستأثرت بالكمال واستعليت في مراتب الجلال واستوليت على محاسن الخلال حتّى خيّلت[1] أنّ يوسف عليه السلام حاسنك فغضضت منه وأنّ امرأة العزيز رأتك فسلت عنه وأنّ قارون أصاب بعض ما كنزت والنطف عثر على فضل ما ركزت وأنّ كسرى حمل غاشيتك وقيصر رعى ماشيتك والإسكندر قتل دارا في طاعتك وأنّ أردشير جاهد ملوك الطوائف بخروجهم عن جماعتك والضحّاك استدعى مسالمتك وجذيمة الأبرش تمنّى منادمتك وبلقيس غايرت الزبّاء عليك وشيرين نافست بوران فيك وأن مالك بن نويرة إنّما ردف لك وعروة بن جعفر إنّما رحل إليك وكليب ابن ربيعة إنّما حمى المرعى بعزّتك وجسّاسًا إنّما قتله بأنفتك ومهلهلاً إنّما طلب ثأره

١ إ: خلت.

This letter is for you—you, stricken of reason, entangled in ignorance, faults glaring, your defects appalling. Tripping in the trailing robes of your own delusion, and blind to manifest truth, you descend like a fly diving into syrup or a moth fluttering into immolation. Vanity is but lies, sir: learn instead to know yourself. 0.1

I received your message aspiring to my favor and venturing my affection. What a futile venture and what fruitless humiliation for the likes of you! And to think you made your own wife[1] convey the proposition, sending this darling of yours as a procuress while you fantasized about replacing her with me! 0.2

> You are not the first whose ambition
> calls him to what he cannot obtain.

Clearly, she hates you deeply and you bore her stiff. For there she was, selling you effusively with no restraint of dignity, expending all effort, means, and energy to solicit the assignation on your behalf. Her assertions painted you as the epitome of virtue and the embodiment—the essence, even—of humanity; she was unequivocal that you possess unique beauty, monopolize perfection, and sit atop the lofty heights of glory with all good virtues subsumed into your person. With all this, she made it seem[2] that when Joseph (eternal peace be his) vied with your beauty, you outshone him; that when she beheld you, Potiphar's wife forgot about him; and that Korah acquired just a part of your riches, while al-Naṭif discovered the mere castoffs from your treasures. According to her, Khosrow carried your saddlecloths, Caesar watched your flocks. Alexander executed Darius in obedience to you, Ardashir battled the Petty Kings for their rebellion against you. Al-Ḍaḥḥāk sued for your peace, Jadhīmah the Speckled aspired to join your entourage. The Queen of Sheba competed with Zenobia for your affection, Shirin vied with Boran over you. Your messenger's puffery lent impressions too that Mālik ibn Nuwayrah was regent only for you, 'Urwah ibn Ja'far set off only to reach you, and that only with your might did Kulayb ibn Rabī'ah defend the pasturelands, only for your honor did Jassās kill

بهمّتك والسموءل إنّما وفى عن عهدك والأحنف إنّما احتبى في بردك وحاتمًا إنّما جاد بوفرك ولقي الأضياف ببشرك وزيد بن مهلهل إنّما ركب بفخذيك والسليك ابن السلكه إنّما عدا على رجليك وعامر بن مالك إنّما لاعب الأسنّة بيديك وقيس بن زهير إنّما استعان بدهائك وإياس بن معاوية إنّما استضاء بمصباح ذكائك وسحبان إنّما تكلّم بلسانك وعمرو بن الأهتم إنّما سحر ببيانك وأن الصلح بين بكر وتغلب تمّ برسالتك والحمالات بين عبس وذبيان أسندت إلى كفالتك وأن احتيال هرم لعلقمة وعامر حتّى رضيا كان عن إشارتك وجوابه لعمر وقد سأله عن أيّهما كان ينفّر وقع عن إرادتك وأنّ الحجّاج تقلّد ولاية العراق بجدّك وقتيبة فتح ما وراء النهر بسعدك والمهلّب أذهب شوكة الأزارقة بأيدك

٣،٠ وأنّ هرمس أعطى بلينوس ما أخذ منك وأفلاطون أورد على أرسطاطليس ما نقل عنك وبطليموس سوّى الاصطرلاب بتدبيرك وصوّر الكرّة على تقديرك وبقراط علم العلل والأمراض بلطف حسّك وجالينوس عرف طبائع الحشائش بدقّة حدسك وكلاهما قلّدك في العلاج وسألك عن المزاج واستوصفك تركيب الأعضاء واستشارك في الداء والدواء وأنّك نهجت لأبي معشر طريق القضاء وأظهرت جابر بن حيّان على سرّ الكيمياء وأعطيت النظّام أصلاً أدرك به الحقائق وجعلت للكنديّ رسمًا استخرج به الدقائق وأنّ صناعة الألحان اختراعك وتأليف الأوتار والأنقار توليدك وابتداعك وأنّ عبد الحميد بن يحيى بارى أقلامك وسهل بن هارون مدوّن كلامك وعمرو بن بحر مستمليك ومالك بن أنس مستفتيك

٤،٠ وأنّك الذي أقام البراهين ووضع القوانين وحدّ الماهية وبيّن الكيفيّة والكميّة وناظر في الجوهر والعرض وميّز الصحّة من المرض وفكّ المعمّى وفصل بين الاسم والمسمّى وضرب وقسّم وعدل وقوّم وصنّف الاسماء والافعال وبوّب الظرف

him, and only with your zeal did Muhalhil avenge his blood. Al-Samawʾal was faithful solely by your pledge, al-Aḥnaf was enrobed strictly in your mantle, and Ḥātim learned charity and hospitality from the example of your bounty and joy. And so it seemed too that Zayd ibn Muhalhil rode with your thighs, al-Sulayk ibn al-Sulakah ran on your legs, ʿĀmir ibn Mālik parried spears with your hands, Qays ibn Zuhayr relied on your sagacity, Iyās ibn Muʿāwiyah shone with the glow of your brilliance, Saḥbān spoke with your tongue, and ʿAmr ibn al-Ahtam dazzled with your eloquence. She made out that it must have been your missive that forged the peace between Bakr and Taghlib, your guarantee that settled the blood feuds of ʿAbs and Dhubyān, your counsel that led Harim to devise the ruse that placated ʿAlqamah and ʿĀmir, and your wish that dictated Harim's answer when ʿUmar asked him about the winner. Al-Ḥajjāj needed your determination to govern Iraq, Qutaybah needed your lucky star to conquer Transoxiana, and al-Muhallab needed your power to break the Blues and your stratagems to disperse their discord.

Your lady's aggrandizement would also have me believe that it was from you that Hermes learned what he taught Apollonius, and you were the source of the wisdom Plato transmitted to Aristotle, that Ptolemy designed the astrolabe with your plans and determined the terrestrial sphere with your calculations, and that your subtle perception taught Hippocrates all the forms of sickness, while Galen learned the nature of herbals from your precise hypotheses, and both of them copied your treatments and consulted you about the humors, the constitution of limbs, and maladies and their cures. For Abū Maʿshar, you blazed the trail of astrological prediction, to Jābir ibn Ḥayyān you revealed the secret of alchemy, to al-Naẓẓām you bequeathed the principles to grasp metaphysical realities, and for al-Kindī you set out the scheme to derive philosophical subtleties. The art of melody is your invention, as well as composition for strings and percussion. ʿAbd al-Ḥamīd pared your pens, Sahl ibn Hārūn recorded your speech, ʿAmr ibn Baḥr took your dictation, and Mālik ibn Anas sought your legal opinion. 0.3

It sounded also as if it was you who established the certainties and laid down all legalities, defined quiddity and ascertained quality and quantity. You investigated substance and accident and distinguished fitness from ailment. You deciphered code, split signifier and signified, minted coins, and resolved monies owed.[3] As if it was you who classified nouns and verbs and categorized adverbials and adverbs. You fixed indeclinable words and declined the others, 0.4

والحال وبنى وأعرب ونفى وتعجّب ووصل وقطع وثنّى وجمع وأظهر وأضمر واستفهم وأخبر وأهمل وقيّد وأرسل وأسند وبحث ونظر وتصفح الأديان ورجّح بين مذهبَيْ ماني وغيلان وأشار بذبح الجعد وقتل بشّار بن برد

٥،٠ وأنّك لو شئت خرقت العادات وخالفت المعهودات فأحلّت البحار عذبة وأعدت السلام رطبة ونقلت غدًا فصار أمسًا وزدت في العناصر فكانت خمسًا وأنّك المقول فيه كلّ الصيد في جوف الفرا

وَلَيْسَ لِلّٰهِ بِمُسْتَنْكِرٍ   أَنْ يَجْمَعَ ٱلْعَالَمَ فِيْ وَاحِدِ

والمعنِيّ بقول أبي تمّام

فَلَوْ صَوَّرْتَ نَفْسَكَ لَمْ تَزِدْهَا   عَلَى مَا فِيْكَ مِنْ شَرَفِ ٱلطِّبَاعِ

والمراد بقول أبي الطيّب

ذُكِرَ ٱلْأَنَامُ لَنَا فَكَانَ قَصِيْدَةً   كُنْتَ ٱلْبَدِيْعَ ٱلْفَرْدَ مِنْ أَبْيَاتِهَا

٦،٠ فكدمت غير مكدم واستسمنت ذا ورم ونفخت في غير ضرم ولم تجد لريح مهزًا ولا لشفرة محزًّا بل رضِيَتْ من الغنيمة بالإياب وتمنّت الرجوع بخفّي حنين لأنّي قلت

لَقَدْ هَانَ مَنْ بَالَتْ عَلَيْهِ ٱلثَّعَالِبُ

وأنشدت

عَلَى أَنَّهَا ٱلْأَيَّامُ قَدْ صِرْنَ كُلُّهَا   عَجَائِبَ حَتَّى لَيْسَ فِيْهَا عَجَائِبُ

showed how to negate and how to express wonders. As if the *hamzah* owes both its forms to you, and you ruled how to express dual and plural too.[4] You decided when words are explicit or implicit and revealed how to interrogate and narrate. As if it was you who in law decreed qualified and strict liability and for legal precedents judged their reliability. In matters of faith, you investigated and speculated: perusing the world's religions, weighing Ghaylanists and Manichaeans, and decreeing for the heretics al-Jaʿd and Bashshār ibn Burd their executions.

Indeed, your power was made out as supernatural: if you so will it, you can 0.5
turn the seas sweet, you can liquefy rocks, and you can even bend time, turning tomorrow into yesterday; and to the four elements, you can add a fifth. In short, when they say, "Everything else is in the wild ass's belly" or

> There is none who doubts that God
> can gather the whole word into one man,

they must mean you! And when Abū Tammām's exlaimed:

> If you described yourself, you could not overstate
> the sum of your noble qualities

he had you in mind! And Abū l-Ṭayyib intended you too:

> If all humanity was depicted in a poem,
> you would be its exquisitely unique verse.

Altogether, though, what your messenger bit off was more than she could 0.6
chew. What she tried selling as a plump morsel is nothing but a blister. Her puffing merely brought bellows to spent ash, her wind swayed nothing, her blade did not cut. She was grateful, in fact, just to steal a safe departure, wishing she could have been in Ḥunayn's slippers, since I quoted to her:

> What an ignominy to be pissed on by foxes![5]

And recited:

> These days everything is so wondrous
> that there's nothing truly wondrous left.[6]

ونخرت وكفرت وعبست وبسرت[١] وأبدأت وأعدت وأبرقت وأرعدت و

هَمَمْتُ وَلَمْ أَفْعَلْ وَكِدْتُ وَلَيْتَنِي

ولولا أنّ للجوار ذمّة وللضيافة حرمة لكان الجواب في قذال الدمستق والنعل حاضرة إن عادت العقرب والعقوبة ممكنة إن أصرّ المذنب

وهبها لم تلاحظك بعين كليلة عن عيوبك ملؤها حبيبها حسن فيها من تودّ وكانت إنّما حلّتك بحلاك ووسمتك بسيماك ولم تعرك شهادة ولا تكلّفت لك زيادة بل صدقت سنّ بكرها فيما ذكرته عنك ووضعت الهناء مواضع النقب فيما نسبته إليك ولم تكن كاذبة فيما أثنت به عليك فالمعيديّ تسمع به خير من أن تراه

هجين القذال أرعن السبال طويل العنق والعلاوة مفرط الحمق والغباوة جافي الطبع سيئ الإجابة والسمع بغيض الهيئة سخيف الذهاب والجيئة ظاهر الوسواس منتن الأنفاس كثير المعايب مشهور المثالب كلامك تمتمة وحديثك غمغمة وبيانك فهفهة وضحكك قهقهة ومشيك هرولة وغناك مسألة ودينك زندقة وعلمك مخرقة

مَسَاوٍ لَوْ قُسِمْنَ عَلَى ٱلْغَوَانِي    لَمَا أُمْهِرْنَ إِلَّا بِٱلطَّلَاقِ

حتّى أنّ باقلاً موصوف بالبلاغة إذا قرن بك وهبنّقة مستوجب اسم العقل إذا أضيف إليك وطويسًا مأثور عنه يمن الطائر إذا قيس عليك فوجودك عدم والاغتباط بك ندم والخيبة منك ظفر والجنّة معك سقر

كيف رأيت لؤمك لكرمي كفاء وضعتك لشرفي وفاء وأنّى جهلت أن الأشياء إنّما تنجذب إلى أشكالها والطير إنّما تقع على ألّافها وهلّا علمت أنّ الشرق والغرب

١ إا: وبسرت وعبست وكفرت.

I snorted, my countenance grew dim, I frowned, I scowled, I mulled over her drivel, thunder and lightning swelled within me:

> Murderous thoughts arose; I did nothing . . . if only I had . . . alas!

Were it not that guests are sacred and suppliants protected, my reply would resemble the message Domestikos relayed via the wounds inscribed on the back of his head. But a sandal is ready and raised if the scorpion revisits, and punishment looms if the guilty persists.

For the sake of argument, let's pretend your lady did not simply behold you with eyes blind to your faults, giving full rein to her imagination as lovers are wont to do. We could then pretend that you do have some charms for her to adorn her descriptions, and that she neither misrepresented nor exaggerated your qualities, and that she was, so to speak, "honest about the camel's age," and she "put the tar on the camel's scabs";[7] but even if we thus pretend that her praise of your character was not just a straight pack of lies, there is nevertheless another saying: "Hearing about the Muʿaydī is better than looking at him." 0.7

So, let's have a look at you: a stooped half-breed head, whiskers drooping ridiculously, and an elongated neck propping an oblong skull; excessively inane; temperament: boorish; responsiveness: sluggish; hateful in appearance, you wander idiotically; obviously mad and your breath's intolerable, your vices are both numerous and infamous. You splutter, murmur, stutter, and guffaw. You're a peripatetic low-life suppliant, a heretic and clumsy incompetent. 0.8

> Not even a raving beauty, given but one of your vices,
> could be betrothed without promise of quick divorce.[8]

You make Bāqil sound eloquent, Habannaqah look sagacious, Ṭuways feel auspicious. Your presence is an absence, to wish you well breeds regret, to lose you is a gain; Heaven, in your company, is Hell.

Wherefore did you consider your ignobleness a match for my dignity, your baseness an equal to my nobility? Are you so ignorant as to not know that only like attracts like—that "birds of a feather flock together"? Do you not agree that east and west cannot associate? Do you not sense that believers 0.9

لا يجتمعان وشعرت أنّ المؤمن والكافر لا يتقاربان وقلت الخبيث والطيب لا يستويان وتمثّلت

أَيُّهَا ٱلْمُنْكِحُ ٱلثُّرَيَّا سُهَيْلًا    عَمْرَكَ ٱللّٰهَ كَيْفَ يَلْتَقِيَانِ

وذكرت أنّي علق لا يباع فيمن زاد وطائر لا يصيده من أراد وغرض لا يصيبه إلّا من أجاد

١٠،٠ ما أحسبك إلّا كنت قد تهيّأت للتهنئة وترشّحت للترفئة[١] ولولا أنّ جرح العجماء جبار للقيت من الكواعب ما لاقى يسار فما هم إلّا ببعض ما هممت به ولا تعرّض إلّا لأيسر ما تعرّضت أين ادّعاؤك[٢] رواية الأشعار وتعاطيك حفظ السير والأخبار أما ثاب إليك قول الشاعر

بَنُو دَارِمَ أَكِفَاؤُهُمْ آلِ مِسْمَع    وَتَنْكِحُ فِي أَكِفَائِهَا ٱلْحَبِطَاتُ

وهلّا عشّيت ولم تغترّ وما أشكّ[٣] أن تكون وافد البراجم أو ترجع بصحيفة المتلمس أو أفعل بك ما فعله عقيل بن علّفة بالجهنيّ حين أتاه خاطبًا فدهن أسته بزيت وأدناه من قرية النمل

١١،٠ ومتّى كثر تلاقينا واتّصل ترائينا فيدعوني إليك ما دعا ابنة الخسّ إلى عبدها من طول السواد وقرب الوساد وهل فقدت الأراقم فأنكح في جنب أو عضلني همّام ابن مرّة فأقول زوج من عود خير من قعود ولعمري لو بلغت هذا المبلغ لارتفعت عن هذه الحطّة ولا رضيت بهذه الخطّة فالنار ولا العار والمنيّة ولا الدنيّة والحرّة تجوع ولا تأكل بثدييها

فَكَيْفَ وَفِي أَبْنَاءِ قَوْمِي مُنْكِحٌ    وَفِتْيَانُ هِزَّانَ ٱلطِّوَالِ ٱلْغَرَانِقَةِ

---

١ (ما أحسبك . . . للترفئة) ساقطة من إ١. ٢ ل١: دعاوك. وما أثبتناه من سائر النسخ. ٣ ل١: أشكو.

and unbelievers will not congregate? Would you not say that the decent never amalgamate with the reprobate? Have you never recited the verse:

> You who aspire to wed the Pleiades to Canopus!
> How in God's name will you get them to meet?[9]

Didn't you mention too that I am a treasure beyond the pockets of high bidders, a bird beyond the reach of all hunters, a target beyond the range of all but the best archers?

Yet, I suppose you were all prepared for a congratulatory celebration of 0.10
felicitous nuptials! Indeed, a feral beast concerns no one,[10] but were it otherwise, you would deserve at least what the girls dealt Yasār, since he hazarded but a fraction of your presumption and misadventure. And to think you allege conversance with poetry and history, yet you cannot recall the poem:

> The Dārim are a fair match for the Misma',
> but the Ḥabiṭāt: they only marry their equals.[11]

So pasture tonight while you can, as upon the morrow you will doubtless go the way of the Barājim bystander or convey your own death warrant like al-Mutalammis. Perhaps I should do unto you as 'Aqīl ibn 'Ullafah did to the Juhanī suitor: oil your anus and drop you atop an anthill.

Should it happen that we begin to frequent the same places, and that our 0.11
glances might more repeatedly meet, do you really think the "long whispers and ready bed cushions" that induced al-Khuss's daughter to lie with her slave will lead me to you? Do you really suppose I am so cut off from the Arāqim that I must marry into the Janb? Has Hammām ibn Murrah concealed me for so long that I'll concede: "a husband of wood beats spinsterhood"? If I ever reach that state, by my life, I will never stoop to such denigration or accede to your machination. May I burn before I am shamed; may I die before I am defamed. A noblewoman will starve before she works as a wet nurse.

> Why you? I have suitors! My own clan's sons,
> And tall, strapping youths of the Hizzān![12]

ما كنتُ لأتخطّى المسك إلى الرماد ولا أمتطي الثور بعد الجواد فإنّما يتيمّم من لم يجد ماءً ويرعى الهشيم من عدم الجميم ويركب الصعب من لا ذلول له

ولعلّك إنّما غرّك من علمت صبوتي إليه وشهدت مساعفتي له من أقمار العصر ١٢،٠
وريحان المصر الذين هم الكواكب علوّ هممٍ والرياض طيب شيم

مَنْ تَلْقَ مِنْهُمْ تَقُلْ لَاقَيْتُ سَيِّدَهُمْ    مِثْلَ ٱلنُّجُوْمِ ٱلَّتِيْ يَسْرِيْ بِهَا السَّارِي

فحنّ قدح ليس منها ما أنت وهم وأين تقع منهم وهل أنت إلّا واو عمرو فيهم وكالوشيظة في العظم بينهم وإن كنت إنّما بلغت قعر تابوتك وتجافيت عن بعض قوتك وعطّرت أردانك وجررت هميانك واختلت في مشيتك وحذفت فضول لحيّتك وأصلحت شاربك ومططت حاجبك ورفعت خطّ عذارك واستأنفت عقد إزارك رجاء الاكتنان فيهم وطمعًا في الاعتداد منهم فظننت عجزًا وأخطأت أستك الحفرة

والله لو كساك محرّق البردَيْن وحلّتك مارية بالقرطين وقلّدك عمرو الصمصامة وحملك الحارث على النعامة ما شككت فيك ولا سترت أباك ولا كنت إلّا ذاك

وهبك ساميتهم في ذروة المجد والحسب وجاريتهم في غاية الظرف والأدب ١٣،٠
ألست تأوي إلى بيت قعيدته لكاع إذ كلّهم عزب خالي الذراع وأين من أنفرد به ممّن لا أغلب إلّا على الأقلّ الأخسّ منه وكم بين من يعتمدني بالقوّة الظاهرة والشهوة الوافرة والنفس المصروفة إليّ واللذّة الموقوفة عليّ وبين آخر قد نضب غديره ونزحت بيره وذهب نشاطه ولم يبق إلّا ضراطه

هل يجتمع لي فيك إلّا الحشف وسوء الكيلة ويقترن عليّ بك إلّا الغدّة والموت في بيت سلولية

تَعَـالَى ٱللهُ يَا سَلْمَ بْنَ عَمْرٍو    أَذَلَّ ٱلْحِرْصُ أَعْنَاقَ ٱلرِّجَالِ

I have no intention to switch sweet musk for ash, or to exchange a stallion to ride an ox. No one ritually cleanses with dust where water is available or opts to pasture on chaff in verdant fields or rides an unbroken steed if a gentle mount is at hand.

Perhaps you were misled by seeing the affection and favor I have shown—but that was meant for someone else:[13] one of the gorgeous greats of our time, one of the bright, high-minded stars and sweetly fragrant gardens: 0.12

Each exudes the presence of lordship,
Shining for travelers like night's guiding stars.[14]

The counterfeit gambling arrow whistles a different tune![15] What are you in comparison to the gallants? How can you compare? You are but the superfluous "w" in their "ʿAmr,"[16] a mere flimsy hanger-on.[17] Now, you might empty your coffers to feign magnanimity, go hungry to clothe yourself in finery, perfume your sleeves, trail your robes, flaunt your gait, primp your beard, tidy your mustache, arch your eyebrows, preen your sideburns, and smarten your outfit, all in the hope of being ranked among them, but this is a vain and fanciful blunder. By God! Even if the Burner wrapped you in his two mantles, and Māriyah pinned her earrings upon you, and ʿAmr affixed al-Ṣamṣāmah on your waist, and al-Ḥārith set you astride Ostrich, you'd still be nothing more than what you are, and with no shadow of a doubt I'd recognize you and your vile lineage!

Even if we pretend that you could compete with the others for the pinnacle of glory and merit, and keep pace with them to the zenith of witty elegance and cultured excellence, don't you nonetheless scurry home to a low-class woman, whereas all the gallants are bachelors and completely free? How can one who offers me but a paltry portion of his time compare to one whom I can enjoy at ample leisure? How great is the difference between someone who can devote his full force and abundant desire for my pleasure alone and another whose pool is dried, whose well is desiccated, whose energy is sapped, and who has nothing left but farts! All you offer me is a brace of bad choices—as they say: "poor-quality dates sold with faulty weights," or the combination of "pestilential goiters and death in a Salūlī woman's tent." 0.13

God is sublime, O Salm ibn ʿAmr!
It's desire that humiliates mankind.

ما كان أخلقك بأن تقدر بذراعك وتربع على ظلعك ولا تكون براقش الدالّة على أهلها وعنز السوء المستثيرة لحتفها فلا[1] أراك إلّا سقط بك العشاء بك على سرحان وبك لا بظبي أعفر

أعذرت إن اغنيت شيئًا وأسمعت لو ناديت حيًا ١٤،٠

إِنَّ ٱلْعَصَا قُرِعَتْ لِذِي ٱلْحِلْمِ وَٱلشَّيْءُ تَحْقِـرُهُ وَقَـدْ يَنْمِي

وإن بادرت بالندامة ورجعت على نفسك بالملامة كنت قد اشتريت العافية لك بالعافية منك وإن قلت جعجعة بلا طحن وربّ صلف تحت الراعدة وانشدت

لَا يُؤْيِسَـنَّكَ مِنْ مُخَـدَّرَةٍ قَوْلٌ تُغَلِّظُهُ وَإِنْ جَرَحَـا

فعدت لما نهيت عنه وراجعت ما استعفيت منه بعثت من يزعجك إلى الخضراء دفعًا ويستحثّك نحوها وكزًا وصفعًا فإذا صرت إليها[2] عبث أكّارُوها بك وتسلّط نواطيرها عليك

فمن قرعة معوجّة تقوّم في قفاك ومن فجلة منتنة يرمى بها تحت خصاك ذلك بما قدّمت يداك[3] لتذوق وبال أمرك وترى ميزان قدرك

فَمَنْ جَهِلَتْ نَفْسُـهُ قَدْرَهُ رَأَى غَيْرُهُ مِنْهُ مَا لَا يَرَى

١ كذا في إ١ ول٢؛ في سائر النسخ: فما. ٢ (إليها) ساقطة من إ١. ٣ (يداك) ساقطة من إ١.

You would be better off testing your grip before you go grasping, and knowing your limits before you start climbing. Otherwise, you will end like Barāqish, who divulged her own campsite, or like the ill-starred goat that prompted her own demise. To me, you seem like the one who went out to pasture in the evening and met Sirḥān; too bad for you, but at least the dust-colored gazelle is fine!

I have done my best to excuse you: if my words have fallen on sentient ears, 0.14
this should be enough:

> A reasoned man understands the staff's knocking;
> A trifle can generate a tumult.[18]

If you now hurry to contrition and focus upon yourself stern admonition, you will secure relief for yourself by relieving me of yourself. However, if you consider my words merely the grinding of a millstone without any grains, or thunderclouds that yield no rains, and if you recite to yourself the verse:

> Never let the harsh words of a privileged girl—
> even if they hurt—discourage your hopes![19]

And if, thenceforth, you revert to your illicit ways and resume the behavior for which, for now, you have been pardoned, I shall dispatch a man who will harry, spur, and slap you into the countryside, where you will be abused and lorded over by the sharecroppers and farmhands. A crooked staff will be straightened on the back of your neck and a stinking black radish will be rammed up your anus, and you will have brought all of this upon yourself, to experience the dire consequences of your actions and to behold the true extent of your worthlessness:

> What one fails to know about oneself
> is plain for all others to see.[20]

# كتاب شرح رسالة ابن زيدون الوزير

# The Genius of Invective

بِسْمِ ٱللَّهِ ٱلرَّحْمَٰنِ ٱلرَّحِيمِ

١،١ الحمد لله الذي لا يجب الحمد إلّا له وصلّى الله على سيّدنا محمّد المخصوص بأشرف رسالة وعلى آله وصحبه فما أفضل وأكرم صحبه وآله وأدام الله أيّام مولانا السلطان الملك المؤيّد العالم العادل عماد الدنيا والدين إدامة متّصلة الجلالة متقبّلة الإيالة ما جنت عسل النصر الشهيّ رماحه العسّالة وأثمرت غصون أقلامه المنعّمة بين ديم أنامله الهطّالة فمن فروض نعمه عليّ وقروض مننه لديّ أن أدعو لأيّامه المكرّمة كما صلّيت على نبيّ المرحمة وأذكر من أصلح لنا أمور الدنيا القائمة كلّما ذكرت من أصلح أمور الدين القيّمة فصلّى الله على سيّدنا محمّد وآله وصحبه وسلّم وأمتعنا ببقاء من سبقت مواهبه الغيث فصلّى وأعجزته فسلّم وبعد

٢،١ فإنّي أُمرت بشرح رسالة أبي الوليد ابن زيدون الآتي ذكرها وإيضاح براهينها الغامض على كثير من سراة الأدب سرّها فقلت ما أنا وصعود هذا الصرح وولوج هذا السرح ومعارضة ذلك البزّ ولست من ذلك الطرح وهل أنا إلّا صاحب أبيات تقيم جدرها قريحتي المطبوعة وكلمات تأتي على العفو فقرها المسجوعة فقيل إنّا نرضى من قسمة الإيضاح ببعض الحصص نقنع من التاريخ القاصّ بأدنى الفرص وإذا كنت من الشعراء فما أنت ببعيد من القصص فقابلت بالطاعة أمرًا قد وجب وقلت إن فاتتني سلوك الأدب المنظومة فإنّ الامتثال من سلوك الأدب ثمّ أمليت هذه النبذة من التاريخ المطلوب عن فكر خامل مسّه القرح وشرحت إلّا أنّني مقصّر وما أطيل للشرح بيد أنّي لم أعتمد إلّا على خبر صحيح ونسب قول صريح

*In the name of God, all and ever merciful.*

Praise God! All praise to Him alone. God bless Muḥammad, our honored leader, the chosen messenger of the most Noble Scripture. Blessings too upon his kin and companions—what virtuous progeny, what noble company! And God prolong the days of our master, the sultan, the king of divine succor, the knowing, the just, the pillar of world and faith![21] Prolong his days in continued glory and felicitous regency for as long as the heads of his spears win the sweet honey of victory and the boughs of his prospering reed pens yield fruit from the nourishing showers of his bounty-filled fingers. The grace he grants and the kindness he bestows oblige my supplication for both him and the Prophet: God prolong the sultan's nobility and God bless the Prophet of mercy! As I pray for the Messenger who restored the True Faith for our hereafter, I pray for the sultan who rights our world in the here and now; God bless our leader, Muḥammad, his descendants and his companions, and God sustain our enjoyment of the favors of the sultan, whose bounty surpasses the succor of rain itself! Blessings! Unmatched gifts! Peace! 1.1

I was asked to elucidate the *Letter* by Abū l-Walīd Ibn Zaydūn, who shall be discussed presently, and to illuminate its intractably difficult allusions, which many a learned savant finds obscure. But—I protested—who am I to climb the heights of that structure, or trespass upon that pasture, or grapple with such armor? I am not of that stature. Am I not just a poet whose natural talent can lay down some lines, and a wordsmith who improvises some prose passages of rhymes? But it was insisted upon: "We should be satisfied with just a partial explication of but a fraction of a share, an explanation of the story howsoever most readily practicable, and since you are a poet, is that so far from your fare?" So, from obedience, I embraced the duty, saying, "Even if the ways of culture escape me, obedience is at least a courtesy," and from meager, ulcerous thoughts, I completed this precis of the explication requested. It is truly brief, and my commentary is nowhere exhaustive; however, what I did write contains 1.2

ولم أخل ترجمة كلّ مذكور من فائدة سارّة ونادرة حارّة وأقوال سديدة وأبيات مشيدة وفقر ما أخطأتها فطنة سعيدة ولم آل في اختيارها جهدًا وما زدت مع صرف الزمان إلّا نقدًا مع تجنّب الإكثار وترك الإجلاب بنظائر الأشعار والتخفيف ممّا لعلّ المباحث تقتضيه من الغبار والله تعالى الموفّق لصواب الإرادة ومعين الخدم على القيام بطاعة السادة وجابر وهنهم بما يتلقّونه من امتثال أوامرهم السادّة بمنّه وكرمه

## ذكر منشئ هذه الرسالة

هو الوزير أبو الوليد أحمد بن عبد الله بن غالب بن زيدون المخزوميّ الأندلسيّ الكاتب الشاعِر المشهور ولد بقرطبة سنة أربع وتسعين وثلاث مائة وكان من أبناء الفقهاء المتعيّنين واشتغل بالأدب وفحص عن نكته ونقّب عن دقائقه إلى أن برع وبلغ من صناعتي النظم والنثر المبلغ الطائل وانقطع إلى أبي الوليد بن جهور أحد ملوك الطوائف المتغلّبين بالأندلس فخفّ عليه وتمكّن من دولته واشتهر ذكره وقدره فاعتمد عليه في السفارة بينه وبين ملوك الأندلس فأعجب القوم وتمنّوا ميله إليهم لبراعته وحسن سيرته واتّفق أنّ ابن جهور نقم عليه أمرًا فحبسه واستعطفه ابن زيدون برسائل عجيبة وقصائد فلم تنجع فهرب واتّصل بعبّاد ابن محمّد صاحب إشبيلية الملقّب بالمعتضد فتلقّاه بالقبول والإكرام وولّاه وزارته وفوّض إليه أمور مملكته وكان جيّد التدبير تامّ الفضل متحبّبًا إلى الناس فصيح المنطق جدًّا ١،٢

حكى ابن بسّام في كتاب الذخيرة عن بعض وزراء إشبيلية يعني كتّابها قال عهدي بأبي الوليد بن زيدون قائمًا على جنازة بعض حرمه والناس يعزّونه على اختلاف طبقاتهم فما سمعته يجيب أحدًا بما أجاب به غيره لسعة ميدانه وحضور جنانه ٢،٢

nothing but correct stories and accurate quotations, and I have provided a biography for each person mentioned in the *Letter*, along with delightful anecdotes, intriguing curiosities, apposite statements, and good poetry. The passages are those that no auspicious perspicacity would fail to mention, and I expended all effort in their selection. And as time wore on, I enhanced my critical inclination, focused on concision, and avoided the diversion of analogous poetic quotation. I refrained from what perhaps a full study would have demanded. But, with His grace and bounty, the Exalted God empowers us to achieve our desired ends, He aids His servants to fulfill the duty they owe their masters, and He resolves their incapacities to discharge the just orders commanded of them.

## The Author of the *Letter*

The author is Ibn Zaydūn, the renowned Andalusian poet, state secretary, and vizier. His full name is Abū l-Walīd Aḥmad ibn ʿAbd Allāh ibn Ghālib ibn Zaydūn of the Makhzūm. Born in Cordoba in 394 [1003] into a family of appointed jurists, he applied himself to learned culture, exploring its repertory and probing its particulars until he shone. His poetry and prose attained vast accomplishment. He joined the court of Abū l-Walīd Ibn Jahwar, one of the Petty Kings among whom Andalusia was parceled, and he met with the king's favor: he was assigned the affairs of state, his renown spread, and the king appointed him as his trusted emissary to the other Petty Kings. Ibn Zaydūn was liked: all craved his attention on account of his brilliance and honest manner, but it so happened that Ibn Jahwar[22] came to harbor a grudge against him for some matter and imprisoned him. Ibn Zaydūn implored clemency with wondrously elegant letters and poems, all to no avail. However, he eventually managed to flee,[23] and a gracious reception greeted him in Seville at the court of its king, al-Muʿtaḍid ʿAbbād ibn Muḥammad. Al-Muʿtaḍid appointed Ibn Zaydūn vizier in charge of the affairs of the kingdom, and he acquitted this task with excellence and virtue. He spoke eloquently and endeared himself to everyone. 2.1

Ibn Bassām reports in *The Treasure Trove* on the authority of one of the "ministers" of Seville (he means one of its state officials) who said: My first acquaintance with Ibn Zaydūn was at a funeral for one of his womenfolk. As people of varying classes each conveyed their condolences, he never once repeated the same expression of appreciation in reply, such was the great expanse of his knowledge and his deftness in plucking from its gardens of eloquence. 2.2

٣،٢ ولم يزل عند عبّاد وعند ابنه المعتمد على الله قائم الجاه وافر الحرمة إلى أن توفّي بإشبيلية سنة ثلاث وستين وأربعمائة

٤،٢ وقد ذكره ابن حيّان وابن بسّام وغيرهما من المؤرّخين وأجروا نبذًا كثيرة من أخباره وفضائله ووقفت على ديوان شعره وكثير من ترسّله ونظمه أمكن عند النقّاد وكان يُسمَّى بحتريّ الغرب لحسن ديباجة لفظه ووضوح معانيه

٥،٢ وأمّا نثره فإنّه أكثر فيه من استعمال أمثال العرب وحلّ أشعار المتقدّمين والمتأخّرين حتّى قِيل إنّ رسائله أشبه بالمنظوم من المنثور وقد دلّ بها على اطّلاع معجب واستحضار معجز وقد اكتفيت منها بسرد هذه الرسالة المشروحة

## ومن شعره

١،٣ قال من قصيدة يخاطب بها ابن جهور أيّام سجنه

مَا جَالَ بَعْدَكِ لَحْظِي فِي سِنَا ٱلْقَمَرِ    إِلَّا ذَكَرْتُكِ ذِكْرَ ٱلْعَيْنِ بِٱلْأَثَرِ
وَلَا ٱسْتَطَلْتُ ذَمَاءَ ٱللَّيْلِ مِنْ أَسَفٍ    إِلَّا عَلَى لَيْلَةٍ سَرَّتْ مَعَ ٱلْقِصَرِ
يَا لَيْتَ ذَاكَ ٱلسَّوَادَ ٱلْجَوْنَ مُتَّصِلٌ    قَدِ ٱسْتَعَارَ سَوَادَ ٱلْقَلْبِ وَٱلْبَصَرِ
جَمَعْتِ مَعْنَى ٱلْهَوَى فِي لَحْظِ طَرْفِكِ لِي    إِنَّ ٱلْحِوَارَ لَمَفْهُومٌ مِنَ ٱلْحَوَرِ

ومنها

لَا يُهْنِئِ ٱلشَّامِتَ ٱلْمُرْتَاحَ نَاظِرُهُ    أَنِّي مُعَنًّى ٱلْأَمَانِي ضَائِعُ ٱلْخَطَرِ
هَلِ ٱلرِّيَاحُ بِنَجْمِ ٱلْأَرْضِ عَاصِفَةٌ    أَمِ ٱلْكُسُوفُ لِغَيْرِ ٱلشَّمْسِ وَٱلْقَمَرِ
إِنْ طَالَ فِي ٱلسِّجْنِ إِيدَاعِي فَلَا عَجَبٌ    قَدْ يُودَعُ ٱلْجَفْنَ حَدُّ ٱلصَّارِمِ ٱلذَّكَرِ
وَإِنْ يُثَبِّطْ أَبَا ٱلْحَزْمِ ٱلرِّضَى قَدَرٌ    عَنْ كَشْفِ ضُرِّي فَلَا عَتْبٌ عَلَى ٱلْقَدَرِ

Until his death in Seville in 463 [1070], Ibn Zaydūn remained in high standing and esteem with ʿAbbād and his son and successor al-Muʿtamid ʿalā Llāh. 2.3

Ibn Ḥayyān, Ibn Bassām, and other historians mention Ibn Zaydūn and relate many stories about his life and virtues. I discovered a copy of Ibn Zaydūn's collected poems and much of his correspondence; critics consider his poetry more accomplished, and he was known as "Buḥturī of the West" for his poetry's beautiful raiment of expression and the clarity of its themes. 2.4

His prose so extensively quotes Arab aphorisms and so dexterously recasts myriad lines of poetry, ancient and modern, that his epistles are said to resemble verse more than prose. They evidence marvelous erudition and phenomenal command of the material, and what I shall relate in the commentary on the *Letter* will stand as ample testament to this. 2.5

## Ibn Zaydūn's Poetry

The following lines are from a poem Ibn Zaydūn composed when he was imprisoned by Ibn Jahwar: 3.1

Nevermore can my glance meet the moon's radiance
without remembrance of you—there's a resemblance.
Never do I yearn for waning nights to linger,
except for that night which was far too short.
If only that night could have lingered longer
by drawing from the deep darkness of my heart and eyes.
All the secrets of love there in your glance—
Beautiful eyes talk without words . . .

(Later on, the poem turns to Ibn Jahwar:)

Let him not rejoice in the repose of a gloat,
to see me hopeless, harassed, hapless.
It's no surprise that I languish imprisoned—
Grass survives a gale:
it's the sun and moon that are eclipsed,
and the sharpest of swords rest in scabbards.
If Fate withholds Ibn Jahwar's grace,[24]
there is no point in blaming Fate.

مَنْ لَمْ أَزَلْ مِنْ تَأَنِّيـهِ[1] عَلَى ثِقَـةٍ    وَلَمْ أَبِتْ مِنْ تَجَنِّيـهِ عَلَى حَـذَرِ

وقال من أبيات في بني جهور ٢،٣

بَنِي جَهْوَرٍ أَحْـرَقْـتُمْ بِجَفَـائِكُمْ    جَنَانِي فَمَا بَالُ ٱلْمَـدَائِحِ تَعْـبَقُ
تَعُـدُّونَنِي كَٱلْعَنْـبَرِ الْوَرْدِ إِنَّمَـا    تَطِيبُ لَكُمْ أَنْفَاسُهُ حِينَ يُحْرَقُ

وقال فيهم من أبيات ٣،٣

إِنَّ ٱلْجَهَاوِرَةَ ٱلْمُـلُوكَ تَبَوَّؤُا    شَرَفًا جَرَى مَعَهُ ٱلسِّمَاكُ جَنِيبَا
فَإِذَا دَعَوْتَ وَلِيدَهُـمْ لِمُـلِمَّـةٍ[2]    لَبَّـاكَ رَقْـرَاقَ ٱلسَّمَاحِ أَرِيبَا
هِمَمٌ تَعَاقَبُهَا ٱلنُّجُومُ وَقَدْ تَلَا    فِي سُؤْدَدٍ مِنْهَا ٱلْعَقِيبُ عَقِيبَا
وَمَحَاسِنٌ تَنْدَى دَقَائِقَ[3] ذِكْرِهَا    فَتَكَادُ تُوهِمُكَ ٱلْمَدِيحَ نَسِيبَا

وقال من قصيدة يمدح بها المعتضد بن عبّاد ٤،٣

أَمَـا فِي نَسِـيمِ ٱلرِّيحِ عَـرْفٌ يُعَـرِّفُ    لَنَا هَلْ لِذَاتِ ٱلْوَقْفِ بِٱلْجِزْعِ مَوْقِفُ
وَلَيْـلَةَ وَافَيْنَـا ٱلْكَثِيبَ لِمَوْعِـدٍ    سُرَى ٱلْأَيْمِ لَمْ يُعْلِمْ بِمَسْرَاهُ مَزْحَفُ

منها

تَهَـادَى أَنَاةَ ٱلْخَطْوِ مُرْتَاعَـةَ ٱلْحَشَا    كَمَا رِيعَ يَعْفُورُ ٱلْفَلَا ٱلْمُـتَشَوِّفُ
فَدَيْتُـكِ أَنَّى زُرْتِ نُورُكِ فَاضِحٌ    وَعَطْـرُكِ نَمَّـامٌ وَحَلْيُـكِ مُـرْجِفُ
هَبِيكِ ٱعْتَسَفْتِ ٱللَّيْلَ[4] وَاشِيكِ هَاجِعٌ    وَفَـرْعُكِ غِـرْبِيبٌ وَلَيْـلُكِ أَغْضَفُ
فَكَيْفَ أَطَقْتِ الْمَشْيَ خَصْرُكِ مُدْمَجٌ    وَرِدْفُـكِ رَجْـرَاجٌ وَقَـدُّكِ أَهْـيَفُ

١ برا: تدانيه؛ إ٣: تأتّيه. ٢ إ٢، إ٣: لعظيمة. ٣ إ٣: رقائق. ٤ إ٢، إ٣: الحي.

I remain hopeful in faith of his clemency,
    and will sleep assured that he'll pardon me.

Some of Ibn Zaydūn's poetry addressed to Ibn Jahwar's clan: 3.2

Sons of Jahwar! Your aloofness burned my heart.
For what then did I praise you so?
You take me as a lump of incense
    that only delights the nose when ablaze.

Lines by Ibn Zaydūn in praise of Ibn Jahwar's family: 3.3

The Jahwar clan—kings one and all,
    their nobility glitters with the brightest stars.
When faced with calamity, one of their children
    rises to your aid, aglow with magnanimity and reason.
Resolute men, they shine with the stars,
    nobility their heirloom and legacy.
Their merits have such beauty
    that praise of them rings like lovers' verse.

One of Ibn Zaydūn's poems praising al-Muʿtaḍid ibn ʿAbbād begins: 3.4

Does the zephyr bear us the sweet scent informing
    that an ivory-bangled one waits at the wadi's bend?[25]
She arrived upon the dune that night at the appointed hour
    like a night-coursing snake; vile scandalmongers saw nothing.

(The poem continues the lovers' encounter:)

She approaches, languid steps but worried breast,
    glancing behind her like an anxious gazelle.
"My life! My love! You made it!
But how did you conceal your glow, your perfume, your jingling jewels?
    You hazarded the night, once the prying gossips slept, but how?
    With your dark locks flowing into the pitch black?
How did you get here?
    Your waist is so slender,
    Your buttocks so heavy, your body so delicate?"

منها

فَمَا قَبْلَ مَنْ أَهْوَى حَوَى ٱلْبَدْرَ هَوْدَجٌ    وَلَا ضَمَّ رِيمَ ٱلْقَصْرِ خِدْرٌ مُسَجَّفُ
وَلَا قَبْلَ عَبَّادٍ حَوَى ٱلْبَحْرَ مَجْلِسٌ    وَلَا حَمَلَ ٱلطَّوْدَ ٱلْمُعَظَّمَ رَفْرَفُ
رَوِيَّتُهُ فِي ٱلْحَادِثِ ٱلْإِدِّ لَحْظَةٌ    وَتَوْقِيعُهُ ٱلْجَالِي دُجَى ٱلْخَطْبِ أَحْرُفُ
عَلَى ٱلسَّيْفِ مِنْ تِلْكَ ٱلصَّرَامَةِ مِيسَمٌ    وَفِي ٱلرَّوْضِ مِنْ تِلْكَ ٱلطَّلَاقَةِ زُخْرُفُ

منها

وَلَمَّا قَضَيْنَا مَا دَعَانَا أَدَاؤُهُ    وَكُلٌّ بِمَا يُرْضِيكَ دَاعٍ فَمُلْحِفُ
رَأَيْنَاكَ فِي أَعْلَى ٱلْمُصَلَّى كَأَنَّمَا    تَطَلَّعَ مِنْ مِحْرَابِ دَاوُدَ يُوسُفُ

وقال من مرثيّة ٥٫٣

يَا مَنْ شَأَى ٱلْأَمْثَالَ مِنْهُ مُهَذَّبٌ    ضُرِبَتْ لَهُ فِي ٱلسُّؤْدَدِ ٱلْأَمْثَالُ
نَقَصَتْ حَيَاتُكَ حِينَ فَضْلُكَ كَامِلٌ    هَلَّا ٱسْتَضَافَ إِلَى ٱلْكَمَالِ كَمَالُ
حَيَّا ٱلْحَيَا مَثْوَاكَ وَٱمْتَدَّتْ عَلَى    ضَاحِي ثَرَاكَ مِنَ ٱلنَّعِيمِ ظِلَالُ
فَلَئِنْ أَذَالَكَ بَعْدَ طُولِ صِيَانَةٍ    قَدَرٌ فَكُلُّ مَصُونَةٍ سَتُذَالُ

وقال في الغزل ٦٫٣

بَيْنِي وَبَيْنَكَ مَا لَوْ شِئْتَ لَمْ يَضِعِ    سِرٌّ إِذَا ذَاعَتِ ٱلْأَسْرَارُ لَمْ يُذَعِ
يَا بَائِعًا حَظَّهُ مِنِّي وَلَوْ بُذِلَتْ    لِيَ ٱلْحَيَاةُ بِحَظِّي مِنْهُ لَمْ أَبِعِ
يَكْفِيكَ أَنَّكَ إِنْ حَمَّلْتَ قَلْبِيَ مَا    لَا تَسْتَطِيعُ قُلُوبُ ٱلنَّاسِ يَسْتَطِعِ
تِهْ أَحْتَمِلْ وَٱسْتَطِلْ أَصْبِرْ وَعِزَّ أَهُنْ    وَوَلِّ أُقْبِلْ وَقُلْ أَسْمَعْ وَمُرْ أُطِعِ

(Further verses:)

My darling is the first full moon to ride in a palanquin,
    the first white gazelle to rest behind curtained quarters;
ʿAbbād is the first to encircle the sea in his assembly,
    the first whose throne is lofty as a mountain.
With a glance, he erases disasters.
With a phrase, he solves grave concerns.
From this lord, the sword learned to cut,
    the garden to bloom.

(Further verses:)

When we pray the obligatory prayer,
    all pray for what pleases him.
When he leads the feast-day prayer, we see
    the apparition of Joseph in David's niche.

An elegy: 3.5

You—unmatched, unprecedented—
    you were the paragon of leadership.
Your virtues perfect, but your lifeblood limited;
    would that it were as perfect as your virtues!
May good rains now nourish your grave,
    and God's grace shade the earth above.
Long had Fate guarded you before it turned perfidious—
    all who feel secure are yet doomed to be trampled.

A love poem: 3.6

Between us is an eternal secret,
    ever hidden, even when all else is known.
They may tempt me with money to relinquish you,
    but I'd rather sell my life.
You can test my heart with the impossible—
    and be sure that it will stay true.
I'll bear your conceit, endure your disdain, submit to your sway,
I'll approach when you avoid; speak and I'll listen; order, I'll obey.

وقال ٧،٣

أَمَّـا رَجَـا قَلْبِي فَأَنْتِ جَمِيعُهُ  يَا لَيْتَنِي أَصْبَحْتُ بَعْضَ رَجَاكِ[1]
يَدْنُو بِوَصْلِكِ حِينَ شَطَّ مَزَارُهُ  وَهْـمٌ أَكَادُ بِهِ أُقَبِّـلُ فَـاكِ

## ذكر سبب إنشاء هذه الرسالة

كان بقرطبة امرأة ظريفة من بنات خلفاء الغرب الأمويّين المنسوبين إلى عبد الرحمن بن المعاوية[2] المعروف بالداخل من بني أميّة تُسمّى ولّادة بنت المستكفي بالله محمّد بن المستظهر بالله عبد الرحمن ابتُذل حجابها بعد قتل أبيها وتغلّب ملوك الطوائف في خبر يطول ثمّ عادت تجلس للشعراء والكتّاب وتعاشرهم وتحاضرهم ويتعشّقها الكبراء منهم وكانت ذات خلق جميل وأدب غضّ ونوادر عجيبة ونظم جيّد ١،٤

فمن نظمها ما كتبت به لابن زيدون وهي راضية عنه ٢،٤

تَـرَقَّبْ إِذَا جَـنَّ ٱلظَّـلَامُ زِيَارَتِي  فَإِنِّي رَأَيْتُ ٱللَّيْـلَ أَكْتَمَ لِلسِّـرِّ
وَبِي مِنْكَ مَا لَوْ كَانَ بِٱلْبَدْرِ لَمْ يُنِرْ  وَبِٱللَّيْلِ لَمْ يُظْلِمْ وَبِٱلنَّجْمِ لَمْ يَسْـرِ

وقولها فيه وهي عليه غضبى ٣،٤

إِنَّ ٱبْنَ زَيْـدُونَ عَلَى فَضْـلِهِ  يَلْهَجُ بِي شَتْمًا وَلَا ذَنْبَ لِي
يَلْحَظُـنِي شَـزْرًا إِذَا جِئْتُـهُ  كَأَنَّمَـا جِئْتُ لِأَخْصِي عَلِي

تعني غلامًا له يُسمّى عليًّا وكان سبب قولها فيه هذا الشعر أنّه اتّهمها بمواصلة أبي عامر بن عبدوس وكان يُلَقَّبُ بالفأر فقال فيه وفيها

---

١ با١: (هواك)؛ إ١ (هواك) وردت في الهامش. ٢ النسخ: الحكم.

More of Ibn Zaydūn's poetry: 3.7

You are the whole of my heart's desire—
if only I could become a part of yours.
Estranged, yet still I feel close, thanks to the vain hope
that imagines me kissing your mouth.

## Why Was the *Letter* Written?

Cordoba was home to a charming woman from the line of the Umayyad caliphs of the West who descended from the Umayyad ʿAbd al-Raḥmān ibn Muʿāwiyah "the Emigré."[26] Her name was Wallādah bint Muḥammad al-Mustakfī bi-llāh ibn ʿAbd al-Raḥmān al-Mustaẓhir bi-llāh. In a series of events that would take too long to detail here, Wallādah's father, the caliph, was killed, the Umayyad caliphate was dismantled by the Petty Kings, and thereafter Wallādah cast off her veil and organized salons with poets and state officials. All the high-ranking attendees tried to woo her since she possessed a beautiful character and impeccable education and could compose marvelous witticisms and excellent poetry. 4.1

Her poetry includes lines written to Ibn Zaydūn when he was in her favor: 4.2

Wait to visit me at the witching hour—
I find darkness keeps secrets best.
What you stir in me would stop
the very cosmos in its tracks.

She also composed poetry against Ibn Zaydūn in anger: 4.3

That Ibn Zaydūn, for all his great virtue,
spreads slander about innocent me!
He eyes my arrival askance,
as if I've come to castrate ʿAlī!

ʿAlī was the name of one of Ibn Zaydūn's servant boys. She composed this poem because Ibn Zaydūn had accused her of granting favor to ʿĀmir ibn ʿAbdūs, he who was nicknamed "the Mouse," and Ibn Zaydūn wrote verses about the pair:

عَيَّرْتُمُونَا بِأَنْ[1] قَدْ صَارَ يَخْلُفُنَا فِيمَنْ نُحِبُّ وَمَا فِي ذَاكَ مِنْ عَارِ
أَكْلٌ شَهِيٌّ أَصَبْنَا مِنْ أَطَايِبِهِ بَعْضًا وَبَعْضًا صَفَحْنَا عَنْهُ لِلْفَارِ

وممّا يُنسب إليها وهو عندي كثير على شعر امرأة ٤،٤

لِحَاظُكُمْ تَجْرَحُنَا فِي ٱلْحَشَى وَلَحْظُنَا يَجْرَحُكُمْ فِي ٱلْخُدُودْ
جُرْحٌ بِجُرْحٍ فَاجْعَلُوا ذَا بِذَا فَمَا ٱلَّذِي أَوْجَبَ جُرْحَ ٱلصُّدُودْ

وممّا يناسبها ما كتبت به على كمّها وقيل على تاجها تقول[2] وهو أنسب شعرها منه ٥،٤

أَنَا وَٱللهِ أَصْلَحُ لِلْمَعَالِي وَأَمْشِي مِشْيَتِي وَأَتِيهُ تِيهَا
وَأُمَكِّنُ عَاشِقِي مِنْ صَفْحِ خَدِّي وَأُعْطِي قُبْلَتِي مَنْ يَشْتَهِيهَا

وكان ابن زيدون شديد الشغف[3] بها والميل إليها وأكثر غزل شعره فيها وفي اسمها ثمّ إنّ الوزير أبا عامر بن عبدوس أيضًا هام بها وكلف بعشرتها وكان قصدهم الظرف والآداب وكانت ولّادة كثيرة العبث به فمن[4] نوادرها الظريفة أنّها مرّت يومًا بدار ابن عبدوس وهو جالس بالباب وحوله جماعة من أصحابه وأمامه بركة تتولّد من مواصي وأقذار فوقفت عليه وقالت أبا عامر ٦،٤

أَنْتَ ٱلْخَصِيبُ وَهٰذِهِ مِصْرُ فَتَدَفَّقَا فَكِلَاكُمَا بَحْرُ

فلم يحر جوابًا ومضت وحُفظت هذه النادرة واشتغل بها الناس وهذا البيت لأبي نواس تمثّلت به ونقلته هذا النقل الحسن من المدح إلى الهجاء

١ إ١: (بمَن) وردت في الهامش. ٢ وقيل . . . تقول: زيادة من بر١. ٣ إ١: الشغب. ٤ وكان . . . فمن: زيادة من إ٦.

You all mocked me when I was supplanted,
  losing the favor of my beloved, but there's no shame:
I had my fill from her delicious offerings,
  and left the scraps for "the Mouse."

Another poem ascribed to Wallādah—which I consider typical of women's poetry—goes as follows: 4.4

Your glances inflict deep wounds;
  ours scratch at your cheek.
A wound for a wound: let's call it even—
  don't add the pain of estrangement.

On the sleeves of her robe (others say on her crown) were inscribed these apposite verses:[27] 4.5

By God, I am best for lofty peaks,
I walk my way and strut as I wish,
I give my lover the side of my cheek,[28]
  and give my kiss to him who desires it.

Ibn Zaydūn was completely infatuated with Wallādah. He composed much amorous verse about her and invoked her name as his poetic beloved, but the Vizier Ibn ʿAbdūs also became smitten, and he yearned for Wallādah's company too. In all this, their intention was to demonstrate their elegance and culture, and Wallādah teased them endlessly. One such witty escapade transpired as she was passing Ibn ʿAbdūs's house. There he was sitting with a group of companions by his gate, before and a pool of wastewater from the laundry and other filth. She stopped and addressed him: "Ibn ʿAbdūs! 4.6

You are the munificent one, and behold here the Nile:
So gush forth, both of you bountiful waters!"

Ibn ʿAbdūs could summon nothing in response, and she walked away. The story spread to everyone's lips. The verse she cited was originally composed as a praise poem by Abū Nuwās;[29] her inversion of its meaning into dispraise was adroit.

وكان كثيرًا ما يخدعها ويبغي التفرّد به وفي ذلك يقول له ابن زيدون ٧،٤

وَغَــرَّكَ مِنْ عَهْــدِ وَلَّادَةٍ  سَرَابٌ تَرَاءَى وَبَرْقٌ وَمَضْ
هِيَ ٱلْمَـاءُ يَأْبَى عَلَى قَابِضٍ  وَيَمْـنَعُ زُبْـدَتَـهُ مَنْ مَخَضْ[1]

أوّل أمرها معه والباعث لابن زيدون على إنشاء هذه الرسالة أنّ ابن عبدوس ٨،٤ لمّا سمع بها أرسل إليها امرأة تستميلها إليه وتعدّد لها محاسنه ومناقبه وترغّبها في التفرّد بمواصلته فكتب ابن زيدون هذه الرسالة جوابًا له عن لسانها تتضمّن هذه الغرائب من سبّه والتهكّم به فبلغت منه كلّمبلغ واشتهر ذكرها في الآفاق وأمسك ابن عبدوس عن التعرّض لولّادة إلى أن انتقل ابن زيدون إلى إشبيلية كما تقدّم في ترجمته وتوفّي بها تغمّدهم الله برحمته هذا معنى ما ذكره ابن حيّان وابن بسّام وغيرهما من المؤرّخين

١ وكان . . . مخض: زيادة من بر١ وإ٦.

Ibn ʿAbdūs was ever endeavoring to trick Wallādah into a private meeting, and Ibn Zaydūn mocked him: 4.7

The promise of Wallādah deceives you—
  a glimmering mirage, a lightning bolt!
She's like liquid running through one's fingers,
  from which no butter can be churned.

What prompted Ibn Zaydūn to write the *Letter* was Wallādah's initial encounter with Ibn ʿAbdūs. When Ibn ʿAbdūs first heard of Wallādah, he aspired to win her and dispatched a woman as a go-between with instructions to extol his virtues and merits with the aim of inspiring Wallādah to devote her favors to him alone. Ibn Zaydūn then wrote the *Letter*, feigning that Wallādah was its author. The *Letter* contains outrageous insults and mockery of the suitor, and it embarrassed him utterly. It spread far and wide, and Ibn ʿAbdūs had to hold back until after Ibn Zaydūn departed for Seville—as noted in our biographical sketch above. Ibn Zaydūn lived there until he died, may God enfold him in His mercy. So the story goes, according to Ibn Ḥayyān, Ibn Bassām, and other historians. 4.8

## ذكر الرسالة وشرح[1] تاريخها كما رسم

٥ أمّا بعد أيّها المصاب بعقله المورّط بجهله البيّن سقطه الفاحش غلطه العاثر في ذيل اغتراره الأعمى عن شمس نهاره الساقط سقوط الذباب على الشراب المتهافت تهافت الفراش في الشهاب فإنّ العجب أكذب ومعرفة المرء نفسه أصوب

وإنّك راسلتني مستهديًا من صلتي ما صفرت منه أيدي أمثالك متصدّيًا من خلّتي لما قرعت دونه أنوف أشكالك مرسلاً خليلتك مرتادة مستعملاً عشيقتك قوّادة كاذبًا نفسك أنّك ستنزل عنها إليّ وتخلف بعدها عليّ

وَلَسْتَ بِأَوَّلِ ذِيْ هِمَّةٍ    دَعَتْهُ لِمَا لَيْسَ بِٱلنَّائِلِ

ولا شكّ أنّها قلتك إذ لم تضنّ بك وملّتك إذ لم تغر عليك فإنّها أعذرت في السفارة لك وما قصّرت في النيابة عنك زاعمة أنّ المروءة لفظ أنت معناه والإنسانية اسم أنت جسمه وهيولاه قاطعة أنّك انفردت بالجمال واستأثرت بالكمال واستعليت في مراتب الجلال واستوليت على محاسن الخلال حتّى خلتَ[2] أنّ يوسف عليه السلام حاسنك فغضضت منه وأنّ امرأة العزيز رأتك فسلت عنه وأنّ قارون أصاب بعض ما كنزت والنطف عثر على فضل ما ركزت

١٫٥ خبر يوسف عليه السلام معروف وجاء في الحديث عن النبيّ صلّى الله عليه وسلّم ذاك الكريم بن الكريم بن الكريم بن الكريم يوسف بن يعقوب بن إسحاق بن إبراهيم وهو أوّل من ضُرب به المثل في الحسن

١ وشرح: زيادة من بر١ ول١.    ٢ إ١، إ٣؛ إ٢: خَيَّلَتْ؛ ل١، ر١، با١: خيلت؛ ت١: خيلتْ ت١: (خِلْتَ) وردت في الهامش.

# The *Letter* and Its Commentary

**This letter is for you—you, stricken of reason, entangled in ignorance, faults glaring, your defects appalling. Tripping in the trailing robes of your own delusion and blind to manifest truth, you descend like a fly diving into syrup or a moth fluttering into immolation. Vanity is but lies, sir: learn instead to know yourself.** 5

**I received your message aspiring to my favor and venturing my affection. What a futile venture and what fruitless humiliation for the likes of you! And to think you made your own wife convey the proposition, sending this darling of yours as a procuress while you fantasized about replacing her with me!**

> **You are not the first whose ambition**
> **calls him to what he cannot obtain.**

**Clearly, she hates you deeply and you bore her stiff. For there she was, selling you effusively with no restraint of dignity, expending all effort, means, and energy to solicit the assignation on your behalf. Her assertions painted you as the epitome of virtue and the embodiment—the essence, even—of humanity; she was unequivocal that you possess unique beauty, monopolize perfection, and sit atop the lofty heights of glory with all good virtues subsumed in your person. With all this, she made it seem that when Joseph (eternal peace be his) vied with your beauty, you outshone him; that when she beheld you, Potiphar's wife forgot about him; and that Korah acquired just a part of your riches, while al-Naṭif discovered the mere castoffs from your treasures.**

Everyone knows the story of Joseph (eternal peace be his).[30] About him, the blessed Prophet reportedly said: "Behold nobility four generations deep: Joseph, son of Jacob, son of Isaac, son of Abraham."[31] Joseph was the first person whose name became a byword for beauty. 5.1

٢،٥ وفي الكتاب العزيز حكاية عن النسوة ﴿فَلَمَّا رَأَيْنَهُۥٓ أَكْبَرْنَهُۥ وَقَطَّعْنَ أَيْدِيَهُنَّ وَقُلْنَ حَٰشَ لِلَّهِ مَا هَٰذَا بَشَرًا إِنْ هَٰذَآ إِلَّا مَلَكٌ كَرِيمٌ﴾ لما ثبت في الطباع أنّ لا شيء أحسن من الملك وقد عاين ذلك قوم لوط في ضيف إبراهيم كما ثبت أيضًا في الطباع أن لا شيء أقبح من الشيطان ولذلك قوله تعالى في صفة جهنّم ﴿طَلْعُهَا كَأَنَّهُۥ رُءُوسُ ٱلشَّيَٰطِينِ﴾ وأرادت النسوة وصف يوسف بالحسن شبّهنه بالملك

٣،٥ وكذلك خبر قارون ويقال إنّه ابن عمّ موسى عليه السلام وهو قارون بن يصهر ابن ناهب[١] وهو أوّل من ضُرب به المثل في كثرة المال وفي الكتاب العزيز ﴿وَءَاتَيْنَٰهُ مِنَ ٱلْكُنُوزِ مَآ إِنَّ مَفَاتِحَهُۥ لَتَنُوٓأُ بِٱلْعُصْبَةِ أُو۟لِى ٱلْقُوَّةِ﴾ أي تنوء بها العصبة تتكلّف بها النهوض وهذا من القلب المستعمل في كلام العرب مثل عرضت الدابّة على الحوض واختلف في مفاتيح فقيل مفاتيح أبواب الخزائن وكانت وقر ستّين بغلاً وهو قول واه وقيل المفاتيح الخزائن نفسها وقد يُسمّى الشيء بما لابسه وقيل المفاتيح العلم والإحاطة لقوله تعالى ﴿وَعِندَهُۥ مَفَاتِحُ ٱلْغَيْبِ لَا يَعْلَمُهَآ إِلَّا هُوَ﴾ والعلم يعنون أنّه أُوتي من الكنوز ما إنّ حفظه والاطّلاع عليه ليثقل على العصبة ﴿أُو۟لِى ٱلْقُوَّةِ﴾ لعجزهم عن حسابها وحفظها

٤،٥ وأمّا النطف فرجل من العرب اختلف القول فيه فبعض من لا يعرف حقيقته يقول إنّه كان يسقي الماء على ظهره فكان ينطف أي يقطر فسُمّي النطف ووجد خبيئة من المال فعظم حاله وبعضهم يقول النطف الرجل المتّهم كأنّ الفقير يجد المال الكثير ويقصد إخفاءه فيُتّهم ويظهر عليه

١ إ ٣؛ وق١: قاهث.

The Holy Qur'an also narrates the bedazzlement of the women whom Potiphar's wife invited to behold Joseph. Exclaiming God's glory, they accidentally cut their hands, crying, «God preserve us! This is no human being but a noble angel!»[32] The women compared Joseph to an angel specifically because, according to nature, nothing can be more beautiful than an angel: Lot's people felt it when they beheld Abraham's angelic guest.[33] In like manner, nothing in nature can be uglier than Satan, hence Almighty God specified him in a simile depicting Hell: «its fruits are like devils' heads.»[34] The women likened Joseph to an angel because they intended to articulate his beauty. 5.2

Korah is also well known. He was the son of Izhar, son of Kohath,[35] and is said to have been the cousin of Moses (eternal peace be his). Korah was the first person whose name become a byword for wealth, and the Holy Qur'an alludes to him thus in the verse: «We had given him such treasures that a band of strong men would have weighed on their keys.»[36] The verse intends that it was the keys that were a heavy load for the band to lift; this is an example of the Arabs' rhetorical style of inverting objects; for example, they might say, "I showed the livestock to the reservoir."[37] There is debate over the precise meaning of "keys" in the verse: some say it literally intends the keys for Korah's storehouse doors, and that the keys alone constituted a heavy load for sixty mules, but this interpretation is unsubstantiated. Others say that the Qur'an uses "keys" figuratively to connote the storehouses themselves (as one may refer to an object via something associated with it); yet others opine that the "keys" refer to knowledge and comprehension, since another Qur'anic verse says: «God holds the keys to the unseen; none knows them but He,»[38] and hence the verse would intend that Korah was given a mass of riches that even a band of strong men would find themselves incapable of tallying and safeguarding. 5.3

Al-Naṭif was an Arab whose identity has been variously described. One narrator who does not know the truth of the matter claims that there was once an individual who distributed water he carried on his back, and because the water would drip, he was called al-Naṭif—that is, "Mr. Trickle"—and one day al-Naṭif discovered a buried hoard of money that transformed him into a man of great means. 5.4

Some others report a different version. They explain that *naṭif* actually means "a person who is suspected"—that is, when a pauper finds a great deal of money, he might try to hide it, and wouldn't be able to keep the secret for long if suspicions of his newfound wealth arose.[39]

٥،٥ والصحيح ما ذكره البلاذريّ في تاريخه أنّه النطف بن خيبريّ[١] بن حنظلة اليربوعيّ كان مقيمًا بالبادية مع بني تميم وكان باذام عامل كسرى على اليمن يحمل ثيابًا من ثياب اليمن وذهبًا ومسكًا وجوهرًا ويرسله إلى كسرى مع خفراء من بني الجعد المراديّين[٢] إلى أن تصير إلى أرض بني تميم فيبعث معها هوذة من يجاوزها أرض بني تميم فلمّا كان في بعض السنين في أرض بني حنظلة تعرّض لها بنو يربوع فأغاروا عليها وقتلوا من بها من العرب وأساورة الفرس وكان النطف مع بني يربوع فعثر على شيء كثير من جملته خرجان مملوءان مناطق ذهبًا محلّاة بالجواهر النفيسة فأباعها متفرّقة وضُرب المثل بما أصابه

٦،٥ وقيل إنّه فرّق على الفقراء من قومه منذ طلعت الشمس إلى أن غابت وفي ذلك يقول بعض ولده

أَبِي ٱلنَّطِفُ ٱلْمُبَارِي ٱلشَّمْسَ إِنِّي   عَرِيقٌ فِي ٱلسَّمَاحَةِ وَٱلْمَعَالِي

٧،٥ ومات النطف حتف أنفه بعد أن جرت بين العرب والفرس حروب طويلة أكثرها بسببه

٦ **وكسرى حمل غاشيتك**

١،٦ كسرى سمة لملوك الفرس وقيصر للروم وخاقان للترك وتبّع لحمير والنجاشي للحبشة

٢،٦ واختلف في نسب الفرس فقيل إنّه فارس بن سام بن نوح وقيل فارس بن أفريدون بن إسحاق عليه السلام وكان في العرب من يفتخر في شعره بفارس على قحطان[٣] والفرس تقول فارس بن كيومرث[٤] وكيومرث عندهم آدم عليه السلام وإنّه أوّل من ملك الفرس وكان منفردًا عن العالم وليس في زمانه ظلم ولا فساد

---

١ إ١: حمري؛ با١: جبيري؛ بر١: جبري.   ٢ إ٣: المرارين؛ إ١ وق١، إ٦، ب: المرادين.   ٣ إ١، بر١، با١: فارس قحطان؛ ل١: فارس وقحطان.   ٤ إ١: كيومرت.

The true account about al-Naṭif, however, is to be found in al-Balādhurī's *History*, where al-Naṭif is identified as the son of Khaybarī ibn Ḥanẓalah al-Yarbūʿī, a Tamīmī denizen of the desert steppe in the days when Bādhām, governor of Yemen for King Khosrow, used to dispatch caravans conveying fine Yemeni textiles, gold, musk, and jewels to Khosrow in Iraq under the protection of the Jaʿd al-Murādī.[40] When the caravan reached the land of the Tamīm, its safe passage was ensured by the tribal leader Hawdhah, who would assign guards,[41] but one year, when the caravan was crossing Ḥanẓalah Tamīm territory, the Tamīm's Yarbūʿ clan attacked and killed the caravan's Arab guards and Persian knights. Al-Naṭif was one of the Yarbūʿ raiders, and he took much plunder, including two saddlebags filled with gilded belts studded with precious jewels. He sold them off one by one, and from the fortune he gained his name became proverbial for wealth. 5.5

It was reported that al-Naṭif sat from dawn to dusk distributing charity among the poor of his kin, and one of his sons memorialized this in a poem: 5.6

> My father, al-Naṭif, rivaled the sun!
> Generosity and virtue run deep in my veins!

Long wars, triggered largely by al-Naṭif's raid, raged between the Arabs and the Persians, but al-Naṭif himself died of natural causes.[42] 5.7

**. . . Khosrow carried your saddlecloths . . .** 6

"Khosrow" was the regnal title for the kings of Persia. The Romans called their emperors "Caesar," the Turks addressed their kings as "Khāqān," Ḥimyar used "Tubbaʿ," and the Ethiopians "Negus." 6.1

There is debate over the lineage of the Persians. Some say they descend from Fāris, the son of Shem, son of Noah; others say Fāris was the son of Feridun, son of Isaac (eternal peace be his); and some Arabs vaunted Fāris over Qaḥṭān in poetry.[43] The Persians themselves, however, claim descent from Fāris son of Gayomard, who, according to them, is Adam (eternal peace be his), who they claim was the first Persian king, and who ruled the whole world at a time when there was neither iniquity nor corruption. But when injustice and iniquity began spreading, the wise men of the age gathered together and declared, 6.2

ففشا البغي والظلم فاجتمع حكماء زمانه وقالوا إنّ صلاح هذا العالم في إقامة ملك يورد الأمور ويصدرها كما أنّ صلاح الجسد بالقلب وإنّ العالم الصغير من جنس العالم الكبير ولا تستقيم أموره إلّا برئيس يدبّره على ما تقتضيه قضايا العقول فصاروا إلى فارس بن كيومرث فقالوا أنت أفضلنا وبقيّة أبينا آدم ولا بدّ من تقديمك علينا وتفويض أمورنا إليك فأخذ عليهم المواثيق والعهود على السمع والطاعة ووضع التاج على رأسه تمييزًا له وهو أوّل من لبسه ثمّ خطب بالسريانيّة وهو لسان آدم ويقال لو تُرك كلّ أحد من بني آدم لتكلّم بالسريانيّة بالطبع فتكلّم بكلام معناه الشكر لله والدعاء والمعونة والهداية ثمّ أقام مدّة طويلة يدبّر الملك وتُوفّي وملك بعده أوشهنج[1] وملوك الفرس تُنسب إليه وللفرس مبالغات عظيمة في وصف كيومرث ومنهم من يزعم أنّه آدم نفسه وأنّه خُلق من الريباس وعاش ألف سنة

٣،٦ وكسرى يقال بفتح الكاف وكسرها وجمع جمعين على غير قياس الأكاسرة والكسور وذلك أنّ حدّ الأفاعلة أن يكون جمعًا لإفعال مثل إسكاف وأساكفة فأمّا الكسور فكأنّه بتقدير حذف الألف مثل جذع وجذوع قال الأعشى

إِنَّهُ كَائِنٌ أَبًا لِلْكُسُورِ

٤،٦ وأظنّ المراد هاهنا كسرى أنوشروان صاحب الإيوان فإنّه أشهر ملوك الفرس وأحسنهم سيرة وأخبارًا وهو ابن قباد[2] بن فيروز وفي أيّامه وُلد النبيّ صلّى الله عليه وسلّم وقال وُلدتُ في زمن الملك العادل يعني كسرى وكان ملكًا جليلًا محسنًا للرعايا تامّ التدبير فتح الأمصار العظيمة في الشرق وأطاعته الملوك وتزوّج ابنة خاقان ملك الترك وقتل مزدك وأصحابه وذلك أنّ أباه قباد قد بايع رجلًا زنديقًا يُسمّى مزدك أحدث مقالات في إباحة الفروج والأموال وقال إنّما الناس فيها سواء وكان

١ إ٣: (هُشنج) وردت في الهامش؛ ت١: (هُوشَنْج) وردت في الهامش. ٢ إ١: قباذ.

"To right this world, we need a king who can institute and regulate order. A body's fitness stems from its heart, and a body is but a microcosm of the workings of the world itself: this world thus cannot proceed soundly without a leader who runs it according to rational laws." Thereupon they approached Fāris son of Gayomard and told him, "You are the most virtuous among us, you carry the vestiges of our father Adam, and so it is you who must lead us and be entrusted with all our affairs." Fāris accepted their pledges and covenants to hear and obey, and he placed a crown upon his head to distinguish himself from them. He was the first king to wear a crown. Fāris then addressed them in Syriac (Syriac was the language of Adam, and it is said that Syriac is every human's innate language) with words to the effect of "Thanks be to God! We make supplications for His succor and right guidance." Fāris reigned for a long time; when he died, Hushang succeeded to the throne, and the kings of Persia trace their lineage from him. The Persians relate grossly exaggerated tales about Gayomard, including claims that he was Adam, that he was created from a rhubarb plant,[44] and that he lived for a thousand years.

In Arabic, the first syllable of the word "Khosrow" (*kisrā*) can be pronounced both with an "a" and with an "i," and the word has two irregular plural forms: *akāsirah* and *kusūr*.[45] They are irregular because the former should only be a plural for words of the *if'āl* pattern (just as the plural of *iskāf* is *asākifah*), and the latter is formed via an irregular dropping of the final "ā" in *kisrā* (a regular example of this plural pattern is *judhū'*, plural of *jidh'*). Al-A'shā's poetry attests the latter plural form:[46] 6.3

He is a father of Khosrows [*kusūr*].

I consider the "Khosrow" in Ibn Zaydūn's *Letter* to be Khosrow Anushirvan, the builder of the Great Vault, for he is the most famous and venerable of all the Persian kings. His father was King Kavad, son of Peroz, and it was during Khosrow's reign that the Prophet (God bless and keep him) was born, as the Prophet reportedly said, "I was born in the days of the Just King" (by whom he meant Khosrow).[47] Khosrow was indeed a sublime king: he was kindly to his subjects and wise in his administration; he conquered great cities in the East, kings obeyed his rule, and he married the daughter of the Turkish Khāqān. Khosrow also executed Mazdak and his followers because of an event that happened during the reign of his father, Kavad. Kavad had been won over[48] by the heretical doctrines concocted by Mazdak—Mazdak neither shed blood nor 6.4

لا يسفك دمًا ولا يأكل اللحم وإنّه دخل يومًا على قباد[1] وعنده زوجته أمّ كسرى وكانت من أحسن النساء وعليها حلي عظيم فأعجبته فقال لقباد إنّي أريد أنكحها لأنّ في صلبي نبيًّا يكون منها فأطاعه قباد[2] لقوله بمقالته فلمّا همّ مزدك بها وكان كسرى صغيرًا فقبّل قدميه وتضرّع له في أن لا يفعل فوهبها له فأوّل ما ملك كسرى بعد موت أبيه قتل مزدك وأصحابه فعظم في عين الفرس وأحبّوه

٥،٦ وسلك سيرة أردشير[3] وتوطّنت مملكته وبنى المباني المشهورة منها السور العظيم على جبل الفتح عند باب الأبواب وأقام الحرس وحسم المادّة من فساد من خلفه ومنها المدينة التي سمّاها باسم روميّة ومنها الإيوان العظيم الباقي الذكر وليس هو المبتدئ ببنيانه وإنّما المبتدئ به سابور وهو الذي رفعه وأتمّه وأتقنه حتّى صار معدودًا من عجائب الدنيا حتّى كان انشقاق مثله من المعجزات النبويّة يُروى أنّ الرشيد هارون أراد هدمه فاستشار يحيى بن خالد البرمكيّ فنهاه وقال في بقائه معجزة باقية فقال الرشيد بل أبيت إلّا تعصّبًا لآبائك يعني الفرس وأمر بهدمه فصرف على هدم شرّافة منه مالاً كثيرًا فكفّ عنه فقال يحيى أرى الآن أن تهدمه لئلّا يتحدّث عنك أنّك عجزت عن هدم ما بناه غيرك فتغافل عن قوله وتركه

٦،٦ وحُكي عن بعض رسل الملوك أنّه دخل الإيوان فرأى فيه اعوجاجًا فسأل عنه فقيل إنّه مكان بيت لعجوز فقيرة سألها الملك بيعه فامتنعت فأرغبها في مال كثير فلم تفعل فتركها وبنى الإيوان على ما هو عليه فقال الرسول هذا الاعوجاج أحسن من الاستواء

١ إ١: قباذ.  ٢ إ١: قباذ.  ٣ بر١ وإ٣ وت١: ازدشير.

ate meat, and advocated the free sharing of wives and property, as he used to proclaim: "Everything for all." One day, Mazdak entered the presence of Kavad, whose wife, the most beautiful of women and the mother of Khosrow, was in attendance, wearing fabulous jewelry. Mazdak was much aroused and told the king, "I desire your wife, for in my loins there is a prophet to whom she will give birth." Kavad consented because he followed Mazdak's creed, and as Mazdak rose to take the queen, Khosrow (who was just a boy at the time) kissed his father's feet, imploring him not to acquiesce, yet Kavad presented the queen to Mazdak regardless. When Khosrow ascended the throne upon his father's death, his very first order was to execute Mazdak and his followers, and for this he won the love of the Persians, who thenceforth held him in great esteem.

Khosrow emulated the kingly traditions of Ardashir:[49] He settled his realm 6.5
and constructed famous edifices, such as the Great Wall of the Caucasus[50] astride the Caspian Gates, and he guarded the borders and secured the realm against the wickedness of those beyond the wall. He also built a city he named Rūmiyyah,[51] and he erected the enduringly renowned Great Vault. Khosrow did not initiate the Vault's construction—it was started by Shapur—but Khosrow completed it to a level of perfection that rendered it a wonder of the world. The fact that something as grand as the Great Vault could be cleft down its middle also testifies to the Prophet's miracles.[52] It is reported that the Caliph Hārūn al-Rashīd wished to demolish the Great Vault, but when he consulted his minister, Yaḥyā ibn Khālid al-Barmakī, Yaḥyā dissuaded him, contending: "Preserving it preserves a miracle." Al-Rashīd retorted, "Nonsense! You only dissuade me because you are partisan to your ancestors" (he meant the Persians), and al-Rashīd ordered the Vault's demolition. He spent a great sum of money, but succeeded only in demolishing one gallery, and so he gave up, whereupon Yaḥyā advised him: "Now I think you should finish the job—otherwise people will say that you were powerless to destroy what someone else had built!" The caliph ignored this counsel and left the Great Vault standing.

Once, a royal ambassador entered the Great Vault and noticed part of its 6.6
wall was crooked. When he asked about it, he was told that the bend marked the location where a poor old woman's house had been. Khosrow had sought to buy her property, but she refused, even after he presented her with a considerable sum of money, so he let her stay, building the Great Vault around her house, with the resultant curve. The ambassador remarked, "In this case, the crooked has the greater rectitude!"

٧،٦ ويُروى أنّ العجوز بعد بناء الإيوان نزلت للملك عن البيت وقالت له إنّما أردت بامتناعي أوّلاً أن يتحدّث الناس بعدلك وتكون لك هذه المأثرة الظاهرة ثمّ صنع كسرى في الإيوان سلسلة عظيمة ذات أجراس وجعل لها طرفًا خارج القبّة وأمر مناديه من كان مظلومًا فليحرّك السلسلة ليعلم به الملك فيزيل ظلامته قال العسكريّ وهذا الأصل في قول الناس حرّك فلان على فلان السلسلة إذا وشى به

٨،٦ وحكي أنّه كان جالسًا بالإيوان وإذا بحيّة قد دبّت تريد عشّ حمامة في بعض سقوف الإيوان لتأكل فراخها فرمى الحيّة بسهم أو ببندقة فقتلها وقال هكذا نفعل بعدوّ من استجار بنا فلمّا كان بعد أيّام جاءت الحمامة بحبّ في منقارها فألقته إليه فأخذه وقال ازرعوه فنبت ريحانًا لم يكن يعرفه فقال نعم ما كافأتنا به الحمامة نسأل الله الذي ألهمها أن يلهمنا الإحسان إلى رعيّته والشكر على نعمته

٩،٦ وخُصّ كسرى هذا بأشياء لم تكن لغيره من الملوك على ما ذكر كثير من الرواة منها القطعة الياقوت المسمّاة لسان الثور تضيء كالسراج بالليل والفلهيد[١] المغنّي واضع العود الخراسانيّ من اثني عشر وترًا كلّ من ضرب به جُرح[٢] إلّا هو والفيل الأبيض النهاية في الطول لركوبه طوله اثنا عشر ذراعًا وكان يعمل له كلّ يوم مع طعامه مهر من الخيل وعناق زرقاء مغذّاة بألبان النعاج يُذبحان بسكين من الذهب ويُسجر التنّور بالعود ويُسمط ما يسمط بالخمر المغلّي ويُطلى بالمسك والملح ويُعلّق في سفّود من ذهب فإذا برد حُمل على خوان من الذهب فيُقدّم إليه فيأكل أكثره ويتحف بالبقيّة من أحبّ من ندمائه ويُكسر التنّور ويُجدّد كلّ يوم مثله واجتمع على بابه سبعون ملكًا

١٠،٦ وله سيرة تشتمل على حكايات حسنة منها أنّ عاملاً له على ناحية كتب إليه يعلّمه بجودة الريع ويستأذنه في الزيادة على الرسوم فأمسك عن إجابته فعاوده العامل في ذلك فكتب إليه قد كان في ترك إجابتك عن كتابك ما حسبتك تنزجر به

١ إ١: فلهند؛ غ: الفلهبد؛ بر١، إ٣، با١، ل٢، ت١: الفلهيد. ٢ إ١: خرج؛ ق٣: جرح.

It is also reported that once the Great Vault was completed, the old woman gave her property to Khosrow, explaining, "I refused to sell it, first, because I wanted people to speak of your justice, and second, so that this would remain a monument to your virtue." Khosrow then ordered a colossal chain with bells attached, with one end hanging outside the Great Vault's dome. He instructed his herald to announce that anyone suffering injustice should pull the chain to alert Khosrow, who would thereupon right the petitioner's wrong.[53] Al-ʿAskarī says that this is the origin of the popular expression: "To pull the chain on someone"—that is, to make accusations about him. 6.7

It is also reported that once, when Khosrow was sitting under the Great Vault, he saw a snake slithering upward to devour chicks in a dove's nest in one of the Vault's ceilings. Khosrow shot the snake dead with an arrow (some say with a pellet), declaring, "This is how we deal with the foe of those under our protection!" A few days later, the dove flew down with seeds in its beak and placed them before Khosrow. He took the seeds and ordered them planted, and up sprouted a variety of aromatic plant he had never seen before. Khosrow exclaimed, "How finely this dove has recompensed us! We ask God Who inspired her to also inspire us to beneficence toward His subjects and to be grateful for His favor." 6.8

Many narrators also distinguish Khosrow Anushirvan for his unique possessions, the like of which no other kings have ever owned. Among them is his ruby, "the Ox's Tongue," which shone like a lamp at night; al-Falhīd, his singing boy, who made a twelve-string Khurasanian oud that injured anyone else who tried to play it;[54] and his white riding elephant, which towered twelve cubits high. Every day, a dish was prepared for Khosrow from the meat of a colt and a gray she-goat kid[55] reared on goat milk, both slaughtered with a golden knife, cooked in a fragrant wood oven, prepared with boiling wine sauce, coated with musk and salt, and fitted on a golden skewer. When the meat cooled, it was placed on a golden tray before the king, and after he ate his fill, he offered the remainders to his favored retinue. Each day, the oven was smashed, and a new one constructed for the morrow. At Khosrow's gate, seventy kings gathered in submission. 6.9

Fine anecdotes about Khosrow's kingship abound. For example, one of his district administrators wrote to him with news of his region's bountiful agricultural yield and requested permission to increase taxes. Khosrow did not respond, and the administrator wrote again. This time, Khosrow 6.10

عن تكلّف ما لم تؤمر به فإذ قد أبيت إلّا تماديًا في سوء الأدب فاقطع إحدى أذنيك واكفف عمّا ليس من شأنك فقطع العامل أذنه وسكت عن ذلك الأمر

١١،٦ ومنها أنّ رجلاً على عهده كان يقول من يشتري ثلاث كلمات بألف دينار فيطنز[١] منه إلى أن اتّصل بكسرى فأحضره وسأله عنها فقال ليس في الناس كلّهم خير فقال كسرى هذا صحيح ثمّ ماذا قال ولا بدّ منهم فقال صدقت ثمّ ماذا قال فألبسهم على قدر ذلك فقال كسرى قد استوجبت المال فخذه قال لا حاجة لي به ولكن إنّما أردت أن أدري من يشتري الحكمة بالمال

١٢،٦ ويُروى أنّه أوّل من جعل لندمائه إشارة ينصرفون بها من مجلسه إذا أراد وذلك أنّه كان يمدّ رجله فيعرفون أنّه يريد قيامهم فينصرفون وتبعه الملوك فكان فيروز الأصغر يعرك عينيه وكان بهرام يرفع رأسه إلى السماء وكان في الإسلام معاوية يقول العزّة لله وعبد الملك بن مروان يلقي المخصرة من يده وعمر بن عبد العزيز يدعو وحُدّث بهذا الحديث عند بعض البخلاء الأملياء وسُئل ما إشارته فقال إذا قلت يا غلام هات الطعام

١٣،٦ ومن كلامه القلوب تحتاج إلى أقواتها من الحكمة كما تحتاج الأبدان إلى أقواتها من الغذاء

١٤،٦ ووقّع في قصّة مرافع أنّ الملوك إذا دبّرت ملكها بمال رعيّتها كان بمنزلة من يعمّر سطح بيته بما ينقضه من أساسه

١٥،٦ وكتب باللؤلؤ على مائدة من الذهب ليهنئه طعام من أكله من حلّه وعاد على ذوي الحاجة بفضله ما أكلته وأنت تشتهيه فقد أكلته وما أكلته وأنت لا تشتهيه فقد أكلك

١٦،٦ وقيل له ما أعظم الكنوز قدرًا وأنفعها عند الحاجة إليه فقال معروف أودعته عند الأحرار وعلم أورثته الأعقاب

١٧،٦ وقال احذروا صولة الكريم إذا جاع واللئيم إذا شبع

---

١ إ١، إ٣: فتطيّر.

replied: "We considered that our silence to your first letter would have restrained you from acting beyond the remit of your duties. It is now clear that you insist on acting in an ill-mannered way, so cut off one of your ears and keep to your own affairs!" The administrator did sever his ear and never raised the matter again.

There is also a story about a man in Khosrow's time who went around asking, "Who will pay a thousand dinars for three sayings?" Everyone mocked him, but when the news reached Khosrow, he summoned the man and bade him pronounce them. The man began: "People are no good." "That's true," replied Khosrow. "What's the next saying?" "You can't live without them." "Also true. So then what?" "Deal with them on that basis." Khosrow responded, "You have earned the money. Take it." But the man replied, "I have no need for it. I only wanted to know who is willing to spend money on wisdom." 6.11

Reportedly, Khosrow was the first king who devised a signal to indicate to his retinue that he wished them to retire from his presence: Khosrow would stretch his leg, and thereupon his courtiers knew it was time to leave. Other kings copied this practice: Peroz the Younger would rub his eyes, and Bahram would lift his gaze up to the sky.[56] In Islamic times, Muʿāwiyah's signal was to say, "Power is God's," ʿAbd al-Malik ibn Marwān would drop his scepter, and ʿUmar ibn ʿAbd al-ʿAzīz would supplicate to God. These signs were once discussed in the presence of a miser who was very wealthy, and he was asked if he too had a signal to indicate to his guests that they should leave. He did: his signal was to order his servant: "Bring in the food!" 6.12

Khosrow's wise words: "Hearts need wisdom just as bodies need food." 6.13

Khosrow would affix the following statement on his replies to petitions:[57] "A king who manages his kingdom by extracting the wealth of his subjects is like a man who digs up his house's foundations for materials to patch the roof." 6.14

Khosrow's golden table bore the following text inscribed in pearl: "Blessed is he who eats reasonably and gives bountifully. He who eats when hungry eats well, but he who stuffs himself will be consumed." 6.15

Khosrow was once asked, "What is the greatest and most useful of treasures?" He replied, "A good deed you render to a nobleman, and knowledge you bequeath to your successors." 6.16

Khosrow's wise words: "Beware the force of a hungry nobleman, and a sated commoner!" 6.17

## وقيصر رعى ماشيتك ٧

قيصر سمة لملوك الروم وسُمّوا الروم لأنّهم ينتسبون إلى روم بن العيص بن إسحاق عليهم السلام وقيل لأنّهم ينتسبون إلى روميّة والصحيح الأوّل لأنّ رومية بُنيت بعد ظهورهم بكثير وكان يقال لها رماس[1] فلمّا سكنوها نُسبت إليهم ١،٧

قال ابن الكلبيّ ولد إسحاق ثلاثين ولدًا منهم الروم وكان أصفر اللون فقيل لولده بنو الأصفر وقيل غارت عليهم الحبشة فولدن[2] لهم بنات أخذن من بياض الروم وسواد الحبشة فكنّ صفرًا لعسًا فنُسبوا إليهنّ ٢،٧

وأوّل من سمّي منهم قيصر بن أنطرطس واسمه قيشر لأنّ أمّه كانت حاملًا به فتعسّرت ولادتها فشقّ بطنها وخرج وكان يفتخر على الناس بأنّ النساء لم تلده وسمّي قيشر ثمّ قيل قيصر وصار هذا اللقب سمة لملوك الروم بعده وكان جبّارًا عاتيًا ٣،٧

وهو أوّل من جمع مملكة الروم واليونان وذلك أنّ أباه أنطرطس لمّا بلغه أنّه لم يبق من ملوك اليونان غير امرأة تسمّى قلاوقطره[3] أرسل يخطبها وكان قد ملك طرفًا من بلادهم حين انقرضوا فعلمت أنّها مغلوبة معه فأجابته ثم قدّمت له طعامًا مسمومًا عند دخوله إليها وأكلت معه فماتا وكان ابنه مع الجيش فسمع بموته فاستولى على بلاد الروم واليونان وبنى قيساريّة الروم وقيل قيساريّة الشام وأقام في الملك خمسين سنة ٤،٧

ومن ظريف أخباره أنّه كان إذا أراد أن يستشير أحدًا من عقلاء دولته أرسل إليه نفقة سنة ليتوفّر ذهنه على الرأي ٥،٧

من بعده اختلفت الروم فتقاسموا البلدان والأطراف إلى ظهور الإسلام وقيصر هذا أعظم ملوكهم ٦،٧

---

١ وكان . . . رماس: زيادة من بر١ وإ٣. ٢ إ١: ولد. ٣ بر١: فلاربطرة؛ ل١: فلاوفطرة؛ إ٣ ول٢: فلارنطره؛ ق٣: فلارنطيره؛ با١ وإ٢: قلاوقطر؛ ق١: ولابظرة؛ ب: جلاانظره.

**. . . Caesar watched your flocks.** 7

"Caesar" is a title of the Roman kings. "Romans" were so named because they descend from Rūm, son of Esau, son of Isaac (eternal peace be theirs). While some claim that the Romans derived their name from the city of Rome, the first opinion is right, given that Rome, then called Rumās, was only built long after the Romans appeared in history; the city took its name from them.[58] 7.1

Ibn al-Kalbī reports that Isaac had thirty sons, one of whom was named al-Rūm. Al-Rūm's skin was pallid, and hence his descendants were known as "the Yellow Folk."[59] Alternatively, it is said that after an Ethiopian invasion, girls were born with a tawny dark-yellow complexion acquired from inheriting the Romans' whiteness and the Ethiopians' blackness, and the Romans descended from them. 7.2

The first Roman to be dubbed "Caesar" was Qayshar, son of Antony.[60] The story goes that his mother experienced complications in labor, so they cut open her belly to extract the baby. Afterward, he would boast that he was not of woman born, and so they named him "Qayshar," which was later pronounced "Qayṣar" (Caesar), and it became the Romans' regnal title after his death. He was a haughty tyrant. 7.3

Caesar was the first to rule Rome and Greece together. This transpired as follows: Caesar's father, Antony, learned that the only surviving Greek ruler was a queen, Cleopatra, and so he wrote to her soliciting marriage, as he had already taken control of parts of Greek territory following the extinction of their other kingly lines. She realized that resistance was futile and consented, but when he took her as his wife, she presented him with poisoned food from which they both ate, and both died together. Caesar was with the army at the time, and upon hearing the news of his father's death, he took control of both Roman and Greek lands. 7.4

Caesar's reign continued for fifty years, and he was the founder of the town known as Roman (or Syrian) Caesarea.

Among the fine stories about Caesar is that when he wished to consult one of his realm's wise men, he would disburse one whole year's stipend to him, so that he could focus wholly on the matter to hand. 7.5

After Caesar died, the Romans squabbled, and their lands and territories became divided until the rise of Islam. This first Caesar was their mightiest king. 7.6

٧.٧ ومن كلامه ما الحيلة فيما أعيى إلّا الكفّ عنه ولا الرأي فيما لا ينال إلّا اليأس منه

## ٨ والإسكندر قتل دارا في طاعتك

١.٨ هو الإسكندر بن قبليس[١] اليونانيّ

٢.٨ واختلف في أصل اليونان فنسبه ابن الكلبيّ إلى إسحاق وقال يعقوب الكنديّ يونان أخو قحطان من العرب من ولد عابر خرج من اليمن فنزل ديار المغرب فأقام بها واستعجم لسانه وتكلّم بلغة من هناك من الروم

٣.٨ وقال الرقاشيّ وهو الأشهر إنّ يونان بن يافث بن نوح وليس من العرب ولا من الروم وإنّما جاور الروم على ساحل البحر الروميّ وكان وسيمًا حسن العقل كبير الهمّة فأقام هناك حتّى كثر ولده فخرج يطلب موضعًا يسكنه فانتهى إلى مدينة بالمغرب يقال لها إثينة[٢] فبنى بها قصورًا وأقام وكثر نسله ثمّ مات فاستولى ولده على بلاد الغرب من ناحية إفرنجة والصقالبة ومن جاورهم ولمّا ظهر بخت نصّر على مصر دخل المغرب ووصل إلى بلاد اليونان وقرّر عليهم أن يؤدّوا الخراج إلى بلاد فارس واستقرّ ذلك إلى أيّام الإسكندر

٤.٨ فأمّا الإسكندر فقيل ابن الصعب[٣] وقيل ابن قبليس[٤] وسُمّي ذا القرنين تشبّهًا بذي القرنين المذكور في الكتاب العزيز لبلوغ ملكه قرني الشمس من المشرق والمغرب وهو صاحب أرسطاطاليس الحكيم كان أبوه قد أسلمه إليه فأقام عنده خمس سنين يتعلّم منه الأدب والحكمة فنال منه ما لم ينل أحد من تلامذته ومرض أبوه فخاف على الملك فاستردّه وعهد إليه

٥.٨ وأمّا دارا فهو دارا الأصغر بن دارا الأكبر بن أردشير أحد ملوك الفرس العظماء المشهورين كانت له قطيعة على أبي الإسكندر في كلّ سنة ألف بيضة من الذهب

١ إ٣: فيلقوس؛ با١: قليس؛ بر١: فيلبس. ٢ إ١: قنينة؛ بر١، با١، ل١، ل٢، ق١: اقنينة؛ ب: افيننة؛ إ٣: اقينية.
٣ ل١؛ إ٣؛ ق٣: المصعب. ٤ ل٢: قِبُلتس؛ ب: قيليس؛ بر١: فيلس؛ ق٢: فيلسوف؛ ق٣، إ٢: فيلفوس.

One of Caesar's wise sayings: "When all attempts fail, the only strategy is to quit. Pondering the unattainable yields only despair." 7.7

**Alexander executed Darius in obedience to you . . .** 8

By "Alexander," Ibn Zaydūn intended Alexander the Great, son of Philip the Grecian. 8.1

Opinions differ over the Greeks' origins. Whereas Ibn al-Kalbī traces their lineage to Yūnān, a descendant of Isaac, Yaʿqūb al-Kindī claims that Yūnān was an Arab, brother of Qaḥṭān and one of the sons of ʿĀbir.[61] According to al-Kindī, Yūnān emigrated from Yemen to the West, where he settled and lost the ability to speak Arabic as he adopted the region's Roman language. 8.2

The established opinion, however, is that of al-Raqāshī: he identifies Yūnān as a handsome, clever, and resolute son of Japheth, son of Noah:[62] neither Arab nor Roman, he merely lived in the vicinity of the Romans on the Mediterranean shore, where he sired many children and then emigrated in search of a new home.[63] Yūnān reached a city in the west called Athens, where he built palaces,[64] and there his offspring multiplied, and in the years after Yūnān's death they expanded across the Western lands along the borders of the Franks and the Slavs. Later, when Nebuchadnezzar conquered Egypt, he marched west, reached the Greek realm, and levied tribute upon them, which they paid to the kings of Persia until the reign of Alexander. 8.3

Some say Alexander's father was named al-Ṣaʿb; others attest he was Philip. Alexander was nicknamed "Two-Horned," for his similarity to the "Two-Horned" mentioned in the Qur'an,[65] because his realm encompassed the whole arc of the sun from east to west. Alexander was the companion of the sage Aristotle: Alexander's father had sent him to Aristotle, where he spent five years learning ethics and wisdom. Alexander excelled above all the other students, but when his father became ill and feared for the future of the realm, he recalled Alexander to succeed him as king. 8.4

Darius the Younger, son of Darius the Elder, son of Ardashir, was one of the great Persian kings. He enjoyed the annual right of tribute from Alexander's father, as all previous Greek kings had paid, of one thousand golden eggs, each weighing one thousand dinars.[66] When Alexander ascended the throne, 8.5

في كلّ بيضة ألف مثقال على عادة آبائهم فلمّا ملك الإسكندر أخّر إرسال القطيعة فكتب إليه دارا يتهدّده وبعث إليه بكرّة وصولجان وخرقة فيها سمسم وقال

> أنت صبيّ فالعب بهذه الكرّة فإن أدّيت الإتاوة وإلّا بعثت إليك بجنود عدد هذا السمسم

فكتب إليه الإسكندر

> أمّا بعد فقد تيمّنت بالكرّة والصولجان فإنّ الدنيا مثل الكرّة وسألعب بها وأضيف ملكك إلى ملكي وأمّا السمسم فقد تيمّنت أيضًا به لأنّه بعيد عن الحرافة والمرارة وأمّا الدجاجة التي كانت تبيض ذلك البيض فقد ذبحتها وأكلت لحمها

٦،٨ فغضب دارا وسار إليه بجموعه وسار الإسكندر بجموعه والتقيا على نصيبين الجزيرة فلمّا همّ دارا باللقاء بعث إليه الإسكندر يقول له

> أيّها الملك لا تفعل فإنّ دماء الملوك لا تحسن إراقتها وهدم البيوت القديمة غير محمود والبغي ذميم وأصحابك قد ملّوك وكرهوك لسوء سيرتك فارجع فإنّك تحمد قولي

٧،٨ فلم يلتفت دارا وأقاما يتحاربان مدّة ثمّ إنّ الإسكندر دبّر حيلة وهو أنّه لمّا وقع الملل بين الفريقين برز منادي الإسكندر وقال يا معشر الفرس قد علمتم ما كان من مكاتبتكم لنا ومكاتبتنا لكم من الأمانات وقد طال القتال فمن كان منكم على العهد فليعتزل وله الوفاء فاتّهمت الفرس بعضها بعضًا واضطربوا وكان من أسباب خذلان دارا ثمّ وثب على دارا رجلان من أصحابه فطعناه من خلفه فوقع وكان الإسكندر نادى من ظفر بدارا فلا يقتله وجاء الرجلان إلى الإسكندر فقالا قد قُتل دارا فجاء إليه ونزل عن فرسه وقعد عند رأسه وبه رمق فقال والله ما هممت بقتلك ولقد نهيت عنه ويعزّ عليّ مصابك فسلني حوائجك فقال تقتل

he delayed payment, and Darius responded with a threat, sending a ball and mallet, some sesame seeds bound in a rag, and a letter:

> "You are a child, so play with this ball and send the tribute; otherwise, I will dispatch against you an army as numerous as these sesame seeds."

Alexander responded:

> "I take the ball and mallet as a good omen since the world is like a ball, and I shall make sport of it, and add your kingdom to mine. I also read a good omen in the sesame seeds since these are far from pungent or bitter to taste. And, moreover, I have slaughtered the chicken that laid those golden eggs, and ate her."

Darius was furious and marched his forces against Alexander. Alexander 8.6
mobilized his armies too, and they met between the upper Tigris and Euphrates at Nisibis. As Darius prepared to attack, Alexander wrote to him:

> "King! Attack not: royal blood ought not be spilled, it is a shame for ancient houses to be destroyed, and injustice is reprehensible. Your followers are weary of you and despise you for your poor leadership, so retreat now and you will appreciate my advice."

Darius paid no heed, and the fighting commenced. On it raged until Alexan- 8.7
der hatched a plot: When it appeared that both sides were exhausted, Alexander's herald stepped forth and proclaimed, "Persians! You know that we have written to each other about a truce. The fighting has been long now: those of you who agreed to that pact may step away, and we will honor it." At this, the Persians began accusing each other and dissent arose. The betrayal of Darius had begun. Then two of his retainers assailed him, stabbing him in the back. Darius fell. Alexander had previously announced, "Whoever apprehends Darius must not kill him!" The two men approached Alexander and reported, "Darius is dead." Alexander rushed to Darius's side, dismounted, and kneeled at his head as he was breathing his last. Alexander told him, "By God, I had no intention to kill you—I actually forbade it, and your suffering grieves me: ask what you wish done!" Darius responded, "Execute the two men who killed me, for I had been beneficent to them, and you must also marry my daughter Roxana." Alexander replied, "I hear and obey!" He summoned the two men

فلانًا وفلانًا اللذين قتلاني فإنّي كنت محسنًا إليهما وتتزوّج ابنتي روسيك[1] فقال سمعًا وطاعة وأحضر الرجلين فقتلهما وقال هذا جزاء من يجترئ على ملكه وتفرّق ملك فارس ثمّ سار الإسكندر إلى بابل وجلس على سرير دارا واستولى على خزائنه وجواهره وسلاحه وتزوّج ابنته ويقال إنّها كانت زوجة دارا وهي ابنته وكانت من أحسن النساء ويقال إنّ الإسكندر لم يجتمع بها وقال أخشى أن أكون غلبت دارا وتغلبني ابنته

٨،٨ ولمّا استولى على ملك فارس عرض جيشه وجيش الفرس فكان ألف ألف أو أكثر وشرع في هدم بيوت النيران وقتل الموابذة وكتب إلى معلّمه أرسطاطاليس يستشيره في من بقي من عظماء الفرس هذا الكتاب

أمّا بعد فإنّ دوائر الأسباب ومواقع الفلك وإن كانت أسعدتنا بالأمور التي أصبح لنا بها الناس دائنين فإنّا مضطرّون إلى حكمتك غير جاحدين فضلك والاجتباء[2] لرأيك لما بلونا من جداء[3] ذلك علينا وذقنا من جنى منفعتك حتّى صار ذلك بتجرّعه فينا وترشيحه بعقولنا كالغذاء لنا فما ننفكّ نعوّل عليه ونستمدّ منه استمداد الجداول من البحار وقوّة الأشكال بالأشكال وقد كان ممّا سبق إلينا من النصر ما يعجز الشكر عن الإنعام به وكان من ذلك أنّا جاوزنا أرض الجزيرة وبابل إلى أرض فارس وقد تلقّانا نفران منهم بقتل ملكهم طلبًا للحظوة عندنا فأمرنا بصلبهما لجرأتهما وقلّة وفائهما ثمّ أمرنا بجميع من هنالك من أبناء ملوكهم وذوي الشرف منهم فرأينا رجالاً عظيمةً أجسامهم وأحلامهم يدلّ ما ظهر من ورائهم على أنّ وراءه من قوّة بأسهم ما لم يكن معه سبيل إلى غلبتهم لولا أنّ القضاء أدالنا[4] منهم ولم نر بعيدًا من الرأي أن نستأصل شأفتهم ونلحقهم بمن مضى من

١ ل١: روسك؛ ق١، إ٣، إ٤، ت١: روشنك؛ ب: روسنك؛ بر١: ورسك؛ ق٣: روشيك. ٢ ب وإ٣ وبر١: الاحتياج؛ ق٣، إ٤: الاجتناء. ٣ بر١: جدوا. ٤ إ١: أداك.

and executed them, declaring, "Behold the fate of men who dare to oppose their king!" The Persian realm disintegrated, and Alexander entered Babylon and sat on Darius's throne, seized his treasuries, jewels, and armaments, and married his daughter. It is said that Roxana was both daughter and wife of Darius and was one of the most beautiful of women.[67] It is also told that Alexander did not lie with her, remarking, "Though I conquered Darius, I fear his daughter will conquer me!"

When Alexander settled on the throne of Persia, he reviewed his own army 8.8
alongside that of the Persians, which numbered a million or more. Alexander set to destroying their fire temples and executing their priests, but he wrote to his teacher Aristotle for advice on how the Persian nobility should fare:

> The celestial bodies and whims of Fortune have favored us in bending the world into our dominion, yet, nonetheless, we have urgent need of your good council. Fully acknowledging your preeminence, we are obligated to your opinion, for often has our experience affirmed your worth, and often have we savored the fruits of your attention. Sipping upon your thoughts is the nourishment of our minds, and our dependence upon you shall never cease; as canals feed from great rivers, or as forms derive potential from others,[68] we ask for your help.
>
> We have secured victories for which no amount of thanks could constitute sufficient gratitude. We crossed Mesopotamia and Babylon and entered Persia. We encountered two individuals who had committed regicide in hope of winning favor with us, and we crucified them for their audacity and perfidy. Then we summoned all their princes and noblemen and beheld a host whose might in body and spirit disclosed that behind them must lie a phenomenal power that we could never have overcome had not Fate ordained a good turn for us. We consider it not imprudent therefore to extirpate their strength and send them all to meet their ancestors, in order that our hearts can rest assured, secure from the risk of their future retrogression. But we shall not hasten to murder without first appealing to your counsel. Send

أسلافهم لتسكن بذلك القلوبُ إلى الأمن من جرائرهم ورأينا أن لا نعجّل ببادية الرأي في قتلهم دون الاستظهار بمشورتك فيهم فارفع إلينا رأيك فيما استشرناك بعد صحّته عندك وتقلبيه على نظرك على عادة آرائك المسعفة وسلام أهل السلام فليكن عليك وعلينا

فكتب إليه أرسطاطاليس ٩،٨

إلى الإسكندر المؤيّد المهدى له من الظفر من أصغر خوله أرسطو أمّا بعد فقد تقرّر عندي من مقدّمات فضل الملك ويمن نقيبته وبروز شأوه ما وقع في فكري أيّام كنت أؤدّي إليه من تعليمي إيّاه ما أصبحت قاضيًا على نفسي بالحاجة إلى تعلّمه منه وقد ورد كتاب الملك بما رسم لي فيه وأنا فيما أشير به على الملك حدّ الطاقة معه كالعدم مع الوجود وغير ممتنع من إجابته فأقول إنّ لكلّ تربة لا محالة قسمًا من كلّ فضيلة وإنّ لفارس قسمتها من النجدة والقوّة وإنّك إن تقتل أشرافهم ترث سفلتهم منازل عليتهم ولم تبتل الملوك قطّ ببلاء أعظم من غلبة السفلة وذلّ الوجوه وأحذر الحذر كلّه أن تمكّن تلك الطبقة من الغلبة فإن نجم منهم ناجم على جندك وأهل بلادك تعدّى ذلك أهل بلادك دهمهم ما لا رويّة ولا منفعة معه فانصرف عن هذا الرأي[1] إلى غيره فاعمد إلى من قبلك من العظماء والأحرار فوزّع بينهم مملكتهم والزم اسم الملك كلّ من ولّيته منهم ناحيةً واعقد التاج على رأسه وإن صغر ملكه فإنّ المتّسم بالملك لازم لاسمه والمعتقد التاج لا يخضع لغيره ولا يلبث ذلك أن يوقع بين كلّ ملك منهم وبين صاحبه تدابرًا وتغالبًا على الملك وتفاخرًا بالمال حتّى ينسوا بذلك أضغانهم عليك ويعود حربهم لك حربًا بينهم ثمّ لا يزدادوا في ذلك بصيرة إلّا

١ أهل بلادك . . . الرأي زيادة من إ٣.

us your opinion at such time of your assurance of its soundness, once it has been sufficiently mulled in your contemplation, as is the usual genesis of your valued assistance. May you and we enjoy the peace of those truly at peace.

Aristotle replied: 8.9

To the heavenly aided, heavenly guided victor, Alexander. From his humblest servant, Aristotle.

I am reminded of His Majesty's virtue, the felicity of his intellect, and the prominence of his supreme ambition, which were revealed to me during the days when I was his teacher, and such memories affirm that it is rather I who am in need of his instruction.

I received His Majesty's letter containing his order. Although my thoughts on His Majesty's question were formed to the best of my capacity, they are merely an empty void compared to physical matter; yet I shall not refrain from responding.

It is inevitable that each plot of earth has its share of good qualities, and the Persians' share is their strength and courage. Should you execute their noblemen, the inheritance of their estates will fall to the commoners. Nothing so sorely tests a king more than an upsurge of the underclass and humiliation of the nobility. Take all precaution to prevent the underclass from victory, for should one of their number rise against your army and your people, that for which there can be no advice or avail will descend upon you.

Set aside the idea of execution and instead put your reliance upon their freeborn nobles. Divide the kingdom among them and bestow the title of "king" upon each whom you grant some territory, and place a crown upon their heads, howsoever small their realms. He who is named a king will never relinquish such a title willingly; he who wears a crown will never willingly submit to another. Very soon, each of these "kings" will begin plotting to defeat the others and to vaunt their possessions. This will cause them to forget their prior resentments of you. Their war against you will thus turn into war among themselves. This will inevitably reveal to them the value of each maintaining his good standing with you. Wherever you go, you will find an ally; if you journey

أحدثوها لك استقامة بك فإن دنوت منهم كانوا لك وإن نأيت عنهم تعزّزوا بك حتّى يثب كلّ منهم على جاره باسمك وفي ذلك شاغل لهم عنك وأمانًا لأحداثهم بعدك ولا أمان للدهر وقد أدّيت للملك ما رأيته لي حظًا وعليّ حقًّا والملك أعلى عينًا فيما استعان عليّ به والسلام الأبديّ فليكن على الملك

فلمّا تأمّل الإسكندر رأيه عرف أنّه الحقّ وفرّق القوم في الملك كما ذكر فسُمّوا ملوك الطوائف

١٠،٨ وسار الإسكندر إلى الشرق فذلّت له الملوك وبنى مدينة إصبهان وهراة وسمرقند ولمّا وصل إلى الهند خرج ملكها في ألف فيل عليها المقاتلة وفي خراطيمها السيوف الهنديّة فلم تثبت خيل الإسكندر فصنع فيلة من نحاس مجوّفة وربط خيله بينها حتّى ألفتها وملأها نفطًا وكبريتًا ثمّ ألبسها السلاح وجرّها على العجل إلى ناحية العدوّ وبينها الرجال فلمّا نشبت الحرب أمر بإشعال النار في أجوافها فلمّا اشتعلت تنحّى الرجال عنها وغشيتها فيلة الهند فضربتها بخراطيمها فاحترقت وولّت هاربة فكانت الدائرة على ملك الهند

١١،٨ ولمّا وصل الإسكندر إلى المانكير وهو من ملوك الصين خرج إليه الملك وأرسل يقول علامَ نفني العالم ابرز إليّ فإن قتلتني فأنت الملك وإن قتلتك فأنا الملك فتيمّن الإسكندر بكونه بدأ بنفسه في ذكر القتل وبرز إليه فقتله ثمّ توغّل في بلاد الصين إلى مقرّ ملكها الأكبر وجرت لهما أخبار طويلة اصطلحا فيها على مهادنات ومهاداة

١٢،٨ وعاد الإسكندَرُ وقد دَوَّخ البلادَ ودانَتْ له الملوك فأقامَ بشهرزور أيّامًا واحتضر بهَا وكانت مدّةُ ملكه ستَّ عشرةَ سنةً واختلف في عمره فقيل ستّ وثلاثون سنة وهو الأكثر وبين وفاته وبين الهجرة ستّمائة سنة وقيل أكثر

> far away, they will seek power via you: each will claim to be fighting his neighbor in your name. This will distract them from your affairs, and so protect against their mischief in the future, though there is no true protection against Time.
>
> I have presented to His Majesty what I could, in fulfillment of my duty. His Majesty knows better than I the answer to the matter for which he sought my assistance. May His Majesty be bestowed eternal peace.

Alexander weighed this advice. He realized its truth, and he doled out kingdoms to the Persian nobles, who became known as the Petty Kings.

Alexander then marched eastward, kings bowed in submission, and he founded the cities of Isfahan, Herat, and Samarqand. But when he reached India, its king met him with a host of a thousand elephants, each carrying warriors and brandishing a sword of Indian steel attached to its trunk. Alexander's horses balked before the beasts, and so Alexander constructed an elephant of his own, made of hollowed bronze. He tethered his horses around the bronze elephant until they became accustomed to it; then Alexander filled it with oil and sulfur, equipped it with weapons, and had it pulled to the front line on wheels, guarded by ranks of infantry. When the fighting reached a frenzy, Alexander ordered that the bronze elephant's hollow core be set alight, and as it began burning, his infantry withdrew. The Indian elephants descended upon it, but they were scorched as they beat it with their trunks, and they stampeded in headlong retreat. Disaster befell the Indian king. 8.10

Alexander next marched upon the Mānkīr, one of the kings of China,[69] who arrayed his army before Alexander and challenged him: "Why destroy the world in our war? Fight me in single combat! If you kill me, then the kingdom is yours. If I kill you, then the kingdom is mine." Alexander thought it auspicious that when the Mānkīr spoke of death, he mentioned himself first, so he agreed, and killed him in the duel. 8.11

Alexander penetrated deeper into China until he reached the seat of their great king. What transpired is a long story; the result was a truce and presentation of gifts.[70] Having thus subjugated the world and established lordship over its kings, Alexander turned homeward, but when pausing in Shahrzūr, he died. His reign had lasted sixteen years. There is disagreement about his age, but most say he was thirty-six. He died about six hundred years (or perhaps more) before the Prophet's Emigration. 8.12

ولمّا حضرته الوفاة كتب إلى أمّه كتابًا يسألها فيه أن تصنع وليمة وتدعو نساء أهل المملكة ولا تأذن إلّا لمن لم تصب بفقد عزيز من أهلها ففعلت ذلك فلم يدخل إليها أحد فعلمت أنّه مات وأنّ ذلك تعزية لها ١٣،٨

ثمّ أوصى أن يُوضع في تابوت من ذهب ويُطلى بالأطلية الممسّكة ويحمل إلى أمّه بالإسكندريّة فلمّا فعل ذلك جمع أرسطاطاليس الحكماء وأمرهم بكلام يكون للخاصّة معزّيًا وللعامّة واعظًا كما فعل بالإسكندر الأوّل وكانوا عشرة ١٤،٨

فقال الأوّل أصبح مستأسر الأسرى أسيرًا ١٥،٨

وقال الثاني هذا الإسكندر طوى الأرض العريضة وهو اليوم يطوى منها في ذراعين

وقال الثالث العجب أنّ القويّ قد غلب والضعفاء لاهون

وقال الرابع ما سافر الإسكندر سفرًا بلا آلة سوى سفره هذا

وقال الخامس سيلحق بك من سرّه موتك كما لحقت بمن سرّك موته

وقال السادس كان يحكم على الرعيّة فصارت الرعيّة تحكم عليه

وقال السابع كنت تأمرنا بالحركة فما بالك ساكنًا

وقال الثامن ربّ حريص على سكوتك وهو اليوم حريص على كلامك

وقال التاسع كم أمات من في[١] هذا الصندوق لئلّا يموت فمات

وقال العاشر كان الإسكندر يعظنا بنطقه وهو اليوم يعظنا بسكوته

وقالت أمّه ممّا يُسلّي عنه المعرفة باللحاق به

وقالت ابنة دارا ما كنت أظنّ أنّ غالب دارا يُغلب

ومن كلام الإسكندر السعيد من لا يعرفنا ولا نعرفه فإنّا إذا عرفناه أطلنا يومه وأطرنا نومه ١٦،٨

---

١ من في: سقطت من إ١ .

On his deathbed, Alexander sent a letter to his mother, asking her to organize a banquet. He told her to extend the invitation to every woman in the kingdom, with the condition that only those who had never suffered the loss of a cherished family member could attend. His mother made all the preparations, but on the day of the banquet no one came. She then knew that Alexander had died and that this was his way of consoling her. 8.13

Alexander instructed that his body be placed in a golden sarcophagus with musk-scented plating, which was to be carried to his mother in Alexandria. Upon its arrival, Aristotle summoned ten sages and instructed each to make a statement that would offer solace to the elite and warning to the commoners, as had been done for a King Alexander in bygone times.[71] 8.14

First sage: "He who took prisoners is now himself a prisoner." 8.15

Second sage: "This is Alexander: he covered the wide world. Now he is covered by a mere six feet of earth."

Third sage: "Isn't it wondrous that the strong can be vanquished, while the weak carry on, oblivious."

Fourth sage: "Alexander never journeyed alone, except for now."

Fifth sage: "Those who are pleased with your death will soon meet you, just as you now meet those whose death pleased you."

Sixth sage: "He who ruled over his subjects is now subject to their judgment."

Seventh sage: "You used to order us into action; how is it now that you stay still?"

Eighth sage: "Many were those who had once wished to silence you, yet now wish they could hear your voice!"

Ninth sage: "How many deaths did the man in this coffin cause in order to avoid his own death?"

Tenth sage: "Alexander used to instruct us with his words; now he does so with his silence."

Alexander's mother spoke: "At least there is consolation in the knowledge that we shall all catch up with him."

Roxana spoke: "Never did I think Darius's vanquisher would be vanquished."

Alexander's own words of wisdom include the following: "Fortunate is he who neither knows us nor is known to us! If we knew of him, we'd pursue him by day and rob his sleep by night." 8.16

وقيل له إنّك عظّمت بمعلّمك أكثر من تعظيم أبيك فقال لأنّ أبي سبب حياتي الفانية ومعلّمي سبب حياتي الباقية

١٧،٨ وقال سلطان العقل على باطن العاقل أشدّ من سلطان السيف على ظاهر الأحمق[١]

وقال النظر في المرآة يري رسم الوجه وفي أقاويل الحكماء يري رسم النفس

وقيل له إنّ فلانًا يثلبك فلو عاقبته قال هو بعد العقاب أعذر

١٨،٨ وأحضر بين يديه لصّ فأمر بصلبه فقال أيّها الملك إنّي فعلت ما قد فعلت وأنا كاره فقال تُصلَب أيضًا وأنت كاره

١٩،٨ وغضب على بعض شعرائه فأقصاه وفرّق ماله في أصحابه فقيل له في ذلك فقال أمّا إقصائي له فلجرمه وأمّا تفريقي ماله في أصحابه فلئلّا يشفعوا فيه

٢٠،٨ وجلس يومًا مجلسًا عامًّا فلم يُسأل فيه حاجة فقال والله ما أعدّ هذا اليوم من ملكي قيل ولِمَ أيّها الملك قال لأنّه لا توجد لذّة الملك إلّا بإسعاف الراغبين وإغاثة الملهوفين ومكافأة المحسنين

٢١،٨ وقال من انتجعك فقد أسلفك حسن الظنّ بك

## ٩ وأردشير[٢] جاهد ملوك الطوائف بخروجهم عن جماعتك

١،٩ أردشير بن بابك من ولد بهمان الملك أبي دارا الأكبر وكان بهمان قد تزوّج بابنته همائي[٣] على عادتهم فحملت منه بدارا الأكبر وسألته أن يعقد التاج على بطنها لولدها ففعل وكان له ولد يسمّى ساسان من امرأة أخرى فلمّا مات بهمان تنسّك

١ وقال سلطان . . . الأحمق: زيادة من إ٢. ٢ كل النسخ إلا بر١ وإ٣ وق٣: ازدشير. ٣ بر١: هماي؛ با١ وإ٢ ومتن إ١: خمائي؛ إ٣: جمائي؛ ل٢، ب: كمافي؛ ق١: خماني؛ ت١: جماني.

Alexander was once asked: "Why have you exalted your teacher more than your father?" He replied, "Because my father is the cause of my mortal existence, whereas my teacher nurtured my immortal soul."

Alexander also said, "Reason's hold over a rational man's mind is far stronger than the sword's control over a fool's body." 8.17

"A mirror shows the features of the face; wise men's words show the lineaments of the soul."

When Alexander was once informed: "So-and-so has slandered you; shouldn't you punish him?" he responded, "Punishment would only give him greater license."

When Alexander ordered the crucifixion of a thief, the thief pleaded, "My Lord! I did it against my will!" Alexander replied, "You will be crucified against your will too!" 8.18

A poet once incurred Alexander's ire, and Alexander banished him, distributing the poet's possessions among the poet's companions. They asked Alexander why he did this, and he responded, "I banished him for his crime, and I dispersed his estate among his companions so that none would make a plea on his behalf." 8.19

Once, Alexander held a court session in which no one made a petition. "By God," he said, "I don't count this as a day of being king." "Lord, why is that?" asked his courtiers. Alexander explained, "One does not taste the sweetness of sovereignty unless one aids the needy, succors the troubled, or rewards the goodly." 8.20

Alexander also said, "A good reputation is what you earn from those who seek your protection." 8.21

**. . . Ardashir battled the Petty Kings for their rebellion against you.** 9

Ardashir, son of Babak, was a descendant of King Bahman, the father of Darius the Elder. In accordance with Persian noble custom, Bahman married his own daughter, Homāy. When Homāy was pregnant with Darius the Elder, she asked Bahman to place the crown on her belly, symbolizing that her son would carry the royal line. By another wife, Bahman had a son named Sassan who, after Bahman's death, took to the ascetic life and wandered in the mountains, though he enjoined his own children to promise that if any of their issue 9.1

ساسان وساح في الجبال وعهد إلى بنيه أنّه من ملك منهم فليقتل من قدر عليه من نسل دارا وكان أردشير هذا من ولد ساسان وهو أوّل الفرس الثانية ومعنى الثانية أنّ الإسكندر لمّا قتل دارا آخر ملوك الفرس وفرّق من بقي منهم وسمّاهم ملوك الطوائف صارت المملكة لليونان فلمّا تُوفّي الإسكندر وتقاصر ملك اليونان بعد مدّة تحرّك أردشير هذا وكان أحد أبناء ملوك الطوائف على إصطخر وخرج طالبًا للملك وأوهم أنّه يطلب بثأر ابن عمّه دارا وجمع الجموع وكاتب ملوك الطوائف بكتاب طويل أوّله

من أردشير بن بابك المستأثر دونه المغلوب على تراث آبائه الداعي إلى الله المستنصر به فإنّه وعد المظلوم الظفر والعاقبة

٢،٩ ثمّ ذكر كلامًا طويلًا معناه الحثّ على المعاونة فمنهم من أطاعه ومنهم من تأخّر عنه فخرج بعساكره فقتل المتأخّر وعطف على البقيّة فقتلهم وعمل بما عهد به جدّه ساسان إلى بنيه ورزقه الله الظفر والنصر وقتل ملك الأردوان مبارزًا ووطئ رأسه وتسمّى من ذلك اليوم شاهنشاه الأعظم ومعناه ملك الملوك

٣،٩ ثمّ قام خطيبًا فقال الحمد لله الذي خصّنا بنعمه وخوّلنا من فضله ومهّد لنا البلاد وها نحن شارعون في إقامة العدل وإدرار[١] الفضل وإنصاف الضعيف من القويّ وسترون في أيّامنا ما يصدّق مقالنا بفعالنا

٤،٩ ثمّ ساس الرعيّة ورتّب الممالك وبه اقتدى الخلفاء والملوك من بعده ورتّب الناس على طبقات فالطبقة الأولى الحكماء والفضلاء كان مجلسهم عن يمينه وهم بطانتة والطبقة الثانية الملوك وأبناؤهم وسمّاهم الخواصّ ومجلسهم عن يساره والطبقة الثالثة الإصهبديّة والمرازبة[٢] وهم بين يديه ولكن ليس فيهم وضيع

١ إ١: إدارة. ٢ سقطت من إ١.

ever became king in the future, that descendant must kill every single one of Darius the Elder's progeny upon whom he could lay his hands. Ardashir was one of Sassan's descendants, and he became the first king of the Persians' Second Kingdom (it was called the "Second Kingdom" because Alexander's defeat of Darius the Younger and division of the realm among the Petty Kings under Greek suzerainty terminated the Persians' First Kingdom). After Alexander's death, Greek power eventually declined, and Ardashir, whose father was the Petty King ruling Iṣṭakhr, rose in revolt, claiming supreme kingship for himself. He contrived to appear as if he was seeking blood revenge against the Greeks on behalf of his cousin Darius, and as he mobilized his forces, he dispatched a long message to the Petty Kings, which began:

> From Ardashir, son of Babak, the Avenger of him who was defeated, the claimant to the rights of his ancestors, the solicitor of God's help and victory: God promises victory and just outcome to the wronged.[72]

The whole letter is quite long: in essence, it lobbied the Petty Kings' support, and some chose to follow Ardashir while others held back. Ardashir marched first against those recalcitrants, and after killing them, he turned on those who had allied with him and eliminated them too, thereby fulfilling his ancestor Sassan's demand for blood revenge. 9.2

God granted Ardashir triumph: Ardashir killed King Artabanus in single combat, and after trampling Artabanus's head underfoot, Ardashir proclaimed himself the Great Shahan Shah—the King of Kings.

When Ardashir ascended the throne, he gave an oration: "Praise the God who favored us with His munificence, endowed upon us His grace, and laid open the world for us. Here we stand, at the inception of a kingdom of justice, munificence, and equity for the weak against the mighty. Under our dominion, our deeds to come shall reveal the sincerity of these words." 9.3

Ardashir governed his subjects well and established such order across the lands that rulers after him, including the caliphs, took him as the exemplar of kingship. Ardashir organized his court into classes: the first, comprising the wise and virtuous men, assembled to the right of his throne and constituted his inner retinue. The second class, comprising client kings and their princes, were named "the nobility," and they assembled to his left. The military commanders[73] sat before Ardashir: although they constituted the third class, none 9.4

ولا دنيء الأصل ثمّ زادهم طبقات أُخَرَ ورتّب لكلّ ربع من أرباع الدنيا قومًا ينفردون بتدبيره وتحريره ودانت له الدنيا وتمكّن من الأرض وكان من الشجعان المشهورين في الفرس يلقى وحده جماعة ويشبه في قوّته وشكله بأردشير الأوّل الذي كان يُدعى طويل الباع

٥،٩ وفي أيّامه بُنِيَت المدن المشهورة كالأبلّة وأستراباذ وكرخ ميسان وغيرها ووضع له النرد تنبيهًا على أنّه لا حيلة للإنسان مع القضاء والقدر وهو أوّل من لعب به فقيل نردشير[1] ويقال إنّه هو الذي وضعه وشبّه به تقلّب الدنيا بأهلها فجعل بيوت النرد اثني عشر بيتًا بعدد شهور السنة وعدد كلابها ثلاثون بعدد أيّام الشهر وجعل الفصّين مثالاً للقضاء والقدر وتقلبيهما بأهل الدنيا وأنّ الإنسان يلعبه فيبلغ بإسعاف القدر ما يريده وأنّ اللاعب الفطن ما يتأتّى له ما يتأتّى لغيره إذا أسعفه القدر فعارضهم الهند بالشطرنج

٦،٩ وأقام في الملك خمسَ عشرة سنة ثمّ فوّضه إلى ابنه سابور وانقطع في بيوت العبادات ثلاث سنين إلى أن تُوفّي

٧،٩ ومن كلامه الدين أساس والملك حارس وما لم يكن له أسّ فمهدوم وما لم يكن له حارس فضائع

٨،٩ وقال لا شيء أضرّ على الملك أو الرئيس من معاشرة وضيع أو مداناة سفيه وذلك لأنّ النفس كما تصلح بمعاشرة الشريف وكذا تفسد بمخالطة السخيف حتّى يقدح ذلك فيها كما أنّ الريح إذا مرّت بالطيب تحمّلت منه رائحة طيّبةً تقوى بها النفس والجوارح فكذا إذا مرّت بالنتن فتحمّلت منه آلمت النفس وأضرّت بها

٩،٩ وكتب إليه متنصّح أنّ قومًا اجتمعوا على سبّك بكذا وكذا فوقّع عليها إن كانوا نطقوا بألسنة شتّى لقد جمعت ما قالوه في ورقتك فجرحك أعجب ولسانك أكذب

١ إ١، ل١، ل٢، بر١، ب، ق٣: نزدشير.

of their members were commoners or of ignoble birth. Ardashir established further classes, and appointed a troop to manage the affairs in each of the four cardinal points. The whole world yielded to Ardashir. He possessed the earth,[74] and was one of the Persians' fabled heroes—he could face an armed band single-handed. His strength and looks drew comparison with Ardashir the First, who had been known as "the Mighty."[75]

Famous cities, including al-Ubulla, Astarabad, and Karkh Maysān, were constructed during Ardashir's reign. He is also credited with inventing backgammon, as a reminder of humanity's impotence against Fate and Destiny. Ardashir was the first to play it, and he was nicknamed "Gamershir."[76] Those who say Ardashir invented it as a means to show the vicissitudes of Fate in this world note that he set the number of points on the table at twelve, equivalent to the months of the year, and the number of counters at thirty, for the days of the month. The two dice represent Fate and Destiny as they roll across this world, and the player is to understand that his progression in the game is ruled by whatever assistance Fate should choose. The skillful player can achieve more than others, but only with the help of Fate. The Indians rivaled the Persians' invention of backgammon with their invention of chess. 9.5

Ardashir reigned for fifteen years, and then, entrusting rule to his son Shapur, he retired to live in temples, where he spent his last three years. 9.6

Ardashir's wise sayings include: "Religion is a foundation, and the king is a guard. Whatever has no foundation will collapse; whatever has no guard will be lost." 9.7

Ardashir observed: "There is nothing worse for a king or leader than fraternizing with base individuals or associating with fools. The soul is improved in the companionship of nobility, as it is spoiled and will degrade when mixed with frivolity. It is like the wind: a breeze that passes over incense brings sweet aroma nourishing the body and spirit, whereas air passing over putridity carries a stench that oppresses and harms the soul." 9.8

An advisor once wrote to Ardashir: "People are unanimously cursing you for all manner of things." Ardashir affixed the following response on the letter: "Many tongues may utter these words, but it is you who have collected their scattered opinions on one sheet. The injury you inflict is the more astonishing—it is your tongue that had spread the most lies." 9.9

## ١٠ والضحّاك استدعى مسالمتك

١،١٠ اختلف في نسب الضحّاك هذا فقيل هو من العرب من قحطان واليمانية تدّعيه وفي ذلك يقول أبو نواس

وَكَانَ مِنَّا ٱلضَّحَّاكُ يَحْذِرُهُ ٱلْـ    حَامِلُ[١] وَٱلْوَحْشُ فِي مَسَارِبِهَا

٢،١٠ وقيل هو الضحّاك بن الأهبوب بن طهمورث بن آدم وزمنه بعد الطوفان وهو ابن أخت جمشيد[٢] بن أوشهنج ملك الأقاليم

٣،١٠ وكان من سيرته أنّ جمشيد ومعناه سيّد الشعاع ملك الأقاليم السبعة وهو أوّل من عمل السلاح واستخرج الإبريسم وألزم أهل الفساد في الأعمال الشاقّة في الصخور واستخراج المعادن وطال عمره وتجبّر وادّعى الربوبيّة فخرج عليه الضحّاك هذا وتبعه خلق كثير لبغضهم في جمشيد فهرب جمشيد بين يديه وظفر به فأمر بنشره بمنشار وقال إن كنت إلٰهًا فادفع عن نفسك

٤،١٠ ثمّ ملك الضحّاك وطغى وتجبّر وفجر ودان بدين البراهمة وهو أوّل من غُنّي له وضرب الدنانير والدراهم ولبس التاج ووضع العشور وكان على كتفيه سلعتان يحرّكهما إذا شاء وادّعى أنّهما حيّاتان يهوّل بهما وذكر أنّهما يضربان عليه فلا يسكنان حتّى يطليهما بدماغَي إنسانين يُذبحان له في كلّ يوم وكان له وزير صالح فكان يستحيي أحدهما في أكثر الأيّام ويضع مكان دماغه دماغ كبش ويأمر الرجل باللحوق بالجبال وأن لا يأوي الأمصار فيقال إنّ الأكراد من تلك القوم لكردهم إلى الجبال

٥،١٠ ثمّ كثر فساد الضحّاك وكان بإصبهان رجل حدّاد يقال له كابي قتل له الضحّاك ولدين فاجتمع عليه خلق كثير وكان له قطعة جلد يتقّي بها حرّ النار فرفعها على رمح وجعلها علمًا وسار إلى الضحّاك والناس معه فخرج إليه فلمّا رأى ذلك العلم

---

١ إ٣: جايلك بر١: جامل. ٢ إ١، ل١، با١: جمشيذ.

**Al-Ḍaḥḥāk sued for your peace . . .** 10

Al-Ḍaḥḥāk's origins are disputed. There are those who say he was an Arab from the Southern lineage of Qaḥṭān, and they adduce a verse by Abū Nuwās as proof: 10.1

Al-Ḍaḥḥāk was one of us too—
he who was feared by wild beasts and the jinn.[77]

Others identify al-Ḍaḥḥāk as the son of al-Ahbūb, son of Tahmurth, son of Adam. Al-Ḍaḥḥāk lived after Noah's Flood, and he was the nephew of Jamshid, son of Houshang, King of the World. 10.2

According to the story, Jamshid (his name means Lord of the Rays)[78] was king of all Seven Climes. He was the first to make weapons, the first to practice sericulture, and the first to compel criminals to perform hard labor by quarrying rocks and mining minerals. Jamshid reigned a prodigiously long time, and toward the end he became tyrannical, claiming divinity for himself. Al-Ḍaḥḥāk rose against him and gathered a great following on account of Jamshid's widespread unpopularity. Although Jamshid initially effected his escape, al-Ḍaḥḥāk captured him and ordered him hewn into pieces, mocking him: "If you really are a god, it is time to defend yourself!" 10.3

Once crowned king, al-Ḍaḥḥāk was himself an oppressive, debauched tyrant. He followed the religion of the Brahmins, and was the first king to have people sing to him, to strike dinars and dirhams, to wear a crown,[79] and to impose tithes on land. He had cysts on each shoulder, and because he was able to wiggle them at will, he claimed that they were two snakes, and in order to inspire fear, he maintained that these "snakes" would torment him ceaselessly unless the brains of two human sacrifices were spread upon them each day. Al-Ḍaḥḥāk had a virtuous vizier who, on most days, would spare one of the sacrifices-to-be and substitute his brain with that of a ram. Each time, the vizier would order the man who had been spared to take refuge in the mountains and stay away from cities. Legend says that the Kurds descend from these men who were driven into the mountains, because the root *k-r-d* means to be "chased away." 10.4

When al-Ḍaḥḥāk's corruption increased, a blacksmith from Isfahan named Kaveh,[80] who had lost two sons to al-Ḍaḥḥāk's sacrifices, raised a great army. Kaveh led them against al-Ḍaḥḥāk, carrying before them a banner he 10.5

ألقى الله تعالى في قلبه الرعب فانهزم وأراد الناس أن يملّكوا كابي فأبى وقال لست من بيت الملك فملّكوا افريدون بن جمشيد[١] وصار كابي عونًا له وقتل الضحّاك وقيل مات منهزمًا وعظم علم كابي ورصّعته الملوك بالدرّ والياقوت وكانوا يقدّمونه أمام الجيوش فينصرون به وكان عندهم كالتابوت في بني إسرائيل ويُعرف هذا العلم بدرفس[٢] كابيان ولم يزل في خزائنهم يتوارثون إلى أيّام يزدجرد بن شهرياز فأخذه المسلمون في وقعة القادسيّة وحُمل إلى عمر بن الخطّاب رضي الله تعالى عنه فقسّم جوهره في الناس

١٠،٦ وممّا اتّفق من الحكايات المستظرفة في أيّام الضحّاك أنّه لمّا طالت مدّته وفساده اجتمع الناس إلى بابه وكابي معهم فلمّا دخل وكان جريئًا قال له أسلّم عليك سلام من يملك الأقاليم كلّها أم سلام من يملك هذا الإقليم قال بل سلام من يملك الأقاليم كلّها فقال إذا كنت تملكها كلّها فلم خصصت هذا الإقليم بنوائبك ومؤونتك وهل لا انتقلت إلى الأقاليم وواسيت بينه وبينهم ثمّ عدّد عليه أشياء وصدّقه الضحّاك ووعد الناس بما يحبّون وانصرفوا

١٠،٧ وكانت له أمّ جبّارة وسمعت ما جرى فلمّا خرجوا أنكرت عليه وقالت لقد جرّأتهم عليك هل لا قتلتهم فقال لها مع عتوّه وتجبّره إنّ القوم بدهوني بالحقّ فلمّا هممت بالسطوة بينهم وقف الحقّ بيني وبينهم كالجبل فحال بيني وبين ما أردت ثمّ كان من أمره بعد ذلك مع كابي ما كان من الهزيمة والموت

١ إ: افريذون بن جمشيذ.  ٢ كلّ النسخ: درفش.

had fashioned by fixing his leather smith's apron atop the head of a spear. Al-Ḍaḥḥāk sallied forth, but when he beheld Kaveh's banner, God struck such fear into al-Ḍaḥḥāk's heart that he submitted in defeat. The crowd then called for Kaveh to be crowned king, but he demurred, saying, "I am not from a royal family," so they crowned Feridun, son of Jamshid. Kaveh became Feridun's aide, and he killed al-Ḍaḥḥāk, though an alternative version relates that al-Ḍaḥḥāk perished while on the run. Kaveh's banner was venerated: subsequent kings studded it with pearls and rubies, and the Persian army would always march behind it as a victory talisman, much like the Ark of the Jews. The banner was known as "Kaveh's Guidon,"[81] and it was placed in the Persian treasury and passed down through the generations until the reign of Yazdegerd III, when it was captured by the Muslims at the Battle of al-Qādisiyyah and sent to the Caliph ʿUmar ibn al-Khaṭṭāb (God be pleased with him), who distributed the banner's jewels among the Muslims.

A fine tale about al-Ḍaḥḥāk's reign relates that when Kaveh and the crowd 10.6
gathered at al-Ḍaḥḥāk's gate, after many years of his corrupt rule, the brave Kaveh confronted al-Ḍaḥḥāk: "Shall I greet you in the way one would the king of all the climes, or in the way one greets the king of just this clime?" "All of them, of course!" replied al-Ḍaḥḥāk, to which Kaveh said, "If you control all the climes, why have you singled out this one to inflict your calamities and hardships? Shouldn't you have traveled among all the climes and distributed your terror evenly?" Kaveh then enumerated the grievances. Al-Ḍaḥḥāk conceded, promising the people what they wanted, and they departed.

In the meantime, al-Ḍaḥḥāk's mother, a real tyrant herself, heard what had 10.7
transpired, and when the crowd dispersed, she scolded him: "You have now emboldened them against you. Why not just kill them?" Though full of pride and haughtiness, al-Ḍaḥḥāk admitted, "They hit me with the Truth unexpectedly. While I seriously considered attacking them, the Truth rose up between us like a mountain, preventing me from reaching what I intended."

It was after this event that al-Ḍaḥḥāk suffered defeat at the hands of Kaveh and died, as noted above.

## وجذيمة الأبرش تمنّى منادمتك ١١

هو وجذيمة بن مالك بن عامر التنوخيّ وقيل الأزديّ أوّل من ساس العرب وملك على قضاعة وكانت منازله الحيرة والأنبار وولايته من قبل أردشير بن بابك وكان أبرص فعُدل عن هذا الاسم فقيل الأبرش والوضّاح فزعم بعضهم أنّه كان لا يأنف من اسم البرص وكذلك كُني بالأبرش وفي العرب من يفتخر بذلك قال الراجز ١،١١

أَبْرَصُ فَيَّاضُ ٱلْيَدَيْنِ أَكْلَفُ وَٱلْبُرْصُ أَدْرَى بِٱللُّهَى وَأَعْرَفُ

وهو أوّل من صُنع له الشمع وأدلج من الملوك وكان ذا رأي وهمّة ويقال له نديمُ الفرقدين كان إذا شرب قدحًا صبّ لهما قدحين ولا ينادم غيرهما وسبب ذلك فيما زعموا أنّه كان قد تكهّن واتّخذ صنمين يقال لهما الضربيان يستسقي بهما وينتصر على أعدائه ٢،١١

كانت إياد قد خرج قوم منهم من الحجاز وانتشروا فيما بين البصرة والكوفة وتمكّنوا على ما يلي الحيرة وكثروا بعين أباغ

فخرج جذيمة غازيًا وكان في إياد رجل يقال له عديّ بن نصر وكان له ظرف وجمال وإليه تُنسَب الملوك من آل نصر فنزل جذيمة بساحتهم فبعثت إياد قومًا منهم إلى صنمي جذيمة فسقوا سدنتهما الخمر وسرقوهما فأصبحوا في إياد فبعثت إياد إلى جذيمة إنّ صنميك قد أصبحا عندنا زهدًا فيك ورغبة فينا فإن عاهدتنا أن لا تغزونا رددناهما إليك فقال جذيمة تعطوني أيضًا عديّ بن نصْر يكون عندي ففعلوا وانصرف عنهم وضمّ عديًّا إلى نفسه وولّاه شرابه وأمر مجلسه ٣،١١

وكان لجذيمة أخت تسمّى رقاش بكرًا فأحبّت عديًّا وأحبّها فسألته أن يخطبها من جذيمة إذا سكر ففعل ذلك وزوّجه بها وشهد عليه من حضر فلمّا أصبح ٤،١١

**...Jadhīmah the Speckled aspired to join your entourage.** 11

Jadhīmah ibn Mālik ibn ʿĀmir of the Tanūkh (or possibly of the Azd) was king of the Quḍāʿah and the first to rule over the Arabs. His homeland was in al-Ḥīrah and al-Anbār, and he was a client king of Ardashir, son of Babak. Jadhīmah was a leper, and he so hated the word "leper" (*al-abraṣ*) that he adjusted his name to "the Speckled" (*al-abrash*), or even "Clear-Face" (*al-waḍḍāḥ*).[82] One narrator, however, alleges that Jadhīmah was actually not offended by being called "the Leper," and likewise he accepted the nickname "the Speckled"—it is indeed the case that some Arabs did mention leprosy in praiseworthy contexts:[83] 11.1

A tawny leper, with bountiful, generous hands—
Lepers! They know how to give gifts!

Jadhīmah was a judicious and resolute king, the first for whom candles were made, and the first to travel by night. He was nicknamed the "Drinking Companion of Ursa and Minor"[84] because he shared his drinking cups exclusively with them. The reason claimed for this is as follows. 11.2

Jadhīmah practiced divination, and he used two idols called the "Interlopers"[85] whenever he prayed for rain or for victory over his enemies. During his reign, groups of the Iyād migrated from the Hijaz and settled between what are now Basra and Kufa. They asserted control and settled in large numbers around ʿAyn Abāgh near al-Ḥīrah, and Jadhīmah marched out to challenge them.

When Jadhīmah neared the Iyād's camps, they sent a party to his shrine, got the custodians drunk with wine, and stole his two idols. The raiders returned to the Iyād by daybreak and sent a message to Jadhīmah: "Your idols arrived here this morning. They have renounced you and they like us better. But if you give us a pledge never to attack us, we will return them to you." Jadhīmah negotiated: "Give me ʿAdī ibn Naṣr in the bargain too." (ʿAdī was a member of the Iyād, and a man of elegant wit and beauty; the Nasrid kings trace their lineage from him.) The Iyād agreed, Jadhīmah withdrew, and he kept ʿAdī by his side, appointing him in charge of drinking ceremonies and court assemblies. 11.3

Jadhīmah had a virgin sister named Raqāsh. She fell in love with ʿAdī, and he with her, so she asked him to request her hand from Jadhīmah when he 11.4

دخل عليه بثياب العرس وكان قد دخل بها تلك الليلة فقال جذيمة ما هذه الآثار يا عديّ قال آثار عرس رقاش قال من زوّجها ويحك قال الملك

٥،١١ فأكبّ إلى الأرض مفكّرًا وهرب عديّ فلم يُعرف له أثر وأرسل جذيمة إلى أخته يقول

خَبِّرِينِي وَأَنْتِ لاَ تَكْذِبِينِي أَبِحُرٍّ زَنَيْتِ أَمْ بِهَجِينِ
أَمْ بِعَبْدٍ فَأَنْتِ أَهْلٌ لَعَبْدٍ أَمْ بِدُونَ فَأَنْتِ أَهْلٌ لِدُونِ

قالت بل أنت زوّجتني امرءًا غريبًا[1] ولم تشاورني في نفسي فكفّ عنها وآلى أن لا ينادم إلّا الفرقدين

٦،١١ وحملت رقاش فولدت غلامًا وسمّته عمرًا فلمّا ترعرع ألبسته وعطّرته ودخلت به على خاله فلمّا رآه أحبّه وجعله مع ولده وخرج جذيمة مبتديًا بأهله في سنة خصبة فأقام في روضة ذات زهر فخرج ولده وعمرو معهم يجتنون الكمأة فكانوا إذا أصابوا كمأة جيّدة أكلوها وإذا أصابها عمرو خبأها وانصرفوا إلى جذيمة يتعادون وعمرو يقول

هٰذَا جَنَايَ وَخِيَارُهُ فِيهِ وَكُلُّ جَانٍ يَدُهُ إِلَى فِيهِ

فضمّه جذيمة إليه وسُرّ به وحلّاه بطوق فكان أوّل عربيّ لبس الطوق

٧،١١ ثمّ إنّ الجنّ استطارته فطلبه جذيمة في الآفاق زمانًا فلم يقدر عليه ثمّ أقبل رجلان من قضاعة يقال لهما مالك وعقيل ابني فارح من الشام يريدان جذيمة وأهديا له طرفًا فبينا هما يأكلان إذ أقبل فتى عريان قد تلبّد شعره فسألاه عن نسبه فعرّفهما نفسه فنهضا وغسلا رأسه وألبساه ثيابًا وقالا ما كنّا لنهدي إلى

[1] إ١ وإ٣: عربيا.

next got drunk. This he did, and the marriage was agreed and witnessed by those present. ʿAdī lay with Raqāsh that night, and in the morning he entered Jadhīmah's court wearing a bridegroom's attire. Jadhīmah asked him, "What's all this finery, ʿAdī?" ʿAdī replied, "It's the suit of Raqāsh's groom!" "Damn you, who gave her to you?" ʿAdī answered, "The king."

Jadhīmah's head drooped low in heavy thought, and ʿAdī fled to where no one knew. Jadhīmah then summoned Raqāsh and addressed her in verse: 11.5

> Tell me truly and don't you lie:
> did you whore with a free man or half-breed?
> Or was it a slave? That's a match for you.
> Or even lower? You're fit for the lowest.

She quipped back: "Indeed! It was you who married me to an outsider,[86] and you never even asked me!"

Jadhīmah relented and swore never to drink again unless it was with "Ursa" and "Minor."

Raqāsh bore ʿAdī a son, whom she named ʿAmr. ʿAmr grew into a fine youth, and one day Raqāsh dressed and perfumed him, and presented him to his uncle Jadhīmah. Jadhīmah loved him at first sight and let him join the company of his own sons. During the pasturing season in one particularly fecund year, Jadhīmah and his kin left for their camps in the desert steppe and settled in a flowery meadow. His sons and ʿAmr went off to pick truffles, and whenever Jadhīmah's boys found good ones, they ate them, but ʿAmr concealed those he found. They all raced each other back to Jadhīmah, and ʿAmr sang: 11.6

> This is my harvest, and it has the best morsels.
> The other harvesters' pickings are in their mouths.

Jadhīmah was delighted: he embraced the boy and provided him with a torque;[87] ʿAmr was the first Arab to don such a torque.

Time passed, and then ʿAmr was abducted by the jinn. Jadhīmah sent out search parties to the far horizons, but time passed and no one could find ʿAmr. But one day, out of the blue, a naked boy, his hair all matted, appeared before two men of the Quḍāʿah, Mālik and ʿAqīl, the sons of Fāriḥ, who had stopped to eat while on their way from Syria bearing gifts for Jadhīmah. They asked the boy his lineage, and he told them. At this, they darted up, washed the boy's 11.7

جذيمة أنفس من ابن أخته وخرجا به إلى جذيمة فسرّ به ورأى الطوق فقال شبّ عمرو عن الطوق فذهبت مثلاً وقال لمالك وعقيل حكمكما فقالا منادمتك ما بقيت وبقينا فمكّنهما من ذلك وهما نديما جذيمة اللّذان يضرب بهما المثل وإيّاهما عني متمّم بن نويرة بقوله

وَكُنَّا كَنَدْمَانَيْ جَذِيمَةَ حِقْبَةً مِنَ ٱلدَّهْرِ حَتَّى قِيلَ لَنْ يَتَصَدَّعَا

وقيل إنّما عنَى الفرقدين

٨،١١ ويحكى أنّ جذيمة سكر مرّة أخرى فقتلهما وبنى عليهما الغريّين[1] وقيل إنّ صاحب الغريبين المنذر الأكبر

٩،١١ ثمّ إنّ جذيمة أرسل يخطب الزبّاء ملكة الحضر الحاجز بين الروم والفرس وكان لها وتر فأجابته واستدعته إليها فأشار أصحابه بالمضيّ فخالفهم قصير بن سعد وكان لبيبًا وقال إنّ النساء يهدين إلى الأزواج فعصاه وسار حتّى إذا كان بمكان يدعى بقّة استشارهم فقالوا بما يعلمون فقال له قصير انصرف ودمك في وجهك فأبى وتقدّم حتّى إذا عاين الكتائب قد استقبلته قال لقصير ما الرأي قال تركت الرأي ببقّة فذهبت مثلاً ثمّ ركب قصير فرسًا لجذيمة يسمّى العصا ونجا وأُخذ جذيمة فلمّا دخل على الزبّاء فأمرت بقطع رواهشه فقطعت والرواهش عروق اليد واستنزفته حتّى مات في خبر طويل مشهور

١ إ، ء، برا: الغريبين.

face, dressed him, and exclaimed, "We could give no better gift to Jadhīmah than his nephew!"

Jadhīmah was overjoyed when they brought ʿAmr to him, and seeing the collar, he remarked, "ʿAmr's outgrown his torque," which became a proverbial expression for children's maturation. Jadhīmah then addressed the two envoys: "Name your terms!" They responded, "May we become your drinking companions for as long as we all live." He fulfilled their wish, and they are the "drinking duo," who became proverbial and to whom the poet Mutammim ibn Nuwayrah referred in a simile:

> For an age, we were inseparable—
> like Jadhīmah's drinking duo.

(Some say that the "drinking duo" intended by Mutammim were actually "Ursa" and "Minor," not the two envoys.)

There is also a story that in another drunken moment, Jadhīmah killed the two boon companions, and then erected a monument to them known as "The Twin Pillars of Blood."[88] However, others report that those pillars were built by King al-Mundhir the Elder. 11.8

Sometime later, Jadhīmah sent a marriage request to Zenobia, queen of Metropolis, a city that lay between the Roman and Persian realms.[89] She harbored an unrevenged blood feud against Jadhīmah,[90] but nonetheless consented to marriage, and invited Jadhīmah to come to her. Most of Jadhīmah's companions urged him to go, but Qaṣīr ibn Saʿd, an astute man, disagreed: "The custom is for women to be presented to their husbands." Jadhīmah ignored Qaṣīr's advice and set off with his companions. When they reached a place called Baqqah, Jadhīmah sought the counsel of his companions, and all endorsed his plan to continue except Qaṣīr, who said, "Turn back while you still have blood running in your veins." Jadhīmah again ignored his counsel, and they advanced until they saw that squadrons of cavalry had come to meet them. Jadhīmah asked Qaṣīr, "What's our plan?" Qaṣīr muttered, "You left the plan behind at Baqqah." This became proverbial. Qaṣīr escaped on Staff, one of Jadhīmah's horses, but Jadhīmah was captured, and when he was presented before Zenobia she ordered his radial and ulnar arteries—that is, the arteries that run into the hand—cut, and he bled to death. The story is longer; it is well known. 11.9

ومن شعره ١٠،١١

أَمْسَى جَذِيمَةُ فِي يَبْرِينَ مَنْزِلَةً قَدْ حَازَ مَا جَمَعَتْ مِنْ قَبْلِهِ عَادُ
مُسْتَعْمِلَ ٱلْخَيْرِ لَا تَفْنِي زِيَادَتُهُ فِي كُلِّ يَوْمٍ وَأَهْلُ ٱلْخَيْرِ يَزْدَادُ

وبلقيس غايرت الزبّاءَ عليك ١٢

١،١٢ بلقيس ابنة الحارث بن سبأ ويُلقّب أبوها بالهدهاد وقيل بنت الشيصبان ملكة بلاد سبأ المذكورة في الكتاب العزيز

٢،١٢ وعن ابن عبّاس قال سئل رسول الله صلّى الله عليه وسلّم عن سبأ أرجل هو أم امرأة أم أرض فقال رسول الله صلّى الله عليه وسلّم بل رجل ولد عشرة سكن منهم اليمن ستّة والشام أربعة فاليمانيّون مذحج وكندة والأنمار والأزد والأشعريّون وحمير وأمّا الشاميّون فلخم وجذام وعاملة وغسّان

٣،١٢ وكانت بلقيس من أحسن نساء العالمين ويقال إنّ أحد أبويها كان جنّيًّا وقال ابن الكلبيّ كان أبوها من عظماء الملوك وولده ملوك اليمن وإنّه اتّفق له زواج امرأة من الجنّ فولدت له بلقيس وتسمّى بلقمة

٤،١٢ ويقال إنّ مؤخّر قدميها كان يشبه حافر الدابّة ولذلك اتّخذ سليمان عليه السلام الصرح الممرّد وكان بيتًا من زجاج يخيّل للرائي أنّه يضطرب فلمّا رأته كشفت عن ساقيها فلم ير غير شعر خفيف ولذلك أمر بإحضار عرشها ليختبر عقلها ثمّ أسلمت وعزم سليمان على تزويجها فأمر الشياطين فاتّخذوا الحمّام والنورة وهو أوّل من اتّخذ ذلك ثمّ تزوّجها وأرادت منه ردّها إلى ملكها ففعل ذلك وأمر الشياطين فبنوا لها باليمن الحصون التي لم يُر مثلها وهي غمدان وبينون وغيرهما وأبقاها على ملكها وكان يزورها في كلّ شهر مرّةً من الشام على البساط والريح وبقي ملكها لى أن تُوفّي فزال بموته

Jadhīmah's poetry: 11.10

Jadhīmah's evening repose is at Yabrīn;
his wealth rivals the fabled possessions of ʿĀd.
Generosity yields to no limit;
the munificent always give more.

**The Queen of Sheba competed with Zenobia for your affection . . .** 12

Bilqīs is the name of the Queen of Sheba, who is mentioned in the Holy Qur'an.[91] Her father's name was al-Ḥārith (known as Hudhād) ibn Saba', or, according to some, Shīṣbān. 12.1

Ibn ʿAbbās reports that the Prophet (God bless and keep him) was once asked about the meaning of "Sheba," and whether it connotes a man, a woman, or a place. He responded, "Certainly it was a man: he had ten sons, six of whom settled in the South and four in the North. The Southerners were Madhḥij, Kindah, al-Anmār, al-Azd, al-Ashʿar, and Ḥimyar; the Northerners were Lakhm, Judhām, ʿĀmilah, and Ghassān."[92] 12.2

The Queen of Sheba was one of the most beautiful women in the world. Some say that one of her parents was a jinni: Ibn al-Kalbī has it that her mother was a jinni who married a great king of Yemen, and from whom the Yemeni royal line traced its descent. The Queen of Sheba is also known by the name Balqamah. 12.3

They say her lower legs resembled hooves, and for that reason Solomon paved his palace floor with smoothed glass,[93] as it would trick the eye into thinking the floor was underwater. When the Queen of Sheba entered and beheld the floor, she lifted her dress, exposing her legs, and Solomon saw their thin feathering of hair. Therefore, he ordered her throne be brought and questioned her so as to gauge her mind. When she converted to Islam, Solomon was determined to wed her: he ordered daemons to build a bathhouse and prepare a depilatory paste of quicklime; he was the first in history to give such an order. He married her, but she wished he would let her return to her kingdom, so Solomon acquiesced and again summoned the daemons, who built palaces for her in Yemen, the likes of which had never been seen before. These include Ghumdān, Baynūn, and others. Solomon allowed her to remain queen, and he visited her once every month, traveling from the Levant on wind-borne carpets. The Queen of Sheba's kingdom collapsed upon Solomon's death. 12.4

٥،١٢ وأمّا الزبّاء فهي فارعة ابنة مليح بن البرّاء كان أبوها ملكًا على الحضر وهو الذي ذكره عديّ بن زيد بقوله

وَأَخُو ٱلْحُضْرِ إِذْ بَنَاهُ وَإِذْ دِجَـ لَةُ تُجْـبَى إِلَيْـهِ وَٱلْخَـابُورُ

فقتله جذيمة الأبرش وطرد الزبّاء إلى الشام فلحقت بالروم وكانت عربيّة اللسان كبيرة الهمّة

٦،١٢ قال ابن الكلبيّ وما رُئِيَ في نساء زمانها أجمل منها وكانت تستحب شعرها وإذا نشرته جلّلها ولذلك سمّيت الزبّاء وهي الكثيرة الشعر

٧،١٢ وبلغ من همّتها أن جمعت الرجال وبذلت الأموال وعادت إلى ديار أبيها ومملكته فأزالت جذيمة عنها وبنت على فرات مدينتين متقابلتين وجعلت بينهما أنفاقًا تحت الأرض وتحصّنت وكانت قد اعتزلت الرجال فهي عذراء وهادنت جذيمة مدّة ثمّ خطبها فاستدعته وقتلته كما تقدّم في ترجمته

٨،١٢ فأمّا مقتلها فإنّ قصيرًا لمّا فارق جذيمة وعاد إلى بلاده تحيّل على قتلها فجدع أنفه وضرب جسده ورحل إليها زاعمًا أنّ عمرو بن[1] عديّ ابن أخت جذيمة صنع به ذلك وأنّه لجأ إليها هاربًا منه واستجار بها ولم يزل يتلطّف لها بطريق التجارة وكسب الأموال إلى أن وثقت به وعلم خفايا قصرها وأنفاقه ثمّ وضع رجالاً من قوم عمرو بن[2] عديّ في غرائر وعليهم السلاح على الإبل على أنّها قافلة متجر إلى أن دخل بهم مدينتها فحلّوا الغرائر وأحاطوا بقصرها[3] وقتلها قبل أن تصل إلى نفقها في حكاية مشهورة وذلك بعد مبعث المسيح عليه السلام

١ عمرو بم: زيادة من إ٣، برا؛ إ١: عدي بن أخت جذيمة. ٢ :عمرو بن: زيادة من إ٣، برا. ٣ :فحلوا . . . بقصرها: زيادة من إ٢ وإ٥ وإ٦ ور٢.

Zenobia is the nickname for Fāriʿah, the daughter of Malīḥ ibn al-Barrāʾ. 12.5
Her father was king of Metropolis, and he is the figure whom ʿAdī ibn Zayd referenced in his verse:

> Where now is the man of Metropolis,
> the builder of the town fed by the Tigris and Khabur?[94]

Jadhīmah the Speckled[95] killed Zenobia's father and expelled Zenobia. She took refuge with the Romans in Syria. She was an Arabic speaker and a most resolute woman.

Ibn al-Kalbī reports that Zenobia outstripped all the beauties of her day. 12.6
Her nickname, "Zenobia," derived from her hair: the word means having abundant hair, and hers was long enough to trail behind her, and even to cover her body when she undid her braids.

Her resolve to recover her father's lands and kingdom drove her to gather 12.7
enough men to mount an invasion, and she forced Jadhīmah off her father's lands. She then built twin fortified cities on opposite sides of the Euphrates, connected by tunnels. She withheld herself from men, and stayed a virgin. As already told,[96] she maintained a truce with Jadhīmah for a period, but when he proposed their marriage, she invited him to her lands and killed him.

Zenobia's murder of Jadhīmah was also her own undoing. After Jadhīmah 12.8
died, Qaṣīr, who had escaped from Jadhīmah's party, returned to his country and plotted revenge. He cut off his nose and further injured his body and then traveled back to Zenobia and begged for asylum, claiming that his wounds had been at the hands of ʿAmr ibn ʿAdī, Jadhīmah's nephew. Qaṣīr then applied himself to trading, and for a long time made money for Zenobia to win her confidence. Eventually she did trust him, and he learned the secrets of her palace, including the tunnels. Thereupon, Qaṣīr concealed an armed band of ʿAmr ibn ʿAdī's warriors in camel saddlebags, feigning that another merchant caravan had arrived in town. Once the caravan was admitted inside the walls, the men broke out of the bags and surrounded Zenobia's palace. Qaṣīr killed Zenobia before she could reach her tunnel. This story is well known; it took place after the time of Jesus (eternal peace be his).

## وشيرين نافست بوران فيك ١٣

شيرين زوجة أبرويز بن هرمز من ولد كسرى أنوشروان كانت يتيمة في حجر رجل من أشراف المدائن وكان أبرويز صغيرًا يدخل منزل ذلك الرجل فيلاعب شيرين وتلاعبه وأخذت من قلبه موضعًا فنهاها ذلك الرجل فلم تنته فرآها وقد أخذت في بعض الأيّام من أبرويز خاتمًا فقال لبعض خواصّه اذهب بها إلى دجلة فغرّقها فأخذها ومضى فقالت وما الذي ينفعك من تغريقي فقال إنّي حالف لا أخالف مولاي فقالت اقذفني في مكان رقيق فإن نجوت لم أظهر ففعل وتوارت في الماء حتّى غاب وصعدت إلى دير فترهّبت فيه وأحسن إليها الرهبان ١،١٣

فلمّا تقرّر الملك لأبرويز بعد أبيه هرمز مرّ بذلك الدير رسل قيصر إلى أبرويز فدفعت الخاتم إلى رئيسهم وقالت ابعث به إلى أبرويز لتحظى عنده فأرسله وعرّفه مكان شيرين فسُرّ بذلك وأرسل إليها فأحضرها وكانت من أظرف النساء ففوّض إليها أموره فهجر نساءه وعاهدها أن لا تمكّن منها أحدًا بعده وبنى لها القصر المعروف بقصر شيرين بالعراق ٢،١٣

فلمّا قتل شيرويه أباه أبرويز راودها على نفسها فامتنعت فضيّق عليها واستأجلها[1] ورماها بالزنا وتهدّدها بالقتل إن لم تفعل فقالت أفعل على ثلاث شرائط قال ما هي قالت تسلّم إليّ قتلة زوجي أقتلهم وتصعد المنبر فتبرّئني ممّا قذفتني به وتفتح لي ناووس أبيك فإنّ له عندي وديعة عاهدني إن تزوّجت بعده ٣،١٣

١ كلّ النسخ: استأصلها.

**. . . Shirin vied with Boran over you.** 13

Shirin was the wife of Khosrow Parviz, the son of Hormizd, son of Khosrow Anushirvan. 13.1

Shirin grew up an orphan under the guardianship of a nobleman from al-Madāʾin. When he was a boy, Khosrow Parviz used to frequent that nobleman's house, and he and Shirin would play together. Shirin won a place in his heart, and against her guardian's wishes she continued to kindle the affection. One day, her guardian noticed that she was wearing a ring gifted by Khosrow Parviz, and he ordered one his householders: "Take the girl and drown her in the Tigris!" The servant seized Shirin and dragged her off. She begged, "What benefit is it to you if you drown me?" The servant answered, "I have sworn not to disobey my master." She pleaded, "Then throw me in a shallow spot, and if I manage to escape, I will conceal myself somehow." This he did, and Shirin hid in the water until he left. She then found her way to a monastery and became a nun. The monks treated her kindly.

Time passed, Khosrow Parviz succeeded his father Hormizd as king, and 13.2
one day a group of Byzantine emissaries was traveling by that very monastery on their way to Khosrow Parviz's court. Shirin presented the ring to their leader and told him, "Give this to Khosrow Parviz. It will be well worth your while." The emissary delivered the ring and revealed Shirin's whereabouts. Khosrow Parviz was thrilled by the news and sent for Shirin. She was a most elegant woman, and Khosrow Parviz shunned all his other wives, assigning Shirin the affairs of state. He made Shirin swear that she would not let another marry her after he died, and the palace in Iraq known as Shirin's Palace was his construction for her.

Later, Sheroe, one of Khosrow Parviz's sons, orchestrated his father's 13.3
murder, and then tried to woo Shirin for himself. She refused, but Sheroe pressed, and when he realized she was dragging her feet, he publicly accused her of adultery and threatened to kill her unless she gave in to him. She at last conceded: "I'll agree on three conditions." "What are they?" "Deliver to me the men who murdered my husband, as I will execute them. Then ascend the pulpit and declare my innocence of the crime for which you have slandered me. Finally, open your father's sarcophagus, as I have a pledge he made me swear I would return to him if I ever married again." Sheroe did as she asked: the murderers were delivered and she executed them, he cleared her of

رددتها عليه فدفع لها قتلة أبيه فقتلتهم وبرّأها ممّا قال وفتح لها ناووس أبيه وبعث الخدم معها فجاءت إلى أبرويز فعانقته ومصّت فصًّا مسمومًا كان معها فماتت من وقتها

٤،١٣ وأمّا بوران فهي ابنة أبرويز المذكور وكانت من أحسن من نشأ بين الترك والفرس من النساء وملكت الناس بعد شهريار بن أبرويز وأصلحت القناطر والجسور ولمّا جلست على السرير قالت ليس ببطش الرجال تدوّخ البلاد ولا بمكايدهم ينال الظفر وإنّما ذلك بعون الله تعالى وقدرته وأقامت سبعة أشهر

٥،١٣ ويقال إنّ فيروز بن رستم صاحب خراسان خطبها فقالت إنّه لا ينبغي للملكة أن تتزوّج علانيّة وواعدته أن يقدم سرًّا في ليلة عيّنتها له فجاءها في تلك الليلة فقتلته فسار إليها أبوه رستم فقتلها وقيل إنّ هذه الواقعة كانت مع أردمرخت[1]

## ١٤ وأنّ مالك بن نويرة إنّما ردف لك

١،١٤ هو مالك بن نويرة بن شدّاد اليربوعيّ التميميّ فارس ذي الخمار وذو الخمار فرسه ويُلقّب مالك بالجفول لكثرة شعره وكان من فرسان العرب وشجعانهم وذوي الردافة في الجاهليّة وكانت لبني يربوع أيّام المنذر

٢،١٤ ومعنى الردف أن يجلس الملك ويجلس الردف على يمينه فإذا شرب الملك شرب الردف بعده وإذا غزا جلس الردف مكانه وللردف إتاوة تؤخذ مع إتاوة الملك وفي ذلك يقول الراجز

وَمَنْ يُنَافِرْ آلَ يَرْبُوعٍ يَخِبْ ٱلْمَجْلِسُ ٱلْأَيْمَنُ وَٱلرِّدْفُ ٱلنُّجُبْ

[1] ق١: أزد مرخت؛ إ٣: اردمي دخت؛ ت١: (آزرْميدُخت) وردت في الهامش.

his accusations, and he had the sarcophagus opened. Sheroe dispatched servants to accompany Shirin, and when she climbed into the sarcophagus, she embraced Khosrow Parviz and sucked on a ring containing poison that she had brought with her, dying instantly.

Boran was the daughter of Khosrow Parviz, and she was one of the best 13.4
women ever born among the Turkish and Persian peoples. Following the death of Shahriyar, son of Khosrow Parviz, Boran ruled the kingdom for seven months herself. During her reign, she repaired bridges and aqueducts, and when she sat on the royal throne she proclaimed, "It is not through the violence of men that the land is subjugated, nor is conquest achieved by their schemes: true victory is through the will and aid of exalted God."

It is told that Piruz, son of Rostam, the ruler of Khurasan, sought Boran's 13.5
hand in marriage. She replied, "It is not decorous for a queen to be married in public," but she promised him marriage if he would come in secret on a night she specified. When Piruz arrived that night, however, she killed him. Then his father, Rostam, killed her in vengeance. There are, however, those who say that this episode involved Queen Azarmidokht, not Boran.[97]

**. . . Mālik ibn Nuwayrah was regent only for you . . .** 14

Mālik ibn Nuwayrah ibn Shaddād hailed from the Yarbūʿ clan of the Tamīm. 14.1
His horse was named the Veiled One, and Mālik was nicknamed "Shaggy," for he had such a head of hair. He was one of the great pre-Islamic Arab mounted warrior heroes and regents. In the days of King al-Mundhir, the privilege of regency was granted to the Yarbūʿ.

"Regent" in this context means the man whom a king permits to sit on his 14.2
right. Whenever the king drinks, the regent is the next for the cup; whenever the king goes raiding, the regent holds court in his stead. The regent was also entitled to a share of the taxes gathered for the king. The Yarbūʿ's right to regency was described by a poet:

Vie against the Yarbūʿ—you lose.
They sit on the right, noble regents.

٣،١٤ وأدرك مالك بن نويرة الإسلام وبعثه رسول الله صلّى الله عليه وسلّم على صدقات قومه من بني يربوع فلمّا تُوفّي رسول الله صلّى الله عليه وسلّم أخّر الصدقة وقيل ارتدّ وبعث أبو بكر رضي الله تعالى عنه خالد بن الوليد رضي الله تعالى عنه لقتال أهل الردّة وأوصاه إذا صبّح قومًا تسمّع الأذان فإن سمعه كفّ عنهم وإن لم يسمعه قتلهم فلمّا مرّ بالبطاح وبه مالك وأصحابه قيل إنّهم لم يسمعوا أذانًا فقاتلهم وأتي بمالك بن نويرة أسيرًا فأمر خالد بن الوليد ضرار بن الأزور بقتله فقتله

٤،١٤ واحتجّ قوم بخالد في قتله وطعن عليه آخرون فأمّا من احتجّ فيزعم أنّ مالكًا مات مرتدًّا وأنّه لمّا وقف بين يدي خالد كان يقول في مخاطبته قال صاحبك وتُوفّي صاحبك يعني النبيّ صلّى الله عليه وسلّم فقال له خالد أوليس هو بصاحبك أيضًا يا عدوّ الله ثمّ قتله ويحتجّون أيضًا بقول أخيه متمّم وذلك أنّ عمر بن الخطّاب رضي الله تعالى عنه لمّا سمع متمّمًا ينشد رثاء أخيه مالك قال وددت لو رثيت أخي زيدًا بمثل ما رثيت به أخاك فقال والله لو علمت أنّ أخي صار إلى ما صار إليه أخوك لم أرثه ولم أحزن عليه يعني الجنّة

٥،١٤ وأمّا الطاعنون فذكروا أنّ خالدًا لمّا احتجّ على مالك بارتداده وأنكر مالك وقال أنا على الإسلام ووالله ما غيّرت ولا بدّلت وشهد أبو[١] قتادة وعبد الله بن عمر ثمّ إنّ خالدًا أمر بقتله فجاءت امرأته ليلى بنت سنان كاشفة وجهها وكانت من الحسان فألقت نفسها عليه فقال لها أنت قتلتني يعني أنّها أعجبت خالدًا وأنّه يريد قتله

---

١ سقطت من إ١.

Mālik was still alive in the early days of Islam, and the Prophet (God bless and keep him) appointed him to collect alms taxes from the Yarbūʿ. After the Prophet (God bless and keep him) died, Mālik delayed payment of the Yarbūʿs' tax, and it was said that he abandoned Islam. The Caliph Abū Bakr (God be pleased with him) dispatched Khālid ibn al-Walīd (God be pleased with him) to wage war on all such apostates, and he counseled Khālid to hold off attacking the camps of suspected apostates until the time of the predawn prayer: if Khālid heard the call to prayer, he was to desist, but if he heard nothing, his orders were to eradicate them. When Khālid was marching through the valley where Mālik and his companions were encamped, it was said that Khālid did not hear the call to prayer, and so attacked. Mālik was brought to Khālid as a prisoner and, on Khālid's order, Ḍirār ibn al-Azwar executed him. 14.3

While some narrators support Khālid's decision to execute Mālik, others censure him. 14.4

Khālid's supporters allege that Mālik was indeed an apostate, and they adduce two anecdotes as evidence.

First, they say that when Mālik was brought before Khālid and interrogated, Mālik used the words "your companion" to refer to the Prophet (God bless and keep him), when he said, "Your companion died." Khālid responded, "Oughtn't he be *your* companion too, you enemy of God?" Thereupon, Khālid ordered Mālik's execution.

Second, they cite a statement allegedly uttered by Mālik's brother Mutammim. Mutammim composed an elegy after Mālik's death, and when ʿUmar ibn al-Khaṭṭāb (God be pleased with him) heard it, he exclaimed to Mutammim, "I would love for you to eulogize my brother Zayd in the way you did for Mālik!" But Mutammim replied, "I mourned for Mālik so much only because I know he isn't destined for the same fate as your brother Zayd." Mutammim intended that Zayd—unlike Mālik—was destined for Paradise.

Khālid's critics, however, report a different version. They say that when Khālid charged Mālik with apostasy, Mālik replied, "I'm on the path of Islam, by God, and have not deviated an inch!" Abū Qatādah[98] and ʿAbd Allāh ibn ʿUmar swore that Mālik said that, but Khālid nonetheless ordered the execution. Right then, Mālik's wife, Laylā bint Sinān, burst in upon them with her head uncovered, and threw herself onto Mālik. She was very beautiful, and Mālik lamented, "My dear, you've just killed me." (Mālik meant that because Khālid found her attractive, he would execute Mālik in order to wed her himself.)[99] Thereupon, 14.5

ليتزوّجها وقام ضرار بن الأزور فقتله وجعل رأسه أثفيّة للقدر ووجهه ممّا يلي النار فنظرت امرأة من قومه وهو على تلك الحال فقالت اصرفوا وجه مالك عن النار فإنّه والله كان غضيض الطرف عن الجارات حديد النظر في الغارات لا يشبع ليلة يضاف ولا ينام ليلة يخاف ثمّ بلغ عمر بن الخطّاب رضي الله تعالى عنه ما صنع خالد فحرّض عليه أبا بكر رضي الله تعالى عنه وقال إنّه قتل مسلمًا وزنا فارجمه ووافقه عليّ بن أبي طالب رضي الله تعالى عنه فقال أبو بكر إنّه تأوّل فأخطأ وما كنت لأشيم سيفًا سلّه رسول الله صلّى الله عليه وسلّم يعني أغمده وما زال عمر رضي الله تعالى عنه حاقدًا على خالد بهذه الواقعة حتّى عزله عن جيش الإسلام فقال والله لا ولي عملاً في أيّامي

٦،١٤ وكان متمّم بن نويرة منقطعًا إلى أخيه مالك مكفي المؤونة فلمّا قتل حزن عليه حزنًا عظيمًا ورثاه بقصائد مشهورة وحضر حين بلغه ذلك إلى مسجد رسول الله صلّى الله عليه وسلّم وصلّى الصبح خلف أبي بكر فلمّا فرغ من صلاته وانفتل قام متمّم واتكأ على قوسه ثمّ أنشد

نِعْـمَ ٱلْقَتِيلُ إِذَا ٱلرِّيَاحُ تَنَاوَحَتْ    خَلْفَ ٱلْبُيُوتِ قَتَلْتَ يَا ٱبْنَ ٱلْأَزْوَرِ

ثمّ أومأ إلى أبي بكر فقال

أَدَعَوْتَـهُ[١] بِٱللهِ ثُـمَّ غَـدَرْتَـهُ    لَوْ هُوَ دَعَـاكَ بِذِمَّـةٍ لَمْ يَغْـدُرِ

٧،١٤ فقال أبو بكر والله ما دعوته ولا غدرته فأنشد بقيّة قصيدته ثمّ بكى وانحطّ على قوسه وكان أعور فما زال يبكي حتّى دمعت عينه العوراء فقام إليه عمر بن

١ إ: (ودعوته) وردت بالهامش.

Ḍirār ibn al-Azwar delivered the blow, and they set up Mālik's severed head as a stand for a cooking pot, placing his face in the direction of the fire. One of Mālik's kinswomen saw this and said, "Turn his face from the fire! By God, he always looked away from women he was protecting, but stared keenly at men he was combating. At night, as a host, he went hungry, and in war he was ever alert and steady." ʿUmar ibn al-Khaṭṭāb (God be pleased with him) was told all of this and sought to incite Abū Bakr (God be pleased with him) against Khālid, saying, "By God, he just killed a Muslim and fornicated with the man's wife! Stone him!" ʿAlī ibn Abī Ṭālib (God be pleased with him) agreed with ʿUmar, but Abū Bakr demurred, saying, "Khālid acted on a presumption, and though wrong, I am loath to sheathe a sword drawn by the Messenger of God (God bless and keep him)." He meant that he would not put "the Sword of God" back in its scabbard.[100] But ʿUmar (God be pleased with him) continued carrying the grudge against Khālid, and when ʿUmar became caliph, he dismissed Khālid from command of the Muslim army, saying, "By God, that man will not be appointed to any command as long as I live!"

Mutammim ibn Nuwayrah had been devoted to his brother Mālik and was materially reliant upon him. Mālik's execution broke Mutammim's heart and moved him to compose now-celebrated elegies of Mālik. The story goes that right after hearing of his brother's death, Mutammim went straight to the Mosque of the Prophet (God bless and keep him) in Medina, where he prayed the predawn prayer right behind the Caliph Abū Bakr. When the prayer was finished, as Abū Bakr turned to leave, Mutammim rose, leaned on his bow, and recited: 14.6

> Where the swirling winds wail, there lies a corpse
> behind the camps. What a good man you felled, Ḍirār!

Mutammim then pointed to Abū Bakr.

> Did you call him in God's name, and then betray him?
> Had you been in his protection, he'd never have betrayed you.

Abū Bakr interjected, "By God, I never called him or betrayed him." Mutammim then completed the poem, slumped over his bow, and wept. He wept until even his blind eye shed tears (Mutammim was one-eyed). This was when ʿUmar ibn al-Khaṭṭāb (God be pleased with him) rose and told Mutammim, "I would love for you to eulogize my brother Zayd," and Mutammim gave the reply noted 14.7

الخطّاب رضي الله تعالى عنه فقال وددت لو رثيت أخي زيدًا فأجابه بما تقدّم ثمّ رثا زيدًا فلم يجد فسُئل عن ذلك فقال والله ليحرّكني لأخي ما لا يحرّكني لزيد

٨،١٤ وسأله عمر عن حزنه فقال والله إنّي لا أنام الليل وما رأيت نارًا رفعت بليل إلّا ظننت أنّ نفسي ستخرج أذكر بها نار أخي إنّه كان يأمر بالنار فتوقّد حتّى يصبح مخافة أن يبيت ضيفه قريبًا منه فمتى رأى النار يأوي إلى الرحل[1] وهو بالضيف يأتي متهجّدًا أسرّ من القوم يقدم عليهم القادم منهم من السفر البعيد فقال عمر أكرم به

٩،١٤ وقال له عمر يومًا حدّثنا عن أخيك فقال أسرت مرّة في حيّ عظيم من أحياء العرب فأقبل أخي فما هو إلّا أن طلع على الحاضر فما كان أحد قاعدًا إلّا قام ولا بقيت امرأة حتّى تطلّعت من خلال البيوت فما نزل عن جمله حتّى تلقّوه بي في رمّتي فحلّني فقال عمر إنّ هذا لهو الشرف

١٠،١٤ ثمّ قال له يومًا إنّك يا متمّم لجزل فكيف كان منك أخوك فقال كان والله أخي في الليلة ذات الأزيز والصرير يركب الجمل الثفال ويجنب الفرس الحرون وفي يده الرمح الثقيل وعليه الشمّلة الفلوت وهو بين المزادتين حتّى يصبح وهو يتبسّم

١١،١٤ ومن جيّد مراثي متمّم له قوله من أبيات

وَقَالُوا أَتَبْكِي كُلَّ قَبْرٍ رَأَيْتَهُ    لِقَبْرٍ ثَوَى بَيْنَ ٱللِّوَى فَٱلدَّكَادِكِ
فَقُلْتُ لَهُمْ إِنَّ ٱلْأَسَى يَبْعَثُ ٱلْأَسَى    دَعُونِي فَهٰذَا كُلُّهُ قَبْرُ مَالِكِ

١٢،١٤ ومن شعر مالك قوله

وَلَقَدْ عَلِمْتُ وَلَا مَحَالَةَ أَنَّنِي    لِلْحَادِثَاتِ فَهَلْ تَرِينِي أَجْزَعُ
أَفْنَيْنَ عَادًا ثُمَّ آلَ مُحَرِّقٍ    فَتَرَكْنَهُمْ بَدَدًا وَمَا قَدْ جَمَّعُو

[1] ل١، إ١، بر١: الرجل.

above.[101] Although Mutammim did comply and composed a eulogy for Zayd, it was not a good poem, and when this was remarked, he explained, "By God, that which stirred me for my brother did not happen for Zayd."

'Umar asked Mutammim about his grief, and Mutammim answered, "By God, I can neither sleep nor see a campfire burning at night without feeling my soul will leap out of me, remembering my brother's hearth. He would command that the fire be lit and stay lit all night, out of worry that someone camping nearby wouldn't know to come unless he saw a fire. Truly, my brother was happier upon receiving a guest in the dead of night than most people would be to see someone returning from a far journey." 'Umar replied, "Honor him." 14.8

One day, 'Umar asked Mutammim to tell a story about Mālik. Mutammim said, "Once, a powerful Arab tribe captured me. But then my brother appeared. As soon as he came into view of their settlement, everyone who had been sitting shot up, and there wasn't a woman in the camp who didn't come to the edge of her tent to look out. He hadn't even descended from his camel before they returned me to him—I was still tied up—and he undid the bonds." 'Umar remarked, "That, sir, is real nobility!" 14.9

On another occasion, 'Umar said, "Mutammim, you're a solid fellow; how did your brother compare?" "By God, on frosty nights so cold that one huddles in extra robes, you could see my brother riding until daybreak, astride a ponderously lumbering camel, leading a restive horse, holding a heavy spear, wearing a wrap barely long enough to cover him, sitting between two provision bags, and he would be smiling." 14.10

One of Mutammim's excellent elegies for Mālik includes these lines: 14.11

They say I cry at every grave I see,
    for a grave between the dunes and al-Dadkādik.
I say: Grief invokes grief—
    Leave me! All graves are those of Mālik.

Mālik's poetry: 14.12

I have always known—forever without doubt—
I'm for confronting Fate—have you ever seen me shudder?
Fate obliterated 'Ād, ended al-Muḥarriq's clan;[102]
    it shattered them, scattered their wealth.

وَعَدَدْتُ آبَائِي إِلَى عِرْقِ ٱلثَّرَى    فَدَعَوْتُهُمْ فَعَلِمْتُ أَنْ لَمْ يَسْمَعُو
ذَهَبُوا فَلَمْ أُدْرِكْهُمْ وَدَهَتْهُمُ    غُولُ ٱللَّيَالِي وَٱلطَّرِيقُ ٱلْمَهْيَعُ

وقوله ١٣،١٤

وَقَالُوا لِيَ ٱسْتَأْسِرْ فَإِنَّكَ آمِنٌ    فَقُلْتُ إِنِ ٱسْتَأْسَرْتُ إِنِّي لَخَائِنُ
عَلَامَ تَرَكْتُ ٱلْمَشْرَفِيَّ مُضَاجِعِي    وَمُطَرَّدًا فِيهِ ٱلْمَنَايَا كَوَامِنُ
فَإِنْ تَقْتُلُونِي بَعْدَ ذٰلِكَ فَإِنَّنِي    أَمُوتُ بِمِقْدَارٍ وَتَبْقَى ٱلضَّغَائِنُ[1]

**وعروة بن جعفر إنّما رحل إليك** ١٥

هو عروة بن عتبة بن جعفر من بني عامر بن صعصعة وأهل بيته يُنسبون إلى جعفر هذا الجعفريّون ولذلك قال ابن زيدون عروة بن جعفر ولم يقل ابن عتبة وكان يُعرف بعروة الرحّال لرحلته إلى ملوك الطوائف وكان من ذوي العقل والشهامة وهو من أرداف الملوك ١،١٥

وللعرب مبالغة عظيمة في وصفه فيزعمون أنّه رحل إلى معاوية بن الجون الكنديّ فغزا معاوية ببني حنظلة قومًا من بني عامر واستصحبه معه فلمّا كان بواردات قال لمعاوية إنّ لي حقّ صحبة ورحلة وأريد أن[2] أنذر قومي من هاهن وبينه وبينهم مسيرة ليلة فعجب معاوية منه وأذن له فصاح ياصباحاه ثلاث مرّات فسمعه قومه من الشعب فاستعدّوا ٢،١٥

وبسبب مقتله قامت حرب الفجار وذلك أنّ النعمان كان يبعث لسوق عكاظ في كلّ عام لطيمة في جوار رجل شريف من أشراف العرب تجيزها له أحياء العرب حتّى تُباع له هنالك ويشتري بثمنها من أدم الطائف وغيره ممّا يحتاج إليه ٣،١٥

---

١ فإن . . . الضغائن: زيادة من برا، باا، ل١. ٢ زيادة من هوامش برا وإ٣.

I can trace my ancestors to the Old Man of Clay;[103]
I summon them—but no, they do not hear;
they departed before my time, ushered
down that well-trodden road by the murderous spirits of night.

Mālik's poetry: 14.13

They cried, "Surrender! We'll spare you!"
I replied, "Surrender is betrayal!
Why should I use my Syrian blade as a pillow
or pasture my havoc-wreaking steed?
If you manage to fell me,
Fate felled me, but the rancor lives on."

**. . . 'Urwah ibn Ja'far set off only to reach you . . .** 15

'Urwah, son of 'Utbah, son of Ja'far was a member of the 'Āmir ibn Ṣa'ṣa'ah. 15.1
His family traced their lineage to their grandfather Ja'far, hence they are called Ja'farīs, and Ibn Zaydūn refers to him as "'Urwah, son of Ja'far," and not "son of 'Utbah." 'Urwah was known as "the Traveler" since he attended the courts of various Client Kings. Wise and astute, he acted as a regent for kings.

The Arabs have spun wildly exaggerated stories about 'Urwah. For exam- 15.2
ple, it is claimed that once, when 'Urwah was residing at the court of King Mu'āwiyah ibn al-Jawn of Kindah, the king requested that 'Urwah accompany him on a raid against the Hanẓalah (one of 'Urwah's kin groups from the 'Āmir). At Wāridāt, 'Urwah told Mu'āwiyah, "I have a claim upon you since I have traveled to join your court: let me warn my kinsmen from this spot." Mu'āwiyah was astonished: they were still one night's journey from their target, so he consented, and 'Urwah thrice cried, "Beware the morn!" His kin heard it through the canyon and readied themselves.

'Urwah's murder was the casus belli of the Fijār War. It happened in con- 15.3
nection with the perfume caravan, which King al-Nu'mān used to dispatch annually to the fair at 'Ukāẓ. Each year, al-Nu'mān would task a noble Arab with securing the caravan's safe passage across the lands of the Arab tribes, and when it reached 'Ukāẓ, its contents would be sold and the proceeds put to purchasing the leather of al-Ṭā'if and other goods al-Nu'mān needed.

وكان سوق عكاظ يقوم في كلّ يوم من ذي القعدة فيتسوّقون إلى حضور الحجّ ثمّ يحجّون وكانت الأشهر الحرم أربعة أشهر ذو القعدة وذو الحجّة والمحرّم ورجب وكانت العرب من ذي الحجّة[١] يتهيّؤون للحجّ ويأمن بعضها بعضًا

٤،١٥ فجهّز النعمان عير اللطيمة ثمّ قال من يجيزها فقال البرّاض بن قيس أنا أجيزها على بني كنانة فقال النعمان ما أريد إلّا من يجيزها على أهل نجد وتهامة فقال عروة الرحّال وهو يومئذ رجل هوازن أهذا الكلب يجيزها أنا أجيزها لك على أهل الشيح والقيصوم من أهل نجد وتهامة فقال البرّاض أعلى بني كنانة تجيزها يا عروة قال وعلى الناس كلّهم

٥،١٥ فدفعها النعمان إلى عروة فخرج بها وتبعه البرّاض وكان فاتكًا عيّارًا وعروة لا يحسّ[٢] منه شيئًا لأنّه كان بين ظهراني قومه من غطفان فنزل بأرض يقال لها أوارة[٣] فشرب الخمر وغنّته قينته ونام فجاء إليه البرّاض فدجل عليه وأيقظه فناشده عروة وقال كانت منّي زلّة فقتله وخرج وهو يرتجز

قَدْ كَانَتِ ٱلْفَعْلَةُ مِنِّي ضَلَّهْ     هَلْ لَا عَلَى غَيْرِي جَعَلْتَ ٱلزَّلَّهْ

وهرب فضربت العرب المثل بفتكة البرّاض وقامت حروب عظيمة بسببه

٦،١٥ ومن شعر عروة

تَعَجَّبَ مِنِّي أُمُّ حَسَّانٍ إِنْ رَأَتْ     نَهَارًا وَلَيْلًا أَبْلَيَانِي فَأَسْرَعَا
وَقَدْ صَارَ إِخْوَانِي كَأَنَّ عَلَيْهِمُ     ثِيَابَ ٱلْمُلَاءِ وَٱلثَّغَامَ ٱلْمُوَزَّعَا

من أبيات وبعض الرواة يرويها لعروة الرجال بالجيم وهو رجل من بني أسد

---

١ با١: القعدة. ٢ ل١، ل٢، با١: يخش. ٣ إ٣: قتاد.

(The ʿUkāẓ fair was held during the month of Dhu'l-Hijjah,[104] and trading occurred daily until the time for hajj, when all performed the pilgrimage. The pre-Islamic Arabs deemed four months sacrosanct: Dhu'l-Qadah, Dhu'l-Hijja, Muharram, and Rajab; during Dhu'l-Qadah, the Arabs would prepare for the hajj and everyone granted mutual security against attacks.)

King al-Nuʿmān prepared his perfume caravan and asked, "Who will convey it?" Al-Barrāḍ ibn Qays boasted, "I can guarantee it safe passage across the lands of the Kinānah!" Al-Nuʿmān answered, "I want one who can convey it across both upland and lowland." ʿUrwah the Traveler (who at that time was the representative of the Hawāzin) interjected, "Does this dog Barrāḍ think he can protect the caravan? I guarantee its safety against bush dwellers, grove dwellers, uplanders, lowlanders, everyone!" Al-Barrāḍ challenged him: "Do you think you can get it past the Kinānah too, ʿUrwah?" "Them and everybody else!" ʿUrwah declared. 15.4

Al-Nuʿmān entrusted the caravan to ʿUrwah, and he set off. Al-Barrāḍ, hot-headed and bellicose as he was, tracked them, but ʿUrwah paid no attention since he was traveling among his kin from the Ghaṭafān. When ʿUrwah and the caravan reached a place called Uwārah, ʿUrwah fell asleep after drinking wine in the company of his singing girl. Al-Barrāḍ then crept in and woke him. ʿUrwah pleaded, "You have caught me at an unguarded moment!" But, unmoved, al-Barrāḍ killed him and left, singing a poem: 15.5

I did the deed—I was out of control—
have your unguarded moments with somebody else.

Al-Barrāḍ escaped, and the Arabs associate him proverbially with hot-blooded belligerence. He was the cause of a great many wars.

ʿUrwah's poetry: 15.6

Umm Ḥassān marvels to see
how quickly rolling days and nights test me.
And all my brothers are as if clad
in wraps beneath the blowing white hyssop.

This is part of a longer poem; some attribute it to ʿUrwah of the Men (*al-rijāl*),[105] a member of the Asad, not ʿUrwah the Traveler (*al-raḥḥāl*).

**١٦ وكليب بن ربيعة إنّما حمى المرعى بعزّتك وجسّاسًا إنّما قتله بأنفتك**

١٦،١ كليب بن ربيعة بن سنان الوائليّ الذي يُضرب به المثل فيقال أعزّ من حمى كليب كان رئيس الحيّين من بكر وتغلب ابني وائل وقاد معدًّا كلّها يوم خزاز وفضّ جموع القوم[١] فاجتمعت عليه معدّ وجعلوا له قسم الملك وتاجه وطاعته

١٦،٢ فغبر بذلك حينًا ثمّ دخله زهو شديد وبغى على قومه بما هو فيه من عزّه واثقًا بانقياد معدّ له حتّى بلغ من بغيه وعتوّه أنّه كان يحمي مواقع السحاب فلا يرعى حماه ويقول وحش كذا وكذا في جواري فلا يهاج ولا يورد أحد مع أبله ولا توقد نار مع ناره ولا يحتبى في مجلسه ولا يتكلّم إلّا بإذنه وفي ذلك يقول أخوه بعد قتله

نُبِّئْتُ أَنَّ ٱلنَّارَ بَعْدَكَ أُوقِدَتْ وَٱسْتَبَّ بَعْدَكَ يَا كُلَيْبُ ٱلْمَجْلِسُ
وَتَكَلَّمُوا فِي أَمْرِ كُلِّ عَظِيمَةٍ لَوْ كُنْتَ حَاضِرَ أَمْرِهِمْ لَمْ يَنْبَسُوا[٢]

١٦،٣ وقيل إنّه كان إذا مرّ بمرعى قذف فيه جروًا فيعوي فلا يرعى أحد من ذلك الكلاء ولذلك قيل كليب وائل يعنون الكلب ويضيفونه إلى وائل وهو اسم الملك ثمّ غلب هذا القول حتّى ظنّوه اسمه

١٦،٤ ومرّ يومًا بحمّرة وهو طائر صغير وقيل قنبرة وقد باضت فلمّا رأته صرصرت وخفقت بجناحيها فقال أمن روعك أنت في ذمّتي ثمّ أنشد

١ إ١، بر١: الروم. ٢ إ١: يدنسوا.

**. . . only with your might did Kulayb ibn Rabīʿah defend the pasturelands, only for your honor did Jassās kill him . . .** 16

The name of Kulayb ibn Rabīʿah ibn Sinān of the Wāʾil has been immortalized in the expression: "More secure than Kulayb's pasturelands." Kulayb was the leader of both the Bakr and the Taghlib, two subtribes of the Wāʾil. He led all the Maʿaddites at the Battle of Khazāz and dispersed their enemies, whereupon the Maʿaddites pledged to him their allegiance, giving him the right to a king's share of the booty and the right to wear a crown.[106] 16.1

So it remained for a time, but the knowledge that all of Maʿadd followed his command gave Kulayb a conviction of strength and impunity that transformed into overweening arrogance, and he began to oppress his own people. His haughtiness and injustice grew so outlandish that he would declare land wherever there were clouds to be his exclusive pasture preserves, preventing anyone else from grazing there. If Kulayb announced, "The wild beasts of such and such a place are under my protection," no one could disturb them, and wherever Kulayb was watering his camels, no one else could approach the water. None were allowed to light a campfire near his, and none could sit or speak at Kulayb's assembly without his permission. Kulayb's brother boasted of this in a poem composed after Kulayb's murder: 16.2

Now that you're gone, I hear that fires are being lit.
Kulayb! Assemblies are rife with discord,
and men speak on momentous matters—
were you presiding, all would be silent.

It is said that Kulayb used to release a puppy into grazing land, and the extent to which its barking was heard marked the bounds within which no one else could pasture.[107] An expression, "the little dog (*kulayb*) of Wāʾil," was coined to describe this practice. "Wāʾil" was Kulayb's actual given name: "Kulayb" initially designated just his puppy, but after the expression's frequent repetition, people began to think "Kulayb" was the king's actual name, and this stuck. 16.3

One day, Kulayb passed a desert lark's nest full of eggs (some say it was a bar-tailed lark), and when the bird saw Kulayb, it chirped and fluttered about. Kulayb told it, "Don't be afraid, you're under my protection!" Then he sang a poem to it:[108] 16.4

يَا لَكِ مِنْ قُنْبَرَةٍ بِمَعْمَرِ
خَلَا لَكِ ٱلْجَوُّ فَبِيضِي وَٱصْفِرِي
وَنَقِّرِي مَا شِئْتِ أَنْ تُنَقِّرِي

فما جسر صاحب بعير يدخل ذلك المرعى

وأمّا جسّاس فهو ابن مرّة بن ذهل كانت أخته تحت كليب وكان بنو جشم وشيبان في دار واحدة قبيلتي كليب وجسّاس وكانت لجسّاس خالة من بني سعد تُسمّى البسوس جاورت بني مرّة فنزلت على ابن أختها جسّاس ومعها ابن لها ولهم ناقة خوّارة من نعم بني سعد ولها فصيل فندّت الناقة ذات يوم فدخلت في إبل كليب ترعى في حماه فنظر إليها فأنكرها فرماها بسهم في ضرعها فولّت حتّى بركت بفناء صاحبتها وضرعها يشخب دمًا ولبنًا فلمّا نظرت إليها برزت صارخة ويدها على رأسها وهي تصيح واذلّاه فلمّا سمع جسّاس قولها سكّتها وقال والله ليُقتلنّ غدًا جمل هو أعظم عقرًا من ناقتك يعني كليبًا ٥،١٦

ثمّ انتجع الحيّ فمرّوا على نهر يقال له شبيث[1] فنهاهم كليب عنه وقال لا تردنّ قطرة منه ثمّ مرّوا على نهر آخر يقال له الأحصّ فنهاهم عنه فمضوا حتّى أتوا الذنائب ونزلوا فمرّ جسّاس بكليب وهو واقف على غدير الذنائب منفردًا فقال طردت أهلنا عن المياه حتّى كدت تقتلهم عطشًا فقال كليب ما منعناهم من ماء إلّا ونحن له شاغلون فقال له جسّاس هذا كفعلك بناقة خالتي فقال وقد ذكرتها أمّا إنّي لو وجدتها في غير إبل مرّة لاستحللت تلك الإبل فعطف عليه جسّاس فرسه فطعنه بالرمح فأرداه ووجد الموت فقال يا جسّاس اسقني فقال هيهات تجاوزت الأحصّ وشبيثًا[2] ثمّ عطف المزدلف فأجهز عليه ٦،١٦

١ إ١، إ٦، بر١، ق١، إ٣، ق٢، ق٣: شبيب. ٢ إ١، ل٢، بر١، ب: شبيب.

What a fine lark at Maʿmar!
The air's clear—lay your eggs and sing,
and peck away! Peck wherever you wish!

No camel herder dared enter that pastureland.

Jassās was son of Murrah ibn Dhuhl, and he had a sister who was one of 16.5
Kulayb's wives. They were all from the same tribe, but Jassās hailed from the Shaybān clan, while Kulayb descended from the Jusham clan.[109]

Jassās had an aunt named al-Basūs from the Saʿd clan who lived under the protection of Jassās's father. Al-Basūs and her son came to stay with Jassās, and they brought with them two camels from the Saʿds' herd: a she-camel, which produced plentiful milk, and her young calf.[110] One day, al-Basūs's she-camel strayed into Kulayb's herd, which was grazing in one of his self-proclaimed pastureland preserves. Kulayb espied the stray and, recognizing she was not from his herd, he shot her in the udder with an arrow. She turned tail and came home, setting down in front of her owner's tent with blood and milk gushing from her udder. When she saw the camel, al-Basūs burst out of her tent calling for help, hands raised to her head and crying, "O the disgrace!" Jassās quieted her, saying, "By God, a bull camel shall die tomorrow, and rest assured, it will be a much graver affair than your mare." (By "bull camel," he meant Kulayb.)

The next day, Jassās's clan departed for new pastures, and as they 16.6
passed a pool called Shubayth,[111] Kulayb forbade them from watering their camels: "None of you will drink even a drop here!" They then rode to the pool at al-Aḥaṣṣ, but Kulayb again barred them, and finally they stopped at al-Dhanāʾib. Kulayb was standing alone at al-Dhanāʾib's well when Jassās rode up to confront him: "You drove our people from the water and well-nigh parched them to death!" Kulayb retorted, "We only prevented them from pools where we ourselves were watering." Jassās grew angrier: "This is just like what you did to my aunt's she-camel!" Kulayb countered, "You bring that up? Listen: if I ever see that camel again in a herd other than your father's, I will kill her!"

At this, Jassās turned his horse upon Kulayb, and with one thrust felled him with his spear. Kulayb felt the coming of death and cried, "Jassās! Give me water!" "Fie for shame! You had your chance at al-Aḥaṣṣ and Shubayth!" Jassās turned upon Kulayb a second time and finished him off.

ثمّ إنّ جسّاسًا لمّا فرغ من قتل كليب أمال يده بالفرس حتّى انتهى إلى أهله فقالت أخته لأبيها إنّ لجسّاس شأنًا قد جاء خارجًا ركبتاه قال والله ما خرجت ركبتاه إلّا لأمر عظيم يعني أنّه كان بركبته وضح لا يظهره فلمّا جاء قال ما وراءك يا بنيّ قال ورائي أنّي طعنت طعنة ليشتغلنّ بها شيوخ وائل زمنًا قال أقتلت كليبًا قال نعم قال وددت أنّك وإخوتك مُتُّم قبل هذا ما بي إلّا أن تسأمني[1] أبناء وائل ثمّ نظر جسّاس إلى أخته نضلة فقال ٧،١٦

وَإِنِّي قَدْ جَنَيْتُ عَلَيْكِ حَرْبًا تُغِصُّ ٱلشَّيْخَ بِٱلْمَاءِ ٱلْقَرَاحِ
مُذَكَّرَةٌ مَتَى مَا يَصْحُ مِنْهَا فَتًى نَشِبَتْ لِآخَرِ غَيْرِ صَاحِي

فأجابته نضلة تطيّب قلبه

وَإِنْ تَكُ قَدْ جَنَيْتَ عَلَيَّ حَرْبًا فَلَا وَاهٍ وَلَا رَثُّ ٱلسِّلَاحِ

ثمّ هرب جسّاس ووقعت بين الحيّين حرب البسوس المشهورة قيل إنّها قامت قريبًا من أربعين سنة ٨،١٦

واختلف في قتل جسّاس فقيل إنّ أبا النويرة قتله هاربًا على طريق الشام بعد حين وقيل إنّ ابن أخته هجرس بن كليب كان عند أمّه وأخواله بعد الفتن فلمّا بلغ مبلغ الرجال وعرف أنّ خاله جسّاسًا قاتل أبيه ركب فرسه وأخذ رمحه وأتى نادي قومه وجسّاس خاله في النادي مع جماعة فقال ورمحي ونصليه وسيفي وزرّيه وفرسي وأذنيه لا يترك الرجل قاتل أبيه وهو ينظر إليه ثمّ طعن جسّاسًا فقتله ولحق بعمومته ٩،١٦

١ سقطت من إ.

Leaving Kulayb dead, Jassās let a loose hand on his reins, and his horse brought him home. As he approached, his sister remarked to their father, Murrah, "Something is up with Jassās—look how his knees point outward!" Murrah exclaimed, "By God, he only rides with his knees out if it's something really serious." This was because Jassās had marks of leprosy on his knees, and he usually wouldn't allow them to be seen. When Jassās arrived, Murrah asked him, "My son, what happened out there?" "Out there I made a thrust that will busy the leaders of the Wā'il for quite some time." "Did you kill Kulayb?" "Yes," Jassās replied. Murrah sighed. "I wish you and your brothers had died before this came to pass. The sons of Wā'il will really have it in for me now." Jassās then looked to his sister Naḍlah and composed a poem: 16.7

My crime has reaped for you a war—
it so disturbs Father that he can't swallow pure water—
A frightening war—should one brave escape its spell,
it will fast bewitch another.

Naḍlah responded, trying to cheer him:

Though your crimes reaped a war for me,
you're not frail, nor are your weapons shabby.

Jassās fled as the fighting between the two tribes flared into the famous al-Basūs War, which reportedly raged for nearly forty years. 16.8

There is disagreement as to how Jassās was killed. One version has it that Jassās attempted to flee to Syria at one point, but Abū l-Nuwayrah killed him on the way. Another version tells that Jassās died at the hand of Hijris, Kulayb's son. When the conflict first broke out, Hijris was young, and lived with his mother and maternal aunts in Jassās's camp,[112] but when he matured to manhood, he learned that Jassās, his maternal uncle, was his father's killer. So he grabbed his spear and went straight to the clan's assembly, where his uncle Jassās sat among the warriors, and Hijris announced to all gathered: "By my spear's edges, my sword's beveled blade, and my horse's ears: I swear that no man allows his father's killer to look him in the eye!" Then and there he stabbed Jassās to death and escaped to join his paternal uncles from Kulayb's clan. 16.9

**ومهلهل إنّما طلب ثأره بهمّتك** ١٧

هو مهلهل بن ربيعة بن الحارث أخو كليب المقدّم ذكره واسمه عديّ ولُقّب مهلهلاً لقوله ١،١٧

لَمَّا تَوَغَّلَ فِي ٱلْكُرَاعِ هَجِينُهُمْ     هَلْهَلْتُ أَثْأَرُ مَالِكًا أَوْ صِنْبِلَا

يعني قاربت وقيل لُقّب مهلهلاً لأنّه أوّل من هلهل نسج الشعر أي أرقّه وهو أوّل من قصّد القصائد وقال فيها الغزل وغنّى بالنسيب من شعره وهو خال امرئ القيس بن حجر ومنه ورث إجادة الشعر

وكان أيضًا كثير المحادثة للنساء حتّى كان أخوه كليب يسمّيه زير النساء ولذلك يقول بعدما قتل كليب وطلب ثأره ٢،١٧

فَلَوْ نُبِشَ ٱلْمَقَابِرُ عَنْ كُلَيْبٍ     لَيَعْلَمُ بِٱلذَّنَائِبِ أَيُّ زِيرِ

وكان خبره في هذه الواقعة وطلبه الثأر أنّ جسّاسًا لمّا قتل كليبًا ومرّ هاربًا كان همّام بن مرّة أخو جسّاس ينادم مهلهل بن ربيعة أخا كليب وكان قد صادقه وآخاه وعاهده أن لا يكتم عنه شيئًا فجاءت إليه أمّه[١] فأسرّت إليه قتل جسّاس كليبًا فقال له مهلهل ما قالت لك فلم يخبره وذكّره العهد فقال أخبرت أنّ أخي قتل أخاك فقال است أخيك أضيق من ذلك فسكت همّام وأقبلا على شربهما فجعل مهلهل يشرب شرب الآمن وهمّام يشرب شرب الخائف فلم تلبث الخمر أن صرعت مهلهلاً فانسلّ همّام فأتى قومه وقد قوّضوا الخيم وجمعوا الخيل والنعم ورحلوا فرحل معهم وظهر أمر قتل كليب ٣،١٧

١ سقطت من إ١.

**. . . only with your zeal did Muhalhil avenge his blood.** 17

Muhalhil ibn Rabīʿah ibn al-Ḥārith was the brother of Kulayb. His given name was ʿAdī, and they called him "Muhalhil," meaning "Almost," after a verse he composed: 17.1

When their half-breed fled into the stony summits at al-Kurāʾ
I almost exacted blood revenge for Mālik or Ṣinbil.

Others, however, say that his nickname, "Muhalhil," instead means "Dextrous," and that he earned the nickname because he was the first to weave delicate poetry.[113] Muhalhil was the first poet to compose long odes, and to incorporate amorous verses and memories of lovers' campsites in his poetry. He was the maternal uncle of Imruʾ al-Qays ibn Hujr, who inherited his poetic genius.

Muhalhil so often dallied with women that his brother, Kulayb, nicknamed him "the Great Flirt," but Muhalhil challenged this when he was seeking to avenge Kulayb's death: 17.2

Were the graves exhumed and Kulayb disinterred,
at al-Dhanāʾib[114] he would see "the Great Flirt's" mettle!

Muhalhil became embroiled in the Basūs War and the revenge for Kulayb's death in the following way. When Jassās killed Kulayb and took flight, Hammām ibn Murrah, Jassās's brother, was carousing with Muhalhil, Kulayb's brother. Hammām and Muhalhil were such friends, they were were like brothers, and Hammām had sworn not to withhold any secret from Muhalhil. When Hammām's mother entered and whispered to Hammām that Jassās had killed Kulayb, Muhalhil asked, "What did she tell you?" Hammām would not say, and Muhalhil reminded him of their pact. So Hammām disclosed it: "She informed me that my brother killed your brother." "Your brother doesn't have the balls to pull off something like that," replied Muhalhil. Hammām said nothing, and the two turned to their drink: Muhalhil drank freely, but Hammām sipped warily. As soon as Muhalhil was floored by the wine, Hammām stole away. By the time he returned to his people, they were already on the run, and had pulled down their tents and rounded up their horses and herds. Hammām followed them. The news of Kulayb's death spread. 17.3

وأفاق مهلهل وصحّح الخبر واجتمعت إليه وجوه قومه فقالوا لا تعجلوا على قومكم حتّى تعذروا بينكم وبينهم ٤،١٧

فانطلق رهط من أشرافهم حتّى أتو مرّة بن ذهل فعظّموا ما بينهم وبينه وقالوا اختر منّا خصالا إمّا أن[١] تدفع إلينا جسّاسًا فنقتله بصاحبنا فلم يظلم من قتل قاتله وإمّا أن تدفع إلينا همّامًا فنقتله وإمّا أن تقيدنا من نفسك فسكت وقد حضرته وجوه بكر فقالوا تكلّم غير مخذول فقال أمّا جسّاس فأنّه غلام حدث السنّ ركب رأسه فهرب حين خاف فلا علم لي به وأمّا أخوه همّام فأبو عشرة وأخو عشرة ولو دفعته لكم لضجّ[٢] بنوه في وجهي وقالوا دفعت أبانا ليقتل في ترة غيره وأمّا أنا فلا أتعجّل الموت وهل تزيد الخيل على أن تجول جولة فأكون أوّل قتيل ولكن هل لكم في غير ذلك هؤلاء بنيّ فدونكم فخذوا أحدهم بنسعه في رقبته فاقتلوه وإن شئتم فلكم ألف ناقة فغضبوا وقالوا إنّا لن نأتك لترذل لنا بنيك أو لتسومنا اللبن ٥،١٧

وتفرّقوا وقام مهلهل فتشمّر للحرب وبدأ القتل واستجرّ بين الفريقين إلى أن كان يوم واردات وقد عظم القتل في بكر فاجتمعوا إلى الحارث بن عباد بن مالك وكان قد اعتزل الحرب وقال لا ناقة لي فيها ولا جمل فذهبت مثلاً فقالوا له قد فني قومك فأرسل ابنه بجيرًا وقيل ابن أخته إلى مهلهل وقال قل له أبو بجير يقرئك السلام ويقول لك قد علمت أنّي قد اعتزلت قومي لأنّهم ظلموك وخلّيتك وإيّاهم وقد أدركت وترك وقتلت قومك ٦،١٧

فأتى بجير مهلهلاً وهو في قومه فقال له خالي يقرئك السلام فقال له من خالك يا غلام ونزا نحوه بالرمح فقال له امرؤ القيس بن أبان التغلبيّ مهلاً يا مهلهل فإنّ أهل بيت هذا قد اعتزلوا حربنا ووالله لئن قتلته ليقتلنّ به رجل لا يُسأل عن خاله ٧،١٧

١ سقطت من إ١. ٢ إ٦: ليصيح.

When Muhalhil roused himself and confirmed that the news was true, the leaders of his people, the Taghlib, gathered around him, urging each other, "Don't hasten to fight your kinsmen—do your utmost to conciliate." 17.4

And so a party of Taghlibī nobles set off to Jassās's father, Murrah of the Bakr. The Taghlibīs explained how grave the rift was and told Murrah, "We give you three options: Hand over Jassās, and we will kill him in compensation for Kulayb, as killing the killer will end the matter. Or deliver Hammām to us, and we'll kill him instead. Or you can settle this affair by killing yourself." Murrah was silent. The nobles of the Bakr had gathered round and urged Murrah, "Answer them strongly." Murrah then spoke: "Jassās is a young lad who acted heedlessly. Now he's fled and I have no idea where he has gone. His brother Hammām has ten sons and ten brothers, and should I relinquish him to you, they will come to me and shout, 'Why did you order the death of our father on account of another man's crime?' I have no wish for suicide: when the cavalry sallies out I'll be the first to perish. Perhaps you would accept an alternative: my other children are here—take your pick, take a rope, collar him, and kill him. Or, you can have one thousand she-camels." The Taghlibīs grew angry. "We didn't come for one of your worthless offspring, nor to strike a deal for milk." 17.5

Everyone dispersed, Muhalhil readied for war, and the killing began. It dragged on between the sides until the Battle of Wāridāt, where the Bakr suffered grievous losses. The Bakr rallied to al-Ḥārith ibn ʿUbād ibn Mālik, who had until then refrained from mobilizing his clan, but he still refused: "I have neither a male nor a female camel in this affair." This became an adage. The Bakr continued to press him: "Your kinsmen are about to be wiped out!" Al-Ḥārith agreed to send his son, Bujayr (alternatively, Bujayr may have been his nephew), to Muhalhil with the instructions: "Tell Muhalhil that I send him my salutations and give him this message: 'You know that I have dissociated myself from my kin in this affair because they wronged you, and so I left it between you and them to resolve. Haven't you now exacted enough blood revenge, and hasn't it already cost enough of your own kinsmen's lives too?'" 17.6

Bujayr set off for Muhalhil's camp, and there announced in the assembly: "My uncle[115] sends his salutations." "Who's your uncle, boy?" Muhalhil responded as he brandished his spear in the boy's direction. Imru' al-Qays ibn Abān of the Taghlib interjected, "Steady, now Muhalhil. This fellow's clan has 17.7

فلم يلتفت مهلهل إلى قوله وشدّ عليه فقتله وقال بؤ بشسع نعل كليب فقال الغلام إن رضيت بهذا بنو تغلب رضيت

٨،١٧ فلمّا بلغ الحارث بن عباد قتله قال نعم الغلام أصلح بين بني وائل وباء بكليب فلمّا سمعوا قول الحارث قالوا إنّ مهلهلاً قال له بؤ بشسع نعل كليب فغضب الحارث ونهض للقتال وعظمت الحروب واستمرّت بين الفريقين دهرًا طويلاً وفني معظمهم وقتل همّام وغيره إلى أن قام في الصلح الحارث بن عوف المرّيّ كما سيأتي عند قوله وأنّ الصلح بين بكر وتغلب تمّ برسالتك

٩،١٧ وآل أمر مهلهل إلى أن وصل إلى أخواله من بني يشكر فريدًا وحيدًا وأقام بين أظهرهم إلى أن مات وقيل قتل وكان سبب قتله كما ذكر ابن الكلبيّ أنّه أسنّ وخرف وكان له عبدان يخدمانه فملّا منه وخرج بهما يريد سفرًا فأناخا به في بعض الفلوات وعزما على قتله فلمّا عرف ذلك كتب على رحل ناقته وقيل أوصاهما

مَنْ مُبْلِغُ ٱلْحَيَّيْنِ أَنَّ مُهَلْهِلَا ... لِلّٰهِ دُرُّكُمَا وَدُرُّ أَبِيكُمَا

١٠،١٧ ثمّ قتلاه ورجعا إلى قومه فقالا مات وأنشداهم[١] قوله ففكّر بعض ولده وقال إنّ مهلهلاً لا يقول هذا الشعر الذي لا معنى له وإنّما أراد

مَنْ مُبْلِغُ ٱلْحَيَّيْنِ أَنَّ مُهَلْهِلًا ... أَمْسَى قَتِيلًا فِي ٱلْفَلَاةِ مُجَدَّلَا
لِلّٰهِ دُرُّكُمَا وَدُرُّ أَبِيكُمَا ... لَا يَبْرَحُ ٱلْعَبْدَانِ حَتَّى يُقْتَلَا

فضربوا العبدين وأقرّا بقتله فقُتلا

١ إ: أنشداهما.

stayed out of our war, and by God, if you kill him now, another man will be killed in retaliation, and there won't be any asking about uncles then!"[116] Muhalhil paid no heed and fatally stabbed the boy, saying, "This will compensate for Kulayb's sandal strap." The boy's last words were: "If the Taghlib think this is fair, then so be it."

Al-Ḥārith exclaimed upon first news of the boy's death: "What a good lad: he reconciled the clans of Wāʾil, and was compensation for the blood debt of Kulayb." But others then corrected al-Ḥārith: "Muhalhil actually said that your lad was only worth the compensation for the value of Kulayb's sandal strap." Fury flared within al-Ḥārith, and he rose straight to battle. Great combats ensued between the two sides for an age, the clans largely annihilated each other, and Hammām was killed before al-Ḥārith ibn ʿAwf of the Murrah finally settled the feud, as will be explained in the section below: "Your missive forged the peace between Bakr and Taghlib."[117] 17.8

In the end, Muhalhil was left solitary and alone, and he settled with his maternal uncles from the Yashkur, with whom he lived until his death. 17.9

It is said that Muhalhil was murdered, and Ibn al-Kalbī tells the story: Muhalhil grew old and senile, and two slaves who served him grew weary of him. One day, Muhalhil left camp with them on a journey, and when they set down their camels in a remote spot in the desert, the slaves resolved to kill him there. Muhalhil grasped their plan and wrote the following verse on his camel saddle (others say he charged the slaves with reciting it):

> Will you inform the two tribes that Muhalhil
> How good you are, and how fine your father!

The slaves murdered him and returned to the camp, saying, "Muhalhil died." 17.10
They recited the verse, and one of Muhalhil's sons said, "Muhalhil wasn't one to sing a meaningless poem: he must have meant:

> 'Will you inform the two tribes that Muhalhil
> was left dead at nightfall in the desert dust.
> How good you are, and how fine your father!
> The two slaves must be killed at once.'"

The slaves were beaten until they confessed, and then were executed.

وشعر مهلهل من أعلى طبقات المتقدّمين ومن ذلك قوله ١١،١٧

بِكُرْهٍ قُلُوبِنَا يَا آلَ بَكْرٍ نُغَادِيكُمْ بِمُرْهَفَةِ ٱلنِّصَالِ
لَهَا لَوْنٌ مِنَ ٱلْهَامَاتِ جَوْنٌ وَإِنْ كَانَتْ تُغَادَى بِٱلصِّقَالِ
وَنَبْكِي حِينَ نَذْكُرُكُمْ عَلَيْكُمْ وَنَقْتُلُكُمْ كَأَنَّا لَا نُبَالِي

هذه الأبيات هي أصل ما اعتمد عليه الشعراء في هذا المعنى وأمهرهم في ذلك البحتريّ في قصيدته العينيّة

ومن ذلك قوله أعني مهلهلاً ١٢،١٧

أَلَيْلَتَنَا بِذِي حُسُمٍ[١] أَنِيرِي إِذَا أَنْتِ ٱنْقَضَيْتِ فَلَا تَحُورِي
فَإِنْ يَكُ بِٱلذَّنَائِبِ طَالَ لَيْلِي فَقَدْ أَبْكِي مِنَ ٱللَّيْلِ ٱلْقَصِيرِ
وَأَنْقَذَنِي بَيَاضُ ٱلصُّبْحِ مِنْهَا لَقَدْ أُنْقِذْتُ مِنْ شَرٍّ كَبِيرِ[٢]
كَأَنَّ كَوَاكِبَ ٱلْجَوْزَاءِ عُوذٌ مُعَطَّفَةٌ عَلَى رُبْعٍ كَسِيرِ
كَأَنَّ ٱلْفَرْقَدَيْنِ يَدَا مُفِيضٍ أَلَحَّ عَلَى إِفَاضَتِهِ قَمِيرِ
فَلَوْ نُبِشَ ٱلْمَقَابِرُ عَنْ كُلَيْبٍ لَخُبِّرَ بِٱلذَّنَائِبِ أَيُّ زِيرِ
وَإِنِّي قَدْ تَرَكْتُ بِوَارِدَاتٍ بُجَيْرًا فِي دَمٍ مِثْلِ ٱلْعَبِيرِ
هَتَكْتُ بِهِ بُيُوتَ بَنِي عُبَادٍ وَبَعْضُ ٱلْغَشْمِ أَشْفَى لِلصُّدُورِ
عَلَى أَنْ لَيْسَ عَدْلًا مِنْ كُلَيْبٍ إِذَا مَا ضِيمَ جِيرَانُ ٱلْمُجِيرِ
عَلَى أَنْ لَيْسَ عَدْلًا مِنْ كُلَيْبٍ إِذَا بَرَزَتْ مُخَبَّأَةُ ٱلْخُدُورِ
كَأَنَّا غُدْوَةً وَبَنِي أَبِينَا بِجَنْبِ عُنَيْزَةٍ رَحَيَا مُدِيرِ

١ إ١، ر١، ق١: جسم. ٢ ب١: كثير.

Muhalhil's poetry ranks among the best of the ancients: 17.11

It's reluctantly, Bakr, that we're compelled
to greet you in the morn with our blades drawn.
Look how your heads have made them deep red;
they had just been sharpened at dawn.
We cry for you when we remember you,
but we kill you as if we don't care.[118]

Later poets who composed verses on this theme all took their inspiration from these lines; al-Buḥturī's "Poem Rhyming in *'Ayn*" is the most skillful adaptation.[119]

Muhalhil's poetry: 17.12

Enough of your darkness, night at Dhū Ḥusum!
Give way to dawn and never return!
When the night at al-Dhanā'ib dragged on,
I wept for the days when once I had thought the nights too short.
Now dawn's shining white rescues me from night,
rescues me from great horror;
at night, Gemini's stars stand unmovable
as a she-camel over her crippled spring newborn,
and Ursa Minor's two stars flicker ceaselessly
as a gambler tossing lots.[120]
Were the graves exhumed and Kulayb disinterred
at al-Dhanā'ib, he would see the "Great Flirt's" mettle!
At Wāridāt, I left Bujayr
caked in blood, like saffron.[121]
And so I despoiled 'Ubād's clan—
a brutal act best clears a troubled chest,
Yet none of this compensates for Kulayb!
When those who are protected are wronged,
Yet none of this compensates for Kulayb!
When the veiled ones rush from their tents.
We and our brethren on the morn of Janb 'Unayzah,
we battered like two crushing millstones.

منها بعد أن كرّر قوله عَلَى أَنْ لَيْسَ عَدْلاً مِنْ كُلَيْبٍ في أبيات كثيرة على عادة العرب في تكرير القول في الأمور العظيمة وتقريرها وبهذه الأبيات استشهد بعض المفسّرين لقوله تبارك وتعالى في سورة الرحمن ﴿فَبِأَيِّ ءَالَآءِ رَبِّكُمَا تُكَذِّبَانِ﴾ وتكرير هذه الآية

كَأَنَّ رِمَاحَنَا أَشْطَانُ بِئْرٍ بَعِيدٌ بَيْنَ جَالِيهَا جَرُورِ
تَظَلُّ ٱلْخَيْلُ عَاكِفَةً عَلَيْهِمْ كَأَنَّ ٱلْخَيْلَ تَنْهَضُ فِي غَدِيرِ
فَلَوْلَا ٱلرِّيحُ أُسْمِعُ مَنْ بِحُجْرٍ صَهِيلَ ٱلْخَيْلِ[1] تَقْرَعُ بِٱلذُّكُورِ

يقال إنّ هذا أوّل كذب ورد في الشعر وأبلغه فإنّ بين الذنائب وحجر سبع ليال

ومن ذلك قوله ١٧،١٣

قَتَلُوا كُلَيْبًا ثُمَّ قَالُوا لَا تَعِثْ كَلَّا وَرَبِّ ٱلْبَيْتِ ذِي ٱلْإِحْرَامِ
حَتَّى يَعَضَّ ٱلشَّيْخُ بَعْدَ حَمِيَّةٍ مِمَّا يَرَى جَزَعًا عَلَى ٱلْإِبْهَامِ
وَتَجُولَ رَبَّاتُ ٱلْخُدُورِ حَوَاسِرًا يَمْسَحْنَ عَرْضَ ذَوَائِبِ ٱلْأَيْتَامِ

وقوله ١٧،١٤

طِفْلَةٌ مَا ٱبْنَةُ ٱلْمُخَلَّلِ[2] بَيْضَا ءُ لَعُوبٌ لَذِيذَةٌ فِي ٱلْعِنَاقِ
ضَرَبَتْ صَدْرَهَا إِلَيَّ وَقَالَتْ يَا عَدِيًّا لَقَدْ وَقَتْكَ ٱلْأَوَاقِي

ومنها يرثي كليبًا ١٧،١٥

إِنَّ تَحْتَ ٱلْأَحْجَارِ حَزْمًا وَعَزْمًا وَخَصِيمًا أَلَدَّ ذَا مِعْلَاقِ
حَيَّةٌ فِي ٱلْوَجَارِ[3] أَرْبَدُ لَا تَنْ فَعُ مِنْهُ ٱلسَّلِيمَ نَفْثَةُ رَاقِ

١ بر١، إ٣: صليل البيض. ٢ إ٣: المجلجل. ٣ إ١: الوجاء؛ إ٣: الوحاء.

(This poem has many lines that each repeat the words "Yet none of this compensates for Kulayb." The Arabs employed this kind of repetition to emphasize great matters, and the Qur'an uses the same rhetorical technique in the Chapter "The Merciful," where it repeats the verse: «Which of your Lord's wonders would you deny?»[122] Some exegetes cite Muhalhil's poem to explain the rhetoric of those Qur'anic verses.)

with lances like tight bucket ropes
trailing taut into deep wells,
upon horses embroiled in the ranks
as if wallowing in a pool.
Were it not for the wind, those at Ḥujr would have heard
our horses' whinnies as they collided upon blades.

(It is said that the above verse is the first and most outlandish lie uttered by a poet: between the battlefield at al-Dhanāʾib and Ḥujr is a seven-night journey.)[123]

Muhalhil's poetry: 17.13

They killed Kulayb, then said, "Don't raise havoc!"
No! By the Lord of the Consecrated House,
it will end when the passion is spent. When the old man
gnaws at his fingers from worry and doubt.
When ladies of the curtained quarters emerge bareheaded,[124]
rubbing the braids of the newly orphaned.

Muhalhil's poetry: 17.14

Soft, the daughter of al-Mukhallal,[125] white,
playful, delectable to embrace.
She beat her breast and cried,
"Muhalhil! The protective spirits preserved you!"

Muhalhil's eulogy for Kulayb: 17.15

Beneath the earth lies resolution and will personified,
stubborn to his foes, an unrelenting advocate.
A dark snake in the rocks[126] with a poison
no sorcerers' spit could undo.

قوله ذَا مِغْلَاقٍ يُروى بالعين وهو الرجل الشديد الخصومة كأنّه يعلق بخصمه ويُروى بالغين كأنّه يغلق على خصمه القول

وجميع شعره في هذه الغاية في التمكين والقوّة ١٦،١٧

والسموءل إنّما وفى عن عهدك ١٨

السموءل بن عادياء بن حباء[١] من يهود يثرب الذي يُضرب به المثل في الوفاء فيقال أوفى من السموءل وسبب ذلك أنّ امرأ القيس بن حجر الكنديّ لمّا قُتل أبوه وكان ملكًا في كندة خرج يستنجد بملك الروم كما سيأتي ذكره[٢] فمرّ على تيماء وبها حصن السموءل المسمّى بالأبلق المذكور في شعره فأودع السموءل مائة درع وسلاح ومضى فسمع الحارث بن ظالم وقيل الحارث بن أبي شمر الغسّانيّ بها فجاء ليأخذها منه فأبى السموءل وتحصّن بحصنه فأخذ الحارث ابنًا للسموءل وناداه إمّا إن تسلّم إليّ الأدراع وإمّا قتلت ولدك فأبى أن يسلّم الأدراع فضرب وسط الغلام بالسيف فقطعه وأبوه يراه وانصرف فقال السموءل في ذلك قصيدة ١،١٨

أَعَاذِلَتِي أَلَا لَا تَعْذِلِينِي ... فَكَمْ مِنْ أَمْرِ عَاذِلَةٍ عَصَيْتُ
وَفَيْتُ بِأَدْرُعِ ٱلْكِنْدِيِّ إِنِّي ... إِذَا مَا ذُمَّ أَقْوَامٌ وَفَيْتُ
وَأَوْصَى عَادِيَا يَوْمًا بِأَنْ لَا ... تُهَدِّمَ يَا سَمَوْءَلُ مَا بَنَيْتُ
دَعِينِي وَٱرْشُدِي إِنْ كُنْتُ أَغْوَى ... وَلَا تَغْوَيْ زَعَمْتِ كَمَا غَوَيْتُ

ومات امرؤ القيس قبل أن يعود إلى تيماء ومنع السموءل الأدراع إلى أن مات هو أيضًا وضُرب به المثل وفي ذلك يقول الأعشى ٢،١٨

١ بياض في إ١. ٢ وردت هذه الجملة في إ١ فقط.

(The word "advocate" (*dhā miʿlāqī*), if written with the letter *ʿayn*, means a man so extremely adversarial that it seems he clings to his opponent; but the word is also narrated with the letter *ghayn—mighlāqī*—which would mean that he shuts up his opponent.)[127]

All of Muhalhil's poetry is just as forceful and energetic as these excerpts. 17.16

**Al-Samaw'al was faithful solely by your pledge . . .** 18

Al-Samaw'al ibn ʿĀdiyā' ibn Ḥabā'[128] was a Jew from Yathrib who was synonymous with fidelity—the saying goes: "More faithful than al-Samaw'al." The story of Samaw'al's fidelity stems from an episode with Imru' al-Qays ibn Ḥujr of the Kindah. Imru' al-Qays's father, the king of Kindah, had been murdered, and Imru' al-Qays was on his way to seek the aid of the Byzantine emperor.[129] En route, Imru' al-Qays passed by al-Samaw'al's fort, called "The Piebald," at Taymā'. (Al-Samaw'al mentions this fort in his poetry.)[130] There he entrusted one hundred sets of armor and weapons to al-Samaw'al's safekeeping, and went on his way. Al-Ḥārith ibn Ẓālim (others say it was al-Ḥārith ibn Abī Shamir of the Ghassān)[131] heard about the deposit of armor and wanted it for himself. Al-Samaw'al refused and barricaded himself in his fort. Al-Ḥārith seized one of al-Samaw'al's sons and threatened him: "Hand over the suits of armor or I'll kill your boy!" Yet al-Samaw'al still refused to deliver them up, so al-Ḥārith took his sword and cleaved the boy in twain, right before his father's eyes. Al-Ḥārith then gave up and made off, and al-Samaw'al composed this poem: 18.1

> Reproachful woman! Why such scolds?
> Don't you know I defy all reproach?
> I protected the Kindite's armor—
>   when others proved faithless, I could be trusted.
> Such was my father's parting advice:
>   "Son, don't destroy what I've built."
> If my act was wrong, let me be: right your own affairs.
>   Don't err, as you allege I have.

Even though Imru' al-Qays died before he could return to Taymā', al-Samaw'al nonetheless kept the armor safe until the day he died. Samaw'al's fidelity became proverbial, and al-Aʿshā commemorated it in verse: 18.2

كُنْ كَٱلسَّمَوْءَلِ إِذَا طَافَ ٱلْهُمَامُ بِهِ    فِي جَحْفَلٍ كَسَوَادِ ٱللَّيْلِ جَرَّارِ
فَقَالَ غَدْرٌ وَثُكْلٌ أَنْتَ بَيْنَهُمَا    فَٱخْتَرْ وَمَا فِيهِمَا حَظٌّ لِمُخْتَارِ
فَشَكَّ غَيْرَ طَوِيلٍ ثُمَّ قَالَ لَهُ    ٱقْتُلْ أَسِيرَكَ إِنِّي مَانِعٌ جَارِي

والسموءل من شعراء الجاهليّة المجيدين وله في الحماسة اللاميّة المشهورة ٣،١٨

إِذَا ٱلْمَرْءُ لَمْ يَدْنَسْ مِنَ ٱللُّؤْمِ عِرْضُهُ    فَكُلُّ رِدَاءٍ يَرْتَدِيهِ جَمِيلُ

وله ٤،١٨

إِنِّي إِذَا مَا ٱلْأَمْرُ بُيِّنَ شَكُّهُ[١]    وَبَدَتْ عَوَاقِبُهُ لِمَنْ يَتَأَمَّلُ
وَتَبَرَّأَ ٱلضُّعَفَاءُ مِنْ إِخْوَانِهِمْ    وَأَلَحَّ مِنْ حَرِّ[٢] ٱلصَّمِيمِ ٱلْكَلْكَلُ
أَدَعُ ٱلَّتِي هِيَ أَرْفَقُ ٱلْخُلَّاتِ بِي    عِنْدَ ٱلْحَفِيظَةِ لِلَّتِي هِيَ أَجْمَلُ

وله ٥،١٨

يَا لَيْتَ شِعْرِي حِينَ أُنْدَبُ هَالِكًا    مَاذَا تُؤَنِّبُنِي بِهِ أَنْوَاحِي
أَيَقُلْنَ لَا تَبْعَدْ فَرُبَّ كَرِيهَةٍ    فَرَّجْتَهَا بِشُجَاعَةٍ وَسَمَاحِ
وَلَقَدْ أَخَذْتُ ٱلْحَقَّ غَيْرَ مُخَاصِمٍ    وَلَقَدْ بَذَلْتُ ٱلْحَقَّ غَيْرَ مُلَاحِ

**والأحنف إنّما احتبى في بردك** ١٩

هو الأحنف المضروب به المثل في الحلم والسيادة واسمه الضحّاك وقيل صخر بن قيس بن معاوية بن حصن السعديّ ويُكنى أبو بحر ١،١٩

---

١ ق٢: شكله. ٢ إ١ ول١ ول٢: حز.

Be like al-Samaw'al: when death swirled around him,
a great battle host descended, vast ranks of blackness.
They cried, "Break your oath or prepare to mourn;
the choice is yours." What a miserable predicament!
He thought but a moment, and then gave a cry back:
"Kill your prisoner, I shall protect my charge."

Al-Samaw'al was one of the finest pre-Islamic poets, and his "Poem Rhyming in *L*," which was included in Abū Tammām's *Valor Anthology*, opens: 18.3

When a man spares his honor from the blemish of shame,
whatever cloak he chooses to don will look handsome.

Al-Samaw'al's poetry: 18.4

When the misgivings prove founded,
the consequences come clear to those who reflect;
the weak find excuses, forsaking their brothers,
and chests balk from scorching heat:
I shun the easy way out—
I choose honor, and head to the fray.

Al-Samaw'al's poetry: 18.5

If only I knew, when I'm dead and eulogized,
how the mourners will reproach me!
Or will they say, "Stay! Your strength and charity
relieved many a misfortune!"
I upheld the right without opposition;
I doled out what's right without complaint.

**... al-Aḥnaf enrobed strictly in your mantle ...** 19

Al-Aḥnaf was the nickname of a man memorialized as the epitome of equanimity and leadership. His given name was either al-Ḍaḥḥāk or Ṣakhr, son of Qays ibn Muʿāwiyah ibn Ḥiṣn[132] of the Saʿd, and he was also known as Abū Baḥr. 19.1

٢،١٩ أدرك النبيّ صلّى الله عليه وسلّم ولم يره ودعا له حدّث الأحنف قال بينما أنا أطوف بالبيت في زمن عمر بن الخطّاب رضي الله تعالى عنه إذ لقيني رجل أعرفه فأخذ بيدي فقال ألّا أبشّرك قلت بلى قال أما تذكّر إذ بعثني رسول الله صلّى الله عليه وسلّم إلى قومك في بني سعد أدعوهم إلى الإسلام فجعلت أدعوهم وأعرض عليهم فقلت إنّه يدعوهم إلى خير ولا أسمع إلّا حسنًا فإنّي رجعت إلى النبيّ صلّى الله عليه وسلّم فأخبرته بمقالتك فقال اللّهمّ اغفر للأحنف

٣،١٩ وسُمّي الأحنف لأنّ أمّه كانت ترقصه وهو طفل وتقول

وَٱللّٰهِ لَوْلَا حَنَفٌ فِي رِجْـلِهِ    مَا كَانَ فِي فِتْيَانِكُمْ مِنْ مِثْلِهِ

يقال تحانف الرجل في مشيته وهو أن يقبل الرجل بالإبهام على الأخرى

٤،١٩ وقال عبد الملك بن عمير وفد علينا الأحنف مع مصعب بن الزبير الكوفة فما رأيت منظرًا يذمّ إلّا رأيته فيه كان ضئيلاً صعل الرأس متراكب الأسنان باخق العينين وكان إذا تكلّم جلّى عن نفسه

٥،١٩ وقال الشعبيّ أوفد أبو موسى الأشعريّ وفد البصرة[1] إلى عمر بن الخطّاب وفيهم الأحنف بن قيس فلمّا قدموا على عمر تكلّم كلّ رجل منهم في حاجة نفسه وكان الأحنف في آخر القوم فحمد الله تعالى وصلّى على نبيّه ثمّ قال

> أمّا بعْد يا أمير المؤمنين فإنّ أهل مصر نزلوا منازل فرعون وأصحابه وأهل الشام نزلوا منازل قيصر وأهل الكوفة نزلوا منازل كسرى ومصانعه في الأنهار العذبة والجنّات المخصبة وفي مثل عين البعير وكالحوار في السلى تأتيهم ثمارهم قبل أن تتغيّر وإنّ أهل البصرة نزلوا في أرض سبخة زعقة نشّاشة طرفها في ملح أجاج والطرف الآخر في

١ البصرة: غير واضحة في إ١.

Al-Aḥnaf and the Prophet (God bless and keep him) were contemporaries, and although they never met in person, the Prophet did bless him. Al-Aḥnaf narrates: Once, during the caliphate of ʿUmar ibn al-Khaṭṭāb (God be pleased with him), I was circumambulating the Kaaba when a man whom I knew took me by the hand and asked me, "Would you like me to impart to you some good tidings?" "Of course!" And he told me, "Do you remember when the Prophet (God bless and keep him) dispatched me to preach Islam to your clan, the Saʿd? And when I explained the faith and invited you all to convert, you said, 'Everything to which this man is calling you sounds good to me.' When I returned to the Prophet (God bless and keep him) and informed him of what you said, he exclaimed, 'Almighty God, be forgiving to al-Aḥnaf!'" 19.2

His nickname, al-Aḥnaf ("Crook-Footed"), derives from his childhood: his mother used to bounce him on her lap while singing: 19.3

By God, if it wasn't for the crook in his foot,
your boys couldn't hold a candle to his flame.

"Crook-footed" indicates a deformation of the foot that causes one to put weight on the side of the little toe when walking.

ʿAbd al-Malik ibn ʿUmayr reports: I saw al-Aḥnaf when he arrived at Kufa in a delegation with Muṣʿab ibn al-Zubayr, and he was truly repulsive to behold: he was slight of frame and small-headed, his teeth were crooked, and one of his eyes was wasted. But when he spoke, he revealed his true worth. 19.4

Al-Shaʿbī reports: Abū Mūsā l-Ashʿarī sent a delegation of Basrans, including al-Aḥnaf ibn Qays, to the Caliph ʿUmar ibn al-Khaṭṭāb. When they presented themselves to the caliph, each man petitioned him on behalf of his personal concerns. Last to speak was al-Aḥnaf: He stood, praised the Exalted God, invoked blessings upon the Prophet, and said: 19.5

> Commander of the Faithful! The Muslims in Egypt settled in the land of Pharaoh and his entourage, the Muslims of Syria settled in the land of Caesar, and the Muslims of Kufa settled in the lands and palaces of Khosrow amid sweet rivers and fertile gardens, moist as a camel's eye or a calf's fetal sack;[133] the fruits of the land reach their tables fresh. But what of the Muslims of Basra? They are settlers in a salt flat. Their water is bitter to the taste. The land drinks it, yet yields nothing. One border is salt marsh; the other is desert

الفلاة لا يأتي الجلب إلّا في مثل حلقوم النعامة فارفع خسيسنا وانعش وكسنا[1] واعدل لنا قفيزنا ودرهمنا ومر لنا بنهر نستعذب منه الماء

فقال عمر أعجزتم أن تكونوا مثل هذا السيّد هذا والله السيّد فما زلت أسمعها منه

٦،١٩ ثمّ حبسه عنده سنة ثمّ قال يا أحنف إنّي قد بلوتك فأعجبتني وإنّما حبستك لأعلم علمك فإنّي سمعت رسول الله صلّى الله عليه وسلّم يقول احذروا المنافق العالم وأشفقت عليك منه فوجدتك بريئًا ممّا تخوّفت عليك وسرّحه وأحسن جائزته

٧،١٩ ولم يزل يُشرّف حتّى مات وساد بعقله وحلمه حتّى كان يُجرّد لأمره مائة ألف سيف وكانت أمراء الأمصار[2] يلتجئون إليه في المهمّات وكان إذا أراد حربًا قال الناس قد غضبت زبراء فصار مثلاً وزبراء جاريته كان مطيعًا لها فكانوا يكنون عن غضبه في الحرب بغضبها

٨،١٩ وكان يقول كنّا نختلف إلى قيس بن عاصم نتعلّم منه الحلم كما نختلف إلى العالم يتعلّم منه العلم

٩،١٩ وحكى خالد بن صفوان قال كنت بالرصافة عند هشام بن عبد الملك فقدم عليه العبّاس بن الوليد فغشيته الناس فدخلت عليه فقال حدّثني عن تسويدكم الأحنف وانقيادكم له فقلت له إن شئت حدّثتك عنه بواحدة تسوّد وإن شئت باثنتين وإن شئت بثلاث وإن شئت حدّثتك عشيّتك ولم تشعر بصومك وكان صائمًا يوم خميس فقال هات الأوّل[3] فقلت كان أعظم من رأينا أو سمعنا سلطانًا على نفسه فيما أراد حملها عليه ودفعها عنه ثمّ أدركني ذهني فقلت غير الخلفاء فقال لقد ذكرتها نجلاء كافية فما الثانية

١٠،١٩ قلت قد يكون الرجل عظيم السلطان على نفسه ولا يكون بصيرًا بالمحاسن والمساوئ ولم نسمع بأحد أبصر منه بالمحاسن والمساوئ فلا يحمل السلطنة ألا

---

١ إ١: وكيسنا. ٢ إ١: الأنصار. ٣ إ١: قال الأولى.

> plain. The land gives no more readily than one could find profit in the neck of an ostrich. Raise us from this misery, relieve us from this privation! Be equitable in our grain measures and coinage weights, and order for us a canal to bring us sweet water.

ʿUmar declared to the others, "You all fell short of this man. This, by God, is a nobleman." ʿUmar was frequently heard repeating this.

ʿUmar then kept al-Aḥnaf with him for a year, at the end telling him, "Aḥnaf, 19.6
I have tested you and I like what I see. I detained you here only because I wanted to know truly who you are: once, I heard the Prophet (God bless and keep him) warn: 'Beware the intelligent hypocrite,' and I was anxious that this might be you. But now I see you are not what I had feared." ʿUmar granted al-Aḥnaf leave to return with a generous reward.

Al-Aḥnaf was held in honor for the rest of his life. He led by virtue of his 19.7
reason and his equanimity: one hundred thousand swords could be unsheathed at his command, and the garrison town commanders relied on his counsel in weighty matters.

Whenever al-Aḥnaf advised war, people would say, "Al-Zabrā''s angry." This became an adage; al-Zabrā' was al-Aḥnaf's slave girl, and he was so under her thumb that people equated his anger in war with her fury.

Al-Aḥnaf said, "We used to frequent Qays ibn ʿĀṣim to learn equanimity, 19.8
just as assiduously as we would frequent a scholar to gain knowledge."

Khālid ibn Ṣafwān told this story: I was attending the Caliph Hishām ibn 19.9
ʿAbd al-Malik at al-Ruṣāfah, and one day al-ʿAbbās ibn al-Walīd arrived. Everyone thronged about al-ʿAbbās, and when I entered he said to me, "Tell us why your kinsmen made al-Aḥnaf their leader and were all so obedient to him." I replied, "If you want, I can explain it with one statement, or with two, or, if you prefer, three. Or I could tell you stories from now until nightfall that will make you forget you're fasting." (Al-ʿAbbās used to fast every Thursday.) "Give us the first," al-ʿAbbās said.

I told him: "We never saw or heard of anyone who had more supreme restraint over his own self-interest before taking decisions . . . excepting, that is"—I quickly caught myself—"the caliphs!" Al-ʿAbbās replied, "That's an amply sufficient answer! What's the second?"

I said, "A man may possess self-control, but he might not be able to perceive 19.10
all advantages and drawbacks of things. No one had sharper foresight than al-Aḥnaf: he never exercised his authority except for benefit, and he always

على حسن ولا يكفّها إلّا عن قبيح فقال قد جئت بصلة الأولى لا تصلح الّا بها فما الثالثة

١١،١٩ قلت قد يكون الرجل عظيم السلطان على نفسه بصيرًا بالمحاسن والمساوئ ولا يكون حظيظًا فلا يُنشر له ذكر وكان الأحنف عند الناس مشهورًا قال وأبيك لقد وصلت الاثنتين فما بقيّة ما يقطع عنّي الصوم

١٢،١٩ قلت أيّامه السالفة مثل فتح خراسان اجتمعت عليه الأعاجم بمرو الرود فجاءه ما لا قبل له به وهو في منزل مضيعة وقد بلغ به الأمر فصلّى العشاء الآخرة ودعا وتضرّع إلى الله تعالى أن يوفّقه ثمّ خرج يمشي في العسكر مثل المكروب متنكّرًا ليسمع ما يقول الناس فمرّ بعبد يعجن وهو يقول لصاحب له العجب لأميرنا يقيم بالمسلمين في منزل مضيعة وقد أطاف بهم العدوّ من نواحيهم واتّخذوه أغراضًا وله متحوّل فجعل الأحنف يقول اللّهمّ وفّق اللّهمّ سدّد فقال العبد للعبد فما الحيلة قال أن ينادي الساعة بالرحيل وإنّما بينه وبين الغيضة فرسخ فيجعلها خلف ظهره فيمنعه الله بها فإذا امتنع ظهره بها بعث بمجنّبتيه اليمنى واليسرى فيمنع الله بهما ناحيتيه ويلقى عدوّه في جانب واحد فسجد الأحنف ثمّ نادى بالرحيل من مكانه حتّى أتى الغيضة فنزل في قبليّها وأصبح فأتاه العدوّ فلم يجدوا سبيلاً إلّا من وجه واحد وهوّلوا بطبول أربعة وركب الأحنف وأخذ اللواء وحمل بنفسه على طبل فشقّه وقتل صاحبه وهو يقول

إِنَّ عَلَى كُلِّ رَئِيسٍ حَقًّا  أَنْ يَخْضِبَ ٱلصَّعْدَةَ أَوْ تَنْشَقَّا

وشقّ بقيّة الطبول فلمّا فقد الأعاجم أصوات طبولهم انهزموا وركب المسلمون أكتافهم وكان الفتح ثمّ عدّد خالد بقيّة أيّامه إلى أن انقضى النهار

desisted where there were pitfalls." "Indeed," al-ʿAbbās remarked, "the first is futile without this! What's the third reason?"

I told him, "A man may have supreme self-restraint, and he may be able to discern advantages from disadvantages, but if he is not lucky, then no one will ever know about him, and al-Aḥnaf, he was a famous man." Al-ʿAbbās exclaimed, "By your father's life, this squares the circle! Now tell me the stories that will make me forget that I'm fasting!" 19.11

I told him, "Listen to the lore about al-Aḥnaf. For instance, during the conquest of Khurasan, the Persians outmaneuvered al-Aḥnaf at Marw al-Rūdh, and he couldn't devise an escape. Things looked grave in this disastrous position, and after al-Aḥnaf prayed the late-evening prayer, he made a supplication and implored God for a successful outcome. He then walked about the camp, anxious and concealing his identity his identity in order to overhear what his men were saying. He passed a slave who was kneading dough. The slave remarked to his companion, 'Isn't it strange that our commander has put the Muslims in this dreadful bind to be surrounded by the enemy and treated like target practice! Especially since there's been a way out all along!' Hearing this, al-Aḥnaf began praying, 'Almighty God, grant us success! Almighty God, show us the way!' And the other slave then asked the first, 'What's the stratagem?' 'Our commander should announce the break of camp right now, as there is but one *farsakh* between us and a swampy thicket. If he places that to his rear, God has provided him a rear guard, and that will free his right and left wings, and so God has thereby guarded his flanks for him too, and the enemy will only be able to attack head-on.' Al-Aḥnaf performed a prostration, and then hastened to announce the departure. They reached the swamp and established themselves with it to their south.[134] In the morning, the enemy appeared, but could find no way to attack except from the front, and they made a terrifying display, beating four signal drums. Al-Aḥnaf rode forth with the banner and charged toward the drums. He slit one, killed the drummer, and sang: 19.12

> Every leader has a duty—
> to dye his lance or break it trying.

"He then slit the rest of their drums. Now the Persians could no longer hear the sound of the signal drums and were lost; the Muslims overran them and carried the day."

Khālid continued recounting al-Aḥnaf's exploits until nightfall.

وللأحنف حكايات حسنة وألفاظ محكمة ومؤاخذات معدودة عليه فمن حكاياته ما حدّث بعض غلمانه قال كان الأحنف يكثر الصلاة بالليل وكان يجيء إلى المصباح فيضع إصبعه فيه ثمّ يقول حسّ[1] ويقول ما حملك على أن صنعت كذا يوم كذا ١٣،١٩

وشكا إليه رجل وجع ضرسه فقال لقد ذهب نور عيني منذ ثلاثين سنة ما علم بذلك أحد ١٤،١٩

وقال له عمر رضي الله تعالى عنه أيّ الطعام أحبّ إليك قال الزبد والكمأة قال عمر ما هما بأحبّ الطعام إليه ولكنّه يحبّ الخصب للمسلمين يعني أنّ الزبد والكمأة لا يكونان إلّا في الخصب ١٥،١٩

وخلا به رجل فسبّه سبًّا قبيحًا فقام الأحنف وهو يتبعه فلمّا وصل إلى قومه وقف وقال يا أخي إن كان قد بقي من قولك فضلة فقل الآن وإلّا يسمعك قومي فتؤذى ١٦،١٩

وقال له رجل بِمَ سدت قومك ولست بأشرفهم فقال بتركي من أمرك ما لا يعنيني كما لم تترك من أمري ما لا يعنيك ١٧،١٩

وقال له رجل لأشتمنّك شتمًا يدخل معك في قبرك فقال في قبرك يدخل والله لا في قبري ١٨،١٩

وقيل له بِمَ سدت قال لو أنّ الناس كرهوا الماء ما شربته ١٩،١٩

ووفد على معاوية مع أهل العراق فقال آذنه إنّ أمير المؤمنين يقسم عليكم أن لا[2] يتكلّم أحد منكم إلّا لنفسه فدخلوا فقال الأحنف لولا عزمة أمير المؤمنين لأخبرته أنّ نازلة نزلت ونائبة نابت وكلّهم به فاقة إلى رفد أمير المؤمنين فقال حسبك يا أبا بحر فقد كفيت من غاب ومن شهد ٢٠،١٩

١ حسّ: بياض في إ١. ٢ سقطت من إ١.

There are many great stories and masterful statements, and a few blameworthy anecdotes, about al-Aḥnaf. 19.13

The praiseworthy stories include one told by one of his household boys: al-Aḥnaf always performed long prayers at night, and afterward he used to take a lamp and put his finger into the flame, saying, "Ouch!" while reproaching himself: "Why on earth did I do that today?"

A man once complained to al-Aḥnaf about a pain in his molar. Al-Aḥnaf 19.14
responded, "I had lost the sight in one of my eyes for thirty years before anyone noticed."

The Caliph ʿUmar ibn al-Khaṭṭāb (God be pleased with him) asked al-Aḥnaf, 19.15
"What is your favorite food?" Al-Aḥnaf replied, "Butter and truffles." ʿUmar would explain what al-Aḥnaf meant: "They are not really his favorite foods: what al-Aḥnaf loves is for Muslims to enjoy abundance." Butter and truffles can only be had in times of bounty.

A man once grossly insulted al-Aḥnaf in private. Al-Aḥnaf walked off, but 19.16
the man followed him. When al-Aḥnaf neared his home, he turned to the man and told him, "Brother, if you have anything more to add, then do so right here; otherwise, my people will hear what you say, and then you might get hurt."

Someone asked al-Aḥnaf, "How did you become your people's leader, given 19.17
that you aren't one of their most nobly born?" "By not involving myself in matters about you that were not my concern, to the same extent that you just now involved yourself in matters about me that are not your concern."

A man once swore at al-Aḥnaf: "I will curse you with an insult so vile that it 19.18
will stay with you in your grave!" Al-Aḥnaf responded, "It will follow you into your grave, by God, not mine."

Another man asked al-Aḥnaf, "How did you become a leader?" Al-Aḥnaf 19.19
told him, "If the people didn't like the water, I didn't drink from it."

An Iraqi delegation, including al-Aḥnaf, once attended the court of the 19.20
Caliph Muʿāwiyah, and the caliph's gatekeeper announced, "The Commander of the Faithful enjoins that each of you must only speak on matters of personal concern." They entered, and al-Aḥnaf spoke: "Were it not for the Commander of the Faithful's strict order, I would have told him that calamity has descended, misfortune has struck, and all in Iraq are in need of the aid of the Commander of the Faithful." The caliph replied, "That's enough! Al-Aḥnaf, you made the case for everyone, present and absent."

وذكّره معاوية يومًا بصحبته لعليّ بن أبي طالب كرّم الله وجهه وأيّام صفّين ٢١،١٩
فقال يا أمير المؤمنين القلوب التي أبغضناك بها بين جنوبنا والسيوف التي قاتلناك بها على عواتقنا وإن شئت استصفيت كدرنا بحلمك فقال أجل

وممّا عيب به وأُخذ إليه أمر الزبير بن العوّام رضي الله تعالى عنه وذلك أنّه ٢٢،١٩
لمّا ترك القتال يوم الجمل ورجع عن الحرب مرّ ببني تميم ذاهبًا إلى دياره فأتى رجل الأحنف فقال هذا الزبير قدم آنفًا فقال ما أصنع به جمع بين المتعادين[١] يقتل بعضهم بعضًا ويريد أن ينجو إلى أهله فتبعه ابن جرموز فقتله غدرًا فقال الناس إنّما قتله الأحنف بكلامه ذلك وإنّ ابن[٢] جزموز إنّما فعل عن رأيه

وحين أتاه كتاب الحسن بن عليّ رضي الله تعالى عنهما يستنصره فقال قد بلونا ٢٣،١٩
حسنًا وآل حسن فلم نجد عندهم إيالة الملك ولا صيانة المال ولا مكيدة الحرب ولم يجبه

وقوله للحتات بن يزيد[٣] اسكت يا آدر وكان الحباب آدر ٢٤،١٩

وطاعته لجاريته زبراء حتّى وقد سئل عن ذلك قال كيف لا أطيع من لي إليه ٢٥،١٩
كلّ يوم حاجة

وأتاه رجل فلطمه فقال لِمَ لطمتني قال جعل لي جعل على أن ألطم سيّد بني تميم ٢٦،١٩
قال لست بسيّدهم وإنّما سيّدهم حارثة بن قدامة فمضى الرجل إليه فلطمه فقطع يده فقال الناس إنّما قطع يده الأحنف

---

١ إ١: الغارين. ٢ سقطت من إ١. ٣ إ١: للحبّاب بن المنذر؛ إ٣ وق٣: الحباب بن يزيد.

One day, Muʿāwiyah brought up al-Aḥnaf's alliance with the former Caliph ʿAlī (God preserve his perfect purity) at the Battle of Ṣiffīn.[135] Al-Aḥnaf responded, "Commander of the Faithful! The hearts that once harbored our hatred for you still beat within us, and the swords with which we fought you are still slung on our backs. If you want, you can erase all our vexation with your equanimity." Muʿāwiyah replied, "But of course." 19.21

People fault al-Aḥnaf for a few cases where he was less judicious. For example, they implicate al-Aḥnaf in the death of al-Zubayr ibn al-ʿAwwām (God be pleased with him). Al-Aḥnaf had desisted from fighting at the Battle of the Camel, and when withdrawing to his homeland, he passed a camp of the Tamīm. A man approached him and said, "Al-Zubayr came by here a little earlier," and al-Aḥnaf scoffed: "What do I want with him? He brought together two armies and they killed one another, and now he wants to escape to his people." Thereupon, Ibn Jarmūz tracked al-Zubayr and deceitfully killed him. People later said, "It was really al-Aḥnaf's words that killed al-Zubayr; Ibn Jarmūz merely acted out al-Aḥnaf's intention."[136] 19.22

Al-Aḥnaf is also faulted for his handling of al-Ḥasan ibn ʿAlī's (God be pleased with both of them) letter soliciting support.[137] Al-Aḥnaf remarked, "We have experience with al-Ḥasan and his clan, and we find him inept in governance, in safeguarding property, and in the wiles of war." Al-Aḥnaf never wrote back. 19.23

People also critique al-Aḥnaf for quipping to al-Ḥutāt ibn Yazīd: "Be quiet, Little Balls!" Al-Ḥutāt was afflicted by swollen testicles.[138] 19.24

Al-Aḥnaf was criticized for his obedience to his slave girl al-Zabrāʾ, and when asked about it, he responded, "How can I disobey one whose help I need every day?" 19.25

People likewise disapproved of al-Aḥnaf's response to a man who once slapped him out of the blue. Al-Aḥnaf asked, "Why did you slap me?" The man confessed, "I was promised a payment if I slapped the leader of the Tamīm." Al-Aḥnaf retorted, "I'm not their leader; that's Ḥārithah ibn Qudāmah."[139] So the man went to Ḥārithah and slapped him, and Ḥārithah ordered his hand chopped off. Everyone remarked, "It was really al-Aḥnaf who cut off the man's hand." 19.26

وأرسل إليه عمرو بن الأهتم رجلاً يكايده فقال ما كان مال أبيك ففطن له ١٩،٢٧
الأحنف فقال صرمة يقري منها ضيفه ويكفي عياله ولم يكن أهتم سلّاحًا

فهذا ما حفظ من سقطاته وقريب منها أنّه خاط عند رجل ثوبًا ثمّ تقاضاه دهرًا ١٩،٢٨
فلمّا ضجر أخذ بيد ولده وجاء إلى الخيّاط فقال إذا متّ فادفع الثوب إلى هذا

ومن كلامه لا خير في لذّة تعقب ندمًا لن يفتقر من زهد اقبلوا عذر من اعتذر ١٩،٢٩
ما أقبح القطيعة بعد الصلة أنصف من نفسك قبل أن تُنتصف منك لا تكوننّ على
الإساءة أقوى منك على الإحسان اعلم أنّ لك من دنياك ما أصلحت به مثواك
فأنفق في حقّ ولا تكوننّ خازنًا لغيرك لا راحة لحسود ولا مروءة لكذوب عجبت
لمن يتكبّر وقد خرج من مخرج البول مرّتين

وقال يومًا ما ردّدت عن حاجة قطّ فقيل له ولم فقال لأنّي لا أطلب المحال ١٩،٣٠

وقال ما نازعني أحد إلّا وأخذت في أمره بثلاث إن كان فوقي عرفت له فضله ١٩،٣١
وإن كان دوني رفعت قدري عنه وإن كان مثلي تفضّلت عليه

وقال له رجل دلّني على المروءة فقال عليك بالخلق الفسيح والكفّ عن القبيح ١٩،٣٢
ثمّ قال ألا أدلّك على أدوأ الداء قال بلى قال اكتساب الذمّ بلا منفعة

وقال يومًا كانت المودّة محضًا فليتها اليوم مذقًا ١٩،٣٣

ومن شعره ١٩،٣٤

لَوْ مَدَّ سَرْوِي[1] بِمَالٍ كَثِيرٍ    لَجُدْتُ وَكُنْتُ لَهُ بَاذِلَا
فَإِنَّ ٱلْمَرُوءَةَ لَا تُسْتَطَاعُ    إِذَا لَمْ يَكُنْ مَالُهَا فَاضِلَا

---

١ إ: ثروي.

Al-Aḥnaf once spoke inappropriately to a man whom ʿAmr ibn al-Ahtam had dispatched to goad al-Aḥnaf into admitting his modest origins. The man asked al-Aḥnaf, "What was your father's property?" Al-Aḥnaf sensed the ploy and replied, "A modest herd of camels from which he could provide for his guests and his dependents. And he wasn't a mangle-toothed shitter."[140] **19.27**

The above are the recorded occasions when al-Aḥnaf did not act with equanimity. Another similar example is the occasion when al-Aḥnaf contracted a tailor to make a robe for him, but the tailor delayed for an age, and when al-Aḥnaf grew exasperated, he brought his son to the tailor and quipped, "See this boy? If I should die, give the robe to him." **19.28**

Al-Aḥnaf's many wise words include the following. There's no good in pleasure followed by regret. The ascetic never suffers lack. Accept apologies. It is wrong to break off a relationship right after a gift. Act justly of your own accord before justice is demanded from you. Be sure to incline more to benevolence than malevolence. Your possessions here are for settling your final dwelling: spend what you have righteously, and don't hoard for someone else. The envious have no rest, liars no virtue. I marvel to think that one who was ejected from two pee holes is able to swagger. **19.29**

Al-Aḥnaf once remarked, "I never had a request rejected." He was asked, "How was that?" "Because I never sought the impossible." **19.30**

Al-Aḥnaf described himself: "When facing an opponent, I adopted one of three strategies. If he ranked higher than me, I conceded his superiority. If he ranked lower than me, I relied on my standing to be aloof from him. If we were equals, I acted graciously." **19.31**

A man once said to al-Aḥnaf, "Tell me the way to virtue." Al-Aḥnaf replied, "Be morally sound and wholly tolerant, and avoid everything ugly." He added, "Would you like me to tell you the worst of ills too?" "Certainly!" "An act that earns you reproach without yielding any benefit." **19.32**

Consider another of al-Aḥnaf's wise sayings: "We used to have friendship like fresh milk; today, we should count ourselves lucky to get it watered down." **19.33**

Al-Aḥnaf's poetry: **19.34**

> Were my magnanimity aided by much wealth,
> I'd generously give with liberality.
> Unless there's capital to spare,
> true virtue there cannot be.

وكان يجالس إليه رجل كثير الصمت فأعجب به الأحنف ثمّ تكلّم يومًا فقال ٣٥،١٩
يا أبا بحر تقدر تمشي على شرف المسجد فقال يا أخي إنّي كبرت ولا أقدر على ذلك ثمّ أنشد

وَكَائِنْ تَرَى مِنْ صَامِتٍ لَكَ مُعْجِبٍ[1] زِيَادَتُهُ أَوْ نَقْصُهُ فِي ٱلتَّكَلُّمِ
لِسَانُ ٱلْفَتَى نِصْفٌ وَنِصْفٌ فُؤَادِهِ فَلَمْ يَبْقَ إِلَّا صُورَةُ ٱللَّحْمِ وَٱلدَّمِ

فرواها قوم له وقيل تمثّل بها وهي لغيره فإنها أرفع طبقة من شعره

ومات بالكوفة سنة تسع وستّين وخرج مصعب بن الزبير في جنازته ماشيًا ٣٦،١٩
بغير إزار وهو أوّل أمير صنع ذلك في جنازة كبير ولمّا وُضع في قبره قامت امرأة فقالت لله درّك من مدرج في كفن نسأل الله الذي ابتلانا بفقدك أن يوسّع في لحدك وأن يكون لك في يوم حشرك أما والذي كنت من أمره إلى مدّة لقد عشت حميدًا مودودًا ومتّ شهيدًا مفقودًا ولقد كنت من الناس قريبًا وفي الناس غريبًا رحمنا الله وإيّاك

وحاتمًا إنّما جاد بوفرك ولقي الأضياف ببشرك ٢٠

هو حاتم بن عبد الله بن سعد الطائيّ وكنيته أبو سفّانة وأبو عديّ وأجواد العرب ١،٢٠
في الجاهليّة ثلاثة حاتم الطائيّ وهرم بن سنان وكعب بن مامة وحاتم أشهرهم ذكرًا أدرك مولد النبيّ صلّى الله عليه وسلّم ومات قبل مبعثه

وحكي عن عليّ بن أبي طالب كرّم الله وجهه أنّه قال يومًا سبحان الله ما أزهد ٢،٢٠
كثيرًا من الناس في خير عجبًا لرجل يجيئه أخوه المسلم في حاجة فلا يرى نفسه للخير أهلًا فلو كان لا يرجو ثوابًا ولا يخاف عقابًا لكان ينبغي له أن يسارع إلى

١ إ: ناطق.

A very laconic man used to attend al-Aḥnaf's assemblies, and al-Aḥnaf was very fond of him, until, that is, one day when the man spoke, saying, "Al-Aḥnaf! Are you able to walk up on the roof of the mosque?" Al-Aḥnaf responded, "My brother, I'm old and cannot do that," and recited: 19.35

Men of few words may win your admiration,
but merit or its absence is measured by speech—
a fellow's tongue is half his worth, the other's his heart;
all else: flesh and bones.

Some narrators ascribe the above verses to al-Aḥnaf, but others say he must have quoted them from another poet, since they are of a higher order than al-Aḥnaf's own poetry.[141]

Al-Aḥnaf died in Kufa in 69 [688–89], and its governor, Muṣʿab ibn al-Zubayr, walked without a mantle during the funeral. That was the first time a commander adopted this deferential comportment at the funeral of a notable. When al-Aḥnaf was placed in his grave, a woman stood up and cried, "What a fine man that shroud encloses! We ask God Who tests us by your passing to make your grave spacious and place you by His side on Judgment Day. I swear by Him to whom I devote myself throughout my allotted time: Aḥnaf, you lived beloved and admired, you die missed and a martyr. You were one of us yet unique among us—may God's mercy be upon us and upon you." 19.36

**. . . Ḥātim learned charity and hospitality from the example of your bounty and joy.** 20

Ḥātim was the son of ʿAbd Allāh ibn Saʿd of the Ṭayyiʾ, and he was known as Abū Saffānah and Abū ʿAdī. Of the three pre-Islamic Arabs famed for generosity—Ḥātim, Harim ibn Sinān, and Kaʿb ibn Māmah—Ḥātim is the best known. He was alive when the Prophet (God bless and keep him) was born, but Ḥātim died before Muḥammad's prophetic mission began. 20.1

It is reported that the Caliph ʿAlī (God preserve his perfect purity) once sermonized: "Glorious God! How reluctant people are to perform good deeds! I am astounded to see that men, when approached by their brother Muslims in need, do not see themselves capable of generosity! Aside from hope for reward or fear of punishment in the Afterlife, one should always be striving after the 20.2

مكارم الأخلاق فإنّها تدلّ على سبيل النجاح فقام إليه رجل فقال يا أمير المؤمنين أسمعته من النبيّ صلّى الله عليه وسلّم قال نعم لمّا أتي بسبايا طيّئ وقفت جارية عيطاء لعساء فلمّا رأيتها أعجبت بها وقلت لأطلبنّها من رسول الله صلّى الله عليه وسلّم فلمّا تكلّمت أنسيت جمالها بفصاحتها فقالت يا محمّد إن رأيت أن تخلّي سبيلي ولا تشمت بي أحياء العرب فإنّي ابنة سيّد قومي وإنّ أبي كان يفكّ العاني ويشبع الجائع ويكسو العاري ويفشي السلام ولم يردّ طالب حاجة قطّ أنا ابنة حاتم الطائيّ فقال النبيّ صلّى الله عليه وسلّم يا جارية هذه صفة المؤمن ولو كان أبوك مات مسلمًا لترحّمنا عليه خلُوا عنها فإنّ أباها كان يحبّ مكارم الأخلاق والله يحبّ مكارم الأخلاق

٣،٢٠ وحكى عديّ بن حاتم للنبيّ صلّى الله عليه وسلّم إنّ أبي كان يطعم المساكين ويعتق الرقاب ويصل الرحم فهل له في ذلك من أجر قال إنّ أباك رام أمرًا فأدركه يعني الذكر

٤،٢٠ وأوّل ما ظهر من جود حاتم أنّ أباه خلّفه في إبله وهو غلام فمرّ به جماعة من الشعراء فيهم عبيد بن الأبرص وبشر بن أبي خازم والنابغة الذبيانيّ يريدون النعمان فقالوا لحاتم هل من قرى ولم يعرفهم فقال تسألون عن القرى وقد رأيتم الإبل والغنم انزلوا فنزلوا فنحر لكلّ واحد منهم وسألهم عن أسمائهم فأخبروه ففرّق فيهم الإبل والغنم فجاء أبوه فقال ما فعلت فقال طوّقتك مجد الدّهر تطويق الحمام وعرّفه فقال أبوه إذًا لا أبالي

٥،٢٠ وحكي عن زوجته النوار قالت أصابتنا سنة اقشعرّت لها الأرض وضنّت المراضع على أولادها فوالله إنّا لفي ليلة صنّبرة بعيدة ما بين الطرفين إذ تضاغى

noblest morals, since they show the way to salvation." One of the audience rose to ask: "Commander of the Faithful! Did you hear this from the Prophet (God bless and keep him)?" ʿAlī responded, "Yes, it was when prisoners from the Ṭayyiʾ were brought in. There was a young girl with an elegant neck and deep-red lips among them. She attracted my attention! I desired her immediately and resolved to ask the Prophet (God bless and keep him) to give her to me, and then, when I heard her speak, her eloquence outshone her beauty! She was pleading, 'Muḥammad! Consider freeing me, so that the Arab tribes will not gloat at my misfortune! I'm from noble stock; my father used to free prisoners, feed the hungry, clothe the naked, and promote peace. Never in his life did he refuse a request. I am the daughter of Ḥātim of the Ṭayyiʾ.' The Prophet (God bless and keep him) replied, 'Girl, this is the description of a Believer; had your father died a Muslim, I would invoke God's mercy upon him. Set her free! Her father prized the noblest morals and God loves the noblest morals.'"

On the other hand, it is reported that Ḥātim's son, ʿAdī, once asked the Prophet (God bless and keep him), "My father used to feed the needy, manumit prisoners, and do right by his kith and kin—will he earn recompense for that?" The Prophet's response: "No. Your father strove for fame, and that's what he obtained." 20.3

The first sign of Ḥātim's generous spirit was noted when he was still a young boy pasturing his father's camels. A group of poets, including ʿAbīd ibn al-Abraṣ, Bishr ibn Abī Khāzim, and al-Nābighah of the Dhubyān, passed by Ḥātim on their way to the court of King al-Nuʿmān, and they asked him, "Is there any hospitality to be had around here?" Ḥātim did not know who they were, and replied, "What sort of question is that? Don't you see these camels and sheep? Dismount!" They dismounted. Ḥātim slaughtered one animal for each man, and then asked them their names. When they informed him, he realized they were famous poets and distributed the whole herd of camels and sheep among them. When his father returned, he was furious: "Ḥātim! What have you done?" Ḥātim responded, "I have bestowed upon you a torque of glory as permanent as the ring of a dove's neck!" He explained all, and his father approved: "In this case, it's fine by me!" 20.4

Ḥātim's wife, Nawār, told the following story: It was a bad year. The ground was absolutely parched, and mothers had scarcely any milk for their suckling babes. By God, that winter, in the middle of a long night of biting cold wind, our children ʿAbd Allāh, ʿAdī, and Saffānah were wailing. Ḥātim attended to 20.5

أولادنا عبد الله وعديّ وسفّانة فقام إلى الصبيّين وقمت إلى الصبيّة فوالله ما سكتوا إلّا بعد هدأة من الليل ثمّ ناموا ونمت أنا وإيّاه فأقبل عليّ يعلّلني بالحديث فعرفت ما يريد فتناومت وما يأتيني نوم فقال ما لها أنامت فسكتّ فلمّا تهوّرت النجوم إذا شيء قد رفع كسر البيت فقال ما هذا قالت جارتك فلانة قال ما بك قالت الشرّ أتيتك من عند صبية يتعاوون تعاوي الذئاب من الجوع قال اعجليهم[1] فهببت إليه فقلت ماذا تصنع فوالله لقد تضاغى صبيتك من الجوع فقال اسكتي وأقبلت المرأة تحمل اثنين ويمشي جانبها أربعة كأنّها نعامة حولها رئالها فقام إلى فرسه جلّاب فنحره وكشط عن جلده ودفع المدية إلى المرأة ثمّ قال ابعثي صبيانك فبعثتهم واجتمعنا فقال سوءة تأكلون دون أهل الصرم ثمّ جعل يأتي بيتًا بيتًا ويقول دونكم النار فاجتمعوا والتفع بثوبه ناحية ينظر إلينا والله ما ذاق منها مزعة وإنّه لأحوجهم وأصبحنا وما على الأرض إلّا عظم أو حافر

٦،٢٠ وحكى ابن الأعرابي قال أُسر حاتم في عنزة فقالت له امرأة يومًا قم فافصد لنا هذه الناقة وكان الفصد عندهم أن يقطع عرق من عروق الناقة ثمّ يجمع الدم فيشوى ويؤكل فقام حاتم إلى الناقة فنحرها فلطمته المرأة فقال لو غير ذات سوار لطمتني فذهبت مثلاً ثمّ قالت له النسوة إنّما قلنا لك افصدها فقال هذا فزدي إنّه يعني فصدي أنا وهي لغة طيّئ

٧،٢٠ وحكى المدائنيّ قال أقبل ركب من بني أسد ومن قيس يريدون النعمان فلقوا حاتمًا فقالوا تركنا قومنا يثنون عليك خيرًا وقد أرسلوا إليك رسالة فقال ما هي فأنشده الأسديّون شعرًا للنابغة فيه فلمّا أنشدوه قالوا إنّا نستحي أن نسألك شيئًا

---

١ إ: أعجلتم.

the two boys while I looked after the girl. And by God, we weren't able to quiet them until a good part of the night had passed. At last they went to sleep, and we went to bed. Ḥātim turned to me and tried to distract me in conversation, but I knew what he was intending, and I pretended to sleep, though I couldn't. He asked himself, "What's with her? Is she asleep?" I stayed silent. When the stars began to plummet under the horizon, the ground flap of our tent lifted. Ḥātim called out, "Who's there?" A woman's voice responded, "It's your neighbor," and she named herself. He asked, "What's your news?" She replied, "Bad. I come to you from a tent of children so starving that they are howling like wolves." "Bring them here, quick!" I shot up to Ḥātim and scolded him: "What in God's name are you doing? Your own children were just now moaning from hunger." He said, "Quiet, you!" and rose as the woman arrived carrying two children, surrounded by four little ones; she looked like an ostrich arriving with her chicks. He fetched his horse, "Stretch Runner," slaughtered it, skinned it, and handed the knife to the woman, saying, "Call your children!" She did, and we all gathered, but he said, "It's terrible that we should eat without the rest of the camp!" And he went around the camp, tent by tent, saying, "Come to the hearth!" Everyone gathered, while he withdrew and wrapped himself in his robe, all the while looking on. By God, he didn't taste a morsel, even though he needed food the most. In the morning, we woke to a scene of bones and hoofs scattered on the ground.

Ibn al-Aʿrābī reports: Ḥātim was captured by the ʿAnazah, and one day one 20.6
of their women ordered him, "Get up and bleed this she-camel!" (By "bleed," she intended for him to cut one of the camel's veins and collect the blood, which would be boiled down and eaten.) Ḥātim went over to the she-camel and slaughtered her. The woman slapped him. Ḥātim remarked, "A slap from a woman who wears no bracelets . . ."[142] This became an adage. Another of their women exclaimed, "We only ordered you to bleed her!" Ḥātim replied, "I don't serve camel's blood without the rest of the camel!" He pronounced "blood" in the accent of Ṭayyiʾ.[143]

Al-Madāʾinī reports: A group from the Asad and Qays met Ḥātim on their 20.7
way to King al-Nuʿmān's court. They announced, "We come from people who speak highly of you, and they send you a message." Ḥātim asked, "What is it?" The riders from the Asad recited poetry by al-Nābighah in praise of Ḥātim, and after their poem, they added, "Though it embarrasses us, we do have one request." Ḥātim asked, "What is it?" "One of our companions is mountless."

وإنّ لنا لحاجة قال ما هي قال صاحب لنا قد أرحل يعني فقدت راحلته فقال حاتم خذوا فرسي هذه فاحملوه عليها فأخذوها وربطت الجارية فلوها بثوبها فأفلت يتبع أمّه واتّبعته الجارية لتردّه فصاح حاتم ما يتبعكم فهو لكم فذهبوا بالفرس والفلو والجارية

ولحاتم أخبار كثيرة وشهرته مغنّية وكانت أمّه عتب بنت عفيف موسرة لا تمسك شيئًا وكانت إخوتها يمنعونها فتأبى فحجروا عليها سنة يطعمونها قوتها لعلّها تكفّ عمّا تصنع ثمّ مكّنوها من صرمة من إبلها وقالوا استمتعي بها فأتتها امرأة من هوازن فسألتها فقالت دونك الصرمة فقد والله ذقت من الفقر ما آليت أن لا أمنع سائلًا شيئًا ٨،٢٠

وحاتم من فحول الشعراء ومن محاسن شعره ٩،٢٠

أَعَاذِلَ إِنَّ ٱلْمَالَ غَيْرُ مُخَلَّدٍ    وَإِنَّ ٱلْغِنَى عَارِيَةٌ فَتَزَوَّدِي
وَكَمْ مِنْ جَوَادٍ يُفْسِدُ ٱلْيَوْمَ جُودَهُ    وَسَاوِسُ قَدْ ذَكَّرْنَهُ ٱلْفَقْرَ فِي غِدِ
وَكَمْ لِيمَ آبَائِي فَمَا كَفَّ جُودَهُمْ    مَلَامٌ وَمِنْ أَيْدِيهِمُ خُلِقَتْ يَدِي

وقوله يخاطب امرأتَهُ ١٠،٢٠

أَمَاوِيَّ إِنَّ ٱلْمَالَ غَادٍ وَرَائِحٌ    وَيَبْقَى مِنَ ٱلْمَالِ ٱلْأَحَادِيثُ وَٱلذِّكْرُ
أَمَاوِيَّ مَا يُغْنِي ٱلثَّرَاءُ عَنِ ٱلْفَتَى    إِذَا حَشْرَجَتْ يَوْمًا وَضَاقَ بِهَا ٱلصَّدْرُ
أَمَاوِيَّ إِنْ يُصْبِحْ صَدَايَ بِقَفْرَةٍ    مِنَ ٱلْأَرْضِ لَا مَاءٌ لَدَيَّ وَلَا خَمْرُ
تَرَيْ أَنَّ مَا أَهْلَكْتُ لَمْ يَكُ ضَرَّنِي    وَأَنَّ يَدِي مِمَّا بَخِلْتُ بِهِ صِفْرُ

(They meant that he no longer had his riding camel.) Ḥātim replied, "Here, take this horse of mine for him." The riders took the mare. One of Ḥātim's slave girls tethered the mare's filly with her shawl, but the filly broke loose and followed its mother. The slave girl ran to catch it, and Ḥātim called out to the riders, "Whatever follows you is also yours!" And so they took the horse, her filly, and the slave girl.

There are many more such stories about Ḥātim, and his generosity is celebrated in song. 20.8

Ḥātim's mother, ʿAtb[144] bint ʿAfīf, a very wealthy woman, had a habit of giving everything away, and though her brothers tried to stop her, she never ceased giving. Eventually, her brothers confined her for a year, providing her with just enough food to survive in the hopes of stemming her habit. After the year was up, they returned to her a small part of her camel herd, telling her, "Make use of these." But when a woman from the Hawāzin approached her and begged assistance, ʿAtb held back nothing: "Take the whole lot: it's yours. By God, I have tasted poverty and I have sworn never to turn down a person in need!"

Ḥātim ranks among the most accomplished poets;[145] examples of his fine poetry include: 20.9

Reproacher! Possessions are not immortal!
Go ahead and hoard, woman! But know: wealth is just borrowed.
Too many magnanimous men have their generosity spoiled
by wanton whispers about future need.
Much reproached were my forefathers, yet their bounty endured,
and from their open hands were mine own created.

Ḥātim's poem addressed to his wife: 20.10

Māwiyah! Money comes and goes between morning and night;
all that remains are reputation and memory.
Māwiyah! What does a fortune do for a man
as he breathes his last, his chest tightening?
Māwiyah! When my corpse[146] comes to lie in an empty desert,
far from all water and wine,
and when my hands no longer grasp what I might have kept,
You'll see that what I spent did me no harm.

وَقَدْ عَلِمَ ٱلْأَقْوَامُ لَوْ أَنَّ حَاتِمًا    أَرَادَ ثَرَاءَ ٱلْمَالِ كَانَ لَهُ وَفْرُ
وَإِنِّي لَا آلُو بِمَالِي صَنِيعَةً    فَأَوَّلُهُ زَادٌ وَآخِرُهُ ذُخْرُ
غَنِينَا زَمَانًا بِٱلتَّصَعْلُكِ وَٱلْغِنَى    وَكُلًّا سَقَانَاهُ بِكَأْسَيْهِمَا ٱلدَّهْرُ
فَمَا زَادَنَا بَغْيًا عَلَى ذِي قَرَابَةٍ    غِنَانَا وَلَا أَزْرَى بِإِحْسَانِنَا ٱلْفَقْرُ

وقوله يصف طارقًا ١١،٢٠

عَوَى آئِسًا شِبْهَ ٱلْجُنُونِ وَمَا بِهِ    جُنُونٌ وَلٰكِنْ كَيْدُ أَمْرٍ يُحَاوِلُهْ
فَأَثْقَبْتُ[1] نَارِي ثُمَّ أَبْرَزْتُ ضَوْءَهَا    وَأَخْرَجْتُ كَلْبِي وَهُوَ فِي ٱلْبَيْتِ دَاخِلُهْ
وَقُلْتُ لَهُ أَهْلًا وَسَهْلًا وَمَرْحَبًا    رَشِدْتَ وَلَمْ أَقْعُدْ إِلَيْهِ أُسَائِلُهْ
وَقُمْتُ إِلَى ٱلْبُزْلِ ٱلْهِجَانِ أُعِدُّهَا    لِوَجْبَةِ حَقٍّ نَازِلٍ أَنَا فَاعِلُهْ

وقوله ١٢،٢٠

حَنَنْتُ[2] إِلَى ٱلْأَجْبَالِ أَجْبَالُ طَيِّئٍ    وَحَنَّتْ قُلُوصِي أَنْ رَأَتْ سَوْطَ أَحْمَرَ
وَإِنِّي لَمِزْجَاءُ ٱلْمَطِيِّ عَلَى ٱلْوَجَى    وَمَا أَنَا مِنْ خُلَّانِكِ ٱبْنَةَ عَفْزَرَ
فَلَا تَسْأَلِينِي وَٱسْأَلِي أَيُّ فَارِسٍ    إِذَا ٱلْخَيْلُ جَالَتْ فِي قَنًا قَدْ تَكَسَّرَ
وَلَا تَسْأَلِينِي وَٱسْأَلِي فِي صُحْبَتِي    إِذَا مَا ٱلْمَطِيُّ فِي ٱلْفَلَاةِ تَضَوَّرَ
وَإِنِّي كَأَشْلَاءِ ٱللِّجَامِ وَلَنْ تَرَيْ    أَخَا ٱلْحَرْبِ إِلَّا سَاهِمَ ٱلْوَجْهِ أَغْبَرَ
أَخُو ٱلْحَرْبِ إِنْ عَضَّتْ بِهِ ٱلْحَرْبُ عَضَّهَا[3]    وَإِن شَمَّرَتْ عَنْ سَاقِهَا ٱلْحَرْبُ شَمَّرَ

---

١ إ: أثبتّ. ٢ إ: خنت. ٣ إ: غضت...غضها.

Had wealth been my aim, they all know:
  "Ḥātim could have had plenty."
But I strove to put wealth to use.
Wealth! One part buys sustenance, the rest surplus.
We've lived poor, we've lived rich—
  Time's cups served both.
Wealth made us no more desirable among kin;
  poverty detracted nothing from our honor.

Ḥātim described a night visitor: **20.11**

A howl . . . of despair, or of madness?
  But no—it's a cry of need.
I kindled my campfire, I stoked its flames high,
  I sent my dog from inside the tent.
  I greeted him: "Welcome! May your stay be easy!
  You've come to the right place." I asked nothing more,
And went straight to my plump, noble white camels reared
  just for this: my duty to visitors. I put on a feast.

Ḥātim's poem:[147] **20.12**

I yearned for the mountains, the mountains of the Ṭayyi'.
My young she-camel went mad[148] seeing the whip of Aḥmar.
I drive my camels till they moan from lacerated feet.
I'm not like your other lovers, Māwiyah:
  Don't ask *me* anything; ask instead which horseman
    in the cavalry charge pierced the spear-bristling rank.
  Don't ask *me* anything; ask my companions
    if any starved on our desert treks.
I'm the iron bit of the bridle: don't expect
  War's brother to be anything but ashen and dusty.
War's brother: when battle bites, he bites back;
  when War rolls up its sleeves, he's ready.

وقوله ١٣،٢٠

وَعَـاذِلَتَـيْنِ هَبَّـتَا بَعْـدَ هَـجْعَـةٍ تَلُومَـانِ مِتْـلَافًا مُفِيـدًا مُـلَوَّمَا
لَحَـا ٱللَّهُ صُعْـلُوكًا مُنَـاهُ وَهَمُّـهُ مِنَ ٱلْعَيْشِ أَنْ يَلْقَى لَبُوسًـا وَمَطْعَمَا
وَٱللّٰهِ صُعْـلُوكٌ يُسَـاوِرُ هَمَّـهُ وَيَمْضِي عَلَى ٱلْأَحْدَاثِ وَٱلْهَوْلِ مُقْدِمَا
إِذَا مَا رَأَى يَوْمًـا مَكَـارِمَ أَعْـرَضَتْ تَيَمَّـمَ كُبْرَاهُـنَّ ثُمَّتَ صَمَّـمَا

## وزيد بن مهلهل إنّما ركب بفخذيك ٢١

١،٢١ هو زيد بن مهلهل بن زيدان الطائيّ فارس مظفّر بعيد الصيت أدرك الإسلام وأسلم وسمّاه رسول الله صلّى الله عليه وسلّم زيد الخير وهو شاعر مفلق مقلّ معدود من الشعراء والفرسان وإنّما سمّي زيد الخيل لكثرة خيله فإنّه لم يكن لكثير من العرب غير الفرس والفرسين وكانت له خيل كثيرة منها المسمّاة المعروفة التي ذكرها في شعره مثل الهطّال وكامل ودؤول ولاحق

٢،٢١ وكان زيد الخيل عظيم الخلقة طويلاً جدًّا ويُسمّى مقبّل الظعن لأنّه كان يقبّل المرأة من الأرض وهي في الهودج وكذلك أبو زبيد الطائيّ وابن جذل الطعّان

٣،٢١ حكى أبو عمرو الشيبانيّ قال وفد زيد الخيل على رسول الله صلّى الله عليه وسلّم ومعه در بن سدوس وغيره من طيّئ فأناخوا ركابهم بباب المسجد ودخلوا ورسول الله صلّى الله عليه وسلّم يخطب فلمّا رآهم قال إنّي أجيركم من العزّى وما حازت[١] مناع[٢] من كلّ ضارّ غير نفّاع ومن الجبل الأسود الذي يعبدونه من دون الله فقام زيد الخيل وكان أتمّ الرجال يركب الفرس ورجلاه تخطّ في الأرض كأنّه على حمار فقال أشهد أن لا إله إلّا الله وأنّك رسول الله فقال ومن أنت قال زيد الخيل بن

١ برا ول١ ول٢ وق١: جارت. ٢ إ١: متاع.

Ḥātim's poetry: 20.13

> Here we go again. Two women stir—
> little sleep, but many scolds for this magnanimous man.
> Despised is the poor fellow who craves nothing,
> for whom a cloak and a meal are enough.
> God help the poor men dueling worry,
> headlong against the blows and terrors of Time,
> At every chance for a noble act,
> they strive for the noblest—on that they're determined.

**. . . Zayd ibn Muhalhil rode with your thighs . . .** 21

Zayd ibn Muhalhil ibn Zaydān[149] of the Ṭayyi' was a champion horse warrior, 21.1
known far and wide. Zayd was a fabulous poet, and, though he only composed a few poems, he is esteemed as one of the great Arab poets and horsemen. He lived into the early Islamic period, and when he converted, the Prophet (God bless and keep him) renamed him "Goodman Zayd"—Zayd had previously been known as "Horseman Zayd" because he owned so many horses. Whereas most Arabs possessed but one or two horses, Zayd had many, and some are famous and mentioned in his poetry, such as Cascade,[150] Perfection, Heavy Trotter, and Overtaker.

Zayd was a gigantic man. He was so extremely tall that he was also nick- 21.2
named "Kiss 'Em as They Go," since he could reach up to kiss a departing woman in her palanquin while he stood on the ground. Abū Zubayd of the Ṭayyi' and Ibn Jidhl al-Ṭa''ān[151] were also "departing kissers."

Abū 'Amr al-Shaybānī reports that Horseman Zayd, together with Wazar 21.3
ibn Sadūs and another member of the Ṭayyi',[152] traveled to meet the Prophet (God bless and keep him). They set down their mounts before the mosque entrance and entered as the Prophet (God bless and keep him) was delivering a sermon. When he saw Zayd and his companions, the Prophet said, "I am better for you than al-'Uzzā,[153] the holy precinct of Manā'i, and the Black Mountain,[154] which you worship instead of Allāh." Zayd then rose—he was one of the tallest men, so tall that when he rode his horse, his feet dragged along the ground as if he was riding a donkey—and he declared, "I swear God is the only god and you are the Messenger of God!"[155] The Prophet asked

مهلهل قال بل أنت زيد الخير ثمّ قال الحمد الله الذي جاء بك من سهلك وجبلك ورقّق قلبك على الإسلام يا زيد ما وُصف لي رجل فرأيته إلّاكان دون ما وُصف لي إلّا أنت فإنّك فوق ما قيل فيك

٤،٢١ وفي رواية أخرى إنّ فيك خصلتين يحبّهما الله ورسوله الأناة والحلم فلمّا ولّى قال رسول الله صلّى الله عليه وسلّم أيّ رجل إن سلم من آطام المدينة فأخذته الحمّى فمكث سبعًا ثمّ اشتدّت به الحمّى فخرج وقال لأصحابه جنّبوني بلاد قيس فقد كانت بيننا حماسات[١] في الجاهليّة ولا والله لا أقاتل مسلمًا حتّى ألقى الله عزّ وجلّ فنزل بماء لجرم يقال له فردة واشتدّت به الحمّى فقال

أَمُرْتَحِلٌ صَحْبِي ٱلْمَشَارِقَ غُدْوَةً　فَأُتْـرَكَ فِي بَيْتٍ بِفَرْدَةٍ مُنْجِدِ
فَلَيْتَ ٱللَّوَاتِي عُدْنَنِي لَمْ يَعُدْنَنِي　وَلَيْتَ ٱللَّوَاتِي غِبْنَ عَنِّي عُوَّدِي

٥،٢١ وكان رسول الله صلّى الله عليه وسلّم كتب معه لبني نبهان كتابًا بفدك فمكث زيد الخيل بفردة سبعًا ثمّ مات فأقام عليه قبيصة بن الأسود المناحة سبعًا ثمّ بعث راحلته ورحله وفيه كتاب رسول الله صلّى الله عليه وسلّم فلمّا نظرت امرأته وكانت على الشرك إلى الراحلة وليس عليها زيد ضربتها بالنار فاحترق الكتاب فيها فلمّا بلغ رسولَ الله صلّى الله عليه وسلّم ضربها الراحلة بالنار وإحراق الكتاب قال ويل لبني نبهان

٦،٢١ وحكى الشيبانيّ عن شيخ من بني عامر قال أصابتنا سنة ذهبت بالأموال فخرج رجل من القوم بعياله حتّى أنزلهم الحيرة فقال لهم كونوا قريبًا من الملك يصبكم من خيره حتّى أرجع إليكم وآلى أليّة لا يرجع حتّى يكسبهم خيرًا فتزوّد زادًا

١ إ: حمانيات.

him, "Who are you?" "I am Horseman Zayd, son of Muhalhil." The Prophet then declared, "Not anymore. You are now Goodman Zayd. We praise God for bringing you here from your lowlands and uplands, and for opening your heart to receive Islam. Zayd! When beheld face to face, men are invariably less impressive than their reputations; you, on the other hand, are the first man I've met who surpasses expectations."

Another version narrates that the Prophet told Zayd, "You possess two traits much valued by God and His Prophet: equanimity and forbearance." 21.4

When Zayd left, the Prophet (God bless and keep him) remarked, "What a man! But will he survive the forts of Medina?" Indeed, Zayd contracted a fever: he stayed in Medina for seven days, but his fever worsened and he departed, instructing his companions: "Don't take me through the lands of the Qays: we sparred mightily in pre-Islamic times, and by God, I dread meeting Almighty God if I fight Muslims now!" They traveled until they reached a watering hole called Fardah, which belonged to the Jarm. There Zayd's fever worsened, and in verse he lamented:

Companions! Do you depart tomorrow whence the sun rises
While I, in a tent at Fardah, am left sweating in grief?
If only these women attending me now would not visit;
If only those women absent from me now could visit.

Zayd had with him a letter that the Prophet (God bless and keep him) intended for the Nabhān camped at Fadak, but Zayd languished at Fardah for seven days and then died. Qabīṣah ibn al-Aswad held a ritual mourning for seven days, and then sent Zayd's camel and saddle homeward, with the Prophet's (peace and blessings upon him) letter still in it. When Zayd's wife, who was still a polytheist, saw the camel approaching without Zayd astride it, she ordered it burned, and along with it went the letter. When the Prophet (God bless and keep him) heard that she had immolated Zayd's camel and burned the letter, he exclaimed, "Alas for the Nabhān!" 21.5

Al-Shaybānī narrates on the authority of an old man from the ʿĀmir: Once, during a bad year that decimated our livestock, one of our men struck out for al-Ḥīrah with his dependents. He settled them there and told them, "Get in good favor with the king; perchance you can benefit from his charity until I return." The man then swore a solemn oath not to return until he could provide something good for his folk. He packed some provisions and walked for 21.6

ثمّ مشى سبعة أيّام حتّى انتهى إلى عطن إبل مع تطفّل الشمس فإذا خباء عظيم وفيه قبّة من أدم

٧،٢١ قال فقلت في نفسي ما لهذا الخباء بدّ من أهل وما لهذا العطن بدّ من إبل فنظرت في الخباء فإذا شيخ قد اختلفت ترقوتاه كأنّه نسر فجلست خلفه مختفيًا فلمّا وجبت الشمس إذا بفارس قد أقبل لم أر قطّ أعظم منه ولا أجسم على فرس مشرف ومعه عبدان يمشيان وإذا مائة من الإبل مع فحلها فبرك الفحل وبركن حوله فقال لأحد عبديه احلب فلانة ثمّ اسق الشيخ فحلب في عسّ حتّى ملأه ثمّ وضعه بين يدي الشيخ وتنحّى عنه فكرع منه الشيخ مرّة أو مرّتين ثمّ نزع وثرت إليه مختفيًا فشربته فرجع العبد فقال يا مولاي قد أتى على آخر العسّ ففرح وقال له احلب فلانة فحلبها ثمّ وضع العسّ بين يدي الشيخ فكرع منه مرّة ثمّ نزع فثرت إليه فشربت نصفه وكرهت أن آتي على آخره وجاء العبد فأخذه ثمّ أمر مولاه بشاة فذبحها وشوي للشيخ منها ثمّ أكل هو وعبداه فأمهلت حتّى إذا ناموا وسمعت الغطيط ثرت إلى الفحل فحللت عقاله واندفع فتبعته الإبل فهمست ليلتي حتّى الصباح

٨،٢١ فلمّا علا النهار إذا أنا بفارس قد أقبل وإذا هو صاحبي فعقلت الفحل ونثلت كنانتي ووقفت بينه وبين الإبل فوقف بعيدًا وقال احلل عقاله فقلت كلّا لقد تركت نسيّات بالحيرة وآليت أن لا أرجع إليهنّ حتّى أفيدهنّ خيرًا أو أموت فقال إنّك ميّت حلّ عقالك لا أبا لك فقلت هو ما قلت فقال إنّك لمغرور ثمّ قال انصب لي خطامه وفيه ثلاث عجر

٩،٢١ ففعلت فقال أين تحبّ أن أضع سهمي فقلت في هذا الموضع فكأنّما وضعه بيده ثمّ رمى الثانية صائبًا فرددت نبلي ووقفت مستسلمًا فدنا منّي وأخذ السيف

seven days. As the sun started to lean downward on the seventh day, he came to a paddock beside a high-topped, leather-domed tent.

The man himself tells the rest of the story: I said to myself, "There's no 21.7
doubt this tent has inhabitants, and no doubt this paddock will have camels!" I looked into the tent, and there sat a solitary old man with a twisted clavicle that made him look like a vulture. I concealed myself behind him, and when the sun had set, a rider appeared astride a towering horse with two slaves walking beside him. I had never seen such an enormous man. Behind them were one hundred camels and one bull camel. The bull sat down and the hundred she-camels settled around him. The rider pointed out a camel and ordered one of the slaves, "Milk her for the old man!" The slave filled a large bowl to the brim and placed it before the old man, who leaned over the bowl and sipped just once or twice, refraining from taking more. I furtively stole to the bowl and finished it off. The slave came back in and cried, "Master! He drank the whole thing!" The man was delighted and said, "Milk so-and-so!" (He named another camel.) The slave milked her and placed the bowl before the old man. He sipped it once, then desisted, and again I stole to the bowl, but only drank half of it, as I was wary of finishing the whole thing. The slave returned and took the bowl, and his master ordered him to slaughter a sheep, which they grilled and presented a portion to the old man. The rider ate with his two slaves, and I stayed concealed until they slept. When I heard their snoring, I jumped up, made for the bull camel, and undid his hobbling rope. He darted off, the herd followed, and I tiptoed after them all night long.

Dawn broke, and first light revealed something following me—a horseman, 21.8
the very same rider from the day before. I hobbled the bull camel, laid out all the arrows from my quiver, and stood between the rider and his camels. He stopped at a distance and shouted, "Undo the hobbling rope!" I replied, "No chance. I have left young women in al-Ḥīrah, and I swore I would not return until I have something for them, or I die." "Well, then you're dead. Watch out! Just undo that rope." I stood my ground. "No. I told you how it is." "You have no idea what you're doing," he countered, and said, "Prop up the camel's bridle for me, as there are three knots in it."

I did as he asked. Then he said, "Where on the rope would you like me to 21.9
shoot my arrow?" I pointed. "This part." He shot and hit it, as if he had placed the arrow right on the spot with his hand. Then he shot three more arrows, each hitting the bridle knots. I gathered my arrows, returned them to their

والقوس ثمّ قال اركب وعرف أنّي الذي شربت اللبن عنده فقال كيف ظنّك بي فقلت أحسن ظن فقال أتراني كنت أروعك وقد بتّ تنادم مهلهلاً قلت أزيد الخيل أنت قال نعم فقلت كن خير آخذ قال لا بأس عليك

١٠،٢١ ومضى بنا إلى موضعه[1] ثمّ قال أما لو كانت هذه الإبل لي لسلّمتها لك ولكنّها لابنة مهلهل فأقم عليّ فإنّي على شرف غارة فأقمت أيّامًا ثمّ أغار على بني نمير بالملح فأصاب إبلاً فأعطانيها وبعث معي خفراء من ماء إلى ماء حتّى وردت الحيرة

١١،٢١ وحكى الأصمعيّ قال أسر زيد الخيل كعب بن زهير والحطيئة الشاعر في حرب فأمّا كعب ففداه قومه وأمّا الحطيئة فشكى الحاجة فقال زيد الخيل

أَقُولُ لِعَبْدِي جَرْوَلٍ إِذْ أَسَرْتُهُ    أَثِبْنِي وَلَا يَغْرُرْكَ أَنَّكَ شَاعِرُ

فقال الحطيئة

إِذَا لَمْ يَكُنْ مَالِي بِآتٍ فَإِنَّهُ    سَيَأْتِي ثَنَائِي زَيْدًا بْنَ مُهَلْهِلِ
فَمَا نِلْتَنَا غَدْرًا وَلٰكِنْ لَقِيتَنَا    غَدَاةَ ٱلْتَقَيْنَا فِي ٱلْمَضِيقِ بِأَخْيُلِ
تَفَادَى حُمَاةُ ٱلْخَيْلِ مِنْ وَقْعِ رُمْحِهِ    تَفَادِي ضِعَافِ ٱلطَّيْرِ مِنْ وَقْعِ أَجْدَلِ

فرضي عنه زيد ومنّ عليه فلمّا رجع الحطيئة إلى قومه قام شاكرًا لزيد ذاكرًا لنعمته

١٢،٢١ فلمّا أسرت طيّئ بني بدر طلبت فزارة من شعراء العرب أن يهجو بني لأم وزيدًا فتحامتهم الشعراء فصاروا إلى الحطيئة فأبى عليهم فقالوا نجعل لك مائة ناقة فقال لو جعلتموها ألفًا ما فعلت ثمّ قال

١ إ: موضعي.

quiver, and stood there in surrender. He came up, took my sword and bow, and told me, "Ride!"

He knew I was the one who had drunk the milk at his tent, and he asked me, "What's your opinion of me?" I replied, "As good as it gets." He said, "You think I'm going to terrify you after you spent a night in the camaraderie of my old man?" "Are you Horseman Zayd?" I asked. "Yes," he replied. I implored him, "Be a good captor." "Don't you worry," he assured me.

We traveled back to his camp and he explained, "If these camels were mine, 21.10
I would hand them over to you, but they belong to my sister. So stay with me awhile, as I am soon about to go raiding." After some days, he raided the Numayr at al-Milḥ, capturing camels, which he gave to me, and sent me back to al-Ḥīrah with an escort of guards to see my safe passage from watering hole to watering hole.

Al-Aṣmaʿī tells that Horseman Zayd once captured Kaʿb ibn Zuhayr and the 21.11
poet al-Ḥuṭay'ah in battle.[156] Kaʿb's people paid his ransom, but al-Ḥuṭay'ah protested poverty, and Zayd retorted:

> To my slave—Ḥuṭay'ah—I said upon his capture:
> "Pay me good ransom! Don't think poets exempt!"

Al-Ḥuṭay'ah replied:

> Though money is not forthcoming,
> praise is on its way—Horseman Zayd!
> You took us fair: caught us in a narrow ravine,
> on a dawn when an ill-omened bird[157] had sung for us.
> Before your spears, our brave horsemen
> were but weak little birds resisting a falcon.

Zayd was satisfied and took mercy on al-Ḥuṭay'ah. When al-Ḥuṭay'ah returned to his people, he continuously expressed gratitude to Zayd and memorialized his benevolence.

Sometime afterward, the Ṭayyi' captured the Badr. The Badr's kinsmen, 21.12
the Fazārah, therefore asked the Arab poets to lampoon the La'm and Zayd, kinsmen of the Ṭayyi',[158] but the poets refused. So the Fazārah approached al-Ḥuṭay'ah, but he also refused, and when they made him an offer: "What if we give you one hundred she-camels?" Ḥuṭay'ah replied, "Not even if you made it one thousand," and sang:

كَيْفَ ٱلْهِجَاءُ وَمَا تَنْفَكُّ صَالِحَةٌ    مِنْ آلِ لَأْمٍ بِظَهْرِ ٱلْغَيْبِ تَأْتِينِي

ومن شعر زيد الخيل ١٣،٢١

بَنِي عَامِرٍ هَلْ تَعْرِفُونَ إِذَا غَدَا    أَبُو مُكْنِفٍ قَدْ شَدَّ عَقْدَ ٱلدَّوَائِرِ
بِجَيْشٍ تَظَلُّ ٱلْبُلْقُ فِي حَجَرَاتِهِ    تَرَى ٱلْأُكْمَ مِنْهُ سُجَّدًا لِلْحَوَافِرِ
أَبَتْ عَادَةٌ لِلْوَرْدِ أَنْ تَكْرَهَ ٱلْقَنَا    وَحَاجَةُ رُمْحِي فِي نُمَيْرٍ وَعَامِرِ

وقوله وقد غزا غزوة فضلع فرس من خيله فلم يتبع الخيل فأخذه بنو الصيداء ١٤،٢١

يَا بَنِي ٱلصَّيْدَاءِ رُدُّوا فَرَسِي    إِنَّمَا يُصْنَعُ هٰذَا بِالذَّلِيلْ
لَا تُذِيلُوهُ فَإِنِّي لَمْ أَكُنْ    يَا بَنِي ٱلصَّيْدَاءِ لِمُهْرِي بِٱلْمُذِيلْ
عَوِّدُوهُ كَٱلَّذِي عَوَّدْتُهُ    دَلَجَ ٱللَّيْلِ وَإِيطَاءَ ٱلْقَتِيلْ

وقوله ١٥،٢١

جَلَبْنَا ٱلْخَيْلَ مِنْ أَجَإٍ وَسَلْمَى    تَخُبُّ نَزَائِعًا خَبَبَ ٱلذِّئَابِ[١]
ضَرَبْنَ بِغَمْرَةٍ فَخَرَجْنَ مِنْهَا    خُرُوجَ ٱلْوَدْقِ مِنْ خَلَلِ ٱلسَّحَابِ
وَقَدْ عَلِمَتْ بَنُو عَبْسٍ وَبَدْرٍ    وَمُرَّةُ أَنَّنِي شَغْبُ عِتَابِي[٢]

١ إ١، بر٢: أحياء سلمى // تحث مراتعا حيث الذباب؛ ق٢: أحياء سلمى // تحب ترابعا جنب الذئاب. ٢ إ١: شعث عقابي.

How can I lampoon the La'm? Those whose good grace
frequents me unbidden.

Zayd's poetry: **21.13**

Sons of ʿĀmir! Don't you know
when Horseman Zayd ties his cuirass cords,
when a mustering army hides piebald chargers deep in thick ranks,
when the hills lie prostrate under trampling hooves,
Then my horse, from habit, will eagerly plunge into spears,
and my spear wants the Numayr—and you too.

Horseman Zayd addressed the following poem to the Ṣaydā' after they cap- **21.14**
tured one of his horses, which had strayed from his troop during a raid:

Sons of al-Ṣaydā'! Return my horse!
Such theft only befalls the lowly.
Sons of al-Ṣaydā', you demean him by keeping him—
colts aren't demeaned by me.
Train my colt in the way I did:[159]
charging through the night and trampling dead bodies.

Zayd's poetry: **21.15**

We gee up the horses from Aja' and Salmā,
let loose, at a canter, rushing like wolves.
In the thicket of the fight, they collide
and burst forth like a storm pouring through the clouds.
The ʿAbs, the Badr, and the Murrah all know:
My reckoning is wicked.[160]

## والسليك بن السلكة إنّما عدا على رجليك ٢٢

هو السليك بن عمرو بن يثربيّ[١] أحد بني مقاعس وأمّه السلكة جاهليّ قديم وهو أحد صعاليك العرب ولصوصهم العدّائين الذين كانوا لا يلحقون ولا تتعلّق بهم الخيل ١،٢٢

حكى ابن شهاب قال كان السليك السعديّ إذا كان الشتاء استودع بيض النعام ماء السماء ثمّ دفنه فإذا كان الصيف وانقطعت إغارة الخيل أغار وكان أدلّ من قطاة فيجيء حتّى يقف على البيضة وكان لا يغير على مضر بل على اليمن فإذا لم يفد أغار على ربيعة وكان يقول اللّهمّ إنّك تهيّئ ما شئت لمن شئت اللّهمّ إنّي لو كنت ضعيفًا لكنت عبدًا اللّهمّ إنّي أعوذ بك من الخيبة فأمّا الهيبة فلا هيبة ٢،٢٢

فذكروا أنّه أملق حتّى لم يبق له شيء فخرج على رجليه رجاء أن يصيب غرّة من بعض من يمرّ به فيذهب بإبله حتّى أمسى في ليلة مقمرة من ليالي الشتاء فاشتمل الصماء ثمّ نام فبينا هو نائم إذ جثم عليه رجل فقعد على جنبه ثمّ قال له استأسر فرفع السليك رأسه وقال الليل طويل وأنت مقمر فذهبت مثلاً فجعل الرجل يلهزه ويقول يا خبيث استأسر فلمّا آذاه أخرج السليك يده فضمّ الرجل ضمّة ضرط منها وهو فوقه فقال السليك أضرطًا[٢] وأنت الأعلى فذهبت مثلاً ثمّ قال السليك ما أنت قال رجل افتقرت فقلت لأخرجنّ فلا أعود إلى أهلي حتّى أستغني قال فانطلق معي فانطلقا فوجدا رجلاً قصّته مثل قصّتهما فاصطحبوا جميعًا ثمّ أتوا جوف[٣] مراد فلمّا أشرفوا إذا فيه نعم كثيرة فهابوا أن يغزوا فيطردوا بعضها فيلحقهم الطلب فقال لهم السليك كونا قريبًا حتّى أتى الرعاء فأعلم لكما علم الحيّ أقريب أم بعيد فإن كان قريبًا رجعت إليكما وإن كانوا بعيدًا قلت لكما ٣،٢٢

١ إ١: تتربي. ٢ إ١: أضارطًا. ٣ إ١: جرف.

**. . . al-Sulayk ibn al-Sulakah ran on your legs . . .** 22

Al-Sulayk was the son of ʿAmr ibn Yathribī.[161] He descended from the Muqāʿis; 22.1
al-Sulakah was the name of his mother. Al-Sulayk lived in ancient pre-Islamic times, and he was one of the Arab desperadoes, one of the Arab thieves, those men who had great prowess as runners—no one could catch them, and they could outrun horses.

Ibn Shihāb[162] tells that during the winter, al-Sulayk of the Saʿd[163] would fill 22.2
ostrich eggs with rainwater and bury them. Al-Sulayk's sense of direction was keener than a sandgrouse's, so in the summer he could find all those eggs and drink from them to sustain his marauding, whereas all other horse-borne raiders had to cease operations until the rains returned. Al-Sulayk predominantly raided Southern tribes, and only if that was not gainful would he attack the Rabīʿah, but he would never plunder the Muḍar.

Al-Sulayk used to say, "Almighty God! You dispose of those whom You wish for the benefit of those whom You wish. Almighty God! If I was weak, I would be a slave. Almighty God! I seek refuge in you from failure. But dread? I have none!"

Narrators tell that al-Sulayk spent all his wealth, and when he was in absolute 22.3
penury he struck out on foot in the hopes of ambushing some passerby whose camels he could steal. That night, with the winter moon shining above him, al-Sulayk bundled up on the hard ground and slept. The next thing he knew, a man had leapt upon him and pinned him down, and was yelling, "Surrender!" Al-Sulayk raised his head and said, "The night is long and the moon shines for you."[164] This became an expression. The man then began beating al-Sulayk on the chest, shouting, "Surrender, you scum!" The beating eventually began to annoy al-Sulayk, and he reached out, grasping the man so tightly that the man passed wind. Al-Sulayk said, "You're on top, yet you fart?" This also became proverbial. Al-Sulayk then asked him, "Who are you?" "I'm an impoverished man who has sworn not to return to my family until I can provide for myself." Al-Sulayk invited him: "Come along with me!" and they set off. Later, they found a third man in a situation similar to theirs, and the trio trekked on together until they reached the Murād Depression. Looking down into it, they espied many camels, but they worried that if they snatched a herd, a search party might catch up with them. So al-Sulayk instructed his companions: "Stay nearby, and I'll approach the herders and find out about this tribe. If the tribe is far enough

قولاً أومئ إليكما به فأغزوا فانطلق حتّى أتى الرعاء فلم يزل يستنطقهم حتّى أخبروه بمكان الحيّ فإذا هو بعيد إن طلبوا لم يدركوا فقال السليك للرعاء ألا أغنّيكم قالوا بلى فرفع صوته وغنّى

يَا صَاحِبَيَّ أَلَا لَا حَيَّ بِٱلْوَادِي ... إِلَّا عَبِيدٌ قِيَامٌ بَيْنَ أَذْوَادِ
هَلْ يَنْظُرَانِ قَلِيلاً رَيْثَ غَفْلَتِهِمْ ... أَمْ تَغْدُوَانِ فَإِنَّ ٱلرَّابِحَ ٱلْغَادِي

فلمّا سمعا ذلك أتيا السليك فطردوا الإبل فذهبوا بأكثرها ولم يبلغ الصريخ إلى الحيّ حتّى فاتوهم

٤،٢٢ وحكى أبو عبيدة قال بلغني أنّ السليك رأى طلائع لبكر بن وائل وكانوا مُنْحدرين ليغزوا على بني تميم ولا يعلم بهم فقالوا إنْ علم السليكُ أنذر بنا قومه فبعثوا له فارسين على جوادين وطارداه فلمّا هايجاه خرج يحضر كانّه ظبيٌ وطارداهُ سحابة يومهم ثمّ قالا إذا كان الليل أعيى وسقط وأقصر عن العدو فنأخذه فلمّا أصبحا وجدا أثره وقد عثر بأصل شجرة فنزا عنها ونذرت قوسه فانحطمت فوجدا[1] قصدة منها قد ارتزّت بالأرض فقالا ما له أخزاه الله وهمّا بالرجوع ثمّ قالا لعلّ هذا كان من أوّل الليل ثمّ فتر فتبعاه فإذا أثره متفجّجًا[2] قد بال ودشّ في الأرض وخدّها فقالا ما له قاتله الله فما رأينا أشدّ منه ولا نتبعه أبدًا وانصرفا

٥،٢٢ ووصل إلى قومه فأنذرهم فكذّبوه لبعد الغاية فقال

يُكَذِّبُنِي ٱلْعَمْرَانِ[3] عَمْرُو بْنُ جُنْدَبٍ ... وَعَمْرُو بْنُ سَعْدٍ فَٱلْمُكَذِّبُ أَكْذَبُ
ثَكِلْتُهُمَا إِنْ لَمْ أَكُنْ قَدْ رَأَيْتُهَا ... كَرَادِيسَ يَهْدِيهَا إِلَى ٱلْحَيِّ مَوْكِبُ

١ إ: قالوا . . . أصبحوا . . . وجدوا. ٢ إ: متفجًّا. ٣ إ: عمروان.

away, I'll give you word, and then we'll attack!" Al-Sulayk approached the herders and drew them into conversation until they volunteered the whereabouts of their tribe—it was sufficiently distant to enable al-Sulayk's band to escape before the search party could arrive. So al-Sulayk next asked the herders, "Shall I sing for you?" "Please do!" And, raising his voice, he sang:

My two companions! There's no tribe in the valley,
  nothing but slaves standing about a herd.
Will you two just stand, gazing at their heedlessness,
  or will you come early? Profit is for the early bird!

Al-Sulayk's companions heard the verses, descended into the depression, and made off with most of the camels. By the time alarm was raised at the tribe's camp, the thieves were out of sight.

Abū ʿUbaydah narrates that the war band of the Bakr ibn Wāʾil was heading for the Tamīm when al-Sulayk caught sight of their advance party. The Bakr warriors remarked, "If al-Sulayk finds out, he'll warn his people." So they sent two horsemen on swift chargers to chase down al-Sulayk, but as they neared him, he sprinted off like a gazelle. They galloped in pursuit for the whole day, and reckoned: "By nightfall, he's bound to have tired, and he'll either have collapsed or slackened his pace, and then we'll catch him!" By dawn, they saw al-Sulayk's tracks: he had stumbled on the roots of a tree, and the force of impact had torn it from the earth, while his bow had broken, and its shattered pieces were stuck in the ground. They exclaimed, "What have we here? May God humiliate him!" They considered turning back, but they thought: "Maybe this happened at the beginning of the night, but now he's tired." And so they continued. Al-Sulayk's tracks were enormously far apart, and the pursuers found a place where he had urinated: his pee had poured forth and made a gulley in the ground. They exclaimed, "What is this! God combat him! How stout he is! By God, we won't pursue him any longer!" They gave up the chase. 22.4

Al-Sulayk continued until he reached his people and warned them of the impending attack, but none believed him since the distances were so far. Al-Sulayk chided his people: 22.5

The two ʿAmrs call me a liar—ʿAmr ibn Jundab
  and ʿAmr ibn Saʿd—but they are the liars!
Damn you both! I truly saw them:
  troops of horses, marching to the camp in formation.

وجاء الجيش فأغاروا

وحكى الأصمعيّ أنّ السليك لقي رجلاً من خثعم ومعه امرأة له فأخذه فقال الخثعميّ أنا أفدي نفسي منك فقال له السليك لك ذلك على أن لا تخيّس[1] بي ولا تطلع عليّ أحدًا من خثعم فحالفه وخلّف عنده امرأته رهنية ورجع إلى قومه فنكحها السليك وجعلت تقول له احذر خثعم فإنّي أخافهم عليك فقال ٦،٢٢

وَمَا خَثْعَمٌ إِلَّا لِئَامٌ أَذِلَّةٌ    إِلَى ٱلذُّلِّ وَٱلْإِسْحَاقِ تَنْمَى وَتَنْتَمِي

وبلغ خبره شبل بن قلادة وأنس بن مدرك الخثعميّ فخالفا إلى السليك فلم يشعر إلّا وقد طرقاه في الخيل وليس له طريق للعدو فقال

مَنْ مُبْلِغٌ قَوْمِي أَنِّي مَقْتُولْ    يَا رُبَّ قِرْنٍ قَدْ تَرَكْتُ مَجْدُولْ
وَرُبَّ زَوْجٍ قَدْ نَكِحْتُ عُطْبُولْ    وَرُبَّ عَانٍ قَدْ فَكَكْتُ مَكْبُولْ

ثمّ عطفا عليه فقتلاه

ومن شعره وقد أغار بقوم ففرّوا فانصرفوا عنه خوفًا من العطش وقد بقي معه رجل يُسمّى صرد فبكى فقال السليك ٧،٢٢

بَكَى صُرَدٌ لَمَّا رَأَى ٱلْحَيَّ أَعْرَضَتْ    مَهَامِهُ رَمْلٍ دُونَهُ وَسُهُوبُ
فَقُلْتُ لَهُ لَا تَبْكِ عَيْنُكَ إِنَّهَا    قَضِيَّةُ مَا يُقْضَى لَنَا فَنَؤُوبُ
سَيَكْفِيكَ صَرْبَ ٱلْقَوْمِ لَحْمٌ مُعَرَّضٌ    وَمَاءُ قُدُورٍ فِي ٱلْقِصَاعِ مَشُوبُ

الصرب اللبن الحامض وماء القدور المرق كأنّه يقول ستستغني وتأكل اللحم بعد اللبن

١ إ١: تحبس بي؛ بر١: تحبسني؛ إ٣: تجيّش لي.

The Bakr's army arrived and they plundered.

Al-Aṣmaʿī reports that a man from the Khathʿam and one of his wives were ambushed by al-Sulayk, who took the man prisoner. The Khathʿamī pleaded, "I will ransom myself." Al-Sulayk said, "I'll accept it, on condition that you must be lenient with me in the future and never let anyone from the Khathʿam attack me." The man swore to the terms, left his wife as a hostage, and returned to his camp. Al-Sulayk lay with the woman. Afterward, she warned, "Beware of the Khathʿam. I fear for you!" But al-Sulayk replied: 22.6

Khathʿam are nothing if not lowly ingrates,
born in ignominy and exile, and they only get worse.

The news reached Shibl ibn Qilādah and Anas ibn Mudrik of the Khathʿam, and they came after al-Sulayk. Catching him unawares, they surrounded him in the night, and with no place to run, al-Sulayk sang these lines:

Who will tell my people of my death?
I, who left heroes in the dust,
who slept with fine girls,
and freed slaves from their bonds.

His assailants then skewered him upon their spears and killed him.

One time, when al-Sulayk was leading a raid, his party abandoned him for fear of dying from thirst on the way. Al-Sulayk was left with only one man, named Ṣurad, who cried, and al-Sulayk consoled him: 22.7

Ṣurad wept. The tribe was far, and he beheld
    endless sand with empty plains beyond.
I told him: Don't you cry;
    this is Fate's decree.
Now you drink sour milk,
    but next you'll have fresh meat and hot bowls of sauce.

(By "sour milk," he means a kind of buttermilk or clabber; "hot bowls of sauce" intends gravy. Al-Sulayk seems to be saying that Ṣurad can look forward to meat after having survived on buttermilk.)

وقوله ٨،٢٢

أَلَا عَتَبَتْ عَلَيَّ فَصَارَمَتْنِي وَأَعْجَبَهَا ذَوُو ٱللِّمَمِ ٱلطِّوَالِ
أَشَابَ ٱلرَّأْسَ أَنِّي كُلَّ يَوْمٍ أَرَى لِي خَالَةً وَسْطَ ٱلرِّجَالِ
يَشُقُّ عَلَيَّ أَنْ يَلْقَيْنَ ضَيْمًا وَيَقْصُرُ عَنْ تَخَلُّصِهِنَّ مَالِي

**وعامر بن مالك إنّما لاعب الأسنّة بيديك** ٢٣

هو عامر بن مالك بن جعفر من بني صعصعة المعروف بملاعب الأسنّة ويُكنى أبو ١،٢٣
براء وأمّه أمّ البنين أنجب امرأة في العرب وذلك أنّها ولدت من مالك بن جعفر
خمسة منهم أبو براء والطفيل أبو عامر بن الطفيل وربيعة أبو لبيد ونزار ومعاوية
ويُسمّى معوّد الحكماء وقد افتخر بها لبيد عند النعمان فقال

نَحْنُ بَنِي أُمِّ ٱلْبَنِينِ ٱلْأَرْبَعَهْ

وإنّما قال الأربعة لضرورة الشعر ونصب بني على المدح

وأبو براء من فرسان العرب المشهورين وكبارهم وإنّما لُقّب بملاعب الأسنّة لقول ٢،٢٣
أوس بن حجر فيه

يُلَاعِبُ أَطْرَافَ ٱلْأَسِنَّةِ عَامِرٌ فَرَاحَ لَهُ حَظُّ ٱلْكَتَائِبِ أَجْمَعُ

وقيل لقول آخر وقد فرّ عنه أخوه في حرب

فَرَرْتَ وَأَسْلَمْتَ ٱبْنَ أُمِّكَ عَامِرًا مُلَاعِبُ أَطْرَافِ ٱلْوَشِيجِ ٱلْمُزَعْزَعِ

Al-Sulayk's poetry: 22.8

Oh, she blames and shuns me,
and fancies the curly-haired boys.
It makes my hair go gray to see
every day my aunts go among men;[165]
it pains me that they are mistreated,
and my funds too little to help them.

**ʿĀmir ibn Mālik parried spears with your hands . . .** 23

ʿĀmir ibn Mālik ibn Jaʿfar was from the Ṣaʿṣaʿah. He was known both as "Spear Brandisher"[166] and "Abū Barāʾ." His mother was nicknamed "the Mother of Sons," since no Arab woman had ever given birth to as many illustrious sons as she. She had five boys with Mālik ibn Jaʿfar: Spear Brandisher, al-Ṭufayl Abū ʿĀmir ibn al-Ṭufayl, Rabīʿah (the father of the poet Labīd), Nizār,[167] and Muʿāwiyah (known as "Exemplar for the Wise"). Labīd boasted about this lineage when he was reciting his poetry to King al-Nuʿmān: 23.1

Us are the Four from the Mother of Sons.

(Labīd referred to "four" sons because to say "five" would have ruined the meter. He says "Us" instead of "We" as this is a grammatical quirk in the style for expressing praise.)

Spear Brandisher was one of the great, famed Arab horse warriors. How he earned his nickname is debated: some say it derives from a verse Aws ibn Ḥajar composed: 23.2

There's ʿĀmir, brandishing spears;
he's worth a whole squadron on his own!

Other say it derives from a verse ʿĀmir composed himself following his brother's flight from a fight:

You fled. You left ʿĀmir, your mother's son,
To parry brandished lances.

وقيل بقول حسّان بن نمير فيه وقد رآه بين فرسان أحاطوا أطافوا به يقاتلهم ما هذا إلّا ملاعب الأسنّة

٣،٢٣ وفد عامر على رسول الله صلّى الله عليه وسلّم ولم يسلم ويزعم بنو جعفر أنّه مات مسلمًا

٤،٢٣ حدّث خالد بن عبد الله قال قدم عامر بن مالك أبو البراء ملاعب الأسنّة على رسول الله صلّى الله عليه وسلّم وأهدى له فرسين وراحلتين فقال له رسول الله صلّى الله عليه وسلّم لو قبلت هديّة مشرك لقبلت هديّتك وعرض عليه الإسلام فلم يسلم ولم يبعد وقال يا محمّد إنّي أرى أمرك هذا حسنًا شريفًا وقومي خلفي فلو أنّك بعثت نفرًا من أصحابك لرجوت أن يجيبوا دعوتك ويتّبعوا أمرك فأن هم اتّبعوا أمرك فما أعزّه فقال رسول الله صلّى الله عليه وسلّم إنّي أخاف عليهم أهل نجد فقال له عامر لا تخف إنّي جار لهم إن تعرّض لهم أحد من أهل نجد فبعث معه أربعين رجلًا من الأنصار وقيل سبعين وأمّر عليهم المنذر بن عمرو فلمّا نزلوا بماء من مياه بني سليم يقال له بئر معونة عسكروا وسرّحوا ظهورهم وبعثوا مع سرحهم الحارث بن الصمّة وعمرو بن أميّة وقدّموا حرام بن ملحان بكتاب رسول الله صلّى الله عليه وسلّم إلى عامر بن الطفيل في رجال من بني عامر

٥،٢٣ فلمّا انتهى حرام لم يقرؤوا الكتاب ووثب عامر بن الطفيل على حرام فقتله واستصرخ عليهم بني عامر فأبوا وقد كان عامر بن مالك خرج قبل القوم إلى ناحية نجد وأخبرهم أنّه جار أصحاب محمّد فلا يعرضوا لهم فقالوا لن يُخفر جوار أبي براء وأبوا أن ينفروا مع ابن الطفيل

٦،٢٣ فاستصرخ قبائل من بني سليم فنفروا معه ورأّسوه عليهم فقال ابن طفيل أقسم بالله ما أقبل هذا وحده فاتبعوا أثره وأقبل بهم حتّى وجدوا القوم فقاتل القوم

Yet others say that Ḥassān ibn Numayr coined the nickname when he observed ʿĀmir surrounded by attacking cavalry and remarked, "That man knows how to brandish spears!"

Spear Brandisher had an audience with the Prophet (God bless and keep him), but it did not result in his conversion. However, his clan, the Jaʿfar, maintain that Spear Brandisher did convert before he died. 23.3

Khālid ibn ʿAbd Allāh narrates that Spear Brandisher presented himself to the Prophet (God bless and keep him) and gave him a gift of two horses and two riding camels. The Prophet (God bless and keep him) replied, "If it was permissible for me to accept gifts from polytheists, I surely would receive yours." Muḥammad preached Islam to Spear Brandisher, and though he did not convert then and there, he didn't reject Islam either, and said, "Muḥammad, I consider your undertaking good and noble, and my kinsmen stand behind me. If you would send them a troop of your companions, I should hope my kin might accept and follow your faith. Wouldn't that be a powerful following!" The Prophet (God bless and keep him) was hesitant: "I fear the people of Najd would do my men harm." But Spear Brandisher assured him, "Don't fear: I promise to protect your companions if any Najdis oppose them." 23.4

The Prophet therefore dispatched forty (some say seventy) of the Allies under the command of al-Mundhir ibn ʿAmr to follow Spear Brandisher to Najd. The Muslim troop reached one of the Sulaym's watering holes, the Maʿūnah Well, and there they set up camp on their own. They sent out their mounts to pasture with two of their men, al-Ḥārith ibn al-Ṣimmah and ʿAmr ibn Umayyah, and they dispatched a third, Ḥarām ibn Milḥān, to deliver a letter from the Prophet (God bless and keep him) to ʿĀmir ibn al-Ṭufayl,[168] who was with warriors of Spear Brandisher's tribe, the ʿĀmir.

Ḥarām reached ʿĀmir and the warriors, but no one read the letter, and ʿĀmir fell upon Ḥarām and murdered him. ʿĀmir then summoned the tribe to fight the Muslims, but because Spear Brandisher had earlier reached Najd and already announced his protection of Muḥammad's companions and forbade his tribe from harming them, the warriors refused ʿĀmir's call, saying, "We will not violate Spear Brandisher's protection guarantee." 23.5

Yet ʿĀmir was undeterred, and he called clans of the Sulaym to arms. They were willing, and mustered under his command. ʿĀmir addressed them, pointing to the murdered Ḥarām: "I swear that this fellow didn't come here alone!"[169] Following Ḥarām's tracks, ʿĀmir and his war band located the Muslims' camp 23.6

حتّى قتل أصحاب رسول الله صلّى الله عليه وسلّم وبقي المنذر بن عمرو فقالوا له إن شئت أمّناك فقال لن أقبل لكم أمانًا حتّى آتي مصرع حرام فأمّنوه حتّى أتى مصرعه ثمّ برئوا من أمانه فقاتلهم حتّى قتل

٧،٢٣ وأقبل الحارث بن الصمّة وعمرو بن أميّة بالسرح وقد ارتابا بعكوف الطير قريبًا من منزلهم فجعلا يقولان قتل والله أصحابنا ثمّ أوفيا على نشز من الأرض فإذا أصحابهم مقتولون والخيل واقفة فقال الحارث لعمرٍو ما ترى قال أرى أن ألحق برسول الله صلّى الله عليه وسلّم فأخبره الخبر فقال الحارث ما كنت لأتأخّر عن موطن قتل فيه المنذر فأقبلا فلقيا القوم فقاتلهم الحارث حتّى قتل منهم اثنين ثمّ أخذوه فأسروه وأسروا عمرو بن أميّة وقالوا للحارث ما تحبّ أن نصنع بك فإنّا لا نحبّ قتلك قال أبلغوا بي مصرع المنذر وبرئت ذمّتكم فبلغوا به ثمّ أرسلوه فقاتلهم فقتل منهم اثنين وشرعوا له الرماح فنظموه فيها ثمّ قال عامر ابن الطفيل لعمرو بن أميّة وهو أسير لم يقاتل إنّه كانت على أمّي نسمة فأنت حرّ عنها وجزّ ناصيته

٨،٢٣ فلمّا جاء رسول الله صلّى الله عليه وسلّم خبر بئر معونة جعل يقول هذا عمل أبي براء قد كنت لهذا كارهًا ودعا على من قتلهم بعد الصبح في الركعة الثانية من الصبح في صبيحة تلك الليلة التي جاءه فيها الخبر فلمّا قال سمع الله لمن حمده قال اللّهمّ اشدد وطأتك على مضر اللّهمّ عليك ببني ذكوان وعصيّة[١] فإنّهم عصوا الله ورسوله قال ذلك خمس عشرة ليلة حتّى نزلت الآية ﴿لَيْسَ لَكَ مِنَ ٱلْأَمْرِ شَيْءٌ﴾

٩،٢٣ ثمّ أقبل أبو براء سائرًا وهو شيخ كبير هِمّ[٢] فأخبر بما فعل ابن الطفيل فشقّ ذلك عليه ولا حركة به من الضعف وقال أخفرني ابن أخي مرّتين وسار حتّى لحق ابن

١ إا وبرا: عُصبيّه. ٢ زيادة من ل١، ل٢، إ٦.

and attacked, killing the Prophet's (God bless and keep him) companions until only al-Mundhir ibn ʿAmr remained standing. They offered al-Mundhir terms: "We'll give you a truce!" But he replied, "I accept your safe passage only to where you murdered Ḥarām." They led him there, al-Mundhir renounced the truce, and he started fighting again until he was cut down.

In the meantime, the two who had been absent from the Muslims' camp pasturing the camels, al-Ḥārith ibn al-Ṣimmah and ʿAmr ibn Umayyah, noticed birds circling over their campsite, and they grew worried. They told each other, "By God! Our companions must have been killed!" They climbed atop a hill that overlooked the campsite, and there they saw the scene: their companions all dead and their horses standing amid the bodies. Al-Ḥārith asked ʿAmr, "What should we do?" ʿAmr replied, "I think we should return to the Prophet (God bless and keep him) and give him the news." But al-Ḥārith disagreed: "I want to go straight to the site of al-Mundhir's murder!" Together they followed the tracks, and al-Ḥārith attacked ʿĀmir's war band, killing two, before both he and ʿAmr were captured. ʿĀmir's men said to al-Ḥārith, "Tell us what you want, since we have no desire to kill you." He replied, "Take me to where you murdered al-Mundhir; after that I have no desire for your protection!" They took him to the spot, and when they set him free, he took up arms and killed two more before they leveled their spears at him and ran him through. ʿAmr remained a captive and refrained from fighting, so ʿĀmir told him, "I will release you in satisfaction of an outstanding oath my mother has sworn to free a prisoner." They cut off ʿAmr's forelock and let him go. 23.7

When news of the Maʿūnah Well incident reached the Prophet (God bless and keep him), he declared, "This is the fault of Spear Brandisher! This is exactly why I opposed the plan!" After the second bow in the following dawn prayer, the Prophet supplicated: "God hears those who praise Him. Good God! Bring down Your might upon the Muḍar! Curse the Dhakwān and the ʿUṣayyah[170] for their transgression against God and His Prophet!" The Prophet repeated this invocation for fifteen days until God revealed the Qurʾanic verse: «You have no say in this affair.»[171] 23.8

Spear Brandisher arrived and was informed of ʿĀmir's actions. Spear Brandisher was an old man, and in anguish at the news he became almost paralyzed, moaning, "My nephew has now betrayed me twice!" Spear Brandisher set forth to find ʿĀmir, and an attempt was made on ʿĀmir's life. People disagree whether Spear Brandisher himself or his son Rabīʿah made the attempt, 23.9

الطفيل فطعنه بالرمح فأخطأ مقتله وقيل كان الطاعن ربيعة ولده فتصايح الناس فقال ابن الطفيل إنّها لم تضرّني وقد وهبتها لعمّي

١٠،٢٣ وانصرف عنه ونزل عامر بن مالك بقومه فدعاهم إلى الارتحال إلى النبيّ صلّى الله عليه وسلّم وطلب ثأر القتلى الذين كانوا في جواره فتثاقلوا عليه وقال له بعض بني أخيه إنّهم يزعمون أنّه حدث لك عارض في عقلك فدعا ابن أخيه لبيدًا وقينة فشرب وقال لها غنّي ثمّ قال يا لبيد لو حدث بعمّك حدث ما كنت قائلاً فإنّ قومك يزعمون أنّ عقله ذهب والموت خير من عزوب العقل فقال لبيد

قُومَا تَجُوبَانِ[1] مَعَ ٱلْأَنْوَاحِ    فَأَبِّنَا مُلَاعِبَ ٱلرِّمَاحِ
أَبَا بَرَاءٍ مِدْرَهَ ٱلشِّيَاحِ    كَانَ غِيَاثَ ٱلْمُرْمِلِ ٱلْمُمْتَاحِ

من أبيات ثمّ شرب أبو براء الخمر صرفًا حتّى مات وهو يقول لا خير في العيش وقد عصتني بنو عامر

١١،٢٣ وبنو جعفر يزعمون أنّه مات مسلمًا وكان شريف بيته يزعمون أنّه لمّا تنافر ابن أخيه عامر بن الطفيل مع علقمة بن علاثة سأل عمّه أبا براء الإعانة على المفاخرة فأعطاه نعليه وقال استعن بهما في مفاخرتك فإنّي ربعت فيهما أربعين مرباعًا مع أنّه كان كارهًا للمنافرة وفي ذلك يقول

أَأُومَرُ أَنْ أَسُبَّ بَنِي شُرَيْحٍ    وَلَا وَٱللّٰهِ أَفْعَلُ مَا حَيِيتُ

١٢،٢٣ ومن أحسن ما سمعت من شعر عامر بن مالك قوله من أبيات

لَحَا ٱللّٰهُ أَنَآنَا عَنِ ٱلضَّيْفِ بِٱلْقِرَى    وَأَلْأَمَنَا عَنْ عِرْضِ وَالِدِهِ ذَبَّا
وَأَدْخَلَنَا لِلْبَيْتِ مِنْ قِبَلِ ٱسْتِهِ    إِذَا ٱلْقُورُ أَبْدَى مِنْ جَوَانِبِهِ رَكْبَا

---

١ إ: بحومان.

but whatever the case, the blow was not fatal, and ʿĀmir declared in the ensuing tumult, "I'm not harmed. I will let pass this act of my uncle."

Spear Brandisher then returned to his people and summoned them to emigrate to the community of the Prophet (God bless and keep him) and seek blood revenge for the murder of those Muslims whom he had promised protection. His clan was unenthusiastic, however, and one of his nephews told him, "The clan is alleging that your mind was impaired there." Spear Brandisher summoned a singing girl and his nephew Labīd and began drinking. He told her, "Sing!" and asked Labīd, "If something were to happen to your old uncle, what would you say? There's talk that he's losing his mind. Death is preferable over senility!" Labīd said: 23.10

> Stand up, women, and tear at your clothes with the wailers!
> Praise him: the Spear Brandisher,
> Abū Barāʾ the battle defender,
> for the needy, the generous giver.

The poem has more verses.[172] Spear Brandisher then began drinking his wine unmixed, mumbling to himself, "What good is life after the ʿĀmir tribe defied me?" until he expired.

The Jaʿfar clan alleges that Spear Brandisher died a Muslim. He was their nobleman, and they purport that when his nephew ʿĀmir ibn al-Ṭufayl had contended in nobility against ʿAlqamah ibn ʿUlāthah, ʿĀmir sought Spear Brandisher's help.[173] Spear Brandisher gave ʿĀmir his sandals, saying, "Rely on these in your dispute: I won the king's share in forty war spoils while wearing them!" Nonetheless, Spear Brandisher disapproved of this competition, and said in verse: 23.11

> Am I to be told to curse the Shurayḥ?
> No, by God! Not as long as I live![174]

One of Spear Brandisher's best poems:[175] 23.12

> God curse us should we begrudge hospitality;
> God revile us should we fail to defend our father's honor
> And drive us into the tent on our backsides
>     when riders appear over the hillocks.

القُور الأكم والجبال الصغار يعني أنّ البخيل إذا كان جالسًا بفناء بيته فرأى راكبًا قد لاح بين الأكم زحف بظهره داخلاً إلى بيته فرارًا من الضيف

**وقيس بن زهير إنّما استعان بدهائك** ٢٤

هو قيس بن زهير بن جذيمة العبسيّ صاحب الحروب بين عبس وذبيان بسبب الفرسين داحس والغبراء كما سيأتي ذلك في موضعه ١،٢٤

كان فارسًا شاعرًا داهيةً يُضرب به المثل فيقال أدهى من قيس ٢،٢٤

حكى المدائنيّ أنّ رجلاً مرّ بحيّ الأحوص فلمّا دنا من القوم بحيث يرونه نزل عن راحلته وأتى بشجرة فعلّق عليها وطبًا من لبن ووضع في بعض أغصانها حنظلة ووضع صرّة من تراب وصرّة من شوك ثمّ أتى راحلته فاستوى عليها وذهب فنظر الأحوص والقوم في أمره فعيّ به فقال أرسلوا إلى قيس بن زهير فجاء فقال له الأحوص ألم تخبرني أنّه لا يرد عليك أمر إلّا عرفت مأتاه ما لم تر نواصي الخيل فقال وما الخبر فأعلموه قال وضح الصبح لذي عينين فصار مثلاً يُضرب في وضوح الشيء ثمّ قال هذا رجل أسره جيش قاصد لكم ثمّ أُطلق بعد أن أُخذت عليه العهود والمواثيق أن لا ينذركم فعرّض لكم بما فعل أمّا الصرّة من التراب فإنّه يزعم أنّه قد أتاكم عدد كثير وأمّا الحنظلة فإنّه يخبر أنّ بني حنظلة قد غزتكم وأمّا الشوك فإنّه يخبر أنّ لهم شوكة وأمّا اللبن فهو دليل على قرب القوم أو بعدهم إن كان حلوًا أو حامضًا فاستعدّ الأحوص وورد الجيش كما ذكر ٣،٢٤

وحكي أنّ النعمان بن المنذر أرسل إلى أبيه زهير يخطب ابنته وسأله أن يبعث إليه ببعض بنيه فأرسل إليه ولده شأسًا فلمّا قدم عليه أكرمه وأحسن جائزته ٤،٢٤

("Hillocks" means little mountains; what he describes is a miser who sits before his tent and, when he espies in the distance a party of camel riders, slinks backward into the tent on his bottom, so as to avoid being seen and thereby having to extend hospitality.)

**. . . Qays ibn Zuhayr relied on your sagacity . . .** 24

Qays ibn Zuhayr ibn Jadhīmah of the ʿAbs was a hero in the war between the ʿAbs and the Dhubyān, which, as will be explained below,[176] broke out on account of two horses, Thrust and the Dusty Mare. 24.1

Qays was a horse warrior, a poet, and a crafty old fox: his name is proverbial for astuteness, as the expression goes: "Shrewder than Zuhayr." 24.2

Al-Madāʾinī tells a story about Qays's shrewdness: One day, a man approached the camp of al-Aḥwaṣ, and when he was near enough for them to see him, he dismounted from his camel and walked up to a tree. He slung a full milk skin on one branch, and on another he suspended a desert gourd and two little bags, one containing earth and the other thorns. This done, he remounted at once and rode out of sight. Al-Aḥwaṣ and his folk looked on in bewilderment, so al-Aḥwaṣ said, "Bring in Qays ibn Zuhayr!" Qays arrived and al-Aḥwaṣ asked him, "Didn't you once tell me that you can discern any situation well before the cavalry comes charging in?" Qays asked, "What's the matter?" When they related to him what happened, Qays said, "The dawn is clear if you have eyes!" (This became a proverb for anything obvious.) Then he explained, "That man had been taken prisoner by an army coming to raid you. They freed him only after he swore solemn oaths, vows, and covenants to not say anything about their plans. So he showed you what will happen. The sack of earth is his way of indicating that the advancing army is a multitude. The desert gourd signifies that the raiders are from the Ḥanẓalah tribe.[177] The thorns mean they'll gash and scratch when they arrive, and the milk skin is an indication of their proximity: depending on the milk's sweetness or sourness, you'll know if they're near or far." Al-Aḥwaṣ prepared his men, and the attack came just as Qays predicted. 24.3

Another story tells that King al-Nuʿmān ibn al-Mundhir requested a daughter in marriage from Qays's father, Zuhayr, and he asked Zuhayr to send one of his sons to arrange it. Zuhayr dispatched Shaʾs, who arrived in al-Ḥīrah and 24.4

وردّه إلى أبيه وعرض عليه أن يرسل معه قومًا يخفرونه فقال لا شيء أمنع لي من نسبتي إلى أبي وخرج وحده فمرّ بماء من مياه بني غنيّ فأكل وشرب ونزل إلى الماء يغتسل وكان رباح ابن الأشلّ الغنويّ نازلًا في بيته على الماء ومعه امرأته فرآها تحدّ النظر إلى جسد شأس وقد شمّا منه رائحة المسك فأخذته غيرة وفوّق إليه سهمًا فقتله وغيّب أثره وأخذ ما معه وكان معه عيبة مملوءة مسكًا وعطرًا من عطر النعمان وحللًا يمانيّة من ثيابه

٥،٢٤ وأبطأ خبر شأس عن زهير فأخبر بما انصرف به من عند النعمان ولم يدر من قتله فقلق لذلك فقال قيس يا أبت أنا أكشف خبر أخي ثمّ دعا بامرأة حازمة من نساء قومه وكانت السنة شديدة فأمرها أن تأخذ لحمًا سمينًا فتقدّده وتخرج به إلى بني عامر وغنيّ فتعرض ذلك عليهم وتقول إنّي قد زوّجت ابنتي وأنا أبغي لها طيبًا وثيابًا ففعلت إلى أن وقعت على امرأة الغنويّ فقالت لها إن كتمت عليّ أعطيتك حاجتك وأخبرتها بأمر شأس وأعطتها طيبًا وثيابًا وباعتها ذلك بما معها من اللحم والشحم وخرجت العبسيّة حتّى أتت قيسًا فأخبرته فأخبر أباه وركب في قوم من بني عبس فأغار على غنيّ فقتلهم وفرّقهم

٦،٢٤ وحكي أنّه في بعض حروبه لبني ذبيان وهو يوم الشعب المشهور صعد بالجيش والنعم إلى الجبل وعقل الإبل عشرة أيّام لا تشرب والماء كثير تحت الجبل فلمّا همّت بنو ذبيان بالصعود إلى الجبل حلّ عقل الإبل وأمسك بذنب كلّ بعير رجل معه سلاحه فمرّت الإبل طالبة الماء لا تمرّ بشيء إلّا طحنته والرجال في أعقابها تضرب من مرّت به فكانت الهزيمة على ذبيان

٧،٢٤ وحكي أنّه لمّا تطاولت الحروب المشهورة بينه وبين ابني بدر حمل وحذيفة الذبيانيّين كما سيأتي ذكره جمعا جمعًا عظيمًا وبلغ بني عبس أنّهم قد ساروا إليهم

was treated munificently by al-Nuʿmān, who, after giving him generous gifts, gave Shaʾs leave to return and offered a bodyguard to accompany him. Shaʾs declined: "Nothing protects me more than my paternal lineage," and he set off alone. On the way, he passed a watering hole of the Ghanī, where he ate, drank, and bathed in a pool. Rabāḥ ibn al-Ashall of the Ghanī was encamped with his wife near the pool. The scent of Shaʾs's musk wafted over them, and Rabāḥ noticed his wife gazing upon Shaʾs's naked body. Jealousy overtook Rabāḥ, and he leveled an arrow at Shaʾs and shot him dead. He covered up all trace of the murder and took Shaʾs's possessions, including a leather bag containing musk, other perfumes, and fine Yemeni robes from al-Nuʿmān.

Time passed without news of Shaʾs. Eventually, Zuhayr was informed about 24.5
the gifts al-Nuʿmān had sent with Shaʾs, but no one knew what had happened to him, and Zuhayr grew troubled. Qays spoke up: "My dear father, I will discover what has happened to Shaʾs." Qays summoned an astute tribeswoman to assist. It had been a bad year, very arid, so Qays instructed the woman to slice up and dry strips of fatty meat and take them around to the ʿĀmir and the Ghanī, offering them under the pretense of an exchange by saying, "My daughter is betrothed, and I need some fine clothes and perfume." The woman did as she was told, and her rounds brought her to the tent of the woman from the Ghanī, who accepted her offer, saying, "If you promise to keep this a secret, I will give you what you need." The Ghanī woman told her the whole story, and exchanged Shaʾs's perfume and clothes for the fatty meat. Qays's clanswoman returned with the news, Qays informed his father, and he mobilized the ʿAbs war band and raided the Ghanī, killing and dispersing them.

It is reported that at the celebrated Battle of the Mountain Pass, during the 24.6
ʿAbs's war against the Dhubyān, Qays led the ʿAbs warriors and camels to the top of the mountain. He hobbled the camels there for ten days with nothing to drink, though there was plenty of water at the foot of the mountain. When the Dhubyān began charging up the mountainside, Qays ordered that the camels be untied, and each of his warriors took hold of a camel by the tail. Down went the thirsty beasts, charging from the mountain toward the water and trampling everything in their path, with Qays's warriors in tow, slashing all the Dhubyānīs within reach. That day, the Dhubyān were routed.

It is told that when Qays's notorious fighting against Ḥamal and Ḥudhayfah, 24.7
the sons of Badr and leaders of the Dhubyān, had dragged on interminably,[178] Ḥamal and Ḥudhayfah mustered an enormous army. When the ʿAbs learned

فقال قيس أطيعوني فوالله لئن لم تفعلوا لأتّكئنّ على سيفي إلى أن يخرج من ظهري قالوا فإنّا نطيعك فأمرهم فسرّحوا السوام والضعاف بليل وهم يريدون أن يظعنوا من منزلهم ذلك ثمّ ارتحلوا في الصبح

٨،٢٤ وأصبحوا على ظهر العقبة وقد مضى أموالهم وضعفاؤهم فلمّا أصبحوا طلعت عليهم الخيل من الثنايا فقال قيس خذوا غير طريق المال فلا حاجة للقوم أن يقعوا في شوكتكم ولا يريدون غير ذهاب أموالكم فأخذوا غير طريق المال فلمّا أدرك حذيفة الأثر ورآه قال أبعدهم الله وما خيرهم بعد ذهاب أموالهم

٩،٢٤ وسارت ظعن عبس والمقاتلة من ورائهم وتبع حذيفة وبنو ذبيان المال فلمّا أدركوه ردّوا أوّله على آخره فلم يفلت منهم شيء وجعل الرجل يطرد ما قدر عليه من الإبل فيذهب بها وينفرد واشتدّ الحرّ فقال قيس يا قوم إنّ القوم قد فرّق بينهم المغنم واشتغلوا فاعطفوا الخيل في آثارهم فلم يشعر بنو ذبيان إلّا بالخيل فلم يقاتلهم أحد إنّما همّ الرجل في غنيمته أن يحوزها ويمضي فوضعت بنو عبس فيهم السلاح حتّى ناشدتهم بنو ذبيان البقيّة ولم يكن لهم همّ غير حذيفة فأرسلوا الخيل تقصّ أثرهُ وكان حذيفة قد استرخى حزام فرسه فنزل عنه ووضع رجله على حجر مخافة أن يقصّ أثره ثمّ شدّ الحزام فعرفوا حنف فرسه والحنف أن تقبل إحدى اليدين على الأخرى وتبعوه

١٠،٢٤ ومضى حتّى استغاث بجفر الهباءة وهو ماء في موضع يُسمّى الهباءة وقد اشتدّ الحرّ فرمى بنفسه ومعه حمل بن بدر أخوه وورقاء بن بلال وقد نزعوا سلاحهم وطرحوا سروجهم ودوابّهم تتمعّك وجعل ربيئتهم يتطلّع فإذا لم ير شيئًا رجع فنظر نظرة فقال إنّي رأيت شخصًا كالنعامة فلم يكترثوا به وبينا هم يتكلّمون إذ دهمهم شدّاد بن معاوية فحال بينهم وبين الخيل ثمّ جاء قيس وقرواش وآخر حتّى تتامّوا خمسةً فحمل بعضهم على خيلهم فطردها وحمل البقيّة على من في

that it was advancing to attack, Qays addressed his kin: "You must obey my next orders, otherwise I shall lean on my sword right now until it comes straight out from my back." The ʿAbs replied, "We are at your command!" Qays then ordered the ʿAbs to send out their herds and noncombatants that night, as they wanted to break camp, but Qays ordered the warriors to tarry behind until dawn.

In the morning, the warriors were still at the top of the mountain track, 24.8
whereas the train of all their herds and noncombatants had already left. At this moment, an enemy cavalry squadron descending from the narrow passes came into view, but Qays ordered his warriors, "Don't join up with the caravan! The Dhubyān don't want a fight, they want plunder." The ʿAbs warriors split from the direction of their property, and when Ḥudhayfah's force arrived and saw their diverging tracks, he exclaimed, "To Hell with them! What will they be worth after they lose all their herds?"

The train continued on, while Qays held back the ʿAbs warriors, and 24.9
Ḥudhayfah and the Dhubyān descended upon the train. The Dhubyān rounded up the whole caravan—nothing escaped—and each Dhubyānī warrior busied himself with taking whatever camels he could get his hands on. The day grew hotter. Then Qays ordered, "My men! The enemy are engrossed in dividing up the plunder. Now's our time! After them with the cavalry!"

Qays and his horsemen caught the Dhubyān completely unawares, and no Dhubyān warriors offered a fight, as each tried to make off with his share of the booty. The ʿAbs wreaked havoc on the Dhubyān, until the survivors pleaded for mercy. Now the main concern was catching Ḥudhayfah, and Qays dispatched horsemen to pursue his tracks. Ḥudhayfah's saddle girth was loose and dangled on the ground, so he dismounted and led his horse to a stony patch where he retightened the girth so as not to leave telltale tracks, but the trackers still recognized his horse's uneven stride—it put one of its hoofs farther in front than the other. The trackers kept up the pursuit.

Ḥudhayfah paused at the Habā'ah well, a large watering hole at the Basin of 24.10
al-Habā'ah. It was terribly hot, and Ḥudhayfah, his brother Ḥamal, and their companion Warqā' ibn Bilāl threw themselves into the water. They had disarmed, and had removed their horses' saddles to allow the mounts to cool in the mud. A scout was sent out with orders to return if the coast was clear. He took a look and reported: "I saw a figure like an ostrich." No one paid any heed. As they were conversing, Shaddād ibn Muʿāwiyah burst upon them and blocked their way to the horses. Qays, Qirwāsh, and another warrior of the ʿAbs arrived next, and altogether they were five. One made for the horses and rustled them;

الجفر فقال حذيفة يا بني عبس فأين الأحلام فضرب أخاه حمل بين كتفيه وقال اتّق مأثور القول فضربها مثلاً يعني أنّك تقول قولاً تخضع فيه وتقتل ويشتهرُ عنك وقتل حذيفة ومن معه وتمزّقت بنو ذبيان وأسرف قيس في النكاية والقتل ثمّ ندم على ذلك ورثى حمل بن بدر بالأبيات المشهورة في الحماسة وهو أوّل من رثى مقتوله

١١،٢٤ ولمّا أطال الحروب بعد ذلك وملّ أشار على قومه بالرجوع إلى قومهم ومصالحتهم فقالوا سر نسر معك فقال لا والله لا نظرت في وجهي ذبيانيّة قتلت أباها وأخاها أو زوجها وولدها ثمّ خرج على وجهه فلحق بالنمر بن قاسط فقال[1] يا معشر النمر أنا قيس بن زهير غريب حريب فانظروا لي امرأة قد أدّبها الغنى وأذلّها الفقر فزوّجوه امرأة منهم ثمّ قال إنّي لأصمّ أبكم حتّى أخبركم بأخلاقي إنّي امرؤ غيور فخور آنف ولست أفخر حتّى أبتلي ولا أغار حتّى أرى ولا آنف حتّى أظلم فرضوا بأخلاقه فأقام فيهم زمنا ثمّ أراد التحوّل عنهم فقال يا معشر النمر إنّي أرى لكم عليّ حقًّا بمصاهرتي لكم ومقامي بين أظهركم وإنّي آمركم بخصال وأنهاكم عن خصال عليكم بالأناة فبها تدرك الحاجة وتسويد من لا تعابون بتسويده والوفاء فيه تتعايشون وإعطاء من تريدون إعطاءه قبل المسألة ومنع من تريدون منعه قبل الإلحاح وخلط الضيف بالإلزام وإيّاكم والرهان فبه ثكلت مالكًا أخي والبغي فإنّه صرع زهيرًا أبي وحملاً والسرف في الدماء فإنّ قتلي أهل الهباءة أورثني العار ولا تعطوا في الفضول فتعجزوا عن الحقوق

١٢،٢٤ ثمّ رحل إلى عمان وأقام بها حتّى مات وقيل إنّه خرج هو وصاحب له من بني أسد عليهما المسوح يسيحان في الأرض ويتقوّتان بما ينبت إلى أن دُفعا ليلة قرّة إلى

١ إ: ثم أراد التحول عنهم فقال.

the others attacked the men in the pool. Ḥudhayfah cried, "'Abs! Have you no restraint?" They struck his brother Ḥamal between his shoulders, and he cried back to Ḥudhayfah, "Speak, but be mindful of its remembrance!" (By this he warns: You are saying something that demeans you, and since you are about to be killed, speak honorably as your statements are what will survive as your sole spokesman.) Ḥudhayfah and his party were all killed, the Dhubyān were shattered, and Qays exacted such a brutal toll on them that he later regretted his acts and composed an elegy for Ḥamal ibn Badr: its well-known verses are included in *The Valor Anthology*. This was the first time a killer eulogized his victim.

The warring continued nonetheless, and Qays grew weary. When he advised his people to return to their clans and make peace, they implored him: "March, and we march with you!" But he demurred: "No, by God. May no woman of the Dhubyān whose father, brother, husband, or son I have killed look me in the eye again." **24.11**

Qays went his own way, alone. Alighting in a camp of the Namir ibn Qāsiṭ, he announced himself: "People of the Namir: I am Qays ibn Zuhayr. I come to you as a war-ragged stranger. From you I ask for a wife who has been both schooled by wealth and humbled by poverty." They gave him a wife, and he spoke again: "I will be but a deaf mute until I tell you about my character. I am a jealous, vaunting, and haughty man. I never boast before I have been put to the test. I never raid without deliberating. I never disdain until I am wronged." They were pleased with his character and he lived among them for a time. When he wished to move on, he addressed them: "People of the Namir! By my marriage into your line and my settlement in your midst, I am obliged to you. So I'll give you some good advice. Be equanimous: it's the most direct path to success. Choose a leader who will not rouse others to critique you. And keep your promises: that is how society is sustained. Give to those whom you want to help before they ask, and withhold from those whom you dislike before they impose upon you. Treat hospitality as an obligation. Beware of all wagering: it cost me my brother Mālik. Beware of iniquity: it brought down my father, Zuhayr, and Ḥamal. Beware of blood lust: my killings at al-Habā'ah brought shame upon me. Finally, don't be unnecessarily generous, lest you find yourself lacking when obligations arise."

Qays traveled to Oman, and there he died. It is said that he found a companion from the Asad, and, with just one camel-hair cloak each, they wandered together, living off the land. One bitterly cold night found them near tents of an Arab people, and in their great hunger, when they smelled burning **24.12**

أخبية لقوم من العرب وقد اشتدّ بهما الجوع فوجدا رائحة القتار فسعيا يريدانه فلمّا قاربا أدركت قيسًا شهامة النفس والأنفة فرجع وقال لصاحبه دونك وما تريد فإنّ لي لبثًا على هذه الأجارع أترقّب داهية القرون الماضية فمضى صاحبه ورجع من الغد فوجده قد لجأ إلى شجرة بأسفل واد فنال من ورقها شيئًا ثمّ مات وفي ذلك يقول الحطيئة من أبيات

إِنَّ قَيْسًا كَانَ مِيْتَتُـهُ ... أَنَفًا وَٱلْحُرُّ مُنْطَلِقُ
فِي دَرِيسٍ لَا يُغَـيِّبُـهُ ... رُبَّ حُرٍّ ثَوْبُهُ خَلَقُ

ومن شعر قيس بن زهير قوله يرثي حمل بن بدر ١٣،٢٤

تَعَلَّمْ أَنَّ خَيْرَ ٱلنَّاسِ مَيْتٌ ... عَلَى جَفْـرِ ٱلْهَبَاءَةِ لَا يَرِيمُ
وَلَوْلَا ظُلْمُـهُ مَا زِلْتُ أَبْكِي ... عَلَيْهِ ٱلدَّهْرَ مَا بَدَتِ ٱلنُّجُومُ
وَلٰكِنَّ ٱلْفَتَى حَمَلَ بْنَ بَدْرٍ ... بَغَى وَٱلْبَغْيُ مَـرْتَعُـهُ وَخِـيمُ
أَظُنُّ ٱلْحِـلْمَ دَلَّ عَـلَيَّ قَوْمِي ... وَقَدْ يُسْتَجْهَلُ ٱلرَّجُلُ ٱلْحَلِيمُ
وَمَارَسْتُ ٱلرِّجَالَ وَمَارَسُونِي ... فَمُعْوَجٌّ عَـلَيَّ وَمُسْـتَقِـيمُ

وقوله ١٤،٢٤

إِذَا أَنْتَ أَقْرَرْتَ ٱلظُّلَامَةَ لِٱمْرِئٍ ... رَمَاكَ بِأُخْرَى شَعْبُهَا مُتَفَاقِمُ
فَلَا تُبْدِ لِلْأَعْـدَاءِ إِلَّا خَشُونَـةً ... فَمَا لَكَ فِيهِمْ إِنْ تَمَكَّنَ رَاحِمُ

وقوله ١٥،٢٤

تَعَـرَّفْنَ مِنْ ذُبْيَانَ مَنْ لَوْ لَقِيتُـهُ ... بِيَوْمِ حِفَـاظٍ طَـارَ فِي ٱللَّهَوَاتِ
وَلَوْ أَنَّ سَافِي ٱلرِّيحِ يَجْعَلُكُمْ قَذًى ... لِأَعْـيُنِنَـا مَـا كُـنْـتُمْ بِقَـذَاةِ

meat, their desires urged them to approach. But as they neared the tents, Qays's honor and pride checked him, and he told his companion, "Go ahead: what you want is right there; but allow me to tarry among these dunes and await what befell the Ancients." His companion entered the camp, and when he returned to the spot in the morning, he found that Qays had taken refuge under a tree at the bottom of the wadi. There he had eaten some leaves and passed away. Al-Ḥuṭay'ah memorialized this in verse:[179]

Qays is dead.
Felled by pride. The free man goes
  forth in meager rags.
Rags, the garment of so many a free man.

An excerpt from Qays ibn Zuhayr's eulogy of Ḥamal ibn Badr: **24.13**

The best of men is dead.
Lying in al-Habā'ah Basin evermore.
I should mourn him across cosmic eternity,
  but for his act of injustice:
    that brave, Ḥamal ibn Badr, he wronged—
    and iniquity leads to barren pasture.
I believe my people know me as patient—
  but the patient can be driven to passion.
I have experience with men, they with me—
  some were crooked, others straight.

Qays's poetry: **24.14**

If you are determined to oppress a man,
know you'll be dealt another from a worse lot.
Treat your enemies harshly,
as none will be merciful to you.

Qays's poetry: **24.15**

The Dhubyān know that should we meet
on the battle day in war's grinding mill.
We wish the billowing gusts blow you into our eyes
as dust for as long as you exist.

## وإياس بن معاوية أنّما استضاء بمصباح ذكائك ٢٥

هو إياس بن معاوية بن قرّة المزنيّ قاضي البصرة وكنيته أبو واثلة صاحب الفراسة ١،٢٥ والأجوبة البديعة المسكتة يضرب به المثل فيقال أزكن من إياس والزكن التفرّس والظنّ قال الشاعر

وَكُنْتُ مِنْهُمْ عَلَى مِثْلِ ٱلَّذِي زَكِنُوا

وبعضهم يقول أذكى من إياس قال أبو تمّام

إِقْدَامَ عَمْرٍو فِي سَمَاحَةِ حَاتِمٍ     فِي حِلْمِ أَحْنَفَ فِي ذَكَاءِ إِيَاسِ

حكى ابن عائشة قال أوّل ما عُرف من ذكاءِ إياس أنّه دخل الشام وهو صغير ٢،٢٥ فقدّم خصمًا له شيخًا إلى قاضي عبد الملك بن مروان وكان القاضي يعرف الخصم فقال لإياس أما تستحي تقدّم شيخًا كبيرًا فقال إياس الحقّ أكبر منه قال له اسكت قال فمن ينطق بحجّتي إذا سكتّ قال ما أحسبك تقول حقًّا حتّى تقوم قال أشهد أن لا إله إلّا الله فقام القاضي فدخل على عبد الملك بن مروان فأخبره الخبر فقال له اقض حاجته واصرفه عن الشام لا يفسد علينا الناس

وحكى غيره قال أوّل ما عرف من ذكاء إياس أنّه كان صبيًّا في المكتب فاجتمع ٣،٢٥ قوم من النصارى يضحكون من المسلمين وقالوا إنّ المسلمين يزعمون أنّه لا يكون في الجنّة ثقل الطعام يعنون الغائط فقال إياس لمعلّمه أليس يزعمون أنّ أكثر الطعام يذهب في البدن قال نعم قال فما يُنكر من أن يكون الباقي يذهبه الله في البدن فسكت النصارى وأعجب به المعلّم

وحكي أنّه دخل إلى الشام مرّة ثانية وأراد الحجّ فقال للمكاري انظر لي إنسانًا ٤،٢٥ غريبًا يعني عديله فأكراهما فلبثا في المحمل ثلاثًا لا يسأل هذا هذا عن شيء فقال

**... Iyās ibn Mu'āwiyah shone with the glow of your brilliance ...** 25

Iyās ibn Mu'āwiyah ibn Qurrah of the Muzaynah, known as Abū Wāthilah, was one of Basra's chief judges. Known for his acute powers of observation and for his brilliant comebacks and withering statements, Iyās's name is proverbially associated with correctly interpreting signs and physiognomy, as in the expression: "More perspicacious than Iyās." This verb for "perspicacity" is attested in a line of poetry: 25.1

> I was one of them, as they had perspicaciously surmised.

Others report an expression: "Smarter than Iyās"; Abū Tammām referred to this in a poem:

> He has 'Amr's bravery, Ḥātim's generosity,
> Iyās's brains, and al-Aḥnaf's equanimity.

Ibn 'Ā'ishah tells that Iyās's intelligence was first noted when he arrived in Syria as a young litigant. He had brought a case against an old man for a hearing before the judge of the Caliph 'Abd al-Malik ibn Marwān, but the judge knew Iyās's adversary and confronted Iyās: "Aren't you ashamed to bring a case against an aged man?" Iyās responded, "Justice is ageless." The judge snapped, "Silence!" Iyās responded, "If I am silent, who will advocate for my rights?" The judge snapped again, "I don't think you will utter a single truthful word in this whole session." Iyās replied, "I swear God is the only god, and Muḥammad is His Prophet!" The judge adjourned the session and informed the caliph, who told him, "Rule in the boy's favor and send him away from Syria before he turns the people here against us!" 25.2

Another account tells that Iyās's intelligence was first noted when he was a small boy attending elementary lessons. A group of Christians entered and ridiculed the Muslims, saying, "Muslims allege that food in Paradise has no consequences" (that is, excrement). Iyās asked his teacher, "Don't they claim that the majority of the food we consume is dissolved into our bodies?" "Yes." "In that case," Iyās continued, "what grounds are there to deny the possibility that God makes all the food consumed in Paradise dissolve?" This silenced the Christians and pleased his teacher. 25.3

It is told that Iyās made a second visit to Syria, and from there he set off for the hajj. He met a camel hirer and told him, "Find for me a stranger"—that is, 25.4

إياس يا عبد الله أخبرني من أنت قال غيلان فقال غيلان القدريّ قال نعم فمن أنت قال إياس قال أبو واثلة قال نعم قال إن شئت سألتني وإن شئت سألتك فقال له غيلان تكلّم قال إن شئت أخبرتك بقول أهل الجنّة وأهل النار والملائكة والشيطان والعرب والعجم فقال غيلان أخبرني بها

٥،٢٥ قال قال أهل الجنّة حين دخلوها ﴿ٱلْحَمْدُ لِلَّهِ ٱلَّذِى هَدَىٰنَا لِهَٰذَا وَمَا كُنَّا لِنَهْتَدِىَ لَوْلَآ أَنْ هَدَىٰنَا ٱللَّهُ﴾ وقال أهل النار حين دخلوها ﴿رَبَّنَا غَلَبَتْ عَلَيْنَا شِقْوَتُنَا﴾ وقالت الملائكة ﴿سُبْحَٰنَكَ لَا عِلْمَ لَنَآ إِلَّا مَا عَلَّمْتَنَآ﴾ وقال الشيطان ﴿رَبِّ بِمَآ أَغْوَيْتَنِى﴾ وقالت العرب

لَا يَمْنَعَنَّكَ ٱلطَّيْرُ شَيْئًا أَرَدْتَهُ فَقَدْ خُطَّ بِٱلْأَقْلَامِ مَا كُنْتَ لَاقِيَا

وقالت العجم هرچه بايد به آن بود همان أز پيش[١]

٦،٢٥ وكان سبب ولاية إياس للقضاء أنّ عمر بن عبد العزيز رضي الله تعالى عنه أرسل رجلاً من أهل الشام وأمره أن يجمع بين إياس والقاسم بن ربيعة الحوشيّ ويولّي القضاء لأنفذهما فجمع بينهما وكان كلّ منهما يمتنع من الولاية فقال إياس للشاميّ سل عنّي وعن القاسم فقيهي المصر الحسن البصريّ وابن سيرين فعلم القاسم أنّه إن سأل عنهما أشارا به فقال للشاميّ لا تسأل فوالله الذي لا إله إلّا هو إنّ إياسًا لأفضل منّي وأعلم بالقضاء فإن كنت ممّن يُصدّق فينبغي لك أن تصدّق قولي وإن كنت كاذبًا فما ينبغي لك أن تولّيني القضاء وأنا كذّاب فقال إياس للشاميّ إنّك جئت برجل فأقمته على شفير جهنّم فافتدى نفسه من النار بيمين

١ إ١: هما داد بيس.

someone to share in the hire of a camel. The camel man found one, and the pair set off in a palanquin together, traveling for three days without asking each other anything. Finally, Iyās asked his companion, "Servant of God, do tell me your name." He replied, "It's Ghaylān." "You're the same Ghaylān as the proponent of free will?" "Yes," Ghaylān replied. "And who are you?" "I am Iyās." Ghaylān asked, "The same Iyās also known as Abū Wāthilah?" "Yes," said Iyās, and then he put it to Ghaylān: "If you would like, ask me your question first, or should I begin?" Ghaylān replied, "You go first." Iyās asked him, "Would you like me to tell you what the Saved in Paradise say? And the Damned in Hell, and the Angels and the Devil and the Arabs and the Persians?" "Do tell!"

And Iyās began:[180] "When the Saved enter Paradise, they say, «All praise belongs to God who has guided us to this. Had God not guided us, we would never have found the way.»[181] When the Damned enter Hell, they say, «Lord, misfortune overcame us and we became an erring people.»[182] As for the Angels, they say, «we have no knowledge except whatever You have taught us,»[183] and the Devil says, «My Lord, since You have made me go astray, I shall make the path of error seem alluring to them on the earth and shall mislead them all.»[184] The Arabs say: 25.5

Fortune's signs have no power to deflect your will:
What's in store for you has already been written.

The Persians say: 'Everything that shall be has always been thus, predestined.'"[185]

The story of Iyās's appointment as judge goes as follows. The Caliph ʿUmar ibn ʿAbd al-ʿAzīz (God be pleased with him) sent a Syrian to Basra with the order to summon both Iyās and al-Qāsim ibn Rabīʿah al-Ḥawshī[186] and appoint the most astute of them as judge. When he assembled the pair, both demurred.[187] Iyās told the Syrian, "Ask the two best jurists of Basra, al-Ḥasan al-Baṣrī and Ibn Sirīn, for their opinion on both of us." Al-Qāsim knew that if they were consulted they would undoubtedly nominate him, so he told the Syrian, "Don't ask them! By God, I swear by Him who is the only true God, Iyās is far superior to me and will make a much more knowledgeable judge. If you think me a man whose opinion is to be trusted, then you must take my word for this; and if I am not telling the truth, then you cannot appoint me as judge, for I am a liar." Iyās responded to the Syrian, "You have summoned this man and placed him at the edge of Perdition,[188] and he only saved himself by swearing a false oath! May he 25.6

كاذبة يستغفر الله عزّ وجلّ منها وينجو من النار فقال الشاميّ أمّا إذا فطنت لها فإنّي أولّيك فاستقضاه فلم يزل على القضاء مدّة ثمّ هرب

٧،٢٥ ولمّا ولّي القضاء دخل عليه الحسن البصريّ فبكى إياس وقال يا أبا سعيد بلغني أنّ القضاة ثلاثة رجل مال به الهوى فهو في النار ورجل اجتهد وأخطأ فهو في النار ورجل اجتهد وأصاب فهو في الجنّة فقال الحسن إنّ فيما قصّ الله تعالى في نبأ داود ما يردّ قول هؤلاء ثمّ قرأ ﴿فَفَهَّمْنَـٰهَا سُلَيْمَـٰنَ وَكُلًّا ءَاتَيْنَا حُكْمًا وَعِلْمًا﴾ فحمد سليمان ولم يذمّ داود

٨،٢٥ وحكى المدائنيّ قال أودع رجل آخر كيسًا فيه دنانير وغاب مدّة طويلة فلمّا طال الأمر شقّ الرجل الكيس وأخذ الدنانير ووضع عوضها دراهم والخيط والخاتم على حاله وثمّ قدم صاحب المال فطلب ماله فدفع له الكيس بخاتمه فلم يقبله وقال هذه دراهم ومالي دنانير فقال هذا كيسك وخاتمك فرفعه لابن هبيرة فقال لإياس انظر بينهما فقال إياس منذ كم أودعك قال منذ عشرة أعوام فقال فضّوا الخاتم ففضّوه ونثروا الدراهم فوجدوا ضرب خمس سنين وستّ سنين وأقل وأكثر فقال إياس قد أقررت أنّه عندك منذ عشر سنين وفي الكيس ضرب خمس سنين فأقرّ بالدنانير وألزم بها

٩،٢٥ ونظر إياس يومًا إلى رجل لم يره قطّ فقال هذا غريب واسطيّ معلّم كتّاب هرب له غلام فوجدوا الأمر كذلك فسئل إياس عن ذلك فقال رأيته يمشي ويلتفت في الأماكن والطرق فعلمت أنّه غريب ورأيت على ثوبه حمرة تراب واسط فعلمت أنّه من أهلها ورأيته يمرّ بالصبيان فيسلّم عليهم ولا يسلّم على الرجال فعلمت أنّه معلّم ورأيته إذا مرّ بذي هيئة لم يلتفت إليه وإذا مرّ بأسود ذي أسمال تأمّله فعلمت أنّه يطلب آبقا

seek God's forgiveness for this and may he be rescued from Hellfire." The Syrian told Iyās, "Since you were able to work out his ruse, I appoint you judge."

Iyās was appointed, but he only served for a while before he fled.

When Iyās was appointed judge, al-Ḥasan al-Baṣrī paid him a visit, and 25.7
there he found Iyās in tears, lamenting: "Ḥasan! I have heard that there are only three possible fates for the judiciary: a judge who favors his whim, and thus enters Hell; a judge who endeavors to discern the truth, but errs, and so also enters Hell; and a judge who endeavors to discern the truth and succeeds, and he is the only one who enters Paradise." Al-Ḥasan corrected him: "God refutes that logic in the story of David when He says: «We gave Solomon the right understanding of the matter, and We bestowed wisdom and knowledge on both of them.»[189] Solomon is praised, yet David is not censured."

Al-Madā'inī tells that a man entrusted a bag full of gold dinars to another 25.8
before leaving on travels. After a long time had passed, the keeper surreptitiously opened the bag without upsetting the original seal and knot, and replaced the gold dinars with silver dirhams. Eventually, the owner of the coins did return and requested his money, and though it was handed back with the seal, he did not accept it. He said, "These are dirhams, and my money was dinars!"[190] The thief replied, "But this is your bag and seal." The matter was raised before Ibn Hubayrah, who ordered Iyās, "Adjudicate between these two." Iyās asked the thief, "How long ago was the bag deposited with you?" He replied, "Ten years." Iyās ordered, "Break the seal." They broke it, and out poured the dirhams. Some had been struck five years previously, some six, others more, and others less. Iyās said, "You confessed that you received the bag ten years ago, but it contains coins that are only five years old!" The thief admitted that it was originally dinars, and he was ordered to repay.

One day, Iyās saw a man whom he had never previously met. He stated, 25.9
"This stranger here is from Wāsiṭ, he teaches elementary lessons, and one of his slave boys has escaped." The man was found to be exactly as Iyās surmised, and they asked him how he knew. He replied, "I saw that he wandered up and down every alley and street he passed, so I knew that he was new to town. I saw that his robes had traces of Wāsiṭ's red earth on them, so I realized that he must be from there. When I saw him pass youths, he would greet them, but he never greeted any grown men, so it was clear that he was a teacher of young boys. And because he scrutinized every rag-wearing black person he passed, I realized that he was searching for a runaway slave."

١٠،٢٥ ووجده يومًا الحكم بن أيّوب عامل[1] البلد فسبّه وقال إنّك خارجيّ منافق فأتني بكفيل فقال أنت أيّها الأمير تكفلني ولا أعلم أحدًا أعرف منك بي فقال وما علمي بك وأنا من أهل الشام وأنت من أهل العراق فقال إياس ففيمَ الشهادة منذ اليوم

١١،٢٥ وتبصّر الناس هلال رمضان فلم يره أحد غير أنس بن مالك وقد قارب المائة سنة فشهد عند إياس فقال له إياس أشر لنا إلى موضعه فجعل يشير ولا يرونه فتأمّل إياس فإذا شعرة بيضاء من حاجب أنس بن مالك قد انثنت وصارت على عينه فمسحها إياس وسوّاها ثمّ قال يا أبا حمزة أرنا موضع الهلال فنظر فقال ما أرى شيئًا

١٢،٢٥ وقيل لإياس إنّ فيك عيوبًا دمامة الشكل وإعجابًا بالقول[2] وعجلة بالحكم فقال أمّا الدمامة فليس أمرها إليّ وأمّا الإعجاب بالقول أفليس يعجبكم ما أقول قالوا نعم فقال فأنا أحقّ بالإعجاب بقولي وأمّا العجلة بالحكم فكم هذه ومدّ أصابع يده فقالوا خمس فقال عجلتم بالجواب ولم تعدّوها إصبعًا إصبعًا قالوا كيف نعدّ ما نعلمه قال فكذلك أنا في الحكم

١٣،٢٥ ودخل إلى واسط فقال يومًا قدمت بلدكم عرفت خياركم من شراركم من غير أن أكشف عنهم قالوا كيف قال معي قوم خيار ألفوا منكم قومًا وقوم شرار ألفوا قومًا فعلمت أن خياركم من ألفه خيارنا وكذلك شراركم

١٤،٢٥ وكان يقول عرفت الزكن من أمّي وكانت خاراسانيّة وأهل بيتها يزكنون أي يتفرّسون ولإياس أخبار كثيرة من هذا الباب مجموعة من كتاب يُسمّى زكن إياس

١٥،٢٥ ومات رحمه الله تعالى سنة إحدى وعشرين ومائة وهو ابن ستّ وتسعين سنة وقال في العام الذي مات فيه رأيت في المنام كأنّي وأبي على فرسين يجريان جميعًا فلم أسبقه ولم يسبقني وكان أبوه قد مات أيضًا وهو ابن ستّ وتسعين سنة

١ إ١: على تلّ. ٢ سقطت من إ١.

The town commander, al-Ḥakam ibn Ayyūb, once located Iyās and swore at him: "You are a Kharijite hypocrite! Produce a guarantor." Iyās told him, "Commander! You can be my guarantor, as no one knows me better than you." Al-Ḥakam said, "What do I know about you, given that I am from Syria and you Iraq?" Iyās replied, "Then on what basis did you ground your allegation just now?" 25.10

People were scanning the sky for sight of the new moon of Ramadan, but no one could discern any trace of it, except for the hundred-year-old Anas ibn Malik, who swore to Iyās that he had seen it. Iyās asked him, "Can you point out where it is?" Anas started pointing, but still no one else saw anything. Iyās pondered for a moment, and then noticed that one white hair from Anas's eyebrow was drooping over his eye. Iyās brushed it up, and asked him, "Anas, show us the crescent moon now." Anas looked again, and replied, "I don't see anything." 25.11

Iyās was once told: "You have three faults: you are ugly, you are enamored with your own eloquence, and you are swift to judgment." Iyās responded, "My ugliness is hardly any of my own doing. I admire my own words; don't you also admire what I say?" "Yes," they responded. "Then they are worthy of admiration, and I should be most entitled to do so. As for my swift judgment, tell me—how many are these?" He stretched out the fingers on his hand. "Five," everyone said. Iyās told them, "That was fast! You answered without counting them finger by finger." They replied, "But why should we count that which we already know?" "That," said Iyās, "is how I am when ruling on a case." 25.12

When Iyās was in Wāsiṭ, he told the locals, "From the very first day, and without any investigation, I knew who in this town is good and who is bad." "How is that?" they asked him. "In my company there are some good people, and they became friendly with a bunch of your folk; I also have wicked associates, and they befriended a different bunch. Thus, I knew your upright citizens as those who befriended my goodly colleagues, and your ne'er-do-wells must be those who befriended my rogues." 25.13

Iyās used to say: "I learned how to interpret signs from my mother, who was from Khurasan; her family was well versed in the art." There are many stories like the above about Iyās, and they are collected in the book *The Perspicacity of Iyās*.[191] 25.14

Iyās died in 121 [739] at ninety-six years of age, God have mercy upon him. In the year in which he died, he said, "I had a dream in which I saw my father. We were both astride galloping horses, but neither of us could overtake the other." His father was also ninety-six when he died. 25.15

## وسحبان إنّما تكلّم بلسانك ٢٦

هو سحبان بن زفر بن إياس الوائليّ وائل باهلة الخطيب المفصح يُضرب به المثل في البيان أدرك الجاهليّة وأسلم ومات سنة أربع وخمسين ١،٢٦

حكى الأصمعيّ قال كان إذا خطب يسيل عرقًا ولا يعيد كلمة ولا يتوقّف ولا يقعد حتّى يفرغ ٢،٢٦

وقدم على معاوية وفد من خراسان فيهم سعيد بن عثمان فطلب سحبان فلم يوجد في منزله فاقتُضب من ناحية اقتضابًا فأدخل عليه فقال تكلّم فقال انظروا لي عصًا تقوّم من أودي فقالوا وما تصنع بها وأنت بحضرة أمير المؤمنين فقال ما كان يصنع بها موسى وهو يخاطب ربّه وعصاه في يده فضحك معاوية وقال هاتوا عصًا فجاؤوا بها فركلها برجله ولم يرضها[١] وقال هاتوا عصاي فأتي بها فأخذها ثمّ قام فتكلّم منذ صلاة الظهر إلى أن قامت صلاة العصر ما تنحنح ولا سعل ولا توقّف ولا ابتدأ في معنى فخرج منه وقد بقي عليه منه شيء فما زالت تلك حالة حتّى أشار معاوية بيده فأشار إليه سحبان أن لا تقطع عليّ كلامي فقال معاوية الصلاة فقال هي أمامك ونحن في صلاة وتحميد ووعد ووعيد فقال معاوية أنت أخطب العرب فقال سحبان والعجم والإنس والجنّ ٣،٢٦

وممّا رُوي من خطبه إنّ الدنيا دار بلاغ والآخرة دار قرار فخذوا من دار ممرّكم لدار مقرّكم ولا تهتكوا أستاركم عند من لا تخفى عليه أسراركم وأخرجوا من الدنيا قلوبكم قبل أن تخرج منها أبدانكم ففيها حييتم ولغيرها خُلقتم إنّ الرجل إذا هلك قالت الناس ما ترك وقالت الملائكة ما قدّم لله آباؤكم قدّموا بعضًا يكون لكم ولا تخلّفوا كلًّا يكون عليكم ٤،٢٦

١ ولم يرضها: زيادة من ل١.

**. . . Saḥbān spoke with your tongue . . .** 26

Saḥbān ibn Zufar ibn Iyās of the Wāʾil branch of the Bāhilah was a most articulate orator whose name is proverbial for eloquence. Born before Islam, he converted, and he died in 54 [674]. 26.1

Al-Aṣmaʿī tells that although Saḥbān would sweat profusely when delivering an oration, he remained standing, never paused, and never repeated so much as a single word throughout his entire speech. 26.2

Once, the Caliph Muʿāwiyah, with an entourage of visiting Khurasanians (including Saʿīd ibn ʿUthmān), sought the company of Saḥbān, but he was not at his home. Eventually, they extracted Saḥbān from where he was,[192] and they presented him before the caliph, who commanded him, "Make a speech!" Saḥbān replied, "First, find me a staff to keep me upright." This surprised them: "You're in the presence of the Commander of the Faithful; what makes you think you should hold a staff?" He replied, "What made Moses think he should hold his staff when he spoke with God?"[193] Muʿāwiyah laughed and said, "Bring a staff!" One was procured, but when Saḥbān gave it a kick, he didn't like it, and said, "Bring mine!" This was done, and with his staff in hand he stood and orated. He spoke from the noon prayer until the afternoon prayer was beginning; he never once cleared his throat, coughed, or paused, nor did he leave a subject broached without having covered every possible angle. He kept on going, and when Muʿāwiyah gave him a signal to stop, he gave a signal back to not interrupt. Muʿāwiyah interjected, "It's prayer time!" But Saḥbān replied, "Later you can perform your prayer, but right now we are discussing prayer and praise, Heaven, Hell, and the End of Days!" Muʿāwiyah conceded: "You are the most articulate of the Arabs!" Saḥbān added, "And of the non-Arabs, and of all humanity and all the jinn too!" 26.3

An excerpt from one of Saḥbān's sermons: "This world is just transit; it's the next that's for settlement. Take from this fleeting world only what you can carry into the permanence of the next. Do nothing that will find you disgraced before Him from Whom no secrets can be kept. Take your minds off worldly things before you cease being part of this world. You were born into this world, but you were created for another. When a man dies, people ask, 'What did he leave?' But the Angels ask, 'What did he offer to God?' Your forefathers left *something* of what they had for you; don't leave *everything*, as it will be counted against you."[194] 26.4

ومن شعره يمدح طلحة الطلحات وهو طلحة بن عبد الله الخزاعيّ ٥،٢٦

يَا طَلْحُ أَكْرَمَ مَنْ بِهَا    حَسَبًا وَأَعْطَاهُمْ لِتَالِدْ
مِنْكَ ٱلْعَطَاءُ فَأَعْطِنِي    وَعَلَيَّ مَدْحُكَ فِي ٱلْمَشَاهِدْ

فيقال إنّ طلحة قال له احتكم قال فرسك الورد وقصرك بكذا قال طلحة أفّ لك لو سألتني على قدري أعطيتك كلّ قصر لي وكلّ فرس ولكن أبيت ألّا بأهليّتك

وعمرو بن الأهتم إنّما سحر ببيانك ٢٧

١،٢٧ هو عمرو بن سنان الأهتم بن سميّ التميميّ المنقريّ وإنّما لُقّب سنان بالأهتم لأنّه هتمت ثنيّته يوم الكلاب وعمرو من أكبر سادات بني تميم وخطبائهم وشعرائهم في الجاهليّة والإسلام بليغ القول طلق العبارة وكان يدعى المكحّل لجماله

٢،٢٧ وفد على رسول الله صلّى الله عليه وسلّم والزبرقان بن بدر فأسلما وكان رسول الله صلّى الله عليه وسلّم يكرمهما وسأل عمرًا يومًا عن الزبرقان بحضوره فقال مطاع في أدنيه[١] شديد العارضة في قومه مانع لما وراء ظهره فقال الزبرقان يا رسول الله إنّه ليعلم منّي أكثر من ذلك ولكنّه حسدني فقال عمرو أمّا والله إنّه لزمر المروءة ضيّق العطن لئيم الخال أحمق الولد ووالله يا رسول الله ما كذبت في الأولى ولقد صدقت في الأخرى ولكنّي رجل رضيت فقلت أحسن ما علمت وغضبت فقلت أقبح ما علمت فقال عليه أفضل الصلاة السلام إنّ من البيان لسحرًا

١ إ: دينه.

He composed poetry, including verses in praise of Ṭalḥah ibn ʿAbd Allāh of the Khuzāʿah, known as "Ṭalḥah the Quintessential": 26.5

Ṭalḥah, the most generous, of the noblest line,
  from venerable legacy you bestow greatest largesse.
Gifting is your prerogative: give to me!
  and I shall praise you in every assembly.

It is reported that Ṭalḥah thereupon asked Saḥbān, "How much do you want?" And Saḥbān said, "Give me Pink, your horse, and an estate of yours." (He specified its location.) "Humph," replied Ṭalḥah. "Had you based your request on the utmost extent of my capacity, I would have given you every estate and every horse I own! But your request was limited to the horizons of your station."[195]

**. . . ʿAmr ibn al-Ahtam dazzled with your eloquence.** 27

ʿAmr ibn Sinān al-Ahtam ibn Sumayy was from the Minqar branch of the Tamīm. His father was nicknamed al-Ahtam ("Broken Teeth") because his front teeth were smashed at the Battle of Kulāb. ʿAmr lived in both the pre-Islamic and the Islamic period; he was one of the most powerful nobles of the Tamīm, and one of their best orators and poets. He spoke eloquently and mellifluously, and was nicknamed "the Kohled One" since he was so handsome. 27.1

ʿAmr presented himself to the Prophet (God bless and keep him) along with al-Zibriqān ibn Badr. Both converted to Islam, and both were honored by the Prophet (God bless and keep him). Later, in the presence of al-Zibriqān, the Prophet asked ʿAmr for his opinion of al-Zibriqān, and ʿAmr said, "He is obeyed by his closest kin, he is a stern force among his people, and he protects those around him." Al-Zibriqān remarked, "Prophet of God! He could have said more about me than that, but he's jealous." ʿAmr then spoke again, "Well then, by God, al-Zibriqān has but little virtue, his camel paddock is meager, his mother's line is ignoble, and his children are idiots. O Prophet of God! I swear by God that my first statement was no lie, and my second was the truth. Such is my way: if I am pleased, I say the best of what I know, and if I am angry, I say the worst." The Prophet (God's greatest blessings be upon him) remarked, "Doesn't eloquence work magic!"[196] 27.2

واختلف قوم في معنى الحديث فقال بعضهم أريد المدح فإنّ البيان الفهم وإنّما سُمّي سحرًا لحدّة عمله وسرعة قبول القلب له والتعجّب منه كما يتعجّب من السحر وقد اتّفق الناس على أنّ تصوير الحقّ في صورة الباطل والباطل في صورة الحقّ من أعلى درجات البلاغة ٣،٢٧

وقال قوم أريد الذمّ لأنّ السحر تمويه والبيان كثرة الكلام والنفاق واحتجّوا بقوله عليه أفضل الصلاة السلام الحياء والعيّ شعبتان من الإيمان والبذاء والبيان شعبتان من النفاق

والأوّل أصحّ وإنّما سُمّي هنا نفاقًا إذا كان من البذاء

وحكى العتبيّ قال وفد الأحنف بن قيس وعمرو بن الأهتم على عمر بن الخطّاب رضي الله تعالى عنه فأراد أن يقرع بينهما في الرياسة فلمّا اجتمعت بنو تميم قال الأحنف وهي من سقطاته ٤،٢٧

ثَوَى قَدَحٌ عَنْ قَوْمِهِ طُولَ مَا ثَوَى فَلَمَّا أَتَاهُـمْ قَـالَ قُومُوا تَفَـاخَـرُوا

فقال عمرو إنّا كنّا وأنتم في دار جاهليّة وكان الفضل فيها لمن جهل فسفكنا دماءكم وسبينا نساءكم ونحن اليوم في دار إسلام والفضل فيها لمن حلم فغفر الله لنا ولك فغُلّب يومئذ عمرو على الأحنف ووقعت القرعة لآل الأهتم فقال عمرُو

وَلَمَّـا دَعَتْـنِي لِلرِّيَاسَـةِ مِـنْقَـرٌ لَدَى مَجْلِسٍ أَضْحَى بِهِ ٱلنَّجْمُ بَادِيَا
شَدَّدْتُ لَهَا أَزْرِي وَقَدْ كُنْتُ قَبْلَهَا لِأَمْثَالِهَـا قِـدْمـًا أَشُـدُّ إِزَارِيَا

وتُوفّي سنة سبع وخمسين وكان يقول أشجع الناس من ردّ جهله بحلمه ٥،٢٧

There is disagreement on the meaning of the Prophet's remark. Some say that he intended praise, since eloquence engenders comprehension, so he likened it to "magic" on account of eloquence's penetrating and quick persuasive effect. The Prophet marveled at 'Amr's words as one would marvel at a magic trick. Furthermore, there is general agreement that the ability to articulate truth in the guise of falsehood and the ability to cloak falsehood in the form of truth are among the highest poetic arts. 27.3

Others say that the Prophet intended disparagement, since magic involves false affectation, and eloquence likewise can be critiqued for indulging in verbosity and hypocrisy. This argument adduces another hadith of the Prophet (God's best blessings be upon him): "Modesty and inexpressiveness are two branches of faith; ribaldry and eloquence are two branches of hypocrisy."[197]

It is most likely that praise was intended, since eloquence is only associated with hypocrisy when it expresses foul things.

Al-'Utbī tells that 'Amr ibn al-Ahtam and al-Aḥnaf ibn Qays presented themselves before the Caliph 'Umar ibn al-Khaṭṭāb (God be pleased with him), and in order to determine which of the two should be appointed leader,[198] 'Umar proposed that they cast lots. The Tamīm mustered, and al-Aḥnaf, in one of his rare slips into hotheadedness, recited the following verse: 27.4

Qadaḥ stayed long, far from his people,[199]
But when he came, he cried, "Stand and vie for glory!"

'Amr responded: "Both of our peoples used to live in the pre-Islamic way, when virtue was won by the most passionate, and so we shed your blood and we captured your women. But now we live in the way of Islam: virtue vests with the most equanimous. May God forgive both you and us." And in this way, 'Amr had the better of al-Aḥnaf. The lots fell in favor of al-Ahtam's clan, and 'Amr recited these lines:

When the Minqar called me to lead,
in a meeting where the brilliant star shone,
I embraced leadership resolutely—
long I have met these matters with resolve.

'Amr died in 57 [676–77]. He used to say: "The bravest are those who can repel passion with forbearance." 27.5

٦،٢٧ ويقول ذامًّا للخمر وكان ممّن حرّمها في الجاهليّة لو كان العقل يُشترى ما كان شيء أنفس منه فالعجب لمن يشتري الحمق بماله فيدخله في رأسه فيقيئ في جيبه ويسلح في ذيله

٧،٢٧ ومن شعره وهو في أعلى الطبقات

وَمُسْتَنْبِحٍ بَعْدَ ٱلْهُدُوءِ دَعَوْتُهُ وَقَدْ حَانَ مِنْ سَارِي ٱلشِّتَاءِ طُرُوقُ
يُعَالِجُ عِرْنِينًا مِنَ ٱللَّيْلِ بَارِدًا تَلُفُّ رِيَاحٌ ثَوْبَهُ وَبُرُوقُ
أَضَفْتُ فَلَمْ أُفْحِشْ عَلَيْهِ وَلَمْ أَقُلْ لِأُحْرِمَهُ إِنَّ ٱلْمَكَانَ يَضِيقُ
وَقُلْتُ لَهُ أَهْلًا وَسَهْلًا وَمَرْحَبًا فَهٰذَا مَبِيتٌ صَالِحٌ وَصَدِيقُ
وَقُمْتُ إِلَى ٱلْبُزْلِ ٱلْهَوَادِجِ فَٱتَّقَتْ مَقَاحِيدُ كُومٌ كَٱلْمَجَادِلِ رُوقُ
بِأَدْمَاءَ مِرْبَاعِ ٱلنِّتَاجِ كَأَنَّهَا إِذَا عَرَضَتْ دُونَ ٱلْعِشَارِ فَنِيقُ
فَقَامَ إِلَيْهَا ٱلْجَازِرَانِ فَٱعْلَمُوا[1] يُطِيرَانِ عَنْهَا ٱلْجِلْدَ وَهِيَ تَفُوقُ
فَجُرَّ إِلَيْنَا ضَرْعُهَا وَسَنَامُهَا وَأَزْهَرُ يَحْبُو لِلْقِيَامِ عَتِيقُ
وَبَاتَ لَنَا مِنْهَا وَلِلضَّيْفِ مَوْهِنًا عَشَاءٌ سَمِينٌ رَاهِنٌ وَغَبُوقُ
وَكُلُّ كَرِيمٍ يَتَّقِي ٱلذَّمَّ بِٱلْقِرَى وَلِلْخَيْرِ بَيْنَ ٱلصَّالِحِينَ طَرِيقُ
لَعَمْرُكَ مَا ضَاقَتْ بِلَادٌ بِأَهْلِهَا وَلٰكِنَّ أَخْلَاقَ ٱلرِّجَالِ تَضِيقُ
نَمَتْنِي عُرُوقٌ مِنْ زُرَارَةَ لِلْعُلَى وَمِنْ فَدَكِيٍّ وَٱلْأَشَدِّ مِنْهُ عُرُوقُ
مَضَارِيبُ يَجْعَلْنَ ٱلْفَتَى فِي أَرُومَةٍ يَفَاعٍ وَبَعْضُ ٱلْوَالِدِينَ دَقِيقُ

١ بياض في إ١؛ إ٢، ب: أعلنوا

ʿAmr disapproved of wine: even during pre-Islamic times he had forbidden drinking, and had this to say: "If it were possible to purchase reason, there would be nothing more valuable. It is thus astounding that a man would spend money on stupidity—pouring it into his head and then vomiting over his clothes and defecating into his robes." 27.6

An excerpt of the finest quality from ʿAmr's poetry: 27.7

Another lost wayfarer. Deep into winter's night, when
even night riders are camped, I called to him.
Frozen in his struggle against the spreading face of darkness,
lightning and wind swirling about his robes.
I called, "Come in" (how abhorrent if I prevented him,
protesting my camp is too small),
With the greeting: "Welcome, may your stay be easy!
Here you find an honest tent and a friend!"
I set to the slumbering fat camels,
fine beasts with towering humps,
who were shielding a white she-camel, massive as a stallion,
preparing to give birth in the spring.
Two butchers clamber atop her; she breathes her last
as they flay her skin straight off.
They brought us her udder and hump,
and premature calf, noble, white, and unsure on its feet.
Our late-night companions:
grilled meat, purest fat, and evening yogurt.
Hospitality. This is how the nobleman parries reproach—
a clear path to goodness for the virtuous.
By your life, it is never the land that causes dearth,
it's men's parsimony.
My descent from Zurārah blood raises me,
as does my lineage from Fadakī and al-Ashadd.
Lofty ancestors becoming of a brave man,
while others have parents who are lowly.

٨،٢٧ وقوله من أبيات

وَذِي لُوثَةٍ شَهِّي ٱلرُّقَادِ بِعَيْنِهِ　فَقَامَ رَخِيمُ ٱلصَّوْتِ أَلْوثُ فَاتِرُ
فَقَالَتْ لَهُ كَمِّشْ ثِيَابَكَ وَٱرْتَحِلْ　وَإِلَّا يَتَكَاءَدْكَ ٱلسُّرَى وَٱلْهَوَاجِرُ[١]
إِذَا مَا نُجُومُ ٱللَّيْلِ صَارَتْ كَأَنَّهَا　هَجَائِنُ يَطْلَعْنَ ٱلْفَلَاةَ صَوَادِرُ
شَآمِيَّةً إِلَّا سُهَيْلٌ كَأَنَّهُ　فَنِيقٌ غَدَا عَنْ شَوْلِهِ وَهُوَ جَافِرُ

٩،٢٧ وقوله وهو أحسن ما للمتقدّمين في هذا المعنى

تَطَاوَحَنِي يَوْمٌ جَدِيدٌ وَلَيْلَةٌ　هُمَا أَبْلَيَا جِسْمِي وَكُلُّ فَتًى بَالِي
إِذَا مَا سَلَخْتُ ٱلشَّهْرَ أَهْلَلْتُ بَعْدَهُ　كَفَى قَاتِلًا سَلْخِي ٱلشُّهُورَ وَإِهْلَالِي

٢٨ وأنّ الصلح بين بكر وتغلب تمّ برسالتك

١،٢٨ بكر وتغلب هم بنو وائل الذين قامت بينهم حرب البسوس كما تقدّم في ذكر جسّاس ومهلهل واستمرّت أعوامًا كثيرة إلى أن تفانى الحيّان وقُتل عظماؤهم فخرج مهلهل إلى أخواله ضجرًا من الحرب ومال من بقي من القوم إلى صلح بعضهم بعضًا وراسلهم الحارث بن عمرو بن معاوية الكنديّ ملك كندة وهو جدّ امرئ القيس الشاعر في الصلح بينهم والتمليك عليهم وقد كانوا قالوا إنّ سفهاءنا قد غلبوا على أمرنا وأكل القويّ الضعيف والرأي أن نملّك علينا ملكًا نعطيه البعير والشاة فيأخذ من القويّ ويردّ الظالم ولا يمكن أن يكون من بعض قبائلنا فيأباه الآخرون ولا تنقطع الحروب فأجابوا الحارث بن عمرو إلى ما

١ وَذِي لُوثَةٍ وَٱلْهَوَاجِر: زيادة من غ.

'Amr's poetry: 27.8

> Many were my nights of dreamy, sweet slumber,
> woken by soft whispers of languorous murmur:
> She says, "It's time you make haste from here,
> lest you struggle against blackness or scorching heat."[200]
> The night stars dwindle like distant white camels
> trailing from a watering hole into the desert plains,
> northward they set, while Canopus dives deep,
> departing Shaulah like a magnificent stallion.

The following lines of 'Amr are the best of what the ancient poets composed on the theme of Fate: 27.9

> I am tossed from day to night to new day,
> constant tests; though does any hero go untested?
> One month passes, another begins:
> Time's march is lethal enough: what's left to fear?

**She made out that it must have been your missive that forged the peace between the Bakr and Taghlib . . .** 28

The Bakr and the Taghlib are the two clans of the Wā'il that fought against each other in the Basūs War, as noted in the biographies of Jassās and Muhalhil.[201] This protracted war nearly annihilated both clans: their great men were killed, and Muhalhil, weary of the fighting, laid down his arms and settled among his maternal uncles. Those who remained began entertaining thoughts of peace, and al-Ḥārith ibn 'Amr ibn Mu'āwiyah, the king of Kindah (and the grandfather of the poet Imru' al-Qays), sent them a message proposing to reconcile their factions by appointing one king over them all.[202] They had said: "Our affairs fell into the hands of our impudent hotheads, and the strong preyed on the weak. The best course would be for us to be ruled by one king to whom we can send tribute of our camels and sheep, and who will distribute the wealth of the strong and punish wrongdoers. The new king must not be from one of our clans, since all the others would reject him, and the warring would just continue." They assented to al-Ḥārith ibn 'Amr's rule: he came and placated the surviving clans, forged peace between them, and busied them 28.1

أراد فقدم عليهم وتلافى بقيّتهم وأصلح أمرهم وشغلهم بغزو اللخميّين من بني غسّان ملوك الشام

وكان الحارث ملكًا جليلًا رفيع الهمّة ويُسمّى آكل المرار وإنّما سُمّي بذلك لأنّ زياد بن الهبولة أحد ملوك الشام غزا أرضه والقوم خلوف بالبحرين فأصاب سبيًا وغنائم وسبى هند بنت ظالم زوجة الحارث بن عمرو فبلغه الخبر فخرج للقاء ابن الهبولة وأرسل سدوس بن سنان وخليع بن وهب يتجسّسان له الخبر في عسكر ابن الهبولة فخرجا حتّى هجما على العسكر ليلًا وقد أمن الطلب وقسّم النهب وأخذ المرباع وأوقد نارًا عظيمة ونادى مناديه من جاء بحزمة حطب فله قدرة[1] من تمر فأخذ كلّ منهما حزمة من الحطب وألقاها عند النار وأخذ التمر فأمّا خليع فقال يكفي هذه آية وانصرف وأمّا سدوس فقال لا أبرح حتّى آتيه بأمر جليّ ٢،٢٨

فلمّا دخل ابن الهبولة قبّته قرب سدوس منها بحيث يسمع كلامه وأقبل الناس يحرسون القبّة فضرب سدوس يده الى جليس له مخافة أن يستنكره فقال من أنت قال فلان ودنا ابن الهبولة من هند امرأة الحارث فقبّلها وداعبها وقال ما ظنّك الآن بالحارث قالت ما هو الظنّ بل هو اليقين إنّه لن يدع طلبك حتّى يعاين القصور الحمر يعني الشام وكأنّي أنظر إليه في فوارس من شيبان يذمّرهم ويذمّرونه وهو شديد الكلب كأنّه بعير أكل مرارًا فسُمّي آكل المرار والمرار نبت فيه مرارة إذا أكلت منه الإبل قلصت مشافرها ٣،٢٨

وقيل بل سمعها سدوس يعني هندًا تقول لابن الهبولة وقد سألها عن حبّها الحارث فقالت ما أبغضت نسمة قطّ بغضي له وما رأيت أحزم منه نائمًا ومستيقظًا وكان إذا أراد النوم أمرني أن أجعل عنده عسًّا من لبن فبينما هو نائم يومًا وأنا قريب منه أنظر إليه إذ أقبل أسود سالخ إلى العسّ فشرب منه ثمّ مجّ فيه فقلت يستيقظ ٤،٢٨

[1] إ: قدرُةُ.

by directing them to fight alongside the Lakhmids in their wars against the Ghassanid kingdom in Syria.

Al-Ḥārith was an illustrious, formidable king, known by his nickname, "Star-Thistle Eater."[203] The story behind this goes as follows. Al-Ḥārith once left his lands unguarded while he campaigned with his warriors in al-Baḥrayn, and at that moment a king of Syria, Ziyād ibn al-Habūlah, invaded. He plundered and took captives, including al-Ḥārith's wife, Hind bint Ẓālim. Al-Ḥārith was informed, and he directly countermarched to intercept Ibn Habūlah, sending ahead two men, Sadūs ibn Sinān and Khalīʿ ibn Wahb,[204] to spy on Ibn Habūlah's camp and verify the reports. They set out, and stole into the camp at night. Ibn Habūlah was feeling secure from counterattack, and he had divided the spoils, taking the king's quarter for himself. He had ordered a giant bonfire lit, telling his herald to announce: "Whoever brings a bundle of firewood will receive its weight in dates." Sadūs and Khalīʿ each gathered a bundle, threw it on the fire, and took their dates. Khalīʿ said, "This is sufficient evidence," and left, but Sadūs said, "I'm staying until I find incontrovertible proof." 28.2

When Ibn Habūlah entered his tent, Sadūs approached to where he could hear what was being said. The tent's guardsmen came by on patrol, and Sadūs gave a man seated next to him a friendly tap so as not to arouse suspicion. The man asked him, "Who are you?" and Sadūs made up a name. Inside the tent, Ibn Habūlah sidled up to Hind, al-Ḥārith's wife, and began kissing and dallying with her. He asked her, "What do you think about al-Ḥārith now?" She replied, "It's not what I think, it's what I know. He will chase you unto the Red Castles themselves." (She meant Syria.) "It is as if I can see him now: charging with horsemen of the Shaybān, each urging each other forward, and he's hopping mad, like a camel that's just eaten purple star thistle." And from then on, al-Ḥārith was known as "Star-Thistle Eater." (Purple star thistle is a plant, and if a camel eats it his muzzle shrinks.) 28.3

However, there is another version of what Sadūs heard. The second story reports that when Ibn Habūlah asked Hind whether she loved al-Ḥārith, she responded, "I have never hated a soul more than I hate him. I have never seen anyone so tenacious as him either, awake or asleep. Whenever he slept, he always ordered me to prepare a large bowl of milk, and during one of his slumbers, while I stayed awake near him, I saw a venomous black snake slither up to the bowl, drink, and spit into it. I said to myself, 'When al-Ḥārith wakes, he'll have a drink, and he'll die. I'll finally be rid of him!' When he roused, he told 28.4

فيشربه فيموت فأستريح منه فانتبه من نومه فقال عليّ بالإناء فناولته إيّاه فشمّه ثمّ ألقاه فهريق ثمّ قال أين ذهب الأسود فقلت ما رأيته قال كذبْت

٥،٢٨ فلمّا سمع سدوس هذه المقالة أمهل حتّى نام الحرس وخرج يسري ليلته حتّى صبّح الحارث فدخل عليه وهو ينشد

أَتَاكَ ٱلْمُرْجِفُونَ بِرَجْمِ ظَنٍّ    عَلَى دَهَشٍ وَجِئْتُكَ بِٱلْيَقِينِ

ثمّ قصّ عليه ما سمع وكان الحارث جالسًا في موضع فيه شيء كثير من نبت المرار فجعل يسمع الحديث ويعبث بالمرار ويأكل منه غضبًا وأسفًا وهو لا يعلم أنّه يأكله من شدّة الغيظ إلى أن[1] فُرغ الحديث ووجد طعمه فسُمّي آكل المرار ثمّ لحق ابن الهبولة فقاتله وظفر به[2] ولم يزل ملكًا على بني وائل بعد ما أصلح بينهم حتّى مات

٦،٢٨ ومن شعره

رُبَّ هَمٍّ جَشَّمْتُهُ فِي هَوَاكُمْ    وَبَعِيرٍ تَرَكْتُهُ مَحْسُورِ
وَغُلَامٍ كَلَّفْتُهُ دَلَجَ ٱللَّيْـ    ـلِ فَأَضْحَى كَأَنَّهُ مَخْمُورُ
إِنَّ مَنْ غَرَّهُ ٱلنِّسَاءُ بِشَيْءٍ    بَعْدَ هِنْدٍ لَجَاهِلٌ مَغْرُورُ
حِلْوَةُ ٱلْعَيْنِ وَٱللِّسَانِ وَمِنْ    كُلِّ مُسِيءٍ نَحْنُ مِنْهَا ٱلضَّمِيرُ
كُلُّ أُنْثَى وَإِنْ بَدَا لَكَ مِنْهَا    آيَةُ ٱلْحُبِّ حُبُّهَا خَيْتَعُورُ

## ٢٩ والحمالات بين عبس وذبيان أسندت إلى كفالتك

١،٢٩ أصل الحروب بين عبس وذبيان أنّ قيس بن زهير المقدّم ذكره كان قد اشترى من مكّة درعًا حسنة تُسمّى ذات الفضول وورد بها إلى قومه فرآها عمّه الربيع

١ سقطت من إ.   ٢ سقطت من إ.

me, 'Bring me the bowl!' I passed it to him, and he sniffed it and threw it to the ground, spilling everything. 'Where did the snake go?' he asked me. 'I didn't see any snake,' I told him. 'You lie,' was his reply."

After Sadūs overheard Hind say this, he loitered about until the guards fell asleep, and then set off into the night, reaching al-Ḥārith by daybreak. He presented himself and recited: **28.5**

When bearers of startling news attend you with speculation—
they bring alarm. I come with the sober truth.

Al-Ḥārith was sitting amid a patch of purple star thistle, and as Sadūs reported what he had heard, al-Ḥārith in his anger and angst fidgeted with the thistles and, as his wrath intensified, he unwittingly began chewing on them. Only when Sadūs finished did al-Ḥārith realize what he was eating, and thereafter he was named "Star-Thistle Eater."

Al-Ḥārith's counterattack against Ibn al-Habūlah was a success, and he continued to reign over the reconciled Wā'il clans until the day he died.

Al-Ḥārith's poetry: **28.6**

For love of you all, I've surmounted trial after trial;
many camels have I left behind, stripped clean;[205]
many lads have I sent out after midnight,
with wine's effects still working upon them at dawn.
Look at Hind: any man hereafter beguiled by a woman
is nothing if not a gullible fool.
Sweet loving glances, soft words,
but harboring all kinds of malice.
Even if they display signs of love,
a woman's love is but a mirage.

**. . . your guarantee that settled the blood feuds of ʿAbs and Dhubyān . . .** **29**

The warring between the ʿAbs and the Dhubyān was triggered by a series of events that began when the aforementioned Qays ibn Zuhayr[206] purchased a fine coat of armor called "the All-Encompassing" in Mecca. When Qays returned to his clan with it, his paternal uncle, al-Rabīʿ ibn Ziyād, leader of the ʿAbs, took a liking to the armor and confiscated it. Qays promptly removed his **29.1**

ابن زياد وكان سيّد بني عبس فأخذها منه غصبًا فانتقل عنه قيس بن زهير بأهله وماله ونزل على بني ذبيان وسيّدهم حمل بن بدر وأخوه حذيفة فأكرموه وأحسنوا جواره

وكانت لقيس خيل كريمة من جملتها داحس وإنّما سُمّي داحسًا لأنّه كان لرجل من بني يربوع يقال له قرواش فرس يُسمّى جلوى ولرجل منهم يقال له حوط فرس يقال له[1] ذو العقّال وكان لا يطرقه شيئًا وإنّهم توجّهوا في نجعة والفحل مع ابنتين لحوط تقودانه فمرّت به جلوى وديقًا فلمّا انتشاها ودى فضحك شابّ[2] منهم فاستحيت الفتاتان فأرسلتا مقوده فوثب على جلوى ثمّ جاء حوط وكان سيئ الخلق فرأى عين فرسه فقال ناز والله فأخبر بالخبر ونادى بني يربوع فاجتمعوا فقالوا والله ما أكرهناه فقال أريد ماء فرسي فقالوا دونك فأوثقها حوط ثمّ جعل في يده ترابًا وسطا[3] عليها فأدخل يده في فرجها وأخرجها فاشتملت الرحم على ما فيها فنتجها قرواش مهرًا فسمّاه داحسًا لسطوة حوط عليه ودحسه إيّاه وخرج داحس كأنّه أبوه ثمّ إنّ قيس بن زهير أغار على بني يربوع فغنم وسبا وركب داحسًا فتيان من بني أزنم فنجوا وقطعا الخيل فلمّا رآه قيس أعجب به فدعا إلى أن يجعل فداء السبي ففعلوا وصار لقيس ٢،٢٩

فتراهن رجلان من بني ذبيان عليه وعلى فرس لحذيفة بن بدر تُسمّى الغبراء أيّهما السابق على عشر قلائص وقد قيل إنّ داحسًا والغبراء فرسا قيس والخطّار والحنفاء فرسا حذيفة وأنّهم أجروا الجميع وقيل تراهنا على فرسي قيس أيّهما أسبق ٣،٢٩

وللرواة في هذه الواقعة أخبار طويلة جدًّا تشتمل على أمثال وأشعار اختصرتها لكثرة ما فيها من الموضوعات

١ حوط . . . يقال له: زيادة من با١، إ٢. ٢ إ٣: شباب. ٣ سقطت من إ١.

clan and herds from al-Rabīʿ's camp and settled among the Dhubyān, who were at the time led by Ḥamal and Ḥudhayfah, the sons of Badr. The Dhubyān welcomed Qays with open, generous arms and offered him mutual protection.

One of the horses Qays brought with him was a stallion of fine pedigree named Thrust. The story of how Thrust got his name goes as follows. There were once two men of the Yarbūʿ: Qirwāsh, who had a mare named Running Clear, and Ḥawṭ, who had a stallion named Limper, which Ḥawṭ never lent to anyone for studding. One day, when the clan was migrating to a new pasture, Ḥawṭ let two of his girls lead Limper. They passed by Running Clear, who was in heat at the time. Limper sniffed her, and some semen splattered from his erect penis. A young boy in the group laughed, and the two girls felt embarrassed and let go of Limper's reins, whereupon he mounted Running Clear. Shortly afterward, Ḥawṭ came riding up—he was of a generally ill temperament—and looking into the eyes of his horse, Limper, he grumbled, "You've been rutting, by God!" Ḥawṭ was told what happened, and he demanded the Yarbūʿ assemble. When they gathered, they told him, "We didn't force Limper to do this, by God!" But Ḥawṭ insisted: "I want my horse's semen back!" They said, "Go for it." Ḥawṭ tied down Running Clear, dusted his hand, and thrust it into her vagina to take back the fluid, but this spread the semen throughout the uterus, and when Running Clear gave birth to a foal, Qirwāsh named him "Thrust" in memory of Ḥawṭ's thrusting hand. Thrust grew up a fine horse just like his father, Limper. 29.2

Sometime later, Qays raided the Yarbūʿ, and as he was rounding up the plunder and captives, two youths of the Aznam clan escaped on Thrust. None of Qays's riders could catch them, and Qays was impressed. He announced that he would free all the captives in return for Thrust alone. This was agreed, and so Thrust became Qays's property.

After Qays had settled with the Dhubyān, two of their tribesmen made a wager of ten young female camels over whether Thrust could outrun Dusty Mare, a horse owned by Ḥudhayfah ibn Badr. 29.3

(There are other narratives concerning the identity of the horses and their ownership: some say Qays owned both Thrust and Dusty Mare, and that they were raced against Ḥudhayfah's two horses, Swisher and Canted. Yet others say that the wager was made just over which of Qays's two horses was the faster.)

About what happened next, narrators tell long stories with many poems and proverbs: from these extensive accounts, I present an abridgment.

٤،٢٩ ثمّ إنّ الرجلين أخبرا حذيفة بن بدر بالرهان على فرسه وفرس قيس فرضي به وأمضاه وأتيا قيسًا فقالا إنّنا راهنّا على فرسك فقال راهنا من شئتما وجنّباني[١] بني بدر فإنّهم قوم يظلمون فقالا قد أوجبنا الرهان مع حذيفة فقال والله لتشعلنّ علينا شرًّا

٥،٢٩ ثمّ جاء قيس إلى حذيفة فقال إنّما جئت لأواضعك الرهان عن صاحبيّ فقال لا والله إلّا بالعشر قلائص فأحفظ ذلك قيسًا وغضب وتزايدا حتّى بلغا مائة قلوص ووضعا الرهان على يد رجل من بني ثعلبة وجعلا الغاية مائة غلوة ثمّ قادا الفرسين وركبهما فتيان منهم وكان حمل بن بدر قد جعل حيسًا في دلاء ووضعه في شعب من شعاب هضب القليب على طريق الفرسين وأكمن فيه فتيانًا وأمرهم إن جاء داحس سابقًا أن يردّوا وجهه إلى أن تسبقه الغبراء فسبق داحس فثار إليه من كان في الشعب فردّ وجهه وجاءت الغبراء وعلم قيس والذي على يده الرهان بذلك فقال قيس لحذيفة أعطني سبقي وقال الذي على يده الرهان أعطوه سبقه فقد سبق داحس فأعطاه السبق

٦،٢٩ ثمّ إنّ جماعة من قوم حذيفة ندّموه على دفعه السبق إلى قيس ونهاه آخرون عن الشرّ وقالوا إنّ قيسًا لم يسبق إلى مكرمة وإنّما سبق دابّة دابّة فأبى وبعث ابنه مالك بن حذيفة إلى قيس يطلب منه السبق فقال له هذا سبقي فكيف أعطيكم إيّاه فتناول ابن حذيفة من عرض قيس وشتمه وأغلظ له وكان إلى جانب قيس رمح فطعنه فدقّ صلبه واجتمع الحيّان وأدّوا دية المقتول فأخذها حذيفة دفعًا للشرّ

٧،٢٩ ثمّ إنّ قومه ندّموه فعاد الشرّ بينهم فتحمّل قيس بمن معه يومئذ ورحل وقامت الفتن بين الحيّيْن والحروب إلى أن قُتل مالك بن زهير أخو قيس وكان الربيع بن زياد عمّهما معتزل الحرب فلمّا سمع بمقتل ابن أخيه مالك شقّ عليه وقاتل وقال

١ إ١: حيًّا في.

The two bettors informed Ḥudhayfah about the wager they had made regarding his horse, Dusty, and Qays's horse, Thrust. Ḥudhayfah was pleased with the wager and sent the men back to Qays. They told Qays, "We've placed a bet on your horse!" Qays replied, "Bet with whomever you like, but don't involve me with the Badr clan, as they don't play fair." The two men confessed: "Actually, we did bet with Ḥudhayfah." Qays was grave: "By God, this will ignite flames of discord upon us." 29.4

Qays approached Ḥudhayfah and told him, "I came to discuss the wager of my two companions." But Ḥudhayfah replied, "No way! Not unless you pay ten young she-camels." This offended Qays, and angrily they argued over the bet, upping the ante until it reached one hundred young she-camels. They placed the wager before a man of the Thaʿlabah and set the racecourse at a length of one hundred bowshots. Thrust and Dusty were led in, and two young boys were to ride them. Ḥamal ibn Badr had placed a mixture of dates and butter in a bucket at one of the defiles of a hill along the racetrack known as Haḍab Qalīb.[207] Ḥamal also hid some braves there and instructed them that if Thrust was leading when he neared their position, they were to divert him until Dusty overtook him. 29.5

During the race, Thrust was in front, and the braves leapt from the defile and diverted him so Dusty was first to the finish. Qays and the man holding the wager both realized what had happened, and Qays told Ḥudhayfah, "I'm the rightful winner. Pay up." The man keeping the wager also told Ḥudhayfah, "Honor the bet! Thrust should have won." Ḥudhayfah duly paid.

But some members of Ḥudhayfah's clan began needling him about having paid. Others tried to stem any ill will, and told Ḥudhayfah, "Qays has not outstripped you in honor; it was just one animal that outran another." Yet Ḥudhayfah was not placated, and he sent his son Mālik to Qays to demand return of the payment. Qays told the boy, "These are my winnings. Why must I give them back?" Ḥudhayfah's son said something that disparaged Qays's honor, and swore at him coarsely. A spear was nearby. Qays grabbed it and ran it through the boy. The two clans gathered and agreed that a blood payment should be made, and Ḥudhayfah accepted it in an effort to stem the rancor. 29.6

But again, Ḥudhayfah's people nagged him for conceding, and rancor began rising between the parties. Qays packed up his clan and left, fighting flared, and Qays's brother, Mālik ibn Zuhayr, was killed. Up to this point, al-Rabīʿ ibn Ziyād, the uncle of Qays and Mālik, had stayed neutral, but the news of Mālik's death so grieved him that he took to arms, singing: 29.7

مَنْ كَانَ مَسْرُورًا بِمَقْتَلِ مَالِكٍ فَلْيَأْتِ نِسْوَتَنَا بِوَجْهِ نَهَارِ
يَجِدِ ٱلنِّسَاءَ حَوَاسِرًا يَنْدُبْنَهُ بِٱلصُّبْحِ قَبْلَ تَبَلُّجِ ٱلْأَسْحَارِ
أَفَبَعْدَ مَقْتَلِ مَالِكِ ٱبْنِ زُهَيْرٍ تَرْجُو ٱلنِّسَاءُ عَوَاقِبَ ٱلْأَطْهَارِ

٨،٢٩ وفي هذه الأبيات معانٍ حسنةٌ لا بأس بالإلماع بذكرها يعني أنّه أخذ ثأر مالك فندبته النساء وكذلك عادة العرب لا تندب القتيل حتّى يُؤْخذ ثاره ولبعض الأدباء اعتراض على قوله بِٱلصُّبْحِ قَبْلَ تَبَلُّجِ ٱلْأَسْحَارِ فإنّ الصبح لا يكون إلّا بعد تبلّجها وأجيب بأقوال منها أنّ المراد بالصبح هاهنا الحقّ الواضح من وصف القتيل الذي هو كالصبح كأنّ النساء يندبنه بأوصافه الحسنة الواضحة والبيت الثالث يستشهد به العروضيّون على دخول الحذف في عروض الطويل كما يدخل في ضربه وهو زوال السبب من مفاعلن المقبوضة ولا يستعمل

٩،٢٩ ثمّ توالت أيّام الحروب وكان أعظمها يوم الهباءة كما تقدّم وسئم قيس من القتال فذهب إلى أخواله كما ذكر في ترجمته في هذا الكتاب وكان الربيع قد مات وأكل بعض القوم بعضًا فقام في الصلح الحارث بن عوف وهرم بن سنان المريّان[1] وحملا الحمالات واجتهدا في إصلاح ذات البين وفي ذلك يقول زهير بن أبي سلمى الشاعر

تَدَارَكْتُمَا عَبْسًا وَذُبْيَانَ بَعْدَمَا تَفَانَوْا وَدَقُّوا بَيْنَهُمْ عِطْرَ مَنْشِمِ

١٠،٢٩ وكانت اليد الطولى للحارث بن عوف أوّلاً وآخرًا والسبب في ذلك أنّ الحارث قال يومًا لخارجة بن سنان أتراني أخطب إلى أحد فيردّني قال نعم قال ومن ذلك قال أوس بن حارثة بن لأم الطائيّ فقال الحارث لغلامه ارحل فركبا حتّى أتيا أوس

١ إ: المريَّين.

You who find joy in Mālik's death,
come witness our women in the early morn!
They stand bareheaded, grieving,
at dawn before the first streaks light the sky.
After the murder of Mālik ibn Zuhayr,
can any women can expect a son like him?[208]

(These lines engage several fine themes worthy of comment. The poet must have composed them after he successfully achieved blood revenge for Mālik, since the women are described as grieving when recalling Mālik's good qualities,[209] and it was the Arabs' custom to only lament the dead in this way after his blood had been requited. Some literary savants take issue with the line "At dawn before the first streaks light the sky," since dawn only begins once streaks of light appear in the sky. One possible rejoinder is that the word "dawn" here implies "clarion truth," and here it is a metaphor for the deceased Mālik—that is, he was true like the dawn, and the women lament him by recounting his shining qualities. Specialists of prosody cite the third line of this poem as an example of the permissibility of elision in the last foot of the first hemistich in the "long" meter, as it appears here in the last foot of the second hemistich whereby the final two-consonant syllable is elided, but this is very rare.[210]) 29.8

The war raged on, with its greatest battle at al-Habā'ah described above.[211] 29.9
Eventually, Qays grew weary of fighting and withdrew to settle with his maternal uncles' clan as mentioned in his biography.[212] Al-Rabīʿ died and the clans consumed each other in violence until peace was brokered by al-Ḥārith ibn ʿAwf and Harim ibn Sinān of the Murrah, who settled the blood payments and strove to resolve the enmity. Their achievement was memorialized by the poet Zuhayr ibn Abī Sulmā:

You both set right the ʿAbs and Dhubyān,
self-annihilators, in war embalmed.[213]

Credit for the peace is fundamentally due to al-Ḥārith ibn ʿAwf, as is 29.10
explained in the following story. Al-Ḥārith once asked Khārijah ibn Sinān, "Do you think any father would turn down my request for his daughter?" Khārijah said, "Yes." "Who would that be?" Khārijah replied, "Aws ibn Ḥārithah ibn La'm of the Ṭayyiʾ." Al-Ḥārith told his slave boy, "We depart!" and al-Ḥārith and Khārijah set out together for Aws's country. They met Aws before his tent,

ابن حارثة في بلاده فوجداه في فناء منزله فلمّا رأى الحارث بن عوف قال مرحبًا بك يا حار قال وبك قال وما حاجتك قال جئتك خاطبًا قال لست هناك

١١،٢٩ فانصرف ولم يكلّمه ودخل أوس إلى امرأته مغضبًا وكانت من عبس فقالت من رجل وقف عليك قال ذاك سيّد العرب الحارث بن عوف قالت فما لك لم تستنزله قال إنّه استحمق قالت وكيف قال جاءني خاطبًا قالت أفتريد أن تزوّج بناتك قال نعم قالت فإذا لم تزوّج سيّد العرب فمن قال قد كان ذاك قالت فتدارك ما كان منك قال بماذا قالت بأن تلحقه فتردّه قال وكيف وقد فرط منّي ما فرط إليه قالت تقول له إنّك لقيتني وأنا مغضب بأمر لم تقدّم فيه قولاً فانصرف ولك عندي ما تحبّ فإنّه سيفعل فركب أوس بن حارثة في أثره

١٢،٢٩ قال خارجة فوالله إنّا لنسير إذ حانت منّي التفاتة فرأيته فأقبلت على الحارث وما يكلّمني غمًّا فقلت له هذا أوس بن حارثة فقال وما تصنع به امض فلمّا رآنا لا نلتفت صاح يا حار اربع عليّ فوقفنا له فكلّمه بذلك الكلام فرجع مسرورًا

١٣،٢٩ فبلغني أنّ أوسًا لمّا دخل منزله قال لزوجته ادعي لي فلانة لأكبر بناته فأتته فقال يا بنيّة هذا الحارث بن عوف سيّد العرب وقد جاءني خاطبًا وقد أردت أن أزوّجك منه فما تقولين قالت لا تفعل قال ولِمَ قالت لأنّي امرأة في وجهي ردّة وفي خلقي بعض العهدة ولست بابنة عمّه فيرعى حقّ رحمي وليس بجارك في البلد فيستحيي منك ولا آمن أن يرى منّي ما يكره فيطلّقني فتكون عليّ وصمة فقال قومي بارك الله فيك

١٤،٢٩ ثمّ دعا الوسطى فأجابته بقريب من هذا الجواب ثمّ دعا الصغرى فقال لها كما قال لأختيها فقالت أنت وذاك فقال إنّي عرضت ذلك على أختيك فأبتاه فقالت

and Aws greeted al-Ḥārith: "May you find here a spacious place, Ḥārith!" "And may it be for you too!" al-Ḥārith replied. Aws then asked him, "What brings you here?" "I have come seeking a bride." "Not around here, you're not."

Al-Ḥārith turned around and left without a further word. Indignant, Aws stormed back into his tent to his wife (who was from the ʿAbs). She asked him, "Who was that man out there?" Aws replied, "That was the lord of the Arabs, al-Ḥārith ibn ʿAwf." "And why did you not invite him to stay?" "Because he wanted something ridiculous." "And what was that?" "He wanted to marry one of my daughters!" Aws's wife asked him, "Are you not looking for grooms for your daughters?" "Of course." "Well, if you are not prepared to marry one of them to the 'lord of the Arabs,' whom exactly do you have in mind?" Aws conceded: "You have a point." His wife told him, "Go and set it right!" "How?" She explained, "Catch up with al-Ḥārith and bring him back!" Aws wondered, "How can I do that, given what I let slip from my tongue?" "Just tell him that I had been arguing with you over something, and don't elaborate. Go now and you will succeed—he will accept." Aws rode out, following their tracks. 29.11

Khārijah tells the rest of the story: 29.12

By God, al-Ḥārith and I were heading off, and I happened to look back, and there I saw Aws. Al-Ḥārith was still very aggrieved and was not speaking to me, so I called to him, "Aws is coming," but al-Ḥārith only said, "What could you want with him? Let's go!"

When Aws saw that we were not going to turn around, he called out, "Ḥārith! Wait for me!" We stopped, and Aws had his talk with al-Ḥārith, who, now very pleased, returned to Aws's camp.

I have been informed that when Aws entered his tent, he asked his wife to summon his eldest daughter. He said to her, "My dear daughter, the lord of the Arabs, al-Ḥārith ibn ʿAwf, is outside. He has come looking for a bride, and I would like to marry you to him. What do you say?" She replied, "Don't do it." "Why not?" "Because my face is not pretty, I have defects, and I'm not his cousin, so I have no uncle there who could uphold my right as his kin, and he isn't under your protection in the territory, so he wouldn't be embarrassed to wrong you. So there is a risk that if he finds something disagreeable in me, he could divorce me, and that would be a disgrace to you." Aws told her, "God bless you, my dear. Return to your tent!" 29.13

He then asked his second daughter, and she said much the same thing. Then he called his youngest and asked her the same question. She responded, 29.14

لكنّي الجميلة وجهًا الصناع يدًا الحسيبة أبًا فإن طلّقني فلا أخلف الله عليه قال بارك الله عليك

١٥،٢٩ ثمّ خرج إلينا فقال قد زوّجتك بهيسة[١] بنت أوس قال قد قبلت فأمر أمّها أن تهيّئها وتصلح من شأنها ثمّ أمر ببيت فضرب له وأنزله إيّاه فلمّا دخلت إليه لبث هنيئةً ثمّ خرج إليّ فقلت أفرغت من شأنك قال لا والله لمّا مددت يدي أليها قالت مه أعند أبي وإخوتي هذا لا يكون

١٦،٢٩ قال فأمر بالرحلة فارتحلنا بها معنا فسرنا ما شاء الله ثمّ قال لي تقدّم فتقدّمت فعدل بها عن الطريق فما لبث أن لحقني فقلت أفرغت قال لا والله قالت لي كما يفعل بالأمة الجليبة والسبيّة الأخيذة لا والله حتّى تنحر الجزر وتذبح الغنم وتدعو العرب وتعمل ما يعمل لمثلي قلت والله لأرى هيئة عقل وإنّي لأرجو أن تكون المرأة النجيبة ثمّ سرنا حتّى دخلنا بلادنا فأحضرنا الإبل والغنم ثمّ دخل إليها وخرج فقلت أفرغت قال لا والله قلت ولم ذاك

١٧،٢٩ قال دخلت عليها أريدها فقلت قد أحضرنا من المال ما ترين قالت والله لقد ذكرت لي من الشرف بما لا أراه فيك قلت كيف قالت أتتفرّغ لنكاح النساء والعرب تقتل بعضها بعضًا يعني عبسًا وذبيان قلت فتقولين ماذا قالت اخرج إلى هؤلاء القوم فأصلح بينهم ثمّ ارجع إلى أهلك فلن يفوتك قلت والله إنّي لأرى عقلاً وهمّةً ولقد قالت قولاً فأخرج بنا فخرجنا حتّى أتينا القوم فمشينا بينهم بالصلح

---

١ إ١، ر١، ب١، إ٢: بهسلة.

"I could do that." Aws was puzzled: "I proposed him to your two older sisters, and they both refused!" She said, "But I have a beautiful face, I'm good with my hands, and I come from an honorable family. If he divorces me, God won't recompense him with anything better." "God bless you!" said Aws.

Aws then came out to al-Ḥārith and me and announced, "I propose to you my daughter Buhaysah."[214] Al-Ḥārith replied, "Agreed!" Aws ordered her mother to prepare her in fine fashion, and he ordered a tent pitched, where he bade al-Ḥārith stay and await his bride. Buhaysah was brought in, but it was only a very short time before al-Ḥārith came out, and I asked him, "Are you done already?" "No," he said. "By God, when I reached out to touch her, she exclaimed, 'Humph! You want to do this in the camp of my father and brothers? It doesn't work that way!'" 29.15

Al-Ḥārith then announced our departure, and we set off with Buhaysah in train and traveled to where God wished us to pause. There al-Ḥārith told me, "Go ahead a little." I did, and he took her off to the side of the track. But it was only a very short time before he caught up with me. "Have you done it now?" I asked. "No," he said. "By God, this time she told me, 'Are you going to do with me as you would an imported slave girl or a ravished captive? No, by God, nothing until the sacrificial camels are slaughtered, the sheep butchered, and all the Arabs are invited. That's what someone like me deserves.'" I told al-Ḥārith, "I see some brains here. I hope she will bear noble sons for you!" 29.16

We traveled on to our own country. Camels and sheep were readied, and he went into the tent with her once more, but again was back out in no time. "Done now?" I asked. "No, by God!" "And why not this time?"

Al-Ḥārith told me, "I entered, and I wanted her. I told her, 'We have produced all the livestock, as you can see.' But she told me, 'By God, I was told you were a nobleman! I don't see any of that in you.' I asked her, 'Why?' And she said, 'How can you find time for sleeping with women while the rest of the Arabs are killing each other?' (She meant the 'Abs and Dhubyān.) I asked her, 'What exactly are you intending?' She told me, 'Go out to those clans and make peace between them. Then come back to your family, and what you want won't escape you.'" 29.17

I told al-Ḥārith, "By God, how smart and resolute! She told you something worthy!"

Al-Ḥārith ordered us to depart, and we met the warring factions. We brought peace between them, and they agreed to end their hostilities by enumerating

فاصطلحوا[١] على أن يحسبوا القتلى من الفريقين ثمّ يؤخذ الفضل ممّن هو عليه فحملنا عنهم الديات فكانت ثلاثة آلاف بعير

وعاش الحارث إلى أن أدرك النبيّ صلّى الله عليه وسلّم ووفد عليه وأسلم وبعث ١٨،٢٩
معه رسول الله صلّى الله عليه وسلّم رجلاً من الأنصار في جواره يدعو قومه إلى الإسلام فقتله رجل من بني ثعلبة فبلغ رسول الله صلّى الله عليه وسلّم الخبر فقال لحسّان قل فيه فقال

يَا حَارِ مَنْ يَغْدِرْ بِذِمَّةِ جَارِهِ ... فِيكُمْ فَإِنَّ مُحَمَّدًا لَا يَغْدِرُ
وَأَمَانَةُ ٱلْمُرِّيِّ حَيْثُ لَقِيتَهُ ... مِثْلُ ٱلزُّجَاجَةِ صَدْعُهَا لَا يُجْبَرُ

فتألّم الحارث لهذا القول وأرسل يعتذّر وبعث بدية الرجل سبعين بعيرًا فقبلها رسول الله صلّى الله عليه وسلّم ومات الحارث عقيب ذلك

ومن شعره قوله ١٩،٢٩

فَإِنْ أَكْبَرْ فَإِنِّي فِي لِدَاتِي ... وَعَاقِبَةُ ٱلْأَصَاغِرِ أَنْ يَشِيبُو
وَمَا كَثَّرْتُ[٢] فَائِدَتِي بِغَدْرٍ ... كَفَانِي فِي ٱلْفَوَائِدِ مَا يَطِيبُ

قوله ولو لم يكن للشاعر غيره لكفاه ٢٠،٢٩

كَمْ مِنْ يَدٍ لَا أُؤَدِّي حَقَّ نِعْمَتِهَا ... عِنْدِي لِمُخْتَبِطٍ طَارٍ وَمِنْ مِنَنِ
إِذْ جَاءَ يَسْعَى إِلَى رَحْلِي لِأُسْعِفَهُ ... أَلَيْسَ قَدْ ظَنَّ بِي خَيْرًا وَلَمْ يَرَنِي[٣]

١ إ١: فما اصطلحوا. ٢ إ١: كررتُ. ٣ قوله ولو . . . ولم يرني: زيادة من بر١، بر٢، ل١، إ٢، إ٦.

the dead on both sides, and whatever deaths did not cancel each other out were paid in blood money. The sum was three thousand camels.

Al-Ḥārith lived into Islamic times. He presented himself to the Prophet (God bless and keep him), converted, and the Prophet (God bless and keep him) sent one of the Allies back with al-Ḥārith to spread the word of Islam among al-Ḥārith's clan. Despite al-Ḥārith's guarantee of safety, the Ally was killed by a man from the Thaʿlabah. News of this reached the Prophet (God bless and keep him), and he commanded his poet Ḥassān: "Compose verses about this." Ḥassān said: **29.18**

Ḥārith! Who among you betrays a covenant of protection?
Muḥammad does not betray his covenants.
The security of a Murrah man, when you entrust him,
is like glass: once broken it cannot be mended.

The poem embarrassed al-Ḥārith, and he sent an apology along with seventy camels as blood payment for the dead man. The Prophet (God bless and keep him) accepted it. Al-Ḥārith died shortly thereafter.

Al-Ḥārith's poetry: **29.19**

I am old, but no older than my contemporaries;
youth's sequel is graying hair.
I have had my gains—and none from deceit;
well-gotten profits are enough for me.

Al-Ḥārith composed the following verses, which on their own are sufficient to rank their composer as a real poet: **29.20**

Were there any hands of needy petitioners desperate for aid,
which I did not fill in full measure from my munificence?
When they come, they hurry to my saddle
before seeing my face; is this not a good reputation?

## وأنّ احتيال هرم لعلقمة وعامر حتّى رضيا كان عن إشارتك ٣٠

١،٣٠ هو هرم بن قطبة بن سيّار الفزاريّ حكم من حكّام العرب يقضي بين السادات فلا يردّ قوله إذا فضّل أحد المنافرين على الآخر ومعنى المنافرة المحاكمة في الحسب والفضل بين الرجلين يقال نافره إذا حاكمه[١] ونفره إذا غلبه

٢،٣٠ وعلقمة هذا هو علقمة بن علاثة بن جعفر من بني صعصعة وعامر هو ابن الطفيل بن مالك بن الأحوص وكلّ منهما سيّد من سادات قومه فارس شاعر وسأورد شيئًا من أخبارهما

٣،٣٠ فأمّا سبب منافرتهما فما حكى أبو عبيدة وغيره قال أوّل ما هاج النفار بين علقمة بن علاثة وعامر بن الطفيل أنّ علقمة كان قاعدًا ذات يوم يبول فبصر به عامر فقال لم أر كاليوم عورة رجل أقبح فقال علقمة إنّها لا تثب على جاراتها ولا تنازل كفّاتها[٢] يعرّض بعامر فقال عامر وما أنت والقروم والله لفرس أبي المسمّى حنوة أذكر من أبيك ولفحل أبي المسمّى الغيهب[٣] أعظم ذكرًا منك فقال علقمة أمّا فرسكم فعارة وأمّا فحلكم فغدرة وكانوا قد استعاروا هذا الفحل من رجل من كلب ليستطرقوه فغلبوا عليه ولكن إن شئت نافرتك فقال عامر قد شئت فقال علقمة والله إنّي لبرّ وإنّك لفاجر وإنّي لوفيّ وإنّك لغادر[٤] فبمَ تفاخرني يا عامر فقال عامر والله إنّي لأنزل منك للقفرة وأنحر للبكرة وأطعن للكثرة[٥] ثمّ تنافروا عن مائة من الإبل يعطيها للحكم من نفّر على صاحبه

٤،٣٠ ثمّ خرج علقمة[٦] بمن معه من بني خالد وخرج عامر بمن معه من بني[٧] مالك وقد أتى عامر بن الطفيل عمّه ملاعب الأسنّة فقال يا عمّاه أعنّي قال يا ابن أخي سبّني قال لا أسبّك وأنت عمّي قال دونك نعليّ فإنّي ربعت فيهما أربعين مرباعًا فاستعن بهما في منفارتك

---

١ إ١: حكّمه. ٢ با١، ل١، ل٢، إ٦، إ٣: كنّاتها؛ بر١: كنانتها. ٣ إ١: الغيث. ٤ إ١: غادر. ٥ بر١، ل١، أز١: للنثرة؛ ل٢: للنزة؛ با١: للثغرة؛ ق١: للثرة. ٦ إ١: على علقمة. ٧ خالد . . . من بني: سقطت من إ١.

**. . . your counsel that led Harim to devise the ruse that placated ʿAlqamah and ʿĀmir . . .** 30

Harim ibn Quṭbah ibn Sayyār of the Fazārah was one of the Arabs' arbiters. The arbiters adjudicated between nobles, determining which was the more honorable, and no one would challenge Harim's rulings. Such arbitration between two men was called *munāfarah*. The verb *nāfara* means "to bring a nobility case against a man," and the verb *nafara* means "to win the arbitration." 30.1

The litigants in the arbitration referred to here were ʿAlqamah, son of ʿUlāthah ibn Jaʿfar of the Ṣaʿṣaʿah, and ʿĀmir, son of al-Ṭufayl ibn Mālik ibn al-Aḥwaṣ. Both were horse warriors, poets, and leading members of their clans, and stories about them follow below.[215] 30.2

Abū ʿUbaydah and other narrators tell the tale of what drove ʿAlqamah and ʿĀmir to seek arbitration to determine who was the more honorable. The dispute arose when ʿĀmir once saw ʿAlqamah squatting to pee, and ʿĀmir quipped: "I've never seen uglier privates than those I see right here!" ʿAlqamah quipped back, "Well, at least it doesn't penetrate the women he is protecting, nor his son's wives"—this was a direct insinuation against ʿĀmir—and ʿĀmir retorted, "Where does your honor rank with the nobles? By God, my father's horse, Basil, is more famous than your father, and my father's stud camel, Night Black, is more famous than you!" ʿAlqamah countered: "Night Black was loaned to you, and Basil was a market leftover." (ʿĀmir's kin used to borrow Night Black to serve as a stud from a man from the Kalb, and it was in this way that Night Black became known as their camel.) ʿAlqamah continued: "If you would like, let's have our nobility judged." ʿĀmir replied, "That I would like." ʿAlqamah exclaimed, "By God, I'm righteous and you commit adultery; I'm trusty and you're full of treachery—how, ʿĀmir, do you count your honor above me?" ʿĀmir followed up: "My camps are more spacious, my giving is more generous, and my fighting is more ferocious than yours!" They set the stake for a contest in honor at one hundred camels, which the arbitrator would award to the winner. 30.3

ʿAlqamah departed with his kin from the Khālid, and ʿĀmir left with his kin from the Mālik clan. When ʿĀmir approached his uncle, Spear Brandisher,[216] and begged, "My uncle! Help me!" Spear Brandisher replied, "My nephew, you revile me!"[217] ʿĀmir responded, "You are my uncle. I can't insult you!" Spear Brandisher said, "Then here are my sandals: I took a king's share from forty war spoils wearing these. Rely on them in your dispute." 30.4

٥،٣٠ وجعلا منافرتهما إلى سفيان بن حرب فلم يقل فيهما شيئًا وكره ذلك لحالهما وحال عشيرتهما فانطلقا إلى هرم بن قطبة حتّى نزلا به فقال هرم لأحكمنّ بينكما ثمّ لأفضلنّ[١] ثمّ لست أثق بواحد منكما فأعطياني موثقًا أطمئنّ إليه أن ترضيا بما أقول وأمرهما بالانصراف ووعدهما ذلك اليوم من قابل فانصرفا حتّى إذا بلغ الأجل خرجا إليه فخرج علقمة ببني الأحوص معهم القباب والجزر والقدور ينحرون في كلّ منزل ويطعمون

٦،٣٠ وجمع عامر بني مالك وخرجوا على الخيل عليهم السلاح فقال رجل من غنيّ يا عامر ما صنعت أخرجت ببني مالك تفاخر بني الأحوص معهم القباب والجزر وليس معك شيء يطعم الناس ما أسوأ ما صنعت فقال عامر لرجلين من بني عمّه أحصيا كلّ شيء مع علقمة من قدر ولقحة وقبّة ففعلا فقال عامر يا بني مالك[٢] إنّما المقاعرة عن أحسابكم فاشخصوا بمثل ما شخصوا ففعلوا وأتوا هرمًا فأقاموا عنده أيّامًا

٧،٣٠ وأرسل إلى عامر فأتي به سرًّا لا يعلم به علقمة فقال يا عامر قد كنت أرى لك رؤيًا وفيك خيرًا وما حبستك هذه الأيّام إلّا لتنصرف عن صاحبك أتفاخر رجلًا لا تفخر أنت وقومك إلّا بآبائه فما الذي أنت به خير منه فقال عامر[٣] نشدتك الله والرحم أن لا[٤] تفضّل عليّ علقمة فوالله إنّ فعلت لا أفلح بعدها هذه ناصيتي جزّها واحتكم في مالي فإن كنت ولا بدّ فاعلًا فسوّ بيني وبينه فقال انصرف فسوف أرى رأيًا فخرج عامر وهو لا يشكّ أنّه ينفّره عليه

٨،٣٠ ثمّ أرسل هرم إلى علقمة سرًّا لا يعلم به عامر فأتاه فقال يا علقمة والله إن كنت لأحسب فيك خيرًا أتفاخر رجلًا هو ابن عمّك في النسب وأبوه أبوك وهو أعظم

١ ثمّ لأفضلنّ: زيادة من ل١. ٢ إ١: يا عامر. ٣ إ١: يا عامر. ٤ سقطت من إ١.

ʿĀmir and ʿAlqamah first approached Abū Sufyān ibn Ḥarb to adjudicate, but Abū Sufyān would not say who was more honorable, as he was wary of their status and the might of their clans. ʿĀmir and ʿAlqamah next traveled to Harim ibn Quṭbah, and when they set down at his camp, he agreed: "I can certainly arbitrate your dispute and declare which of you is the most honorable. But I trust neither of you: give me a pledge so I can be sure you will accept my judgment." He then ordered them to leave and set the contest exactly one year hence. 30.5

The parties left, and when the appointed day approached, ʿAlqamah set out with clan al-Aḥwaṣ in a caravan of high-topped tents, with camels for slaughter and cauldrons, and they served up banquets of fresh camel meat at each place they stopped along the track.

ʿĀmir set off with clan Mālik, and they rode out on their horses, bristling with weapons. When they passed a man of the Ghanī, he was astonished. "ʿĀmir, what are you doing? You parade clan Mālik to vie with clan al-Aḥwaṣ in honor, yet you bring nothing, while clan al-Aḥwaṣ have brought out high-topped tents and camel banquets to feed everyone! You couldn't be going about this any worse!" ʿĀmir ordered two of his kinsmen, "Go and count every pot, camel, and tent ʿAlqamah has with him!" They did, and ʿĀmir said, "Clan Mālik! The contest is about our virtue. Let's not fall short!" The Mālik did as ordered, and they all arrived before Harim, where everyone camped for several days. 30.6

Harim sent for ʿĀmir to come in secret without letting ʿAlqamah know. When ʿĀmir arrived, Harim told him, "ʿĀmir! I have considered your case, and you have much virtue, but after what's transpired these days, I think you should withdraw. How can you trade boasts with ʿAlqamah? You and your clan can only prove your honor by bragging about ʿAlqamah's forefathers, so in what way can you be better than him?"[218] ʿĀmir pleaded, "I beg you for God's mercy! Please do not declare ʿAlqamah more honorable than me—I would never recover. Just cut off my forelock right now and take whatever you want of my possessions! At the very least, can't you say we're equal?" Harim said, "Go. I will decide something." ʿĀmir departed, certain that Harim would declare him the loser. 30.7

Without letting ʿĀmir know, Harim then sent for ʿAlqamah in secret. ʿAlqamah presented himself, and Harim told him, "ʿAlqamah. By God, I see virtue in you, but how can you hope to out-boast a man who is the son of your uncle, who shares the same forefathers as you, and who has more money and receives more 30.8

منك غناءً وأحمد لقاءً فما الذي أنت به خير منه فقال له علقمة ناشدتك الله أن لا[1] تنفّره عليّ وأجابه بما أجابه عامر وانصرف

٩،٣٠ ثمّ إنّ هرمًا أحضر بنيه وقال إنّي قائل غدًا بين هذين الرجلين مقالةً فإذا فعلت ذلك فليطرد بعضكم عشر جزائر فينحرها عن علقمة ويطرد بعضكم عشر جزائر فينحرها عن[2] عامر فرّقوا بين الناس لئلّا يكون لهم جماعة وأصبح هرم فجلس في مجلسه وأقبل الناس وأقبل علقمة وعامر حتّى جلسا وقام لبيد فقال

يَا هَـرِمَ بْنَ ٱلْأَكْرَمَيْنِ مَنْصِبَا    إِنَّكَ قَدْ وَلِيتَ حُكْمًا مُعْجِبَا
فَٱحْكُمْ وَصَوِّبْ رَأْيَ مَنْ تَصَوَّبَا

١٠،٣٠ فقام هرم فقال يا بني جعفر قد تحاكمتما عندي ووالله إنكما كركبتي البعير الآدم يقعان معًا على الأرض وليس منكما أحد إلّا وفيه ما ليس في صاحبه وكلاكما سيّد كريم وعمد بنو هرم إلى الجزر فنحروها وفرّقوا الناس[3] وكره أن يفضّل بينهما وهما ابنا عمّ فيوقع بذلك عداوة بين الحيّين وخرجا من عنده راضيين

١١،٣٠ وقد قيل إنّه قال لهما إنّكما كغربي السيف وكان الأعشى يدّعي أنّهما حكّماه وحكم لعامر على علقمة وله في ذلك قصائد منها التي أوّلها

عَلْقَمَ لَا تُنْسَبْ إِلَى عَامِرِ

١٢،٣٠ ومات علقمة مسلمًا وله وفادتان إحداهما على النبيّ صلّى الله عليه وسلّم أسلم فيها والثانية على عمر بن الخطّاب رضى الله تعالى عنه وجرت له حكاية ظريفة كان علقمة صديقًا لخالد رضي الله تعالى عنه وكان عمر يشبّه بخالد فالتقاه في الليل فقال يا خالد أعزلوك من جيش الشام وهو يظنّ أنّه خالد وكان عمر قد عزل

١ سقطت من إ١.   ٢ علقمة ويطرد . . . فينحرها عن: سقطت من إ١.   ٣ إ٢: وفرقوا على الناس؛ ق٢: وفرقوا بين الناس.

praise than you? How can you claim greater honor than him?" 'Alqamah replied, "I beg you, for the sake of God, please do not declare him more honorable than me!" Harim responded as he did to 'Āmir, and 'Alqamah departed.

Harim next gathered his sons and told them, "I will make a statement regarding these two men tomorrow. When I do that, one of you must drive ten camels and slaughter them by 'Alqamah's camp, and another must drive ten camels and slaughter them by 'Āmir's camp. Ensure that the people are kept apart." **30.9**

In the morning, Harim sat in his assembly, with 'Alqamah, 'Āmir, and everyone in attendance. When they were seated, Labīd rose and sang:

> Doubly ennobled Harim,
> entrusted with an extraordinary judgment:
> Judge! And bring shame upon the loser![219]

Harim rose and spoke: "Clan Ja'far! Both of your noble lines have sought my ruling. By God, you are like two riders astride one shining white camel. You cover the same ground. Whatever one of you lacks is found in the other; you are both noble leaders." Harim's sons then made for the camels and slaughtered them as planned, thereby dispersing the people. **30.10**

Harim did not want to declare in favor of one of the men since they were cousins, and to make a preference would sow seeds of discord between the tribes. Both left his camp satisfied.

Others report that Harim worded his pronouncement: "You are like the two edges of a sword." **30.11**

Al-A'shā claimed that he himself adjudicated between 'Āmir and 'Alqamah, and found in favor of 'Āmir; he mentions this in several poems, including one that begins:

> 'Alqamah, don't claim lineage from 'Āmir!

As for 'Alqamah, he lived into the Islamic period and died a Muslim. He formally presented himself twice in Medina: once to the Prophet (God bless and keep him) when 'Alqamah converted to Islam, and on the second occasion to the Caliph 'Umar ibn al-Khaṭṭāb (God be pleased with him). There is an amusing anecdote about the second visit. 'Alqamah ran into the Caliph 'Umar on the street in Medina at night: 'Umar looked similar to Khālid ibn al-Walīd (God be pleased with him), and Khālid was a close friend of **30.12**

خالدًا عن جيش الشام غيظًا منه بسبب قتل مالك بن نويرة كما تقدّم فقال عمر نعم فقال علقمة والله ما هو إلّا نفاسة عليك وحسدًا لك فقال عمر فما عندك معونة على ذلك فقال معاذ الله إنّ لعمر علينا سمعًا وطاعة وما نخرج عليه ولا نخالفه وانصرفا فلمّا أصبح دخل علقمة على عمر وعنده خالد فقال عمر ويه يا علقمة أنت القائل البارحة لخالد ما قلت فقال علقمة لخالد أفعلتها فقال والله ما لقيتك البارحة ولا رأيتك إلّا في هذه الساعة ففطن علقمة وعرف أنّه إنّما لقي عمرًا وظنّه خالدًا فقال يا أمير المؤمنين ما سمعت إلّا خيرًا قال أجل ثمّ ولّاه حوران وخرج إليها فقصده[1] الحطيئة الشاعر مادحًا له فمات علقمة قبل أن يصل إليه فقال

لَعَمْرِي لَنِعْمَ ٱلْمَرْءُ مِنْ آلِ جَعْفَرٍ    بِحَوْرَانَ أَمْسَى عُلِّقَتْهُ ٱلْحَبَائِلُ
وَمَا كَانَ بَيْنِي لَوْ لَقِيتُكَ سَالِمًا    وَبَيْنَ ٱلْغِنَى إِلَّا لَيَالٍ قَلَائِلُ

فلمّا وصل وجد علقمة قد أوصى له بسهم من ماله

فأمّا عامر فهو ابن الطفيل وكان شجّاعًا مشهورًا شاعرًا مقدّمًا قال أبو عبيدة ١٣،٣٠ اجتمع العكاظيّون على أنّ فرسان العرب ثلاثة ففارس تميم عتيبة[2] بن الحارث بن شهاب أحد بني ثعلبة[3] صيّاد الفرسان وفارس ربيعة بسطام بن قيس وفارس قيس عامر بن الطفيل

وفد على رسول الله صلّى الله عليه وسلّم ومعه أربد بن قيس مع قوم من بني ١٤،٣٠ عامر فقال يا محمّد إن أسلمت ما لي قال رسول الله صلّى الله عليه وسلّم لك ما للمسلمين وعليك ما عليهم قال لا إلّا أن تجعل لي الأمر من بعدك قال ليس لقومك

١ سقطت من إ. ٢ إ: ربيعة. ٣ إ: تغلب.

ʿAlqamah, so ʿAlqamah, thinking he had met Khālid, said, "Khālid! Have you really been sacked from the Syrian army?" (ʿUmar had just relieved Khālid from command in retribution, since ʿUmar had been harboring resentment against Khālid for killing Mālik ibn Nuwayrah and marrying his wife, as noted above.)[220] ʿUmar, not giving anything away, responded to ʿAlqamah, "Yes." ʿAlqamah said, "By God, it was only out of jealousy that he deemed you unworthy!" ʿUmar asked, "Can you be of any help in this?" But ʿAlqamah balked: "I seek refuge in God! We owe ʿUmar the duty to hear and obey! We can neither dissent nor resist." The two went their separate ways, and in the morning ʿAlqamah entered before ʿUmar, and Khālid was also in attendance. ʿUmar said, "ʿAlqamah, too bad about what you said to Khālid last night!" ʿAlqamah asked Khālid, "What have you done?" Khālid answered, "By God, I didn't see you yesterday; I haven't seen you before just now!" ʿAlqamah then understood everything: he had confused ʿUmar for Khālid the night before. He then addressed the caliph: "Commander of the Faithful! Wasn't everything I said good?" "Indeed!" ʿUmar replied, and appointed him governor of Ḥawrān. ʿAlqamah departed to take up his post. The poet al-Ḥuṭayʾah traveled there to praise him, but by the time al-Ḥuṭayʾah arrived, ʿAlqamah had died, and al-Ḥuṭayʾah sang:

> By my life! What a man from clan Jaʿfar,
> at Ḥawrān he found his end awaiting.
> Only a few nights stood between me
> and meeting him, and finding wealth!

When al-Ḥuṭayʾah arrived, he found that ʿAlqamah had left him a share of his estate.

ʿĀmir was the son of al-Ṭufayl, and a famous warrior and accomplished poet. Abū ʿUbaydah reports that the men of ʿUkāẓ agree that there were three great Arab horse warriors: one from the Tamīm, ʿUtaybah ibn al-Ḥārith ibn Shihāb, the "Hunter Horseman" of clan Thaʿlabah; another from the Rabīʿah, Bisṭām ibn Qays; and the third from the Qays, ʿĀmir ibn al-Ṭufayl.[221] 30.13

ʿĀmir formally presented himself, along with Arbad ibn Qays and a delegation of clan ʿĀmir, to the Prophet (God bless and keep him), and he asked, "Muḥammad, what's in it for me if I convert?" The Prophet (God bless and keep him) replied, "You receive the same rights and obligations as every Muslim." ʿĀmir said, "No. I will only convert if you appoint me your successor." "That 30.14

قال فتجعل لي الوبر ولك المدر قال لا ولكن أجعل لك أعنّة الخيل قال أو ليست لي ثمّ قال يا محمّد والله لأملأها عليك خيلاً ورجلاً ولأربطنّ بكلّ نخلة فرسًا وولّى فقال رسول الله صلّى الله عليه وسلّم اللّهمّ اكفني عامرًا وأربد واهد بني عامر وأغن الإسلام عن عامر

١٥،٣٠ ثمّ انصرفوا حتّى إذا كانوا ببعض الطريق بعث الله تعالى على عامر بن الطفيل الطاعون في عنقه فاندلع لسانه في فيه كضرع الشاة فمال إلى بيت امرأة من سلول وجعل يقول غدّة كغدّة البعير وموت في بيت سلوليّة ثمّ مات فواراه أصحابه وجعلوا على قبره أنصابًا ميلاً في ميل وجعلوه حمًى فقيل إنّ بعض ولده رأى ذلك فيما بعد فقال لقد ضيّقتم على أبي والله

١٦،٣٠ أمّا أربد فأرسل الله عليه صاعقة قتلته وفي ذلك يقول أخوه[1]

أَخْشَى عَلَى أَرْبَدَ ٱلْحُتُوفَ وَلَا    أَرْهَبُ نَوْءَ ٱلسِّمَاكِ وَٱلْأَسَدِ[2]

١٧،٣٠ ولعامر بن الطفيل شعر جيّد سريّ فمن ذلك قصيدته الرائيّة التي ذكر فيها عور عينه حين غدر به بعض أصحابه وطعنه فيها وهرب وذلك أنّ مسهر بن يزيد كان فارسًا شريفًا فجنى جناية على قومه فلحق ببني عامر فشهد يوم فيف الريح[3] مع عامر بن الطفيل وكان عامر يتعهّد[4] القوم يومئذ فيقول يا فلان ما رأيتك ويا فلان ما صنعت فيقول الرجل الذي أبلى انظر إلى سيفي وما فيه وإنّ مسهرًا أقبل في تلك الهيئة فقال يا أبا عليّ يعني عامر بن الطفيل انظر إلى ما صنعت اليوم وإلى سنان رمحي حتّى إذا أقبل عليه عامر أي ضربه[5] وجأه بالرمح في وجهه ففلق الوجنة وانشقّت عين عامر ففقأها وترك مسهر الرمح في عينه وضرب فرسه ولحق بقومه

١ إ: أبُو لبيد.  ٢ أرهب . . . الأسد: سقطت من إ.  ٣ فشهد . . . الريح: بياض في إ.  ٤ إ: متعهّد.
٥ زيدت من إ فقط.

is not to be for your people."[222] 'Āmir then suggested, "Appoint me over the Bedouins, and you can run the settlements." The Prophet replied, "No. But I can appoint you in charge of the cavalry." But 'Āmir said, "Don't I already control those?" He then added, "Muḥammad, by God, I could summon so many soldiers and cavalry against you that I'd need every palm tree here to tether them!" He turned and left, and the Prophet (God bless and keep him) prayed, "Almighty God! Spare me from 'Āmir and Arbad! Guide clan 'Āmir to Islam! Make Islam rise above 'Āmir!"

The delegation departed, and when they had progressed a little down the track, the Exalted God sent a pox on 'Āmir in his neck; his tongue lolled out like a sheep's udder, and he took refuge in the tent of a women from the Salūl. He began muttering, "What's worse: pestilential goiters or death in a Salūlī woman's tent?"[223] and there he died. His companions buried him and erected memorial stones on his grave for a mile in each direction, which they then declared a sanctuary. It is said that afterward one of 'Āmir's children saw the markers and moaned, "By God, this is too narrow for my father!" 30.15

As for Arbad, he was killed by a thunderclap sent by God. Arbad's brother references this in a poem: 30.16

Though I dreaded the descent of death upon Arbad,
I never feared the storms brought by Pisces and Leo.[224]

'Āmir composed excellent, mellifluous poetry, including his *r*-rhyming poem[225] in which he mentions that he lost an eye from an act of treachery committed by one of his companions, who then fled. The companion's name was Mushir ibn Yazīd, a noble horse warrior. Mushir had perpetrated a crime among his own kin and sought refuge with clan 'Āmir, and fought for them at the Battle of Fayf al-Rīḥ under the command of 'Āmir. In the aftermath of the battle, 'Āmir inspected each of his warriors, challenging them: "You, I didn't see you out there! What did you do?" Warriors who had fought would respond, "Come, look at my sword!" When Mushir came up, 'Āmir put the same question to him, and Mushir responded, "Hey 'Āmir, look at my spear to see what I did today!" When 'Āmir approached to inspect it, Mushir jabbed him in the face, splitting open 'Āmir's cheek and putting out his eye. Leaving the spear hanging from 'Āmir's blinded eye, Mushir kicked his horse and bolted off back to his own kin. 30.17

قالوا وإنّما دعا مسهرًا إلى الغدر بعامر أنّه كان يراه يصنع بقومه هذا فقال هذا ١٨،٣٠
والله مبير[١] قومه فأراد قتله وإراحتهم منه فقال عامر

لَقَدْ عَلِمَتْ عُلْيَا هَوَازِنَ أَنَّنِي    أَنَا ٱلْفَارِسُ ٱلْحَامِي حَقِيقَةَ جَعْفَرِ
وَقَدْ عَلِمَ ٱلْمَزْنُوقُ أَنِّيَ أَكُرُّهُ    عَلَى جَمْعِهِمْ كَرَّ ٱلْمَنِيحِ ٱلْمُشَهَّرِ
أَلَسْتَ تَرَى أَرْمَاحَهُمْ فِيَّ شُرَّعًا    وَأَنْتَ حَصَانٌ مَاجِدُ ٱلْعِرْقِ فَٱصْبِرِ
لَعَمْرِي وَمَا عَمْرِي بِهَيِّنٍ    لَقَدْ شَانَ حُرَّ ٱلْوَجْهِ طَعْنَةُ مُسْهِرِ
فَبِئْسَ ٱلْفَتَى إِنْ كُنْتُ أَعْوَرَ عَاقِرًا    جَبَانًا فَمَا عُذْرِي لَدَى كُلِّ مَحْضَرِ

ومن ذلك قوله ١٩،٣٠

وَكَمْ مُظْهِرٍ بُغْضًا لَنَا وَدَّ أَنَّنَا    إِذَا مَا ٱلْتَقَيْنَا كَانَ أَخْفَى ٱلَّذِي أَبْدَى
مَطَاعِيمُ فِي ٱللَّأْوَا مَطَاعِينُ فِي ٱلْوَغَى    شَمَائِلُنَا تُتْلَى وَأَيْمَانُنَا تَنْدَى

وقوله ٢٠،٣٠

وَصَاحِبِ صِدْقٍ قَدْ أَخَذْتُ بِضَبْعِهِ    وَقُلْتُ لَهُ وَازِرْ أَخَاكَ فَآزَرَ
ضَرُوبٌ بِنَصْلِ ٱلسَّيْفِ خَلْفَ صِحَابِهِ    إِذَا ٱغْبَرَّ أَوْلَادُ ٱلْمَقَارِيفِ أَسْفَرَا[٢]

---

١ إ١: يَسُر.   ٢ إ١: الماريف اصفرا.

They say Mushir's treachery was prompted by his disgust at seeing ʿĀmir's mistreatment of his own men. Mushir exclaimed, "This man will wipe out his own kin, by God!"[226] and he attempted the murder to rid them of ʿĀmir once and for all. 30.18

In response, ʿĀmir composed his *r*-rhyming poem:

The nobles of Hawāzin all know
  I am the horseman, protector of the Jaʿfar.
My horse knows too—on him I charge and countercharge
  the ranks. He's the blank gaming arrow thrown in every round.[227]
See their spears leveled at me?
You are a noble steed—be steady!
By my life—and I don't sell it cheap—
Mushir's thrust has marred my face.
  I lost an eye, but not my mettle.
I need make no excuse—in the assemblies I will still stand brave.

ʿĀmir's poetry: 30.19

How many people who have shown us hate
  regret it on the day we battle them.
We give feasts at home, we give thrusts in battle;
our left hands strike, our right hands give.

ʿĀmir's poetry: 30.20

Another honest man, I took him by the arm
and cried, "Stand by your brother!" and he fought
  furiously at the blade point, shielding his companions:
  when vile dogs are left sprawling in the dust, he emerges
    unvanquished.

**وجوابه لعمر وقد سأله عن أيّهما كان يُنفّر وقع عن إشارتك[1]** ٣١

١،٣١ يعني هرم بن قطبة المقدّم ذكره وذلك أنّه كان أسلم وكان عمر بن الخطّاب رضي الله تعالى عنه يقرّبه[2] فقال يا أبا عمرو أيّهما كان ينفّر عندك يعني علقمة وعامرًا ومن كان الأفضل منهما فقال يا أمير المؤمنين لو قلت الآن فيهما كلمة لعادت جذعة يعني الحرب بين الحيّين فأعجب بهذا القول منه فقال بحقّ حكّمتك العرب

**وأنّ الحجّاج تقلّد ولاية العراق بجدّك** ٣٢

١،٣٢ الجدّ الحظّ والجِدّ[3] الاجتهاد في الأمور وكلا الوجهين يصلح هاهنا

٢،٣٢ وهذا المذكور هو الحجّاج بن يوسف بن أبي عقيل الثقفيّ السفّاك المشهور ولد سنة إحدى وأربعين ونشأ بالطائف وزعم بعض الرواة أنّه كان أوّل أمره معلّمًا للصبيان ويُسمّى كليبًا وفيه يقول الشاعر

أَيَنْسَى كُلَيْبٌ زَمَانَ ٱلْهِزَالِ وَتَعْلِيمَهُ سُورَةَ ٱلْكَوْثَرِ
رَغِيفٌ لَهُ فَلْكَةٌ مَا تُرَى وَآخَرُ كَٱلْقَمَرِ ٱلْأَزْهَرِ

يشير إلى خبز المعلّمين فإنّه مختلف في الصغر والكبر على قدر بيوت الصبيان

٣،٣٢ ثمّ صار دبّاغًا ويستدلّ على ذلك بحكايته مع كعب الأشقريّ أيّام ولايته وذلك أنّ المهلّب بن أبي صفرة لمّا طال قتال الأزارقة في ولاية الحجّاج كتب إليه يستبطئه في مناجزة الأزارقة ويعجّزه فقال المهلّب لرسوله قل له إنّ الشاهد يرى ما لا يرى الغائب وقام كعب الأشقريّ وكان من جند المهلّب فأنشد

---

١ إ١: إرادتك؛ با١: بعد مشورتك. ٢ برا وإ٣: يحبّه. ٣ سقطت من إ١.

**... your wish that dictated Harim's answer when 'Umar asked him about the winner.** 31

After the aforementioned Harim ibn Quṭbah[228] had converted to Islam, he became a close confidant of the Caliph 'Umar ibn al-Khaṭṭāb (God be pleased with him), and one day 'Umar asked him, "Harim, which of those two contestants actually won"—that is, 'Alqamah or 'Āmir—"and who was the more honorable?" Harim replied, "Commander of the Faithful! If I were to say now, the sparks would be rekindled." (In other words, there would be war between the two tribes.) 'Umar was impressed by his response and said, "The Arabs were right to make you their adjudicator." 31.1

**Al-Ḥajjāj needed your determination to govern Iraq ...** 32

You can read the above line either as "your determination" (*jidd*) or "your good fortune" (*jadd*); either suits the meaning. 32.1

The infamous al-Ḥajjāj ibn Yūsuf ibn Abī 'Aqīl of the Thaqīf, "the Bloody," was born in al-Ṭā'if in 41 [661], and there he was raised. Some narrators allege that he first worked as a teacher for young boys, and in those days was nicknamed "Little Dog"; as attested by a poet: 32.2

Does "Little Dog" remember the lean years
when he taught elementary Qur'an?[229]
In return for a little round loaf,
or perchance a big one, fulsome like the moon!

(Elementary teachers used to be paid in bread, the amount of which depended on the means of the children's households.)

They say al-Ḥajjāj next became a tanner. They deduce this from a poem Ka'b of the Ashqar composed in the days when al-Ḥajjāj was governor of Iraq. At that time, al-Ḥajjāj's lieutenant, al-Muhallab ibn Abī Ṣufrah, was engaged in a very protracted war against the rebellious Blues,[230] and al-Ḥajjāj had sent a missive to al-Muhallab, chiding him for his delay in confronting the Blues and insinuating that he was incompetent. Al-Muhallab told al-Ḥajjāj's messenger: "Tell him that those present see what those absent do not." Ka'b of the Ashqar, who was one of al-Muhallab's soldiers, then rose and addressed the messenger: 32.3

إِنَّ ٱبْنَ يُوسُفَ غَرَّهُ مِنْ غَزْوِكُمْ خَفَضُ ٱلْمَقَامِ بِجَانِبِ ٱلْأَمْصَارِ
لَوْ شَاهَدَ ٱلصَّفَّيْنِ حِينَ تَلَاقَيَا ضَاقَتْ عَلَيْهِ رَحِيبَةُ[1] ٱلْأَقْطَارِ
وَرَأَى مُعَاوَدَةَ ٱلدَّبَاغِ غَنِيمَةً أَيَّامَ كَانَ مُحَالِفَ ٱلْإِقْتَارِ

٤،٣٢ فبلغت أبياته الحجّاج فكتب إلى المهلّب بإشخاص كعب فأعلم[2] كعبًا بذلك وأوفده من ليلته إلى عبد الملك بن مروان وكتب إليه يستوهبه منه فقدم كعب برسالة المهلّب إلى عبد الملك فاستنطقه واستنشده فأعجبه ما سمع منه وكتب إلى الحجّاج يقسم عليه أن يعفو عنه فلمّا دخل كعب على الحجّاج قال إيّه يا كعب

وَرَأَى مُعَاوَدَةَ ٱلدَّبَاغِ غَنِيمَةً

فقال أيّها الأمير والله لوددت في بعض ما شاهدت من تلك الحروب وما يوردناه المهلّب من خطرها أن أنجو منها وأكون حجّامًا أو حائكًا فضحك الحجّاج وقال أولى لك لو لا قسم أمير المؤمنين لما نفعك ما أسمع فالحق بصاحبك

٥،٣٢ وبعض الرواة ينكر هذه الأقوال ويقول هذه من أكاذيب الشعراء ويزعم أنّ الحجّاج لم يزل في كنف أبيه وكان أبوه نبيلاً جليل القدر إلى أن اتّصل يعني الحجّاج بروح بن زنباع ثمّ بعبد الملك بن مروان ولم يزل يترقّى إلى أن ولّي العراق والمشرق وعظم سلطانه

٦،٣٢ وأوّل ما عرف من شهامته وجوره أنّ أباه خرج من مصر يريد عبد الملك بن مروان ومعه ابنه الحجّاج فأقبل سليم بن عمرو القاضي وكان من أورع الناس وأتقاهم فقام إليه يوسف فسلّم عليه وقال إنّي أريد أن آتي أمير المؤمنين فإن كانت لك حاجة فأعلمني قال نعم حاجتي أن تسأله أن يعزلني عن القضاء فقال يوسف والله لوددت بقضاة المسلمين كلّهم مثلك فكيف أسأله هذا ثمّ انصرف فقال ابنه

١ إ١: رحبة. ٢ إ١: فارسل.

Al-Ḥajjāj's sumptuous repose in the towns
misleads his opinion of our war.
Let him come to the front lines and see them collide,
and feel the world close in on all sides;
Then, wouldn't flight back to the tannery seem a fine outcome,
back to those days when he was thoroughly skint.

The poem worked its way to al-Ḥajjāj, and he wrote again to al-Muhallab, summoning Kaʿb. Muhallab let Kaʿb know what was likely in store for him, and dispatched him by night—not to al-Ḥajjāj, but to the Caliph ʿAbd al-Malik ibn Marwān with a letter asking the caliph for a favor. Kaʿb presented al-Muhallab's letter, and ʿAbd al-Malik questioned Kaʿb and asked him to recite poetry. ʿAbd al-Malik took a liking to Kaʿb and wrote to al-Ḥajjāj ordering him to swear to pardon Kaʿb. Kaʿb then traveled to al-Ḥajjāj's court. When he entered, al-Ḥajjāj addressed him: "What's this all about, Kaʿb: 32.4

Then, wouldn't flight back to the tannery seem a fine outcome?"

Kaʿb replied, "Commander! In the midst of the furor of some of those battles through which al-Muhallab led us, I found myself wishing I was a cupper[231] or a tailor!" Al-Ḥajjāj laughed, but said, "To Hell with you. It was not what you just said that saved you, but the caliph's order. Now, get back to the front."

Some narrators reject all these stories about al-Ḥajjāj's origins, considering them to be the fabrications of poets, and they allege instead that al-Ḥajjāj lived under the care of his father, a nobleman of means, until al-Ḥajjāj served with Rawḥ ibn Zinbāʿ, and then Caliph ʿAbd al-Malik ibn Marwān, after which he steadily rose in the ranks until he wielded great authority as governor of Iraq and the East. 32.5

The first reported incident in which al-Ḥajjāj manifested his forceful and tyrannical character occurred during his childhood, when his father, Yūsuf, took him along on travels from Egypt to visit the Caliph ʿAbd al-Malik.[232] Before they departed Egypt, the judge Sulaym ibn ʿItr,[233] a most devout man, presented himself to them, and al-Ḥajjāj's father rose in greeting and said, "I intend to visit the caliph, so tell me if there is any message you would like me to deliver." Sulaym replied, "Yes, there is. Tell him to discharge me from my judicial post." Al-Ḥajjāj's father replied, "By God, I should be so grateful if all the judges in Islam were like you! How can I possibly petition your dismissal?" 32.6

الحجّاج من هذا الذي قمت إليه فقال يا بنيّ هذا سليم بن عمرو قاضي أهل مصر وقاصّهم فقال يغفر الله لك يا أبت أنت ابن أبي عقيل تقوم إلى رجل من كندة أو تجيب[١] فقال يا بنيّ إنّي أرى الناس ما يرحمون إلّا بهذا وأشباهه فقال والله ما يفسد الناس على أمير المؤمنين إلّا هذا وأشباهه يقعدون وتقعد إليهم أحداث الناس[٢] فيذكرون سيرة أبي بكر وعمر فيخرجون على أمير المؤمنين والله لو صفا لي هذا الأمر لسألت أمير المؤمنين أن يجعل لي السبيل فأقتل هذا وأشباهه فقال أبوه والله يا بنيّ إنّي لأظنّ أنّ الله تعالى خلقك شقيًّا

٧،٣٢ وأوّل ما أعجب عبد الملك بن مروان منه أنّه كان قد اتّصل بروح بن زنباع وصار من جملة شرطته وكان روح بمنزلة نائب عبد الملك ثمّ إنّ عبد الملك توجّه إلى الجزيرة لقتال زفر بن الحارث عندما عصى عليه بقرقسيا فأمر روح بن زنباع جماعة من أصحاب شرطته يحثّون المتأخّرين من أهل العسكر في كلّ منزلة وكان الحجّاج من جملتهم فكان يجتهد في ذلك إلى أن مرّ يومًا بعد رحيل العسكر بجماعة من خواصّ غلمان روح في خيمة يأكلون فأمرهم بالرحيل فسخروا منه إذلالًا بمحلّهم ومحلّ سيّدهم وقالوا له انزل كل واسكت فضرب بسيفه أطناب الخيمة فسقطت عليهم وأطلق فيها نارًا وأحرقت أثاثهم فقبضوا عليه وأتوا به إلى روح وسمع عبد الملك الخبر فطلبه وقال من فعل هذا بغلمان روح فقال أنت يا أمير المؤمنين أمرتنا بالجهاد في ما ولّيتنا[٣] ففعلنا ما أمرت وبهذه الفعلة يرتدع من بقي من أهل العسكر وما على أمير المؤمنين أن يعوّض[٤] عليهم ما ذهب وقد تمّت الحرمة وتمّ المراد فأعجب منه عبد الملك وقال إنّ شرطيّكم لجلد ثمّ أقرّه على ما هو عليه فأوصى روحًا به

٨،٣٢ ولمّا طال القتال والحصار بينه وبين زفر بن الحارث أرسل عبد الملك رجاء بن حيوة وجماعة منهم الحجّاج إلى زفر بكتاب يدعوه إلى الصلح فأتوا بالكتاب وقد

---

١ إ، ل٣، بر٢: تحيب؛ با١: يجاب. ٢ سقطت من إ. ٣ إ: ولينا. ٤ إ: يعرض.

Sulaym departed, and al-Ḥājjāj asked his father, "Whom did you rise to greet?" "My son, that was Sulaym ibn ʿItr, the chief judge and preacher of Egypt." Al-Ḥajjāj replied, "Father! God forgive you! You're the son of Abū ʿAqīl and you stood up for a Kindite!" (Or he said, "a Tujībī.")[234] "My son! It is men like him who preserve the people's faith." Al-Ḥajjāj countered, "No, by God. It is men like him who corrupt people's opinion of the Commander of the Faithful. This sort of man abstains from fighting, and fools follow suit. They preach about the lives of the ideal caliphs Abū Bakr and ʿUmar, and then everyone rebels against our Commander of the Faithful. By God, if I had charge of this, I'd ask the Commander of the Faithful to let me kill this man and all his ilk!" "By God, my son, I sense that God created you a wretch."

The Caliph ʿAbd al-Malik first took a liking to al-Ḥajjāj when al-Ḥajjāj was serving as a special security constable under Rawḥ ibn Zinbāʿ. Rawḥ had the rank of ʿAbd al-Malik's deputy, and when ʿAbd al-Malik advanced his forces to the Jazīrah to combat Zufar ibn al-Ḥārith's rebellion in Circesium, Rawḥ ordered his constables to round up all the laggards of any rank and send them to join ʿAbd al-Malik. Al-Ḥajjāj, selected as one of those constables, worked tirelessly to fulfill the order. At one point, after the general departure had been completed, al-Ḥajjāj came upon a group of Rawḥ's personal retainers dining in a tent. He ordered them to join the march, but they ridiculed him, asserting their superior rank and privileged standing with their master. They told him, "Sit down, eat, and shut up!" At that, al-Ḥajjāj slashed their tent cords with his sword, and as the whole structure collapsed upon the retainers, al-Ḥajjāj set it on fire. Their possessions burned, and they arrested al-Ḥajjāj, dragging him off to Rawḥ. But ʿAbd al-Malik heard about the incident and summoned al-Ḥajjāj for questioning. "Who would do such a thing to Rawḥ's retainers?" Al-Ḥajjāj responded, "Commander of the Faithful! I did as you ordered, and exerted myself in performing my duty. This action will prevent anyone else in the camp from tarrying. There is no need for the Commander of the Faithful to reimburse those retainers for what they have lost—their goods were no longer inviolable. The intent of your orders has been carried out." ʿAbd al-Malik liked this and remarked, "This constable here is tough!" ʿAbd al-Malik reinstated al-Ḥajjāj and advised Rawḥ to take good care of him. 32.7

ʿAbd al-Malik's assault on Zufar ibn al-Ḥārith developed into a siege, and as it dragged on, ʿAbd al-Malik entrusted Rajāʾ ibn Ḥaywah and a group including al-Ḥajjāj to deliver an entreaty for peace. The group arrived with their letter 32.8

حضرت الصلاة فقام رجاء فصلّى مع زفر وصلّى الحجّاج وحده فسئل عن ذلك فقال لا أصلّي مع منافق خارج على أمير المؤمنين وعن طاعته فسمع عبد الملك ذلك فزاد عجبًا بالحجّاج ورفع قدره[1] فولّاه بلدًا تُسمّى تبالة وهي أوّل ما ولي فخرج إليها فلمّا قرب سأل عنها فقيل إنّها وراء هذه الأكمة فقال أفّ لبلد[2] تسترها أكمة ثمّ رجع فقيل في المثل أهون من تبالة على الحجّاج

٩،٣٢ ثمّ قدم على عبد الملك ملازمًا خدمته فلمّا فرغ عبد الملك من قتاله مصعب ابن الزبير ورجع إلى الشام قال من لابن الزبير يعني عبد الله القائم بالحجاز وندب الناس إلى قتاله فقام الحجّاج فقال أنا يا أمير المؤمنين له فأعرض عنه ثمّ أعاد المقال فقال الحجّاج ابعثني يا أمير المؤمنين إليه وقد رأيت في المنام كأنّي أخذته فسلخته[3] فبعثه إليه وجهّزه معه جيشًا فقدم إلى مكّة ونصب المنجنيق على الكعبة وفعل ما فعل حتّى قتل ابن الزبير وصفت الخلافة لعبد الملك

١٠،٣٢ فسُرّ باجتهاده وأرسل إليه عهده على مكّة والمدينة والطائف فاستخفّ أهل الحرمين وأهانهم ثمّ كتب إلى عبد الملك يقول إنّي قد حزت الحجاز بشمالي وبقيت يميني فارغة يعرّض بالعراق فبعث إليه عهده بالعراق وهذه أحد الأقوال في سبب ولايته العراق

١١،٣٢ والقول الآخر أنّه وفد[4] على عبد الملك ومعه إبراهيم بن محمّد بن[5] طلحة بن عبد الله التيميّ وكان من رجال قريش علمًا ونبلًا وزهدًا ومهابة وكان الحجّاج مسخّرًا له لا يترك من إجلاله شيئًا فلمّا قدما على عبد الملك أذن للحجّاج في الدخول فلمّا دخل سلّم ولم يبدأ بشيء إلى أن قال يا أمير المؤمنين قدمت عليك برجل من أهل الحجاز ليس له نظير في كمال المروءة والديانة وحسن المذهب والطاعة مع القرابة ووجوب الحقّ[6] فقال ومن هو قال إبراهيم بن طلحة التيميّ فليفعل أمير المؤمنين ما يفعله بأمثاله فقال عبد الملك ذكّرتنا حقًّا واجبًا ورحمًا قريبة ثمّ أذن له

١ في إ١: يده. ٢ إ١، بر١، با١: اموت ببلدة. ٣ إ١: فنكحته. ٤ إ١، بر١، با١، إ٦: ثم وفد. ٥ محمد بن: سقطت من كلّ النسخ. ٦ وحسن المذهب . . . ووجوب الحق: زيادة من إ٦.

during prayer time, so Rajā' rose and prayed with Zufar. Al-Ḥajjāj, however, prayed apart. He was asked about this and explained, "I'll never pray with a rebellious hypocrite who defies the Commander of the Faithful."

'Abd al-Malik heard about this and liked al-Ḥajjāj even more. Al-Ḥajjāj's star ascended. 'Abd al-Malik appointed him governor of Tabālah, the first governorship of al-Ḥajjāj's career, but when he neared Tabālah, he asked where it was and they told him, "Behind this hill!" Al-Ḥajjāj was unimpressed. "What sort of town can be concealed by a single hill?" He turned back. Hence the proverb: "More contemptible than Tabālah was to al-Ḥajjāj."

Al-Ḥajjāj returned to 'Abd al-Malik's retinue. After 'Abd al-Malik defeated 32.9
Muṣ'ab ibn al-Zubayr and returned to Syria, he addressed his men, "Who will take on Ibn al-Zubayr?" (he meant 'Abd Allāh ibn al-Zubayr, the rival caliph in the Hijaz), and 'Abd al-Malik urged his men to war. Al-Ḥajjāj spoke up: "Commander of the Faithful! I can do it!" 'Abd al-Malik turned away from al-Ḥajjāj and asked the question a second time. Again, al-Ḥajjāj spoke up: "Send me, Commander of the Faithful! I dreamt that I captured Ibn al-Zubayr and flayed him!" 'Abd al-Malik consented and sent al-Ḥajjāj with an army to attack Mecca. Al-Hajjāj deployed siege engines against the Kaaba and did what he did, killing Ibn al-Zubayr and leaving the caliphate for 'Abd al-Malik alone.

The caliph was very pleased with al-Ḥajjāj's efforts and formally appointed 32.10
him governor over Mecca, Medina, and al-Ṭā'if. Al-Ḥajjāj belittled and humiliated the residents of the Holy Sanctums, and he wrote to 'Abd al-Malik: "My left hand grips the Hijaz, but the right is empty" (insinuating his desire for Iraq), and 'Abd al-Malik appointed him its governor. This is one version explaining how al-Ḥajjāj came to govern Iraq.

An alternative version goes as follows: Al-Ḥajjāj once traveled to 'Abd 32.11
al-Malik's court, bringing with him Ibrāhīm ibn Muḥammad ibn Ṭalḥah ibn 'Ubyad Allāh of the Taym,[235] one of the most learned, noble, ascetic, and revered men of the Quraysh. Al-Ḥajjāj was deferential to Ibrāhīm and held him in awe. Upon their arrival, al-Ḥajjāj was admitted to the caliph's presence first. He offered his salutations, and then straightaway said, "Commander of the Faithful! I have brought you a peerless native of the Hijaz, a man of perfect virtue and faith, an adherent of the proper creed and allegiance, combining a noble lineage and probity." The caliph asked, "Who is he?" "Ibrāhīm ibn Ṭalḥah of clan Taym. May the Commander of the Faithful treat him according to his station." 'Abd al-Malik replied, "You have reminded us of the duties we owe him and his rights of kinship," and Ibrāhīm was admitted.

١٢،٣٢ فلمّا دخل قرّبه وأدناه ثمّ قال له إنّ أبا محمّد ذكرنا ما نعرفك به من الفضل وحسن المذهب فلا تدع من حاجة إلّا ذكرتها فقال إبراهيم إنّ أولى الأمور أن يفتتح به الحوائج ما كان لله فيه رضى ولحقّ رسول الله صلّى الله عليه وسلّم أداء ولجماعة المسلمين نصيحة قال وما هو قال لا يمكن القول إلّا وأنا خال فأخلني قال أو دون أبي محمّد قال نعم

١٣،٣٢ فأشار عبد الملك إلى الحجّاج وإلى من كان حاضرًا فخرج وقال قل قال يا أمير المؤمنين إنّك عهدت إلى الحجّاج مع تغطرسه وتعجرفه وبعده عن الحقّ وركونه إلى الباطل فوليّته الحرمين وفيهما من أبناء المهاجرين والأنصار من قد علمت يسومهم الخسف و يقودهم[1] بالعنف ويطؤهم بطغام أهل الشام ورعاع لا رويّة لهم في إقامة حقّ ولا في إزاحة باطل ثمّ تظنّ أنّ ذلك ينجيك من عذاب الله فكيف بك إذا جاء بك محمّد صلّى الله عليه وسلّم غدًا للخصومة بين يدي الله تعالى أمّا والله إنّك لا تنجو هناك إلّا بحجّة تضمن لك النجاةَ فاتقّ[2] لنفسك أو دع

١٤،٣٢ وكان عبد الملك متّكئًا فاستوى جالسًا وقال كذبت ومنت فيما جئت به ولقد ظنّ بك الحجّاج ظنًّا لم يجده فيك وربّما ظنّ الخير بغير[3] أهله قم فأنت المائن الحاسد

١٥،٣٢ قال إبراهيم فقمت ووالله ما أبصر شيئًا فلمّا جاوزت الستر لحقني لاحق فقال للحاجب امنع هذا من الخروج وأذن للحجّاج فدخل فلبثا مليًّا وما أشكّ أنّهما في أمري ثمّ خرج الإذن لي فدخلت فلمّا كُشف الستر إذا أنا بالحجّاج خارجًا فاعتنقني وقبّل ما بين عينيّ وقال إذا جزى الله المتواخيين بفضل تواصلهما فجزاك الله أفضل الجزاء أمّا والله لئن بقيت لأرفعنّ ناظريك ولأتبعنّ الرجال غبار قدميك قال فقلت في نفسي إنّه ليسخر بي فلمّا وصلت إلى عبد الملك أدنى مجلسي كما فعل في الأوّل ثمّ قال يا ابن طلحة هل[4] أعلمت الحجّاج بما جرى أوشاركك أحد

---

١ إ١، بر١: يقصدهم. ٢ إ١، بر١، أز١، إ٣: ابق. ٣ بغير: زيادة من إ٤ وإ٧. ٤ إ١: قد.

The caliph permitted Ibrāhīm to approach the throne, and then addressed him: "Al-Ḥajjāj reminded us about your virtue and impeccable faith, so please tell us everything that is on your mind." Ibrāhīm replied, "The most deserving matter to petition first is that which pleases God, upholds the right of His Prophet (God bless and keep him), and guides all Muslims." "And what would that be?" Ibrāhīm replied, "It is a matter that can only be discussed in complete privacy." The caliph asked, "Even without al-Ḥajjāj?" "Yes." 32.12

'Abd al-Malik motioned to al-Ḥajjāj and all those present to leave. Then he said, "Speak." Ibrāhīm said, "Commander of the Faithful! Despite al-Ḥajjāj's arrogance, haughtiness, perversity, and malfeasance, you have seen fit to appoint him governor over God's Holy Sanctums, home of the descendants of the Emigrants and Allies. You know how this man abuses them and piles humiliation upon disgrace: he threatens them with violence and has them trampled underfoot by brutes and ingrates from Syria who have no consideration for maintaining right or forbidding wrong. And you suppose that this man can save you from God's torment? What will you do when Muḥammad (God bless and keep him) challenges you upon the morn before the Hands of the Exalted God? By God, then only a truly just plea can protect you. Save yourself, or let it be as it is!" 32.13

'Abd al-Malik had been reclining. When Ibrāhīm finished, he sat up: "You lie! You came bearing base calumny! Al-Ḥajjāj was deluded in his opinion of you; perhaps he trusts the wrong people. Take your lying, envious presence and begone!" 32.14

Ibrāhīm himself tells the rest of the story: I rose. By God, everything was a blur, but when I passed the curtain, someone caught up with me and told the chamberlain, "Prevent him from leaving!" Al-Ḥajjāj was then ushered in and stayed with the caliph for quite some time; I was certain they were discussing me. Eventually I was summoned, and as I entered, the curtain was pulled back, and there was al-Ḥajjāj, on his way out. He embraced me, kissed my forehead, and said, "God rewards two men of opposite natures via His grace in making them associate with each other. May God reward you with the best recompense. By God, for so long as I live I will enjoin you to keep your head raised, and I will order men to march in the dust of your footprints!" I said to myself, "He's surely mocking me!" and when I presented myself before the caliph, he again bade me approach the throne. He then spoke: "Ibrāhīm, did you inform al-Ḥajjāj of what happened or did you collude with anyone in 32.15

في نصيحتك فقلت لا والله ولا أعلم أحدًا أظهر يدًا عندي من الحجّاج ولو كنت محابيًا أحدًا بديني لكان هو ولكنّي آثرت الله ورسوله والمسلمين فقال قد علمت صدق مقالتك ولو آثرت الدنيا لكان لك في الحجّاج أمل وقد عزلته عن الحرمين لما كرهت ولايته عليهما وأخبرته أنّك أنت الذي استنزلتني له[١] عنهما استصغارًا للولاية وولّيته العراق لما هنالك من الأمور التي لا يدحضها إلّا أمثاله وأعلمته أنّك أنت سألتني له في ذلك لعظمها[٢] وإنّما قلت له ذلك ليؤدّي ما يلزمه من ذمامك فاخرج معه فإنّك غير ذامّ لصحبته مع يدك عنده

١٦،٣٢ فخرجت مع الحجّاج فأكرمني أضعاف إكرامه واستدللت على مكارم عبد الملك وأخلاقه واعترافه بالحقّ وتلطّفه بالأمور

وهذا أحد الأقوال في سبب ولاية الحجّاج للعراق

١٧،٣٢ ثمّ دخل الكوفة وخطب خطبته المشهورة وأخاف القوم وأثبت مهابته في قلوب أهل عمله وتحكّم في رقابهم وكان القاسم بن سلّام[٣] يقول قاتل الله أهل الكوفة أين قبائلهم وعشائرهم وأهل الأنفة منهم وأين تجبّرهم[٤] قتلوا عليًّا وطعنوا الحسين وقاتلوا المختار وعجزوا عن قتل هذا الملعون الدميم الصورة وقد جاءهم في اثني عشر راكبًا وهم في مائة ألف ولكن ظهر تصديق قول أمير المؤمنين عليّ رضي الله تعالى عنه اللّهمّ سلّط عليهم الغلام الثقفيّ

١٨،٣٢ ثمّ أقام الحجّاج بالعراق يرهب ويفتك حتّى استوثقت له الأمور ثمّ خرج عليه عبد الرحمن بن الأشعث بأهل العراق فأمدّه عبد الملك بأهل الشام فكانوا شيعته واستمرّت بينه وبين ابن[٥] الأشعث الوقائع حتّى هزمه الحجّاج بعد ثمانين وقعة في ستّة أشهر بدير الجماجم وكان مع ابن الأشعث أكثر من مائتي ألف فلمّا هُزموا قال الحجّاج لأصحابه اتركوهم فليتبدّدوا ولا تتبعوهم ثمّ نادى مناديه من رجع فهو

١ إ١: استنزلته. ٢ إ١: أعلمتني لعظمهما. ٣ إ١: القايم بنُ السلاطم. ٤ إ١: مجيرهم. ٥ سقطت من إ١.

your advice?" "No, by God! I know no one kinder to me than al-Ḥajjāj, and if I would be partial to anyone, it would be to him; but I preferred what is good for God, His Prophet, and the Muslims." ʿAbd al-Malik replied, "I realized the honesty of your words: if you preferred worldly things, al-Ḥajjāj would have fulfilled your hopes. I have relieved him of his governorship of the Holy Sanctums for the reasons of your complaint. However, I informed him that you asked me to relieve him because you consider it too trifling a post for a man like him, and I appointed him over Iraq. Only a man of his mettle can quell the situation there, but I informed him that you petitioned me to appoint him on account of the prominence of the post. I explained it to him in this way so that he would continue to uphold the protection he owes you, so leave with him now, and rebuke not his companionship, for he is obliged to you."

I departed with al-Ḥajjāj, and he treated me even more generously than 32.16
before. The experience also revealed to me the extent of ʿAbd al-Malik's noble manners, his recognition of what is right, and his subtle ways of managing affairs.

This is one of several stories about how al-Ḥajjāj came to govern Iraq.

Al-Ḥajjāj then entered Kufa and gave his famous oration, terrifying the 32.17
population, instilling awe in the hearts of his subjects, and asserting absolute control over their lives. Al-Qāsim ibn Sallām used to say, "My goodness, you Kufans! What became of your tribes, your clans, your pride, and the might you used to assert? You killed ʿAlī, stabbed al-Ḥusayn, and fought al-Mukhtār, yet you, in your myriads, were impotent to kill that accursed, repulsive man when he turned up with a dozen horsemen! This indeed is the fruition of the Caliph ʿAlī's (Exalted God be pleased with him) invocation: 'Good God! Subject the Kufans to the boy from the Thaqīf!'"[236]

Al-Ḥajjāj ruled Iraq with brutal terror and lethal force until he felt cer- 32.18
tain that matters were under control. But then ʿAbd al-Raḥmān ibn al-Ashʿath roused the Iraqis into revolt, and, with a force of over two hundred thousand, waged war on al-Ḥajjāj, who could only rely on Syrian soldiers dispatched by ʿAbd al-Malik as reinforcements. After eighty clashes over a six-month period, al-Ḥajjāj finally defeated Ibn al-Ashʿath at Dayr al-Jamājim, but announced to his own men: "Desist from fighting! Let the survivors disperse and do not give chase." Then he had his herald announce: "Immunity for all who return." Al-Ḥajjāj entered Kufa, and as the remnants of the defeated came in to swear their allegiance, al-Ḥajjāj ordered each of them, "You must swear

آمن ودخل الكوفة وجاء الناس من المنهزمين يبايعونه فكان يقول لمن جاء يبايعه لتشهد على نفسك بالكفر وخروجك عن الجماعة ثمّ تب فإن شهد وإلّا قتله

١٩،٣٢ فأتاه رجل من خثعم فقال اشهد على نفسك بالكفر فقال إن كنت عبدت ربّي ثمانين سنة ثمّ شهدت على نفسي بالكفر لبئس[١] العبد أنا والله ما بقي من عمري إلّا ظمء حمار وإنّي أنتظر الموت صباحًا ومساء فأمر به فضربت عنقه وقدّم بعده شيخ آخر فقال الحجّاج ما أظنّ الشيخ يشهد على نفسه بالكفر فقال يا حجّاج أتخادعني[٢] أنت عن نفسي أنا أعرف بها منك وإنّي لأكفر من فرعون وهامان وضحك الحجّاج وخلّى سبيله

٢٠،٣٢ وكان في الحجّاج خلال حسنة امتاز بها في وقته وهي الكرم والفصاحة والدهاء وجوره[٣] والحلم في بعض الأوقات

٢١،٣٢ وأمّا كرمه فحُكي أنّه لمّا دخل المدينة[٤] قال لأهلها أتيناكم وقد غاض الماء لكثرة النوائب فاعذرونا فقال رجل لا عذر الله من يعذرك وأنت أمير المصرين وابن عظيم القريتين فقال صدقت واقترض أموال كثيرة من هناك من التجّار وكان شيئًا عظيمًا ففرّقها

٢٢،٣٢ ولمّا ولّي العراق كان يطعم في كلّ يوم على ألف مائدة يجمّع على كلّ مائدة عشرة أنفس ويطاف به في محفّة على أيدي الرجال ليشرف على القوم ويقول يا أهل الشام اهشموا الخبز لئلّا يعاد عليكم وكان يرسل الرسل إلى الناس لحضور الطعام فكثر[٥] عليه ذلك فقال أيّها الناس رسولي إليكم الشمس إذا طلعت فهي رسولي إليكم فاحضروا للغداء وإذا غربت فاحضروا للعشاء فكانوا يفعلون ذلك واستقلّ الناس يومًا فقال ما بال الناس قد قلّوا فقال رجل أيّها الأمير إنّك أغنيت الناس في بيوتهم عن الحضور إلى مائدتك فأعجبه ذلك وقال له اجلس بارك الله عليك

١ إ١: ليس. ٢ إ١، إ٢، إ٣، با٢، أز١: أخادعي. ٣ وجوره: زيادة من بر١، با١، إ٦، ل١، ر٢. ٤ إ١، إ٢، بر١، با١، ق٢، ل١، إ٦، ر٢: مكّة. ٥ إ١: كبر.

and confess that you were a nonbeliever, that your revolt was a rejection of Muslim community, and that you have now repented." Any who refused the oath were killed.

A man of the Khath'am was brought in and told, "Confess that you were a nonbeliever!" He replied, "What a miserable believer I would be if I confessed to nonbelief after having worshipped God for eighty years! By God, there's but a drop of life left in me, and I expect death's call any morning or night." Al-Ḥajjāj ordered him executed on the spot. Next, another old man was brought forward. Al-Ḥajjāj observed, "I can't see this grandad confessing to nonbelief either," but the man replied, "Hajjāj! Do you cheat me out of my life? I know myself better than you, and I most certainly am an unbeliever—more unbelieving than Pharaoh and his High Priest!"[237] Al-Ḥajjāj laughed and set him free. 32.19

Alongside his despotism, al-Ḥajjāj had some fine qualities: generosity, eloquence, shrewdness, and even, at times, equanimity. 32.20

As for al-Ḥajjāj's generosity, they relate that when he entered Mecca he announced, "We arrive after many tribulations! Pardon us, for our pockets are empty." But when someone cried, "May God not pardon anyone who pardons you! You are commander of the 'Two Towns' and son of the 'Two Villages,'"[238] al-Ḥajjāj conceded, "You're right," and he borrowed a vast sum of money from merchants to distribute among the people. 32.21

Also, as soon as al-Ḥajjāj became governor of Iraq, he ordered that every day one thousand tables, each laid for ten persons, be set up, and he moved around them carried upon a sedan, inspecting and ordering his soldiers to serve: "Syrians! Break all the bread! Let not a crumb remain!" Initially, he sent out messengers to invite the populace, but since there were so many, al-Ḥajjāj eventually just made a general proclamation: "People! Treat the sun as my messenger to you: when it rises, come for breakfast, and when it sets, come for dinner!" This arrangement stuck. One day, al-Ḥajjāj noted the gathering had decreased and asked, "Why have so few people come?" One attendee said, "Commander! It is you who so enriched the people in their homes that they no longer need your tables!" Al-Ḥajjāj was pleased and said, "Take a seat, God bless you!" 32.22

٢٣،٣٢ وأمّا دهاؤه فحكى عبيد الله بن زياد بن[1] ظبيان قاتل مصعب بن الزبير قال كنت يومًا واقفًا على باب الحجّاج فإذا به قد خرج وحده وكانت القائلة وما بالباب أحد فوقع في نفسي أن أقتله فنظر إليّ وقال لقيت يزيد بن أبي مسلم يعني كاتبه قلت لا قال القه فإنّ عهدك على الريّ معه فطمعت وكففت عنه وتوجّهت إلى يزيد فلم يكن معه عهد ولا شيء من ذلك وإنّما قال الحجّاج ذلك حذرًا واشتغالاً لي عمّا أردته

٢٤،٣٢ وبنى هو وعبد الملك في بعض المساجد بابين فوقعت صاعقة أحرقت باب عبد الملك فداخله حسد للحجّاج فكتب إليه الحجّاج إنّما مثل أمير المؤمنين ومثلي كمثل ابني آدم ﴿إِذْ قَرَّبَا قُرْبَانًا فَتُقُبِّلَ مِنْ أَحَدِهِمَا وَلَمْ يُتَقَبَّلْ مِنَ ٱلْآخَرِ﴾

٢٥،٣٢ ودخل يومًا على عبد الملك فأكل معه ثمّ دعاه[2] للشرب فقال يا أمير المؤمنين أعفني فإنّي أنهى أهل عملي عنه وأكره أن أخالف قول العبد الصالح حين قال ﴿وَمَآ أُرِيدُ أَنْ أُخَالِفَكُمْ إِلَىٰ مَآ أَنْهَىٰكُمْ عَنْهُ﴾ فقال عبد الملك إنّه نبيذ الرّمان يشهّي الطعام ويزيد في الباه فقال الحجّاج أمّا كونه يشهّي الطعام فوالله لوددت أنّ هذه الأكلة تكفيني إلى أن أموت وأمّا كونه يزيد في الباه فحسب الرجل أن يصرع في الشهر مرّة

٢٦،٣٢ وصعد يومًا المنبر فأراد أن يختبر طاعة الناس له فقال ألا إنّ الحجّاج كافر فلم يردّ عليه أحد شيئًا[3] فقال بللّات والعزّى والبغلة الشهباء ويوم الأربعاء

٢٧،٣٢ ودخل عليه قاتل الحسين رضي الله تعالى عنه فقال له أنت قاتل الحسين قال نعم قال كيف قتلته قال دسرته بالرمح دسرًا[4] ثمّ هبرته بالسيف هبرًا ووكلت أمر رأسه إلى امرئ غير وكل[5] فقال الحجّاج له أمّا ولله لا تجتمعان في الجنّة وكان قصده

١ زياد بن: سقطت من النسخ. ٢ إ١، بر١: ثم أمر فدعاه. ٣ إ١ وإ٢: عليه حديثا. ٤ إ١: دبرته بالرمح دبرًا.
٥ إ١: امرٍ رد غير.

Among the stories told about al-Ḥajjāj's shrewdness is one told by 'Ubayd Allāh ibn Ziyād ibn Ẓabyān, the warrior who killed Muṣ'ab ibn al-Zubayr: One day, in the hot part of the afternoon when nobody was around, I was standing at al-Ḥajjāj's door. Al-Ḥajjāj came out alone, and a feeling came over me to murder him. When he saw me, he said, "Did you find Yazīd ibn Abī Muslim?" (Yazīd was al-Ḥajjāj's secretary.) I said, "No." "Go find him—he has the papers for your promotion to the governorship of Rayy." I liked the sound of that, so I let al-Ḥajjāj go on his way, and I went straight to Yazīd. But he had no commission for me at all, and I realized that al-Ḥajjāj had concocted this ruse on the spot to divert me from my intention. 32.23

Al-Ḥajjāj and 'Abd al-Malik each funded a door for a mosque, but a lightning strike incinerated 'Abd al-Malik's door. Envy began to work upon the caliph, so al-Hajjāj wrote to him: "This event concerning the Commander of the Faithful and me resembles the parable of Adam's two sons: «When they both presented an offering, it was accepted from one of them and not from the other.»"[239] 32.24

On one of al-Ḥajjāj's visits to 'Abd al-Malik's court, the caliph called for wine at dinner, but al-Ḥajjāj demurred: "Commander of the Faithful. Do excuse me: I forbid my subjects from drinking wine, and I'd hate to contradict the Righteous Believer's words: «I have no desire to do, out of opposition to you, what I am asking you not to do.»"[240] 'Abd al-Malik said, "It's only pomegranate wine: it makes food tastier, and it's good for the libido too!" But al-Ḥajjāj replied, "In terms of appetite, by God, my hope is that your food is enough for me until I die, and in terms of libido, once a month is enough for a man to be overcome by that!" 32.25

Al-Ḥajjāj once ascended the pulpit wanting to test his subjects' obedience. He began by saying, "Is al-Ḥajjāj not an unbeliever?" No one said a word, so he continued: "I swear by the goddesses al-Lāt and al-'Uzzā, by the Gray Mule and by Holy Wednesday!"[241] 32.26

One day al-Ḥusayn's (God be pleased with him) killer had an audience with al-Ḥajjāj. Al-Ḥajjāj asked him, "Are you the one who killed al-Ḥusayn?" The man replied, "Yes, sir!" Al-Ḥajjāj asked, "How did you kill him?" "First I skewered him on my spear, then I cleaved him with my sword, and I entrusted his head to a good man." To this, all al-Ḥajjāj said was, "Well, by God, you won't be meeting each other in Paradise." Al-Ḥajjāj's response was intended to please everyone: the Iraqis left thinking: "By God, al-Ḥajjāj spoke the 32.27

رضا أهل العراق أهل الشام فخرج أهل العراق يقولون صدق الحجّاج لا يجتمع والله ابن رسول الله صلّى الله عليه وسلّم وقاتله في الجنّة وخرج أهل الشام يقولون صدق الأمير لا يجتمع من شقّ عصا المسلمين وخالف أمير المؤمنين هو وقاتله في طاعة الله في الجنّة

٢٨،٣٢ وأمّا جوره وسفكه الدماء فقد اشتهر أنّه قتل أكثر من مائة ألف صبرًا آخرهم سعيد بن جبير رضي الله تعالى عنه ومات في حبسه أكثر من عشرين ألفًا لم يجب على أحد منهم حدّ وكان حبسه بغير سقف ولا مستراح والناس بعضهم على بعض ومرّ عليهم يومًا فاستغاثوا به فقال ﴿ٱخْسَـُٔوا۟ فِيهَا وَلَا تُكَلِّمُونِ﴾

٢٩،٣٢ وقال أبو عمرو بن العلاء كنت أقرأ ﴿إِلَّا مَنِ ٱغْتَرَفَ غُرْفَةًۢ بِيَدِهِۦ﴾ بالفتح وبلغ الحجّاج وكان يقرأ بالضمّ فطلبني فهربت إلى واد بصنعاء فأقمت زمانًا فسمعت أعرابيًّا يقول لآخر قد مات الحجّاج فقال الأعرابيّ

رُبَّمَا تَجْزَعُ ٱلنُّفُوسُ مِنَ ٱلْأَمْرِ لَهَا فَرْجَةٌ كَحَلِّ ٱلْعِقَالِ

فلم أدر بأيّ شيء[1] كنت أشدّ فرحًا بموت الحجّاج أم بسماع البيت أستشهد به على القراءة

٣٠،٣٢ وحكى بعض القرّاء قال قرأ الحجّاج في سورة هود ﴿إِنَّهُۥ عَمَلٌ غَيْرُ صَٰلِحٍ﴾ فلم يدر أيقول ﴿عَمِلَ﴾ أم ﴿عَمَلٌ﴾ فقال ائتوني بقارئ فأتي بي وقد قام من مجلسه فحبست ونسيني الحجّاج حتّى عرض السجن بعد ستّة أشهر فلمّا انتهى إليّ قال فيما حُبست قلت في ابن نوح فضحك وأطلقني

٣١،٣٢ وحُكي أنّه أراد سفرًا فصعد المنبر فقال إنّني قد عزمت على السفر وخلّفت عليكم ابني محمّدًا وأوصيته بخلاف ما أوصى به العبد الصالح أن لا يُتقبّل من محسنكم ولا

١ إ١: ما بي من.

truth: the son of the Prophet of God (God bless and keep him) will not meet his killer in Paradise," while the Syrians left thinking: "The commander spoke the truth: in Paradise, the one who split the staff of Muslim unity and rebelled against the Commander of the Faithful will not meet the man who, in obedience to God, killed him."

As for al-Ḥajjāj's tyranny and murder, it is well known that he executed more than one hundred thousand captives, the last of whom was Saʿīd ibn Jubayr (Exalted God be pleased with him), while another twenty thousand who were not charged with any capital offence died in his prisons. Al-Ḥajjāj's prisons had neither roof nor any form of shelter, and prisoners were piled on top of one another. One day, as al-Ḥajjāj passed by the prisoners and they implored mercy, he replied, "«Begone and do not address Me.»"[242] **32.28**

Abū ʿAmr ibn al-ʿAlāʾ says: Once, when I read the Qurʾanic verse: «one who sips only a handful of it,»[243] I pronounced the word"handfal" with an "a,"[244] and al-Ḥajjāj heard about it. He pronounced it "handful," with a "u," and summoned me. I fled to a wadi near Sanaa, where I stayed for some time. One day, I overheard a Bedouin saying to his companion, "Al-Ḥajjāj died," and the Bedouin sang a verse: **32.29**

> Sometimes the soul is burdened by a matter,
> but ralief[245] is as easy as undoing a hobbling rope.

I didn't know what made me happier at that moment: hearing that al-Ḥajjāj was dead, or hearing a line of poetry that corroborated my Qurʾan reading!

A Qurʾan reciter tells: Al-Ḥajjāj was reading a verse from Surah Hūd: «he was unrighteous in his conduct,»[246] and he didn't know if the word "conduct" should be read as a noun or as a verb.[247] Al-Ḥajjāj ordered, "Summon a Qurʾan reciter!" and they brought me in, but by the time I arrived, al-Ḥajjāj had left the assembly, and they ended up putting me in prison. Al-Ḥajjāj forgot about me until he reviewed the inmates six months later. When he turned to me and asked, "What did you do?" I replied, "I was imprisoned on account of Noah's son."[248] Al-Ḥajjāj laughed and released me. **32.30**

It is told that once, before leaving on a journey, al-Ḥajjāj mounted the pulpit and announced, "I am set on departure, and I have appointed my son Muḥammad over you. I have instructed him to follow the opposite of the advice given by the Righteous Believer: I told him to spurn the righteous among you, **32.31**

يتجاوز[1] عن مسيئكم ألا وإنّي أعلم أنكم تقولون لا أحسن الله له الصحابة ألا وإنّي معجّل لكم الجواب فأقول لا أحسن الله عليكم الخلافة

٣٢،٣٢ وحدّث رجل قال هربت من الحجّاج حتّى مررت بقرية فأجد كلبًا نائمًا في ظلّ جبّ فقلت في نفسي ليتني كنت هذا الكلب وكنت مستريحًا من خوف الحجّاج ومررت ثمّ عدت من ساعتي فأجد الكلب مقتولاً فسألت عنه فقيل جاء أمر الحجّاج بقتل الكلاب فعجبت من عموم جوره

٣٣،٣٢ وأمّا حلمه فحكي أنّه خرج يومًا إلى ظاهر الكوفة منفردًا فرأى رجلاً فقال ما تقول في أميركم قال الحجّاج قال نعم قال زعموا أنّه من ثمود وكفى بسوء سيرته شرًّا فعليه لعنة الله فقال الحجّاج أتعرفني قال لا قال أنا الحجّاج قال الرجل أتعرفني أيّها الأمير قال لا قال أنا مولى بني عامر أجنّ في كلّ شهر ثلاثة أيّام هذا اليوم أشدّها فضحك الحجّاج وصفح عنه

٣٤،٣٢ وأتي بقوم من أصحاب ابن الأشعث فأمر بضرب أعناقهم فقام رجل فقال أيّها الأمير إنّ لي عندك يدًا قال وما هي قال شتمك رجل بحضرة ابن الأشعث فرددت عنك قال ومن يشهد لك بهذا قال هذا وأشار إلى رجل منهم فقال صدق أيّها الأمير فقال ما منعك أن تفعل كما فعل قال بغضي لك فقال الحجّاج أطلقوا هذا ليده عندنا وهذا لصدقه في مثل هذا الوقت

٣٥،٣٢ وقال يومًا لأحمد بن يوسف فكّرت في أمرك فوجدت دمك ومالك لي حلالاً فقال أيّها الأمير أشدّ ما في القضيّة أنّ هذا الرأي بعد الفكر فضحك وعفا عنه

٣٦،٣٢ وكان عنده يومًا بعض ندمائه وقد أدركته سنة فعطس النديم عطسة منكرة ففزع الحجّاج وقام مغضبًا وقال ما أردت بهذه العطسة إلّا أن تروّعني فقال أيّها الأمير هذه والله عادتي فقال والله إن لم تأتني بشاهد على ذلك وإلّا ضربت عنقك

---

١ إ١: يعفو.

and not to forgive the errant.[249] I know full well that you will say, 'May God not grant him good companionship,' and I promptly give you my reply: May God not grant you the caliphate!"

A man once narrated: I fled from al-Ḥajjāj, and when I passed a village I saw a dog sleeping in the shade of a well. I said to myself, "If only I could be that dog, free from fear of al-Ḥajjāj!" I continued on my way. Shortly after, I returned to the spot, and there I saw the dog, dead. I asked and was told, "An order came in from al-Ḥajjāj to kill all dogs." I was astonished by the breadth of his tyranny. 32.32

As for al-Ḥajjāj's equanimity, there is a story that he once went walking alone about the outskirts of al-Kufah and questioned a passerby: "What do you think of your governor?" The man asked, "You mean al-Ḥajjāj?" "Yes," replied al-Ḥajjāj. The man said, "They allege that he is a survivor from Thamūd,[250] but whatever the case, his horrid behavior is evil enough on its own. God curse him!" Al-Ḥajjāj then asked him, "Do you know who I am?" "No," he confessed. "I'm al-Hajjāj!" The man then asked, "Do you know who I am?" Al-Ḥajjāj admitted, "No." The man told him, "I'm one of the affiliates of the 'Āmir. I am possessed three times a month, and today my madness is at its peak!" Al-Ḥajjāj laughed and walked on his way. 32.33

A troop of prisoners from Ibn al-Ash'ath's army was presented to al-Ḥajjāj, and he ordered all of them executed. But one interjected, "Commander! You owe me a favor!" "And why is that?" The man explained, "Once, in the presence of Ibn al-Ash'ath, a man cursed you and I stood up for you." Al-Ḥajjāj demanded, "Can anyone here vouch for you?" The man pointed to another, who said, "It's true, Commander." Al-Ḥajjāj questioned that witness: "What prevented you from standing up for me then too?" The man replied, "My hatred for you." Al-Ḥajjāj ordered, "Free the first man, as we owe him a favor, and free the second for his honesty in a moment like this." 32.34

Al-Ḥajjāj once told Aḥmad ibn Yūsuf,[251] "I have deliberated upon your case, and I've decided that I can lawfully spill your blood and seize your property." Aḥmad replied, "Commander! What's worst is that you came to this decision after deliberation!" Al-Ḥajjāj laughed and pardoned him. 32.35

One day during an assembly, al-Ḥajjāj was snoozing when one of his confidants let out an unholy sneeze, and al-Ḥajjāj shot up angrily: "The only reason for that sneeze was to frighten me!" The man protested: "Commander! By God, that's how I sneeze." Al-Ḥajjāj said, "By God, you will bring me a witness to 32.36

فخرج الرجل فوجد بعض أصحابه فقصّ عليه الأمر فقال أنا أشهد لك فدخلا على الحجّاج فقال لصاحبه بِمَ تشهد فقال أيّها الأمير أشهد أنّه عطس يومًا عطسة وقع ضرسه منها فضحك الحجّاج حتّى استلقى وقال حسبك وأمر بهما فأخرجا وكان قليل الضحك إلّا أن يغلب على نفسه

وأمّا فصاحته وبلاغته فمنها خطبته المطوّلة المشهورة المذكورة في الكتب ٣٧،٣٢
بأيدي الناس وفصوله الموجزة في المكاتبات وعلى المنابر قال مالك بن دينار والله لربّما رأيت الحجّاج على المنبر ويذكر حسن صنيعه إلى أهل العراق وسوء صنيعهم له حتّى يخيّل لي أنّه مظلوم

وقال الحسن البصريّ لقد وقذتني كلمة سمعتها من الحجّاج يقول على هذه ٣٨،٣٢
الأعواد إن امرؤًا ذهبت ساعة من عمره في غير ما خُلق له لجدير أن تطول حسرته

وخطب يومًا فقال أيّها الناس اقدعوا هذه الأنفس فإنّها أسأل شيء إذا ٣٩،٣٢
أعطيت وأعطى شيء إذا سُئلت فرحم الله امرؤًا جعل لنفسه خطامًا وزمامًا فقادها بخطامها إلى طاعة الله وعطفها بزمامها عن معصية الله فإنّي رأيت الصبر على محارم الله أيسر من الصبر على عذابه

وبلغه وفاة أخيه وابنه فصعد المنبر وقال محمّدَانِ في يوم أمّا والله ما كنت ٤٠،٣٢
أحبّ أن يكونا معي في الدنيا لما أرجو لهما من ثواب الله وايم الله ليوشكنّ الباقي منّا ومنكم أن يفنى والجديد أن يبلى وستدال الأرض منّا فتأكل من لحومنا وتشرب من دمائنا كما أكلنا من ثمارها وشربنا من مائها

وخطب يومًا فقال إنّ الله أمرنا بالعمل وكفانا الرزق فليتنا لو أمرنا بالرزق ٤١،٣٢
وكفينا العمل

وقال أيّها الناس والله ما أحبّ أنّ ما مضى من الدنيا بعمامتي هذه ولما بقي منها ٤٢،٣٢
أشبه بما مضى[1] من الماء بالماء

١ برا: (بقي) وردت في الهامش.

attest to that, otherwise your head will roll!" The man left, and found one of his friends. He explained the situation, and his friend offered: "I'll testify for you." They both presented themselves to al-Ḥajjāj and he asked the witness, "What's your evidence?" He replied, "Commander! I swear that this man once sneezed so violently that he blew out his molar tooth!" Al-Ḥajjāj laughed until he couldn't sit upright and cried, "Enough!" He exonerated them, and they were led out.

Al-Ḥajjāj seldom laughed, but when he did, he was unable to control himself.

Al-Ḥajjāj's eloquence and persuasive rhetoric are evidenced in his famous 32.37
long speech, which you can find in books,[252] together with excerpts of his letters and pulpit orations. Mālik ibn Dīnār said: "By God, if al-Ḥajjāj were to ascend the pulpit and describe how beneficent he had been to the Iraqis and how wicked they had been to him, he could convince me that he was the one who was oppressed!"

Al-Ḥasan al-Baṣrī reports how he was struck by one of al-Ḥajjāj's pulpit 32.38
speeches: "Anyone who wastes a moment of his life on something other than that for which he was created truly deserves to suffer long distress."

A sermon by al-Ḥajjāj: "Listen, everyone! Practice self-control! We invari- 32.39
ably desire more than we receive, and we give more prodigally than is ever required. God shows mercy to the man who fixes muzzle and halter upon himself, hauling himself toward obedience to God and yanking himself away from disobedience. Know this: it is far easier to endure abstinence from what God has forbidden now than it will be to endure His punishment later."

Al-Ḥajjāj was informed of the death of both his brother and son on the 32.40
same day. He ascended the pulpit and spoke: "Two Muḥammads in one day. But, by God, however much I would love them to still be with me in this world, stronger is my hope that God gives them just rewards in the next. I swear by God: those of us who remain are but quick on the brink of annihilation; the young but on the verge of decrepitude. Soon it will be the earth's turn to consume our flesh and drink our blood, just as we in our time nibbled its fruits and sipped its waters."

A sermon by al-Ḥajjāj: "God commands us to work, and the sustenance we 32.41
receive is up to Him. Would that He commanded us to find sustenance, and spared us from the work!"

He once said, "Listen, everyone! By God, I wouldn't trade this turban of 32.42
mine for all that's past in this world. The days in store will be no different from the days past, more alike than water is to water."

٤٣،٣٢ ولمّا قتل عبد الله بن الزبير ارتجّت مكّة بالبكاء فصعد الحجّاج المنبر وقال ألا إنّ ابن الزبير كان من أحبار هذه الأمّة حتّى رغب في الخلافة ونازع فيها وخلع طاعة الله واستكنّ بحرم الله ولو كان شيء مانعًا للعصاة لمنعت آدم حرمة الجنّة لأنّ الله تعالى خلقه بيده وأسجد له ملائكته وأباحه جنّته فلمّا عصاه أخرجه منها بخطيئته وآدم على الله أكرم من ابن الزبير والجنّة أعظم حرمة من الكعبة

٤٤،٣٢ وأرجف قوم بموته فخرج متحاملاً حتّى صعد المنبر فقال ألا إنّ أهل العراق أهل النفاق نفخ الشيطان في مناخرهم فقالوا مات الحجّاج ولئن متّ فمه والله ما يرجى الخير إلّا بعد الموت وما رضي الله تعالى ذكره بالتخليد لأحد من خلقه إلّا لأخبثهم[١] وأهونهم عليه إبليس ولقد سأل سليمان عليه السلام ربّه فقال ﴿رَبِّ﴾ ﴿هَبْ لِى مُلْكًا لَّا يَنۢبَغِى لِأَحَدٍ مِّنۢ بَعْدِىٓ﴾ ففعل ثمّ اضمحلّ كأن لم يكن أستغفر الله لأمير المؤمنين ولي للمسلمين ثمّ نزل

٤٥،٣٢ وكتب إلى قتيبة بن مسلم إنّي نظرت في سنّي فإذا أنا قد بلغت خمسين سنة وأنت نحو منّي في السنّ وإنّ امرءًا قد سار خمسين حجّة إلى مورد لقمن أن يرده

٤٦،٣٢ ولمّا حضرته الوفاة كان يقول اللّهمّ اغفر لي فإنّ الناس يزعمون أنّك لا تفعل

٤٧،٣٢ ومات بواسط سنة خمس وتسعين وهي مدينته التي أنشأها وكان يوم موته يسمّى عرس العراق ولم يُعلم بموته حتّى أشرفت جارية من القصر وهي تبكي وتقول ألا إنّ مطعم الطعام ومفلق الهام قد مات ثمّ دفن فسمع جرّ السلاسل من قبره فقال كاتبه رحمك الله أبا محمّد ما تدع القراءة حيًّا ولا ميّتًا فضحك الناس من قوله ووقف رجل من أهل الشام على قبره فقال اللّهمّ لا تحرمنا شفاعة الحجّاج

---

١ بر١، إ٣: أخسّهم.

When ʿAbd Allāh ibn al-Zubayr was killed and Mecca quaked in lamentation, al-Ḥajjāj ascended the pulpit: "Indeed, Ibn al-Zubayr was one of this community's eminent learned men. But then he desired the caliphate. He struggled for it, he forsook his obedience to God, and then he hid in the midst of God's Sanctum. If anything could protect those who disobey God, then surely the sanctum of Paradise would have protected Adam. Adam—he whom the Exalted God created with His own hands, he before whom the Angels prostrated, and he whom God granted enjoyment of Paradise! But then Adam forsook his obedience to God, and God cast him out for his sin. Was not Adam nobler before God than Ibn al-Zubayr? Is not Paradise a greater sanctum than the Kaaba?" 32.43

A group was spreading false rumors that al-Ḥajjāj had died. Al-Ḥajjāj struggled and hauled himself up the pulpit:[253] "Are not the Iraqis a hypocritical brood? The Devil puffed up their nostrils and they're saying, 'Al-Ḥajjāj is dead.' If I die, so be it. By God, the only good is what's after death. To whom did God give the satisfaction of immortality? To the Devil only, the most miserable, most vile of creation. Peace upon Solomon—he prayed, «Oh God! Grant me such power as no one after me will have,»[254] and God gave it, but then it all crumbled to nothing as if it had never been. Good God! I seek God's forgiveness for the Commander of the Faithful, for myself, and for all Muslims." Al-Ḥajjāj then descended from the pulpit. 32.44

Al-Ḥajjāj wrote to Qutaybah ibn Muslim: "I considered my age and realize I have reached fifty, and you are nearly the same. Shouldn't any man who strives for fifty years to reach water be able to drink from it?" 32.45

On his deathbed, al-Ḥajjāj was heard to say, "Good God! Forgive me! The people allege that you will not!" 32.46

In the year 95 [714], Al-Ḥajjāj died in Wāsiṭ, the city he founded. The day of his death was named "Iraq's Wedding Day." His death was not known until a girl surmounted the roof of his palace in tears, crying aloud, "Alas! The feast-giver, the head-chopper is dead." 32.47

A sound of clinking chains was heard from al-Ḥajjāj's grave when he was being buried, and his secretary said, "God have mercy upon you, Ḥajjāj! You never stopped reciting the Qur'an in life or in death!" People chuckled at this. One of the Syrians stood over his grave and cried, "Good God! Deny us not al-Ḥajjāj's intercession!"

وحلف رجل بالطلاق أنّ الحجّاج في النار فاستفتى طاووس فقال يغفر الله لمن يشاء وما أظنّها إلّا طلّقت فاستفتى الحسن البصريّ فقال اذهب لزوجتك وكن معها فإن لم يكن الحجّاج في النار فما يضرّكما أنكما في الحرام ٤٨،٣٢

وقتيبة فتح ما وراء النهر بسعدك ٣٣

هو قتيبة بن مسلم بن عمرو الباهليّ وكنيته أبو صالح نشأ في الدولة المروانيّة وترقّى وتولّى الإمارة وفتح الفتوحات العظيمة وعبر ما وراء النهر مرارًا وأبلى في الكفّار وكان شجّاعًا جوّادًا دمث الأخلاق ولم يكن يعاب إلّا أنّه باهليّ وكان أصحابه يمازحونه بذلك ويحتمل ويحلم ١،٣٣

حكى أبو عبيدة قال قدم رجل من بني سلول على قتيبة بن مسلم بكتاب عامله على الريّ وهو المعلّى المحاربيّ فرآه على الباب قدامة بن جعدة بن هبيرة[١] وكان صديقًا لقتيبة كثير الإدلال عليه فدخل على قتيبة فقال ببابك ألأم العرب فقال ومن هو فقال سلوليّ رسول محاربيّ إلى باهليّ فتبسّم قتيبة تبسّم غيظ والتفت إلى مرداس الأسديّ فقال أنشدني شعرًا للأقيشر ففهم مرداس مراده فأنشده شعرًا للأقيشر فيه تعريض بقدامة ٢،٣٣

قُلْتُ قُمْ صَلِّ فَصَلَّى قَاعِدًا    يَتَغَشَّاهُ سَمَادِيرُ ٱلسُّكُرْ

فتغيّر وجه قدامة فقال قتيبة هذه بتلك والبادئ أظلم

ويُروى أنّه مازح أعرابيًّا جافيًّا فقال أيسرّك أن تكون مثلي باهليًّا أميرًا فقال لا والله فقال فتكون باهليًّا خليفة فقال لا والله ولو أنّ لي ما طلعت عليه الشمس ٣،٣٣

١ كل النسخ: قدامة بن جعفر.

A man swore that he would divorce his wife if al-Ḥajjāj was not in Hell. He consulted Ṭāwūs about this, who advised him: "God may forgive anyone He wishes, so my judgment is that you must divorce her." The man then sought al-Ḥasan al-Baṣrī's opinion, who advised: "Go back to your wife and live with her. If al-Ḥajjāj is not destined for Hell, then what does it matter if you live in adultery?" 32.48

**. . . Qutaybah needed your lucky star to conquer Transoxiana . . .** 33

Qutaybah ibn Muslim ibn ʿAmr of the Bāhilah, known as Abū Ṣāliḥ, was a military man of the Marwanid dynasty. Qutaybah rose to the rank of commander and waged campaigns of conquest, crossing the Oxus several times and laying waste to the unbelievers. He was brave, generous, and mild-tempered; his only shortcoming was his Bāhilah lineage—his companions used to chide him about it and he would bear it patiently.[255] 33.1

Abū ʿUbaydah tells that Qutaybah once received a letter from his lieutenant in charge of Rayy. The lieutenant, named al-Muʿallā, was of Muḥāribī lineage, and the messenger who delivered the letter was of Salūlī descent. Qudāmah ibn Jaʿdah ibn Hubayrah,[256] a friend of Qutaybah and one who often teased him, espied the messenger at Qutaybah's door and announced, "The most ignoble of the Arabs is at your door." Qutaybah asked, "Who might that be?" Qudāmah quipped, "It's a man from the Salūl sent by one of the Muḥārib with a message to a Bāhilite." Qutaybah's smile was more of a grimace, and he turned to Mirdās of the Asad and said, "Sing to us a poem by al-Uqayshir!" Mirdās knew exactly what Qutaybah meant, and he sang a verse that al-Uqayshir had once composed to lampoon Qudāmah: 33.2

I told him, "Get up and pray!" He did pray,
sitting, bleary-eyed from drunkenness.

Qudāmah's face changed color, and Qutaybah quipped, "Tit for tat; the one who started is the ruder."

It is reported that Qutaybah once joked with an ill-mannered Bedouin, asking him, "Would you accept having Bāhilah lineage if it meant you could be a commander like me?" "No, not at all!" was the Bedouin's reply. Qutaybah then asked, "What if accepting Bāhilah lineage meant you could be the 33.3

قال فيسرّك أن تكون باهليًّا وتكون في الجنّة فأطرق ثمّ قال بشرط أن لا يعلم أهل الجنّة أنّي باهليّ فضحك قتيبة من قوله

٤،٣٣ وكان قتيبة من أكبر أمراء الدولة المنتمين إلى الحجّاج وهو الذي كاتب عبد الملك بن مروان في أمره حتّى ولّاه خراسان وذلك أنّ يزيد بن المهلّب كان قد[١] ولي خراسان بعد أبيه وظهرت مناقبه وعظمت آثاره فحسده الحجّاج فعمل على عزله وتولية قتيبة وكان ممّا أكّد أمر يزيد عنده أنّ الحجّاج وفد على عبد الملك ثمّ عاد إلى العراق فمرّ في طريقه بدير فيه راهب عالم بالكتب وعلوم الأوّلين فسأله هل تجدون أمرنا في كتبكم قال نعم قال ما تقول في عبد الملك قال نجده في زماننا الذي نحن فيه قال ومن يقوم بعده قال رجل يُسمّي الوليد قال فهل تعلم ما لي يعني عمله قال نعم قال فمن يليه قال يزيد قال في حياتي أم بعد مماتي قال لا أعلم فوقع في نفسه أنّه يزيد بن المهلّب ثمّ جلس يومًا وفكّر وعنده عبيد بن يونس وهو ينكت[٢] في الأرض فقال له ما الذي بك فقال إنّ أهل الكتاب يذكرون أنّ ما تحت يدي يليه رجل يُسمّى يزيد وإنّي نظرت في هذا الاسم فذكرت جماعة منهم يزيد بن أبي كبشة ويزيد بن الحصين ويزيد بن دينار وليس فيهم من يصلح لهذا الأمر وما ثمّ غير يزيد بن المهلّب قال فأخلق به فلم يجد شيئًا يعزله به فكتب إلى عبد الملك بن مروان يذمّ من يزيد ويقول إنّه يميل إلى آل الزبير فكتب إليه عبد الملك إنّ ذلك وفاء لآل زبير من آل المهلّب وإنّ وفاءهم لأولئك يدعوهم إلى الوفاء لنا فكتب إليه الحجّاج يخوّفه غدر يزيد وآل المهلّب فكتب إليه عبد الملك قد أكثرت في يزيد فسمّ لي رجلاً يصلح لخراسان فسمّى له مجّاعة بن سعر[٣] ولم يكن يصلح وإنّما جعل ذلك دهاء منه حتّى لا يعرف ميله إلي قتيبة ويعلم أنّ عبد الملك لا يرضى مجّاعة

١ قد: زيادة من إ٢، إ٣. ٢ إ١، بر١، ق٣: ينكث. ٣ في النسخ: مسعر.

caliph?" "No! By God, not even if I could rule all lands under the sun!" Then Qutaybah asked, "Would you accept Bāhilah lineage if it got you straight to Paradise?" The Bedouin lowered his head in thought, and then said, "All right, but only on condition that no one else in Paradise was told that I was from the Bāhilah." This made Quytabah laugh.

Qutaybah was one of al-Ḥajjāj's most prominent lieutenants. It was al-Ḥajjāj 33.4
himself who petitioned the Caliph ʿAbd al-Malik to appoint Qutaybah as governor of Khurasan, replacing Yazīd ibn al-Muhallab, who had inherited the governorship from his father.[257] Yazīd had showed himself a praiseworthy leader and attained such great renown that al-Ḥajjāj grew envious and strove to contrive Yazīd's dismissal and appoint Qutaybah in his stead. Yazīd's fate was sealed when al-Ḥajjāj, upon returning to Iraq from an audience with ʿAbd al-Malik in Syria, passed a monastery where a learned monk well versed in the ancient books of prophesy lived. Al-Ḥajjāj asked the monk, "Do your books prophesy about us?" "Yes." "What do they say about ʿAbd al-Malik?" al-Ḥajjāj asked. "It was foretold that he would rule in this time." "Who do your books say will rule next?" "A man named al-Walīd."[258] Al-Ḥajjāj then asked, "Do you know about my affairs?"—he meant his governorship. The monk answered, "Yes." "Who will succeed me?" "A man named Yazīd." "Will it be in my lifetime or after?" The monk replied, "I don't know." Al-Ḥajjāj got it in his head that this "Yazīd" was certainly Yazīd ibn al-Muhallab. A little while later, al-Ḥajjāj sat with his secretary ʿUbayd ibn Yūnus,[259] lost in thought and tapping the ground with his staff. ʿUbayd asked, "What's the matter?" Al-Ḥajjāj told him, "The People of the Book prophesy that what I control will pass into the hands of a 'Yazīd,' and I've mulled all the possibilities: there's Yazīd ibn Abī Kabshah, Yazīd ibn al-Ḥaṣīn, and Yazīd ibn Dīnār, and none of them seem suitable candidates. So that just leaves Yazīd ibn al-Muhallab." His secretary suggested, "Fabricate some charge against him." Al-Ḥajjāj pondered, and though he was unable to find any ready excuse to justify dismissing Yazīd, he disparaged him in a letter to ʿAbd al-Malik, saying, "Yazīd is partial to the Zubayrids." ʿAbd al-Malik replied, "This is merely an expression of the Muhallabid clan's faithfulness to the Zubayrids. That trait of fidelity will prompt their faithfulness to us in turn."[260] Al-Ḥajjāj wrote back, fearmongering that Yazīd and the Muhallabid clan were plotting, and ʿAbd al-Malik finally responded: "You keep harping on about Yazīd; name someone who is worthy of commanding Khurasan in his stead." Al-Ḥajjāj proposed Mujjāʿah ibn Siʿr, though al-Ḥajjāj knew that Mujjāʿah was not a suitable

ابن سعر[1] فكتب إليه عبد الملك يسفّه رأيه ولم يرض ابن سعر[2] فسمّى له قتيبة بن مسلم فقال ولّه فولّاه

٥،٣٣ وكره أن يواجه ابن المهلّب بالعزل فكتب إليه اقدم عليّ واستخلف أخاك ففعل وعند قدومه سار قتيبة إلى خراسان فدخلها وصعد المنبر فسقطت العصا من يده فتطيّر الناس فأخذها وقال ليس كما ساء الصديق وسرّ العدوّ ولكن كما قال الشاعر

فَأَلْقَتْ عَصَاهَا وَٱسْتَقَرَّتْ بِهَا ٱلنَّوَى    كَمَا قَرَّ عَيْنًا بِٱلْإِيَابِ ٱلْمُسَافِرُ

٦،٣٣ ثمّ نهض قتيبة لغزو ما وراء النهر فجمع جيوشه وخطبهم خطبة بليغة وقطع النهر فتلقّاه من الطالقان رسل الملوك وهداياهم أوّلهم صاحب طخارستان وهو من ملوك الترك وأرسل إليه مفتاح بلده وغيره ذلك من الهدايا فصالحه وأقام قتيبة على بلخ لأنّ بعضها كان عاصيا عليه فقاتل أهلها وسباهم وكان فيمن سبى امرأة برمك جدّ البرامكة فصارت إلى عبد الله بن مسلم أخي قتيبة فواقعها فيقال إنّها حملت منه بخالد وقيل كانت حاملاً به

٧،٣٣ ثمّ غزا قتيبة بيكند وهي أوّل مدائن بخارى إلى النهر ويقال لها مدينة التجّار وهي على رأس المفازة من بخارى فلمّا نزل بهم استنصروا بالصغد واستنجدوا من حولهم فأتوهم في جمع كثير وأخذوا على قتيبة الطرق والمضايق فلم يصل إليه رسول ولا قدر على إنفاذ رسول مدّة شهر وأبطأ على الحجّاج خبره فأشفق عليه وعلى من معه من المسلمين فأمر الناس بالدعاء وكتب بذلك إلى الأمصار وأقام قتيبة يقاتلهم كلّ يوم

٨،٣٣ وكان لقتيبة عين فيهم يقال له تندر[3] أعجميّ فدفع إليه أهل بخارى مالاً على أن يدفع عنهم قتيبة فأتاه فقال أخلني فأخلى له المجلس فقال قد عزل الحجّاج عن

١ في النسخ: مسعر. ٢ في النسخ: مسعر. ٣ إ، برا: بنذ'ر.

candidate—al-Ḥajjāj only proposed him as a ruse to deflect attention from his real partiality to Qutaybah. ʿAbd al-Malik duly rejected the idea, and wrote back chiding al-Ḥajjāj for the poor suggestion. Then al-Ḥajjāj proposed Qutaybah, and ʿAbd al-Malik wrote back: "Appoint him."

Al-Ḥajjāj was wary of bluntly dismissing Yazīd, so he wrote instead: "Present yourself to us, and deputize your brother." Yazīd did as ordered, and as he arrived in Iraq, Qutaybah entered Khurasan. Qutaybah ascended the pulpit to make his address, but he dropped his staff, and the congregation considered it an ill omen. Qutaybah picked it up and said, "This is not a case of bad news for the friend and good news for the enemy. No! It is as a poet once said: 33.5

> She threw down her staff—the journey's ended—
> a traveler's return brings repose."[261]

Qutaybah immediately applied himself to conquest. He gathered his armies, delivered them a stirring speech, and marched across the Oxus. Near Taloqan, he met the emissaries of kings bearing gifts. First were the Tokharians, a Turkish kingdom, who presented him the key to their city among other gifts. Qutaybah made peace with them and took up residence in Balkh, as the region's population was resistive. Qutaybah battled them and took captives, including the wife of Barmak, the ancestor of the Barmakids. She was given to ʿAbd Allāh ibn Muslim, Qutaybah's brother, who lay with her, and she became pregnant with Khālid the Barmakid; though it is said that she was already pregnant before her capture.[262] 33.6

Qutaybah next marched against Paykent, a merchant city near the Oxus at the edge of the desert, and the conduit to Bukhara. The townsfolk appealed to the Sogdians for relief, and a large host of reinforcements arrived, surrounding Qutaybah's army and completely cutting him off. For a month, Qutaybah fought them every day, but since no messenger could get in to, or out from, Qutyabah's position, al-Ḥajjāj grew anxious about Qutaybah and his Muslim soldiers. Al-Ḥajjāj directed everyone to make supplications to God, and wrote to all the cities of the realm to make supplications too. 33.7

A local spy named Tundar[263] worked for Qutaybah, but the Bukharans bribed him to devise a way of getting Qutaybah to withdraw. Tundar went to Qutaybah's assembly and requested, "Can I speak privately?" Qutaybah bade his companions retire, and Tundar told him, "Al-Ḥajjāj has been relieved of governorship over Iraq. A new official is coming and you are to retreat 33.8

العراق وهذا عامل جديد يقدم عليك فارجع بالناس إلى مرو وكان عند قتيبة ضرار الضبّيّ فقال قتيبة لغلامه اقتل تندر فضرب عنقه فقال لضرار والله لئن علم أحد بهذا الحديث قبل أن يُقضى حربنا لألحقنّك به فإنّ انتشار مثل هذا الحديث يفتّ في أعضاد المسلمين

٩،٣٣ ثمّ أصبح الناس على راياتهم وأنكروا قتل تندر[1] وقالوا كان ناصحًا للمسلمين فقال قتيبة ظهر لي غشّه فأخذه الله بذنبه ثمّ تقدّم وأنزل الله النصر على المسلمين فهزموهم وفتح قتيبة أكنافهم[2] ووصل إلى بيكند ففتحها عنوة وأصاب بها من الأموال والجواهر من لم يصبه في بلد آخر وكان بها صنم فأذابوه فخرج منه مائة ألف[3] وخمسون ألف مثقال من الذهب

١٠،٣٣ ثمّ توجّه إلى سمرقند فقاتل وثلّم السور فطلبوا الصلح فصالحهم على ألف ألف مائتي ألف في كلّ سنة وعلى أن يعطوه ثلاثين ألف رأس ليس فيهم طفل ولا شيخ ولا عاجز[4] وعلى أن يخلو المدينة ويخرجوا منها المقاتلة ويدخلها قتيبة فيبني فيها مسجدًا ويصلّي فيه ويخطب ويتغدّى ويخرج فأجابوه فقال ابعثوا إلينا ما صالحناكم عليه فبعثوا المال والرؤوس فقال الآن ذلّوا حين صار أولادهم وإخوانهم في أيدينا ثمّ بنوا جامعًا ونصبوا منبرًا وأخلوا المدينة وانتخب قتيبة من أراد من فرسانه ودخلها فأتى المسجد فصلّى وخطب ثمّ تغدّى وأرسل إلى أهلها لست بخارج منها فخذوا ما أعطيتمونا وكان قتيبة يُعيَّر بالغدر بأهل سمرقند ثمّ حرّق الأصنام وبيوت النيران ووجد جارية من بنات يزدجرد فقال قتيبة ابن هذه يكون هجينًا فقالت نعم من قبل أبيه فأرسل بها إلى الحجّاج فبعث بها إلى الوليد بن عبد الملك فولدت له يزيدًا

١١،٣٣ ثمّ غزا قتيبة الصين وكاشغر فبعث إليه ملك الصين ابعث لنا رجلًا من قومك نسائله عن دينكم فانتدب له عشرة من أشراف القبائل لهم هيئة وجمال

---

١ إ١، بر١: بنذ̇ر. ٢ إ١، إ٤، إ٥، ل٢، ت١: منح قتيب اكتافهم. ٣ إ١، إ٦، بر١، با١: ألف ألف. ٤ ولا عاجز: زيادة من با١، إ٦.

to Marw." Only Ḍirār of the Ḍabbah and a young slave remained in Qutaybah's presence, and Qutaybah ordered the slave, "Kill Tundar!" Tundar was executed on the spot, and Qutaybah told Ḍirār, "The news Tundar brought will devastate the Muslims' morale: by God, if any word of it gets out before our current battles are concluded, you will be joining Tundar forthwith, I can assure you."

In the morning, the soldiers in their battle formations were dismayed to hear of Tundar's execution: "He helped us with good counsel!" But Qutaybah corrected them: "I found out he was double-crossing us, and God took him for his sin." Qutaybah then advanced once again, and this time God bestowed victory on the Muslims. Qutaybah and the Muslims got the better of the Sogdians and stormed Paykent, taking it by force and seizing such property and jewels as had never been captured in any previous conquest. Among the spoils was an idol, which they melted down into 150,000 mithkals of gold.[264] 33.9

Qutaybah next turned to Samarqand, and after a fight before its walls, he made a breach and its populace sued for peace. Terms were set at an annual tribute of 1.2 million,[265] plus the surrender of thirty thousand sound-bodied adult captives, and the people of Samarqand were to temporarily evacuate from their town and vacate their soldiers, so that Qutaybah could enter and build a mosque where he could give a sermon, lead prayers, and hold a midday banquet before quitting town. They agreed. Qutaybah ordered them: "Fulfill your treaty payment," and they sent the money and captives. Qutaybah remarked, "Now they're brought low—their children and brothers are in our hands!" The people of Samarqand built the mosque, installed a pulpit, and vacated the city.[266] Qutaybah selected a troop of his cavalry and entered, prayed in the mosque, delivered a sermon, ate his meal, and then sent word to the Samarqandis: "I will not leave this city, so I will return to you all the treaty payments you made." Qutaybah has been critiqued for cheating the Samarqandis in this way. He then set about torching their idols and fire temples, and he found a young princess who was a daughter of the last Sassanian shah, Yazdegerd. Qutaybah asked her, "Can the son of one such as you be of ignoble blood?" "Yes," she replied, "but only from its father's side." Qutaybah sent her to al-Ḥajjāj, who delivered her to the future caliph al-Walīd ibn ʿAbd al-Malik, for whom she bore a son, Yazīd. 33.10

Qutaybah then marched on China. When he raided Kashgar, the Chinese king wrote: "Send us one of your men who can tell us about your religion." 33.11

فدخلوا عليه وعليهم ثياب رقيقة فلم يكلّمهم أحد فنهضوا ودخلوا عليه في اليوم الثاني وعليهم البيض والمغافر والسلاح كأنّهم الجبال فسأل الملك أحدهم عن صنيعهم أمس واليوم فقالوا ذاك لباسنا في أهلنا وهذا في حربنا فقال انصرفوا إلى صاحبكم وقولوا له ينصرف فقد عرفت قلّة أصحابه وإلّا بعثت له من يهلكه ومن معه فقالوا كيف تقول هذا لمن أوّل خيله في بلادك وآخرها في منابت الزيتون يعنون الشام قد غزاك في بلادك ودوّخها وهو في طلبك لا تردّ له راية قال وما الذي يريد قال إنّه أقسم أن لا يرجع حتّى يطأ أرضك ويختم على أعناق أولاد الملوك ويأخذ الجزية قال الملك فنحن نبرّ قسمه ثمّ دعا بصحاف من ذهب وجعل فيها ترابًا كثيرًا واستدعى صبيانًا من أبناء الملوك ومالاً عظيمًا[1] وقال ليطأ هذا التراب ويختم على أعناق هذه الغلمة ويأخذ منّا المال ففعل قتيبة ذلك وقرّر عليهم مالاً ومضى

١٢،٣٣ وقد أذعنت له ممالك ما وراء النهر واشتهرت فتوحاته حتّى سمع معبد المغنّي أنّه فتح سبعة حصون بالمشرق لا يرتقى إليها فصنع سبعة أصوات صعبة المآخذ وسمّاها مدن معبد معارضة لقتيبة

١٣،٣٣ وأقام قتيبة بالمشرق واليًا عليه ثلاث عشرة سنة عظيم الرتبة مرهوب الجانب وكان شرف بيته ثمّ عمل على خلع سليمان بن عبد الملك لمّا سمع أنّه عازم على ولاية يزيد بن المهلّب حكى الجاحظ قال لمّا بلغ قتيبة أنّ سليمان يريد عزله عن خراسان كتب إليه ثلاث صحائف وقال للرسول ادفع إليه هذه فإن دفعها إلى يزيد بن المهلّب فادفع له هذه فإن شتمني فادفع إليه الثالثة فلمّا دفع له الكتاب الأوّل إذا فيه يا أمير المؤمنين إن من بلائي في طاعتك وطاعة أبيك كذا وكذا

١ إ: جماعة من أولاد الملوك.

Qutaybah selected ten striking and handsome tribal notables, and they presented themselves wearing fine clothes. No one gave them an audience, and the next day they donned their helmets, coats of armor, and weapons, and in this towering mien, they presented themselves again. This time, the king asked them about their change of deportment, and they replied, "Yesterday we were in our garb of peace; today we come in our garb of war." The king replied, "Go back to your commander and tell him to leave. We know how small his forces are: if he does not retreat, I will send an army to annihilate the lot of you." The Muslims responded, "How can you say that to a man who commands a column of cavalry whose front rank stands on your territory, and whose rear stretches all the way to the Land of Olives?" (They meant Syria.) "He has marched this force against you, he has subjugated your land, and he has his sights set on you. No army can repel him." The king asked them, "What does he want?" "He has sworn not to return until he has marched on your soil, affixed the seal of subjugation upon the necks of your princes, and imposed the unbeliever tax upon you." The king told them, "We will enable him to fulfill his oath." The king ordered sheets of gold and covered them with earth. He then summoned several princes and amassed a great sum of money, and told the Muslims, "Let your man stamp on this earth, let him impress a seal on the necks of these boys, and take this money." Qutaybah did all this, then established payment terms from the Chinese, and turned back.

Thus were the kings of Transoxiana subjugated by Qutaybah. His conquests 33.12
garnered wide renown, such that when the singer Maʿbad heard of Qutaybah's reduction of seven unscalable citadels in the East, he composed seven songs that were extremely difficult to play, naming them the "Seven Cities of Maʿbad," paralleling Qutaybah's conquest.

For thirteen years, Qutaybah ruled as governor of the East; both power- 33.13
ful and awed, he brought nobility to his clan. When the Caliph Sulaymān ibn ʿAbd al-Malik resolved to replace Qutaybah with Yazīd ibn al-Muhallab, Qutaybah resisted him, as explained by al-Jāḥiz: When Qutaybah learned that Sulaymān intended to sack him from the governorship of Khurasan, Qutaybah wrote three letters, giving the following instructions to the messenger: "Give the first letter to the caliph. If he hands it to Yazīd, give him the second one. If the caliph curses me when he reads it, give him the third." The messenger arrived and presented the first letter. It said: "Commander of the Faithful! I have endured many hardships"—which he listed—"in the service of you and

فدفعه إلى يزيد فدفع إليه الرسول الكتاب الثاني وفيه عجبًا كيف تأمن ابن دحمة على أسرارك ولم يكن أبوه يأمنه على أمّهات أولاده يعني يزيد بن المهلّب فشتم قتيبة فدفع إليه الرسول الكتاب الثالث وفيه من قتيبة بن مسلم إلى سليمان أمّا بعد والله لأوثقنّ لك أخيّة لا ينزعها المهر الأرنّ فقال سليمان جدّدوا له عهدًا على عمله

١٤،٣٣ ثمّ فسدت على قتيبة بطانته فقتلوه في خلافة سليمان وقام العزاء في المشرق عليه وقال رجل من الأعاجم يا معشر العرب قتلتم قتيبة والله لو كان فينا ومات لجعلناه في تابوت واستفتحنا به غزونا

١٥،٣٣ ولقتيبة أخبار وألفاظ تدلّ على غزارة علمه وعقله وفصاحته كتب إليه الحجّاج إنّي قد طلّقت بنت قطن الهلاليّة عن غير ريبة فتزوّجها فكتب إليه ليس كلّ مطالع الأمير أحبّ أن أطّلع فقال الحجّاج ويل أمّ قتيبة كيف أُلام عليه

١٦،٣٣ وكتب إليه الحجّاج إنّ أمير المؤمنين كتب إليّ يقول أنت عندي قدح ابن مقبل فلم يدر ما أراد فقال قتيبة إنّ ابن مقبل نعت قدحًا له كثير الفوز فقال

غَـدَا وَهُوَ مَجْـدُولٌ فَـرَاحَ كَأَنَّهُ    مِنَ ٱلْمَسِّ وَٱلتَّقْلِيبِ بِٱلْكَفِّ أَفْطَحُ
إِذَا ٱمْتَـحَنَتْـهُ مِنْ مَعَـدٍّ قَبِيـلَةٌ    غَدَا رَبُّـهُ قَبْـلَ ٱلْمُفِيضِـينَ يَقْدَحُ

وصف بهذا القدح وهو السهم الذي يُستقسم به على عادتهم العرب من الميسر وهو الاصطلاح على نوع من أنواع القمار معروف فيقول إنّه هذا القدح[1] لكثرة

---

١ القدح: زيادة من إ٣.

your father." The caliph did hand the letter to Yazīd, so the messenger gave him the second. It said: "Commander of the Faithful! It is a wonder that you can trust the son of Daḥamah with your secrets, while his own father couldn't even trust him near his concubines!" (Daḥamah was Yazīd's mother.) The caliph cursed Qutaybah, so the messenger presented the third letter. It said: "From Qutaybah ibn Muslim to Sulaymān. By God, I guarantee you a tether so strong that no sprightly colt can break it." The caliph then gave his order: "Renew Qutaybah's governorship over his province!"

Later during Sulaymān's caliphate, Qutaybah's own retinue mutinied and killed him. Mourning was announced across the East, and one of the Persians said, "Arabs! You have killed Qutaybah! By God, if he was one of us, we would have placed his body in a sarcophagus and carried him before us for good fortune in battle." 33.14

Qutaybah's profound knowledge, reason, and eloquence are amply evidenced in the record of his actions and sayings. For example, al-Ḥajjāj once wrote to him: "I have divorced the daughter of Qaṭan of the Hilāl; I had no particular misgivings about her—you should marry her." Qutaybah wrote back: "I am not desirous of scaling every height surmounted by my commander." Al-Ḥajjāj remarked, "Damn Qutaybah's mother! Thanks to her son, I'm going to be roundly rebuked!" 33.15

On another occasion, al-Ḥajjāj wrote to Qutaybah with a question: "The Commander of the Faithful wrote to me and said: 'To me, you are like Ibn Muqbil's gaming arrow.'" Al-Ḥajjāj did not understand the analogy, but Qutaybah did, and explained: "Ibn Muqbil composed verses describing a gaming arrow with which he frequently won bets: 33.16

It went out, bound tight, but it came back
with head flattened from the many throws.
If any Maʿaddite tribe could borrow it,
they'd light their fires before the first toss."

Ibn Muqbil describes his gaming arrow: a headless arrow, which the Arabs used to toss as lots in the game of *maysir*, a form of gambling. The poet intends that this particular arrow was always victorious; the poet admired the lucky arrow and frequently threw it. The expression "light their fires" intends that victory to the arrow's thrower was guaranteed: before the game even begins,

فوزه[1] وخروجه دون قداح الجماعة يكثر تقليبه والتعجّب منه ويقدح صاحبه النار قبل خروجه ثقة[2] بفوزه وقال قتيبة إنّ هذا القدح فاز ستّين مرّة لم يخب منها مرّة واحدة حتّى ضُرب به المثل

ولمّا دخل قتيبة خراسان قام إليه بعض الشعراء فأنشده ١٧،٣٣

شَدَّ ٱلْعِصَابَ عَلَى ٱلْبَرِيِّ وَمَا جَنَى   حَتَّى يَكُونَ لِغَيْرِهِ تَنْكِيلَا
وَٱلْجَهْلُ فِي بَعْضِ ٱلْأُمُورِ وَإِنْ عَلَا   مُسْتَخْرِجٌ لِلْجَاهِلِينَ عُقُولَا

فقال قتيبة قبّحك الله من مشير والله لا أقمت معي في بلد ثمّ أخرجه من خراسان

ونظر في بعض مغازيه إلى رجل من الأزد معه ترس ىن جلد بعير قد تشعّث من جميع نواحيه فقال يا أخا الأزد ترس ابن أبي ربيعة خير من ترسك يريد قول ابن أبي ربيعة في قصيدته المشهورة وقد تستّر بنسوة من الحيّ ١٨،٣٣

فَكَانَ مِجَنِّي دُونَ مَنْ كُنْتُ أَتَّقِي   ثَلَاثُ شُخُوصٍ كَاعِبَانِ وَمُعْصِرُ

فقال الرجل أيّها الأمير هذا المجنّ أوفى من ذاك[3] المجنّ

ومن كلام قتيبة لا تستعن على من تطلب إليه حاجة بمن له عنده طعمة فإنّه لا يؤثرك على نفسه ولا بكذّاب فإنّه يقرّب لك البعيد ويبعّد القريب ولا بأحمق فإنّه ربّما أراد نفعك فضرّك ١٩،٣٣

ومرّ يومًا بكناسة فيها عظام وأقذار فقال إنّ الذي يبخل بما يصير آخره إلى هذا لبخيل ٢٠،٣٣

---

١ إ: نغيره. ٢ إ: لله در. ٣ إ: هذا.

the lucky arrow's thrower could confidently light his fire in anticipation of winning the meat.[267]

Qutaybah's letter continued: "This arrow won sixty times straight without losing once, and hence it became the stuff of proverbs."

When Qutaybah first arrived in Khurasan, a poet rose and recited: 33.17

Harshly punish the innocent, though he committed no crime!
This shall be a stern lesson for all!
Sometimes it's a vehement approach, even severe,
that brings recalcitrant churls to their senses.

Qutaybah replied, "What bad advice, God disfigure you! You will not stay with me in my land." He expelled the poet from Khurasan.

During one of his invasions, Qutaybah beheld a man from the Azd who 33.18
carried a camel-leather shield tattered on all sides, and Qutaybah called out, "'Umar ibn Abī Rabī'ah's shield was stouter than this one here!"

Qutaybah intended 'Umar's famous poem in which he described how he hid behind women of the tribe:

My shield, behind which I sheltered from those I feared,
was made of three: two comely lasses and one just pubescent.

The Azdī replied, "But my lord, this shield here is more faithful!"

Qutaybah's sayings include: "Never ally with a man who has dealings with 33.19
your opponent—your ally will always look to his own interests before he attends to yours. Never rely on a liar, for he will make what is difficult seem easily within your grasp, and what is actually easy seem out of reach. And never rely on a fool: even his attempts to help may bring you harm."

Qutaybah remarked when passing a rubbish dump full of bones and filth, 33.20
"Anyone who is stingy over things that eventually end up here is truly a miser."

والمهلّب إنّما أوهن شوكة الأزارقة بجدّك وأفسد ذات بينهم بكيدك[1] ٣٤

١،٣٤ هو المهلّب بن أبي صفرة واسمه ظالم بن سرّاق بن صبح الأزديّ العتكيّ البصريّ أمير كبير مشهور الذكر شجّاع جوّاد نشأ في دولة آل أبي سفيان ثمّ أمّره مصعب ابن الزبير على البصرة نيابة عنه في أيّام أخيه عبد الله بن الزبير ثمّ ولّاه عبد الله خراسان وقتال[2] الخوارج واستمرّ على ذلك إلى أن مات في زمن الحجّاج وهو أوّل من اتّخذ الركب الحديد وكانت قبل ذلك من الخشب

٢،٣٤ وكان يقال ساد الأحنف بحلمه ومالك بن مسمع بمحبّة للعشيرة وقتيبة بدهائه وساد المهلّب بهذه الخصال جميعها وسيأتي في آخر الترجمة نبذة من أخباره وألفاظه

٣،٣٤ فأمّا الأزارقة فهم الخوارج القائلون بمذهب نافع بن عبد الله بن الأزرق الخارجيّ خرجوا معه من البصرة والأهواز وغيرها من بلدان فارس واتّبعوه وعظمت شوكتهم وتملّكوا الأمصار وكانت له آراء ومذاهب دانوا بها معه

٤،٣٤ منه أنّه أكفر عليًّا رضي الله تعالى عنه بسبب التحكيم المشهور وقال أنّ الله تعالى أنزل في حقّه ﴿وَمِنَ ٱلنَّاسِ مَن يُعْجِبُكَ قَوْلُهُۥ فِى ٱلْحَيَوٰةِ ٱلدُّنْيَا وَيُشْهِدُ ٱللَّهَ عَلَىٰ مَا فِى قَلْبِهِۦ وَهُوَ أَلَدُّ ٱلْخِصَامِ وَإِذَا تَوَلَّىٰ سَعَىٰ فِى ٱلْأَرْضِ لِيُفْسِدَ فِيهَا وَيُهْلِكَ ٱلْحَرْثَ وَٱلنَّسْلَ وَٱللَّهُ لَا يُحِبُّ ٱلْفَسَادَ وَإِذَا قِيلَ لَهُ ٱتَّقِ ٱللَّهَ أَخَذَتْهُ ٱلْعِزَّةُ بِٱلْإِثْمِ فَحَسْبُهُۥ جَهَنَّمُ وَلَبِئْسَ ٱلْمِهَادُ﴾

٥،٣٤ وأنزل في حقّ ابن ملجم لعنه الله و﴿ وَمِنَ ٱلنَّاسِ مَن يَشْرِى نَفْسَهُ ٱبْتِغَآءَ مَرْضَاتِ ٱللَّهِ وَٱللَّهُ رَءُوفٌۢ بِٱلْعِبَادِ﴾[3]

١ وأفسد بكيدك: زيادة من با١، ر٢، إ٣. ٢ إ١، بر١: قتل. ٣ (وقال إن الله . . . بالعباد) زيادة من با١، إ٥، إ٦، ر٢.

**. . . al-Muhallab needed your power to break the Blues and your stratagems to disperse their discord.** 34

Al-Muhallab was the son of Abū Ṣufrah Ẓālim ibn Sarrāq ibn Ṣubḥ of the ʿAtak clan of the Azd. He was from Basra and was a celebrated, brave, and magnanimous military commander who first served the Sufyanid caliphs. Under the caliphate of ʿAbd Allāh ibn al-Zubayr, the caliph's brother, Muṣʿab appointed al-Muhallab as deputy over Basra, and Ibn al-Zubayr himself subsequently appointed al-Muhallab as governor of Khurasan and commander of the war against the Kharijites. He served in these capacities until he died during the governate of al-Ḥajjāj. He was the first to ride with metal stirrups; previously, horsemen had used wooden ones. 34.1

They used to say that al-Aḥnaf[268] became a leader because of his equanimity, Mālik ibn Mismaʿ because of his love for his clan, Qutaybah because of his shrewdness, and al-Muhallab for all three reasons. Some stories about al-Muhallab and sayings ascribed to him are included at the end of this section.[269] 34.2

The "Blues" were a sect of the Kharijites who followed the creed of Nāfiʿ ibn ʿAbd Allāh, "son of the Blue." Nāfiʿ and his Blues rebelled in Basra, Ahwaz, and the neighboring regions of southwestern Iran. They gained a following, and with their formidable power they seized cities. 34.3

The creed of Nāfiʿ, which the Blues embraced, included the following views: Nāfiʿ deemed the Caliph ʿAlī (God be pleased with him) a non-Muslim because ʿAlī agreed to the famed Arbitration Hearings.

Nāfiʿ claimed that ʿAlī is the precise person intended by the following Qurʾanic verses: «From among humanity there is one whose views on the affairs of this life may please you. He even calls on God to witness whatever is in his heart, yet he is the most contentious of quarrelers. In reality, he turns away and sets out to spread corruption in the land, destroying crops and cattle. God does not love corruption. When he is told, "Have fear of God," he is seized by pride, which drives him to wrongdoing. Hell shall be enough for him. A dreadful resting place.»[270] 34.4

Nāfiʿ believed that another Qurʾanic verse was revealed to describe Ibn Muljam (God curse him), the Kharijite who assassinated ʿAlī: «There is another who dedicates himself to seeking the pleasure of God. God is compassionate to His servants.»[271] Nāfiʿ held that anyone who did not follow his creed was a non-Muslim whose blood could be spilled lawfully. 34.5

ومنها أنّه أكفر من لم يقل برأيه واستحلّ دمّه وأكفر القعدة عن القتال معه وتبرّأ ممّن قعد عنه وحكمه أنّ من ارتكب كبيرة خرج عن الإسلام وكان مخلّدًا في النار مع سائر الكفّار واستدلّ بكفر إبليس وقال ما ارتكب إلّا كبيرة واحدة حيث أُمر بالسجود فامتنع وإلّا فهو عارف بوحدانيّة الله تبارك وتعالى إلى غير ذلك من المذاهب التي اجتمعت عليها الأزارقة ٦،٣٤

حُكي عن خالد بن خداش[1] قال لمّا تفرّقت آراء الخوارج ومذاهبهم أقام نافع ابن الأزرق بسوق الأهواز يعترض الناس وكان متشكّكًا في ذلك فقالت له امرأته إن كنت كفرت بعد إيمانك وشككت فدع نحلتك ودعوتك وإن كنت قد خرجت من الكفر للإيمان فاقتل الكفّار حيث لقيتهم تعني المسلمين المخالفين لمذهبه وأثخن في النساء والصبيان كما قال نوح عليه السلام ﴿رَّبِّ لَا تَذَرْ عَلَى ٱلْأَرْضِ مِنَ ٱلْكَـٰفِرِينَ دَيَّارًا﴾ فقبل قولها وبسط سيفه فقتل الرجال والنساء فإذا وطئ بلدًا كان ذلك دأبه إلى أن يجيبه أهلها فيضع عليهم الجباية والخراج ٧،٣٤

واشتدّت شوكته ونشأ عمله في السواد فارتاع لذلك أهل البصرة ومشوا إلى الأحنف بن قيس وشكوا إليه أمرهم وقالوا ليس بيننا وبين القوم إلّا ليلتان فقال لهم الأحنف إنّ سيرتهم في مصركم إن ظفروا بكم مثل سيرتهم في سوادكم فخذوا في جهاد عدوّكم وحرّضهم الأحنف فاجتمعوا إليه زهاء عشرة آلاف في السلاح وأمّر عليهم مسلم بن عبيس[2] وكان شجاعًا ديّنًا فخرج بهم فلمّا صار بموضع يُعرف بدولاب خرج إليه نافع بن الأزرق على الشراة وكانوا ستمائة نفر فاقتتلوا قتالًا شديدًا فقُتل في المعركة ابن عبيس[3] وهو أمير على البصرة وقُتل نافع بن الأزرق أيضًا فعجب الناس من قتل الاثنين ثمّ أمّر غيرهما وعاد القتال وانهزم البصريّون وتبعهم الخوارج فألقوا نفوسهم في دجيل فغرق منهم خلق كثير أكثرهم من الأزد وفي ذلك يقول شاعر الأزارقة ٨،٣٤

---

١ إ: حراش. ٢ إ: مسلمة بن عنبس. ٣ إ: عنبس.

Nāfiʿ also deemed anyone who abstained from joining his army to be a non-Muslim too, and he disclaimed all association with them. Furthermore, Nāfiʿ claimed that if a Muslim committed a single major sin, he was forever expelled from the Muslim fold and was destined for eternal torment in Hell alongside all other non-Muslims. To substantiate this claim, Nāfiʿ adduced the example of Satan: "Satan only committed one major sin: his refusal to prostrate before Adam;[272] otherwise, Satan knew the oneness of the Exalted and Glorious God." 34.6

Nāfiʿ promulgated sundry related doctrines, which all the Blues followed.

It is reported on the authority of Khālid ibn Khidāsh that when the Kharijite groups splintered into various sects, Nāfiʿ Son of the Blue took a position in the market of Ahwaz and harangued passersby, but he had some misgivings about his creed. His wife told him, "If you have become an unbeliever after you were once a believer, then go ahead and doubt to your heart's content and quit your sect now. But if you have become a believer after having been an unbeliever, then set forth and kill the unbelievers wherever you find them"—by "unbelievers" she meant the Muslims who did not adhere to his creed—«and slaughter their women and children! Pray like Noah, eternal peace be his: "O my Lord! Do not leave on earth a single one of those who deny the truth!"»[273] Nāfiʿ took her advice and laid forth with his sword. Whenever he entered a region, he killed men and women until the population acquiesced to his creed, and then he burdened the survivors with tithes and land taxes. 34.7

As Nāfiʿ's might grew, his operations spread across the Iraqi countryside, and fear gripped the people of Basra. They gathered before al-Aḥnaf ibn Qays and bemoaned, "The Blues are now but two nights' journey from us!" Al-Aḥnaf advised them: "If they conquer you, they will do to your town exactly as they have across all your countryside. Wage jihad against them now!" Al-Aḥnaf stirred the Basrans to war, and once they mustered a force of about ten thousand men, he appointed Muslim ibn ʿUbays,[274] a brave warrior and devout Muslim, to lead them. Ibn ʿUbays marched the Basran force out, and they encountered Nāfiʿ and six hundred Zealot Blues at Dūlāb.[275] All fought ferociously, and both Ibn ʿUbays and Nāfiʿ were killed. Both sides were shocked at the deaths of their leaders, but they selected new commanders on the field and the battle raged on. The Basrans were eventually defeated, and with the Blues in hot pursuit, they fled, hurling themselves into the Dujayl canal, where many drowned. Most were from the Azd, and one of the Blues' poets chided them: 34.8

يَرَى مَنْ جَاءَ يَنْظُرُ فِي دُجَيْلٍ    شُيُوخَ ٱلْأَزْدِ طَافِيَةً لِحَاهَا

٩،٣٤ وقلق أهل البصرة لذلك ودخل في قلوبهم الرعب من الخوارج فبينما هم كذلك إذ ورد المهلّب بن أبي صفرة متوجّهًا إلى خراسان وقد كتب له عبد الله بن الزبير عهده بها فلمّا مرّ بالبصرة قال الأحنف لوجوه أهل البصرة والله ما للخوارج غير المهلّب فكلّموه في ذلك فقال هذا عهدي على خراسان وما كنت لأدع أمر أمير المؤمنين يعني عبد الله بن الزبير فاتّفق أهل البصرة مع الأحنف على أن يفتعلوا كتابًا عن ابن الزبير يأمره فيه بقتال الخوارج فكتبوه وفيه أمّا بعد فإنّ الحارث[1] بن عبد الله كتب إليّ يخبرني أنّ الأزارقة أصابوا جندًا من المسلمين وأنّهم قد أقبلوا نحو البصرة وكنت قد كتبت عهدك على خراسان ووجّهتك وقد رأيت أن تبتدئ بقتال الخوارج فإنّ الأجر فيه أعظم من سيرك إلى خراسان

١٠،٣٤ فلمّا قرأ المهلّب الكتاب قال والله ما أسير إليهم حتّى تجعلوا لي ممّا غلبت عليه وتقوّوني من بيت المال وأنتخب من فرسانكم ورجالكم من شئت فأجابوه إلّا طائفة من بني مسمع فحقدها عليهم المهلّب وسار إلى الخوارج فكان عليهم أشدّ من كلّ من قاتلهم وبلغ ابن الزبير افتعال الكتاب فلم يقل شيئًا وأقرّه على ذلك

١١،٣٤ ثمّ إنّ المهلّب أخذ بالحزم في القتال وإعمال الرأي والمطاولة فأذكى العيون وأقام الحرس وخندق ولم يزل الجند على مصافّهم والناس على راياتهم وأخماسهم فكانت الأزارقة إذا أرادوا بيات المهلّب وجدوا أمرًا محكمًا ثمّ خرج المهلّب يومًا على تعبئة حسنة وخرج الخوارج على مثل ذلك إلّا أنّهم أحسن عدّة وأكرم خيلًا وأكثر سلاحًا من أهل البصرة وذلك أنّهم كانوا قد أكلوا ما بين كرمان إلى الأهواز فجاؤوا في المغافر والدروع يسحبونها فالتقى الناس واشتدّ القتال ثمّ شدّت الخوارج على الناس شدّة منكرة فأجفل الناس وانصاعوا منهزمين وأسرع المهلّب حتّى سبقهم

١ كلّ النسخ: الحسن.

Come, onlookers, look at the Dujayl;
See the old men of al-Azd, beards afloat.

News of the defeat rocked the Basrans with fear of their impending doom at the hands of the Blues. But amid their woes, Muhallab ibn Abī Ṣufrah arrived. He was on his way to Khurasan bearing a letter of his appointment as governor from the Caliph Ibn al-Zubayr. As he passed through Basra, al-Aḥnaf told the town's leaders, "By God, al-Muhallab is your only hope!" They entreated al-Muhallab, but he replied, "My commission is Khurasan, and I wouldn't want to disobey the Commander of the Faithful's order!" (that is, the Caliph Ibn al-Zubayr). The Basrans and al-Aḥnaf colluded to forge a letter, pretending it to be an order from Ibn al-Zubayr to combat the Kharijites. Their letter read: "Al-Ḥārith[276] ibn ʿAbd Allāh wrote informing me that the Blues inflicted a defeat on the Muslim army and that they are advancing toward Basra. Though I had written you with a commission over Khurasan and dispatched you to there, I now think you should start with the Kharijites, for it entails greater reward from God than your march to Khurasan." 34.9

When al-Muhallab read the letter, he told the Basrans, "I will only fight them if you allow me to keep all the land I take, if you fund my campaign from your treasury, and if you allow me to select from your horsemen and infantry the men I want." Everyone consented except a clan of the Mismaʿ, and al-Muhallab resented them for this. 34.10

Al-Muhallab then marched against the Kharijites and fought them more tenaciously than anyone had before. Ibn al-Zubayr was informed about the forged letter, but said nothing, and confirmed al-Muhallab's appointment to battle the Kharijites.

Al-Muhallab was cautious in the war, pondering each move and favoring a Fabian strategy. He spread spies, kept constant, vigilant guard, and entrenched his camp with soldiers in ranks at the ready, grouped by cohort under their battle standards. The Blues launched surprise attacks by night, but could find no weak spots. And by day, al-Muhallab advanced in fine battle formation and met the Blues similarly arrayed, but because the Blues exploited the wealth of the whole territory between Ahwaz and Kerman, they had better equipment, finer steeds, and more weapons than the Basrans. Wearing helmets and heavy suits of trailing armor, the Blues confronted al-Muhallab's men in a terrifying clash. In despair, al-Muhallab's forces broke ranks and turned heel in defeat. Al-Muhallab raced to an elevated point and called out, "Worshippers of God! 34.11

إلى مكان يفاع ثمّ نادى الناس إليّ إليّ عباد الله فثاب إليه جماعة من قومه حتّى اجتمع إليه نحو من ثلاثة آلاف فلمّا نظر إلى من اجتمع رضي جماعتهم فحمد الله تعالى وأثنى عليه ثمّ قال أمّا بعد فإنّ الله يكل الجمع الكثير إلى أنفسهم فينهزمون وينزل النصر على الجمع القليل فيظهرون ولعمري إنّي الآن بجماعتكم لراض وأنتم والله أهل الصبر وفرسان النصر وما أحبّ أنّ أحدًا ممّن انهزم معكم ﴿لَوْ خَرَجُواْ فِيكُم مَّا زَادُوكُمْ إِلَّا خَبَالًا﴾ عزمت على كلّ نفر منكم لما أخذ عشرة أحجار معه ثمّ امشوا بنا نحو معسكرهم فإنّهم الآن آمنون وقد خرجت خيلهم في طلب إخوانكم

١٢،٣٤ فقبلوا منه ثمّ أقبل بهم زحفًا فما شعرت الخوارج إلّا بالمهلّب فصار بِهم في جانب عسكرهم ثمّ استقبلوا أميرهم عبد الله بن الماحوز وأصحابه وعليهم الدروع والسلاح فجعل الرجل من أصحاب المهلّب يستعرض وجه الرجل بالحجارة حتّى يشخنه ثمّ يضربه بسيفه فلم يقاتلهم إلّا ساعة حتّى قُتل ابن الماحوز وصرف الله وجوه أصحابه وأخذ المهلّب عسكر القوم وما فيه ومضى المنهزمون إلى كرمان وإصبهان

١٣،٣٤ ثمّ وُلّي مصعب بن الزبير العراق ورجع إليه المهلّب فقاتل معه المختار بن أبي عبيد إلى أن قتل ورجع إلى الأزارقة فلم يزل يغاديهم القتال ويراوحهم وهو مع ذلك شديد الاحتراز على عسكره والتحفّظ إلى أن مضت مدّة طويلة وبلغ الخوارج قتل مصعب بن الزبير أمير العراق واستيلاء عبد الملك بن مروان قبل أن يبلغ المهلّب وأصحابه فناداهم الخوارج ما تقولون في مصعب قالوا إمام هدى ولينا في الدنيا والآخرة قالوا فماذا تقولون في عبد الملك قالوا ذاك ابن اللعين قالوا فأنتم منه برّاء في الدنيا والآخرة قالوا نعم ونحن له أعداء كعداوتنا لكم قالوا فإنّ إمامكم مصعب قد[١] قتله عبد الملك وإنّكم ستجعلون عبد الملك غدًا إمامكم وأنتم اليوم تتبرّؤون منه وتلعنون أباه قالوا كذبتم يا أعداء الله

١ سقطت من إ.

Rally to me! To me!" Some three thousand answered his call. Al-Muhallab surveyed the troops and liked what he saw. He addressed them, praising God and saying, "God lets mighty forces think their own numbers make them invincible, but they find themselves beaten, for if God wills victory for a small party, it will prevail. By my life! I am most pleased with your number: you are men of grit and horse warriors of triumph, and I would not want a single one of those who have fled to come and join us: «Had they gone forth with you, they would only have proved a source of evil.»[277] My order is that each of you take ten stones and charge with the rest of us toward the Blues' camp. Right now they feel secure, and their cavalry is distracted by the chase of your comrades."

They accepted al-Muhallab's plan. All advanced, and they burst into the camp, catching the Kharijites' leader, ʿUbayd Allāh ibn al-Māḥūz,[278] and his heavily armed and equipped retainers totally unawares. Al-Muhallab's men hurled their stones with deadly accuracy at the heads of the Kharijites, and then charged with their swords. After a short fight, Ibn al-Māḥūz was felled and God drove off the surviving Blues in defeat. Al-Muhallab plundered everything in the camp, while the Blues beat a retreat to Kerman and Isfahan. 34.12

After the battle, Muṣʿab ibn al-Zubayr was appointed governor over Iraq, and al-Muhallab returned to support him in another war: this one against al-Mukhtār ibn Abī ʿUbayd. Once al-Mukhtār was killed, al-Muhallab turned again to prosecute the campaign against the Blues. Day and night he fought, while always maintaining extreme vigilance in protecting his own camp. The fighting was long and unabated. 34.13

In the meantime, in Iraq, the Caliph ʿAbd al-Malik defeated Muṣʿab ibn al-Zubayr: Muṣʿab was killed and ʿAbd al-Malik conquered the province. The Kharijites heard the news before it reached al-Muhallab's army, and they called to al-Muhallab's men across the battle lines, "What is your opinion of Muṣʿab?" Al-Muhallab's men cried back, "He is our imam of right guidance! Our overlord in the affairs of this world and the next!" The Kharijites asked, "And what do you think about ʿAbd al-Malik?" "Nothing but the son of a damned man!" The Kharijites asked further, "So do you renounce him in this world and the next?" "Of course: he is our enemy just as much as you are!" The Kharijites then revealed the news: "Know that your imam Muṣʿab has been killed by ʿAbd al-Malik, and tomorrow you will proclaim ʿAbd al-Malik your new imam, even though today you renounce him and curse his father!" Al-Muhallab's men were incredulous: "You lie, you enemies of God!"

١٤،٣٤ فلمّا كان من الغد تبيّن لهم قتل مصعب فبايع المهلّب الناس لعبد الملك فنداهم الأزارقة يا أعداء الله بالأمس تتبرّؤون منه واليوم تبايعونه بالخلافة وقد قتل إمامكم الذي كنتم توالونه[1] فأيّهما المهديّ فأيّهما الضالّ فقالوا رضينا بذاك ونرضى بهذا إذ كلّ منهما أمرنا فقالوا لا والله ولكنّكم إخوان الشياطين وطلبة الدنيا

١٥،٣٤ ثمّ ولي عبد الملك وأمّر الحجّاج على العراق وأمره بإمداد المهلّب فشمّر الحجّاج لذلك وتتابع المدد إلى أن قال المهلّب لقد ولي العراق وال ذكر

١٦،٣٤ ثمّ إنّ الحجّاج كتب إلى المهلّب يستبطئه في مناجزة الأزارقة ويستعجزه فحبس المهلّب رسول الحجّاج أيّامًا حتّى رأى صنيع الخوارج وجلدهم وثباتهم وكتب إلى الحجّاج يقول إنّ الشاهد يرى ما لا يرى الغائب فإن كنت نصبتني لحرب هؤلاء القوم على أن أدبّرها كما أرى فإذا أمكنتني فرصة انتهزتها وإن لم تمكّني توقّفت فأنا أدبّر ذلك بما يصلحه وإن أردت منّي أن أعمل وأنا حاضر برأيك وأنت غائب فإن كان صوابًا فلك وإن كان خطًأ فعليّ فابعث من أردت مكاني والسلام

١٧،٣٤ ولمّا طالت الحروب بين المهلّب وبينهم ورأى اتّفاق أهوائهم وثباتهم علم أنّه لا يُظفر إلّا باختلاف يقع بينهم وكان في عسكرهم حدّاد يُسمّى إبزن يصنع نصالًا مسمومة يرمى بها أصحاب المهلّب فوجّه المهلّب رجلًا من أصحابه بكتاب وألف درهم إلى عسكر الخوارج وقال ألق الكتاب في العسكر واحذر على نفسك وكان في الكتاب إلى الحدّاد أمّا بعد فإنّ نصالك قد وصلت وقد وجّهت إليك بألف درهم فاقبضها وزدنا من هذه النصال فوقع الكتاب إلى قطريّ فدعا إبزن وقال ما هذا الكتاب قال لا أدري قال فما هذه الدراهم قال لا أعلم علمها فأمر به فقتل فجاءه

١ إ: تنالوه.

In the morning, the news of Muṣʿab's death was confirmed and al-Muhallab ordered his men to swear allegiance to ʿAbd al-Malik. Soon the Blues were shouting again: "You enemies of God! Yesterday you disclaimed the man to whom today you pledge obedience as caliph, even though he killed the man whom you had followed as your imam! Tell us, which of them is the rightly guided and which is the false imam?" Al-Muhallab's men cried back, "They are our leaders. We were satisfied with one and now are satisfied with the other!" The Kharijites responded, "No, by God! You are the party of Devil. All you care for is worldly gain!" 34.14

ʿAbd al-Malik appointed al-Ḥajjāj as governor over Iraq, commanding him to support al-Muhallab. Al-Ḥajjāj applied himself with vigor. He sent such constant trains of supplies and reinforcements that al-Muhallab remarked, "Now Iraq has a real man in charge." 34.15

As al-Muhallab's campaign dragged on, al-Ḥajjāj wrote, chiding him for his delay in confronting the Blues and insinuating that he was incompetent. Al-Muhallab detained the messenger for a few days so he could observe the Kharijites' mettle and tenacity for himself. Al-Muhallab also wrote to al-Ḥajjāj: "Those present see what those absent do not. You have appointed me to wage war against these people according to the strategy I see fit: if I espy an opportunity, I snatch it, but if there is none, I hold back; I consider this the right approach. If you intend to command me yourself, while I am present on the front line and you are absent, then if I succeed, all will congratulate you, and if I fail, they will blame me. If this is what you prefer, send whomever you would like to replace me. Peace be upon you." 34.16

Al-Muhallab continued the interminable campaign. He was aware that the Blues' steadfastness stemmed from their unified commitment to their creed, and he realized that he could only triumph if he kindled division among their ranks. The Blues had in their camp a blacksmith named Ibzan[279] who made poison-tipped arrows, which they shot at al-Muhallab's forces. One day, al-Muhallab gave one of his men a forged letter with a thousand dirhams, and instructed him: "Steal into the Blues camp, drop this letter, and take care of yourself!" The letter read: "To the blacksmith: your arrowheads arrived, and we have sent you one thousand dirhams. Take it, and make more arrowheads for us." The letter fell into the hands of the Blues' leader, Qaṭarī, and he summoned Ibzan: "What's this letter about?" Ibzan replied, "No idea, sir." "And what about this money?" "I know nothing about it." Qaṭarī gave the order 34.17

عبد ربّه الصغير وكان من كبار القوم فقال له أقتلت رجلاً على غير بيّنة[1] قال فما حال هذه الدراهم فقال يجوز أن يكون أمرها كذبًا ويجوز أن يكون حقًّا قال قطريّ فقتل رجل في صلاح الناس غير منكر وللإمام أن يحكم بما يراه صلاحًا وليس للرعيّة أن تعترض عليه فتنكّر له عبد ربّه ومن معه ولم يفارقوه

١٨،٣٤ فبلغ ذلك المهلّب فدسّ إليه رجلاً نصرانيًّا فقال له إذا رأيت قطريًّا فاسجد له فإذا نهاك فقل إنّما سجدت لك ففعل النصرانيّ ذلك فقال له قطريّ إنّما السجود لله فقال ما سجدت إلّا لك فقال له رجل من الخوارج قد عبدك من دون الله وتلا ﴿إِنَّكُمْ وَمَا تَعْبُدُونَ مِن دُونِ ٱللَّهِ حَصَبُ جَهَنَّمَ أَنتُمْ لَهَا وَٰرِدُونَ﴾ فقال قطريّ إن هذه النصارى عبدوا عيسى بن مريم فما ضرّ عيسى بن مريم ذلك فقام رجل من الخوارج إلى النصرانيّ فقتله فأنكر ذلك عليه وقال قتلت ذمّيًّا فاختلفت الكلمة

١٩،٣٤ فبعث إليهم المهلّب رجلاً يسألهم عن شيء تقدّم به إليه فأتاهم الرجل فقال أرأيتم رجلين خرجا مهاجرين إليكم فمات أحدهما في الطريق وبلغكم الآخر فامتحنتموه فلم يجز المحنة ما تقولون فيهما فقال بعضهم أمّا الميّت فهو من أهل الجنّة وأمّا الذي لم يجز المحنة فكافر حتّى يجيزها فقال قوم آخرون بل هما كافران حتّى يجيزا المحنة وكثر الخلاف فخرج قطريّ إلى حدود إصطخر وأوقع المهلّب بمن بقي منهم مع صالح بن مخراق وزحف إلى البقيّة وخندق عليهم[2] ثمّ أقام أيّامًا وأوقع بينهم الفتنة حتّى وقع بين قطريّ وعبد ربّه وانحاز إلى عبد ربّه جماعة وولّوه عليهم وذهب قطريّ بأصحابه وقاتل المهلّب جيش عبد ربّه وقتله[3] بعد وقائع طويلة وانفلّ حدّ الأزارقة وتشتّتوا في البلاد وتخطّفهم الناس

١ إ٣: غير ثقة ولا تبيّن. ٢ إ١، ر١، إ٢، إ٣: عليه. ٣ زيادة من بر١.

and Ibzan was executed, prompting ʿAbd Rabbihi "the Small," who was one of the Blues' greatest leaders, to say, "You just killed a man without conclusive evidence!" Qaṭarī replied, "What about the money here?" ʿAbd Rabbihi said, "It might indicate the truth of the matter. On the other hand, it might not." Qaṭarī was unmoved: "Executing one man for the good of the collective is legitimately within the powers vested in the imam. He can act as he sees best for the group, and its members have no right to challenge him." ʿAbd Rabbihi and his men disapproved, but did not break rank.

Al-Muhallab heard the outcome, and he next contrived to slip a Christian into the Blues' camp, instructing him: "When you see Qaṭarī, prostrate before him, and when he forbids you, insist and tell him, 'I prostrate only to you.'" The Christian did as he was ordered, and Qaṭarī told him, "We can prostrate only to God." But the Christian repeated, "I prostrate to you!" One of the Kharijites cried, "He's worshipping you instead of God!" and recited the Qur'an: «Both you and what you worship instead of God will be fuel for Hell: to it you shall all come.»[280] Qaṭarī retorted, "No: Jesus son of Mary is not destined for Hell just because he is worshipped by these Christians." But another Kharijite stepped forward and struck the Christian dead, and Qaṭarī exclaimed in reproach, "You have killed one protected under the law!"[281] There were mumblings of dissent. 34.18

Al-Muhallab then sent a third man into the Blues' camp, this one to question them on a point of doctrine. He entered and asked them, "What is the ruling in the case of two men who set out to join the movement, one of whom dies on the way, while the second fails when you test his faith?" Some of the Blues said, "The one who died on the way will enter Paradise, whereas the one who was tested is an unbeliever until such time as he can pass our trial." But another group of Blues disagreed: "Absolutely not! They are both unbelievers—only those who pass the trial of faith can enter Paradise." This time the disagreement spread, and Qaṭarī was forced to withdraw to Iṣṭakhr. Al-Muhallab then overwhelmed the remaining Blues under the command of Ṣāliḥ ibn Mikhrāq, and advanced on the rest, once again entrenching his position. Al-Muhallab remained thus for several days, stoking discord among their ranks until he finally caused a rift between ʿAbd Rabbihi and Qaṭarī. ʿAbd Rabbihi's companions declared him their leader, Qaṭarī and his contingent then quit the camp, al-Muhallab assaulted ʿAbd Rabbihi's army, and, after a long series of battles, al-Muhallab finally killed him. With this, the Blues' power was sapped. They dispersed throughout the countryside, and locals captured them piecemeal. 34.19

وكتب المهلّب إلى الحجّاج بالفتح كتابًا أوّله ٢٠،٣٤

الحمد لله الكافي بالإسلام فقد ما سواه بأن حكم[١] أن لا ينقطع المزيد منه حتّى ينقطع الشكر من عباده أمّا بعد فقد كنّا وعدوّنا على حالين مختلفين يسرّنا منهم أكثر ما يسوءنا ويسوءهم منّا أكثر ما يسرّهم على اشتداد شوكتهم فقد كان علن[٢] أمرهم حتّى ارتاعت الفتاة ويتم به الرضيع[٣] فانتهزت منهم الفرصة في وقت إمكانها وأدنيت السواد حتّى تعارفت الوجوه فلم يزل ذلك حتّى بلغ الكتاب أجله ﴿فَقُطِعَ دَابِرُ ٱلْقَوْمِ ٱلَّذِينَ ظَلَمُواْ وَٱلْحَمْدُ لِلَّهِ رَبِّ ٱلْعَٰلَمِينَ﴾

فكتب إليه الحجّاج يشكره ويذكر بلاءه ويأمره بالقدوم عليه واستخلاف أحد ٢١،٣٤
بنيه فقدم على الحجّاج فأجلسه على السرير إلى جانبه وأظهر إكرامه وبرّه وقال يا أهل العراق أنتم عتقاء المهلّب ثمّ قال أنت والله كما قال لقيط الإياديّ

وَقَلِّدُوا أَمْرَكُمْ لِلَّهِ دَرُّكُمُ   رَحْبَ ٱلذِّرَاعِ بِأَمْرِ ٱلْحَرْبِ مُضْطَلِعَا
لَا يَطْعَمُ ٱلنَّوْمَ إِلَّا حَيْثُ يَبْعَثُهُ   هَمٌّ يَكَادُ حَشَاهُ يَقْصِمُ[٤] ٱلضِّلَعَا
حَتَّى ٱسْتَمَرَّ عَلَى شَزْرٍ مَرِيرَتُهُ   مُسْتَحْكِمُ ٱلرَّأْيِ لَا قَحْمًا وَلَا ضَرَعَا

فقام رجل فقال أصلح الله الأمير والله لكأنّي أسمع قطريًّا وهو يقول المهلّب كما قال لقيط ثمّ أنشد هذا الشعر فسُرّ الحجّاج حتّى ظهر عليه

وسُئل المهلّب ما أعجب ما رأيت من قتال الأزارقة قال رأيت رجلاً منهم ٢٢،٣٤
يطعن في أحدهم فيمشي في الرمح إلى طاعنه ليضربه وهو يقول ﴿وَعَجِلْتُ إِلَيْكَ رَبِّ لِتَرْضَىٰ[١]﴾

١ إ١: وبان لا حكم. ٢ بر١، إ٦: علا. ٣ ويتم به الرضيع: زيادة من بر٢، أز٢، ق٢. ٤ إ١: سداه يفطم.

Al-Muhallab announced the victory in a letter to al-Ḥajjāj: 34.20

> Praise be to God Whose Islam is good recompense for the loss of everything else, and Who decrees continued good recompense for so long as His worshippers give thanks. We and our enemy subsisted in different conditions. We got the better of them more than we suffered, and they suffered from us more than they got the better of us. The vehemence of the enemies' might had been manifest, causing young girls to fear and suckling babes to become orphans. But I seized the opportunity when it arose and pressed forward toward their sprawling, swarming ranks until I could see the whites of their eyes. The battle lasted till the preordained time for its predetermined outcome: «The wrongdoers were annihilated. All praise be to God, the Lord of the Worlds.»[282]

Al-Ḥajjāj replied, expressing gratitude and lauding al-Muhallab's valor, and he ordered al-Muhallab to attend court and to deputize one of his sons as commander over the forces. Al-Muhallab arrived, al-Ḥajjāj showed him honor and respect, seating him at his side on the elevated throne. Al-Ḥajjāj announced, "People of Iraq! You were as slaves and al-Muhallab has manumitted you." To al-Muhallab, al-Ḥajjāj added, "You, by God, are as the poet Laqīṭ al-Iyādī described: 34.21

> How right it will be! Entrust your war
> to a powerful man, well versed in its arts.
> He takes no rest so long as he faces
> distress that gnaws at his innards.
> He confronts it: tightly wound torque at point of force,
> with decisive mind: this is no frail coward!"

A man rose and exclaimed, "God save the Commander! By God, I once heard Qaṭarī saying exactly the same thing about al-Muhallab: Qaṭarī said, 'Al-Muhallab is as Laqīṭ described,' and recited that very poem!" Al-Ḥajjāj was so impressed with this that everyone could see his pleasure.

Al-Muhallab was asked, "What was the most astounding thing you saw in war against the Blues?" He replied, "Once, I saw that one of our men had stabbed a Blue with a lance, but the Blue still managed to plunge through the length of the lance to slash our man, all the while reciting the Qur'an: «I have hastened to You, my Lord, to please You.»"[283] 34.22

وكانت مدّة إقامة المهلّب على قتال الخوارج ومصابرته لهم تسع عشرة سنة إلى أن فتح الله على يديه وطهّر منهم الأرض ومات على فراشه ٢٣،٣٤

ومن أخباره المستحسنة أنّه أقبل يومًا من بعض غزواته فتلقّته امرأة فقالت أيّها الأمير إنّي نذرت إن أقبلت سالما أن أصوم يومًا وتهب لي جاريةً وألفَ درهم فضحك وقال قد وفّينا نذرك فلا تعاودي فليس كلّ أحد يفي لك ٢٤،٣٤

ووقف له رجل فقال أريد منك حويجة فقال اطلب لها رجيلاً يعني أن مثلي لا يُسأل إلّا حاجة عظيمة[1] ٢٥،٣٤

ومرّ يومًا في البصرة فسمع رجلاً يقول هذا الأعور ساد الناس ولو أُخرج إلى السوق لمّا ساوى أكثر من مائة درهم فبعث إليه مائة درهم وقال لو زدتنا في الثمن زدناك في العطيّة ٢٦،٣٤

ولمّا هزم قطريّ بن الفجاءة دخل إليه رجل فأنشده ٢٧،٣٤

أَمْسَى ٱلْعِبَادُ لَعَمْرِي لَا غِيَاثَ لَهُمْ　　إِلَّا ٱلْمُهَلَّبُ بَعْدَ ٱللهِ وَٱلْمَطَرُ
هٰذَا يَجُودُ وَيَحْمِي عِنْ دِيَارِهِمْ　　وَذَا يَعِيشُ بِهِ ٱلْأَنْعَامُ وَٱلشَّجَرُ

فقال هذا والله الشعر وأمر له بعشرين ألفًا

ومن كلامه عجبت لمن يشتري العبيد بماله ولا يشتري[2] الأحرار بإفضاله ٢٨،٣٤

وكان يقول لولده إذا غدا عليكم الرجل وراح مسلّمًا[3] فكفى بذلك تقاضيًا ٢٩،٣٤

وتذاكروا عنده الثياب فقال أحسن ثيابكم ما رأيتموه على غيركم ٣٠،٣٤

وكان كثيرًا ما يأمر بصلة الرحم والمكيدة في الحرب ٣١،٣٤

وحكي أنّ عبد الرحمن بن الأشعث لمّا خرج على الحجّاج كاتب المهلّب وهو بخراسان يدعوه إلى خلع الحجّاج فقال المهلّب لا أغدر بعد سبعين سنة ثمّ كتب ٣٢،٣٤

---

١ ووقف له . . . عظيمة: زيادة من بر١ ول١ وبا١. ٢ العبيد . . . يشتري: سقطت من إ١. ٣ سقطت من إ١.

It took nineteen years of steady conflict for al-Muhallab to defeat the Kharijites and purify the land of their wickedness. Al-Muhallab died in his bed. 34.23

Commendable anecdotes about al-Muhallab include a story of a woman who approached him when he returned from one of his victorious campaigns and said, "Commander! I swore a solemn oath to God that if He returned you safe and sound from the war, I would fast for one month, and you would give me a slave girl and one thousand dirhams." Al-Muhallab laughed and told her, "We will satisfy your vow, but don't do this again: not everyone will be so generous." 34.24

A man stopped al-Muhallab and said to him, "I have just a little request of you." Al-Muhallab replied, "Then ask a little man." What al-Muhallab meant was that men like him are for serious requests only. 34.25

Al-Muhallab once overheard someone in Basra saying, "This one-eyed man commands the people, yet if he was up for sale here in the market, he wouldn't fetch more than a hundred dirhams!" Al-Muhallab sent the Basran one hundred dirhams with the message: "If you had valued us more greatly, you would have earned more." 34.26

When Qaṭarī ibn al-Fujā'ah was defeated, a man presented himself to al-Muhallab and recited: 34.27

There is no aid for the humble,
beyond God and the rain, except for al-Muhallab.
Al-Muhallab: generosity and protection that saves their land;
God and His rains: succor for the plants and animals.

Al-Muhallab told him, "This, by God, is real poetry!" and gave him twenty thousand.

Al-Muhallab's wise words include: "I am astonished that a man will spend his money to buy a slave, but gives nothing to win the hearts of the well-born." 34.28

Al-Muhallab used to tell his sons: "If a man comes to you in the morning and leaves in the evening wishing you well,[284] consider that sufficient settlement." 34.29

The topic of clothing was raised in al-Muhallab's assembly, and he said, "Your best clothes are the ones you see others are wearing." 34.30

Al-Muhallab exhorted people to maintain good family relations. 34.31

In war, he frequently took recourse to crafty stratagems.

It was reported that when ʿAbd al-Raḥman ibn al-Ashʿath launched his revolt against al-Ḥajjāj, al-Muhallab was in Khurasan, and Ibn al-Ashʿath sent him a 34.32

إلى الحجّاج أمّا بعد فإنّ أهل العراق مع ابن الأشعث قد أقبلوا إليك وهم مثل السيل المنحطّ من عل ليس يردّه شيء حتّى ينتهي إلى قراره ولأهل العراق شدّة في أوّل[1] حربهم ولهم صبابة إلى نسائهم وأبنائهم فليس يردّهم شيء دون أهلهم فلا تستقبلهم وخلّ لهم السبيل حتّى يأتوا البصرة فيضاجعوا نساءهم ويتشمّموا[2] أبناءهم فترقّ قلوبهم ويخلدوا إلى المقام في منازلهم ويتفرّقوا عن ابن الأشعث فأوقع بمن حاربك منهم فإنّ الله ناصرك عليهم فلمّا قرأ الحجّاج كتابه قال ويلي على ابن المرويّ والله ما لي نظر وإنّما نظر لابن عمّه ولم يقبل منه وكان ذلك مراد المهلّب وتلطّف له في طيّ هذه النصيحة

٣٣،٣٤ ومن شعره

إِنَّا إِذَا أَنْشَأَتْ قَوْمًا لَنَا نِعَمٌ　　قَالَتْ لَنَا أَنْفُسٌ أَزْدِيَّةٌ عُودُو
لَا يُوجَدُ ٱلْجُودُ إِلَّا عِنْدَ ذِي كَرَمٍ　　وَٱلْمَالُ عِنْدَ لِئَامِ ٱلنَّاسِ مَوجُودُ

٣٥ **وأنّ هرمس أعطى بلينوس ما أخذ منك**

١،٣٥ هرمس هذا هو الذي يزعم قوم من الصابئة أنّه نبيّ مرسل وأنّه إدريس عليه السلام ويسندون إليه شرائعهم من تعظيم الكواكب السبعة والبروج الاثنى عشر والتقريب إليها بالذبائح وما أشبه ذلك من مذاهبهم

٢،٣٥ قال أبو معشر البلخيّ هو أوّل من تكلّم في الأشياء العلويّة من الحركات النجوميّة وجدّه كيومرث وهو آدم عليه السلام علّمه ساعات الليل والنهار وهو أوّل من بنى الهياكل ومجّد الله فيها وأوّل من نظر في الطبّ وتكلّم فيه وصنّف لأهل زمانه كتبًا

١ سقطت من إ. ٢ إ، برا: ويرشفوا.

letter asking him to renounce his allegiance to al-Ḥajjāj. Al-Muhallab replied: "For seventy years I have never acted perfidiously, and I will not do so now." Then al-Muhallab wrote to al-Ḥajjāj: "The people of Iraq support Ibn al-Ashʿath, and they are advancing upon you like a raging torrent from high ground: nothing can divert them until they hit the plain. Know, however, that the Iraqis are ferocious at the outset of their campaigns, but their adoration of their women and children is greater. Nothing holds them back like their families, so do not march out to meet them. Leave them be until they enter Basra and sleep with their wives and savor time with their children. Their hearts will soften, they will decide to remain forever in their homes, and they will desert Ibn al-Ashʿath. Then strike those who still fight you, for God will grant you victory." Al-Ḥajjāj read the letter and exclaimed, "Blazes! The son of Marw will be my damnation! By God, he didn't look to my interests; he was thinking of the interests of his cousins." Al-Ḥajjāj did not accept al-Muhallab's advice, yet this was precisely what al-Muhallab had subtly intended between the lines of his message.

Al-Muhallab's poetry: 34.33

Granting favors made people favor us;
  Azdī voices called out, "Grant more!"
Contemptible men may possess wealth;
  generosity, though, is only found among the noble.

**. . . it was from you that Hermes learned what he taught Apollonius . . .** 35

Some of the Sabians allege that this Hermes[285] was a prophet who received divine revelation, and that he is one and the same as Enoch (eternal peace be his). Those Sabians trace various tenets of their creed to Hermes, including their rites of venerating and sacrificing to the seven celestial bodies and the twelve constellations. 35.1

Abū Maʿshar al-Balkhī says: Hermes was the first to prognosticate about celestial matters by observing the movement of the stars. Hermes's grandfather, Gayomard—that is, Adam (eternal peace be his)[286]—taught him the reckoning of the hours of the day and night, and Hermes was the first man to construct temples for the worship of God. He was also the first to explore and 35.2

كثيرة بأشعار موزونة بلغتهم في معرفة الأشياء العلويّة والأرضيّة أوّل من أنذر بالطوفان ورأى أنّ آفة[1] سماويّةً تلحق الأرض من الماء والنار

٣،٣٥ وكان مسكنه مصر فعند ذلك بنى الأهرام ومدائن التراب وخاف ذهاب العلم بالطوفان فبنى البرابيَ وهو في[2] الجبل المعروف ببرباة أخميم وصوّر فيها الصناعات وصنّاعها نقشًا وأشار إلى صفات العلوم لمن بعده حرصًا على تخليدها من بعده

٤،٣٥ وتزعم الصابئة أنّ النبوّة بعده لإسقبلينوس[3] وأصل اسمه بلينوس فزيد في اسمه تعظيمًا له وكذلك يقال في أرسطو زيد في اسمه تعظيمًا فقيل أرسطوطاليس ومذهبهم في ذلك أنّه كلّما مهر وعظم زيد حرفًا أو حرفين وكان بلنيوس قد أخذ العلوم والأسرار عن هرمس هذا وهو هرمس الهرامسة

٥،٣٥ وزعم آخرون أنّ هرمس صاحب بلنيوس كان بعد الطوفان قال يعقوب الكنديّ وهو صاحب كتاب الحيوان ذوات السموم وكان طبيبًا فيلسوفًا عالمًا بطبائع الأدوية جوّالًا في الأرض عالمًا بنصبة المدائن وطبائعها وطبائع أهلها وأدويتها وهو صاحب الطلّسمات الأندلسيّة مثل السودانيّة النحاس وغيرها وكان بلنيوس هذا تلميذه سافر معه البلاد فلمّا خرجا من الهند إلى فارس خلّفه ببابل

٦،٣٥ وكان قد أخذ عنه جميع علومه وظهرت له في الطبّ وإبراء المرضى وقائع معجزة إلى أن كثرت فيه أقاويلهم وقالوا هو نبيّ وقال قوم هو ملك وزعموا أنّ مولده روحانيّ وأنّ الله تعالى رفعه في عمود من نور

٧،٣٥ وإقليدس يُنسب إليه وهو الذي وضع علم الطبّ في هيكل يعرف بهيكل إسقنبلنيوس ويدلّ على ذلك قول جالينوس في بعض كتبه إنّ الله تعالى لمّا خلّصني من دبيلة قتّالة كانت عرضت لي حججت إلى بيته المسمّى بهيكل

---

١ إ١؛ آية. ٢ هو في: سقطت من إ١. ٣ إ١: أسفنبلينوس؛ إ٦: إسقلينوس؛ بر١: اسقنبلنيوس.

expound upon the science of medicine, and he compiled numerous versified books in his people's language about matters celestial and terrestrial. Hermes was also the first to warn about the Great Flood, as he observed astral signs that indicated flood and fire were to be inflicted on the world.

Hermes lived in Egypt, and was the builder of the Pyramids and the cities made of earth. He feared that a great flood would obliterate all knowledge, and so he built the temples at Mount Birbā' near Akhmim[287] in which he inscribed illustrations of every craft and its craftsmen, in the hope that future generations could recover knowledge by examining his detailed depictions. 35.3

The Sabians also allege that prophecy passed from Hermes to Apollonius. His name was originally Apollonius, but as an honorific, they added letters to his name and it became Asclepius.[288] The same was the case for Aristotle: his given name was Aristo, and it was expanded to Aristoteles to honor him. The ancients used to express their esteem for men who achieved great things by adding a syllable or two to their names. The Sabians believe that Hermes taught Apollonius all knowledge and the mysteries, and they identify this Hermes as Hermes Trismegistus. 35.4

Others claim that Hermes was the teacher of Apollonius and that they both lived after the Flood. Yaʿqūb al-Kindī says: Hermes was the writer of *The Book of Poisonous Animals*, and he was a doctor and philosopher well versed in the science of herbals. He was well traveled too, and knew the natural conditions and humors of lands and populations, as well as of medicines. He was creator of the Andalusian Talismans, including, among others, the Bronze Starling.[289] Hermes and his student Apollonius traveled through the lands. Together they visited India, and when they quit it for Persia, Hermes chose Apollonius as his successor in Babylon. 35.5

Apollonius had mastered all of Hermes's knowledge and attained miraculous powers in medicine and healing the sick. His fame spread, and some said, "He's a prophet!" while others said, "He's an angel!" They alleged that he had a mystical birth and that Exalted God raised Apollonius to the Heavens on a column of light.[290] 35.6

One of Asclepius's descendants, Euclid, built the temple of medical science known as the Temple of Asclepius. We know the temple existed, since Galen mentioned it in one of his books: "After the Exalted God had cured me from an affliction of a potentially fatal abdominal disease, I made a pilgrimage to His shrine known as the Temple of Asclepius." It is said that this temple was in 35.7

إسقنبلنيوس ويقال إنّ هذا الهيكل بمدينة روميّة كانت فيه صورة تكلّم الناس مركّبة على حركات نجوميّة وإنّه كان فيها روحانيّة كوكب من الكواكب السبعة

٨،٣٥ وحكى جالينوس أنّ الله تعالى أوحى إلى إسقنبلنيوس أنّي لأن أسمّيك ملكًا أقرب من تسميتك إنسانًا

٩،٣٥ وكان معظّمًا عند اليونان يستسقون بقبره ويوقدون عليه كلّ ليلة ألف قنديل وخلّف ابنين ماهرين في صناعة الطبّ وعهد إليهما أن لا يعلّما الطبّ إلّا لأولادهما وأهل بيتهما ولا يدخلا في هذه الصناعة غريبًا وكان تعليم الطبّ تلقينًا إلى أن وضع أبقراط الكتب وهو السادس عشر من ولده

١٠،٣٥ قال جالينوس وأمّا صورته يعني الصورة في الهيكل فصورة رجل ملتح قائمًا مشمّرًا مجموع الثياب يدلّ بهذا الشكل على أنّه ينبغي للأطبّاء أن يستعدّوا في جميع الأوقات آخذًا بيده عصًا معوجّةً ذات شعب يدلّ كذلك على أنّه يمكن في صناعة الطبّ أن يبلغ بمن استعملها من السنّ أن يحتاج إلى عصًا يتوكّأ عليها وقيل إنّما صوّر العصا لأنّها من شجر الخطميّ وأنّه يطرد بها الأمراض وأمّا شعبها فتدلّ على كثرة أصناف الطبّ والتفنّن فيه ثمّ صوّر على تلك العصا صورة حيوان طويل العمر وهو التنّين ويقرب هذا الحيوان منه لأشياء كثيرة أحدها أنّه حيوان حادّ البصر كثير السهر وكذلك ينبغي للطبيب أن يكون في المعرفة والاجتهاد والثاني أنّه يسلخ لباسه الذي يسمّونه الشيخوخة وكذلك يمكن الطبيب أن يسلخ الشيخوخة بما يفيده من الصحّة والثالث أنّه طويل العمر وعلى ذلك يحرص بعض الأطبّاء

١١،٣٥ ويُروى أنّه عاش تسعين سنة ومن كلامه الصنيعة عند الكفور إضاعة للنعمة والمتعبّد بغير معرفة كحمار الطاحون يمشي ولا يبرح ولا يعرف ما هو فاعل

Rome, and it contained an automaton constructed to correspond with astral movements, which could speak to the temple visitors: it was inhabited by the spirit of one of the seven Celestial Spheres.

Galen reports that Exalted God revealed to Asclepius: "I am closer to calling you an angel than a human." 35.8

Asclepius was revered among the Greeks: they used to pray at his grave for rain and lit one thousand candles before it every night. Asclepius passed on his knowledge of medicine to two of his sons who showed mastery of the science, and he made them swear a solemn oath never to teach medicine to anyone other than their own descendants, nor admit any outsider to the profession. Thus was medical knowledge transmitted only via oral instruction within the family for sixteen generations, until Hippocrates recorded the knowledge in books. 35.9

Galen says: The image of Asclepius in his temple depicts a bearded man standing and gathering up his robes: this symbolizes that doctors must be ready to practice their art at all times. The statue holds in its hand a crooked staff with several branches at its head, symbolizing that knowledge of medicine enables its practitioner to reach such an advanced age that he needs a staff; others say the staff represents a branch of the althea hibiscus, since it has healing properties. The staff's several limbs represent the many branches of medical knowledge requiring specialization. A serpent, an animal distinguished by its long life, is depicted coiled on the staff, and this symbolizes several things: first, the serpent has keen eyesight and remains alert at night, symbolizing that doctors must possess knowledge and stamina; second, the serpent sheds its skin, which is called "old age," and likewise the doctor can shed old age by granting health; and third, the serpent lives to a ripe old age, and some doctors endeavor to achieve this as well. 35.10

It is narrated that Asclepius lived to be ninety. His wise words: "A good turn done unto an ingrate is a waste of the blessing." 35.11

"A pious believer without knowledge is like a miller's donkey: he walks endlessly turning the stone, unaware of what he is doing."

## وأفلاطون أورد على أرسطاطليس ما نقل عنك ٣٦

١،٣٦ هو أفلاطون بن أرسطن الإلٰهيّ آخر المتقدّمين الأوائل معروف بالتوحيد والحكم ولد في زمان أردشير الأوّل وتتلمّذ لسقراط ولمّا اعتلّ سقراط ومات مسمومًا قام مكانه وجلس على كرسيّه وقد أخذ العلم عن سقراط وطيماوس وفيثاغورس وغيرهم[١] وضمّ إلى العلوم الإلٰهيّة العلوم الطبيعيّة والرياضيّة وهو أحد المشّائين المشهورين ومعنى المشّائين أنّه كان من رأيه الرياضة للبدن بالسعي المعتدل لتحليل الفضول ومدارسة الحكمة في تلك الحال

٢،٣٦ ويقال إنّه أمر الملوك باتّخاذ بيوت الحكمة لتعليم أولادهم وكانوا يتّخذون البيوت المذهّبة المزخرفة ويصوّرون فيها أصناف الصوّر المستحسنة التي ترتاح إليها النفوس ثمّ يتعلّم فيها الصبيّ فإذا حفظ علمًا أو وحكمة صعد يوم عيد على درج إلى مجلس بديع وقد اجتمع كبار أهل المملكة فتكلّم بالحكمة التي حفظها على رؤوس الأشهاد وعليه التاج ويُسمّى حكيمًا كلّ ذلك ترغيب للصبيّ في الاشتغال لما يحصل له من التشريف والسرور في يوم من هذه الأيّام ظهر أمر أرسطوطاليس كما سيأتي ذكره

٣،٣٦ ولأفلاطون آراء ومذاهب أخذها عنه أرسطو وخالفه في بعضها مثل حدوث العالم وغيره

٤،٣٦ وكان يُصوَّر للأفلاطون الصورة ويؤتى بها إليه فيقول من خلق صاحب[٢] هذه الصورة كذا وكذا فصُوّرت صورته وسُئل عنها فقال من خلق صاحب هذه الصورة كذا وكذا وهو محبّ للزنا فقيل إنّها صورتك فقال نعم ولولا أنّي أحبس نفسي عن الزنا لفعلت

٥،٣٦ ومن كلامه إنّ الله تعالى بقدر ما يعطي من الحكمة يمنع من الرزق فقيل ولم قال لأنّ الحكمة حظّ النفس الناطقة والمال حظّ النفس الشهوانيّة والناطقة غالبة على الشهوانيّة[٣] فالمال والحكمة متغايران ولا يجتمعان

---

١ وفيثاغورس وغيرهم: زيادة من بر١ وإ٦؛ إ١ وبا١ ول٢: وغيره. ٢ سقطت من إ١، إ٢. ٣ والناطقة . . . الشهوانية: سقطت من إ١.

**. . . you were the source of the wisdom Plato transmitted to Aristotle . . .** 36

Plato, son of Ariston, "the Divine,"[291] was the last of the great sages of the ancients and is famed for his wisdom and monotheism. He was born in the time of Ardashir the First,[292] he studied under Socrates, and when Socrates became sick and died from poisoning, Plato assumed his chair. Plato also studied under Timaeus,[293] Pythagoras, and others, and he integrated theology with the natural sciences and mathematics. Plato was an adherent of the celebrated Peripatetic school, a term designating those who believe that walking at a gentle pace facilitates the moderation of excess and the study of wisdom. 36.1

It is said that the Greek kings used to construct academies for the education of their children, and that these buildings would be gilded and decorated with pretty images to soothe the mind. Children would study in this environment, and once a student had memorized a tract of a discipline or philosophy, he would ascend to a marvelous platform where the great men of the kingdom gathered each feast day, and the student would repeat what he had memorized before the assembly. The student would be crowned and called "sage," and all these honors and pomp were intended to inspire diligence in their studies. Aristotle rose to prominence within this system, as will be detailed presently.[294] 36.2

Aristotle followed Plato's opinions and doctrines, but also disagreed in some respects, such as his theories of the material world's origin. 36.3

People used to present Plato with pictures of individuals, from which he would infer: "The person depicted here has x, y, and z characteristics." One day, he was presented with a picture of himself and observed, "The person depicted here has a proclivity to fornicate." They told him, "This is a picture of you!" He replied, "Yes indeed. If I did not hold myself in check, I would be guilty of it."[295] 36.4

Plato's wise sayings include the following: "To the extent which the Exalted God grants a man wisdom, he denies him wealth." When asked, "Why is that?" he replied, "Because wisdom is the share of the rational soul, whereas wealth is the share of the appetitive soul.[296] The rational axiomatically overcomes the appetitive: wealth and wisdom are contradictory, and they will not combine in one body." 36.5

٦،٣٦ وقال لا ينبغي إذا فعلت شيئًا ما إذا عُيّرت به غضبت فإنّك إذا فعلت ذلك كنت أنت القاذف لنفسك

٧،٣٦ وقال عقول الناس مدوّنة في رؤوس أقلامهم وظاهرة في اختياراتهم

٨،٣٦ وقيل له بماذا ينتصف الإنسان من عدوّه قال بأن يزداد فضلاً في نفسه

٩،٣٦ وقال في معنى الملك هو كالبحر تستمدّ منه الأنهار فإن كانت عذبًا عذبت وضدّ ذلك[1]

١٠،٣٦ وقال ينبغي للذين يأخذون على أيدي الأحداث أن يدعوا لهم موضعًا للعذر لئلّا يُضطرّوا إلى القحة[2] بكثرة التوبيخ

١١،٣٦ وقيل له فلان لا يعرف الشرّ فقال فإذًا لا[3] يعرف الخير يريد أن تكون الأمور متميّزة عند الإنسان فإنّه بعد تمييزها يختار منها وإذا لم يوضّحها التمييز بطل اختياره ومتى بطل اختياره خيف عليه أن يقع في مهلكاتها

١٢،٣٦ وقال من القبيح أن يمتنع من الطعام اللذيذ لتصحّ أبداننا ولا تمتنع من القبائح لتصفو أنفسنا

١٣،٣٦ فأمّا أرسطوطاليس فهو ابن منقوماخوس[4] المعروف بالمعلّم الأوّل وإنّما سُمّي بذلك لأنّه أوّل من وضع التعاليم المنطقيّة وأخرجها من القوّة إلى الفعل وحكمه حكم واضع النحو والعروض

١٤،٣٦ وكان سبب محبّة أفلاطون له وإلقاء علومه إليه أنّ أباه كان أسلمه لأفلاطون صغيرًا ومات فاستمرّ أرسطو يتيمًا في خدمته وكان روفسطالس[5] الملك قد اتّخذ لولده نطافورس[6] بيتًا للحكمة وأمر أفلاطون بتعليمه وكان غلامًا متخلّفًا قليل الفهم وأرسطو غلامًا ذكيًا حادًّا فكان أفلاطون يعلّم نطاقورس الآداب والحكمة وأرسطو يعي ذلك سرًّا ويرسّخ في صدره حتّى إذا كان يوم العيد زُيّن بيت الذهب الذي هو بيت الحكمة وألبس نطافورس التاج وحضر الملك وأهل المملكة على

١ وقال . . . وضد ذلك: سقطت من إ١. ٢ بياض في إ١. ٣ سقطت من إ١. ٤ إ١: سقوماخوس. ٥ إ١: روقسطاليس. ٦ إ٣: نطاقورس.

Plato said: "If you're likely to get angry if rebuked for an act, don't do it. Were you to follow through with it, you would become your own slanderer." 36.6

Plato also said: "People's reason is recorded on the nibs of their pens, and made manifest in their choices." 36.7

Plato was once asked, "How should one get even with an enemy?" Plato told them, "By increasing one's own virtue." 36.8

On the topic of kings, Plato said, "They are like the big bodies of water from which rivers derive: if the source is sweet, so will be the rivers, and also the contrary."[297] 36.9

Plato said: "When you scold the youth, give them some scope for excuses, otherwise you will impel them to become insolent from over-scolding." 36.10

When Plato was once told, "There is a man who knows no evil," he responded, "Then that man knows no good, either." He meant that people must be able to draw distinctions, since decisions are made by differentiating between available options. One who cannot differentiate cannot make sound choices, and one who makes unsound choices can, it is feared, commit mortal mistakes. 36.11

Plato said: "It is shameful that we withhold tasty food from ourselves for the sake of our bodies, yet we do not refrain from immoral acts for the sake of our souls." 36.12

Aristotle, the son of Nicomachus, is known as the "First Teacher" since he established logic as a discipline: he brought it from potentiality to reality and he determined its fundamental principles with the exactitude of those who established the rules of grammar and prosody. 36.13

The reason why Aristotle became Plato's most beloved student, and why Plato paid special attention to his instruction, is explained as follows. When Aristotle was a young boy, his father sent him to study under Plato, but shortly after, Aristotle's father died, and Aristotle stayed on as one of Plato's servants. At the same time, King Rufistanes had enrolled his son, Nitaforas,[298] in an academy and ordered Plato to teach him. Nitaforas was dim-witted and slow, whereas Aristotle was sharp and intelligent. When Plato instructed Nitaforas in philosophy and the fields of cultured knowledge, Aristotle used to listen surreptitiously, absorbing everything and committing it to memory. On the festival day, the academy was adorned and gilded, Nitaforas was crowned, 36.14

العادة وصعد أفلاطون وولد الملك إلى مجلس الحكمة والشرف على رؤوس الأشهاد فلم يورد الغلام شيئًا ولا نطق بحرف فأطرق أفلاطون ثمّ اعتذر بأنّه لم يقصر في الإلقاء عليه[1] وقال يا معشر التلامذة من فيكم من ينوب عن نطافورس فبدر أرسطو وصعد إلى المجلس وأخذ يسرد جميع ما ألقاه أفلاطون إلى ابن الملك ولم يغادر منه حرفًا فقال أفلاطون أيّها الملك هذه الحكمة التي ألقيتها على ولدك قد حفظها هذا اليتيم فما احتيالي في الرزق والحرمان ثمّ انصرف الجمع وقد اغتبط أفلاطون بأرسطو واعتنى به بعد ذلك ومكث عنده نيّفًا وعشرين سنة

١٥،٣٦ وكان كثير التعليم له بحيث أنّه كان إذا جلس فاستدعي منه الكلام يقول اصبروا وحتّى يحضر الناس وربّما قال حتّى يحضر العقل فإذا حضر أرسطو قال تكلّموا

١٦،٣٦ ثمّ مات أفلاطون وقد أخذ عنه أرسطو جميع علومه وخالفه في مسائل استدركها عليه وكان يقول إنّا لنحبّ أفلاطون ونحبّ الحقّ فإذا افترقا[2] كان الحقّ أولى بالمحبّة

١٧،٣٦ ثمّ وضع علم المنطق وأصوله وقال إنّما فضّل الناس على البهائم بالمنطق فأحقّهم بالإنسانيّة أبلغهم منطقًا وأوصلهم إلى عبارات ذات نفسه[3] بالإيجاز

١٨،٣٦ وله في ذلك مسائل ومصنّفات معروفة وكذلك في جميع علوم الحكمة والفلسفة وكان قد تسلّم الإسكندر بن قبليس[4] من أبيه وعلّمه وهذّبه وولي الإسكندر المملكة فكان لا يبرم أمرًا ولا ينقضه إلّا بإشارته فكان بمنزلة الوزير والمشير إلى أن تُوفّي الإسكندر وعاش بعده قليلاً ومات فوُضعت جثّته في إناء من نحاس وقيل فِي خشبة كالتابوت وعلّقت في جزيرة صقّليّة وكان أهل البلد يجتمعون إليها عند المشاورة والمدارسة في فنون الحكمة ويقولون إنّ مجيئهم إلى ذلك الموضع يذكّي عقولهم ويصحّح فكرهم وربّما استسقوا به في الجدب

١ بأنه . . . عليه زيادة من برا وبا١ ول٢ وإ٦. ٢ إ١: اقترنا. ٣ بياض في إ١. ٤ إ٣: فيلقوس.

and in the presence of the king and kingdom, he ascended the venerated platform with Plato, as was the custom. But the prince couldn't recite anything. He couldn't say so much as a word, and Plato hung his head, protesting that he had expended all effort in instructing the boy. He then addressed his students, "Pupils! Who among you can stand in for Nitaforas?" Aristotle rose, ascended the platform, and recited verbatim everything Plato had taught to the prince. Plato exclaimed, "King! This is the wisdom I taught your son, yet it was the orphan who memorized it all. I have no power over how knowledge is or is not learned!" All departed, but Plato was overjoyed with Aristotle and paid particular attention to him. Aristotle remained in Plato's academy for twenty-some years.

Plato would most often teach only when Aristotle was present: when Plato sat and was entreated to teach, he would say, "Wait until there are people here," or "Wait until reason attends." When Aristotle came, Plato would say, "Let's begin!" **36.15**

By the time of Plato's death, Aristotle had learned all his teachings and articulated corrections to precepts upon which they disagreed, saying, "We love Plato, and we love Truth, but wherever they diverge, Truth has precedence." **36.16**

Aristotle established the discipline of logic and expounded its principles. He said, "It is speech alone that renders humans superior to beasts; the more eloquent and more capable of concise expression are thus the more deserving of being called human." **36.17**

Aristotle composed famous discourses and compilations covering the whole ambit of wisdom and philosophy. King Philip entrusted Aristotle with teaching and cultivating the mind of his son Alexander, and when Alexander ascended the throne himself, he neither undertook nor annulled any matter without first consulting Aristotle. Aristotle remained in the position of Alexander's vizier until the king's death, and Aristotle only briefly outlived him. When Aristotle died, they placed his body in a copper vessel (some say wooden) resembling a sarcophagus, and they suspended it at a place in Sicily. The locals used to gather underneath it when seeking counsel or studying the fields of wisdom, since they claimed the place sharpened their minds and righted their thoughts. In times of drought, they often gathered there to pray for rain. **36.18**

ومن كلامه ما كتب به إلى الإسكندر وهو في غاية البلاغة أيّها الملك لا تنخدع للهوى وإن خُيّل لك أنّ في انخداعك له خداعة فقد يسترسل الإنسان وهو يظنّ أنّه متحفّظ واجمع في سياستك بين بدار لا حدّة فيه وريث لا غفلة معه[1] وامزج كلّ شيء[2] بشكله حتّى تزداد قوّة وكن عبدًا للحقّ فعبد الحقّ حرّ وليكن وكدك[3] الإحسان إلى الخلق ومن الإحسان وضع الإساءة في موضعها وكن نصيح نفسك فليس أحد أرأف بك منك وإذا أشكل عليك أمر فاضرع إلى الله تعالى الذي بلّغك هذه الغاية فإنّه يفتح لك المرتج وإذا فاتك شيء فاعلم أنّ ذلك لسهو عرض لك في الشكر على ما أفادك ومهما أخطأك شيء فلا يخطئك الفكر في الرحيل عن هذه الدار ١٩،٣٦

وقال لكلّ شيء صناعة وصناعة العقل حسن الاختيار ٢٠،٣٦

وقال سلوا القلوب عن المودّات فإنّها شهود لا تقبل الرشا ٢١،٣٦

وقال من علم أن الفناء مستول على كونه هانت عليه المصائب ٢٢،٣٦

وأكثر الأمثال المستجادة من شعر المتنبّي مأخوذة من كلامه وقد أُفرد في ذلك رسائل للحاتميّ وغيره ٢٣،٣٦

وحكى عبد الله بن طاهر أنّ المأمون قال رأيت في المنام رجلًا قد جلس مجلس الحكماء فقلت له من أنت فقال أرسطو الحكيم فقلت أيّها الحكيم ما أحسن الكلام قال ما يستقيم في الرأي قلت ثمّ ماذا قال ما يستحسن سامعه قلت ثمّ ماذا قال ما لا تخشى عاقبته قلت ثمّ ماذا قال ما عدا هذا هو ونهيق الحمار سواء قال المأمون ولو كان حيًّا ما زاد على هذا وقد قيل إن هذا الكلام وُجد في كتبه ٢٤،٣٦

١ سقطت من إ١.   ٢ إ١، با١، إ٦، إ٢، إ٣: شكل.   ٣ اللفظة غير واضحة في النسخ، المثبتة من إ٦.

Records of Aristotle's sayings include his extremely eloquent letters to Alexander: "King! Yield not to desires, even if you imagine that yielding to them will benefit you, for it is easy for a man who believes himself heedful to act unrestrained. In affairs of state, be both quick to act (without ceding to impatience) and take your time (without becoming neglectful). Balance matters in harmony, for that achieves greater strength. Give yourself in servitude to Truth, for a slave to Truth is free. Set beneficence to all as your goal, but know that beneficence also requires exercising malice where appropriate. Admonish yourself, as no one will be more compassionate to you than you yourself. When faced with difficulty, submit to the Exalted God, for He has brought you this far and will open the way for you. If you see an opportunity pass from your grasp, know that it was because of your laxity in expressing gratitude for what you do possess. Should you ever manage to dodge harm, never dodge contemplation of your departure from this world." 36.19

Aristotle's wisdom: There is an art in all things. The art of reason is choosing well. 36.20

Aristotle's wisdom: To know about love, ask the heart directly, for it is an unimpeachable witness. 36.21

Those who recognize the inevitability of the end bear troubles well. 36.22

Indeed, most of the admired maxims in al-Mutanabbī's poetry are derived from Aristotelian aphorisms; there are several epistles on this topic, including one by al-Ḥātimī.[299] 36.23

ʿAbd Allāh ibn Ṭāhir tells that the Caliph al-Maʾmūn said: In a dream, I saw a man seated at the Assembly of Wise Men, and I asked him, "Who are you?" He replied, "I am Aristotle the Sage." I said to him, "Wise one! Tell us what constitutes the best speech." He said, "That which stands to reason." "What's the second best?" "That which listeners find good." "And the third?" "That which can be said without fear of consequences." "And fourth?" "Everything else is but the braying of donkeys." Al-Maʾmūn told us, "If he was here with us, he certainly wouldn't add anything further." 36.24

It is said that this dialogue is recorded in one of Aristotle's books.

**وبطليموس[١] سوّى الأسطرلاب بتدبيرك وصوّر الكرّة على تقديرك** ٣٧

١،٣٧ هو بطليموس صاحب كتاب المجسطي الكبير وجغرافيا والاسطرلاب وكتاب اللحون الثمانية وغير ذلك وهو أوّل من شرح القول على هيئات الفلك وأخرج علم الهندسة من القوّة إلى الفعل[٢]

٢،٣٧ وأكثر الرواة يقولون إنّه ثالث ملوك اليونان بعد الإسكندر وبطليموس لقب ملوكهم وكان رجلاً حكيماً[٣] وسبب ملكه أنّه لمّا مات بطليموس الصانع ملك اليونان لم يكن في أهل بيت هذا الملك من يصلح فذكر لليونان رجل يصلح فقال بطليموس إنّه لا يصلح للملك قالوا ولِمَ قال لأنّه كثير الخصومة وليس يخلو في خصومته أن يكون ظالمًا أو مظلومًا فإن كان ظالمًا لم يصلح للملك لظلمه وإن كان مظلومًا لم يصلح لضعفه قالوا صدقت وأنت أولى بالملك فملّكوه عليهم

٣،٣٧ وقال بعض محقّقي التاريخ ليس بطليموس الحكيم من ملوك اليونان بل هو رجل حكيم كان في زمن أنطيسوس أحد ملوك الروم بعد اليونان بملوك كثيرة والدليل على أنّه ليس من ملوك اليونان أنّه ذكر في كتاب المجسطي أنّه رصد الشمس بالإسكندريّة سنة ثمان مائة وثمانين لبخت نصّر وكان من بخت نصّر إلى قتل دارا أربع مائة وتسع وعشرون سنة ومن قتل دارا إلى زوال ملك اليونان على يد أوغسطيس[٤] مائتا سنة وثمانون سنة ومذ غلبة أوغسطيس إلى أن ملك أنطيسوس مائة وسبعين سنة فيكون ذلك موافقًا لما حكاه بطليموس في كتابه

٤،٣٧ ومثّل بطليموس الاسطرلاب كرّة مطبوعة على هيئة الفلك كأنّها من شمع ضمّت عليها اليدان وزعم أنّ الأفلاك تسعة فأوّلها أقربها إلى الأرض وأصغرها وهو فلك القمر ثمّ الذي يليه فلك عطارد ثمّ الزهرة ثمّ الشمس ثمّ المرّيخ ثمّ المشتريّ ثمّ زحل الثامن فلك البروج وفيه سائر الكواكب الثابتة التاسع الأعظم الحاكم على

١ إ١، إ٥، إ٦، ل٢: بطلميوس. ٢ إ١: العقل. ٣ إ١: حليما. ٤ إ١: أوغطيس.

**. . . Ptolemy designed the astrolabe with your plans and determined the terrestrial sphere with your calculations . . .** 37

Ptolemy's books include the *Almagest*, the *Geography*, and *Harmonics*. He invented the astrolabe, he was the first to expound upon astronomy,[300] and he elevated the science of geometry from theory to practice. 37.1

Most narrators say that Ptolemy was a wise man who became the third of the Greek kings after Alexander; "Ptolemy" is the Greeks' regnal title.[301] They say that King Ptolemy the Builder died without suitable heirs from his household, and the Greeks proposed a man whom they considered fit, but Ptolemy the Sage disagreed: "He is not suitable for kingship." They asked him, "Why not?" He replied, "That man is forever involved in disputes, and disputes inevitably result in one either doing wrong or being wronged. If he does wrong, he should never be king on account of his injustice, and if he is wronged, he should never be king on account of his weakness." The Greeks agreed: "You are absolutely right. And thus you are the most suitable monarch!" They crowned Ptolemy the Sage king. 37.2

However, one of the diligent historians contends that Ptolemy the Sage was not one of the Greek kings but was instead a wise man who lived during the time of Antonius, a Roman emperor who reigned long after the fall of the Greek kingdom.[302] The argument that Ptolemy the Sage could not have been a Greek king is corroborated by Ptolemy's own book, *Almagest*, in which he describes observations he took of the sun at Alexandria in the year 880 of the Era of Nebuchadnezzar. This confirms he was contemporary with Antonius, since there were 429 years between Nebuchadnezzar and the death of Darius, 280 years between Darius's death and Augustus Caesar's conquest of the Greeks, and 170 more years to the reign of Antonius.[303] 37.3

Ptolemy constructed the astrolabe in the form of the celestial sphere stamped flat, like wax flattened between two hands. He alleges that there are nine concentric celestial spheres: the smallest, and nearest to the Earth, is the sphere of the Moon, the second is the sphere of Mercury, then Venus, the Sun, Mars, Jupiter, and Saturn, and the eighth is the sphere of the Constellations in which all other fixed stars are situated. The ninth, the greatest sphere, which 37.4

جميع الأفلاك ويُسمّى الأثير لأنّه يؤثّر في غيره وغيره لا يؤثّر فيه والقسريّ لأنّه يدير الأفلاك دورة قسريّة في كلّ يوم وليلة

٥،٣٧ وحكى أبو حيّان التوحيديّ قال كان ابن بكير يخالف بطليموس ويقول دون فلك القمر فلكان هما سبب المدّ والجزر ويقطعان الفلك كلّ يوم وليلة مرّتين وهذا من آرائه التي انفرد بها ولم أجد أحدًا يوافقه عليها والصناعة برهانيّة ولا أعرف أيّ برهان قام له على هذه الدعوى

٦،٣٧ ومن كلام بطليموس ما أحسن بالإنسان أن يصبر عمّا يشتهي وأحسن منه أن لا يشتهي إلّا ما ينبغي

٧،٣٧ وقال ينبغي للعاقل أن ينظر كلّ يوم في المرآة فإن رأى وجهه حسنًا لم يشنه بقبيح وإن رآه دميمًا لم يجمع بين قبيحين

٨،٣٧ وكان يقول إنّما نحن كائنون في الزمن الذي يأتي بعد هذا رمزًا إلى المعاد إذ الكون الحقيقيّ ذلك الكون

٣٨ وبقراط علم العلل والأمراض بلطف حسّك

١،٣٨ هو أبقراط بن إيرقليدس كان في زمن بهمان بن اسفنديار ويقال إنّه سابع الأطبّاء الذين أوّلهم أسفنبلنيوس[١] وهو قبل سقراط وأفلاطون وهو الذي نظر في صناعة الطبّ فوجدها قد كادت تبيد لقلّة أبناء المورّثين لها من آل أسفنبلنيوس فإنّهم كانوا يلقّنونها لأبنائهم ولا يكتبونها فيتعلّمها غيرهم فبثّ أبقراط هذه الصناعة في الناس وعلّم الغرباء وعهد إلى الأطبّاء عهدًا طويلاً مشهورًا

٢،٣٨ وقال جالينوس في بعض كتبه إنّ أبقراط كان يعلم مع ما كان يعلمها في الطبّ من أمر النجوم ما لم يكن يدانيه أحد من أبناء زمانه وكان يعلم أمر الأركان التي منها تركيب أبدان الحيوان وكون جميع الأجساد التي تقبل الكون والفساد وفسادها وهو الذي يرى كيف يكون المرض والصحّة في جميع الحيوان والنبات

١ إ:٣: اسقيليبيوس.

controls all the rest, is called the Ether, so named since it affects everything but is itself not affected;[304] it is also called the Prime Mover, since it compels all the spheres to move in their fixed path each day and night.

Abū Ḥayyān al-Tawḥīdī reports: Ibn Bukayr[305] disagreed with Ptolemy's model and proposed that there was one further sphere between the Earth and the Moon, which causes high and low tides that cut across this sphere twice every day and night. This is one of the various opinions unique to Ibn Bukayr, as I have not found anyone else embracing the view. Astronomy is an evidential science, and I am unaware of any evidence that can be adduced to prove Ibn Bukayr's claim. 37.5

Ptolemy's wisdom: "Very good is the man who abstains from his desires, but even better is he who desires only what he needs." 37.6

Ptolemy's wisdom: "The reasoned man ought to look into the mirror each day. If he sees that his face is beautiful, he must keep it unsullied by vice, and if he sees that it is repulsive, he must be sure not to add any vices!" 37.7

Ptolemy's wisdom: "We exist for a time that is yet to come." He alludes to the Resurrection, since true existence comes in the Hereafter. 37.8

**. . . your subtle perception taught Hippocrates all the forms of sickness . . .** 38

Hippocrates, son of Heracleides, lived before Socrates and Plato during the reign of Bahman, son of Esfandiar. It is said that Hippocrates was the seventh of the great Greek doctors (the first was Asclepius),[306] and he rescued the knowledge of medical practice from the brink of oblivion. Up until Hippocrates's time, medicine had been taught orally, and exclusively within the family of Asclepius: nothing was written down, so no one else could learn it. By Hippocrates's day, almost no descendants of the family remained, so Hippocrates recorded and disseminated the family's medical knowledge. He taught nonfamily members and made them swear his long and famous Hippocratic oath. 38.1

Galen says in one of his books: Hippocrates outstripped all his contemporaries with his combination of medical knowledge and astrological understanding. He knew the fundamental elements from which animate bodies are composed, the essences of all kinds of bodies that can subsist, and all the ailments and how they corrupt bodies. He understood how health and malady occur in 38.2

واستنبط أجناس الأمراض وجهات مداواتها وهو أوّل من اتّخذ البيمارستان وذلك أنّه عمل بالقرب من داره موضعًا منفردًا للمرضى وجعل لهم خدمًا يقومون بمداواتهم وسمّاه أخسدوكن[1] أي مجمع المرضى

٣،٣٨ ولم يكن يرغب في الاتّصال بالملوك حتّى أنّ ملك الفرس كتب إلى عامله من بلاد اليونان يأمره بحمل أبقراط إليه لأجل وباء عرض في بلاده وأن يحمل إليه مائة قنطار ذهبًا وكتب إلى ملك اليونان في ذلك الوقت يستعين به على إخراجه إليه وضمن إليه مهادنته خمس سنين فلم يجب أبقراط إلى هذا وقال أهل المدينة[2] إن خرج أبقراط خرجنا كلّنا وقُتلنا دونه

٤،٣٨ وتفسير أبقراط ضابط الخيل[3] وكتبه جليلة وأخباره نفيسة ومن ظريف حكاياته أنّ ولد أحد الملوك عشق جاريةً من حظايا أبيه فنحل بدنه واشتدّت علّته وهو كاتم خبره فأحضر أبقراط فجسّ نبضه ونظر إلى بشرته فلم ير عليه علّة فذاكره حديث العشق فرآه يهتزّ لذلك ويطرب فاستخبر الحال من حاضنته فلم يكن عندها خبر فقال هل خرج من الدّار فقالت لا[4] فقال لأبيه مر رئيس الخصيان بطاعتي فأمره بذلك فقال أخرج عليّ النساء فخرجن وأبقراط واضع إصبعه على نبض الصبيّ فلمّا خرجت الحظيّة اضطرب عرقه وحار طبعه فعلم أبقراط أنّها المعيّنة فصار إلى الملك فقال إنّ ابن الملك عاشق لمن الوصول إليها صعب قال الملك ومن ذلك قال هي زوجتي قال انزل عنها ولك عنها بدل فتمنّع أبقراط وقال هل رأيت أحدًا كلّف أحدًا طلاق امرأته ولا سيّما الملك في عدله ونصفته يأمرني بمفارقة زوجتي وهي عديلة روحي فقال الملك إنّي أوثر ولدي عليك وأعوّضك أحسن منها فامتنع حتّى بلغ الأمر إلى التهديد والسيف فقال أبقراط إنّ الملك لا يُسمّى عادلاً حتّى ينصف من نفسه ما ينصف من غيره أرأيت لو كانت

١ اللفظة غير واضحة في النسخ وفي إ٣: اخشيدكن. ٢ إ١: البلدان. ٣ إ١،إ٣: الحيل. ٤ قالت لا: سقطت من إ١.

animals and plants, and he could deduce the forms of sickness and determine the right approaches for cures. Hippocrates was the first man to build a hospital: in a secluded spot near his house, he established a place for the sick, staffed with servants to administer medication. He called it "Xenodocheion," which means assembly for the sick.[307]

Hippocrates had no desire to serve kings. Once, during a time of pestilence 38.3
in the Persian lands, the Persian king wrote to his administrator over the Greek lands to send Hippocrates in return for a very hefty sum of gold.[308] The Persian king also wrote to the Greek king, entreating him to deliver Hippocrates in return for a five-year truce. Yet Hippocrates would not be moved. One resident of Hippocrates's city exclaimed, "If Hippocrates leaves, we all leave with him and will lay down our lives for him."[309]

The name "Hippocrates" means "controller of horses";[310] his books are 38.4
invaluable and the anecdotes about him are fascinating. One excellent story tells about a prince who fell in love with one of his father's young concubines. The lovesick prince pined away to nothing and his illness worsened, yet he never revealed his secret. Hippocrates was summoned. He examined the prince's pulse and complexion, and could see no signs of illness, but when he told the prince a love story, the youth began to shake with delight. Hippocrates made inquiries with the prince's nursemaid, but she knew nothing, and when Hippocrates asked her, "Has the prince ever left the palace?" she replied, "No." So Hippocrates asked the king for permission to give orders to the chief eunuch, and thus empowered, Hippocrates commanded the eunuch, "Bring out all the palace women!" As each lady filed past, Hippocrates placed his hand on the prince's wrist to check his pulse, and when the prince's beloved came into view, his veins quivered and he became confused. Hippocrates was now certain which harem girl the youth loved, and he informed the king, "His Majesty's son is in love with a woman who's rather hard to obtain." The king asked, "Who is she?" Hippocrates answered, "My wife!" The king proposed: "Relinquish her and I will give you a replacement." Hippocrates declined: "Has it ever been that one man demanded another to divorce his wife? And to think that a king, charged with justice and equity, would order me to abandon my wife, my soulmate!" The king replied, "I look to my son's interests over yours, and I promise you an even better woman in return!" But Hippocrates resisted until the king began threatening execution. At this point, Hippocrates said, "His Majesty cannot be called just unless he is willing to charge himself with what he would demand from

العشيقة حظيّة الملك ففهم الملك المراد وقال يا أبقراط عقلك أتمّ من معرفتك ونزل عن الحظيّة لابنه وشفى الفتى

٥،٣٨ ومن كلامه الإقلال من الضارّ خير من الإكثار من النافع

٦،٣٨ وسئل كم ينبغي للإنسان أن يجامع فقال في كلّ سنة مرّة قيل فإن لم يقدر قال في كلّ شهر قيل فإن لم يقدر قال في كلّ أسبوع قيل فإن لم يقدر قال هي روحه متى شاء أخرجها

## ٣٩ وجالينوس عرف طبائع الحشائش بدقّة حدسك

١،٣٩ جالينوس هو آخر الحكماء المشهورين ويسمّى خاتم المعلّمين وذلك أنّه عندما ظهر وجد صناعة الطبّ قد كثرت فيها أقوال الأطبّاء السوفسطائيّين ومحيت محاسنها فانتدب لذلك وأبطل آراءهم وشيّد آراء أبقراط والتابعين له ونصرها

٢،٣٩ وساح فتطلّب الحشائش وجرّب وقاس أمزجتها وطبائعها وشرّح الأعضاء ووضع الكتب النفيسة في هذه الصناعة وهو مادّة الأطبّاء إلى اليوم وأشهرها الكتب الستّة التي شرحها الإسكندرانيّون ولم يأت بعده إلّا من هو دون منزلته وكانت وفاته بعد مبعث المسيح عليه السلام ولم يره

٣،٣٩ وحُكي أنّه لمّا بلغه من دعوة المسيح صلوات الله عليه إحياء الموتى وخلق الطير وإبراء الأكمه والأبرص قال لمن حوله من التلامذة إن عُلم من هذا المدّعي بما لا تستقلّ به الطبيعة سفه قبل ما ادّعاه لا يُخاطب ويُحمل فيما ادّعاه على ما تقدّم به العلم من السفه وإن لم يُعلم منه سفه تقدّم دعواه يُطالب بالبيان لإمكانه من علم ما وراء عالم الطبيعة وذلك سبيل كلّ ناطق يقوم في ابتداء كلّ قرن يأتي في الزمان للاضطرار إليه عند ظهور الفساد في الأرض سبيله الدعوى بما لا تستقلّ

others. How would His Majesty respond if I told him the prince was in love with one of His Majesty's concubines?" The king now understood and remarked, "Hippocrates! Your intelligence is even greater than your knowledge." The king gave his harem girl to the prince, and the youth made a full recovery.

Hippocrates's sayings include: "Better to refrain from what harms than to 38.5
indulge in what helps."

Hippocrates was once asked, "How often should a man have intercourse?" 38.6
He replied, "Once a year." "What if he can't abstain that long?" "Then once a month." "What if he can't abstain that long either?" "Then once a week." "But what if even that's too long?" Hippocrates said, "Intercourse is his soul, so he should let it out whenever he wishes."

**. . . Galen learned the nature of herbals from your precise hypotheses . . .** 39

Galen was the last of the great sages of the ancients. When he became a 39.1
doctor, he saw that the benefits of medicine were being lost among a sea of quacks' nostrums,[311] and Galen dedicated himself to debunking those views and reestablishing the principles of Hippocrates and his school. He championed Hippocrates's learned approach, and for that Galen became known as the "Seal of the Scholars."

Galen traveled far and wide. He studied and trialed herbals, evaluated 39.2
temperaments and natures, performed anatomical dissection of the body's limbs, and compiled invaluable books that are to this day the basis for medical practice. The most famous are the Six Books[312] upon which the Alexandrians wrote commentaries.

No doctors after Galen ever attained his stature. Galen died after the coming of Jesus (eternal peace be his), but they did not meet.[313]

They say that when Galen heard about Jesus's (God's blessings be upon him) 39.3
divine mission and that Jesus was raising the dead, creating birds,[314] and healing lepers and the blind, Galen remarked to the pupils gathered around him, "If this man who claims supernatural powers was known to be a fool prior to making these present claims, then no one should talk to him, as what he claims now can be assumed as more of his old foolishness. But if he was not previously known as a fool, then proof should be demanded of how he was enabled to acquire this metaphysical knowledge. At the outset of every century, God

به الطبيعة لانقياد الناس إلى طاعته بعد القيام بصحّة ما ادّعاه فمن سلك طريقه بعد ذلك تمّت حركته

٤،٣٩ ثمّ تجهّز للاجتماع به وسار إليه فمات في طريقه بمدينة الفرما وهي على شاطئ بحيرة تنّيس وبها قبره ولمّا اشتدّ به مرضه قيل له ألا تتداوى قال إذا نزل قدر الربّ بطل حذر المربوب ونعم الدواء الأجل ومات مبطونًا ومات أرسطوا بالسلّ ومات أفلاطون مبرسمًا ومات أبقراط مفلوجًا[١]

٥،٣٩ ومن حكاياته عن نفسه قال مررت بشيخ يزرع شجرة فقلت يا شيخ ما تزرع قال شجرة ثمرتها لي ولك قلت وما هي قال شجرة المشمش ثمرتها لي لأنّي آخذ ثمنها ولك لأنّها تكثر المرضى فتأخذ من أموالهم

٦،٣٩ وحكي عن نفسه في معرفة التشريح قال أعرف رجلًا شكا ضعف شهوته للطعام فوضعت على رقبته أدوية فبرئ لأنّ في العصبتين المجاورتين للعرقين شعبة إلى فم المعدة تنال منها الحسّ وكان في رقبة ذلك الرجل خنازير فقطعها الأطبّاء فأضرّ ذلك بتلك العصبة[٢] التي منها الشعبة وبرئت رقبته وصار ضعيف الشهوة عن الطعام فوضعت عليها الأدوية المقوّية فبرئ

٧،٣٩ ومن كلامه الإنسان سراج ضعيف كيف يدوم ضوؤه بين رياح أربع يعني الطبائع

٨،٣٩ وقال الإنسان إلى تجنّب ما يضرّه أحوج منه إلى تناول ما ينفعه

٩،٣٩ وقال من كان له درهم فليجعل نصفه في النرجس فإنّ النرجس راعي الدماغ والدماغ راعي العقل

١٠،٣٩ ورأى مصارعًا كان لا يرمي أحدًا قد صار طبيبًا فقال الآن كما صرعت الناس

١ ومات أرسطوا . . . مفلوجًا: زيادة من با١ وإ٦ ول٢ وحاشية بر١. ٢ إ١: القصبة.

endows a man with supernatural abilities to mend the corruption in the land, and once the veracity of his claims is established, people will submit to him. Those who follow him from that point on bring his mission to fruition."

Galen set out to meet Jesus, but he passed away at the city of Pelusium on the shores of Lake Tinnīs, and there he was buried.[315] As his sickness worsened, he was asked, "Don't you want to take any medicine?" but he replied, "Upon the strike of Fate set by the Lord, His minions have no recourse. The coming of death is a fine cure." 39.4

Galen died from a stomach malady, Aristotle died of tuberculosis, Plato from pleurisy, and Hippocrates from hemiplegia.

Galen told the following story about himself: When once I passed an old man planting a tree, I asked him, "What's the fruit, old man?" He replied, "It's for the both of us." "What's that?" "It's an apricot tree: when people buy the fruit, I'll get money, and because the fruit causes sickness, you'll get their money when you treat them."[316] 39.5

In another story, Galen reveals his knowledge of anatomy: I know a man who was complaining of reduced appetite for food, and I cured him by applying medicines on his neck. This worked because between the two nerves alongside the two parts of the neck[317] is a branch of nerves that extends down to the mouth of the stomach, and this is what stimulates the sensation of hunger. The man had suffered from scrofula on his neck, and doctors had excised them, but their treatment damaged that nerve branch leading to the stomach. The doctors thereby made the man's appetite decline by the way they cured the scrofula on his neck, and so, by applying a stimulant to his neck, I cured the lack of appetite. 39.6

Galen's wise words include: "People are but dim little lamps; how could they possibly survive gusts of the four winds?" He meant the effects of the four humors.[318] 39.7

Galen's wisdom: "An ounce of prevention is better than a pound of cure." 39.8

Galen's wisdom: "If you have but one dirham, spend half of it on narcissi, for the narcissus soothes the brain, and the brain looks after your reason." 39.9

To a wrestler who, after never succeeding in throwing anyone to the mat, became a doctor, Galen remarked, "Now it's as if you have floored everyone!" 39.10

٤٠ **وكلاهما قلّدك في العلاج وسألك عن المزاج واستوصفك تركيب الأعضاء**
**واستشارك في الداء والدواء وأنّك نهجت لأبي معشر طريق القضاء**

١،٤٠ المراد بالقضاء هاهنا حكم المنجّمين وقولهم بتأثّر الكواكب قال الشاعر

يَقْضُونَ بِٱلْأَمْرِ عَنْهَا وَهِيَ غَافِلَةٌ

٢،٤٠ وأبو معشر هذا هو جعفر بن عمر البلخيّ المنجّم المشهور في علم النجامة كان في الأوّل من أصحاب الحديث ببغداد وكان يشنّع على الكنديّ الفيلسوف بعلوم الفلسفة ويغري به العامّة فدسّ إليه الكنديّ من حسّن له النظر في علم الحساب والهندسة فدخل في ذلك ثمّ عدل إلى أحكام النجوم فتفنّن وبهر وانقطع شرّه عن الكنديّ لأنّه من جنس علوم الكنديّ

٣،٤٠ ويقال إنّه اشتغل بالنجوم بعد سبع وأربعين سنة من عمره وصنّف الكتب الحسنة في هذا العلم مثل كتاب الألوف وكتاب المدخل وكتاب المذاكرات وغير ذلك وظهرت له إصابات عجيبة وحُكي عنه فيها حكايات بديعة

٤،٤٠ قال في كتاب المذاكرات حضرت وشيلمة[١] الزياديّ عند الموفّق وكان الزياديّ أستاذ زمانه في النجوم فأضمر الموفّق ضميرًا فقال الزياديّ أضمر الأمير فقد أمر جليل رفيع فقال له كذبت فقال الهشاميّ قولاً قريبًا منه فقال الموفّق كذبت ثمّ قال لي هات ما عندك فقلت أضمر الأمير الله عزّ وجلّ فقال أحسنت والله ويلك من أين لك هذا قلت الرأس يرى فعله ولا يرى نفسه وكان في أرفع درجة الفلك في الضمير ولم أعرف له مثلاً إلّا الله عزّ وجلّ فإنّ الله تعالى يُرى فعله ولا يُرى هو وهو فوق كلّ ذي سلطان وعزّة وليس فوقه شيء

١ إ: وشملة

**... both of them copied your treatments, and consulted you about the humors, the constitution of limbs, and maladies and their cures. For Abū Maʿshar, you blazed the trail of astrological prediction ...** 40

"Astrological prediction" here refers to the astrologers' conviction that the stars really do influence events; however, a poet once said:[319] 40.1

Astrologers predict, but the stars are oblivious.

Abū Maʿshar is the nickname of the famous astrologer Jaʿfar ibn ʿUmar al-Balkhī. Initially, he was trained as a Hadith specialist in Baghdad, and in those days he used to revile the philosophical inquiries of the thinker al-Kindī, and even incited mobs against him.[320] In response, al-Kindī surreptitiously arranged for a man to extol the virtues of mathematics and geometry to Abū Maʿshar. The scheme worked: Abū Maʿshar's interest was piqued; he began studying, and took a particular liking to astrological speculation, which he studied exhaustively and became a great practitioner. Since astrology is a similar discipline to al-Kindī's specialization, Abū Maʿshar no longer had any grounds to chastise him. 40.2

They say that Abū Maʿshar was forty-seven when he began studying astrology. He wrote excellent books on the subject, including *The Book of Thousands*, *The Introduction*, and *Dialogues*, among others. Some of his predictions were amazingly accurate and make for wondrous stories. 40.3

In *Dialogues*, Abū Maʿshar tells the following story: Prince al-Muwaffaq once invited al-Ziyādī, the preeminent astrologer of his day, along with Shaylamah, al-Hāshimī,[321] and me, to his court. The prince asked each of us to guess what he was thinking. Al-Ziyādī said, "The prince is thinking about a highly important agreement."[322] Al-Muwaffaq replied, "Wrong!" Al-Hāshimī guessed something similar, and al-Muwaffaq again replied, "Wrong!" Then he turned to me: "Tell us what you think!" I said, "The prince is thinking about God, Great and Glorious." "Absolutely right, by God! How on earth did you work it out?" I answered him, "The head can see its action, but it cannot see itself. Your idea was at the highest celestial sphere, and I couldn't think of anything apt other than the Great and Glorious God. The acts of the Exalted God can be seen, although He cannot be seen, since He is higher and more powerful than all other authorities: there is nothing above Him." 40.4

٥،٤٠ وحُكي عنه أنّه كان قد تقلّب في البلاد فاتّصل ببعض ملوك العجم وأنّ الملك طلب رجلاً من أتباعه وأكابر دولته ليطالبه بجريمة وقعت منه فاستخفى الرجل وعلم أنّ أبا معشر يدلّ عليه بالطريق التي يستخرج بها الخفايا والأشياء الكامنة فأراد أن يصنع شيئًا لا يهتدى إليه ويُبعد عنه الحدس فأخذ طشتًا وملأه دمًا وجعل في الدم هاون ذهب كبيرًا يتمكّن من القعود عليه ثمّ جلس عليه أيّامًا وتطلّب الملك ذلك الرجل فأعياه فأحضر أبا معشر وقال له عرّفني بموضعه كما جرت عادتك فعمل المسألة التي يستخرجها وسكت زمانًا حائرًا فقال له الملك ما سبب حيرتك قال أرى شيئًا عجيبًا قال وما هو قال أرى الرجل المطلوب على جبل من ذهب والجبل في بحر دم ولا أعرف موضعًا في العالم على هذه الصفة فلمّا يئس الملك من القدرة عليه نادى في البلد بأمان الرجل ومن أخفاه فلمّا اطمأنّ الرجل بذلك ظهر وحضر بين يدي الملك فسأله عن الموضع الذي كان فيه فأخبره بما اعتمد عليه فأعجبه حسن احتياله وإصابة أبي معشر في استخراجه

٦،٤٠ ولأبي معشر من هذا الباب أخبار كثيرة والله أعلم بحقيقتها وكان مع تقدّمه في هذه الصناعة يصيبه الصرع عند امتلاء القمر في كلّ شهر وكان لا يعرف لنفسه مولدًا ولكن كان قد عمل مسألة عن عمره وأحواله وسأل عنها الزياديّ المنجّم ليكون أصحّ دلالة إذا اجتمع عليها طبيعتان طبيعة المسئول وطبيعة السائل فخرج طالع تلك المسألة السنبلة والقمر في العقرب في مقابلة الشمس والمريخ ناظر إلى القمر من الدلو وهذه الصورة توجب الصرع

٧،٤٠ ومات سنة اثنتين وسبعين ومائتين وكان سبب موته أنّ المستعين ضربه أسواطًا لأنّه أخبر بشيء قبل كونه فأصاب وخيف من الشناعة[1] فكان يقول أصبت فعوقبت

١ وخيف . . . الشناعة: زيادة من با١، إ٦، ل٢، ر٢، غ.

Another story tells that Abū Maʿshar's travels once took him to a king in Iran, who at that time was searching for a high-ranking courtier of his retinue who had fled after committing a crime and was in hiding. Because the courtier knew that Abū Maʿshar's subtle perception of the unseen could expose his hideout, he contrived a plan to confound Abū Maʿshar and throw him off the scent. He filled a large basin with blood and placed inside it a golden pestle large enough to sit on, and there he sat for days. The king's search came to naught and, frustrated, he summoned Abū Maʿshar: "Figure out, in the way you do, where the man is." Abū Maʿshar said, "I see something very odd." "What is it?" "I see the man you're after: he is living on a mountain of gold that sits in the midst of a sea of blood, and I have no clue where in the world matches that description!" The king despaired of ever finding his man, and so proclaimed amnesty for him and all those abetting his concealment. Once the courtier was reassured, he came out of hiding and presented himself before the king. The king asked him where he had been hiding, and the man told him the ruse: the king marveled at the stratagem and at how well Abū Maʿshar had guessed it. 40.5

There are many similar stories about Abū Maʿshar, and God knows best if they are true. His advanced powers in astrology enabled him to determine his own birthday—it had not been recorded, but he suffered seizures every month upon the full moon, and the astral coincidence of his seizures led him to guess his age and conditions of his birth. For greater certainty, he asked the astrologer al-Ziyādī' to corroborate the calculation. The horoscope was in the sign of Ceres when the Moon was in Scorpio, opposite the Sun, with Mars as the Moon's guardian in Aquarius—this combination necessarily induces seizures.[323] 40.6

Abū Maʿshar died in 272 [886]. His death stemmed from the effects of a severe flogging ordered by the Caliph al-Mustaʿīn:[324] Abū Maʿshar had so correctly predicted an event that some feared he was possessed by devils. Abū Maʿshar used to say, "I was punished for guessing correctly!" 40.7

**وأظهرت جابر بن حيّان على سرّ الكيمياء** ٤١

١،٤١ جابر بن حيّان هذا لا أعرف له ترجمة صحيحة في كتاب يُعتمد عليه وهو دليل على قول أكثر الناس فيه إنّه اسم موضوع وضعه المصنّفون في علم الكيمياء وزعموا أنّه كان في زمن جعفر الصّادق وأنّه إذا قال في كتبه قال لي سيّدي وسمعت من سيّدي فإنّه يعني بقوله جعفر الصادق عليه الصلاة والسلام

٢،٤١ وليعقوب الكنديّ رسالة بديعة سمّاها إبطال دعوى المدّعي صنعة الذهب والفضّة وفيها إبطال هذا الاسم والله أعلم[١]

**وأعطيت النظّام أصلاً أدرك به الحقائق** ٤٢

١،٤٢ هو إبراهيم بن سيّار بن هانئ البصريّ المعروف بالنظّام ويُكنى أبا إسحاق شيخ من كبار المعتزلة وأئمّتهم متقدّم في العلوم شديد الغوص على المعاني وإنّما أدّاه إلى المذاهب التي استبشعت منه تدقيقه وغوصه فأنّه كان قد اطّلع على كثير من كتب الفلاسفة

٢،٤٢ ومال في كلامه إلى الطبيعيّين والإلهيّين فاستنبط من كلامهم مسائل وخلطها بكلام المعتزلة وانفرد بها عنهم مثل قوله إنّ الله تبارك وتعالى لا يوصف بالقدرة على الشرور والمعاصي خلافًا لأصحابه فإنّهم قضوا بأنّه قادر عليها لكنّه لا يفعلها ومثل قوله إنّ الجوهر مؤلّف من أعراض اجتمعت وقوله إنّ الله تعالى خلق الموجودات دفعة واحدة على ما هي عليه الآن معادن ونباتًا وحيوانًا وإنسانًا ولم يتقدّم خلق آدم على خلق أولاده غير أنّ الله تعالى أكمن بعضها في بعض وهذا قول أهل الكمون من الفلاسفة وقوله في القرآن إنّ في قوى البشر أن تأتي بمثله

١ والله أعلم: زيادة من بر١.

**. . . to Jābir ibn Ḥayyān you revealed the secret of alchemy . . .** 41

I know of no truthful biography of Jābir ibn Ḥayyān in any reliable book, and this supports the majority opinion that his identity was invented by the practitioners of alchemy. They allege that he lived in the time of Jaʿfar al-Ṣādiq, and that the phrases "my master told me" and "I heard from my master," which appear in books ascribed to Jābir, mean that he was narrating from Jaʿfar al-Ṣādiq (God bless and keep him). 41.1

Yaʿqūb al-Kindī has an excellent epistle entitled *Debunking the Alchemists' Claims to Make Gold and Silver*, which includes a refutation of the claims that Jābir was a real person. God knows best. 41.2

**. . . to al-Naẓẓām you bequeathed the principles to grasp metaphysical realities . . .** 42

Al-Naẓẓām is the nickname of Abū Isḥāq Ibrāhīm ibn Sayyār ibn Hāni' al-Baṣrī. He was one of the great thinkers and leaders of the rationalist Muʿtazilī theologians, and a great scholar possessing deep conceptual insight in manifold disciplines. Some elements of his creed are considered grossly aberrant, but this is merely the result of his intensive study and engagement with a wide range of philosophical writings. 42.1

Al-Naẓẓām was partial to the views of natural philosophers and metaphysical theologians, and by melding their precepts with those of the rationalist Muʿtazilīs, he emerged with views unique to himself. For example, al-Naẓẓām believed that Exalted God could not be associated with the capacity to do evil or to ordain disobedience, and therein he differed from his fellow Muʿtazilīs, for they opined that while God is technically capable of evil, He never performs it. Another example of al-Naẓẓām's pseudo-Muʿtazilism is his view that substance is created from a collection of accidents. Al-Naẓẓām also opined that Exalted God created all things at once in their current forms, be they minerals, plants, animals, or people, and that the creation of Adam did not precede the creation of his descendants: al-Naẓẓām considered that God just hid them until their time. The precept concurs with the branch of speculative theologians who argue that all things exist as hidden potential until they are made manifest. Al-Naẓẓām also considered that it was within human capacity 42.2

إلّا أنّ الله تعالى صرف أذهانهم عن ذلك إلى غير ذلك من مسائله المذكورة في كتب الأصوليّين

٣،٤٢ ومراد ابن زيدون بالحقائق غير ذلك من مسائله المعجبة الحسنة فإنّها كثيرة وإنّما عُدّت سقطات النظّام لكثرة إصابته[1]

٤،٤٢ وكان من صغره يتوقّد ذكاء ويتدفّق فصاحة حُكي أنّ أباه جاء به وهو صغير إلى الخليل بن أحمد ليعلّمه فقال الخليل يمتحنه وفي يده قدح زجاج يا بنيّ صف لي هذه الزجاجة فقال أبمدح أم بذمّ قال بمدح قال نعم تريك القذى ولا تقبل الأذى ولا تستر ما وراء قال فذمّها قال يسرع إليها الكسر ولا تقبل الجبر قال فصف لي هذه النخلة وأومأ إلى نخلة في داره قال بمدح أو ذمّ قال بمدح قال هي حلو جناها باسق منتهاها ناضر أعلاها قال فذمّها قال صعبة المرتقى بعيدة المجتنى محفوفة بالأذى فقال يا بنيّ نحن إلى التعليم منك أحوج

٥،٤٢ ثمّ اشتغل على أبي الهذيل العلّاف بمذهب الكلام إلى أن بهر وظهر في أيّام المعتصم وتبعه خلق كثير وكان أصل مذهبهم أنّ من زعم أنّ الله تعالى شيء فهو كافر ثمّ ناظر شيخه أبا الهذيل وظهر عليه مرارًا وقيل له أتناظر أبا هذيل قال نعم وأطرح له رخًّا من عقلي

٦،٤٢ وحكى الجاحظ عنه وكان من أكبر تلامذته وأصحابه قال دخل أبو إسحاق النظّام على أبي الهذيل وقد أسنّ وبعد عهده بالمناظرة وأبو إسحاق حدث السنّ فقال يا أبا الهذيل أخبرني عن قراركم أن يكون جوهرًا مخافة أن يكون جسمًا فهل لا قرّرتم أن يكون جوهرًا مخافة أن يكون عرضًا والعرض أضعف من الجوهر فبصق أبو الهذيل في وجهه فقال أبو إسحاق قبّحك الله من شيخ ما أضعف حجّتك

---

١ وإنما . . . إصابته: زيادة من إ٦، إ٥، با١، ل٢، ر٢، غ.

to create something like the Qur'an, but Exalted God diverts our minds from being able to do so. Further views unique to al-Naẓẓām can be found in theological texts.

When Ibn Zaydūn mentions the "metaphysical realities" in the *Letter*, he intends the excellent and brilliant opinions of al-Naẓẓām: those are plentiful; I only mentioned his few mistakes above as counterpoints to his many apposite views. 42.3

The light of al-Naẓẓām's brilliance and the ease of his eloquence showed themselves already in his childhood. It is told that when al-Naẓẓām was a boy, his father brought him to the philologist al-Khalīl ibn Aḥmad for lessons. Al-Khalīl first tested al-Naẓẓām, and, as he was holding a glass in his hand, he said, "Dear boy, describe this glass." Al-Naẓẓām asked him, "In terms that praise it or that fault it?" "Start with praise." "Yes, sir. It reveals what's impure, yet itself stays pure, and nothing within it is obscure." Al-Khalīl then said, "Now dispraise it." "Quick to shatter; impossible to put back together." Pointing to a palm tree in his courtyard, al-Khalīl next said, "Describe this palm to me." "In terms of praise or dispraise?" "Praise first." Al-Naẓẓām said, "Its fruit is sweet, and it towers lofty, with a verdant peak." "Now dispraise it." "Its trunk is unscalable, its harvest inaccessible, and what surrounds it is painful." Al-Khalīl responded, "Dear boy, we need your instruction more than you need ours!" 42.4

Al-Naẓẓām first studied theology under Abū l-Hudhayl "the Feed Merchant."[325] He shone, and by the time of al-Muʿtaṣim's caliphate, al-Naẓẓām had a large following of his own. The basis of his creed was that God cannot be described as a thing, and that anyone who alleges otherwise is an unbeliever. Al-Naẓẓām then started debating against Abū l-Hudhayl, and bested him several times. He was once asked, "Do you really challenge Abū l-Hudhayl in debate?" and he replied, "Yes indeed! And I checkmate him with my mind's rook!" 42.5

Al-Jāḥiẓ,[326] one of al-Naẓẓām's greatest pupils and colleagues, tells that al-Naẓẓām, when still young, once visited Abū l-Hudhayl, who by that time had aged and had long passed his debating days, and asked him, "Abū l-Hudhayl! Tell me about your assertion that it is a substance, lest it be taken to be a body, whereas you did not assert that it is a substance lest it be taken to be an accident, whereas an accident is ultimately weaker than a substance."[327] Abū l-Hudhayl responded by spitting in al-Naẓẓām's face. Al-Naẓẓām retorted, "God disfigure this old man! What a weak argument!" 42.6

وحُكي عنه قال مات لصالح بن عبد القدّوس ولد فمضى إليه أبو الهذيل والنظّام معه وهو غلام حدث كالتبع له فرآه محترقًا فقال له أبو الهذيل لا أعرف لجزعك وجهًا إذا كان الناس عندك كالزرع فقال صالح يا أبا الهذيل إنّما أجزع عليه لأنّه لم يقرأ كتاب الشكوك فقال أبو الهذيل وما كتاب الشكوك[1] قال كتاب وضعته من قرأه شكّ فيما كان حتّى يتوهّم أنّه لم يكن وفيما لم يكن حتّى يظنّ أنّه قد كان فقال له النظّام فشكّ أنت في موت ابنك واعمل على أنّه لم يمت وشكّ أيضًا في أنّه قد قرأ هذا الكتاب وإن كان لم يقرأه فحصر صالح وكان مذهبه مذهب السوفسطائيّة فإنّهم يزعمون أنّ الأشياء لا حقيقة لها وأنّ ما نستبعده يجوز أن يكون على ما نشاهده ويجوز أن يكون على غير ما يشاهده[2] وإنّ حال اليقظان كحال النائم ٧،٤٢

وحكى الجاحظ قال تجاذبت[3] أنا وإيّاه حديث الطيرة فقال أخبرك أنّي جعت حتّى أكلت الطين وما صرت إلى ذلك حتّى قلّبت قلبي أيذكر هل ثمّ رجل أصيب عنده غداء أو عشاء فما قدرت وكان عليّ جبّة وقميص فبعت القميص[4] فقصدت الأهواز وما أعرف بها أحدًا وما كان ذلك إلّا شيئًا أمر به الضجر فوافيت الفرضة فلم أجد بها سفينة فتطيّرت من ذلك ثمّ إنّي رأيت سفينة في صدرها خرق وهشم فتطيّرت أيضًا فقلت للملّاح ما اسمك قال ديوزاد[5] بالفارسي وهو اسم الشيطان فتطيّرت وركبت معه فلمّا قربنا من الفرضة صحت بحمّال ومعي لحاف سمل وبعض ما لا بدّ لي منه فكان أوّل حمّال أجابني أعور فقلت لبقّار بكم تكريني ثورك هذا إلى الخان فلمّا أدناه منّي فإذا هو أعضب[6] فازددت طيرة وقلت في نفسي الرجوع أسلم ثمّ ذكرت حاجتي إلى أكل الطين وقلت من لي بالموت فلمّا صرت إلى الخان وأنا حائر ما أصنع إذ سمعت قرع باب البيت الذي أنا فيه فقلت من هذا ٨،٤٢

١ فقال أبو هذيل . . . شكوك: سقطت من إ١. ٢ ويجوز . . . يشاهده: زيادة من بر١ وإ٣. ٣ إ١: تجاريت.
٤ فما قدرت . . . قميص: زيادة من من إ٦، إ٥، ل٢، غ. ٥ إ١: دازداذ. ٦ فقلت لبقار..أعضب: زيادة من بر١ وبا١ وإ٦.

When al-Naẓẓām was a young boy, Abū l-Hudhayl brought him along when he went visiting Ṣāliḥ ibn ʿAbd al-Quddūs to offer condolences upon the death of one of Ṣāliḥ's sons. They found Ṣāliḥ in utter despair, and Abū l-Hudhayl remarked to him, "I see no justification for your distress: your family is so numerous, it's as if they sprout like crops!" Ṣāliḥ replied, "Abū l-Hudhayl, the reason for my distress is only that my boy never read *The Book of Doubts*." Abū l-Ḥudhayl asked, "What is *The Book of Doubts*?" Ṣāliḥ told him, "It's a treatise I wrote: whoever reads it will be so full of doubts that he will think that things which really exist do not, and that things which do not really exist actually do!" Al-Naẓẓām piped up: "Then you should doubt that your son died, and proceed on the basis that he might be alive, and doubt too that your son didn't read your book, and think that he might have." Ṣāliḥ was speechless. 42.7

Ṣāliḥ's creed was that of the Sophists: they allege that there is no underlying reality to things, and that things which one considers unlikely could nonetheless exist, whether or not they can be seen. They also allege that the state of being awake is no different from the state of being asleep.

Al-Jāḥiẓ reports: Al-Naẓẓām and I were competing over who could tell the better story about evil omens, and al-Naẓẓām told the following: Once, my poverty was so dire that I would be forced to eat dirt, and as I reached that state, I wracked my brain to recall if there was anyone out there from whom I could get a lunch or a dinner. But there was no one. I did own a tunic and robe, so I sold the tunic and went down to try my luck in Ahwaz. I didn't know anyone there either, but my desperation compelled me to go. When I reached the dock, there wasn't a boat to be seen. I considered that a bad omen. Then I did spot a boat, a rickety affair with holes amidships—this seemed another bad omen. When I asked the sailor, "What's your name?" he replied, "Dīvzād," a Persian name for the Devil.[328] Clearly, another bad omen. Nevertheless, I boarded, and as we approached the next dock I called for a porter, as I had a bundle of my necessities wrapped in a threadbare shawl. The first porter to answer was one-eyed.[329] On shore, I found a bullock driver and asked him, "How much to rent this bullock to the inn?" He brought the bullock closer, and I saw it had just one horn.[330] With all these bad omens, I said to myself, "Prudence suggests turning back," but I remembered that I had nothing but dirt to eat back home, so I said, "What do I care about death!" and I pushed on to the inn. Once inside, I had no idea what to do next, but suddenly there was a knock at the door of my room. 42.8

قال رجل يريدك فقلت من أنا قال إبراهيم بن سيّار النظّام فقلت هذا عدوّ أو رسول سلطان ثمّ إنّي تحاملت وفتحت له الباب فقال أرسلني إليك إبراهيم بن عبد العزيز الكاتب ويقول لك وإن كنّا اختلفنا في المقالة فإنّا نرجع بعد ذلك إلى حقوق الأخلاق والحرّيّة وقد رأيتك حيث مررت على حال كرهتها وينبغي أن تكون نزعت بك حاجة فإن شئت فأقم مكانك مدّة شهر أو شهرين فعسى نبعث لك بعض ما يكفيك زمنًا من دهرك وإن اشتهيت الرجوع فهذه ثلاثون دينارًا فخذها وانصرف أنت أحقّ من عذر قال فورد عليّ أمر أذهلني أمّا واحدة فإنّي لم أكن ملكت قطّ ثلاثة دنانير والثانية أنّه لم يطل مقامي وغيبتي عن أهلي والثالثة ما تبيّن لي من الطيرة أنّها باطل

٩،٤٢ وتُوفّي النظّام سنة إحدى وعشرين[١] ومائتين وله من العمر ستّ وثلاثون سنة وله كلام حسن وشعر رقيق

١٠،٤٢ فمن كلامه العلم شيء لا يعطيك بعضه حتّى تعطيه كلّك فإذا أعطيته كلّك فأنت من إعطائه لك البعض على خطر

١١،٤٢ وقال كنّا نلهو بالأمانيّ ونعد أنفسنا بالمواعيد فذهب من كان ينجز ثمّ شغلنا بالهموم عن الأمانيّ

١٢،٤٢ وقال إذا كانت في جيرانك جنازة وليس في بيتك دقيق فلا تحضر الجنازة فإنّ المصيبة عندك أكثر منها عند القوم وبيتك أولى بالمآتم

١٣،٤٢ وقال أبو العيناء أنشدت النظّام

إِذَا هَمَّ ٱلنَّدِيمُ لَهُ بِلَحْظٍ    تَمَشَّتَ فِي مَفَاصِلِهِ ٱلْكُلُومُ

فقال ما ينبغي أن ينادم هذا إلّا الأعمى ثمّ نظم المعنى في شعره

١ سقطت من إ.

I asked, "Who is it?" The visitor replied, "A man who wants you." "Who am I, then?" "You're Ibrāhīm ibn Sayyār al-Naẓẓām." I thought this must be either an enemy or an agent of the state, but regardless I braced myself and opened the door to the man, and he announced, "Ibrāhīm ibn ʿAbd al-ʿAzīz, the state secretary, sent me to you with this message: 'Though we had disagreed with you on a point of theology, we have now returned to our sense of decency and respect, and just now we saw you arriving here in a condition we hate to see, and we realize it must be penury that has compelled you to this. Thus, if you would like, you can stay in this inn for a month or two and we can send you enough to suffice you for a time; or, if you prefer to return home, take these thirty dinars and leave: you have no need to make any excuses.'" Al-Nazzām summed up his story, saying, "There were several astonishing things about this: first, never previously in my life had I even three dinars to my name; second, I had only just arrived at the inn and had not been away from my family for any length of time; and third, I learned that bad omens clearly mean nothing at all!"

Al-Naẓẓām died in 221 [836] at the age of thirty-six.[331] Fine sayings and elegant poems are ascribed to him. **42.9**

His sayings include: "Knowledge does not give you a part of itself until you give it all of yourself. And once you have given all of yourself, your possession of just a part of knowledge is dangerous." **42.10**

We used to distract ourselves with hope and make promises for the future, but then those who could realize our hopes passed away, and so now we use worries to distract ourselves from our hopes. **42.11**

If there is a funeral in your neighborhood but no flour in your house, then don't attend the funeral: your misfortune is the greater, and it's really your house that should be mourned. **42.12**

Abū l-ʿAynāʾ said: I recited this verse to al-Naẓẓām: **42.13**

> If this fellow drinker shoots you a glance,
> pangs will shoot through your joints.

Al-Naẓẓām observed: "In that case, only blind men should be allowed to drink with him!" And he composed some verses on the topic.

ومن شعره ١٤،٤٢

ذَكَرْتُكَ وَٱلرَّاحُ فِي رَاحَتِي    فَشُبْتُ ٱلْمُدَامَ بِدَمْعٍ غَزِيرِ
فَإِنْ يُنْفِدْ ٱلدَّمْعَ فَرْطُ ٱلْأَسَى    بَكَتْكَ ٱلْحَشَا بِدُمُوعِ ٱلضَّمِيرِ

ومنه ١٥،٤٢

يَا تَارِكِي جَسَدًا بِغَيْرِ فُؤَادِ    أَسْرَفْتَ فِي ٱلْهِجْرَانِ وَٱلْإِبْعَادِ
إِنْ كَانَ يَمْنَعُكَ ٱلزِّيَارَةَ مَعْشَرٌ    فَٱدْخُلْ عَلَيَّ بِعِلَّةِ ٱلْعُوَّادِ
إِنَّ ٱلْعُيُونَ عَلَى ٱلْقُلُوبِ إِذَا جَنَتْ    كَانَتْ جِنَايَتُهَا[1] عَلَى ٱلْأَجْسَادِ

ومنه ١٦،٤٢

أُرِيدُ ٱلْفِرَاقَ فَأَشْتَاقُكُمْ    كَأَنَّا ٱفْتَرَقْنَا وَلَمْ نَفْتَرِقْ
وَأَسْتَغْنِمُ ٱلْوَصْلَ كَيْ أَشْتَفِي    وَهَلْ يَشْتَفِي أَبَدًا مَنْ عَشِقْ

ومنه ١٧،٤٢

يَرُوعُ مُنَاجِيهِ بِهَارُوتِ لَفْظِهِ    وَيُؤْنِسُهُ مِنْهُ بِصُورَةِ آدَمِ
تَرَى فِيهِ[2] لَامًا فَرْدَةً فَوْقَ وَرْدَةٍ    وَفَصًّا مِنَ ٱلْيَاقُوتِ مِنْ فَوْقِ خَاتِمِ

ومنه ١٨،٤٢

وَشَادِنٍ يَنْطِقُ بِٱلظَّرْفِ    يَقْصُرُ عَنْهُ مُنْتَهَى ٱلْوَصْفِ
رَقَّ فَلَوْ بَزَّتْ سَرَابِيلَهُ    عَلَّقَهُ ٱلْجَوُّ مِنَ ٱللُّطْفِ
يَجْرَحُهُ ٱللَّحْظُ بِتَكْرَارِهِ    وَيَشْتَكِي ٱلْإِيمَاءَ بِٱلطَّرْفِ
أَفْدِيهِ مِنْ مَغْرًى بِمَا سَاءَنِي    كَأَنَّهُ يَعْلَمُ مَا أُخْفِي

---

١ با١، إ٦، إ٣: بليتها. ٢ إ١، بر١: منه.

Al-Naẓẓām's poetry: 42.14

Wine in hand, I remember you,
and my wine is mixed with copious tears.
If an excess of grief can exhaust the tears,
I'll shed my soul's tears within me.

Al-Naẓẓām's poetry: 42.15

You left my body a vacant shell—
    Your separation has gone too far.
If it's a crowd that prevents your return,
    come visit—say you're attending an invalid.
When eyes perpetrate crimes against hearts,
    bodies suffer.

Al-Naẓẓām's poetry: 42.16

Though I want us to part, I yearn for you.
We've parted ways, yet we are still bound.
I seize your coming as a chance for relief,
    but can there be relief for one in love?

Al-Naẓẓām's poetry: 42.17

His form is delightfully human,
    but he enthralls with devilish whispers;
His mouth is the curve of a *lām* atop a rose,[332]
    a ruby stone atop a ring.

Al-Naẓẓām's poetry: 42.18

Like a little gazelle fawn, his elegance speaks—
    yet there are no words to describe him.
So thin—take off his baggy pants,
    he's so refined the air will lift him upward.
Stares wound him;
    glances cause him to complain.
Releasing him from seduction pains me,
    as if he knows what I hide.

وقيل له وهو في[1] مرضه وفي يده قدحُ دواء ما هذا فقال ١٩،٤٢

أَصْبَحْتُ فِي دَارِ بَلِيَّاتِ    أَدْفَعُ آفَاتٍ بِآفَاتِ

وجعلت للكنديّ رسمًا استخرج به الدقائق ٤٣

١،٤٣ هو يعقوب بن إسحاق بن الصبّاح الكنديّ المسمّى في وقته فيلسوف الإسلام من ولد الأشعث بن قيس كان أبوه ابن الصبّاح من ولاة الأعمال بالكوفة وغيرها في أيّام المهديّ والرشيد وانتقل يعقوب إلى بغداد فاشتغل بعلم الأدب ثمّ بعلوم الفلسفة جميعها فأثبتها وحَلّ مشكلات كتب الأوائل وحذا حذو أرسطاطليس وصنّف الكتب الجليلة الجمّة وكثرت فوائده وتلامذته وكانت دولة المعتصم تتجمّل به وبمصنّفاته وهي كثيرة جدًّا ومن كتاب العقل الإنسيّ وكتاب الجوامع الفكريّة وكتاب الفلسفة الأولى وله أخبار حسنة ونوادر في البخل وغيره

٢،٤٣ فمن أخباره أنّه كان حاضرًا عند أحمد بن المعتصم وقد دخل أبو تمّام فأنشده قصيدته السينيّة فلمّا بلغ إلى قوله

إِقْدَامَ عَمْرٍو فِي سَمَاحَةِ حَاتِمٍ    فِي حِلْمِ أَحْنَفَ فِي ذَكَاءِ إِيَاسِ

قال الكنديّ ما صنعت شيئًا قال كيف قال ما زدت على أن شبّهت ابن أمير المؤمنين بصعاليك العرب وأيضًا إنّ شعراء دهرنا تجاوزوا بالممدوح من كان قبلهم ألا ترى إلى قول العكوّك في أبي دلف

رَجُلٌ أَبَرَّ عَلَى شَجَاعَةِ عَامِرٍ    بَأْسًا[2] وَغَبَّرَ فِي مُحَيَّا حَاتِمِ

[1] سقطت من إ١. [2] إ١: كرما.

When al-Naẓẓām was sick with his mortal illness and was holding a cup of medicine, someone asked him, "What is that?" He replied: 42.19

I awoke in a world of pains,
fending off harm with more harm.

**. . . for al-Kindī you set out the scheme to derive philosophical subtleties.** 43

Yaʿqūb ibn Isḥāq ibn al-Ṣabbāḥ al-Kindī was known in his day as the "Philosopher of Islam." He was a descendant of al-Ashʿath ibn Qays; his father, Ibn al-Ṣabbāḥ, had served as one of the district governors of Kufa and over other regions during the caliphates of al-Mahdī and al-Rashīd. Yaʿqūb al-Kindī moved to Baghdad and applied himself first to studying learned culture, and then turned to philosophy in all its fields, affirming philosophy's validity and solving conundrums from the books of the ancients. Al-Kindī was like a second Aristotle: he wrote many seminal books, was greatly valued, and attracted a large following of students. His presence and learned output lent glory to al-Muʿtaṣim's caliphate. Al-Kindī's works include *On the Human Intellect*, *Collected Discourses on Thought*, and *On First Philosophy*, among many others. Fine and witty anecdotes are told about al-Kindī, including stories about his miserliness. 43.1

One story recounts al-Kindī at the court of Prince Aḥmad, son of the Caliph al-Muʿtaṣim. Abū Tammām was at court to recite his *s*-rhyme poem in praise of the prince, and when he reached the verse: 43.2

He has ʿAmr's bravery, Ḥātim's generosity,
Iyās's brains, and al-Aḥnaf's equanimity . . .

al-Kindī interrupted, "This is nothing!" Abū Tammām asked, "Why not?" Al-Kindī explained, "All you've done is compare the son of the Commander of the Faithful with a bunch of Arab paupers! Furthermore, contemporary poetic style is to elevate their patrons beyond all the great men of the past. Haven't you heard al-ʿAkawwak praising Abū Dulaf:

ʿĀmir's bravery is no match for his—
He outshines the magnanimous face of Ḥātim."

فأطرق أبو تمّام ثمّ أنشد ٣،٤٣

لَا تُنْكِرُوا ضَرْبِي لَهُ مِنْ دُونِهِ     مَثَلًا شَرُودًا فِي ٱلنَّدَى وَٱلْبَاسِ
فَٱللّٰهُ قَدْ ضَرَبَ ٱلْأَقَلَّ لِنُورِهِ     مَثَلًا مِنَ ٱلْمِشْكَاةِ وَٱلنِّبْرَاسِ

ولم يكن هذا في القصيدة فتعجّب منه ثمّ طلب أن تكون الجائزة ولاية عمل فاستُصغر عن ذلك فقال الكنديّ ولّوه فإنّه قصير العمر لأنّ ذهنه ينحت من قلبه فكان كما قال وقد يكون ظهرت له دلائل في شخصه في ذلك الوقت على قرب أجله والله أعلم[1]

وسمع الكنديّ إنسانًا ينشد ٤،٤٣

وَفِي أَرْبَعٍ مِنِّي حَلَتْ مِنْكَ أَرْبَعٌ     فَمَا أَنَا أَدْرِي أَيُّهَا هَاجَ لِي كَرْبِي
خَيَالُكَ فِي عَيْنِي أَمِ ٱلذِّكْرُ فِي فَمِي     أَمِ ٱلنُّطْقُ فِي سَمْعِي أَمِ ٱلْحُبُّ فِي قَلْبِي

فقال والله لقد قسّمها تقسيمًا فلسفيًّا

ومن نوادره وكلامه في البخل كان يقول من شرف البخل أنّك تقول للسائل لا ورأسك إلى فوق ومن ذلّ العطاء أنّك تقول نعم ورأسك إلى أسفل ٥،٤٣

وكان يقول سماع الغناء برسام حادّ لأنّ الإنسان يسمع فيطرب فينفق فيسرف فيقتصر فيغتمّ فيعتلّ فيموت ٦،٤٣

وقال عمرو بن ميمون تغدّيت يومًا عند الكنديّ فدخل جار له فدعوته إلى الطعام فقال الرجل والله تغدّيت فقال الكنديّ ما بعد الله شيء فكتفه كتافًا لو نشط ليأكل معه لكان كافرًا ٧،٤٣

---

١ وقد يكون . . . أعلم: زيادة من بر١، با١.

Abū Tammām paused for a moment with his head sunk in thought, and then recited: 43.3

Don't reprove my comparison with the prince's inferiors
 in generosity and bravery:
God described His own Light by comparison
 with a lamp and its niche.[333]

All marveled at Abū Tammām's ability to compose these new verses on the spot. Abū Tammām asked to be given the tax revenues of a district as his prize; this was deemed beyond the poet's station, but al-Kindī disagreed: "Appoint him, since he has but a short time left to live: his mind is wearing out his heart." And it transpired exactly so—it seems al-Kindī saw signs in Abū Tammām indicating his time was almost up; God knows best.

Al-Kindī heard a man recite the following verses: 43.4

Four sweet things about you match four in me,
but I don't know which provoked my pangs:
 your apparition in my eyes, your name on my tongue,
 your voice in my ear, or the love for you in my heart.

Al-Kindī congratulated him: "By God, that's a perfect metaphysical categorization!"

The droll stories and sayings about al-Kindī's miserliness include his comment: Miserliness confers nobility inasmuch as you say no to a beggar while keeping your head aloft, whereas generosity confers ignobility inasmuch as you have to look down to him when saying yes. 43.5

Al-Kindī once remarked: Listening to music is a form of chronic pleurisy. When you listen to music, you quiver with delight; when you quiver with delight, you remunerate singers; when you remunerate singers, you spend too much; when you spend too much, you become poor; when you become poor, you worry; when you worry, you get sick; when you get sick, you die. 43.6

ʿAmr ibn Maymūn[334] tells: Once, I was having lunch with al-Kindī when one of his neighbors entered.[335] I extended an invitation for the neighbor to eat with us, but when he said, "No thank you, by God, you're too kind!" al-Kindī quickly interjected, "Well then, after God, there's nothing more to say!" This stymied the neighbor: if he made a move to eat, he would have become an unbeliever.[336] 43.7

٨،٤٣ ومن وصيّته لولده يا بنيّ كن مع الناس كلاعب الشطرنج تحفظ شيئك وتأخذ من شيئهم فإنّ مالك إذا خرج عن يدك لم يعد إليك واعلم أنّ الدينار محموم فإذا صرفته مات[١] واعلم أنّه ليس شيء أسرع فناء من الدينار إذا كسر والقرطاس إذا نشر ومثل الدرهم كمثل الطائر الذي هو لك ما دام في يدك فإذا طار صار لغيرك وقال المتلمّس

قَلِيلُ ٱلْمَالِ تُصْلِحُهُ فَيَبْقَى وَلَا يَبْقَى ٱلْكَثِيرُ مَعَ ٱلْفَسَادِ
لَحِفْظُ ٱلْمَالِ خَيْرٌ مِنْ بَغَاهُ وَسَيرٍ فِي ٱلْبِلَادِ بِغَيْرِ زَادِ

وأعرف بيتًا بيّت أكثر من مائة ألف في المساجد وهو هذا

فَسِرْ فِي بِلَادِ ٱللهِ وَٱلْتَمِسِ ٱلْغِنَى تَعِشْ ذَا يَسَارٍ أَوْ تَمُوتَ فَتُعْذَرَا

فاحذر يا بنيّ أن تلحق بهم[٢]

٩،٤٣ ومن كلامه في الفلسفة علوم الفلسفة ثلاثة فأوّلها العلم الرياضيّ في التعليم وهو أسفلها في الطبع والثاني علم الطبيعيّات وهو أوسطها في الطبع والثالث علم الربوبيّة وهو أعلاها في الطبع وإنّما كانت العلوم ثلاثة لأنّ المعلومات ثلاثة إمّا علم ما يقع عليه الحسّ وهو ذوات الهيوليّ وإمّا علم ما ليس بذي هيوليّ إمّا أن يكون لا يتّصل بالهيوليّ البتّة وإمّا أن يكون قد يتّصل بها فأمّا ذوات الهيوليّ فهو المحسوسات وعلمها وهو العلم الطبيعيّ وإمّا أن يتّصل بالهيوليّ فإنّ له انفرادًا بذاته كعلم الرياضيّات التي هي العدد والهندسة والتنجيم والتأليف وإمّا ما لا يتّصل بالهيوليّ البتّة وهو علم الربوبيّة

١٠،٤٣ ومن شعره في وصف قصيدة

١ سقطت من إ١. ٢ فاحذر . . . بهم: سقطت من إ١.

Al-Kindī's final words of admonition to his son include the following: "My dear son, in the world you must operate like a chess player: guard your pieces jealously and snatch those of others. Money that leaves your hand will never return. Gold coins are infirm: if you send them out, they will die, and nothing in this world disappears faster than a gold coin after it's first clipped[337] or a promissory note after it's unfurled to be cashed. The silver coin is like a bird: while you clutch it, it's yours, but once you let it fly, it becomes someone else's. Remember the poem of al-Mutalammis: 43.8

Little sums, well maintained, remain,
while fortunes, treated carelessly, are lost.
It's easier to save money than to seek it,
traveling the land without provisions.

"I know a verse that has busied more than one hundred thousand minds by night in the mosques:

Go forth into God's green earth and seek riches;
you'll either live easy or die excused.

"Beware, my dear son, of becoming like these people."

One of al-Kindī's philosophical statements: "Philosophy is divisible into three disciplines: the first to learn is mathematics, for it is the closest to the natural disposition; the second, the intermediate discipline, is the physical sciences; the third, the loftiest, is divinity. The disciplines are tripartite because the objects of knowledge are likewise of three kinds: (1) knowledge that can be obtained by the senses—this is material reality; (2) knowledge of immaterial reality, which is of two subsets: that which can never be perceived materially, and that which may have a potential connection to the material world. Material reality constitutes things that can be perceived, and these constitute the physical sciences. Knowledge that has a potential connection to material reality is unique and self-subsistent, such as mathematics, which is divided into arithmetic, geometry, astrology, and composition. (3) Knowledge totally disconnected from material reality is knowledge of the divine." 43.9

Al-Kindī composed the following poem to describe poetry: 43.10

يُقَصِّرُ عَنْ مَدَاهَا ٱلرِّيحُ جَرْيًا    وَتَعْجِزُ عَنْ مَوَاقِعِهَا ٱلسِّهَامُ
تَنَاهَبَ حُسْنَهَا حَادٍ وَشَادٍ    فَحَثَّ بِهَا ٱلْمَطَايَا وَٱلْمُدَامُ

ومنه ١١،٤٣

أَنَافَ ٱلذُّنَابَى عَلَى ٱلْأَرْؤُسِ    فَغَمِّضْ جُفُونَكَ أَوْ نَكِّسِ
وَعِنْدَ مَلِيكِكَ فَٱبْغِ ٱلْعُلُوَّ    وَبِٱلْوَحْدَةِ ٱلْيَوْمَ فَٱسْتَأْنِسِ
فَإِنَّ ٱلْغِنَى فِي قُلُوبِ ٱلرِّجَالِ    وَإِنَّ ٱلتَّعَزُّزَ بِٱلْأَنْفُسِ
وَكَائِنْ تَرَى مِنْ أَخِي عُسْرَةٍ    غَنِيٍّ وَذِي ثَرْوَةٍ مُفْلِسِ
وَمَنْ كَاتِمَ شَخْصَهُ مَيِّتًا    عَلَى أَنَّهُ بَعْدُ لَمْ يُرْمَسِ

وسمع رجلًا ينشد قول ربيعة الرقّيّ ١٢،٤٣

لَوْ قِيلَ لِلْعَبَّاسِ يَا ٱبْنَ مُحَمَّدٍ    قُلْ لَا وَأَنْتَ مُخَلَّدٌ مَا قَالَهَا

فقال ليس يجب أن يقول الإنسان في كلّ شيء نعم وكان الوجه أن يستثني فيقول

هَجَرْتُ فِي ٱلْقَوْلِ لَا إِلَّا لِعَارِضَةٍ    تَكُونُ أَوْلَى بِلَا فِي ٱللَّفْظِ مِنْ نَعَمِ

**وإنّ صناعة الألحان اختراعك وتأليف الأوتار والإنقار توليدك وابتداعك** ٤٤

أوّل من صنّف في الألحان كتابًا مخترعًا بطليموس وقد ذكر وأوّل من غنّى في الإسلام بألحان الفرس طويس وقيل ابن مسجح وسيأتي ذكره وذلك أنّ عبد الله ابن الزبير لمّا وهى بناء الكعبة رفعها وجدّد بناءها وكان فيها صاغ من الفرس يغنّون بألحانهم[1] فوقّع عليها طويس وابن مسجح الغناء العربيّ ١،٤٤

---

١ وكان فيها . . . بألحانهم: زيادة من بر١، با١.

It spreads beyond the gusts of the wind.
It flies farther than arrows can reach.
Its beauty is grasped by camel driver and crooner,
  who use it to encourage beasts and drinkers.

His poetic compositions also include the following: 43.11

The rabble now tower over their leaders,
  so avert your gaze or close your eyes;
Climb only the heights that ascend to your Lord;
  find in solitude good companionship.
True wealth is what's in the heart,
  and true glory is only in the soul.
You see the poor man prosper,
the moneymen go bust;
all forms conceal a corpse,
bodies of the yet unburied.

A man was reciting a verse by Rabīʿah al-Raqqī: 43.12

Had al-ʿAbbās been told: you'll win immorality if you say no,
  he would still never refuse a request.[338]

When al-Kindī interjected: "One does not necessarily have to say yes to everything; there are exceptions," and he recited the following verse:

I took recourse in "No!" in circumstances
  when no felt more apt than yes.

**The art of melody is your invention, as well as composition for strings and percussion.** 44

The first to write a book about melody was Ptolemy.[339] Reportedly, the first to sing Persian melodies in Islamic times was Ṭuways,[340] though there are those who say it was Ibn Misjaḥ. The inspiration stems from the songs of the Persian craftsmen whom ʿAbd Allāh ibn al-Zubayr had brought to work on his rebuilding and enlargement of the Kaaba, which had become structurally weak at that time. 44.1

٤٥ **وأنّ عبد الحميد بن يحيى باري أقلامك**

١،٤٥ هو عبد الحميد بن يحيى بن سعيد العامريّ الكاتب البليغ المقدّم[1] يقال إنّه في أوّل عمره كان معلّم صبيان بالكوفة ثمّ اتّصل بمروان الجعديّ قبل أن تصل إليه الخلافة وصحبه وانقطع إليه فلمّا جاء الخبر بالخلافة سجد مروان وسجد من معه من أصحابه إلّا عبد الحميد فقال له مروان لِمَ لا سجدت فقال ولم أسجد أعلى أن كنت معنا فطرت عنّا يعني بالخلافة فقال إذًا تطير معي قال الآن طاب السجود وسجد

٢،٤٥ وكان كاتب مروان طول خلافته وهو أوّل من اتّخذ التحميدات في صدور الكتب واستعمل في بعضها الإيجاز البليغ وفي بعضها الإسهاب المفرط على ما اقتضاه الحال

٣،٤٥ فمن الإيجاز أنّ بعض عمّال مروان أهدى إليه عبدًا أسود فأمره بالإجابة ذامًّا مختصرًا فكتب لو وجدت لونًا شرًّا من السواد وعددًا أقلّ من الواحد لأهديته

٤،٤٥ وأمّا الإسهاب فإنّه لمّا ظهر أبو مسلم الخراسانيّ بدعوة بني العبّاس كتب إليه عن مروان كتابًا يستميله ويضمّنه ما لو قرئ لأوقع بين أصحاب أبي مسلم وكان من كبر حجمه يحمل على جمل ثمّ قال لمروان قد كتبت كتابًا متى قرأه بطل تدبيره فإن يكن ذاك وإلّا فالهلاك

٥،٤٥ فلمّا ورد الكتاب على أبي مسلم لم يقرأه وأمر بنار فأحرقته وأبقى جزازة منه فكتب عليها إلى مروان

مَحَا ٱلسَّيْفُ أَسْطَارَ ٱلْبَلَاغَةِ وَٱنْتَحَى    عَلَيْكَ لُيُوثُ ٱلْغَابِ مِنْ كُلِّ جَانِبِ

٦،٤٥ ولمّا اشتدّ الطلب على مروان وتتابعت هزائمه[2] المشهورة قال لعبد الحميد القوم محتاجون إليك لأدبك وإنّ إعجابهم بك يدعوهم إلى حسن الظنّ بك فاستأمن

١ إ: المتقدم.   ٢ إ: عزائمه.

## ʿAbd al-Ḥamīd pared your pens . . . 45

ʿAbd al-Ḥamīd ibn Yaḥyā ibn Saʿīd of the ʿĀmir was a preeminent, gifted writer and state secretary. His career is said to have begun as an elementary teacher in Kufa before he joined the retinue of the future caliph Marwān the Jaʿdite, and became his devoted confidant. When news came that Marwān had been proclaimed as caliph, Marwān and all his retinue prostrated in prayer, except ʿAbd al-Ḥamīd. Marwān asked him, "Why did you not pray?" He replied, "Do you expect me to prostrate in thanks for your departure after our time together?" (He lamented that Marwān would depart to assume the caliphate.) Marwān responded, "Then come and depart with me!" ʿAbd al-Ḥamīd then said, "Now I'm happy to pray!" And he did. 45.1

ʿAbd al-Ḥamīd was Marwān's secretary for the duration of his caliphate. He was the first letter writer to begin his missives with elaborate praises of God. At times, ʿAbd al-Ḥamīd's style employed highly expressive concision, at other times dense prolixity—all according to what the context required. 45.2

An example of ʿAbd al-Ḥamīd's concision can be seen in a letter Marwān ordered as a curt rebuke to one of his administrators who had given him a black slave. ʿAbd al-Ḥamīd wrote on Marwān's behalf: "If I could find a color worse than black and a number more paltry than one, I'd send you that." 45.3

An example of ʿAbd al-Ḥamīd's prolixity is the letter he wrote when Abū Muslim al-Khurāsānī proclaimed the Abbasid Revolt. ʿAbd al-Ḥamīd wrote on behalf of Marwān in an effort to win over Abū Muslim, and had the letter's contents circulated among Abū Muslim's camp, they would surely have stoked wide dissent. The letter was so voluminous that a camel was needed to carry all its pages, and ʿAbd al-Ḥamīd told the caliph, "If Abū Muslim reads the letter, his plans will be confounded, but if he does not, there's no hope for us." 45.4

Abū Muslim did not read the letter. Instead, he ordered it incinerated, retaining just a slip of its paper, on which he wrote a verse as his reply: 45.5

Let the sword efface the best-composed lines
and lions of the thicket approach you from all sides.

As is well known, Marwān then suffered a series of defeats. As his pursuers began closing in, he told ʿAbd al-Ḥamīd, "Because of your erudition, the foe will need you, and since you impress them, they will think well of you. You should seek their mercy now and make it appear that you're willing to betray 45.6

إليهم وأظهر الغدر بي فلعلّك تنفعني في حياتي أو بعد مماتي في حرمي فقال عبد الحميد

أُسِرُّ وَفَاءً ثُمَّ أُظْهِرُ غَدْرَةً فَمَنْ لِي بِعُذْرٍ يُوسِعُ ٱلنَّاسَ ظَاهِرُهْ

ثمّ قال يا أمير المؤمنين إنّ الذي أمرتني به أنفع الأمرين لك وأقبحهما بي ولكنّي أصبر حتّى يفتح الله عليك أو أُقتل معك

٧،٤٥ فلمّا قُتل مروان استخفى عبد الحميد فغمز عليه بالجزيرة عند ابن المقفّع وكان صديقه وفاجأهما الطلب وهما في بيت فقال الذين دخلوا أيّكما عبد الحميد فقال كلّ واحد منهما أنا خوفًا على صاحبه إلى أن عُرف عبد الحميد فأُخذ وسلّمه السفّاح إلى عبد الجبّار صاحب شرطته وكان يحمي له طستًا ويضعه على رأسه إلى أن مات وذلك في سنة اثنيتن وثلاثين ومائة

٨،٤٥ وكان أبو جعفر المنصور يقول غلبنا بنو أميّة بثلاثة أشياء بالحجّاج وعبد الحميد والمؤذّن البعلبكيّ

٩،٤٥ وقيل لعبد الحميد ما الذي مكّنك من البلاغة قال حفظ كلام الأصلع يعني أمير المؤمنين عليّ ابن أبي طالب كرّم الله وجهه

١٠،٤٥ وقيل له أيّما أحبّ إليك أخوك أم صديقك قال إنّما أحبّ أخي إذا كان صديقي

١١،٤٥ وقال أكرموا الكتّاب فإنّ الله تعالى أجرى الأرزاق على أيديهم

١٢،٤٥ وقال القلم شجرة ثمارها الألفاظ

١٣،٤٥ وكان إبراهيم بن جبلة يكتب خطًّا رديئًا فقال له عبد الحميد أطل جلفة القلم وأسمنها وحرّف قطّتك وأيمنها يصلح خطّك وإلى هذا أشار ابن زيدون بقوله وعبد الحميد باري أقلامك

١٤،٤٥ ومن رسائله ما كتب به عن مروان إلى هشام يعزّيه بحظيّة من حظاياه

me: in this way, you might help my own cause, or perhaps assist my family after I am dead." But ʿAbd al-Ḥamīd replied:

> If I keep faith in my heart, but express perfidy,
> who will voice my excuse before the world?

ʿAbd al-Ḥamīd continued: "Commander of the Faithful, what you have ordered me is a better option for your interests, but worse for mine; I will persevere until either God opens a way to victory for you or I am killed with you."

When Marwān was killed, ʿAbd al-Ḥamīd went into hiding with his friend, Ibn al-Muqaffaʿ, in Mesopotamia, but his pursuers were tipped off and surprised them both in their house. The troops burst in and shouted, "Which of you is ʿAbd al-Ḥamīd?" Both men, hoping to protect the other, said, "I am!" Eventually ʿAbd al-Ḥamīd was recognized, and the Caliph al-Saffāḥ delivered him to his chief constable, ʿAbd al-Jabbār, who had a basin heated and placed on top of ʿAbd al-Ḥamīd's head until it killed him. This was in the year 132 [750]. 45.7

The Caliph ʿAbū Jaʿfar al-Manṣūr said: The Umayyads had three things over us: al-Ḥajjāj,[341] ʿAbd al-Ḥamīd the Secretary, and the Baʿalbakī prayer caller.[342] 45.8

ʿAbd al-Ḥamīd was once asked, "What made you such an eloquent writer?" He replied, "I memorized the words of the Bald One." (He meant the Caliph ʿAlī, God preserve his perfect purity.) 45.9

Someone asked ʿAbd al-Ḥamīd, "Whom do you love more: your brother or your friend?" ʿAbd al-Ḥamīd replied, "I love my brother if he is also my friend." 45.10

ʿAbd al-Ḥamīd said: "Treat the chancellery secretaries well, for Exalted God has placed the apportionment of salaries in their hands." 45.11

He also said: "The pen is a tree that bears the fruit of words." 45.12

Ibrāhīm ibn Jabalah had terrible handwriting, and ʿAbd al-Ḥamīd advised him: "To improve your penmanship, lengthen and broaden the cut of your pen, and cut the nib obliquely to the right."[343] This is the saying Ibn Zaydūn had in mind in the *Letter*'s line: "ʿAbd al-Ḥamīd pared your pens." 45.13

An example of ʿAbd al-Ḥamīd's letters is one he wrote on behalf of Marwān to the Caliph Hishām consoling him on the death of one of his concubines: 45.14

إنّ الله تعالى أمتع أمير المؤمنين من أنيسته وقرينته متاعًا مدّة إلى أجل مسمًّى فلمّا أتمّت له مواهب الله وعاريته قبض إليه العارية ثمّ أعطى أمير المؤمنين من الشكر عند بقائها والصبر عند ذهابها أنفس منها في المنقلب[1] وأرجح في الميزان وأسنى في العوض[2] والحمد لله ربّ العالمين وإنّا لله وإنّا إليه راجعون

١٥،٤٥ وكتب موصيًّا لشخص حقّ موصّل كتابي إليك كحقّه عليّ إذ جعلك موضعًا لأمله ورآني أهلاً لحاجته وقد أنجزت حاجته فصدّق أمله

١٦،٤٥ وكتب رسالة يعرّض بشعار بني العباس الأسود برسالة فرويدًا حتّى ينصبّ السيل ويمحو الله آية الليل

١٧،٤٥ وكتب من رسالة إلى أهله وهو مهزوم مع مروان

أمّا بعد فإنّ الله تعالى جعل الدنيا محفوفة بالكره والسرور فمن ساعده الحظّ فيها سكن إليها ومن عضّته بأنيابها ذمّها ساخطًا وشكاها مستزيدًا لها وقد كانت أذاقتنا أفاويق استحليناها ثمّ جمحت بنا نافرة ورمحتنا موليّة فملح عذبها وخشن ليّنها فأبعدتنا عن الأوطان وفرّقتنا من الإخوان فالدار نازحة والطير بارحة وقد كتبت إليكم والأيّام تزيدنا منكم بعدًا وإليكم وجدًا فإن تتمّ البليّة إلى أقصى مدّتها يكن آخر العهد بنا وبكم وإن يلحقنا ظفر جارح من أظفار من يليكم نرجع إليكم بذلّ الإسار والذلّ شرّ جار نسأل الله الذي يعزّ من يشاء ويذلّ من يشاء أن يهب لنا ولكم ألفة جامعة في دار آمنة تجمع سلامة الأبدان والأديار فإنّه ربّ العالمين وأرحم الراحمين

١ إ٣: المتقلّب. ٢ إ١ ول٢ وبر١ وإ٦ وب وق١ وإ٣: عرض.

> The Commander of the Faithful enjoyed the pleasure of his companion and consort as a grant from God until the allotted time. When God completes the term of His gifts and loans, all that was borrowed is returned unto Him, but He then grants the Commander of the Faithful both the sense of gratitude for her life, and the power of acceptance to endure her passing. These gifts are the more valuable in the final reckoning, a more propitious weight on the scales of one's deeds, and a nobler recompense. Praise be God, Lord of the Worlds. We are from Him and to Him we return.

Someone requested a letter of recommendation from ʿAbd al-Ḥamīd, and he wrote: "What you owe the person who conveys this letter is the same as what I owe him, inasmuch as he considers you an object of his hope, and he considers me worthy of writing his request. As I have fulfilled his request, please grant him his hope." 45.15

In a letter disparaging the Abbasid Revolt's signature black flags, ʿAbd al-Ḥamīd wrote: "Wait a little while until the flood pours; then God will efface that sign of the night." 45.16

As he was fleeing with Marwān in defeat, ʿAbd al-Ḥamīd wrote to his family: 45.17

> The Exalted God fills this world with pains and delights. Those upon whom fortune smiles find repose; those whom this world gnaws deride it with curses and complain, demanding it provide them something more. This world had succored us with rains we found sweet, but it bolted from us, and then galloped back against us: what had been sweet turned bitter, what had been soft turned hard. It cast us from our lands, separated us from friends: home is now distant, the birds bring ominous signs, and as I write to you, each passing day pushes us farther apart in the same measure that it increases our yearning for you. If our trials end with the worst, then this shall be our last contact, but if the talons of those now around you snatch us, we shall return with the ignominy of imprisonment; ignominy is the worst protector. We ask God, who exalts and abases those He wills, to grant us a meeting in serenity where bodies and abodes are at peace. He is Lord of the Worlds and Most Merciful.

**ومن شعره** ١٨،٤٥

تَرَحَّلَ مَا لَيْسَ بِٱلْقَافِلِ[1]    وَأَعْقَبَ مَا لَيْسَ بِٱلزَّائِلِ
فَلَهْفِي لِذِي سَلَفٍ قَادِمٍ    وَلَهْفِي عَلَى سَلَفٍ رَاحِلِ
سَأَبْكِي عَلَى ذَا وَأَبْكِي لِذَا    بُكَاءَ مُوَلَّهَةٍ ثَاكِلِ
تُبَكِّي مِنِ ٱبْنٍ لَهَا قَاطِعٍ    وَتَبْكِي عَلَى ٱبْنٍ لَهَا وَاصِلِ[2]

**ومن شعره** ١٩،٤٥

كَفَى حُزْنًا أَنِّي أَرَى مَنْ أُحِبُّهُ    قَرِيبًا وَلَا غَيْرُ ٱلْقُلُوبِ يُتَرْجِمُ
فَأُقْسِمُ لَوْ أَبْصَرْتَنَا حِينَ نَلْتَقِي    وَنَحْنُ سُكُوتٌ خِلْتَنَا نَتَكَلَّمُ

## وسهل بن هارون مدوّن كلامك ٤٦

هو سهل بن هارون بن راهيون[3] ويكنى أبو عمرو من أهل نيسابور نزل البصرة فنُسب إليها ويقال إنّه كان شعوبيًّا والشعوبيّة فرقة تبغض العرب وتتعصّب عليها للفرس وافترد سهل في زمانه بالبلاغة والحكمة وصنّف الكتب معارضًا بها كتب الأوائل حتّى قيل له بزرجمهر الإسلام ومن محاسن كتبه كتاب ثعله وعفراء يعارض به كتاب كليلة ودمنة وهو موجود في أيدي الناس ورأيت للقاضي الفاضل رحمه الله رسالة في وصفه يقول فيها ما معناه من أراد أن يعرف مقدار هذا الرجل فليتأمّل كتابه المسمّى ثعله وعفراء[4] وله اليد الطولى في النظم والنثر ١،٤٦

وكان في أوّل أمره خصيصًا بالفضل بن سهل ثمّ قدّمه إلى المأمون فأعجب ببلاغته وعقله وجعله كاتبًا على خزانة الحكمة وهي كتب الفلاسفة التي نقلت للمأمون من جزيرة قبرص[5] وذلك أنّ المأمون لمّا هادن صاحب هذه الجزيرة أرسل ٢،٤٦

١ إ١: بالغافل. ٢ إ١: راحل. ٣ إ١: راهون. ٤ ومن محاسن . . . عفرة: زيادة من با١، ل١، ل٢، إ٦، غ.
٥ با١، إ٦: جزيرة صقلية.

ʿAbd al-Ḥamīd's poetry: 45.18

What passed shall never return;
what's to come shall never cease to be.[344]
I fret for those whose successors are yet to arise,
as I grieve for those whose successors have passed.
I lament the past and weep for the future,
bewildered weeping of the bereaved—
mourning over a son lost,
or mourning for a son about to come.

ʿAbd al-Ḥamīd's poetry: 45.19

It is sad enough for me to see one I love
nearby, but we cannot speak except through our hearts.
I swear, if you could see us when we meet,
you'd see us silent, yet you'd think we're talking.

**... Sahl ibn Hārūn recorded your speech ...** 46

Sahl ibn Hārūn ibn Rāhyūn,[345] known as Abu ʿAmr, hailed from Nīshāpūr, but he settled in Basra and became known as a Basran. He is said to have been one of the Persian-partisan Arab haters. Sahl was the most brilliant mind of his day, and the best writer: his books rival the wisdom of the ancients, and hence he was nicknamed "Bozorgmehr of Islam." One of his best books, still extant, is *Thaʿlah and ʿAfrāʾ*,[346] a text that rivals *Kalīlah and Dimnah.* I have read an epistle about it by al-Qāḍī l-Fāḍil (God have mercy upon him), which in short says that anyone wishing to know Sahl's merit simply need ponder *Thaʿlah and ʿAfrāʾ*. Sahl's writings decisively influenced Arabic prose and poetry. 46.1

At the beginning of his career, Sahl was the private confidant of al-Faḍl ibn Sahl. Al-Faḍl presented Sahl to the Caliph al-Maʾmūn, who was so impressed by Sahl's eloquence and intelligence that he appointed him to oversee the House of Wisdom, the depository of philosophical books that al-Maʾmūn acquired from Cyprus. The books came into al-Maʾmūn's possession when he signed a truce with the ruler of Cyprus and requested Greek books that 46.2

إليه يطلب خزانة كتب اليونان وكانت مجموعة في بيت لا يظهر عليها أحد ولم يكن لهم بها نفع لأنّهم نصارى أهل شريعة[1] فجمع صاحب الجزيرة بطانته وذوي الرأي واستشارهم في حمل الخزانة إلى المأمون فكلّهم أشاروا بعدم الموافقة إلّا مطران واحد فإنّه قال الرأي أن تعجّل بإنفاذها إليه فما دخلت هذه العلوم العقليّة على دولة شرعيّة إلّا أفسدتها وأوقعت بين علمائها فأرسلها إليه واغتبط بها المأمون وسلّمها إلى سهل فتصفّحها ونسج على منوالها وصنّف كتاب عفراء وثعله في معارضة كتاب كليلة ودمنة

٣،٤٦ ووضع كتابًا في مدح البخل وأهداه للحسن بن سهل واستماحه فكتب إليه الحسن قد مدحت ما ذمّ الله وحسّنت ما قبّحه الله وما يقوم بفساد معناك صلاح لفظك وقد جعلنا ثوابك فيه قبول قولك فما نعطيك شيئًا

٤،٤٦ وكان سهل من أبخل الناس وله في البخل وغيره نوادر حسنة حكى الجاحظ قال لقي رجل سهل بن هارون فقال هب لي مالًا مرزية عليك فيه قال وما هو قال درهم قال لقد هوّنت الدرهم وهو طابع الله في أرضه الذي لا يعصى وهو عشر العشرة والعشرة عشر المائة والمائة عشر الألف والألف عشر دية المسلم ألا ترى إلى أين انتهى الدرهم الذي هوّنته وهل بيوت لأموال إلّا درهم على درهم فانصرف الرجل ولو لم ينصرف لم يسكت

٥،٤٦ وحكى دعبل الخزاعيّ قال أقمنا يومًا عند سهل بن هارون وأطلنا الحديث حتّى أضرّ به الجوع إلى أن دعا بغدائه وأتي بصحفة فيها مرق تحته ديك هرم فأخذ كسرة وتفقّد ما في الصحفة فلم يجد رأس الديك فبقي مطرقًا ثمّ قال للغلام أين الرأس قال رميت به قال ولم قال لم أظنّك تأكله قال ولم ظننت ذلك فوالله إنّي لأمقت من يرمي برجله فكيف برأسه والرأس رئيس يتفاءل[2] به وفيه الحواس

١ ولم . . . شريعة: زيادة من با١، ل١، ل٢، إ٦، غ. ٢ إ١: يتغالي.

the Cypriots held in a disused depository—after all, the books were of no use to the Cypriots since they had embraced Christian monotheistic laws. The Cypriot ruler assembled his retinue and wise men to consult about transferring the archive. All opposed the idea, except one bishop who said, "The right opinion is to send them at once! Whenever a monotheistic community comes into contact with the rational sciences, they corrupt it and sow dissention among its scholars. Send the books to him!"[347]

Al-Ma'mūn was delighted to receive the books, and he delivered them to Sahl. Sahl perused them and began writing in their style, and at this juncture he wrote *Tha'lah and 'Afrā'* to rival *Kalīlah and Dimnah.*

Sahl also wrote a book in praise of miserliness, which he gifted to the Vizier al-Ḥasan ibn Sahl, seeking favors, but the vizier wrote back: "You have praised that which God reviles; you have gilded that which God denounces. The rectitude of your language does not correct the depravity of your intention, and the mere acceptance of the book is all the recompense we shall offer. You will receive no gift." 46.3

Sahl was one of the most miserly men imaginable, and many droll stories are told about this. Al-Jāḥiẓ relates one: A man once said to Sahl, "Give me a sum of money you would find contemptible!" Sahl asked, "How much would that be?" "One dirham," the man replied. Sahl exclaimed, "You make light of the dirham! The bearer of the stamp of God on His Earth[348] where He is not to be disobeyed! A single dirham is one-tenth of ten dirhams, which is one-tenth of a hundred, and the hundred is a tenth of a thousand, and that is the tenth of ten thousand, which is the sum of blood money payable for killing a Muslim. Do you now see the ultimate fate of the one dirham you so belittled? And are not the state treasures merely one dirham placed upon another . . . ?" The man left; had he not, Sahl would have kept on going. 46.4

Di'bil al-Khuzā'ī relates: Once, when visiting Sahl, we prolonged our conversation for so long that finally he couldn't bear his own hunger anymore and had to call for lunch. Out came a plate containing a decrepit rooster covered in gravy. Sahl took a piece of bread and began rooting about in the gravy. He couldn't find the rooster's head, and he looked down for a while, then called to the servant, "Where's the head?" "I threw it away." "Why?" "I didn't think you'd eat it." Sahl then laid into him: "And why in God's name would you think that! Given how much I would abhor throwing away the rooster's drumstick, how could I discard the head? The head! The very leader 46.5

الخمس ومنه يصيح الديك ولولا صوته ما أريد وفيه فرقه الذي يتبرّك به وعينه التي يُضرب بصفائها المثل ودماغه عجيب لوجع الكلية ولم يُرَ عظم قطّ أهشّ من عظم رأسه فإن كان بلغ من نبلك أن لا تأكله فعندنا من يأكله أو ما علمت أنّه خير من طرف الجناح والسّاق انظر أين رميته قال لا والله لا أدري قال لكنّي أدري أنّك رميت به في بطنك

٦،٤٦ وحكى الجاحظ أنّ أبا الهذيل العلّاف المتكلّم سأله رقعة يكتب بها إلى الحسن ابن سهل يستعينه على ضائقة لحقته فكتب رقعة وختمها ودفعها إليه فأوصلها إلى الحسن فلمّا رآها ضحك وأوقف عليها أبا الهذيل وإذا فيها

إِنَّ ٱلضَّمِيرَ إِذَا سَأَلْتُكَ حَاجَةً لِأَبِي ٱلْهُذَيْلِ خِلَافُ مَا أُبْدِي
فَٱمْنَعْهُ رَوْحَ ٱلْيَأْسِ ثُمَّ ٱمْدُدْ لَهُ حَبْلَ ٱلرَّجَاءِ بِمُخْلِفِ ٱلْوَعْدِ
حَتَّى إِذَا طَالَتْ شَقَاوَةُ ٱلْجَدِّ وَعَنَائِهِ فَٱجْبَهْهُ بِٱلرَّدِّ
وَإِنِ ٱسْتَطَعْتَ لَهُ ٱلْمَضَرَّةَ فَٱجْتَهِدْ فِيمَا يَضُرُّ بِأَبْلَغِ ٱلْجُهْدِ

٧،٤٦ ثمّ قال الحسن هذه صفته لا صفتنا وأمر لأبي الهذيل بمال فعاد إليه فعاتبه فقال سهل ترى أين عزب عنك الفهم أما سمعت قولي إِنَّ ٱلضَّمِيرَ خِلَافُ مَا أُبْدِي فلو لم يكن ضميري الخير ما قلت هذا وهذه من مغالطات سهل وبلاغته وسيأتي في ترجمة الجاحظ حكاية مثل هذا

٨،٤٦ ومن محاسن تعريضات سهل أنّه خاطب بعض الأمراء فقال له كذبت فقال أيّها الأمير وجه الكذّاب لا يقابلك يعني الأمير نفسه لأنّ وجه الإنسان لا يقابله

from which all good omens are derived, the organ of the rooster's five senses. From his head the rooster crows, and were it not for his crowing, he would be unwanted. The head also holds the rooster's comb, for which he is admired. It holds his eyes too, and haven't you heard the proverb for purity: 'as clear as a rooster's eye'?[349] His head holds his brains as well, so wondrously beneficial for kidney pains. And I have never seen so tender a bone as a rooster's skull. If you fancy yourself too fancy to eat the head, there are people here who will. Don't you know the head is tastier than the wing or thigh? Find where you tossed it!" The boy said, "I swear I have no idea." Sahl replied, "Nay, I know what happened to it: you tossed it into your belly!"

Al-Jāḥiẓ reports that a misfortune had befallen the theologian Abū l-Hudhayl, "the Feed Merchant," and he asked Sahl to write a petition on his behalf to the Vizier al-Ḥasan ibn Sahl, asking for assistance. Sahl wrote the petition, sealed it, and handed it to Abū l-Hudhayl, who presented it to al-Ḥasan. But when al-Ḥasan read it, he burst out laughing, and told Abū l-Hudhayl what it said. Sahl had written: 46.6

When I ask you to aid Abū l-Hudhayl,
I desire the opposite in my heart—
Withhold, make him desperate, then dangle
a hope, a vain hope—
dangle it long, as he faces fortune's misery and pain,
then smack him with a flat refusal.
If you can distress him, use all your efforts
to bring it to the maximum.

Al-Ḥasān then said, "This is his way, but not ours," and he ordered money for Abū l-Hudhayl. Abū l-Hudhayl stormed back to Sahl, upbraiding him, but Sahl said, "Don't you see how your analysis erred? Didn't you hear me say, 'What my heart desires is the opposite of what I say'? I thus wouldn't have written that message unless in my heart I wished you well!" Though rhetorically elegant, this was one of the cases where Sahl overstepped the bounds of decency; a similar story will be narrated in the biography of al-Jāḥiẓ.[350] 46.7

Among Sahl's cleverly equivocal one-liners was his response to one of the ruling elite who had confronted him, saying, "You lied to us!" Sahl responded, "My lord! The face of the liar is not facing you." He meant that the aristocrat was the liar, since one cannot face one's own face. 46.8

٩،٤٦ ويُروى أنّ المأمون كان قد انحرف عن سهل إلى أن دخل عليه يومًا فقال يا أمير المؤمنين إنّك ظلمتني وظلمت فلانًا الكاتب قال ويلك وكيف قال رفعته فوق قدره ووضعتني دون قدري إلّا أنّك له في ذلك أشدّ ظلمًا قال وكيف قال إنّك أقمته مقام هزؤ وأقمتني مقام رحمة فضحك المأمون وقال قاتلك الله ما أهجاك ثمّ رضي عنه

١٠،٤٦ وقد حُكي عن سبب رضا المأمون عنه أنّه تكلّم بكلام حسن في حفل فقام سهل فقال ما لكم تسمعون ولا تعون فلا تعجبون أمّا والله إنه ليقول ويفعل في اليوم القصير مثل ما[١] قالت وفعلت بنو مروان في الدهر الطويل فأعجب المأمون قوله ورضي عنه

١١،٤٦ ومن كلامه يعزّي التهنئة على آجل الثواب أَوْلى من التعزية على عاجل المصيبة

١٢،٤٦ وقال في المعنى[٢] ومصيبة في غيرك لك أجرها خير لك من مصيبة فيك لغيرك ثوابها

١٣،٤٦ وكتب إلى صديق له أبلّ من ضعف بلغني خبر الفترة في إلمامها وانحسارها والشكاة في حلولها وارتحالها فكاد يشغل القلق بأوّله عن السكون لآخره وتذهل الحيرة في ابتدائه عن المسرّة بانتهائه وكان تصرّفي في الحالين بقدرهما ارتياعًا في الأولى وارتياحًا للأخرى

١٤،٤٦ وكتب لآخر أمّا بعد فالسلام على عهدك وداع ذي ظنّ بك في غير مقلية لك ولا سلوة عنك بل استسلام للبلوى في أمرك وإقرار بالعجز عن استعطافك إلى أوان فيئتك أو يجعل الله لنا دولة من رجعتك[٣]

١٥،٤٦ وقال يفضّل الزجاج على الذهب[٤] من رسالة

الزجاج مجلوّ نوريّ والذهب متاع سائر[٥] والشراب في الزجاج أحسن منه في كل معدن ولا يُفقد معه وجه النديم ولا يُثقل اليد ولا يرتفع

١ سقطت من إ١. ٢ وقال . . . المعنى: زيادة من إ٢، إ٣. ٣ وكتب . . . رجعتك: زيادة من با١، إ٦، ل١، بر٢.
٤ إ١: الذهب على الزجاج. ٥ إ١: ساتر.

It is narrated that Sahl fell somewhat out of the Caliph al-Ma'mūn's favor, until one day Sahl entered the caliph's presence and announced, "Commander of the Faithful! You have wronged both me and one of the secretaries." (Sahl identified the man by name.) Al-Ma'mūn replied, "What the Hell do you mean by that?" Sahl said, "You have promoted him above his competence and demoted me below my aptitude; though to him you have been more unjust." "And why is that?" Sahl explained, "You exposed him to ridicule, whereas you put me in a position deserving of compassion." Al-Ma'mūn laughed and said, "My goodness! How vicious you are!" He returned Sahl to favor. 46.9

Another version explaining Sahl's return to al-Ma'mūn's favor relates that when al-Ma'mūn made a fine speech at an assembly, Sahl rose and announced, "What is wrong with all of you? You heard but understood nothing, so you have no appreciation. By God, what he says and accomplishes in but one day equals what the Marwanid caliphs said and accomplished in all their days!" Al-Ma'mūn liked what he heard and was pleased with Sahl. 46.10

In a condolence letter, Sahl said, "I offer you congratulations for the good recompense you will receive in the future, as this is more apposite than offering condolences over your present loss." 46.11

On the same theme, Sahl also said, "A loss of another for which you are the beneficiary is better than a loss of yours from which others benefit." 46.12

Sahl wrote to a convalescing friend: "The news that infirmity had called and ailment had settled upon you aroused such anxiety within me that the news of infirmity's departure and ailment's decampment has but scarcely relaxed or gladdened me. My delight to hear the outcome is equal in measure to the fright I felt at the outset." 46.13

To another,[351] Sahl wrote: "Our erstwhile peace be upon you. Discount any misapprehensions of dislike or disregard: it is but surrender in the face of the trials you can inflict, and acknowledgment of incapacity to entreat your return, or to hope God would give us the power to bring you round." 46.14

The following is an excerpt from an epistle Sahl wrote on the merits of glass over gold: 46.15

> "Glass is clear and belongs to the realm of light, while gold is a market chattel. Glass reveals the beauty of wine more than any other material; it neither obscures the face of your drinking

في السوم واسم الذهب يُتطيّر منه ومن لؤمه سرعته إلى اللئام وهو فاتن[1] قاتل لمن صانه وهو أيضًا من مصائد إبليس ولذلك قالوا أهلك الرجال الأحمران والزجاج لا يحمل الوضر ولا يتداخله الغمر ومتى غسله بالماء وحده عاد جديدًا وهو أشبه شيء بالماء وصنعته عجيبة وصناعته أعجب

وهي طويلة وكان سبب قولها أنّ شدّاد الحارثيّ كان وصف الذهب فأطنب وكان النظّام قد ذمّ الزجاج

١٦،٤٦ وقال تعلّموا العلم فلأن يُذمّ الزمان لكم خير من أن يُذمّ بكم

١٧،٤٦ وقال يومًا ثلاثة من المجانين الغضبان والغيران والسكران فقال شخص من العوامّ فما تقول في المنعظ فضحك حتّى استلقى وأنشد

وَمَا شَرُّ ٱلثَّلَاثَـةِ أُمَّ عَمْرٍو بِصَاحِبِكِ ٱلَّذِي لَا تَصْبَحِينَا

١٨،٤٦ ومن كلامه في كتاب عفراء وثعله اجعلوا أداء الحقوق مقدّمًا قبل الذي تجودون به من تفضّلكم فإنّ تقديم النافلة مع الإبطاء في أداء الفريضة شاهد على وهن العقيدة وتقصير الرويّة ومضرّ بالتدبير ومخلّ بالاختيار وليس في نفع محمدته عوض من فساد المروءة ولزوم النقيصة

١٩،٤٦ ومن شعره قوله

أَعَانَ طَرْفِي عَلَى جِسْمِي وَأَعْضَائِي بِنَظْـرَةٍ وَقَفَتْ جِسْمِي عَلَى دَائِي
وَكُنْتُ غِـرًّا بِمَا تَجْنِي عَلَيَّ يَدِي لَا عِلْمَ لِي أَنَّ بَعْضِي بَعْضُ أَعْدَائِي

---

١ إ: قاس

companion, nor weighs down the hand, nor costs you dearly. Gold's very name is ill omened,[352] and as indication of its ignominy, consider how quickly it goes into the hands of the ignoble. Gold incites discord, murders its keeper, and is one of Satan's traps—as the saying goes: 'Men are wasted by the two reds.'[353] Glass neither carries filth, nor is penetrated by rotting smells. Washing it with water alone returns it as good as new. No material more resembles water; its workmanship can be marvelous and the process of its production even more so."

It is a long epistle: Sahl wrote it as a response both to the long-winded praise of gold by Shaddād al-Ḥārithī and to al-Naẓẓām's disparagement of glass.[354]

Sahl's wise words include: "Study and learn: if you can't make a living off knowledge, then it's your society that's to blame, but if you don't apply yourself to study, then your society will be blamed on account of you!"[355] 46.16

Once, Sahl said: "There are three kinds of madmen: those driven mad by anger, by jealousy, or by drunkenness." One of the commoners listening interjected: "What about sexual desire?" Sahl collapsed in laughter and quoted a verse: 46.17

Umm ʿAmr, your companion is not the worst
of the three, yet you served him no drink![356]

An excerpt from Sahl's *Thaʿlah and ʿAfrāʾ*: Fulfill your obligations before dispensing bonuses from your bounty. Performing the supererogatory before the obligatory is suggestive of weak faith, insufficient reflection, detrimental planning, and faulty judgment. Though the supererogatory is commendable per se, its benefit does not compensate for corrupted virtue and persistent defects. 46.18

Sahl's poetry: 46.19

My glance cast an evil eye upon my body and limbs;
my gaze saw my body struck with infirmity.
Would that I had considered what my hands were reaping—
little did I know that my enemy was within me!

وقوله ٢٠،٤٦

إِنْ كُنْتُ أَخْسطَأْتُ أَوْ أَسَأْتُ فَفِي فَضْـلِكَ مَـأْوًى لِلْعَفْوِ وَٱلْمِنَنِ
أَتَيْتُ مَا أَسْتَحِقُّ مِنْ خَطَإٍ فَجُدْ بِمَا تَسْتَحِقُّ مِنْ حَسَنِ

وقوله ٢١،٤٦

هُدًى لَا يَسْتَرِيحُ وَلَا يُرِيحُ وَقَلْبٌ مِنْ جَوَانِبِهِ جَرِيحُ
فَإِنْ يَكُ سِرُّ قَلْبِكَ أَعْجَمِيًّا فَإِنَّ ٱلدَّمْعَ نَمَّامٌ فَضُوحُ
سَأَجْمَحُ فِي ٱلْهَوَى وَأُلِحُّ فِيهِ وَلَيْسَ أَخُو ٱلْهَوَى إِلَّا ٱلْجَمُوحُ
عَلَى أَنَّ ٱلْهَوَى لَمْ يُبْقِ مِنِّي سِوَى كَبِدٍ عَلَى بَدَنٍ يَنُوحُ

وقوله يهجو رجلاً ذا بيتا ٢٢،٤٦

مَنْ كَانَ يَعْمُرُ مَا شَادَتْ أَوَائِلُهُ فَأَنْتَ تَهْدِمُ مَا شَادُوا وَمَا سَمَكُوا[1]
مَا كَانَ فِي ٱلْحَقِّ أَنْ تَأْبَى فَعَالَهُمُ وَأَنْتَ تَحْوِي مِنَ ٱلْمِيرَاثِ مَا تَرَكُوا

وقوله ٢٣،٤٦

تَكَنَّفَنِي هَمَّانِ قَدْ كَسَفَا بَالِي وَقَدْ جَعَلَا قَلْبِي مَحَلَّةَ بَلْبَالِ
هُمَا أَذْرَيَا دَمْعِي وَلَمْ تَذْرِ أَدْمُعِي رَبِيبَةُ خِدْرٍ ذَاتُ سِمْطٍ وَخَلْخَالِ
وَلٰكِنَّمَا أَبْكِي بِعَيْنٍ سَخِينَةٍ عَلَى خَلَلٍ تَبْكِي لَهُ عَيْنُ أَمْثَالِي
فِرَاقُ خَلِيلٍ فَقْدُهُ يُورِثُ ٱلْأَسَى وَخَلَّةُ حُرٍّ لَا يَقُومُ لَهَا مَالِي
فَوَاحَرْبَا حَتَّى مَتَى أَنَا مُوجَعٌ بِفَقْدِ حَبِيبٍ أَوْ تَعَذُّرِ إِفْضَالِ

---

١ إ: شركوُا

Sahl's poetry: 46.20

If I erred or did you wrong, remember this—
    Your virtue is a forgiving refuge of good will.
I made every mistake expected of me.
Please bestow every goodness expected of you.

Sahl's poetry: 46.21

Guidance that gives you no repose,
    a heart all which ways injured—
Your heart's secret mumbles indecipherable,
    though your tears are gossips revealing all.
I'll run wild with love and press on—
    a lover is nothing if not defiant.
Though love leaves me nothing
    but a heart in mourning.

Sahl disparaged a man who owned a house: 46.22

There are those who enliven what their ancestors built,
    and then there's you: destroyer of your forefathers' house.
You've no right to reject their example,
    while you take all that they left.

Sahl's poetry: 46.23

Two worries envelop me; they darken my thoughts,
    fill my heart with confusion,
    and wrench tears from my eyes.
Not tears for a secluded girl, in necklace and anklets.
No, my hot tears flow for privations without redress,
    cried over by many an eye as mine—
    loss of a friend, grief his legacy,
    and poverty of one wellborn, when my funds aren't enough to help.
Such anguish! How much longer must I suffer from
    losing a beloved, and excusing my poverty?

وقوله ٢٤،٤٦

إِذَا ٱمْرُؤٌ ضَاقَ عَنِّي لَمْ يَضِقْ خُلُقِي    مِنْ أَنْ يَرَانِي غَنِيًّا عَنْهُ بِٱلْيَأْسِ
لَا أَطْلُبُ ٱلْمَالَ كَيْ أَغْنَى بِفَضْلَتِهِ    مَا كَانَ مَطْلَبُهُ فَقْرًا إِلَى ٱلنَّاسِ

## وعمرو بن بحر مستمليك ٤٧

١،٤٧ هو عمرو بن بحر بن محبوب ويُكنى بأبي عثمان ويُعرف بالجاحظ وبالحدقيّ والأوّل أشهر إمام الفصحاء والمتكلّمين الذي ملأت الآفاق أخباره وفوائده حتّى قيل ممّا فضّل الله أمّة محمّد صلّى الله عليه وسلّم على غيرها من الأمم عمر بن الخطّاب بسياسته والحسن البصريّ بعلمه والجاحظ ببيانه

٢،٤٧ ولد بالبصرة ونشأ ببغداد واشتغل على النظّام المقدّم ذكره بمذهب الاعتزال وتأمّل كتب الفلاسفة ومال إلى الطبيعيّين منهم وساد على المتكلّمين بفصاحة لسانه وبلاغة فكره

٣،٤٧ وممّا تفرّد به القول بأنّ بالمعرفة طباع وهي مع ذلك فعل العباد على الحقيقة وكان يقول في سائر الأفعال إنّها إنّما تُنسب إلى العباد على أنّها وقعت منهم طباعًا وأنّها وجبت بإرادتهم وليس بجائز أن يبلغ أحد ولا يعرف الله تعالى والكفّار عنده بين معاند وعارف قد استغرقه حبّه لمذهبه وعصبيّته فهو لا يشعر بما عنده من المعرفة بخلافه إلى غير ذلك من آرائه التي تبعه عليها أصحابه المعروفون بالجاحظيّة

٤،٤٧ فأمّا مصنّفاته الأدبيّة مثل كتاب الحيوان وكتاب الأمصار وكتاب البيان والتبيين وغيرها من الرسائل فكثيرة جدًّا مشحونة بالفضائل مع إسهاب كثر وكان ذلك مذهبه في القول

Sahl's poetry: 46.24

> If a man is stingy with me, my character
> will not let him see me helpless and in need.
> I don't seek money from gifts of scraps—
> coins gained by fawning are not for me.

**. . . 'Amr ibn Baḥr took your dictation . . .** 47

'Amr ibn Baḥr ibn Maḥbūb was the leading literary figure and theologian of his day. Most called him Abū 'Uthmān, but he also went by the nicknames Goggle-Eyed (al-Jāḥiẓ) and Stary.[357] Al-Jāḥiẓ is famed far and wide, such that they count him one of the three men through whom God elevated Muḥammad's (God bless and keep him) people above all others: the Caliph 'Umar ibn al-Khaṭṭāb for his statecraft, al-Ḥasan al-Baṣrī for his knowledge, and al-Jāḥiẓ for his eloquence. 47.1

Al-Jāḥiẓ was born in Basra and grew up in Baghdad. He studied the rationalist Mu'tazilite doctrine under the aforementioned al-Naẓẓām,[358] and he pondered the books of the philosophers, generally favoring natural philosophy. He prevailed over all other theologians with his eloquence and the excellence of his expressions. 47.2

Among the suppositions unique to al-Jāḥiẓ is his opinion that knowledge of God is both innate and an actual act undertaken by worshippers. Al-Jāḥiẓ similarly opined that all the other acts ascribed to the agency of worshippers are innate but necessitated by the worshippers' own will. 47.3

Al-Jāḥiẓ did not believe anyone could reach the age of majority without knowing that the Exalted God exists.

As for unbelievers, al-Jāḥiẓ viewed them as occupying a state between knowledge of God and stubborn defiance: submersed in zealous infatuation with their own creed, the unbelievers are unable to perceive that they are opposing their own innate knowledge of God.

Al-Jāḥiẓ espoused other such opinions, which were embraced by his followers, known as the "Jahizians."

Al-Jāḥiẓ's literary output was copious: it includes his books, such as *Living Things*, *The Cities*, and *Eloquence and Exposition*, and various epistles. All brim with manifold merit, and with lengthy tangential elaborations, as was his signature style. 47.4

٥،٤٧ وكان منقطعًا إلى الوزير محمّد بن عبد الملك بن الزيّات منحرفًا عن ابن أبي دؤاد فلمّا قبض ابن الزيّات هرب الجاحظ فقيل له لم هربت قال خفت أن أكون ثاني اثنين إذ هما في التنّور يريد ما صنعوا بابن الزيّات من إدخاله تنّورًا من نحاس فيه مسامير محميّة كان هو صنعه ليعذّب الناس فيه فعذّب فيه حتّى مات

٦،٤٧ ثمّ أتي بالجاحظ بعد موت ابن الزيّات وفي عنقه سلسلة وهو مقيّد في قميص سمل فلمّا نظر إليه ابن أبي دؤاد قال والله ما علمتك إلّا كفورًا للنعمة معدّدًا للمساوئ في كلام يقرّعه به فقال الجاحظ خفّض عليك أيّدك الله فوالله لأَن يكون لك الأمر عليّ خير من أن يكون لي عليك ولأن أسيئ فتحسن أحسن في الأحدوثة عنك من أن أحسن وتسيئ ولأن تعفو عنّي في حال قدرتك أجمل بك من الانتقام منّي فقال ابن أبي دؤاد قبّحك الله فوالله ما علمتك إلّا كثير تزويق اللسان يا غلام صر به إلى الحمّام

٧،٤٧ فأُدخل إلى الحمّام وحُمل إليه تخت من ثياب طويلة فلبس ذلك وأتاه فصدّره في مجلسه ثمّ أقبل عليه وقال هات الآن أحاديثك يا أبا عثمان ولم يزل عزيز الجانب موفور المال والجاه من مبتدأ أمره إلى أن مات سنة خمس وخمسين ومائتين بعد أن بلغ أكثر من تسعين سنة

٨،٤٧ وله أخبار ظريفة ونثر كامل طائل ونظم ضعيف

٩،٤٧ فمن أخباره ونوادره قال أتيت منزل صديق لي فطرقت الباب فخرجت إليّ جارية سنديّة فقلت قولي لسيّدك الجاحظ بالباب فقالت أقول الجاحد بالباب على لغتها فقلت لا قولي الحدقيّ فقالت أقول الحلقيّ فقلت لا تقولي شيئًا ورجعت

Al-Jāḥiẓ was a devoted servant of the Vizier Muḥammad ibn ʿAbd al-Malik ibn al-Zayyāt, and was disinclined to the chief judge Ibn Abī Du'ād. When Ibn al-Zayyāt was arrested, al-Jāḥiẓ initially fled. When he was later questioned about it: "Why did you run away?" he responded, "I was afraid to be the second of the two in the oven."[359] Al-Jāḥiẓ alluded to Ibn al-Zayyāt's fate: they killed him by stuffing him into a copper oven fitted with heated spikes—the very oven Ibn al-Zayyāt had invented to torture his victims. 47.5

After Ibn al-Zayyāt's execution, al-Jāḥiẓ was hauled before the judge Ibn Abī Du'ād with a chain around his neck, shackled, and wearing only a tattered shirt. When Ibn Abī Du'ād beheld him, he vituperated him: "All I've heard about you is that you are a thankless wretch who stubbornly persists in wrongdoing," and so on and so forth—he carried on the diatribe until al-Jāḥiẓ responded, "Calm down, God aid you! By God, is it not better for you that you have power over me, rather than the other way around? People can speak well of you if I do wrong and you do what's right, whereas they wouldn't say the same if it was I who did right and you who did wrong. Exercising your capacity to forgive will exhibit more grace than if you exact your revenge upon me." Ibn Abī Du'ād replied, "God disfigure you! By God, I know all about your finely adorned speech!" and he commanded one of his retainers, "Boy—take the man to the bathhouse!" 47.6

They dragged al-Jāḥiẓ into the bathhouse. There, they fitted him in abundant flowing robes and brought him back to Ibn Abī Du'ād's assembly, placing him in the seat of honor. Ibn Abī Du'ād addressed him: "Now, Jāḥīẓ, tell us your stories!" 47.7

From this point onward, al-Jāḥiẓ enjoyed full favor, and was well remunerated and well regarded until he died in 255 [868–69], when he was over ninety years old.

There are delightful stories about al-Jāḥiẓ: his immense prose output is perfect, though his poetry is weak. 47.8

Among the droll anecdotes is a story al-Jāḥiẓ tells about himself: I visited the house of a friend, and when I rapped on the door, a Sindi slave girl came out and I told her, "Inform your master that al-Jāḥiẓ is at the door." She replied, "You want me to say an infidel is at the door?" Her accent mispronounced my name as *al-jāḥid* (infidel), so I told her, "No, no, say it's al-Ḥadaqī." "You want me to say the man in rags (*al-khalaqī*)?" I told her, "No. Don't say anything," and I left. 47.9

١٠،٤٧ وقال ما أخجلني أحد مثل امرأتين رأيت إحداهما في العسكر وكانت طويلة القامة وكنت على طعام فأردت أن أمازحها فقلت انزلي كلي معنا فقالت اصعد أنت حتّى ترى الدنيا وأمّا الأخرى فإنّها أتتني وأنا على باب داري فقالت لي إليك حاجة وأريد أن تمشي معي فقمت معها إلى أن أتت بي إلى صائغ يهوديّ فقالت له مثل هذا وانصرفت فسألت الصائغ عن قولها فقال إنّها أتت إليّ بفصّ وأمرتني أن أنقش لها فيه صورة شيطان فقلت ما رأيت الشيطان فأتت بك وكان الجاحظ بشع المنظر إلّا أنّ بيانه يجلي عنه

١١،٤٧ وقال دخلت ديوان المكاتبات ببغداد فرأيت قومًا قد صقلوا ثيابهم وصفّوا عمائمهم ووشّوا طرزهم ثمّ اختبرتهم فوجدتهم كما قال الله تبارك وتعالى ﴿فَأَمَّا ٱلزَّبَدُ فَيَذْهَبُ جُفَآءً﴾ ظواهر نظيفة وبواطن سخيفة ﴿فَوَيْلٌ لَّهُم مِّمَّا كَتَبَتْ أَيْدِيهِمْ وَوَيْلٌ لَّهُم مِّمَّا يَكْسِبُونَ﴾

١٢،٤٧ وقال وقفت يومًا على قاصّ[١] فأردت الولع به فقلت لمن حوله إنّه رجل صالح لا يحبّ الشهرة فتفرّقوا عنه فنظر إليّ وقال حسبك الله

١٣،٤٧ وقال قلت يومًا لعبيد الكلابيّ أيسرّك أن تكون هجينًا ولك ألف دينار قال لا أحبّ اللؤم بشيء قلت فإنّ أمير المؤمنين ابن أمة قال أخزى الله من أطاعه قلت نبيّا الله محمّد وإسماعيل كانا ابني[٢] أمة قال لا يقول هذا إلّا قدريّ قلت وما القدريّ قال لا أدري إلّا أنّه رجل سوء

١٤،٤٧ وقال أتاني بعض الثقلاء فقال سمعت أنّ لك ألف جواب مسكت فعلّمني منها فقلت إنّها لا تتعلّم فإنّ الجواب على قدر الكلام فقال على كلّ حال فقلت نعم فقال إذا قال لي شخص يا زوج القحبة يا ثقيل الروح أيش الذي أقول له قلت قل له صدقت

١ إ١، إ٢: قاض ٢ إ١، ل٣: نبي الله إسماعيل كان.

Al-Jāḥiẓ also tells: My two most embarrassing moments were at the hands of women. The first involved a tall woman whom I saw in al-ʿAskar; I was having food and wanted to tease her, and so I said, "Come down and eat with us!" But she replied, "Climb up so you can see the world!" The second was a woman who approached me while I was at the door of my home. She said, "I need you for something; would you come walk with me?" I rose and followed her to the shop of a Jewish jeweler, and she told him, "Just like this one," and left. I asked the jeweler what she meant, and he replied, "That woman brought a jewel to me and asked me to inscribe an image of Satan on it. I told her, 'I don't know what he looks like,' and then she brought you." 47.10

Al-Jāḥiẓ was ugly to behold, but his eloquence revealed his true worth.

Al-Jāḥiẓ said: Once, when I entered the chancellery bureau in Baghdad, I saw an immaculately bedecked crowd with neatly wrapped turbans and sumptuous, finely embroidered garments. But when I put some questions to them, I found them actually like the Qur'anic verse: «The scum is cast away»[360]—outwardly spotless, but inwardly useless—«Woe to them because of what their own hands have written, and woe to them for what they have earned.»[361] 47.11

Al-Jāḥiẓ also recounted: I once stood before a public preacher and wanted to stir up some trouble. So I announced to the whole assembly: "This is an honest man, and he doesn't seek fame." At that, everyone left. He looked at me and said, "God take vengeance on you!"[362] 47.12

Al-Jāḥiẓ said: Once, I asked ʿUbayd al-Kilābī, "Would you be happy if you were a half-caste, but also in possession of a thousand dinars?" He replied, "No, I couldn't live with the ignominy." I then said, "But the Commander of the Faithful is a son of a concubine." ʿUbayd replied, "May God disgrace any who pledge allegiance to him!" Then I told him, "But two prophets of God, Muḥammad and Ishmael, were also sons of concubines."[363] ʿUbayd responded, "Only a proponent of free will would say something like that!" I asked him, "What is free will?" And he answered, "I have no idea, but it surely must be a bad thing."[364] 47.13

Al-Jāḥiẓ also relates: An oaf once said to me, "I hear you have a thousand crushing comebacks. Can you teach me some?" I told him, "They cannot simply be learned; each response must come according to what is said." He said, "So there's a different one for each case?" I told him, "Yes." Then he asked, "If someone says to me, 'You're a bore and your wife's a whore,' what's the comeback?" I told him, "Say: 'You're right.'" 47.14

١٥،٤٧ وقال أنشدت أبا شعيب القلّال[١] شعرًا لأبي نواس فقال هذا شعر لو نقرته لطنّ فقلت ويلك ما تخالف الجرار والخزف

١٦،٤٧ واشترى الجاحظ خصيًّا أسود فقيل له في ذلك فقال أخذته أسود لئلّا يُتّهم بي وخصيًّا لئلّا أُتّهم به

١٧،٤٧ واجتمع في البصرة بالجمّاز في مجلس فقال له الجمّاز كم نارًا في اللغة فقال نار الحرب ونار الشجر ونار الحباحب ونار المعدة والنار المعروفة قال تركت أبلغ النيران قال وما هي قال نار حر أمّك التي ﴿كُلَّمَآ أُلْقِىَ فِيهَا فَوْجٌ سَأَلَهُمْ خَزَنَتُهَآ﴾ فقال الجاحظ أمّا نار أمّي فقد قضيت أنّ لها خزّانًا الشأن في نار حر أمّك التي[٢] يقال لها ﴿هَلِ ٱمْتَلَأْتِ وَتَقُولُ هَلْ مِن مَّزِيدٍ﴾

١٨،٤٧ وسأله شخص كتابًا إلى بعض أصحابه بالوصيّة فكتب له رقعة وختمها فلمّا خرج الرجل من عنده فضّها فإذا فيها كتابي إليك مع من لا أعرف ولا أوجب حقّه فإن قضيت حاجته لم أحمدك وإن رددته لم أذمّك فرجع إليه الرجل فقال الجاحظ كأنّك فضضت الورقة قال نعم قال لا يضرّك ما فيها فإنّه علامة لي إذا أردت العناية بشخص فقال الرجل قطع الله يديك ورجليك ولعنك فقال ما هذا قال علامة لي إذا أردت أن أشكر شخصًا

١٩،٤٧ وقال نزلت على صديق لي فلم آكل عنده لحمًا فعرّضت له فقال إنّي لا أكثر من اللحم مذ سمعت الحديث أنّ الله يكره البيت اللحم فقلت يا أخي إنّ الحديث إنّما أراد البيت الذي تؤكل فيه لحوم الناس بالغيبة فلم يؤخّر حضور اللحم من ذلك اليوم

٢٠،٤٧ واعتلّ الجاحظ في آخر عمره علّة طويلة وكان سببها أنّه حضر مائدة ابن أبي دؤاد وفي الطعام سمك ولبن وكان ابن بختيشوع الطبيب حاضرًا فنهاه عن الجمع بينهما فقال الجاحظ إنّ السمك إن كان مضادًّا للبن فإنّي إذا أكلتهما دفع كلّ منهما ضرر صاحبه وإن كانا متساويين فكأنّي أكلت شيئًا واحدًا فقال ابن بختيشوع أنا لا

١ إ: الهلال. ٢ كلّما ألقى . . . التي: سقطت من إ.

Al-Jāḥiẓ tells: I recited a poem by Abū Nuwās to Abū Shuʿayb "the Jug Maker," and he responded, "That rings well when you tap on it!" I replied, "To Hell with you! You just can't get out of the potters' world, can you?" 47.15

When al-Jāḥiẓ was chided for buying a black eunuch, he said, "I chose a black man so he wouldn't be shamed on account of me, and I chose a eunuch so I wouldn't be shamed on account of him!" 47.16

Al-Jāḥiẓ held an assembly in Basra with al-Jammāz, who asked him, "How many types of fire are there in Arabic?" Al-Jāḥiẓ replied, "There is the fire of war, the fire plow,[365] the firefly, the fire of hunger, and the familiar physical flame." Al-Jammāz then said, "You left out the fieriest one of all!" "Which one is that?" "The fire of your mother's vulva, which, whenever a troop of men are tossed in, «its storekeepers ask them 'Were you not warned?'»"[366] Al-Jāḥiẓ replied, "Thus you concede that my mother's fire is limited by a storekeeper, whereas when they ask your mother's vulva, «'Are you now full?' it will answer, 'Are there any more?'»"[367] 47.17

Someone once asked al-Jāḥiẓ to support him by writing a petition to one of his companions, and al-Jāḥiẓ wrote one and sealed it. The man broke the seal after he left and read the contents: "I write to you on behalf of a man whom I do not know, and whose rights I cannot affirm. If you satisfy his request, I will not praise you, and if you refuse him, I will not blame you." The man went straight back, and al-Jāḥiẓ remarked, "It seems as if you've unsealed the letter!" "Yes, I did," he replied. Al-Jāḥiẓ explained, "Its contents do you no harm. It is my signature way of indicating I want to help someone." The man told him, "May God cut off your hands and your feet and damn you!" Al-Jāḥiẓ asked, "What's that all about?" The man said, "It is my signature way of thanking someone." 47.18

Al-Jāḥiẓ tells: Once, I stayed with a friend who never served me any meat, and when I alluded to this, he said, "I haven't eaten much meat since I heard the hadith 'God dislikes the carnivorous house.'"[368] I explained to him, "Brother! The hadith only intends houses in which people are 'eaten' by slander." From that day forth, he was ever quick to serve meat. 47.19

At the end of his life, al-Jāḥiẓ suffered from a protracted illness that began when he attended a dinner given by Ibn Abī Du'ād. The fare included fish and yogurt, and one of the attendees, the physician Ibn Bukhtīshūʿ, forbade him from eating the two together, but al-Jāḥiẓ reasoned: "If fish is of an opposing nature to yogurt, then if I eat the two together, one will counterbalance against any ill effects of the other. So, if I eat from both in equal measure, it is as though 47.20

أحسن الكلام ولكن إن شئت أن تجرّب فكل فأكل فأصابه فالج عظيم ونقرس حتّى دخل عليه بعض أصحابه فقال له كيف حالك فقال كيف حال من اصطلحت عليّ الأعلال لو جُرح شقّي الأيسر ما أحسست به من الفالج ولو مرّت على شقّي الأيمن ذبابة أوجعتني وأشدّ ما أشكو التسعون

٢١،٤٧ وحكى بعض أبناء البرامكة قال تقلّدت السند وحصل لي ما شاء الله ثمّ صرفت عنها وكنت قد كسبت بها ثلاثين ألف دينار فصغتها عشرة آلاف إهليلجة[١] وجاء الصارف فركبت البحر وانحدرت إلى البصرة فخُبّرت أنّ الجاحظ بها وأنّه عليل بالفالج وأحببت أن أراه قبل وفاته فصرت إليه وقرعت الباب فخرجت لي خادم صفراء فقلت رجل غريب أحبّ أن أنظر إلى الشيخ فبلّغته فسمعته يقول ما يصنع بشقّ مائل ولعاب سائل ولون حائل فبلّغتني الجارية فقلت لا بدّ من النظر إليه فسمعته يقول هذا رجل ورد البصرة وسمع بي ويريد أن يقول رأيت الجاحظ فأذن لي ودخلت فسلّمت فردّ ردًّا جميلاً وقال لي من تكون أعزّك الله فانتسبت له فقال رحم الله أسلافك وآباءك السمحاء فلقد كانت أيّامهم رياض الدهر ولقد رأى بهم الخلق خيرًا كثيرًا فسقيًا لهم ورعيًا فدعوت له وقلت أنشدني شيئًا فقال

لَئِنْ قُدِّمَتْ قَبْلِي رِجَالٌ فَطَالَمَا    مَشَيْتُ عَلَى رِسْلِي فَكُنْتُ ٱلْمُقَدَّمَا
وَلٰكِنَّ هٰذَا ٱلدَّهْرَ تَأْتِي صُرُوفُهُ    فَتُبْرِمُ مَنْقُوضًا وَتَنْقُضُ مُبْرَمَا

٢٢،٤٧ ثمّ نهضت فلمّا قربت من الباب قال يا فتى أرأيت مفلوجًا ينفعه الإهليلج قلت لا قال فإنّ الإهليلج الذي معك ينفعني فابعث منه فقلت نعم وعجبت من وقوعه على خبري مع كتمي له وبعثت له منه شيئًا

١ إ١ وإ٣: هليلجة.

I have eaten one dish." Ibn Bukhtīshūʿ replied, "I am not such a clever rhetorician; if you want to try eating them, go ahead." Al-Jāḥiẓ did this and then suffered severe hemiparesis and gout.[369] When one of his friends paid him a visit and asked him, "How are you feeling?" he replied, "How do you think I feel? Sicknesses have become reconciled in me: if my left side is injured, I feel nothing because of the hemiparesis, and if even a fly lands on my right side, I'm in pain—and the worst of my complaints is that I am ninety."

One of the Barmakids' descendants tells: I was appointed to an administra- 47.21
tive position in Sind, and it was profitable for me for so long as God wished. By the time I was dismissed, I had earned thirty thousand dinars, and I concealed them in ten thousand black myrobalan nuts. When the order of my dismissal arrived, I took to the sea and landed in Basra, where I was informed that al-Jāḥiẓ was residing and suffering from hemiparesis. I wanted to see him before he died, so I went to his house, and when I knocked on the door a black slave girl emerged and I told her, "A stranger to these parts would like to see the master." She informed al-Jāḥiẓ, and I heard him respond, "What does he want with someone who's half drooping, who's drooling, and whose complexion is waning?" She conveyed the message, but I insisted: "I must see him." I heard him respond, "This man arrived in Basra, heard about me, and wants to be able to say, 'I met al-Jāḥiẓ.'" I was permitted to enter, and when I greeted him, he elegantly returned my greeting and said, "God give you strength! Who are you?" I told him my lineage, and he said, "God have mercy on your magnanimous ancestors: their days were a golden age when people benefited from them most handsomely. God be with them and grant them succor!" I blessed him and said, "Please recite me a poem." He complied:

> Though men had been advanced ahead of me,
> I walked at my leisure and reached the front.
> But Time brings vicissitudes,
> reversing all that has been.

I rose to leave, and as I neared the door, he called out, "Young man, have 47.22
you ever known black myrobalan nuts to help a patient of hemiparesis?" I said, "No." But he added, "Indeed, but those particular black myrobalan nuts of yours would benefit me: can you spare my any?"[370] I said, "Yes," and was amazed that he had worked out my ruse to conceal money in the nuts! I sent him some.

٢٣،٤٧ ومن كلام الجاحظ من رسالة أبقاك الله بقاء أياديك ولا نُقلنا عن ظلّك ولا أضلّنا عن سبلك فما صان وجه الأحرار سواك ولا أخذ الملهوف مظلمته في دهره إلّا بعدواك

٢٤،٤٧ وكتب إلى قليب المغربيّ والله يا قليب لو لا أنّ كبدي في هواك مقروحة وروحي بك مجروحة لساجلتك هذه القطيعة وماددتك حبل المصارمة وأرجو أنّ الله تعالى يديل تصبّري من جفائك فيردّك إلى مودّتي وأنف القلى راغم فقد طال العهد بالاجتماع حتّى كدنا نتناكر عند اللقاء

٢٥،٤٧ وكتب إلى ابن أبي دؤاد يستعطفه ليس عندي أعزّك الله سبب ولا أقدر على شفيع إلّا ما طبعك الله عليه من الكرم والرحمة والتأميل الذي لا يكون إلّا من نتاج حسن الظنّ وإثبات الفضل لحال المأمول وأرجو أن أكون من العتقاء الشاكرين فتكون خير معتب[١] وأكون أفضل شاكر ولعلّ الله أن يجعل هذا الأمر سببًا لهذا الإنعام وهذا الإنعام سببًا للانقطاع إليكم والكون تحت أجنحتكم فيكون لا أعظم بركة ولا أيمن نقيبة من ذنب أصبحت فيه وبمثلك جُعلت فداك عاد الذنب وسيلة والسيئة حسنة جُعلت فداك من عاقب فقد أخذ حظّه وإنّما الأجر في الآخرة وطيب الذكر في الدنيا على قدر الاحتمال وتجرّع المرائر فأرجو أن لا أضيع وأهلك فيما بين عقلك وكرمك وما أكثر من يعفو عن صغير ذنب وإنّما الفضل والثناء العفو عن عظيم الجرم ضعيف الحرمة وإن كان العفو العظيم مستطرفًا من غيركم فهو تلاد فيكم حتّى ربّما دعا ذلك كثيرًا من الناس إلى مخالفة أمركم فلا أنتم عن ذلك تنكلون ولا على سالف أخباركم تندمون وما مثلكم إلّا كمثل عيسى بن مريم حين كان لا يمرّ بملأ من بني إسرائيل إلّا أسمعوه شرًّا وأسمعهم خيرًا فقال له شمعون الصفا ما رأيت كاليوم كلّما أسمعوك شرًّا أسمعتهم خيرًا فقال

١ إ: فيكون خير معتبة.

Examples of al-Jāḥiẓ's compositions include the following excerpt from a letter: God keep you, preserving your benevolence, and may He never remove us from the canopy of your bounty or divert us from you. Only your protection preserves the dignity of those wellborn, and only by petitioning you can the wronged find redress. 47.23

To Qulayb al-Maghribī, al-Jāḥiẓ wrote: "By God, Qulayb, I would compete with you to see who can maintain our estrangement the longest, and I would vie with you in withholding all connection, but my liver is lacerated and my soul wounded out of love for you. So I hope that the Exalted God will reward my endurance of your estrangement by restoring your affection for me. Ignoble is the face of hatred, and it has now been so long that we may almost not recognize each other upon meeting." 47.24

Al-Jāḥiẓ wrote the following with the intention of conciliating the judge Ibn Abī Du'ād: "God grant you strength! I lack all hope and means of intercession other than from the nobility and mercy that God has made innate in you, and from the optimistic expectation that springs from the high regard in which you are held and the acknowledged certainty of your grace. Thus I hope to be among the grateful men freed by your hand, that you shall be the best sustainer and I the most grateful recipient. Perhaps God shall make this matter an opportunity for you to bestow favor, and make your favor an opportunity to inspire my devotion to you and exist under your wing. Therefore, may the offence I committed be counted a great blessing and a felicitous act. I implore you! You are among those who can turn an offense into a chance for favor, to turn an ill deed into a good outcome. I beg you to consider! Those who punish have satisfaction in the here and now, but those who patiently forbear unpleasantness receive the true reward in the Hereafter and good reputation in the here and now. Thus, I hope not to be lost and perish somewhere between your legitimate reason to punish and your benevolent nature to forgive. So often we see little offenses forgiven, but true merit and praise derive from forgiving major offenses committed by the weak. Exceptional lenience is seldom found, but it is the longstanding way of you and your ancestors. Perhaps someone deliberately opposed you, yet you never desisted from forgiveness or ever had cause to regret your generous acts of forgiveness. I find your likeness only in Jesus, son of Mary: no matter how much he was reviled by the Israelite crowd, hearing nothing but bad things from them, his words were only ever good. Thereupon, Simon Peter remarked, 'Never before have I beheld such a day: 47.25

كلّ امرئ ينفق ممّا عنده وليس عندكم إلّا الخير ولا في أوعيتكم إلّا الرحمة وكلّ إناء بالذي فيه ينضح

٢٦،٤٧ ومن فصوله القصار قال البخل والجبن غريزة واحدة يجمعهما سوء الظنّ بالله تعالى

٢٧،٤٧ وقال من رسالة من العدل المحض أن تحطّ عن الحاسد نصف عقابه لأنّ ألم حسده لك قد كفاك شطر مؤنة غيظه عليك

٢٨،٤٧ وقال لمّا مسخ الله الإنسان قردًا تُرك في مشابهَ من الإنسان ولمّا مسخ زماننا لم يُترَك في مشابه من الأزمان

٢٩،٤٧ ومن شعره

يَطِيبُ ٱلْعَيْشُ أَنْ تَلْقَى حَكِيمًا    غَذَاهُ ٱلْعِلْمُ وَٱلْفَهْمُ ٱلْمُصِيبُ
فَيَكْشِفُ عَنْكَ حَيْرَةَ كُلِّ جَهْلٍ    وَفَضْلُ ٱلْعِلْمِ يَعْرِفُهُ ٱللَّبِيبُ
سَقَامُ ٱلْحِرْصِ لَيْسَ لَهُ شِفَاءٌ    وَدَاءُ ٱلْجَهْلِ[١] لَيْسَ لَهُ طَبِيبُ

٣٠،٤٧ ومنه

إِنْ حَالَ لَوْنُ ٱلرَّأْسِ عَنْ حَالِهِ    فَفِي خِضَابِ ٱلْمَرْءِ مُسْتَمْتَعُ
هَبْ أَنَّ مَنْ شَابَ لَهُ حِيلَةٌ    فَمَا ٱلَّذِي يَحْتَالُهُ ٱلْأَصْلَعُ

٣١،٤٧ ومنه يمتدح من أبيات

بَدَا حِينَ أَثْرَى بِإِخْوَانِهِ    يُفَلِّلُ عَنْهُمْ شَبَاةَ ٱلْعَدَمْ
وَذَكَّرَهُ ٱلْحَالُ صَرْفَ ٱلزَّمَانِ    فَبَادَرَ قَبْلَ ٱنْتِقَالِ ٱلنِّعَمْ
فَتًى خَصَّهُ ٱللَّهُ بِٱلْمَكْرُمَاتِ    فَمَازَجَ مِنْهُ ٱلْحَيَا بِٱلْكَرَمْ

---

١ إ: الموت.

malevolence returned with benevolence!' And Jesus told him, 'We give from that which is in ourselves.' In you, there is only goodness. In your vessels, there is only mercy, and it is inevitable that a vessel must pour forth its contents."

One of al-Jāḥiẓ's sayings: Miserliness and cowardliness are of the same nature: they both stem from a lack of faith in the Exalted God. 47.26

In an epistle, al-Jāḥiẓ wrote: True justice should spare the envious person half of the punishment due to him, for the pain he inflicts upon himself and suffers through his envy of you compensates you for half of the trouble of his anger against you. 47.27

Al-Jāḥiẓ said: When God transformed people into apes,[371] he left them in a state somewhat resembling human forms, whereas when God transformed our age, he left it devoid of resemblance to any previous age. 47.28

Al-Jāḥiẓ's poetry: 47.29

Life goes well if you meet a wise man
who fed on knowledge and understanding.
He will keep you free of ignorant confusion;
the virtue of knowledge is known to the intelligent.
The malady of greed has no cure;
no doctor can remedy the disease of ignorance.

Al-Jāḥiẓ's poetry: 47.30

If the hair's color should change,
there is still happy recourse in dye.
Allow the gray-haired this ploy,
but what scheme is there for the bald?

Al-Jāḥiẓ's poetry of praise: 47.31

When he got rich, it was his friends who gained wealth;
he dulled poverty's prick upon them.
His felicity reminded him of Time's misfortunes;
he hurried to help before his boon passed.
Ordained by God for noble deeds—
his generosity is mixed with modesty.

ومنه ٣٢،٤٧

وَكَمْ كَانَ مِنْ أَصْدِقَاءَ لَهُ وَأَعْدَاءٍ تَفَانَوْا فَمَا خَلَدُو
تَسَاقَوْا جَمِيعًا كُؤُوسَ ٱلرَّدَى فَمَاتَ ٱلصَّدِيقُ وَمَاتَ ٱلْعَدُو

أورد له الشريف المرتضى وهو أعلى من طبقة شعر ٣٣،٤٧

رُبَّ فَتَاةٍ مِنْ بَنِي هِلَالِ قَدْ عَجِلَتْ إِلَيَّ بِٱلسُّؤَالِ
مَا لِي أَرَاكَ قَانِئَ ٱلسِّبَالِ كَأَنَّمَا كَرَعْتَ فِي جِرْيَالِ
تَنَحَّ عَنْ فِكْرِي وَعَنْ خَيَالِي

**ومالك بن أنس مستفتيك** ٤٨

هو مالك بن أنس بن أبي عامر التيميّ وكنيته أبو عبد الله إمام دار الهجرة وُلد بالمدينة سنة سبع وتسعين ويقال إنّه أقام في بطن أمّه ثلاث سنين وكان يقول قد يكون الحمل ثلاث سنين وقد حُمل ببعض الناس ثلاث سنين[١] يعني نفسه ١،٤٨

وكان طويلاً شديد البياض مائلاً إلى الشقرة مهيبًا سري اللباس والمجلس وهو أوّل من صنّف في الفقه كتابًا فوضع الموطّأ كذا قال العسكريّ في الأوائل ولعلّه أراد بالمدينة وكان مالك إذا أراد أن يحدّث عن رسول الله صلّى الله عليه وسلّم اغتسل وتبخّر وتطيّب فإذا رفع أحد صوته قال اخفض صوتك فإنّ الله تعالى يقول ﴿يَٰٓأَيُّهَا ٱلَّذِينَ ءَامَنُواْ لَا تَرْفَعُوٓاْ أَصْوَٰتَكُمْ فَوْقَ صَوْتِ ٱلنَّبِيِّ﴾ فمن رفع صوته عند حديثه فكأنّما رفعه عند صوته ٢،٤٨

وقال زيد بن داود رأيت في المنام كأنّ القبر انفرج وإذا رسول الله صلّى الله عليه وسلّم قاعدًا والناس مصفوفون فصاح صائح أين مالك بن أنس فجاء مالك حتّى ٣،٤٨

١ وقد حمل . . . سنين: سقطت من إ١.

Al-Jāḥiẓ's poetry: 47.32

> So many friends he had, and enemies too—
> all passed away now, none immortal.
> The cup of death is handed round—
> dies the friend, dies the enemy, die all.

Al-Sharīf al-Murtaḍā ascribes the following poem to al-Jāḥiẓ, but it seems of 47.33
higher quality than al-Jāḥiẓ's poetry.

> There was once a girl of the Hilāl
> who pressed me with an urgent question:
> "I see your whiskers are ever so red,
> as if you've been sipping wine!
> Forget about me, don't even dream."[372]

**. . . Mālik ibn Anas sought your legal opinion.** 48

Mālik ibn Anas ibn Abī ʿĀmir of the Taym, known as Abū ʿAbd Allāh, was the 48.1
great Islamic jurist of Medina. There he was born in 97 [715–16], after, so they say, a three-year gestation. Mālik is said to have been referring to his own gestation when he opined: "Pregnancy can last up to three years, as one person was born after such a term."[373]

Mālik was tall, his skin was extremely white, his hair almost blond, and he 48.2
was a solemn man who took great care with his clothes and comportment when in studious or judicial assemblies. According to al-ʿAskarī's *Book of Firsts*, Mālik was the first to compile a book of Islamic law, which he entitled *The Well-Trodden Path*, but perhaps al-ʿAskarī meant it was the first such book written in Medina. Whenever Mālik intended to narrate hadiths from the Prophet (God bless and keep him), he would bathe and perfume himself with incense and oils, and should anyone in attendance speak loudly, Mālik would say, "Lower your voice, for God says: «Believers, do not raise your voices above the voice of the Prophet»;[374] raising one's voice when narrating the Prophet's sayings is tantamount to raising one's voice before him in person."

Zayd ibn Dāwūd says: In a dream I saw as if the graves had been opened: 48.3
the Prophet of God (God bless and keep him) was seated and the people were arrayed in rows. A voice cried out, "Where is Mālik ibn Anas?" Mālik appeared

انتهى إلى رسول الله صلّى الله عليه وسلّم فأعطاه شيئًا فقال فرّقه على الناس فإذا هو مسك

٤،٤٨ وقال الشافعيّ رضي الله تعالى عنه ورحمه قال لي محمّد بن الحسن أيّهما أعلم صاحبنا أم صاحبكم يعني أبا حنيفة ومالكًا رضي الله تعالى عنهما فقلت على الإنصاف قال نعم فقلت ناشدتك الله من أعلم بالقرآن قال اللّهمّ صاحبكم قلت فمن أعلم بالسنّة قال اللّهمّ صاحبكم قلت فمن أعلم بأقاويل الصحابة قال اللّهمّ صاحبكم قلت فلم يبق إلّا القياس والقياس لا يكون إلّا على هذه الأشياء فعلى أيّ شيء نقيس

٥،٤٨ وقال ابن[١] وهب سمعت مناديًا ينادي ألا لا يفتي الناس إلّا مالك وابن أبي ذئب[٢]

٦،٤٨ وقال محمّد بن جعفر لمّا دُعِي مالك وأشار وقبل منه حسده الناس وبغوه بكلّ شيء فلمّا ولّي جعفر بن سليمان سعوا به إليه وقالوا إنّه لا يرى أيمان بيعتكم[٣] هذه بشيء ويأخذ بحديث رواه الأحنف في طلاق المكره أنّه لا يجوز فدعا جعفر بمالك وقد غضب فاحتجّ عليه بما قيل عنه ثمّ جرّده وضربه بالسياط ومُدت يده حتّى خُلع كتفاه فوالله ما زال مالك بعد ذلك في رفعة من الناس وعلوّ من قدره وإعظام الخلق له حتّى كأنّما كانت تلك السياط التي ضرب بها حليًا حُلّي به

٧،٤٨ وقيل إنّما ضُرب مالك لأنّه سأل عن سيرة عبد الرحمن بن معاوية الأمويّ الداخل إلى المغرب والمتملّك بجزيرة الأندلس فقيل له إنّه يأكل خبز الشعير ويلبس الصوف ويجاهد في سبيل الله وعددت مناقبه فقال مالك ليت أنّ الله زيّن حرمنا بمثله فنقم إليه بنو العبّاس هذا القول فضُرب[٤] وبلغ عبد الرحمن قول مالك فسُرّ به وجمع أهل الأندلس على مذهب مالك فهذا سبب اجتماع المغاربة على مذهبه

١ سقطت من إ١. ٢ إ١، إ٢، ل١، ل٢، إ٦، ب: ذؤيب. ٣ بياض في إ١. ٤ فضرب: زيادة من بر١، إ٦، ل٢.

and went all the way up to the Prophet (God bless and keep him), who gave him something, saying, "Distribute this among the congregation." It was musk.[375]

Al-Shāfiʿī (God be pleased with him and show him mercy) narrates: Muḥammad ibn al-Ḥasan asked me, "Who is more knowledgeable, our teacher or yours?" Muḥammad meant his teacher, Abū Ḥanīfah, and my teacher, Mālik (God be pleased with them both). I asked Muḥammad, "In all fairness?" He said, "Yes." So I began: "Swear by God's name: who is the most knowledgeable of the Qur'an?" He conceded: "By God, your teacher is." Next, I asked, "Who is the most knowledgeable of the Sunnah?" He conceded, "By God, your teacher." Next, I asked, "Who is the most knowledgeable about the sayings of the Companions?" He conceded, "By God, your teacher." I then said, "Only juridical reasoning by analogy remains, and this can only be performed correctly when based on the material I've just asked about, so on what grounds can our teachers be compared?"[376] 48.4

Ibn Wahb says: I once heard a crier announce: "There are but two men entitled to pronounce legal opinions: Mālik ibn Anas and Ibn Abī Dhi'b."[377] 48.5

Muḥammad ibn Jaʿfar[378] relates: When Mālik was invited to court and his counsel was accepted, some people grew envious and tried to scheme against him in any way they could. So, when Jaʿfar ibn Sulaymān was appointed governor, those enviers slandered Mālik, telling Jaʿfar: "Mālik considers the oaths of allegiance given to the Abbasid caliphs to be void, and he substantiates this by citing the hadith narrated by al-Aḥnaf that divorce by compulsion is invalid."[379] Jaʿfar reacted angrily and summoned Mālik. He cited what had been said as evidence against him, and ordered Mālik stripped bare and whipped, and then had his arm stretched until his shoulder was dislocated. But by God, from then onward, everyone else held Mālik in high esteem and all were enormously impressed; in their eyes, he wore the scars of his whipping as adornments. 48.6

Alternatively, the whipping of Mālik is explained as a result of Mālik's inquiry about ʿAbd al-Raḥmān ibn Muʿāwiyah "the Emigré," who founded Umayyad rule in Andalusia. Mālik was told, "ʿAbd al-Raḥmān eats barley bread, wears wool, and wages jihad for God," and they recounted more of ʿAbd al-Raḥmān's virtues, which prompted Mālik to say, "If only God would adorn Medina with such a man!"[380] The Abbasids held this against Mālik and ordered him beaten. When Mālik's words reached ʿAbd al-Raḥmān, however, he was well pleased and instructed the Andalusians to follow Mālik's jurisprudence, and this is the reason why the Muslims of the West embraced Mālikī law.[381] 48.7

وتوفّي رحمه الله سنة تسع[1] وسبعين ومائة ٨،٤٨

ومن أخباره ما حكى الشافعيّ رضي الله تعالى عنه قال رأيت على باب مالك كراعًا من أفراس خراسان وبغال مصر قلّ ما رأيت مثله فقلت لمالك ما أحسنه قال هو هديّة منّي إليك فقلت يا أبا عبد الله دع لنفسك منها ما تركبه قال أنا أستحيي من الله أن أطأ تربة فيها رسول الله عليه وسلّم بحافر دابّة ٩،٤٨

ووجّه الرشيد إلى مالك رضي الله تعالى عنه ليأتيه فقال مالك إنّ العلم يُؤتى إليه فصار الرشيد إلى منزله واستند إلى الجدار فقال مالك يا أمير المؤمنين من إجلال رسول الله صلّى الله عليه وسلّم إجلال العلم فقام فجلس بين يديه فحدّثه وبعث الرشيد إلى سفيان بن عيينة فأتاه سفيان بن عيينة فقعد بين يديه فحدّثه فكان الرشيد يقول يا مالك تواضعنا لعلمك فانتفعنا به وتواضع لنا علم سفيان فلم ننتفع به ١٠،٤٨

وحكى ابن حمدون في تذكرته أنّ الحسين بن دحمان قال كنت بالمدينة فجلا لي الطريق نصف النهار فجعلت أتغنّى في شعر ذي يزن ١١،٤٨

مَا بَالُ قَوْمِكِ يَا رَبَابُ    خُزْرًا[2] كَأَنَّهُمُ غِضَابُ

فإذا كوّة قد فُتحت وإذا وجه قد بدا فيها وجه تتبعه لحيّة حمراء فقال يا فاسق أساءت التأدية وتمنّعت القائلة وأذعت الفاحشة ثمّ اندفع فغنّى الصوت غناء لم أسمع بمثله فقلت أصلحك الله من أين لك هذا الغناء فقال نشأت وأنا غلام يعجبني الأخذ عن المغنّين فقالت أمّي يا بنيّ إنّ المغنّي إذا كان قبيح الوجه لم يُلتفت إلى غنائه فدع الغناء واطلب الفقه فتركت المغنّين وتبعت الفقهاء فبلّغ الله بي إلى ما ترى فقلت أعد الصوت جُعلت فداك فقال لا ولا كرامة تريد أن تقول أخذته عن مالك بن أنس فإذا به مالك رضي الله عنه

١ كل النسخ إلّا با١: سبع. ٢ بياض في إ١.

Mālik died in 179 [796], God have mercy on him. 48.8

Among the stories about Mālik is one told by al-Shāfiʿī (God be pleased with him): At the door of Mālik's house, I saw Khurasanian horses and Egyptian mules of uncommon excellence, and I complimented him: "What fine animals!" He replied, "They're my present to you." I replied, "Mālik! Keep at least one for yourself to ride!" But he said, "I would stand in shame before God if I allowed an animal's hoof to trod on the ground in which the Prophet (eternal peace be his) lies buried." 48.9

The Caliph al-Rashīd sent a summons to Mālik (Exalted God be pleased with him) to present himself, but Mālik declined: "Knowledge does not visit, it is visited." And so al-Rashīd went in person to Mālik's house. As al-Rashīd sat down, leaning against a wall, Mālik told him, "Commander of the Faithful! Showing respect for knowledge is showing respect for the Prophet (God bless and keep him)." Al-Rashīd stood up, and then sat before Mālik, who recited hadith to him. Al-Rashīd also sent a summons to Sufyān ibn ʿUyaynah, who presented himself straightaway, and sat before the caliph to recite hadith. Al-Rashīd remarked, "Mālik, we humbled ourselves before your knowledge, and we benefited from it; Sufyān's knowledge humbled itself before us, and we received no benefit." 48.10

Ibn Ḥamdūn tells in his *Compendium*: Al-Ḥasan[382] ibn Daḥmān tells: Once, in the middle of the day when the streets in Medina were all empty, I began singing lines by Dhū Yazan:[383] 48.11

> Rabāb! What's wrong with your folk,
> all sideways glances as if they're irate . . .

Suddenly a wall flap sprang open and a red-bearded face emerged, rebuking me: "You profligate! You botched the song, you interrupted our siestas, and you spread a story about fornication!" Then he burst into song, singing the same lines in a style I had never heard before. I exclaimed, "God bless you! Where did you learn that song?" He told me, "When I was a young boy, I used to love imitating singers, but my mother told me, 'My dear son, people only listen to singers with pretty faces, so leave off song and apply yourself to jurisprudence instead!' I replaced the company of singers with jurists, and God brought me to where I am now." I said, "Please repeat the song, I beg you!" But he refused: "No thanks. You want to say that you learned a song from Mālik!" And indeed, it was Mālik himself, God be pleased with him.[384]

١٢،٤٨ وحُكي أنّ أبا يوسف القاضي حضر مجلس مالك فقال أبو يوسف من جملة كلام الإنسان تارة يخطئ وتارة لا يصيب فقال مالك هكذا عرّفنا مشايخنا فضحك بعض الحاضرين فلمّا خرجوا قال بعض أصحاب مالك إنّ أبا يوسف قال كذا ولعلّه متعمّدًا وأجبت كذا فخجل مالك ودعا على أبي يوسف أن لا يُنتفع بعلمه فكان كذلك مع جودة كتبه عند الحنفيّة

١٣،٤٨ ومن كلام مالك إذا ترك العالم قول لا أدري[١] أُصيبت مقاتله

١٤،٤٨ وقال ليس العلم بكثرة الرواية وإنّما هو نور يقذفه الله في القلب

١٥،٤٨ وسأله رجل عن قوله تعالى ﴿ٱسْتَوَىٰ عَلَى ٱلْعَرْشِ ٱلرَّحْمَٰنُ﴾ فقال الاستواء معقول والكيف مجهول وما أظنّك إلّا رجل سوء

٤٩ **وأنّك الذي أقام البراهين ووضع القوانين وحدّ الماهيّة وبيّن الكيفيّة والكمّيّة وناظر في الجوهر والعرض وميّز الصحّة من المرض وفكّ المعمّى وفصل بين الاسم والمسمّى وصرّف وقسّم وعدّل وقوّم وصنّف الأسماء والأفعال وبوّب الظرف والحال وبنى وأعرب ونفى وتعجّب ووصل وقطع وثنّى وجمع وأظهر وأضمر واستفهم وأخبر وأهمل وقيّد وأرسل وأسند وبحث ونظر وتصفّح الأديان ورجّح بين مذهبيْ ماني وغيلان**

١،٤٩ هو ماني بن ماتن الثنويّ الذي تُنسَب إليه المانويّة كان راهبًا بحرّان قائلًا بنبوّة المسيح عليه السلام معظّمًا في أساقفة النصارى محمود السيرة فيهم فزنى فسقطت رتبته وكان له حسدة من بطارقة زمانه فوجدوا السبيل إلى ما أرادوا

---

١ سقطت من إ

It is told that the judge Abū Yūsuf attended Mālik's study circle, and among other things, Abū Yūsuf said, "People occasionally err, and occasionally are incorrect." Mālik replied, "This is what our teachers had taught us."[385] Some of the assembly laughed, and when they dispersed, one of Mālik's companions told him, "Abū Yūsuf may have said this intentionally, and your answer fell into his trap." Mālik was embarrassed and cursed Abū Yūsuf, asking that God prevent him from benefiting from his knowledge, and that is what transpired, notwithstanding the excellence of Abū Yūsuf's books among the Ḥanafīs. 48.12

Mālik's sayings include: "The scholar's demise occurs when he no longer says, 'I don't know.'" 48.13

Mālik also said: "Knowledge is not just memorizing and reciting; it is light that God projects into the heart." 48.14

Someone once questioned Mālik on the Qur'anic verse: «the All Merciful settled on the throne.»[386] Mālik answered, "The 'settling' is understandable, but the way He does it is unknown; you appear to be a rather wicked fellow." 48.15

**It sounded also as if it was you who established the certainties and laid down all legalities, defined quiddity and ascertained quality and quantity. You investigated substance and accident and distinguished fitness from ailment. You deciphered code, split signifier and signified, minted coins, and resolved monies owed. As if it was you who classified nouns and verbs and categorized adverbials and adverbs. You fixed indeclinable words and declined the others, showed how to negate and how to express wonders. As if the hamzah owes both its forms to you, and you ruled how to express dual and plural too. You decided when words are explicit or implicit and revealed how to interrogate and narrate. As if it was you who in law decreed qualified and strict liability, and for legal precedents judged their reliability. In matters of faith you investigated and speculated: perusing the world's religions, weighing Ghaylanists and Manichaeans . . .** 49

Mānī, son of Pattikios,[387] was a believer in Dualism and founder of the religion called Manichaeanism. Mānī had been a priest in Ḥarrān; he believed in the prophethood of Jesus (eternal peace be his), and Christian bishops held him in high esteem and praise.[388] However, some bishops were envious of Mānī, and they tarred his reputation by charging him with adultery. When 49.1

منه فلمّا رأى حاله أخذ في الردّ على أصحابه وقال لم أزن ولكنّهم حسدوني وأنكروا مخالفتي لهم في أصل مذهبهم إذ كانوا يقرّون بالمسيح اللاهوتي ويأخذون شرائعهم عن رسول الشيطان[1]

٢،٤٩ وكان ماني في الأصل مجوسيًّا عارفًا بمذاهب القوم فأحدث دينًا ودعا إليه وظهر في أيّام سابور بن أردشير وتبعه خلق عظيم من المجوس وادّعوا نبوّته ونُسبوا إليه إلى أن قُتل في زمان بهرام بن سابور كما سيأتي ذكره

٣،٤٩ حدّث النوبختيّ وغيره قال زعم ماني وأصحابه أنّ صانع العالم اثنان ففاعل الخير نور وفاعل الشرّ ظلمة وهما قديمان لم يزالا ولن يزالا حسّاسين سميعين بصيرين وهما مختلفان في النفس والصورة متضادّان في الفعل والتدبير فجوهر النور فاضل حسن نيّر ونفسه خيّرة حليمة نفّاعة منها الخير والسرور والصلاح وليس منها شيء من الشرور وجوهر الظلمة ضدّ ذلك جميعه والنور مرتفع في ناحية الشمال والظلمة منحطّة في ناحية الجنوب وزعموا أنّ لكلّ واحد منهما أجناسًا خمسة أربعة منها أبدان وخامس هو الروح فأبدان النور النار والماء والهواء[2] والنور وروحه الشبح المتحرّك في هذه الأبدان وأبدان[3] الظلمة الحريق والسموم والضباب والظلام وروحه الدخان وسمّوا أبدان النور ملائكة وأبدان الظلمة شياطين وبعضهم يقول أبدان النور تتولّد ملائكة وأبدان الظلمة تتولّد شياطين[4] وأنّ النور لا يقدر على الشرّ ولا يجوز منه والظلمة لا تقدر على الخير ولا تجوز منه

٤،٤٩ وردّ عليهم بعض المتكلّمين في قولهم إنّ النور يفعل الخير والظلمة تفعل الشرّ بأنّه لو هرب مظلوم فاستتر بالظلمة فهذا خير وقع من شرّ ومنه قول المتنبّي

وَكَمْ لِظَلَامِ ٱللَّيْلِ عِنْدِي مِنْ يَدٍ    تُخَبِّرُ أَنَّ ٱلْمَانَوِيَّةَ تَكْذِبُ

١ ويأخذون . . . الشيطان: زيادة من ل١، إ٢. ٢ في سائر النسخ: الريح. ٣ سقطت من إ١. ٤ وبعضهم . . . شياطين: سقطت من إ١.

Mānī realized their plot, he swore to his companions: "I did not commit adultery. Those bishops resent me because I critique the principles of their faith: particularly their belief in Jesus's divinity and their adoption of rules learned from the messenger of Satan."

Mānī was originally a learned Zoroastrian, but he formed his new religion and proselytized during the reign of Shapur son of Ardashir. Multitudes of Zoroastrians followed him, claiming Mānī was himself a prophet, and his followers named themselves "Manichaeans." But in the reign of Bahram, son of Shapur, Mānī was executed, as we shall recount presently. 49.2

Al-Nawbakhtī and others relate: Mānī and his companions allege that the creator of the world is the combination of two forces: one of light that does good, and the other of darkness that does evil. The pair are elemental, they always have been, and will never cease to exist, perceptible, audible, and visible. They are together mixed in the soul and in form, and they oppose each other in act and thought. The substance of light is good, virtuous, and spreads light. The soul of light is virtuous, forbearing, and beneficial, engendering goodness, happiness, and probity. Nothing evil can be associated with it. The substance of darkness is the exact opposite of the above. Light resides above in the north, and darkness lies below in the south. The Manichaeans allege that each of the two elements has five forms: four are corporeal and the fifth is spiritual. Light's corporeal bodies are fire, water, air, and light, and light's spirit is the spirit that inhabits these forms. Darkness's bodies are destructive wind, poison, fog, and darkness, and its spirit is smoke. They call the bodies of light "angels" and the bodies of darkness "devils"; some Manichaeans hold that the bodies of light in turn manifest as angels, while the bodies of darkness manifest as devils. They also categorically reject that light can engender ill, as they categorically reject that darkness has any capacity to do good. 49.3

To disprove the Manichaean doctrine that only light does good and darkness only does evil, some theologians cite the case of an oppressed person who flees and is concealed by darkness: the safety he achieves thereby is a "good" outcome that was produced by the "evil" darkness. Al-Mutanabbī echoed this: 49.4

> So often, night's darkness came to my aid:
> The Manichaeans lie.

وقال الجاحظ المانويّة تزعم أنّ العالم بما فيه مركّب من عشرة أجناس خمسة منها خير ونور وخمسة شرّ وظلمة والإنسان مركّب من جميعها فمن نظر نظرة رحمة فتلك النظرة من النور ومن نظر نظرة قساوة فتلك النظرة من الظلمة وكذلك جميع الحواسّ ٥،٤٩

وكان المأمون يسأل المانويّة مسألة قريبة المأخذ قاطعة ناظر أحدهم فقال أسألك عن حرفين فقط هل ندم مسيء على إساءته قال بلى قد ندم كثير قال فخبّرني عن الندم على الإساءة أإساءة أم إحسان قال إحسان قال فالذي ندم هو الذي أساء قال نعم قال فأرى صاحب الخير هو صاحب الشرّ وقد بطل قولكم إنّ الذي ينظر نظر الوعيد غير الذي ينظر نظر الرحمة قال فإنّي أزعم أنّ الذي أساء غير الذي ندم قال فندم على شيء كان من غيره أو على شيء كان منه فقطعه ٦،٤٩

ولماني وأصحابه في امتزاج النور والظلمة وحدوث الشمس والقمر والنجوم لاستصفاء النور من الظلمة إلى أن لا يبقى شيء منه في هذا العالم وتنطبق السماء على الأرض ويرجع كلّ شكل إلى شكله أقوال عجيبة إلى غير ذلك من أنّه لا يرى المناكح ليستعجل فناء العالم ويسرع بجمع الأشكال ٧،٤٩

ولم تزل أتباعه تكثر وشوكته تقوى إلى أن أحضره بهرام بن سابور وأراد قتله باتّفاق الموابذة فأمر أدرياد موبذ موبذان فناظره في مسألة قطع النسل وتعجيل فراغ العالم قال الموبذ أنت ألذي تقول بتحريم النكاح لتستعجل فناء العالم ويرجع كلّ شكل إلى شكله وأنّ ذلك حقّ واجب فقال ماني واجب أن يعان النور على خلاصه بقطع النسل ممّا هو فيه من الامتزاج فقال أدرياد فمن الواجب أن يعجّل لك هذا الخلاص الذي تدعو إليه وتعان على إبطال هذا الامتزاج المذموم ٨،٤٩

Al-Jāḥiẓ says: The Manichaeans allege that the world is entirely constituted from ten elements, five of them goodness and light, and the other five darkness and evil. They allege too that humanity is created from all these elements: our merciful glances are light acting through us, and our callous glances are from the forces of darkness within us. The Manichaeans apply the same dichotomy to all sensory acts. 49.5

The Caliph al-Ma'mūn used to pose a very simple but decisive question to refute the Manichaeans. Once, when debating with one of them, he said, "I will pose a simple question: does the evildoer feel remorse?" The Manichaean replied, "Of course. Many are remorseful!" Al-Ma'mūn then asked, "So tell me about remorse for an evil deed: is it in itself a good thing or bad thing?" The Manichaean said, "A good thing." Al-Ma'mūn then asked, "Is not the person who feels remorse one and the same as the person who acted evilly?" "Yes." Al-Ma'mūn then concluded, "I thus see that the one who does good is the same person as the one who does evil, and this confounds your assertion that the one who adopts an aggressive stance is different from the one who adopts a merciful one." The Manichaean countered, "I would claim that the one who does evil is not the same as the one who feels remorse." Then al-Ma'mūn said, "So then what? Does he feel remorse over something somebody else did, or does he feel remorse over something he did?" The Manichaean was stumped. 49.6

Mānī and his companions also held bizarre beliefs about how light and dark could be mixed, how the sun, moon, and stars were created to purify light from darkness until no light would be left in this world, at which point the sky would collapse upon the earth and everything would return to its elemental form. Mānī also strongly opposed marriage, in order to hasten the end of the world and the reunification of all things in their elemental state.[389] 49.7

Mānī's followers grew, and their influence became so powerful that King Bahram son of Shapur, in collusion with the Zoroastrian priests, summoned Mānī with the intention of executing him. Bahram called for the head priest, Adriyād,[390] and he debated with Mānī on the connection between ceasing procreation and the end of the world. The priest said, "You yourself forbid marriage in order to hasten the end of the world by reunifying all things in their elemental state. Do you consider this an obligation?" Mānī replied, "It is a duty to assist the liberation of light from darkness by refraining from procreation, since procreation prolongs the mixture of light and dark." The priest replied, "Is it then not equally a duty for us to hasten the liberation you claim 49.8

فانقطع ماني فأمر بهرام بصلبه على الخشبة فجعل يسبّح ويقول أيّها المعبود النورانيّ بلّغت ما أمرتني به وهذه عادتهم فيّ وأنت الحليم وها أنا مارّ إليك وما آذيت صامتًا ولا ناطقًا فتباركت أنت وعالمك النورانيّون الأزليّون[1] فكان آخر قوله ثمّ سلخ جلده ومُلئ[2] تبنًا

وكان بهرام في الأوّل قد أظهر مشايعته حتّى أحاط علمًا بمن تبعه فلمّا قتله أمر بقتل أصحابه وظهر ممّن يسلك مسلكهم في الإسلام بشر عظيم يُسمّون الزنادقة فقتلهم المهديّ وأبادهم ٩،٤٩

وأمّا غيلان فهو ابن يونس الدمشقيّ القدريّ كان أبوه مولى لعثمان بن عفّان رضي الله تعالى عنه وغيلان أوّل من تكلّم في القدر وخلق القرآن في الإسلام وقيل أوّل من تكلّم في القدر رجل من أهل العراق كان نصرانيًّا فأسلم ثمّ تنصّر وأخذ عنه معبد الجهنيّ وغيلان الدمشقيّ ١٠،٤٩

وروي أنّ مكحولاً قال لغيلان ويلك يا غيلان ألم أجدك[3] ترامي النساء بالتفّاح في شهر رمضان ثمّ صرت حارثيًّا تخدم امرأة الحارث الكذّاب وتزعم أنّها أمّ المؤمنين ثمّ تحوّلت قدريًّا زنديقًا ١١،٤٩

وقيل لغيلان من كان أشدّ عليك قال عمر بن عبد العزيز كأنّما كان يلقّن من السماء ١٢،٤٩

وحكى ابن مهاجر قال بلغ عمر بن عبد العزيز أنّ غيلانًا وفلانًا نطقا في القدر فأرسل إليهما فقال ما الأمر الذي تنطقان فيه قال غيلان هو ما قال الله يا أمير المؤمنين قال وما قال الله قال يقول ﴿هَلْ أَتَىٰ عَلَى ٱلْإِنسَـٰنِ حِينٌ مِّنَ ٱلدَّهْرِ لَمْ يَكُن شَيْـًٔا مَّذْكُورًا إِنَّا خَلَقْنَا ٱلْإِنسَـٰنَ مِن نُّطْفَةٍ أَمْشَاجٍ نَّبْتَلِيهِ فَجَعَلْنَـٰهُ سَمِيعًۢا بَصِيرًا إِنَّا هَدَيْنَـٰهُ ٱلسَّبِيلَ إِمَّا شَاكِرًا وَإِمَّا كَفُورًا﴾ ثمّ سكت فقال عمر اقرآ فقرآ ١٣،٤٩

١ إ١: الأولون. ٢ سلخ . . . وملئ: زيادة من بر١، ل١. ٣ إ١: أجد.

by putting an end to the objectionable mixture of light and dark within your body too?" Mānī was flummoxed, and Bahram ordered him crucified. On the cross, Mānī began exalting his deity: "Worshipful Light! I delivered the message with which you entrusted me, and this is how they have always treated me. You are the forbearing one, and here I am, coming to you: I have harmed no living thing; I glorified you and your illuminous eternal world." These were his last words. They skinned him and then stuffed his skin with straw.

Previously, Bahram had pretended to adhere to Mānī's creed, but only for 49.9
as long as it took him to uncover the identities of all his followers, and once Bahrām executed Mānī, he ordered the death of all his adherents too.

In Islamic times, there were also large numbers of adherents to Manichaeanism. They were called "heretics," and the Caliph al-Mahdī executed them and extinguished their movement.[391]

Ghaylān the Damascene propounded deviant beliefs. His father, Yūnus,[392] 49.10
was a non-Arab under the protection of the Caliph ʿUthmān (God be pleased with him). They say Ghaylān was the first in Islam to theorize about free will and the createdness of the Qur'an, though others contend that the first to do this was an Iraqi Christian who converted to Islam, but then reverted to Christianity, and instructed both Ghaylān and Maʿbad of the Juhaynah.[393]

It is narrated that Makḥūl told Ghaylān: "To Hell with you, Ghaylān! First 49.11
I saw you tossing apples to the ladies during Ramadan; then you became an adherent of al-Ḥārith the Liar and served his wife, claiming she was the 'Mother of the Believers'; and now you've become a heretic proponent of free will!"

Someone once asked Ghaylān, "Who was hardest on you?" Ghaylān an- 49.12
swered, "The Caliph ʿUmar ibn ʿAbd al-ʿAzīz; it was as if he was inspired by instruction from Heaven."[394]

Ibn Muhājir narrates: ʿUmar ibn ʿAbd al-ʿAzīz was informed that Ghaylān 49.13
and an accomplice were promulgating free-will doctrine, and he summoned the pair. ʿUmar asked them, "What is this matter you are discussing?" Ghaylān answered, "Commander of the Faithful! We are discussing God's words." "And what did God say?" asked ʿUmar. Ghaylān recited from the Qur'an: «Was there not a period of time when man was nothing worth mentioning? We created man from a drop of mingled fluid so that We might try him; We gave him hearing and sight; We showed him the way, whether he be grateful or ungrateful.»[395] He stopped reciting, and ʿUmar commanded, "Recite the next verses, both of you!" They did, until they reached the verse «This is a reminder. Let

حتّى إذا بلغا ﴿إِنَّ هَٰذِهِۦ تَذْكِرَةٌ فَمَن شَآءَ ٱتَّخَذَ إِلَىٰ رَبِّهِۦ سَبِيلًا وَمَا تَشَآءُونَ إِلَّآ أَن يَشَآءَ ٱللَّهُ﴾ إلى آخر السورة قال كيف تريا يا ابني الأتانة تأخذان الفروع وتدعوان الأصول

١٤،٤٩ قال ابن مهاجر ثمّ بلغ عمر بن عبد العزيز أنّهما أسرفا فأرسل إليهما وهو مغضب فقام عمر وكنت خلفه قائمًا حين دخلا عليه وأنا مستقبلهما فقال لهما ألم يكن في سابق علم الله حين أمر إبليس بالسجود أن لا يسجد قال فأومأت إليهما برأسي أن قولا نعم وإلّا فهو الذبح فقالا نعم فقال ألم يكن في سابق علم الله حين نهى آدم وحوّاء عن الشجرة أن لا يأكلا منها أنّهما يأكلان منها فأومأت إليهما برأسي فقالا نعم فأمر بإخراجهما وأمر بالكتاب إلى سائر الأعمال بخلاف ما يقولان وأمسكا عن الكلام فلم تلبث الأقدار حتّى مرض عمر[١] ومات ولم يفد الكتاب وسال منهما بعد ذلك السيل

١٥،٤٩ وكان غيلان قد تاب[٢] على يد عمر بن عبد العزيز فقال عمر اللّهمّ إن كان كاذبًا فلا تمته حتّى تذيقه حرّ السيف فقُطعت يداه ورجلاه وصلب في أيّام هشام بن عبد الملك

١٦،٤٩ حدّث ابن عيّاش[٣] قال أرسل هشام بن عبد الملك إلى غيلان فقال يا غيلان ما هذه المقالة التي تبلغني عنك في القدر قال هو ما بلغك يا أمير المؤمنين فأحضر من يحاجّني فإن غلبني ضربت رقبتي[٤] فأحضر الأوزاعيّ فقال له الأوزاعيّ إن شئت ألقيت عليك سبعًا وإن شئت خمسًا وإن شئت ثلاثًا فقال له ألق ثلاثًا فقال أقضى الله على عبد ما نهى عنه قال ما أدري ما تقول قال فأمر بأمر حال دونه قال هذه

١ سقطت من إ. ٢ إ: مات. ٣ إ: عباس. ٤ سقطت من إ.

whoever wishes take the right path to his Lord. But you cannot will it unless God wills,»[396] and they continued to the end of the chapter. ʿUmar then challenged them: "What do you say now that you've recited the whole passage, you sons of asses? You focus on the minutiae and skip over the essence!"

Ibn Muhājir's story continues: Sometime later, ʿUmar ibn ʿAbd al-ʿAzīz was informed that Ghaylān and his colleague were now making even more exaggerated claims. ʿUmar angrily summoned them. I was standing behind ʿUmar when they were brought in, so I directly faced the pair. ʿUmar began the interrogation: "Did God not have foreknowledge that when he ordered Satan to prostrate, Satan would not comply?" I gave a nodding signal to both Ghaylān and his colleague to indicate they should agree or otherwise face execution. They both nodded: "Yes." Then ʿUmar asked, "Did God not have the foreknowledge that when he forbade Adam and Eve from eating from the tree, they would disobey?" Again I nodded at them, and they said, "Yes." ʿUmar then dismissed them and ordered that a letter refuting their doctrine be written and dispatched to all districts. Ghaylān and his associate immediately refrained from theological discussion, but it was only a short time before ʿUmar became sick and died, and his letter was never sent. However, matters came to a head for the pair in due course. 49.14

After Ghaylān had made the abovementioned show of repentance before ʿUmar, the caliph made a supplication: "Good God! If his repentance was a sham, don't let him die until you let him taste the searing heat of the sword!" Ghaylān indeed had his hands and feet chopped off and was crucified during the caliphate of Hishām ibn ʿAbd al-Malik. 49.15

Ibn ʿAyyāsh[397] tells: The Caliph Hishām summoned Ghaylān and said, "Ghāylan, tell me about the doctrine I hear you're espousing about free will." Ghaylān responded, "It is as the Commander of the Faithful has heard; summon someone to debate with me, and if he defeats me, then execute me!" Al-Awzāʿī was summoned, and he proposed to Ghaylān: "If you want, I can challenge you on seven precepts; or, if you prefer, five; or, if you prefer, only three." Ghaylān replied, "Set out the three." Al-Awzāʿī opened: "Did God ever ordain that his worshippers perform something He had forbidden them to do?" Ghaylān replied, "I don't understand what you say!" Al-Awzāʿī put the second question: "Did God ever command something that was impossible to perform?" Ghaylān said, "This is more severe than the first case!" Then al-Awzāʿī put the third question: "Has God ever prohibited something before making it permissible?" 49.16

أشدّ من الأولى قال فحرّم الله حراماً ثمّ أحلّه قال ما أدري ما تقول قال فأمر هشام فقُطعت يداه ورجلاه فمات فصُلب على باب كيسان بدمشق

١٧،٤٩ ثمّ قال هشام للأوزاعيّ يا أبا عمر فسّر لنا ما قلت قال قضى الله على عبد ما نهى عنه نهى آدم أن يأكل من الشجرة ثمّ قضى عليه فأكل منها وأمر إبليس أن يسجد لآدم وحال بين إبليس السجود وقال ﴿حُرِّمَتْ عَلَيْكُمُ ٱلْمَيْتَةُ﴾ ثمّ قال ﴿فَمَنِ ٱضْطُرَّ﴾ فأحلّه بعد ما حرّمه

١٨،٤٩ ومّما كان أيضًا يميل إلى هذا المذهب ممّن اسمه غيلان ذو الرمّة غيلان بن عقبة الشاعر حكى أبو الفرج قال اختصم ذو الرمّة ورؤبة الراجز عند بلال بن أبي بردة فقال رؤبة والله ما فحص طائرًا فحوصًا ولا تقرمص سبع قرموصًا إلّا لقضاء من الله وقدر فقال ذو الرمّة والله ما قدر الله على الذئب أن يأكل حلوبة عيابيل ضرائك فقال رؤبة أفبقدرته أكلها هذا[1] كذب على الذئب ثان فقال ذو الرمّة الكذب على الذئب خير من الكذب على ربّ الذئب

١٩،٤٩ وعن إسحاق بن سعد قال أنشدني ذو الرمّة قوله

وَعَيْنَانِ قَالَ ٱللهُ كُونَا فَكَانَتَا    فَعُولَانِ بِٱلْأَلْبَابِ مَا تَفْعَلُ ٱلْخَمْرُ

فقلت له فعولين خبر الكون فقال لي لو سبّحت ربحت إنّما قلت فعولان وإنّما تحرّز ذو الرمّة بهذا الكلام من القول بخلاف مذهبه

٥٠ وأشار بذبح الجعد

١،٥٠ هو الجعد بن درهم مولى بني الحكم كان يسكن دمشق ويعلّم مروان بن محمّد آخر خلفاء بني أميّة فنُسب إليه وقيل مروان الجعديّ ويُروى أنّ أمّ مروان كانت أمة

---

١ إ: على.

Ghaylān replied, “I don’t understand what you are saying.” Hishām gave the order, and Ghaylān’s hands and feet were chopped off. He died from these wounds and was crucified on the Kaysān Gate in Damascus.

Hishām said to al-Awzāʿī, “Explain your argument to us.” Al-Awzāʿī said, 49.17
“First, God did ordain that a worshipper perform that which He forbade him when He prohibited Adam from eating from the tree, and then he ordained that Adam eat from it. Second, he commanded Satan to prostrate before Adam, but He prevented Satan from doing so. And third, God says in the Qur’an: «You are forbidden carrion,» but He also says: «if anyone is forced by hunger to eat something which is forbidden, not intending to commit a sin, he will find God forgiving and merciful»;[398] hence, God did permit something after prohibiting it.”

There was a second “Ghaylān,” who also inclined toward the doctrine of 49.18
free will: the poet Ghāylān ibn ʿUqbah, known as Dhū l-Rummah. Abū l-Faraj reports: Dhū l-Rummah and Ru’bah the Rajaz poet were disputing before Bilāl ibn Abī Burdah, and Ru’bah said, “Not a bird scratches at the ground to lay eggs, nor any predator crawls into a hole, without God having first ordained it. All is predestined.” Dhū l-Rummah replied, “By God, God didn’t ordain the wolf to eat the milk camels of poor men with big families!” Ru’bah responded, “Did the wolf do it all on its own, then? This is calumny against the wolf!” Dhū l-Rummah replied, “Better to calumniate the wolf than calumniate the wolf’s Lord.”

Isḥāq ibn Saʿd[399] says: Dhū l-Rummah recited one of his verses to me: 49.19

Her two eyes: God told them, “Be,” and they were—
seizers of one’s reason, just like wine.

I told him, “‘Seizers’ should be in the accusative case,” and he said, “If you glorify God, you obtain a reward. I intended them to be nominative.” Dhū l-Rummah only said this as a precaution to hide his actual creed, which held the opposite.[400]

**. . . and decreeing for the heretic al-Jaʿd . . . [his] execution . . .** 50

Al-Jaʿd ibn Dirham was a non-Arab, affiliated with the al-Ḥakam tribe. He lived 50.1
in Damascus and was a teacher of Marwān ibn Muḥammad, the last of the Umayyad caliphs. The caliph is sometimes identified as Marwān “the Jaʿdite” on account of this. Some aver that al-Jaʿd’s sister was the concubine who gave

وكان الجعد أخاها وهو أوّل من تكلّم بخلق القرآن من أمّة محمّد صلّى الله عليه وسلّم بدمشق ثمّ طلب فهرب ثمّ نزل الكوفة فتعلّم منه الجهم بن صفوان وهو الذي تُنسب إليه الجهميّة

٢،٥٠ وقيل إنّ الجعد أخذ ذلك من أبان بن سمعان وأخذه أبان من طالوت بن أعصم اليهوديّ الذي سحر النبيّ صلّى الله عليه وسلّم وكان يقول بخلق القرآن وكان طالوت زنديقًا وهو أوّل من صنّف في ذلك ثمّ أظهره الجعد بن درهم فقتله خالد ابن عبد الله

٣،٥٠ ودخل عليه بهلول يومًا فقال أحسن الله عزاءك في ﴿قُلْ هُوَ ٱللَّهُ أَحَدٌ﴾ فقد ماتت قال كيف تموت قال لأنّك تقول إنّها مخلوقة وكلّ مخلوق يموت

٤،٥٠ ولم يزل الجعد على مذهبه إلى أن قتله خالد بن عبد الله القسريّ يوم الأضحى بالكوفة وكان واليًا عليها خطب ثمّ قال في آخر الخطبة انصرفوا وضحّوا تقبّل الله منّا ومنكم فإنّي أريد أن أضحّي اليوم بالجعد بن درهم فإنّه يقول ما كلّم الله موسى تكليمًا ولا اتّخذ إبراهيم خليلًا[1] تعالى الله عمّا يقول الجعد علوًّا كبيرًا ثمّ نزل وقدم إليه الجعد في وثاقه فحزّ رأسه بالسكّين بيده وانطفأت نائرته إلى أن نشأت في أيّام ابن أبي دواد[2]

٥،٥٠ فأمّا خالد هو ابن عبد الله ابن يزيد القسريّ البجليّ كان من أمراء الدولة بني أميّة وُلّي اليمن ومكّة ثمّ ولّي العراقين من قبل هشام بعد عمر بن هبيرة ثمّ عزله هشام لمّا بلغه من كثرة أمواله وبلاده وأنهاره وله مع ابن هبيرة مكايدات وأخبار فمن أعجبها ما حكي أنّ ابن هبيرة لمّا هرب من سجن خالد ووفد على هشام وأمّنه أرسل خالد مائة من خيل المضمار قد انتخبها وأمر السوّاس أن يعارضوا بها هشامًا إذا ركب وكان هشام معجبًا بالخيل لا يشتهي أن يكون عند غيره من

---

١ ولا . . . خليلا: سقطت من إ١. ٢ وانطفأت . . . دواد: زيادة من بر١، با١، إ٥، إ٦، غ.

birth to Marwān. Al-Jaʿd was the first Muslim in Damascus to propagate the idea that the Qur'an had been created. Al-Jaʿd was summoned, but he fled to Kufa, where he studied under al-Jahm ibn Ṣafwān, to whom the Jahmite creed of theology is ascribed.[401]

It is said that al-Jaʿd learned his creed about the createdness of the Qur'an from Abān ibn Samʿān, who had learned it from the Jew Ṭālūt, nephew of Labīd ibn Aʿṣam, the man who bewitched the Prophet (God bless and keep him).[402] Ṭālūt, a heretic, was the first to write books about the Qur'an's createdness. When al-Jaʿd publicly proclaimed this creed, he was executed by Khālid ibn ʿAbd Allāh. 50.2

Buhlūl once met al-Jaʿd and exclaimed, "May God grant you good solace! Did you know that Chapter 112 of the Qur'an has passed away?"[403] Al-Jaʿd said, "But how could the verses die?" Buhlūl responded, "Because you say that the Qur'an is created, and everything created must pass away." 50.3

Al-Jaʿd held to his creed until the very end, when Khālid ibn ʿAbd Allāh al-Qasrī executed him in Kufa on the Feast of the Sacrifice. Khālid was then governor of Kufa, and at the feast prayer he gave a sermon, at the end of which he announced, "Depart and make your sacrifices, and may God accept ours and yours! Today I want to sacrifice al-Jaʿd ibn Dirham since he claims that God never directly spoke to Moses or took Abraham as his chosen companion—may God be exalted far above what al-Jaʿd claims!" 50.4

Khālid then descended the pulpit, al-Jaʿd was presented in bonds, and Khālid, with his own hands, decapitated al-Jaʿd with a knife.[404] Thus ended al-Jaʿd's heresy until it resurfaced in the days of Ibn Abī Du'ād.

Khālid was the son of ʿAbd Allāh ibn Yazīd al-Qasrī of the Bajīlah, and he was one of the lieutenants of the Umayyad caliphs, serving as governor of Yemen and Mecca during his career. The Caliph Hishām subsequently appointed him governor of the Two Iraqs, replacing ʿUmar ibn Hubayrah. Hishām later dismissed Khālid when he heard that Khālid had amassed a vast fortune of money, land, and waterways. 50.5

There are many stories about how Khālid and Ibn Hubayrah plotted and schemed against each other, and the following tale is a great example. Khālid had imprisoned Ibn Hubayrah, but he managed to escape and was granted asylum by the Caliph Hishām. When Khālid heard about this, he personally selected one hundred racing horses and sent them to Hishām, ordering the grooms to parade them in front of Hishām when he went out to ride. Khālid

جيّدها شيء فلمّا ركب هشام نظر إلى خيل راقته فسأل القوم عنها لمن هي فقالوا لابن هبيرة فاستشاط غيظًا وقال واعجبني اختان ما اختان ثمّ قدم فوالله ما رضيت عنه بعد وهو يوائمني في الخيل عليّ بعمر فدعا به وهو يسير في عرض الموكب فجاء مسرعًا فقال له هشام ما هذه الخيل فكأنّه فطن لما صنع خالد فقال خيل يا أمير المؤمنين اخترتها وطلبتها من مظانها حتّى جمعتها لك فمر بقبضها فأعجبه ذلك وسكت خالد عن أمرها وفسدت مكيدته ولم يزل ابن هبيرة يبغي به الغوائل إلى أن عُزل وأقام بالشام برهة ثمّ عُذّب إلى أن مات سنة ستّ وعشرين ومائة في خلافة الوليد ابن يزيد[١]

## وقتل بشّار بن برد ٥١

١،٥١ هو بشّار بن برد بن يرجوخ الشاعِر من مخضرمي الدولتين الأمويّة والعبّاسيّة كان جدّه من طخارستان من سبي المهلّب ويدّعي أنّه مولى بني عقيل وحدّث عن نفسه قال لمّا دخلت على المهديّ قيل لي فيمن تعتدّ يا بشّار فقلت أمّا اللسان فعربيّ وأمّا الأصل فعجميّ كما قلت في شعري يا أمير المؤمنين

وَنُبِّـئْتُ قَوْمًا بِهِمْ جِنَّـةٌ يَقُولُونَ مَنْ ذَا وَكُنْتُ ٱلْعَلَمْ
أَلَا أَيُّهَا ٱلسَّائِلِي جَاهِلًا لِيَعْرِفَنِي أَنَا أَنْفُ ٱلْكَرَمْ
نَمَتْ فِي ٱلْكِرَامِ بَنِي عَامِرٍ فُرُوعِي وَأَصْلِي قُرَيْشُ ٱلْعَجَمْ

---

١ فأما خالد . . . يزيد: زيادة من بر١، با١، إ٥، إ٦، غ.

knew that Hishām was mad about horses and hated anyone to have better ones than his. When Hishām rode, he espied Khālid's horses, and they delighted him. Hishām asked, "Who owns those horses?" The grooms claimed, "They're Ibn Hubayrah's." Hishām burst into rage: "Unbelievable! This Ibn Hubayrah acts perfidiously and then starts showing off! By God, I'm not yet pleased with him, and he's already trying to rival my horses! Bring him to me!" Ibn Hubayrah was summoned—he was also out inspecting the horse parade, so he was soon produced. Hishām questioned him: "What's the story with these horses?" Immediately, Ibn Hubayrah realized that Khālid was scheming against him, and he said, "Commander of the Faithful! They are chosen horses I requested from their paddocks so I could gather them for you. Give the order, and they shall be yours!" Hishām was pleased. Khālid never mentioned the matter again—his ploy had failed. Afterward, Ibn Hubayrah machinated Khālid's downfall until Khālid was finally dismissed. Khālid lived on for a short time in Syria before he was tortured to death in 126 [743–44] during the caliphate of al-Walīd ibn Yazīd.

**... and for Bashshār ibn Burd ... [his] execution ...** 51

Bashshār ibn Burd ibn Yarjūkh was a poet whose career spanned the end of 51.1
the Umayyad and the beginning of the Abbasid eras. His grandfather hailed from Tukharistān and was captured during one of al-Muhallab's campaigns. They claim Bashshār was a non-Arab affiliate of the ʿUqayl, but Bashshār himself described his lineage thus: "When I entered the presence of the Caliph al-Mahdī, I was asked, 'Whom do you count as your kin, Bashshār?' I said, 'Commander of the Faithful! In terms of language, I'm an Arab; in terms of origin, I'm a Persian—it is as I said in my poem:

> I'm told some madmen are asking, 'Who's this?'
> though I'm a household name!
> Ignorant questioner! You want to know who I am?
> I'm the peak of nobility:
> I rose among the patricians of the ʿĀmir,
> and my roots are the Quraysh of the East.'"

وكان يتلوّن في ولائه فتارة يفتخر بقيس وتارة بغيرهم وتارة يقول ٢،٥١

أَصْبَحْتَ مَوْلَى ذِي ٱلْجَلَالِ وَبَعْضُهُم    مَوْلَى ٱلْعُرَيْبِ فَخُذْ بِفَضْلِكَ وَأَظْهِرِ
وَٱرْجَعْ إِلَى مَوْلَاكَ غَيْرَ مُدَافَعٍ    سُبْحَانَ مَوْلَاكَ ٱلْعَلِيِّ ٱلْأَكْبَرِ

وكان يُلقّب بالمرعّث لرعاث في أذنه وهو صغير والرعاث القرط وقيل لبيت ذكر فيه الرعاث ٣،٥١

ووُلد أعمى وكان يقول أشدّ ما هجيت به قول الباهليّ ٤،٥١

وَعَبْدِي فَقَا عَيْنَيْكَ فِي ٱلرَّحْمِ أَيْرُهُ    فَجِئْتَ وَلَمْ تَعْلَمْ لِعَيْنَيْكَ فَاقِئَا

وكان[١] يشبّه الأشياء بما لا يقدر البصراءُ عليه وسئل عن ذلك فقال عدم النظر يقوّي ذكاء القلب ويقطع عنه الشغل بما ينظر إليه من الأشياء فيتوفّر حسّه ٥،٥١

وسئل أبو عبيدة من أشعر عندك بشّار أمّ مروان بن أبي حفصة فقال إنّ بشّارًا حكم لنفسه بأمور لم يعطها غيره وذلك أنّه قال لي اثنا عشر ألف بيت جيّد فقيل له كيف ذاك فقال لي اثنا عشر ألف قصيدة إن لم يكن في كلّ قصيدة بيت جيّد فلعنها الله ولعن قائلها ٦،٥١

وكان يُتّهم بالزندقة وروى الجاحظ قوله ٧،٥١

ٱلْأَرْضُ مُظْلِمَةٌ وَٱلنَّارُ مُشْرِقَةٌ    وَٱلنَّارُ مَعْبُودَةٌ مُذْ كَانَتِ ٱلنَّارُ

وقال بهذا البيت وجد واصل بن عطاء السبيل إلى تكفير بشّار وخطب فيه خطبته المحذوفة الراء

وحكى سعيد قال كان بالبصرة ستّة من أصحاب الكلام عمرو بن عبيد وواصل ابن عطاء وبشّار الأعمى وصالح بن عبد القدّوس وعبد الكريم بن أبي العوجاء ٨،٥١

١ سقطت من إ.

However, Bashshār was also known to masquerade under several lineages: sometimes he boasted of descent from the Qays, sometimes others, and once he addressed himself in verse: 51.2

Others align with puny Arabs; your master is God!
How much more excellent! Show it off!
Return to your Lord. Undisputed—
Glory to your Lord, the Great, the Most High.

Bashshār was nicknamed "the Earringed," either because he wore an earring when he was a youth or because he mentioned a rare word for "earring" in one of his verses. 51.3

Bashshār was born blind, and he once remarked, "The worst I was ever lampooned was in a poem al-Bāhilī composed against me: 51.4

My slave's penis poked out your eyes when you were in the womb.
You emerged with no idea who put your eyes out."

Bashshār was able to draw analogies that no sighted person could have perceived, and when someone questioned him about this talent, he replied, "Inability to see strengthens the heart's acumen; when freed from the distractions of sight, the heart's senses are enhanced." 51.5

Someone once asked Abū 'Ubaydah, "Who do you think is a better poet: Bashshār or Marwān ibn Abī Ḥafṣah?" He replied, "Bashshār ruled in his own favor with an exceptional argument, inasmuch as he reasoned: 'I have composed twelve thousand good lines of poetry.' And when he was asked, 'How is that?' he replied, 'I have composed twelve thousand poems, and if each poem does not contain at least one good line, then may God curse the poet and his poems!'" 51.6

Bashshār was accused of Manichaean heresy: consider the verse of poetry ascribed to Bashshār as narrated by al-Jāḥiẓ: 51.7

The earth, dark; the fire, luminous—
fire was worshipped since its first flame flickered.

Al-Jāḥiẓ explains: Wāṣil ibn 'Aṭā' used this verse as grounds to accuse Bashshār of being non-Muslim; Wāṣil mentioned this in his famous *r*-less oration.[405]

Sa'īd tells: Jarīr ibn Ḥāzim used to host five other Basran theologians in his house: 'Amr ibn 'Ubayd, Wāṣil ibn 'Aṭā', Bashshār the blind, Ṣāliḥ ibn 'Abd al-Quddūs, and 'Abd al-Karīm ibn Abī l-'Awjā'. The six would argue about 51.8

وجرير بن حازم فكانوا يجتمعون في منزل جرير ويختصمون عنده فأمّا عمرو وواصل فصارا إلى الاعتزال وأمّا عبد الكريم وصالح فصحّحا الثنويّة وأمّا جرير فمال إلى السمنيّة وهو مذهب من مذاهب الهند وأمّا بشّار فبقي متحيّرًا فقيل إنّه قال بعد بمذهب الثنويّة وعدم الرجعة

٩،٥١ قال أحمد بن خلّاد كنت أكلّم بشّارًا وأردّ[1] عليه مذهبه بميله إلى الإلحاد[2] فكان يقول لا أعرف إلّا ما عاينت أو عاينه معاين وكان يطيل الأمر بيننا فقال لي ما أظنّ الأمر بيننا يا أبا مخلّد إلّا كما يقال إنّه خذلان ولذلك أقولُ

طُبِعْتُ عَلَى مَا فِيَّ غَيْرَ مُخَيَّرٍ هَوَايَ وَلَوْ خُيِّرْتُ كُنْتُ ٱلْمُهَذَّبَا
أُرِيدُ فَلَا أُعْطَى وَأُعْطَى وَلَمْ أُرِدْ وَغُيِّبَ عَنِّي أَنْ أَنَالَ ٱلْمُغَيَّبَا
وَأُصْرَفُ عَنْ عِلْمِي وَعِلْمِي مُبْصِرٌ فَأُمْسِي وَمَا أَعْقَبْتُ إِلَّا ٱلتَّعَجُّبَا

١٠،٥١ وروى المازنيّ قال قائل لبشّار أتأكل اللحم وهو مباين لمذهبك فقال إنّما أدفع به شرّ هذه الظلمة وبمثل هذه الحكايات المنسوبة إليه دبّر عليه يعقوب وزير المهديّ حتّى قُتل

١١،٥١ حكى ابن نصر قال قدم بشّار من البصرة إلى بغداد وقد مدح المهديّ بقصيدته الرائيّة وأنشده إياها فلم يحظ منه بشيء فقيل إنّه لم يستجد شعرك فقال والله لقد مدحته بمدح لو مدحت به الدهر لم يُخش[3] صرفه على أحد ولكنّا نكذب في القول فنكذب في الأمل[4] ثمّ مدح وزيره يعقوب فلم يحفل به ولم يعطه شيئًا وأقام ينتظر جائزته فمرّ يعقوب يومًا ببشّار فقام بشّار إليه وقال

طَالَ ٱلثَّوَاءُ عَلَى رُسُومِ ٱلْمَنْزِلِ

١ إ: أذود. ٢ بميل . . . الإلحاد: سقطت من إ. ٣ إ: يُدِرْ. ٤ إ: العمل.

theology, and ʿAmr and Wāṣil ended up becoming Muʿtazilites; ʿAbd al-Karīm and Ṣāliḥ embraced Dualism;[406] and Jarīr leaned toward Buddhism, one of the Indian religions;[407] but Bashshār remained undecided, and some claim that after adhering to Dualism for a time, he then rejected the notion of the afterlife altogether.

Aḥmad ibn Khallād relates that his father, Khallād, told:[408] In theological debate with Bashshār, I would always challenge his errant leanings toward unbelief, and he would always reply, "I only believe in that which I can see or that which is visible."[409] After long discussion, Bashshār told me, "Khallād,[410] I see no resolution for us, and so I say: 51.9

"I have no choice in beliefs; they were given to me innate—
had I been permitted the choice, I'd be put right.
What I want I'm not given; I'm given what I don't want—
I have no insight into the secrets of the Divine.
I'm diverted from what I know, yet my knowledge is insightful—
and here I am: all I've achieved is astonishment."

Al-Māzinī narrates: When someone said to Bashshār, "You eat meat, yet it's in breach of your creed?" he replied, "With it I repel the evil of the Dark." The attribution of Manichaean-heretical statements like these to Bashshār were what enabled Yaʿqūb, vizier of the Caliph al-Mahdī, to plot Bashshār's execution. 51.10

Ibn Naṣr recounts the story: When Bashshār composed his *r*-rhyming poem praising al-Madhī, he came up to Baghdad from Basra to recite it before the caliph. He was given no reward, and was told, "The caliph didn't consider it good." Bashshār responded, "By God, I praised him so effusively that if I had praised Time in those same terms, no one would fear its calamities! Well, my hopes were just as false as my praise was." 51.11

Bashshār then praised al-Mahdī's vizier Yaʿqūb, but also to no avail. Bashshār stayed, waiting to receive a reward, and when Yaʿqūb passed him one day, Bashshār rose and recited a half-verse:

At the remains of the camp, we've lingered long . . .

فقال يعقوب

فَإِذَا تَشَاءُ أَبَا مُعَاذٍ فَٱرْحَلِ

فغضب بشّار وقال يهجوه ١٢،٥١

بَنِي أُمَيَّةَ هُبُّوا طَالَ نَوْمُكُمُ    إِنَّ ٱلْخَلِيفَةَ يَعْقُوبُ ٱبْنُ دَاوُدِ
ضَاعَتْ خِلَافَتُكُمْ يَا قَوْمِ فَٱلْتَمِسُوا    خَلِيفَةَ ٱللهِ بَيْنَ ٱلنَّايِ وَٱلْعُودِ

ثمّ رحل وحضر حلقة يونس النحويّ فقال هاهنا من نحتشمه فقال لا فأنشد هجاء في المهديّ وهجا يعقوب فسعى به إلى يعقوب ١٣،٥١

وكان المهديّ قد دخل البصرة فدخل عليه فقال إنّ بشّارًا زنديق وقد قامت عليه البيّنة وقد هجا أمير المؤمنين فأمر ابن نهيك وهو صاحب الشرطة بأمره ثمّ أزف خروجهم فأخرجه ابن نهيك معه في زورق فلمّا كانوا بالبطيحة ذكره المهديّ فأرسل إلى ابن نهيك أن يضربه بالسياط ضرب التلف ويلقيه بالبطيحة فأمر به فأقيم في صدر السفينة وأمر الجلّادين أن يضربوه ضربًا متلفًا فجعل يقول كلّما وقع عليه السوط حسّ وهي كلمة تقولها العرب عند الألم فقال بعضهم انظروا إلى زندقته ما تراه يحمد الله تعالى فقال بشّار ويلك أهو ثريد أحمد الله عليه فلمّا بلغ سبعين سوطا أشرف على[1] الموت ألقي في صدر السفينة فقال ليت عين أبي الشمقمق تنظر إليّ حين يقول ١٤،٥١

إِنَّ بَشَّارَ بْنَ بُرْدٍ    تَيْسٌ أَعْمَى فِي سَفِينَهْ

ثمّ مات في ساعته فألقي في خرّارة البطيحة فحمله الماء إلى البصرة فأخذه أهله فدفنوه ١٥،٥١

١ سبعين . . . على: سقطت من إ١.

Yaʿqūb responded, completing the verse:

Then if you want, Bashshār, hit the road.

This piqued Bashshār's ire, and he composed a lampoon of Yaʿqūb: 51.12

Rise, Umayyads! You've slumbered too long.
Yaʿqūb ibn Dāwūd is the caliph!
Your caliphate is ruined! Behold God's caliph now:
reveling amid flutes and lutes.

Bashshār then returned to Basra and attended the circle of Yūnus the 51.13
Grammarian, and asked, "Is anyone here partisan to Yaʿqūb?" "No," they said, and Bashshār recited his lampoons of both al-Mahdī and Yaʿqūb. Slanderous reports reached Yaʿqūb.

Soon afterward, the Caliph al-Mahdī visited Basra, and Yaʿqūb started 51.14
working on him: "This Bashshār is a heretic, and we have proof: he has lampooned the Commander of the Faithful!" Al-Mahdī ordered Ibn Nahīq, the commander of his constabulary, to apprehend Bashshār. The time came for al-Mahdī to depart, and Ibn Nahīq marched Bashshār out and they took him with them in a boat. When they reached the marshes, al-Mahdī remembered the matter of Bashshār and ordered Ibn Nahīq to whip Bashshār to death and throw him into the marshes. Bashshār was brought to the prow of the ship and the executioners were ordered to begin a fatal lashing. After each lash, Bashshār cried, *"Ḥas!"!* (the word the Arabs utter when in pain). One of the executioners scorned him: "Look at this heretic; he doesn't even praise the Exalted God!" Bashshār responded, "Go to Hell! Am I receiving a fine dish of *tharīd* for which I should praise Him?"

After seventy lashes, Bashshār was on the point of expiring, and they threw him down on the prow. He muttered, "If only old Abū l-Shamaqmaq could see me now when he recites:

Bashshār ibn Burd:
a blind goat in a boat."

Bashshār died, and they tossed him into a quick-flowing channel in the 51.15
marshland. The water carried him back to Basra, where his family collected his body and buried him.

وحكى ابن خلّاد قال لمّا ضرب بشّار بعث المهديّ إلى منزله من يفتّشه على كتب الزندقة فوجدوا طومارًا فيه ١٦،٥١

> بسم الله الرحمن الرحيم إنّي أردت هجاء آل سليمان بن عليّ فذكرت قرابتهم من رسول الله صلّى الله عليه وسلّم فتركتهم إجلالاً له صلّى الله عليه وسلّم

فلمّا قرأه المهديّ بكى وندم على قتله[١] وقال لحا الله يعقوب ولا جزاه خيرًا فإنّه لمّا هجاه لفق عليه شهودًا على أنّه زنديق فقتله وندمت حيث لا تنفع الندامة ١٧،٥١

ومن مستظرف أخبار بشّار قال له هلال بن عطيّة يمازحه وكان صديقًا له إنّ الله تعالى لم يذهب عيني أحد إلّا عوّضه عنها فما الذي عوّضك قال الطويل العريض أن لا أراك ولا أمثالك من الثقلاء ثمّ قال يا هلال أتطيعني في نصيحة أنصحك بها قال ما هي قال إنّك كنت[٢] تسرق الحمير ثمّ تبتّ وصرت رافضيًّا فعد إلى سرقة الحمير فهي خير لك من الرفض ١٨،٥١

ومرّت به نسوة حسان فقلن له أيسرّك يا أبا معاذ أنّنا بناتك قال نعم والدين كسرويّ ويقال إنّه كفر في هذا اللفظ فإنّه أراد يسرّني أيضًا أنّ الدين كسرويّ[٣] ١٩،٥١

ودخل يومًا الحمّام وفيه بعض ولد قتيبة فقال يا بشّار وددت أنّك تبصر وتراني في الحمّام فتعرف كذبك في قولك ٢٠،٥١

عَلَى أَسْتَاهِ سَادَتِهِمْ كِتَابٌ     مَوَالِي عَامِرٍ وَسْمٌ بِنَارِ

فقال بشّار يا ابن أخي ذهب عليك الصواب إنّما قلت سادتهم ولست منهم

وكان يومًا في مجلس المهديّ ينشد شعرًا وشيخ من أخوال المهديّ حاضر وكانت منه غفلة فقال لبشّار ما صناعتك قال أثقب اللؤلؤ وضحك المهديّ وكلّ من حضر[٤] ٢١،٥١

١ على قتله: سقطت من إ٣. ٢ إ١، أز١، ق١، ب: عهدتك. ٣ ويقال إنه . . . كسروي: زيادة من بر١.
٤ وكان يومًا . . . حضر: زيادة من بر١ وإ٦.

Ibn Khallād tells that when al-Mahdī ordered Bashshār's execution, he sent a party to Bashshār's house to search for evidence of his heresy. They found a scroll upon which Bashshār had written: 51.16

> In the name of God, all and ever merciful. I wanted to lampoon the family of Sulaymān ibn ʿAlī, but I recalled their descent from the family of the Prophet (God bless and keep him), so I desisted out of respect for the Prophet (God bless and keep him).

After al-Mahdī read the letter, he wept, regretting Bashshār's execution, and lamented, "God's plague on Yaʿqūb! May God never reward him! When he was lampooned by Bashshār, he fabricated false evidence of heresy and had him killed. All my regret cannot bring him back." 51.17

As for the witty stories about Bashshār's life, there was an exchange he had with Hilāl ibn ʿAṭiyyah,[411] a friend with whom Bashshār used to jest. Hilāl said, "When the Exalted God deprives someone of sight, He always recompenses them with something. What did you get?" Bashshār told him, "Very ample recompense! I'm spared seeing you and all the other oafs." 51.18

Bashshār also told Hilāl, "Hilāl! Do you want some advice?" "What is it?" "In the past you used to be a donkey thief, then you reformed and became a Shiʿi.[412] Go back to stealing donkeys—it's better for you."

One day, some pretty girls walked past Bashshār and called out to him, "Bashshār! Would you like it if we were your daughters?" He replied, "Oh yes, and our religion, Khosrow's!" Some say that this statement confirms his unbelief, as he meant that he would be pleased if the people's religion was that of the pre-Islamic Persians.[413] 51.19

One day, Bashshār entered a bathhouse where a son of Qutaybah was washing. He called out, "Bashshār! It's a pity you can't see! If you could, you'd see me here in the bathhouse and realize that you lied when you said: 51.20

> Their noblemen's backsides bear the message
> 'Affiliates of the ʿĀmir,' branded by fire."

Bashshār responded, "No my boy, you're the one who's wrong. I specifically said, 'their noblemen'; that doesn't include you!"

Once, Bashshār was reciting poetry at al-Mahdī's court. An absent-minded, aged uncle of al-Mahdī was present and asked Bashshār, "What is your profession?" Bashshār responded, "I'm a pearl borer." Al-Mahdī and all present laughed.[414] 51.21

وجلس إليه رجل فاستثقله فضرط فظنّ الرجل أنّها أفلتت منه ثمّ ضرط أخرى ٢٢،٥١
وأخرى فقال له ما هذا فقال مه أرأيت أم سمعت قال بل سمعت صوتًا قبيحًا قال
فلا تصدّق حتّى ترى فقام الرجل وتركه

وحكى أبو عبيدة قال كان حمّاد عجرد يُتّهم بالزندقة وكان يعيّر بشّارًا بقبح ٢٣،٥١
خلفته فلمّا قال فيه حمّاد[1]

وَٱللهِ مَا ٱلْخِنْزِيرُ فِي نَتْنِهِ بِرُبْعِهِ فِي ٱلنَّتْنِ أَوْ خُمْسِهِ
بَلْ شَكْلُهُ أَحْسَنُ مِنْ شَكْلِهِ وَنَفْسُهُ أَشْرَفُ مِنْ نَفْسِهِ

قال بشّار ويلي على الزنديق لقد نفث بما في صدره قيل له وكيف قال ما أراد الزنديق إلّا قول الله تعالى ﴿لَقَدْ خَلَقْنَا ٱلْإِنسَـٰنَ فِىٓ أَحْسَنِ تَقْوِيمٍ﴾ فأخرج الجحود بها فخرج الهجاء وهذا خبث شديد من بشّار وتغلغل

وقد وقع بشّار أيضًا في مثل هذه الوقعة حدّث السريّ بن الصبّاح قال دخلت ٢٤،٥١
على بشّار بالبصرة فقال أمّا إنّي قد أوجعت صاحبكم وبلغت منه يعني حمّاد عجرد
فقلت بماذا يا أبا معاذ قال بقولي

يَا ٱبْنَ نِهْيَا رَأْسٌ عَلَيَّ ثَقِيلُ وَٱحْتِمَالُ ٱلرَّأْسَيْنِ خَطْبٌ جَلِيلُ
فَٱدْعُ غَيْرِي إِلَى عِبَادَةِ رَبَّيْـ نِ فَإِنِّي بِوَاحِدٍ مَشْغُولُ

فقلت له قد بلغ حمّادًا هذا الشعر وهو يرويه على غير هذا قال كيف قلت يرويه

فَٱدْعُ غَيْرِي إِلَى عِبَادَةِ رَبَّيْـ نِ فَإِنِّي عَنْ وَاحِدٍ مَشْغُولُ

فلمّا سمعه أطرق وقال والله لقد أجاد ابن الفاعلة ثمّ كان يقول إذا سُئل عن هذين بيتين ليس هما لي

---

١ حمّاد: زيادة من برا.

Bashshār once found himself sitting with someone whom he found obnoxious, so he farted. The man thought Bashshār had done it inadvertently, but then Bashshār farted again, and again. At last the man said, "What's this?" Bashshār replied, "Hmph, is it something you saw or heard?" "Indeed, I heard a repugnant sound." Bashshār said, "Don't believe anything until you see it." The man got up and left. 51.22

Abū 'Ubaydah tells: Ḥammād 'Ajrad, another poet who was suspected of heresy, used to insult Bashshār for being ugly. When Ḥammād recited the poem: 51.23

> The pig, by God, for all its stench,
> is four or five times sweeter than Bashshār.
> The pig is better looking too,
> and of nobler soul.

Bashshār responded, "Alas, this heretic spat out what he truly believes within his breast." "How is that?" someone asked. Bashshār explained, "This heretic knows that the Qur'an says: «We have indeed created man in the best of forms,»[415] and with this lampoon he intends to refute the Qur'an!" This was a very nasty and deep jibe against Ḥammād.

Bashshār himself fell into a similar trap, as narrated by al-Sirrī ibn al-Sabāḥ: 51.24
I visited Bashshār in Basra, and he told me, "I really pained your man Ḥammād and caused him havoc!" I asked Bashshār, "How is that?" He explained, "By composing these lines:

> Ḥammād![416] Listen: one head is heavy for me—
> the prospect of two, that's a serious matter.[417]
> Call someone else to the worship of two Lords—
> I am busy with one."

I told Bashshār: "Ḥammād has heard your poem, but he narrates it differently." "How so?" "He narrates it:

> Call someone else to the worship of two Lords—
> I'm too busy to worship just one."

When Bashshār heard this, he hung his head, saying, "Damn it! That son of a whore did it well!"[418] Afterward, if anyone asked Bashshār about these verses, he would say, "They're not mine."

٢٥،٥١ ومن كلام بشّار وكان الجاحظ يعدّه من الخطباء مع شعره قوله لقد عشت في زمان فأدركت أقوامًا لو احتفلت الدنيا ما تجمّلت إلّا بهم وإنّي لفي زمان ما أرى فيه عاقلًا حصيفًا ولا جوادًا شريفًا ولا جليسًا ظريفًا ولا من يساوي على الخيرة رغيفًا

٢٦،٥١ وقال الأصمعيّ قلت لبشّار إنّ الناس يعجبون من أبياتك في المشورة يعني قوله

وَلَا تَجْعَلِ ٱلشُّورَى عَلَيْكَ غَضَاضَةً مَكَانُ[١] ٱلْخَوَافِي عُــدَّةٌ لِلْقَوَادِمِ

فقال يا أبا سعيد إنّ المشاور بين صواب يفوز بثمرته أو خطأ يُشارَك في مكروهه

٢٧،٥١ ومن محاسن شعره قوله من قصيدة

حَــرَّمَ ٱللّٰهُ أَنْ تَــرَى كَٱبْنِ سَلْــمٍ عُقْبَـةِ ٱلْخَيْرِ مُطْعِـمِ ٱلْفُقَـرَاءِ
مَـالِكِيٌّ تَنْشُقُّ عَنْ وَجْهِـهِ ٱلْحَرْ بُ كَمَا ٱنْشَقَّتْ ٱلسَّمَاءُ عَنْ ذُكَاءِ
لَيْسَ يُعْطِيـكَ لِلرَّجَـاءِ وَلَا ٱلْخَوْ فِ وَلٰكِنْ يَلَذُّ طَعْـمَ ٱلْعَطَـاءِ
لَا وَلَا أَنْ يُقَـالَ شِـيمَتُـهُ ٱلْجُو دُ وَلٰكِنْ طَبَائِعَ ٱلْآبَـاءِ

٢٨،٥١ وقوله من قصيدة في المهديّ

تَسَلَّى عَنِ ٱلْأَحْبَابِ صَرَّامَ خُـلَّةٍ وَوَصَّـالَ أُخْـرَى[٢] مَا يُقِيمُ عَلَى أَمْـرِ
وَرَكَّاضَ أَفْـرَاسِ ٱلصَّبَابَـةِ وَٱلْهَوَى جَرَتْ حِجَجًا ثُمَّ ٱسْتَقَّلَتْ فَلَا تَجْرِي
إِلَى مَـلِكٍ مِـنْ هَـاشِـمٍ فِي نُبُوَّةٍ وَمِنْ حِـمْـيَرٍ فِي ٱلْمُلْكِ وَٱلْعَـدَدِ ٱلدَّثْـرِ
مِنَ ٱلْمُشْـتَرِينَ ٱلْحَمْدَ تَنْدَى مِنَ ٱلنَّدَى يَدَاهُ وَيَنْـدَى عَـارِضَـاهُ مِنَ ٱلْعِطْـرِ
فَأَلْزَمْتُ حَبْـلِي حَـبْلَ مَنْ لَا تُغِبُّـهُ عُفَاةُ ٱلنَّدَى مِنْ حَيْثُ يَدْرِي وَلَا يَدْرِي

١ إ١: فإنّ. ٢ كلّ النسخ: وصال خلة وصرام أخرى.

Al-Jāḥiẓ counted Bashshār as one of the excellent orators in addition to his poetic talent; Bashshār's sayings include the following: "There was a time when I met men of peerless quality, the true assets of this world. But now I live in an age devoid of rational, judicious, magnanimous, and noble men. There are no elegant companions, nor anyone whom one would choose over a loaf of bread." **51.25**

Al-Aṣmaʿī says: I told Bashshār, "People are impressed by your verses about consultation." (He meant the lines: **51.26**

Don't consider consultation a disgrace:
The coverts of a bird's wing support the primaries.)

Bashshār replied, "A counselor is either correct and wins the fruits, or he errs and shares in the adversity."

Bashshār's best poetry includes this excerpt: **51.27**

God prohibits us from seeing another ʿUqbah ibn Salm:
Bastion of goodness, provider for the poor.
Descendant of the noble clan Mālik, an irresistible force in war.
He breaks upon battle like dawn, overcomes the night sky.
He gives, not for considerations or out of fear,
but because he savors the taste of giving.
Not to hear them say "generosity is his good trait";
No, his giving is innate; it runs in his blood.

Bashshār praised the Caliph al-Mahdī: **51.28**

Dwell no more on lovers—
apply yourself to a different aim:
the years of racing on chargers of passion and love
are over; they gallop no more.
Turn now to a king, prophecy-endowed from clan Hāshim,
with a legacy of dominion and warrior hosts from Ḥimyar.[419]
His giving hands reap praise;
his soft cheeks are a profusion of perfume.
On him alone I pin my heart, he from whom
supplicants receive unceasing gifts, expected and unexpected.

وقوله في البائيّة المشهورة ٥١،٢٩

إِذَا كُنْتَ فِي كُلِّ ٱلْأُمُورِ مُعَاتِبًا  صَدِيقَكَ لَمْ تَلْقَ ٱلَّذِي لَا تُعَاتِبُهْ
فَعِشْ وَاحِدًا أَوْ صِلْ أَخَاكَ فَإِنَّهُ  مُقَارِفُ ذَنْبٍ مَرَّةً وَمُجَانِبُهْ
إِذَا أَنْتَ لَمْ تَشْرَبْ مِرَارًا عَلَى ٱلْقَذَى  ظَمِئْتَ وَأَيُّ ٱلنَّاسِ تَصْفُو مَشَارِبُهْ

يقول فيها

وَلَمَّا تَوَلَّى ٱلْحَرُّ[1] وَٱعْتَصَرَ ٱلثَّرَى  لَظَى ٱلْقَيْظِ مِنْ نَجْمٍ تَوَقَّدَ لَاهِبُهْ
غَدَتْ عَانَةٌ تَشْكُو بِأَبْصَارِهَا ٱلصَّدَى  إِلَى ٱلْجَأْبِ إِلَّا أَنَّهَا لَا تُخَاطِبُهْ

ومنها

إِذَا ٱلْمَلِكُ ٱلْجَبَّارُ صَعَّرَ خَدَّهُ  مَشَيْنَا إِلَيْهِ بِٱلسُّيُوفِ نُعَاتِبُهْ
كَأَنَّ مُثَارَ ٱلنَّقْعِ فَوْقَ رُؤُوسِنَا  وَأَسْيَافَنَا لَيْلٌ تَهَاوَى كَوَاكِبُهْ

وقوله في خالد البرمكيّ ويقال إنّ خالدًا كتب هذه الأبيات في صدر مجلسه ٥١،٣٠

أَخَالِدُ إِنَّ ٱلْحَمْدَ يَبْقَى لِأَهْلِهِ  جَمَالًا وَلَا يَبْقَى ٱلْكَثِيرُ عَلَى ٱلْكَدِّ
فَأَطْعِمْ وَكُلْ مِنْ عَارَةٍ مُسْتَرَدَّةٍ  وَلَا تُبْقِهَا إِنَّ ٱلْعَوَارِي لِلرَّدِّ

وقوله ٥١،٣١

رُبَّمَا يَثْقُلُ ٱلْجَلِيسُ وَإِنْ كَا  نَ خَفِيفًا فِي كَفَّةِ ٱلْمِيزَانِ
وَلَقَدْ قُلْتُ حِينَ وَتَّدَ فِي ٱلْأَرْ  ضِ ثَقِيلٌ أَرْبَى عَلَى كَيْوَانِ
كَيْفَ لَا تَحْمِلُ ٱلْأَمَانَةَ أَرْضٌ  حَمَلَتْ فَوْقَهَا أَبَا مَرْوَانِ

---

١ إ: البرد.

His famous *b*-rhyming poem contains the lines: 51.29

If it's your intention to berate every fault in your friends,
know that you'll never find a man without flaw.
So live alone! Or stand by your brother
with his mix of blunder and rectitude.
If you can't accept a few specks in your water,
you will go thirsty—none serve from flawless cups.

An excerpt from the same poem:

The Dog Star is set alight, the hot season burns,
the earth baked dry.
A mute onager jenny makes her thirst known
by glances to her jack.

An excerpt:

When a haughty tyrant shows us disdain,[420]
we march forth; our swords express our rebuke.
When clouds of war dust blacken the day,
our swords shine like stars in battle's night.

Bashshār also praised Khālid al-Barmakī, and it is said that Khālid had the 51.30
following verses inscribed prominently in his assembly:

Khālid: praise keeps the worthy in beauty,
while miserliness never preserves a fortune.
So give and eat from your borrowed chattels
and keep none: all that remains must be returned.

Bashshār's poetry: 51.31

This man, though light in the scales that measure men,
may yet prove the heaviest to bear.
I said when his mass was pegged into the earth:
"He is heavier than Saturn!"[421]
Why did the land refuse to bear God's Trust,
given that it can bear the weight of Abū Marwān?[422]

وقوله ٣٢،٥١

أُرْفُقْ بِعَمْرٍو إِذَا حَرَّكْتَ نِسْبَتَهُ فَإِنَّـهُ عَـرَبِيٌّ مِـنْ قَوَارِيـرِ

وإنّك لو شئت خرقت العادات وخالفت المعهودات فأحلّت البحار عذبة وأعدت السلام رطبة ونقلت غدًا فصار أمسا وزدت في العناصر فكانت خمسًا وأنّك المقول فيه كلّ الصيد في جوف الفَرَاْ ٥٢

لَيْسَ لِلّٰهِ بِمُسْتَنْكِرٍ أَنْ يَجْمَعَ ٱلْعَالَمَ فِيْ وَاحِدِ

والمعنيّ بقول أبي تمّام

فَلَوْ صَوَّرْتَ نَفْسَكَ لَمْ تَزِدْهَا عَلَى مَا فِيْكَ مِنْ شَرَفِ ٱلطِّبَاعِ

والمراد بقول أبي الطيّب

ذُكِرَ ٱلْأَنَامُ لَنَا فَكَانَ قَصِيْدَةً كُنْتَ ٱلْبَدِيْعَ ٱلْفَرْدَ مِنْ أَبْيَاتِهَا

فكدمت غير مكدم واستسمنت ذا ورم ونفخت في غير ضرم ولم تجد لريح مهزًا ولا لشفرة محزًّا بل رضِيَتْ من الغنيمة بالإياب وتمنّت الرجوع بخفّي حنين

اختلف في حنين هذا فقال قوم إنّه كان رجلاً ادّعى أنّه من بني أسد بن هاشم بن عبد مناف فأتى عبد المطّلب وعليه خفّان أحمران فقال يا أبا عمرو أنا ابن أسد ابن هاشم فقال عبد المطلب لا وثياب هاشم ما أعرف فيك شمائله فارجع فرجع وصار مثلاً يُضرب للراجع بالخيبة ١،٥٢

وقال قوم كان حنين إسكافًا من أهل الحيرة ساومه أعرابيّ بخفّين ولم يشتر منه شيئًا فغاظه فخرج فعلّق أحد الخفّين على شجرة في طريقه وتقدّم قليلاً ٢،٥٢

Bashshār's poetry: 51.32

Be gentle with ʿAmr—if you handle his lineage,
his Arabness is fragile blown glass.

**Indeed, your power was made out as supernatural: if you so will it, you can turn the seas sweet, you can liquefy rocks, and you can even bend time, turning tomorrow into yesterday; and to the four elements, you can add a fifth. In short, when they say, "Everything else is in the wild ass's belly" or** 52

**There is none who doubts that God**
**can gather the whole word into one man,**

**they must mean you! And when Abū Tammām's verse exclaimed,**

**If you described yourself, you could not overstate**
**the sum of your noble qualities,**

**he had you in mind! And Abū l-Ṭayyib intended you too:**

**If all humanity was depicted in a poem,**
**you would be its exquisitely unique verse.**

**Altogether, though, what your messenger bit off was more than she could chew. What she tried selling as a plump morsel is nothing but a blister. Her puffing merely brought bellows to spent ash, her wind swayed nothing, her blade did not cut. She was grateful, in fact, just to steal a safe departure, wishing she could have been in Ḥunayn's slippers . . .**

There is debate over Ḥunayn's identity. Some say he was a man who claimed descent from Asad ibn Hāshim ibn ʿAbd Manāf, and that once, wearing a pair of red slippers, he approached ʿAbd al-Muṭṭalib and told him, "I am the son of Asad ibn Hāshim!" ʿAbd al-Muṭṭalib replied, "No you're not. I swear on Hāshim's robes, you have not a single one of his characteristics. Go home!" Ḥunayn turned tail in his slippers, and the anecdote became proverbial for anyone departing in failure. 52.1

Others say Ḥunayn was a shoemaker from al-Ḥīrah with whom a Bedouin once struck a deal to make a pair of slippers. The Bedouin, however, did not 52.2

وطرح الآخر وكمن فجاء الأعرابيّ فرأى أحد الخفّين فوق الشجرة فقال ما أشبهه بخفّ حنين لو كان معه آخر لتكلّفت أخذه ثمّ تقدّم فرأى الخفّ الآخر مطروحًا فنزل وعقل بعيره وأخذه ورجع ليأخذ الأوّل فخرج حنين من الكمين فأخذ بعيره وذهب ورجع الأعرابيّ إلى أهله بخفّى حنين

وقال قوم كان حنين يهوديًّا نخس بامرأة مسلمة حمارًا فقمص فصرعها ٣،٥٢
فتكشّفت فكُتب بخبره إلى عمر فقال عمر ليس على هذا صالحناهم وقد خلع ربقة الذمّة من عنقه فاصلبوه حيًّا[١] ولمّا نُصب على خشبته أتت امرأته وعليه خفّان فقالت الآن تموت فما تصنع بالخفّين فأخذتهما من رجليه فقال الناس انقلبت بخفّي حنين

لأنّي قلت ٥٣

لَقَدْ هَانَ مَنْ بَالَتْ عَلَيْهِ ٱلثَّعَالِبُ

وأنشدت

عَلَىٰ أَنَّهَا ٱلْأَيَّامُ قَدْ صِرْنَ كُلُّهَا    عَجَائِبَ حَتَّى لَيْسَ فِيهَا عَجَائِبُ

ونخرت وكفرت وعبست وبسرت[٢] وأبدأت وأعدت وأبرقت وأرعدت و

هَمَمْتُ وَلَمْ أَفْعَلْ وَكِدْتُ وَلَيْتَنِي

١ سقطت من إ.   ٢ إ: وبسرت وعبست وكفرت.

go through with the purchase. Much vexed, Ḥunayn went out and hung one of the slippers from a tree on the desert track along which the Bedouin would be passing, and, a little farther along, Ḥunayn placed the second on the ground. Ḥunayn then concealed himself and waited. The Bedouin came riding up and saw the first slipper in the tree. He said to himself, "My, this is just like Ḥunayn's slipper! If its partner is around, I'd take the trouble of taking this one down." The Bedouin continued down the road, and saw the second slipper in the dust. He dismounted from his camel to pick it up, and then he hobbled his camel and ran back to fetch the first. At that point, Ḥunayn emerged from hiding, took the camel, and rode it back to town. The Bedouin returned to his camp with the two slippers.

There are yet others who say Ḥunayn was a Jew who once saw a Muslim 52.3
woman riding a donkey, and gave the animal a prod. It bucked back and threw the woman off, uncovering her. The incident reached the ears of the Caliph ʿUmar, who exclaimed, "We didn't grant the Jews a peace treaty for them to act like this! The man's actions have voided our promise of protection. Crucify him alive!" When the cross was erected, the woman came, and seeing Ḥunayn was wearing slippers, she said, "Since you're about to die, what good can these slippers do you?" She took them from his feet, and the people said, "She returned with Ḥunayn's slippers."

**I quoted to her:** 53

> **What an ignominy to be pissed on by foxes!**

**And recited:**

> **These days everything is so wondrous**
> **that there's nothing truly wondrous left.**

**I snorted, my countenance grew dim, I frowned, I scowled, I mulled over her drivel, thunder and lightning swelled within me:**

> **Murderous thoughts arose; I did nothing . . . if only I had . . . alas!**

**ولولا أنّ للجوار ذمّة وللضيافة حرمة لكان الجواب في قذال الدمستق**

هو الدمستق بن بردس[1] الأعور بطريق كان في زمن سيف الدولة بن حمدان أرسله ملك الروم مقدّمًا على جيش فقاتل سيف الدولة بطريق سمندو فهزمه سيف الدولة هزيمة مشهورة ثمّ إنّ ملك الروم كاتب سيف الدولة بعد ذلك يطلب الهدنة فمدحه المتنبّي بقصيدة ومن جملتها ١،٥٣

رَأَى مَلِكُ ٱلرُّومِ ٱرْتِيَاحَكَ لِلنَّدَى    فَقَامَ مَقَامَ ٱلْمُجْتَدِي ٱلْمُتَمَلِّقِ
وَلَمْ يَثْنِكَ ٱلْأَعْدَاءُ عَنْ مُهَجَاتِهِمْ    بِمِثْلِ خُضُوعٍ فِي كَلَامٍ مُنَمَّقِ
وَكُنْتَ إِذَا كَاتَبْتَهُ قَبْلَ هٰذِهِ    كَتَبْتَ إِلَيْهِ فِي قَذَالِ ٱلدُّمُسْتُقِ

يعني أنّك هزمت الدمستق فرأى ملك الروم آثار ضربك في قفاه وذلّ الهزيمة فقرأ منها أحوالك وشجاعتك فكأنّك كتبت إليه خبرك في قذال الدمستق وقيل إنّ كلّ بطريق تقدّم على جيش يُسمّى الدمستق ٢،٥٣

**والنعل حاضرة إن عادت العقرب والعقوبة ممكنة إن أصرّ المذنب** ٥٤

**وهبها لم تلاحظك بعين كليلة عن عيوبك ملؤها حبيبها حسن فيها من تودّ وكانت إنّما حلّتك بحلاك ووسمتك بسيماك ولم تعرك شهادة ولا تكلّفت لك زيادة بل صدقت سنّ بكرها فيما ذكرته عنك ووضعت الهناء مواضع النقب**

---

١ إ١، با١، ق١، ل١، ب: بودس.

**Were it not that guests are sacred and suppliants protected, my reply would resemble the message Domestikos relayed via the wounds inscribed on the back of his head . . .**

Domestikos was the son of Bardas the "One-Eyed," a *patrikios*[423] contemporary with Sayf al-Dawlah ibn Ḥamdān.[424] The Byzantine emperor dispatched Domestikos in command of the army that was famously routed by Sayf al-Dawlah at Samandu.[425] The Byzantine emperor then sued for peace, and al-Mutanabbī composed his praise poem of Sayf al-Dawlah, which included the following lines: 53.1

The Roman[426] knew your delight in giving,
so he adopted the mien of a humble beggar.
But the enemy's fine words of submission
will not divert you from spilling their blood.
When you last corresponded,
you inscribed your note on the back of Domestikos's head.

Al-Mutanabbī meant that after Sayf al-Dawlah defeated Domestikos, the Byzantine emperor would have been able to infer Sayf al-Dawlah's message either physically, in the marks of the wounds struck on the back of Domestikos's head, or metaphorically, in the shame of the defeat—either way, the emperor could "read" about Sayf al-Dawlah's prowess and bravery by looking upon the back of Domestikos's head. 53.2

It is said that the word *domestikos* is a title given to any *patrikios* leading an army.

**A sandal is ready and raised if the scorpion revisits, and punishment looms if the guilty persists.** 54

**For the sake of argument, let's pretend your lady did not simply behold you with eyes blind to your faults, giving full rein to her imagination as lovers are wont to do. We could then pretend that you do have some charms for her to adorn her descriptions, and that she neither misrepresented nor exaggerated your qualities, and that she was, so to speak, "honest about the camel's age," and she "put the tar on the camel's scabs" . . .**

**فيما نسبته إليك ولم تكن كاذبة فيما أثنت به عليك فالمعيديّ تسمع به خير من أن تراه**

هو شقّة بن ضمرة المعيديّ ومعيد اسم قبيلة قال الشاعر ١،٥٤

سَتَعْلَمُ مَا يَقْضِي مُعَيْدٌ وَمُعْرِضُ

وكان فاتكًا يغير على مال النعمان ويطلب فلا يقدر عليه إلى أن أمّنه النعمان ٢،٥٤
وكان يعجبه ما يسمع عنه من الشجاعة والإقدام[١] فلمّا استحضره بعد خبر طويل ورآه[٢] استزرى منظره لأنّه كان دميم الخلقة[٣] وقال لأن تسمع بالمعيديّ خير من أن تراه فقال أبيت اللعن إنّ الرجال ليست بجزر وإنّما يعيش المرء بأصغريه قلبه ولسانه فأعجب النعمان كلامه وعفا عنه وجعله من خواصّه وصار كلام النعمان مثلاً يُضرب به لمن كان خبره دون خبره

**هجين القذال** ٥٥

الهجين من الناس الذي في نسبه هجنة أي قبح والقذال مؤخّر الرأس فالهجين يطأطأ رأسه حياء[٤] ١،٥٥

**أرعن السّبال طويل العنق والعلاوة مفرط الحمق والغباوة جافي الطبع سيئ الإجابة والسمع بغيض الهيئة سخيف الذهاب والجيئة ظاهر الوسواس منتن الأنفاس كثير المعايب مشهور المثالب كلامك تمتمة وحديثك غمغمة وبيانك فهفهة وضحكك قهقهة ومشيك هرولة وغناك مسألة ودينك زندقة وعلمك مخرقة** ٥٦

١ من الشجاعة والإقدام: سقطت من إ١. ٢ استحضره . . . ورآه: سقطت من إ١. ٣ لأنه . . . الخلقة: سقطت من إ١. ٤ الهجين من حياء: زيادة من ل٢ وإ٦.

**Even if we thus pretend that her praise of your character was not just a straight pack of lies, there is nevertheless another saying: "Hearing about the Muʿaydī is better than looking at him."**

"The Muʿaydī" is a reference to Shuqqah ibn Ḍamrah. 54.1

(Muʿāyd was the name of a tribe, as evidenced in the poet's line:

You will learn what the Muʿayd and the Muʿriḍ will do.)

Shuqqah "the Muʿaydī" was a bellicose raider who used to plunder the herds of King al-Nuʿmān, always eluding capture. Eventually, al-Nuʿmān granted him amnesty, given how impressed he was with what he heard about Shuqqah's bravery and nerve. To cut a long story short, when Shuqqah was presented before al-Nuʿmān, the king thought little of his looks, since Shuqqah was of repulsive appearance, and remarked, "Hearing about the Muʿaydī is better than looking at him!" Shuqqah replied, "May the king never desire a cursed deed![427] Don't judge a man like you would a slaughter camel—a man's worth resides in his two smallest parts: his tongue and his heart." Al-Nuʿmān so liked the response that he pardoned Shuqqah and made him one of his retainers. Al-Nuʿmān's statement became a proverb for situations when hearsay about someone does not reveal his true character. 54.2

**A stooped half-breed head . . .** 55

"Half-breed" connotes someone whose lineage includes some shameful ancestry. The word for "head" in this phrase (*qidhāl*) specifies the back of the head, as the half-breed always keeps his head lowered in shame. 55.1

**. . . whiskers drooping ridiculously and an elongated neck propping an oblong skull; excessively inane; temperament: boorish; responsiveness: sluggish; hateful in appearance, you wander about idiotically; obviously mad and your breath's intolerable, your vices are both numerous and infamous. You splutter, murmur, stutter, and guffaw. You're a peripatetic low-life supplicant, a heretical clumsy incompetent.** 56

مَسَاوٍ لَوْ قُسِمْنَ عَلَى ٱلْغَوَانِي    لَمَا أُمْهِرْنَ إِلَّا بِٱلطَّلَاقِ

حتّى أنّ باقلاً موصوف بالبلاغة إذا قرن بك

١،٥٦ هو باقل بن عمرو بن ثعلبة الإياديّ الذي يُضرب به المثل في العيّ فيقال أعيى من باقل قال أبو عبيدة بلغ من عيّه أنّه اشترى ظبيًا بأحد عشر درهمًا فلقيه شخص فقال بكم اشتريته ففتح كفّيه وفرّق أصابعه وأخرج لسانه يشير بذلك إلى أحد عشر درهمًا فهرب الظبي وله أخبار معروفة من هذا الباب وهو جاهليّ قديم والله أعلم[1]

٥٧ وهبنّقة مستوجب اسم العقل إذا أضيف إليك

١،٥٧ هو يزيد بن ثروان أحد بني قيس بن ثعلبة الملقّب هبنّقة والمكنّى بأبي الودعات لأنّه نظم ودعًا في سلك وجعله في عنقه علامة لنفسه لئلّا يضيع وهو أيضًا جاهليّ يُضرب به المثل في الحمق

٢،٥٧ ومن أخباره أنّه كان إذا رعى غنمًا أو إبلاً جعل مختار المراعي للسّمان ونحّى المهازيل وقال لا أصلح ما أراد الله فساده

٣،٥٧ ومنها أنّه اختصم إليه بنو راسب وبنو طفاوة في شخص يدّعونه فقال هبنّقة ارموه في البحر فإنّ رسب فهو من بني راسب وإنّ طفا فهو من طفاوة

٤،٥٧ ومنها أنّه رأى مع الناس جرادًا قد أقبل فقال لا يهولنّكم ما ترون فإنّ أكثرها موتى

٥،٥٧ واشترى له أخوه بقرة بأربعة أعنز فركبها فأعجبه عدوها فالتفت إلى أخيه فقال زدهم عنزًا فضُرب بهذا المثل للمعطي بعد إمضاء البيع ثمّ سار بها[2] فرأى أرنبًا تحت شجرة ففزع منها فركضت[3] البقرة فقالَ

١ وله أخبار . . . أعلم: زيادة من بر١ وبا١ وق١ وإ٦. ٢ سقطت من إ١. ٣ إ١: ركض.

**Not even a raving beauty,[428] given but one of your vices,**
**could be betrothed without promise of quick divorce.**

**You make Bāqil sound eloquent . . .**

Bāqil ibn ʿAmr ibn Thaʿlabah of the Iyād was proverbial for inarticulateness: one can say, "He stammers worse than Bāqil." Bāqil's utter inarticulateness is exemplified in an anecdote narrated by Abū ʿUbaydah: Once, after Bāqil had bought a gazelle for eleven dirhams, he met someone who asked him, "How much did you pay?" Bāqil showed the fingers of both his hands and then stuck out his tongue to indicate "eleven." In doing thus, he had to let go of the gazelle, and it escaped. Bāqil features in various stories like this; he lived in the deep pre-Islamic past. God knows best. 56.1

**. . . Habannaqah look sagacious . . .** 57

Habannaqah was the nickname of Yazīd ibn Tharwān, a clansman of the Qays ibn Thaʿlabah. He was also nicknamed "Mr. Shell Amulet," as he strung seashells on a string, which he wore around his neck as a marker of his identity in case he got lost. He was another character from the deep pre-Islamic past; his name is proverbial for stupidity. 57.1

For example, they tell that when Habannaqah took sheep or camels out to graze, he used to pasture the fat animals on the best grazing fields and drive away the scrawny animals, explaining, "I will not mend what God wants to ruin." 57.2

It is narrated that the Rāsib and the al-Ṭufāwah[429] clans were each claiming a certain individual as belonging to them, and they sought Habannaqah to resolve their dispute. Habannaqah told them, "Throw him in the water. If he sinks, he's from the Rāsib, and if he floats, he's from the al-Ṭufāwah."[430] 57.3

Another story tells that Habannaqah and a group of people observed a locust approaching, and Habannaqah said, "Don't be distressed by what you see; most of them are dead."[431] 57.4

Habannaqah's brother once bought him a cow, for which he paid four goats. Habannaqah rode the cow and liked its gait, so he called to his brother, "Give them one more goat!" (This became proverbial for a purchaser who pays further consideration after a deal is concluded.) They rode off and passed by a rabbit under a tree. The rabbit frightened Habannaqah and the cow bolted. About this, Habannaqah composed a poem: 57.5

ٱللَّهُ نَجَّانِي وَنَجَّى ٱلْبَقَرَهْ مِنْ جَاحِظِ ٱلْعَيْنَيْنِ تَحْتَ ٱلشَّجَرَهْ

٦،٥٧ وروي أنّ مالك بن مسمع قال للأحنف بن قيس مازحًا وهو يفتخر بالربعيّة على المضريّة لأحمق بكر بن وائل أشهر من سيّد بني تميم يعني بالأحمق هبنّقة القيسيّ فقال الأحنف لتيس بني تميم أشهر من سيّد بكر بن وائل يعني تيس بني حمّان الذي يقال فيه أغلم من تيس بني حمّان يزعمون أنّه نزا على سبعين عنزًا وترًا وعلى عنز بعد أن فريت أوداجه

٥٨ وطويسًا مأثور عنه يمن الطائر إذا قيس عليك

١،٥٨ هو عيسى بن عبد الله مولى بني مخزوم وكنيته أبو عبد النعيم كان مخنّثًا ماجنًا ظريفًا يسكن المدينة وهو أوّل من غنّى بها على الدفّ بالعربيّة ويُضرب به المثل في الشؤم وذلك أنّه وُلد يوم قبض رسول الله صَلّى الله عليه وسلّم وفُطم يوم مات أبو بكر وخُتن يوم قُتل عمر وكانت أمّه تمشي بالنميمة بين نساء الأنصار

٢،٥٨ وله أخبار تدلّ على فطنة ومكر حكى أبو الفرج[١] الإصفهاني قال كان عبد الله بن جعفر معه حدّاث له في عشيّة من عشايا الربيع فراحت عليهم السماء بمطر جود أسال كلّ شيء فقال عبد الله هل لكم في العقيق وهو منتزه أهل المدينة في الربيع والمطر فركبوا ثمّ أتوا العقيق[٢] فوقفوا على شاطئه وهو يرمي بالزبد وإنّهم لينظرون إذ جاءت السماء فقال عبد الله لأصحابه ليس معنا جنّة نستجنّ بها وهذه سماء خليقةٌ أن تبلّ ثيابنا فهل لكم في منزل طويس فإنّه قريب منّا فنسكن فيه ويحدّثنا ويضحّكنا قال وطويس في النظّارة يسمع كلام ٱبن جعفر وأصحابه ولم يروه فقال

١ أبو الفرج: سقطت من إ. ٢ سقطت من إ.

God saved me and saved the cow
from the bug-eyed thing under the tree.

It is narrated that Mālik ibn Misma' and al-Aḥnaf ibn Qays teased each other over the relative merits of the Rabīʿah and the Muḍar. Mālik said, "The idiot from Bakr ibn Wā'il is more famous than the lord of the Tamīm" (by "the idiot," he meant Habannaqah), whereupon al-Aḥnaf quipped, "The billy goat of the Tamīm is more famous than the lord of the Bakr ibn Wā'il." Al-Aḥnaf intended the billy goat of the Ḥammān—there is a proverb: "Lustier than the Ḥammān's goat"—it is claimed that the billy mounted seventy nannies one after another, and that even when they slaughtered him and had slit his neck veins, he still was able to mount one final time. 57.6

**... Ṭuways feel auspicious ...** 58

Ṭuways was one of the nicknames of ʿĪsa ibn ʿAbd Allāh.[432] His other nickname was Abū ʿAbd al-Naʿīm, and he was a non-Arab client of the Makhzūm. Ṭuways was one of the "Effeminates" of Medina, an elegant and saucy wag,[433] who was the first to sing songs in Arabic to the accompaniment of a tambourine. His name is proverbial with ill omen, since he was born on the very day the Prophet Muḥammad (God bless and keep him) died, he was weaned on the same day the Caliph Abū Bakr died, and he was circumcised on the day the Caliph ʿUmar was assassinated.[434] Moreover, Ṭuways's mother used to spread gossip among the women of Medina. 58.1

Ṭuways was perspicacious and cunning, as evidenced by several stories. Abū l-Faraj al-Iṣbahānī narrates one example: ʿAbd Allāh ibn Jaʿfar and his companions once set out on a spring evening and were surprised by the onset of heavy rains that threatened extensive flooding. ʿAbd Allāh suggested, "Shall we go up to al-ʿAqīq?" (a pleasure spot frequented by the Medinans during the spring rains). They set off, but when they reached al-ʿAqīq, they found that its banks were flooded by a frothy torrent, and they saw the portent of yet more rain. ʿAbd Allāh told his companions, "There's no cover for us here, and this is the sort of sky that will soak us to the bone. Shall we head for Ṭuways's house? It's close by, and there we can rest in the company of his jocular banter." Ṭuways himself overheard this, since he was sheltering in a lookout within earshot of ʿAbd Allāh's party, though they couldn't see him. 58.2

عبد الرحمن ابن حسّان جُعلت فداك ما لنا ومنزل طويس عليه غضب الله[1] مخنّث شائن لمن عرفه فقال عبد الله لا تقل ذلك فإنّه خفيف لنا فيه أنس[2]

٣،٥٨ فلمّا استوفى طويس الكلام تعجّل إلى منزله فقال لامرأته ويحك قد جاءك أكرم الناس عبد الله بن جعفر فما عندك قالت نذبح هذه العناق وكانت قد ربّتها باللبن واختُبز رقاقًا فبادر وذبحها وعجنت ثمّ خرج فتلقّاه مقبلاً إليه فقال له طويس بأبي أنت وأمّي هذا المطر فهل لك في المنزل فتسكن إلى أن تكفّ السماء قال إيّاك أريد قال فامض يا سيّدي على بركة الله ثمّ مشى بين يديه إلى أن نزلوا فتحدّثوا إلى أن[3] أدرك الطعام فاستأذنه عليه فأذن به وأتى بعناق سمينة فأكل وأكل القوم وأعجبهم طعامه ثمّ قال بأبي أنت وأمّي ألا أغنّيك قال بلى فأخذ الدفّ وتغنّى

يَا خَلِيلَيَّ نَابَنِي سُهُدِي    لَمْ تَنَمْ عَيْنِي وَلَمْ تَكَدِ
كَيْفَ تَلْحُونِي عَلَى رَجُلٍ    آنِسٍ تَلْتَذُّهُ كَبِدِي

٤،٥٨ فطرب القوم وقالوا أحسنت ثمّ قال يا سيّدي أتدري لمن هذا الشعر قال لا قال لفارعة بنت حسّان وهي تعشق عبد الرحمن ابن الحارث المخزوميّ وتقوله فيه فسكت القوم وضرب عبد الرحمن صدره بذقنه وتمنّى لو ساخت الأرض به وعلم عبد الله أنّه اقتصّ من عبد الرحمن

٥،٥٨ ولطويس شعر ركيك لا فائدة في ذكره

---

١ عليه . . . الله: سقطت من إ١. ٢ إ١: وفيه كَيْسٌ. ٣ إلى أن: زيادة من بر١، ق١.

ʿAbd al-Raḥmān ibn Ḥassān disagreed with ʿAbd Allāh: "I beg you! Please, let's not go to Ṭuways's house! That effeminate disgraces all who know him. May God bring wrath down upon him!" ʿAbd Allāh said, "Don't say that. He's lighthearted and companionable with us!"

When Ṭuways heard this, he rushed home and called to his wife, "Hell's bells! The greatest of noblemen, ʿAbd Allāh ibn Jaʿfar, is about to come here. What do you have for him?" She suggested, "We can slaughter this little she-goat." Ṭuways's wife had reared the she-goat on milk and fed it loaves of fine bread. Ṭuways straightaway slaughtered the goat while his wife made flour-based dishes. Then Ṭuways strode out to meet ʿAbd Allāh on the track, and greeted him, "It's rainy. I would be so honored if you would come and stay with me until the rain stops." ʿAbd Allāh replied, "It's precisely you we've come to visit!" Ṭuways told him, "My lord, come with God's blessing!" They all walked together, and once they arrived at Ṭuways's house they conversed until the food was ready. Ṭuways invited them to eat, they agreed, the fattened goat was presented, and they all ate and found the food delicious. When they were finished, Ṭuways said to ʿAbd Allāh, "It would be such an honor if I could sing for you!" "Of course," replied ʿAbd Allāh, and Ṭuways took up his tambourine and sang: 58.3

> Listen, my dears: sleeplessness overwhelmed me,
> my eye saw no rest, not a wink.
> But can you blame me? The man's
> a darling, he turns me on.[435]

Everyone quivered with joy upon hearing it and cried, "Bravo!" Ṭuways replied, "My lord, do you know who composed this poem?" "No," said ʿAbd Allāh. Ṭuways told him, "It's by Fāriʿah, daughter of Ḥassān, singing about how she's in love with ʿAbd al-Raḥmān ibn al-Ḥārith of the Mazkhzūm." Everyone was silent, and ʿAbd al-Raḥmān ibn Ḥassān clapped his hands over his face, wishing the earth would swallow him up.[436] ʿAbd Allāh realized that Ṭuways had intended revenge on ʿAbd al-Raḥmān. 58.4

Ṭuways also composed poetry, but it was of feeble quality, and there is no point in relating any here. 58.5

٥٩ فوجودك عدم والاغتباط بك ندم والخيبة منك ظفر والجنّة معك سقر كيف رأيت لؤمك لكرمي كفاء وضعتك لشرفي وفاء وأنّى جهلت أنّ الأشياء إنّما[١] تنجذب إلى أشكالها والطير إنّما تقع على ألّافها وهلّا علمت أن الشرق والغرب لا يجتمعان وشعرت أن المؤمن والكافر لا يتقاربان وقلت الخبيث والطيب لا يستويان[٢] وتمثّلت

أَيُّهَا ٱلْمُنْكِحُ ٱلثُّرَيَّا سُهَيْلاً عَمْرُكَ ٱللهَ كَيْفَ يَلْتَقِيَانِ

وذكرت أنّي علق لا يباع فيمن زاد وطائر لا يصيده من أراد وغرض لا يصيبه إلّا من أجاد

ما أحسبك إلّا كنت قد تهيّأت للتهنئة وترشّحت للترفئة[٣] ولولا أنّ جرح العجماء جبار للقيت من الكواعب ما لاقى يسار

١،٥٩ يسار اسم عبد كان أسود دميمًا سمّته العرب في الجاهليّة[٤] يسار الكواعب لأنّ النساء إذا رأينه يضحكن منه لقبحه[٥] فكان يظنّ أنّهن يضحكن بعجبهنّ به حتّى نظرت إليه امرأة مولاه فضحكت فظنّ أنّها خضعت له فقال لصاحب له أسود كان يكون معه في الإبل قد والله عشقتني مولاتي فلأزورنّها الليلة فقال له صاحبه يا يسار اشرب لبن العشار وكل لحم الحوار وإيّاك وبنات الأحرار فقال له يا صاحب أنا يسار الكواعب والله ما رأتني حرّة إلّا عشقتني

٢،٥٩ فلمّا أمسى قال لصاحبه احفظ على الإبل حتّى أنصرف وأعود[٦] إليك فنهاه فلم ينته حتّى[٧] دخل على امرأة مولاه يراودها عن[٨] نفسها فقالت له مكانك فإنّ للحرائر طيبًا أشمك إيّاه فقال هاتيه فأتته بطيب وموسى خذمة أيّ قاطعة فأشمّته الطيب ثمّ أنحت بالموسى على أنفه فقطعته وقيل وضعت تحته بخورًا وقطعت مذاكيره

---

١ سقطت من إ١ ٢ سقطت من إ١. ٣ ما أحسبك . . . للترفئة: سقطت من إ١. ٤ إ١: قيل له. ٥ لقبحه: زيادة من بر١، با١، ل٢، إ٦. ٦ وأعود: زيادة من بر١، با١، ل٢، إ٦. ٧ حتى: زيادة من بر١، با١، ل٢، إ٦. ٨ إ١: يريدها على.

**Your presence is an absence, to wish you well breeds regret, to lose you is a gain; Heaven, in your company, is Hell.** 59

**Wherefore did you consider your ignobleness a match for my dignity, your baseness an equal to my nobility? Are you so ignorant as to not know that only likes attract—that "birds of a feather flock together"? Do you not agree that east and west cannot associate? Do you not sense that believers and unbelievers will not congregate? Would you not say that the decent never amalgamate with the reprobate? Have you never recited the verse:**

> **You who aspire to wed the Pleiades to Canopus!**
> **How in God's name will you get them to meet?**

**Didn't you mention too that I am a treasure beyond the pockets of high bidders, a bird beyond the reach of all hunters, a target beyond the range of all but the best archers?**

**Yet, I suppose you were well prepared for a congratulatory celebration of felicitous nuptials! Indeed, a feral beast concerns no one, but were it otherwise, you would deserve at least what the girls dealt Yasār . . .**

Yasār was an ugly black slave who lived before Islam. The Arabs named him 59.1
"Yasār the ladies' man," since whenever women saw Yasār they laughed at his ugliness, though he interpreted their giggling as flirting. Once, the wife of Yasār's master saw him and laughed, and, as was his wont, Yasār believed she desired him. Yasār told his fellow black slave tending the camels with him, "By God, my mistress loves me! I shall pay her a visit tonight." His companion warned him: "Yasār, stay here, drink the camels' milk, and eat the calves' tender meat. Keep far away from the freeborn ladies." Yasār replied, "My friend, I'm 'Yasār the ladies' man' himself, by God! There isn't a single freeborn woman who sees me and isn't smitten!"

In the evening, Yasār announced, "I'm off. Take care of the camels till I 59.2
come back." His friend tried strongly to dissuade him, but Yasār paid no heed and entered his master's wife's tent to woo her. When she saw him, she said, "Stay where you are! Freeborn women have a special perfume. I'll fetch it so you can smell it." He said, "Bring it on!" And she brought him the perfume, concealing a poniard (a sharp knife), and as she let him smell the perfume, she sliced the blade across his nose and cut it off (some say she placed a censer

فصاح فقالت صبرًا على مجامر الكرام ثمّ خرج هاربًا حتّى أتى صاحبه ودمه سائل فضُرب به المثل

٣،٥٩ وقيل اسم المرأة منشم وإنّها التي ضُرب بها المثل بقولهم عطر منشم على أحد الأقوال في ذلك

٦٠ فما همّ إلّا ببعض ما هممت به ولا تعرّض إلّا لأيسر ما تعرّضت أين ادّعاؤك رواية الأشعار وتعاطيك حفظ السير والأخبار أما ثاب إليك قول الشاعر

بَنُو دَارِمَ أَكِفَاؤُهُمْ آلِ مِسْمَع     وَتَنْكِحُ فِي أَكِفَائِهَا ٱلْحَبِطَاتُ

١،٦٠ دارم هو ابن مالك بن حنظلة التميميّ وآل مسمع هم بيت بكر بن وائل والحبطات بنو الحارث بن عمرو بن تميم يجمعهم البيت مع بني دارم وإنّما نقص قدر الحبطات عنهم لقول الشاعر

وَجَدْنَا ٱلنَّيِّبَ مِنْ شَرِّ ٱلْمَطَايَا     كَمَا ٱلْحَبِطَاتِ شَرُّ بَنِي تَمِيمٍ[1]

٦١ وهلّا عشّيت ولم تغترّ وما أشكّ أن تكون[2] وافد البراجم

١،٦١ هو عمّار بن صخر التميميّ والبراجم خمسة من أولاد حنظلة والعرب تضرب المثل بوافد البراجم وذلك أنّ الملك عمرو بن هند أحرق تسعة وتسعين رجلًا من بني تميم لثأر له[3] عندهم وقد كان آلَى أن يحرّق منهم مائة فبينا هو[4] يلتمس بقيّة المائة إذ مرّ عمّار هذا ولا علم له فاشتمّ رائحة القتار فظنّ أنّ الملك قد اتّخذ طعامه فعدل إليه فأخذ فقيل له من أنت قال من البراجم فألقي في النار

١ دارم هو ابن . . . تميم: زيادة من بر.  ٢ إ: انك.  ٣ إ: لنازلة.  ٤ سقطت من إ.

underneath him and cut off his genitals). As Yasār screamed, she told him, "Can't you endure the braziers of the noble?" Yasār fled back to his companion, dripping blood, and his story became proverbial.

According to some, the woman's name was Manshim, and her act was the origin of the proverb: "Manshim's perfume." 59.3

**. . . since [Yasār] hazarded but a fraction of your presumption and misadventure. And to think you allege conversance with poetry and history, yet you cannot recall the poem:** 60

**The Dārim are a fair match for the Misma',**
**but the Ḥabiṭāt: they only marry *their* equals.**

The Dārim are a lineage group descended from Mālik ibn Ḥanẓalah of the Tamīm. The Misma' are a clan of the Bakr ibn Wā'il. Al-Ḥabiṭāt is the name of the Ḥārith ibn 'Amr clan of the Tamīm. The Ḥabiṭāt and the Dārim thus hail from the same stock, but the Ḥabiṭāt lost status when a poet lampooned them: 60.1

I find aged camels to be the worst of mounts,
just as the Ḥabiṭāt are the worst of the Tamīm.[437]

**So pasture tonight while you can, as upon the morrow you will doubtless go the way of the Barājim bystander . . .** 61

The "Barājim bystander" was 'Ammār ibn Ṣakhr of the Tamīm. The Barājim clan descended from the five sons of Ḥanẓalah. The Arabs coined the expression "Barājim bystander" from the following story. King 'Amr ibn Hind had sworn to immolate one hundred men of the Tamīm in blood revenge, but when he attacked them, he found only ninety-nine, and burned them alive. 'Amr was looking for one more to complete the hundred, when along rode 'Ammār, who had no knowledge of what was transpiring. 'Ammār smelled the scent of his compatriots' burning flesh and, thinking it was meat being prepared for the king's feast, he turned toward them. When he was asked, "Who are you?" he replied, "I'm from the Barājim." They threw him onto the fire. 61.1

وقيل في المثل إنّ الشقيّ وافد البراجم ومن هنالك عيّرت بني تميم بحبّ الطعام وسيأتي ذكر الملك عمرو بن هند في تسميته محرّقًا ٢،٦١

أو ترجع بصحيفة المتلمّس ٦٢

هو جرير بن عبد المسيح أحد بني ضبيعة شاعر مجيد من شعراء الجاهليّة وفد هو وابن أخته طرفة بن العبد على عمرو بن هند أحد ملوك الحيرة فنزلا منه في خاصّته حتّى نادماه فبينما طرفة يومًا يشرب معه وفي يده جام من ذهب فيه شراب أشرفت أخت عمرو فرآها طرفة وقيل إنّما رآها في الإناء فقال ١،٦٢

أَلَا بِأَبِي ٱلظَّبْيُ ٱلَّذِي يَبْرُقُ شَنْفَاهُ
وَلَوْلَا ٱلْمَلِكُ ٱلْقَاعِدُ قَدْ أَلْثَمَنِي فَاهُ

فسمعها عمرو فاضطغنها عليه وأمسكها في نفسه ثمّ خرج عمرو يتصيّد ومعه عبد عمرو بن بشر وكان طرفة هجاه فرمى عمرو حمارًا قال لعبد عمرو انزل فاذبحه فنزل إليه فعالجه فأعياه فقال عمرو عرفك طرفة حين يقول فيك ٢،٦٢

لَا خَيْرَ فِيهِ غَيْرَ أَنَّ لَهُ غِنًى وَأَنَّ لَهُ كَشْحًا إِذَا قَامَ أَهْضَمَا

فقال له عبد عمرو وما هجاك به أشدّ قال وما هو قال قوله

فَلَيْتَ لَنَا مَكَانَ ٱلْمُلْكِ عَمْرٍو رَغُوثًا حَوْلَ قُبَّتِنَا تَدُورُ

There is an expression: "Wretched as the Barājim bystander." The story is also cited to reproach the Tamīm for their fatal infatuation with food. In the biography of King ʿAmr ibn Hind below, we explain why he was called "the Burner."[438] 61.2

**. . . or convey your own death warrant like al-Mutalammis.** 62

Al-Mutalammis was the nickname of Jarīr ibn ʿAbd al-Masīḥ, one of the Ḍubayʿah, and one of the great poets of pre-Islam. He and his cousin Ṭarafah ibn al-ʿAbd presented themselves to the court of ʿAmr ibn Hind, one of the kings of al-Ḥīrah, where they stayed in his retinue, eventually becoming his drinking companions. One day, when Ṭarafah was drinking with ʿAmr from a golden goblet filled with wine, ʿAmr's sister appeared on a balcony above and Ṭarafah saw her (some say he only saw her reflection in the cup). There and then, he sang: 62.1

By my father's life! Look at that gazelle!
How her earring shines!
If the king wasn't sitting nearby,
  that gazelle would give me a kiss.

ʿAmr heard this and began harboring hatred toward Ṭarafah, though he didn't show it. Later, ʿAmr went on the hunt with ʿAbd ʿAmr ibn Bishr (whom Ṭarafah had earlier lampooned in a poem). When ʿAmr shot an onager, he told ʿAbd ʿAmr, "Dismount and slaughter it!" ʿAbd ʿAmr did, but he had difficulty finishing the job, and ʿAmr called to him, "Ṭarafah indeed knew you well when he said: 62.2

The only good in him is that he's rich,
  and when he rises, you see his svelte waist."

ʿAbd ʿAmr responded, "His lampoon of you was worse!" ʿAmr asked, "How does it go?" ʿAbd ʿAmr recited:

Wouldn't it be better if we had a ewe about the tent,
  instead of King ʿAmr?"

٣،٦٢ فهمّ بقتل طرفة وخاف من هجاء المتلمّس له وأن يجتمع عليه بكر بن وائل متى قتلهما ظاهرًا فقال لهما يومًا أظنّكما قد اشتقتما إلى الأهل[١] قالا نعم فكتب لهما كتابين إلى عامل[٢] البحرين وقال إنّي قد كتبت لكما بصلة فاقبضاها من عامل البحرين

٤،٦٢ فخرجا من عنده والكتابان في أيديهما فمرّا بشيخ جالس على ظهر الطريق متكشّفًا يقضي حاجته وهو مع ذلك يأكل ويتفلّى فقال أحدهما لصاحبه أرأيت أعجب من هذا الشيخ فسمع الشيخ مقاله فقال ما ترى من عجبي أخرج خبيثًا وأدخل[٣] طيّبًا وأقتل عدوًّا وإنّ أعجب منّي من يحمل حتفه بيده وهو لا يدري فأوجس المتلمّس في نفسه خيفة وارتاب بكتابه فلقيه غلام من أهل الحيرة فقال له أتقرأ يا غلام قال نعم ففضّ كتابه فقرأه فإذا فيه إذا أتاك المتلمّس فاقطع يديه ورجليه واصلبه حيًّا

٥،٦٢ فقال لطرفة والله لقد أمر في كتابك بمثل هذا فادفعه إلى الغلام يقرأه فقال كلّا ما كان ليجسر على قومي بمثل هذا وأنا أقدم عليهم فأكون أعزّ منه فألقى المتلمّس صحيفته في نهر الحيرة وقال

رَضِيتُ لَهَا لَمَّا رَأَيْتُ مَدَادَهَا    يَجُولُ بِهِ ٱلتَّيَّارُ فِي كُلِّ جَدْوَلِ

ثمّ قال يخاطب طرفة

أَطُرَيْفَةُ بْنُ ٱلْعَبْدِ إِنَّكَ حَائِنٌ    أَبِسَاحَةِ ٱلْمَلِكِ ٱلْهُمَامِ تُمَرِّسُ
أَلْقِ ٱلصَّحِيفَةَ لَا أَبَا لَكَ إِنَّهُ    يُخْشَى عَلَيْكَ مِنَ ٱلْحِبَاءِ ٱلنِّقْرِسُ

٦،٦٢ ثمّ مضى طرفة بكتابه إلى صاحب البحرين فقتله فقال المتلمّس

١ إلى الأهل: سقطت من إ١. ٢ عامل: زيادة من بر١ وبا١. ٣ إ١: آكل.

After this, ʿAmr was determined to kill Ṭarafah; however, he feared being lampooned by al-Mutalammis, and if he killed both of them openly, he feared reprisal from their tribe, the Bakr ibn Wāʾil. So, one day, ʿAmr told Ṭarafah and al-Mutalammis, "I sense you miss your own people." "Yes," they both replied, and ʿAmr wrote a letter for each, addressed to his administrator over al-Baḥrayn, and he told the pair, "In this letter I have ordered a disbursement for each of you; present it to my administrator in al-Baḥrayn." 62.3

Al-Mutalammis and Ṭarafah departed together, each carrying his letter. On their way, they passed an old man who was sitting by the side of the road, uncovered and defecating, while delousing himself and eating at the same time. Al-Mutalammis and Ṭarafah said to each other, "Have you ever seen anything stranger than this old man?" The man overheard them and called back, "What do you find so strange? I am evicting what's bad and eating what's good, while I kill my enemies. To me, what's really strange is seeing someone blithely carrying his death in his own hands!" 62.4

A sense of dread came over al-Mutalammis, and he began to have doubts about his letter. Next, they met a boy from al-Ḥīrah, and al-Mutalammis asked him, "Boy! Can you read?" The boy replied, "Yes." Al-Mutalammis broke the letter's seal and the boy read it: "When al-Mutalammis arrives, cut off his hands and feet and crucify him alive."

Al-Mutalammis told Ṭarafah, "By God, he must have made the same order in your letter! Give it to the boy to read." But Ṭarafah paid no heed: "Impossible. The king wouldn't dare risk something like that against *my* people. I am traveling to them and will be in a more powerful position than him." 62.5

Al-Mutalammis threw his letter into the river of al-Ḥīrah and sang:

I liked the letter when I saw its ink
  run in streaks with the currents of the stream.

He then warned Ṭarafah:

Ṭarafah ibn al-ʿAbd! You're fatally misled,
  to think of mingling with the resolute king.
Look out! Just throw away your letter—
  I fear the gift you're promised is death.

Ṭarafah carried on with his letter to al-Baḥrayn, where ʿAmr's administrator executed him. Al-Mutalammis composed the following lines: 62.6

عَصَانِي فَمَا لَاقَى رَشَادًا وَإِنَّمَا    تَبَيَّنُ مِنْ أَمْرِ ٱلْغَوِيِّ عَوَاقِبُهُ
فَأَصْبَحَ مَحْمُولًا عَلَى ظَهْرِ آلَةٍ    تَمُجُّ نَجِيعُ ٱلْجَوْفِ مِنْهُ تَرَائِبُهْ
فَإِلَّا تُجَلِّلْهَا يُعَالُوكَ فَوْقَهَا    وَكَيْفَ تَوَقَّى ظَهْرَ مَا أَنْتَ رَاكِبُهْ

٧،٦٢ ثمّ لحق بالشام وهجا عمرًوا وبلغه أنّ عمرًوا يقول حرام عليه حبّ العراق يُطعَم منه حبّة ولئن وجدته لأقتلنّه فقال

آلَيْتَ حَبَّ[1] ٱلْعِرَاقِ ٱلدَّهْرَ أَكْلُهُ    وَٱلْحَبُّ يَأْكُلُهُ فِي ٱلْقَرْيَةِ ٱلسُّوسُ
أَغْنَيْتُ شَأْنِي فَأَغْنُوا ٱلْيَوْمَ شَأْنَكُمُ    وَٱسْتَحْمِقُوا فِي مِرَاسِ ٱلْحَرْبِ أَوْ كِيسُو

٨،٦٢ ومن جيّد شعر المتلمّس قوله

أَلَمْ تَرَ أَنَّ ٱلْمَرْءَ رَهْنُ مَنِيَّةٍ    صَرِيعٌ لِعَافِي ٱلطَّيْرِ أَوْ حِينَ يُرْمَسُ
فَلَا تَقْبَلَنْ ضَيْمًا مَخَافَةَ مِيتَةٍ    وَمُوتَنْ بِهَا حُرًّا وَجِلْدُكَ أَمْلَسُ

٩،٦٢ وقوله يمدح البخل[2]

لَحِفْظُ ٱلْمَالِ خَيْرٌ مِنْ بُغَاهُ    وَسَيْرُكَ فِي ٱلْبِلَادِ بِغَيْرِ زَادِ
وَإِصْلَاحُ ٱلْقَلِيلِ يَزِيدُ فِيهِ    وَلَا يَبْقَى ٱلْكَثِيرُ مَعَ ٱلْفَسَادِ

١٠،٦٢ وقوله

إِلَى كُلِّ قَوْمٍ سُلَّمٌ يُرْتَقَى بِهِ    وَلَيْسَ إِلَيْنَا فِي ٱلسَّلَالِمِ مَطْلَعُ
وَيَهْرُبُ مِنَّا كُلُّ وَحْشٍ وَيَنْتَمِي    إِلَى وَحْشِنَا وَحْشُ ٱلْفَلَاةِ فَيَرْتَعُ

١١،٦٢ وقوله وهو أحسن ما ورد في المستنبحات

---

١ إ: حرَبَّ. ٢ يمدح البخل: سقطت من إ.

He disobeyed me and went astray.
  Misguidedness's consequences come clear.
He found himself carried on a bier,
  Blood flowing from his chest.
Either accept Fate, or have it hoisted upon you;
  There's no protection from the very beast you're riding.

Al-Mutalammis fled to Syria and lampooned ʿAmr. When ʿAmr heard about 62.7
it, he declared, "He shall not eat so much as a single grain of Iraq's crop: if I see
him, he dies!" Al-Mutalammis responded in verse:

So you swear: you'll forever keep Iraq's grain from me,
  but worms will still eat the grains stored in villages.
I've restrained myself, so restrain yourselves too!
Rush like fools into war or come to your senses.

Al-Mutalammis's excellent poetry includes the following: 62.8

Don't you see? Death has a lien on all men,
  collected, whether the corpse is buried or lies bare for the birds.
Never choose dishonor to stave off death—
Face death freely with dignity unblemished.

Al-Mutalammis praised miserliness: 62.9

It's easier to save money than to seek it,
  traveling the land without provisions.
Little sums, well maintained, all remain,
while fortunes, treated carelessly, are all lost.

Al-Mutalammis's poetry:[439] 62.10

Some have their ladders by which they ascend,
  but our ladder leads nowhere.
Wild beasts run from us. All we can gather
  are desert creatures, pasturing.

Al-Mutalammis's description of a wayfarer seeking hospitality is among the 62.11
best of this theme:[440]

وَمُسَتَنْبَحٍ يَسْتَكْشِطُ ٱلرِّيحُ ثَوْبَهُ    لِيَسْقُطَ عَنْهُ وَهُوَ بِٱلثَّوْبِ مُعْصِمُ
عَوَى فِي سَوَادِ ٱللَّيْلِ بَعْدَ ٱعْتِسَافِهِ    لِيَنْبَحَ كَلْبٌ أَوْ لِيُوقَظَ نُوَّمُ
فَجَاوَبَهُ مُسْتَسْمِعٌ لِلصَّوْتِ لِلنَّدَى    لَهُ عِنْدَ إِتْيَانِ ٱلْمُهِيبِينَ مَطْعَمُ
يَكَادُ إِذَا مَا أَبْصَرَ ٱلضَّيْفَ مُقْبِلاً    يُكَلِّمُهُ مِنْ حُبِّهِ وَهُوَ أَعْجَمُ

٦٣ **أو أفعل بك ما فعله عقيل بن علّفة[١] بالجهنيّ إذ جاءه خاطبًا فدهن أسته بزيت وأدناه من قرية النمل**

١،٦٣ هو عقيل بن علّفة[٢] بن الحارث اليربوعيّ يُكنى أبا العملّس وأمّه عمرة بنت الحارث ابن عوف المرّيّ وأمّها بنت بدر بن حصن بن حذيفة شاعر من شعراء الدولة الأمويّة وكان أهوج جافيًا شديد الغيرة والعجرفيّة البذخ بنسبه وهو في بيت شرف في قومه من كلا طرفيه وكان لا يرى أنّ له كفوًا

٢،٦٣ وكانت قريش ترغب في مصاهرته وتزوّج إليه من خلفائها وأشرافها وخطب إليه عبد الملك بن مروان لبعض ولده فأطرق ساعة ثمّ قال إن كان ولا بدّ فجنّبني هجناءك فضحك عبد الملك وعجب من كبر نفسِه على ضائقته وشدّة عيشه بالبادية وتزوّج يزيد بن عبد الملك بعض بناته وأقبل بها ماسكًا بخطام جملها إلى أن سلّمه من يده ليد يزيد[٣]

٣،٦٣ ودخل على عثمان بن حيّان وهو أمير المدينة فقال له عثمان زوّجني بعض بناتك فقال أبكرة من إبلي تعني فقال له عثمان أمجنون أنت قال أي شيء قلت لي قال قلت لك زوّجني بعض بناتك قال إن كنت تريد بكرة من إبلي فنعم فأمر به فوُجئت عنقه فخرج وهو يقول

١ إ١، ق٢، أز١، ب: علقمة.  ٢ إ١، ق٢، أز١، ب: علقمة.  ٣ وأقبل . . . يزيد: زيادة من بر١ ول٢ وإ٦.

Another lost wayfarer, clutching his robes
against blasts of tearing wind;
Lost, he howled into the blackness
to rouse a dog's bark or stir a slumberer.
An alert ear answered him with a bark—
Hospitality for guests feeds the dogs too!
As he espied the approaching guest,
though speechless, the dog's love expressed welcome.

**Perhaps I should do unto you as 'Aqīl ibn 'Ullafah did to the Juhanī suitor: oil your anus and drop you atop an anthill.** 63

'Aqīl ibn 'Ullafah ibn al-Ḥārith of the Yarbū', an Umayyad-era poet known as Abū l-'Amallas, was a most impudent and coarse individual. He was haughty, intensely jealous, and full of overweening pride in his lineage since he was noble on both his father's and mother's side. 'Aqīl's mother was 'Amrah, daughter of al-Ḥārith ibn 'Awf of the Murrah, and her father was Badr, son of Ḥiṣn ibn Ḥudhayfah. 'Aqīl thus represented his clan's noblest family. He was convinced that none were his equal. 63.1

'Aqīl's daughters were sought by the highest-born men of their day: caliphs and noblemen of the Quraysh secured their marriages. One time, the Caliph 'Abd al-Malik proposed that one of his sons marry 'Aqīl's daughter. When 'Aqīl received the message, he looked down for a time, and then reluctantly conceded: "Okay, if I must—but don't give the girl to one of the caliph's mongrels."[441] 'Abd al-Malik laughed in amazement at 'Aqīl's conceit, especially given 'Aqīl's poverty and meager subsistence in the desert. The marriage was agreed for 'Abd al-Malik's son Yazīd, and 'Aqīl brought his daughter himself, not letting go of her camel's bridle until he handed her to Yazīd in person. 63.2

The governor of Medina, 'Uthmān ibn Ḥayyān, once proposed to 'Aqīl: "Marry one of your girls to me." "Do you mean one of my baby camels?" 'Aqīl asked. 'Uthmān replied, "Are you out of your mind?" "What did you ask me, then?" "I said, 'Marry one of your girls to me'!" "If it's one of my baby camels you want, then that's fine." 'Uthmān had 'Aqīl apprehended, and they struck him on the neck. Then they let him go, and 'Aqīl departed, singing: 63.3

لَحَى ٱللّٰهُ دَهْرًا ذَعْذَعَ ٱلْمَالُ كُلَّهُ    وَسَوَّدَ أَبْنَاءَ ٱلْإِمَاءِ ٱلْعَوَارِكِ

٤،٦٣ وكان له جار جهنيّ فخطب إليه ابنته فغضب عقيل وأخذ الجهنيّ فكتفه ودهن استه بزيت وشحم وأدناه من قرية النمل فأكل النمل خصيتيه حتّى ورم جسده ثمّ حلّه وقال أيخطب إليّ عبد الملك وأردّه وتجترئ أنت على أن تخطب إليّ

٥،٦٣ وممّا حكي عنه أنّه خرج هو وابناه جثّامة وعملّس وأختهما ا الحوراء حتّى أتوا ابنة له ناكحًا في بني مروان بالشام ثمّ قفلوا حتّى إذا كانوا ببعض الطريق قال عقيل

قَضَتْ وَطَرًا مِنْ دَيْرِ سَعْدٍ وَطَالَمَا    عَلَى عُرُضٍ نَاطَحْنَهُ بِٱلْجَمَاجِمِ

ثمّ قال أجز يا جثامة فقال

وَأَصْبَحْنَ بِٱلْمَوْمَاةِ يَحْمِلْنَ فِتْيَةً    نَشَاوَى مِنَ ٱلْإِدْلَاجِ مِيلَ ٱلْعَمَائِمِ

٦،٦٣ ثمّ قال أجز يا عملّس فقال

إِذَا عَلَمٌ غَادَرْنَهُ بِتَنُوفَةٍ    تَذَارَعْنَ بِٱلْأَيْدِي لِآخِرِ طَاسِمِ

ثمّ قال يا الحوراء أجيزي فقالت

كَأَنَّ ٱلْكَرَى سَقَّاهُمْ صَرْخَدِيَّةً    تَدُبُّ دَبِيبًا فِي ٱلْمَطَا وَٱلْمَنَاسِمِ

٧،٦٣ فقال عقيل شربتها وربّ الكعبة ثمّ شدّ عليها بالسيف ليقتلها فقال أخوها ما ذنبها إنّما أجازت شعرًا فشدّ عليه فخدشه أحدهم بسهم فوقع يتمعّك في دمه ويقول

God curse these times, when money moves the earth
and princes are sired from menstruating slaves.

A man from the Juhaynah who was under ʿAqīl's protection once asked ʿAqīl for a daughter in marriage. ʿAqīl grabbed the man, trussed him up, spread oil and lard in his anus, and sat him down by an anthill. The ants worked on his genitals until his whole body was swollen, and then ʿAqīl set him free, saying, "How dare you! You ask for one of my girls! I've even refused the Caliph ʿAbd al-Malik!" 63.4

Another story tells that ʿAqīl, along with his two sons, Jaththāmah and al-ʿAmallas, and his daughter al-Ḥawrāʾ,[442] set out to visit another of his daughters, who had married into the Marwanid family in Syria. On the way back along the road, ʿAqīl broke into song: 63.5

The camels finished at Saʿd Monastery[443]
and powered through to Jamājim . . .

ʿAqīl then turned to his son: "Complete the next line, Jaththāmah!" Jaththāmah sang:

Their morning broke upon them on the blank sheet of desert plain;
bewildered from night travel, with turbans asway, they carried a girl . . .

ʿAqīl then called to his next son, "Complete another line, ʿAmallas!" ʿAmallas sang: 63.6

Leaving waymarks behind, entering a featureless waste,
passing by a campsite, effaced . . .

ʿAqīl next addressed his daughter: "Finish the poem, al-Ḥawrāʾ!" She sang:

Drowsy, as if they had been served the wine of Ṣarkhad,
which crawls its way through the back and feet.

ʿAqīl exclaimed, "By the Lord of the Kaaba! You've dabbled in drink!" He was about to come down upon her with his sword to kill her, but her brother interjected, "What's her crime? She merely completed the verse!" As ʿAqīl turned on him with his sword, his other son shot an arrow in defense. It wounded ʿAqīl, and he tumbled from his mount. Rolling on the ground in his blood, ʿAqīl chanted a poem in *rajaz* meter: 63.7

إِنَّ بَنِيَّ ضَرَّجُونِي بِٱلْدَمِ مَنْ يَلْقَ أَبْطَالَ ٱلرِّجَالِ يُكْلَمِ
شِنْشِنَةٌ أَعْرِفُهَا مِنْ أَخْزَمِ

والشنشنة السجيّة وأخرم فحل منجب لرجل من العرب وقيل أخرم جدّ حاتم الطائي[1]

٨،٦٣ ثمّ توجّه ولده إلى الطريق فلمّا مرّوا ببني القين قالوا لهم هل لكم في جزور انكسرت قالوا نعم قالوا فألزموا أثر هذه الرواحل حتّى تجدوه فخرج القوم حتّى انتهوا إلى عقيل فاحتملوه وعالجوه حتّى برئ ولحق بهم

٩،٦٣ وحُكي أنّ عمر بن عبد العزيز رضي الله تعالى عنه عاتب رجلاً من قريش أمّه أخت عقيل بن علّفة[2] فقال له قبّحك الله لقد أشبهت خالك في الجفاء فبلغت عقيلاً فرحل من البادية حتّى دخل على عمر فقال له أمّا وجدت لابن عمّك شيئًا تعيّره به إلّا خؤلتي قبّح الله شرّكما خالاً فقال عمر إنّك لأعرابيّ جاف أمّا لو كنت تقدّمت إليك لأدّبتك والله ما أراك تقرأ من كتاب الله شيئًا قال بلى إنّي لأقرأ ثمّ قرأ إنّا بَعَثْنَا نُوحًا فقال عمر ألم أقل إنّك لا تقرأ فقال ألم أقرأ فقال إنّ الله تعالى قال ﴿إِنَّآ أَرْسَلْنَا نُوحًا﴾ فقال عقيل

خُذَا بَطْنَ هَرْشَى أَوْ قَفَاهَا فَإِنَّهُ كِلَا جَانِبَيْ هَـرْشَى لَهُنَّ طَرِيقُ

فجعل القوم يضحكون من عجرفيّته يعجبون منه

١٠،٦٣ وقدّم عقيل المدينة فدخل المسجد وعليه خفّان غليظان فجعل يضرب برجليه فضحكوا منه فقال ما يضحككم فقال له ابن الحكم وكانت ابنة عقيل عنده وكان أميرًا على المدينة إنّهم يضحكون من خفّيك وضربك برجليك وجفائك فقال لا ولكنّهم يضحكون من إمارتك فإنّها أعجب من خفّيّ

١ والشنشنة . . . الطائيّ: زيادة من بر١، با١، إ٦. ٢ إ١، ق٢، أز١: علقمة.

My sons daubed me in blood—
those who tangle with heroes get hurt.
I know this nature: like father, like son.

By "nature" in the poem, ʿAqīl meant "natural disposition," and "like father, like son" is an adage invoked by reference to the name "Akhzam," either a stud camel owned by an Arab, or the grandfather of Ḥātim of the Ṭayyi'.[444]

ʿAqīl's sons and daughter went on their way, and when they passed a camp 63.8
of the al-Qayn, they asked, "Do any of you want a maimed camel for slaughter?"[445] The al-Qayn replied, "Of course!" The sons told them, "Retrace our path, and you'll find it." The al-Qayn followed the tracks, and there they found ʿAqīl. They carried him back and nursed him to health, and he returned home.

It is told that the Caliph ʿUmar ibn ʿAbd al-ʿAzīz (God be pleased with him) 63.9
censured a Qurayshite who was the son of ʿAqīl's sister, telling him, "God disfigure you! You are just like your boorish uncle!" ʿAqīl heard about this, and he rode in from the desert at once, entered ʿUmar's court, and said, "Were his maternal uncles the only fault you could find with your cousin? Let God disfigure the one who has the worst maternal uncles!"[446] ʿUmar responded, "You are an uncouth Bedouin. If I had come to you, I would teach you a lesson! By God, I don't imagine you even know any verses of the Qur'an!" ʿAqīl replied, "I damn well do!" And he began reciting: "We dispatched Noah out..." ʿUmar interjected, "Didn't I say you know none? The actual verse goes «We sent Noah forth»!"[447] ʿAqīl responded:

Ride up Harshā from either the front or the back,
both sides of Harshā are a passable track.

Everyone laughed and marveled at ʿAqīl's arrogant manner.

One day, ʿAqil traveled to Medina and entered the mosque wearing a pair of 63.10
rough-cut slippers, and he stomped about, making everyone laugh. He asked, "What's so funny?" Ibn al-Ḥakam, the governor of Medina, who was married to one of ʿAqīl's daughters, told him, "They laugh at your funny slippers, your stomping, and your boorishness." ʿAqīl responded, "No, they're laughing at your governorship—it's more bizarre than my slippers!"

وحُكي أنّ يحيى بن الحكم حين خطب ابنة عقيل بعث إليها جارية من عنده لتنظر إليها فغمزت الجارية عضدها فرفعت يدها فدقّت أنف الجارية فرجعت إلى يحيى فقالت بعثتني إلى أعرابيّة مجنونة فصنعت فيّ ما ترى فلمّا اتّصلت بيحيى قال لها ما لك مع الخادم فقالت أردت أن يكون نظرك إليّ قبل كلّ ناظر فإن كان حسنًا كنت أوّل من رآه وإن كان قبيحًا كنت أولى من واراه ١١،٦٣

ومن شعر عقيل يرثي ولده ١٢،٦٣

لَعَمْرِي قَدْ جَاءَتْ قَوَافِلُ أَخْبَرَتْ بِأَمْرٍ مِنَ ٱلدُّنْيَا عَلَيَّ ثَقِيلِ
لَتَسْعَى ٱلْمَنَايَا حَيْثُ شَاءَتْ فَإِنَّهَا مُحَلَّلَةٌ بَعْدَ ٱلْفَتَى ٱبْنِ عُقَيْلِ
فَتًى كَانَ مَوْلَاهُ يَحُلُّ بِنَجْوَةٍ فَحَلَّ ٱلْمَوَالِي بَعْدَهُ بِمَسِيلِ
كَأَنَّ ٱلْمَنَايَا تَبْتَغِي مِنْ خِيَارِنَا لَهَا تِرَةً أَوْ تَهْتَدِي بِدَلِيلِ

ومنه يحرّض قومه بسبب جار لهم ١٣،٦٣

أَمَّا هَلَكْتُ فَلَمْ آتِكُمْ[١] فَأَبْلِغْ أَمَاثِلَ سَهْمٍ رَسُولَا
أَذُلَّ ٱلْحَيَاةِ وَذُلَّ ٱلْمَمَاتِ وَكُلًّا أَرَاهُ وَخِيمًا وَبِيلَا
فَإِنْ لَمْ يَكُنْ غَيْرُ إِحْدَاهُمَا فَسِيرُوا إِلَى ٱلْمَوْتِ سِيرًا جَمِيلَا
وَلَا تَقْعُدُوا وَبِكُمْ مُنَّةٌ كَفَى بِٱلْحَوَادِثِ لِلْمَرْءِ غُولَا

ومنه وقد خطب إليه رجل كثير المال يُغمز في نسبه فامتنع ١٤،٦٣

لَعَمْرِي لَئِنْ زَوَّجْتُ مِنْ أَجْلِ مَالِهِ هَجِينًا لَقَدْ حُبَّتْ إِلَيَّ ٱلدَّرَاهِمُ
أَبَى لِيَ أَنْ أَرْضَى ٱلدَّنِيَّةَ أَنَّنِي أَمُدُّ عِنَانًا لَمْ تَخُنْهُ ٱلشَّكَائِمُ

١ سقطت من إ.

It is told that when Yaḥyā ibn al-Ḥakam proposed to marry a daughter of 'Aqīl, he sent one of his maidservants to have a look at her. The maid prodded her in the arm, and the girl promptly slapped her back and bruised her nose. The maid returned and told Yaḥyā, "You sent me to a crazy Bedouin girl and look what she did!" 63.11

When the marriage was agreed and the girl arrived, Yaḥyā asked her, "What was all that with the maid about?" She told him, "I wanted you to be the first person to look upon me. If I'm beautiful, you should be the first to see it, and if I'm ugly, then you're the one most suitable to cover it up."

'Aqīl composed a poem to eulogize one of his sons: 63.12

By my life, a caravan has brought news,
a matter of this world that weighs heavy upon me—
The Fates strike fast wherever they wish:
they've settled here and taken 'Aqīl's brave son:
He who gave protection on the high ground;
those needing protection now are left in a torrent's path.
The Fates were desirous of our best.
They had a score to settle, or were led here by a guide.

He composed the following poem to urge his people to war on account of a man he was protecting: 63.13

If I perish before meeting my people,
then inform the nobles of the Sahm:
There's disgrace in life and disgrace in death;
I find both unhealthy, unwholesome.
If I'm forced to choose,
then it's for death, nobly!
If you have any strength, do not sit idly:
Time itself will kill you soon enough.

About another wealthy suitor whom he rejected because he belittled his lineage, 'Aqil sang: 63.14

On my life, would I marry my daughter for money
to a mongrel who comes tempting with dirhams?
Infamy can never please my soul;
even if I loosen my halter, the bridle bit holds firm.

ومتى كثر تلاقينا واتّصل ترائينا فيدعوني إليك ما دعا ابنة الخسّ إلى عبدها من طول السواد وقرب الوساد ٦٤

هي هند بنت الخسّ ويقال الخصّ والخسف الإياديّ قديمة في الجاهليّة أدركت العملّس أحد حكّام العرب الذي يقال إنّه أوّل من وصل الوصيلة وسيّب السّائبة وتحاكمت هي وأختها جمعة إليه في كلام لهما ومدحته بأبيات منها ١،٦٤

إِذَا ٱللّٰهُ جَازَى مُنْعِمًا بِوَفَائِهِ فَجَازَاكَ عَنِّي يَا عَمَلَّسُ بِٱلْكَرَمِ

وبعض الرواة يزعم أنّها ماتت في زمن النعمان بن المنذر[1] عند هند ابنته ويستشهد على ذلك بقول الفرزدق ٢،٦٤

وَفَيْتَ بِعَهْدٍ كَانَ مِنْكَ تَكَرُّمًا كَمَا لِٱبْنَةِ ٱلْخُسِّ ٱلْإِيَادِيِّ وَفَتْ هِنْدُ

وليس الأمر كذلك وإنّما مراد الفرزدق أنّ[2] هندًا هي التي وفت لأختها جمعة لا أنّها هند ابنة النعمان

وكانت ابنة الخسّ قد زنت بعبد لها أسود فليمت وقيل لها ما حملك على الزنا فقالت قرب الوساد وطول السواد والسواد السرار يقال ساودته إذا ساررته وفي الحديث السواد من السحر وألحق بعض الرواة في قولها وحبّ السفاد لأنّ أباها كان قد[3] منعها من الزواج ٣،٦٤

ولها أسجاع كثيرة وشعر قليل ٤،٦٤

١ ابن المنذر: سقطت من إ١. ٢ مراد الفرزدق أن: زيادة من إ٢، إ٣. ٣ قد: زيادة من بر١، إ٦، با١.

**Should it happen that we begin to frequent the same places, and that our glances might more repeatedly meet, do you really think the "long whispers and ready bed cushions" that induced al-Khuss's daughter to lie with her slave will lead me to you?** 64

The daughter of al-Khuss (whose name is also spelled al-Khuṣṣ and al-Khusf) of the Iyād was named Hind. She lived in ancient pre-Islamic times. She was a contemporary of al-ʿAmallas, the Arab arbiter who reportedly first sanctified the *waṣīlah* and the *sāʾibah* animals.[448] After bringing a case before al-ʿAmallas with her sister, Jumʿah, Hind praised al-ʿAmallas in a poem, which includes the verse: 64.1

As God rewards benefactors for their good faith
for your good turn to me, He'll reward you, al-ʿAmallas, with nobility.

Some claim that Hind was not from such ancient times, since one narrator alleges that she died in the days of King al-Nuʿmān ibn al-Mundhir, at the side of his daughter, who was also named Hind. A line of poetry by al-Farazdaq is cited to support this opinion: 64.2

You kept your gracious promise,
like Hind's fidelity to al-Khuss's daughter.

However, this verse by al-Farazdaq does not actually prove that Hind was contemporary with King al-Nuʿmān. The "Hind" mentioned by al-Farazdaq is not al-Nuʿmān's daughter; rather, al-Farazdaq alludes to the very ancient Hind's fidelity to her own sister, Jumʿah, the other daughter of Khuss.

Hind was once shamed for committing fornication with one of her black slaves, and when she was asked, "What could have driven you to fornication?" she quipped, "Long whispers and ready bed cushions." 64.3

(The word she used for whispers (*siwād*) has the same connotation as "secret speech" (*sirār*); both words convey a sense of "exchanging secret whispers"; a hadith reports: "Secret whispers are a form of magic.")[449]

Some say that because Hind's father had prevented her from marrying, what she really said was: "Long whispers, ready bed cushions, and craving passions."

Various statements in rhymed prose and a few poems are ascribed to Hind. 64.4

وكانت تحاجي الرجال إلى أن مرّ بها رجل فسألته المحاجاة فقال لها كاد فقالت كاد العروس يكون أميرًا فقال كاد فقالت كاد المنتعل يكون راكبًا فقال كاد فقالت كاد البخيل يكون كلبًا وانصرف فقالت له حاجيتك فقال قولي فقالت عجبت فقال عجبت للسّبخة لا يجفّ ثراها ولا ينبت مرعاها فقالت عجبت فقال عجبت للحجارة لا يكبر صغيرها ولا يهرم كبيرها فقالتعجبت فقال عجبت لحفرة بين فخذيك لا يُملأ حفرها ولا يُدرك قعرها فخجلت وتركت المحاجاة ٥،٦٤

ومن أسجاعها قيل لها أيّ الخيل أحبّ إليك قالت ذو الميعة الصنيع السليط التليع[١] الآيد الضليع الملهّب السريع فقيل لها أيّ الغيوث أحبّ إليك قالت ذو الهيدب المنبعق الصخب المنبثق الأضخم المؤتلق فقيل لها أيّ الأيور أحبّ إليك فقالت الذي إذا حفز حفر وإذا أخطأ قشر وإذا أخرج عقر ٦،٦٤

وقيل لها من أعظم في عينك قالت من كانت لي إليه حاجة ٧،٦٤

ومن شعرها ٨،٦٤

أَشَمُّ كَنَصْلِ ٱلسَّيْفِ جَعْدٌ مُرَجَّلٌ  شُغِفْتُ بِهِ لَوْ كَانَ شَيْءٌ مُدَانِيَا
وَأُقْسِمُ لَوْ خُيِّرْتُ بَيْنَ لِقَائِهِ  وَبَيْنَ أَبِي لَا ٱخْتَرْتُ أَنْ لَا أَبَا لِيَا

١ إ: الابد الشليع.

Hind used to engage in verbal competitions with men. This all ended when a man came to challenge her and began by saying, "Almost." She replied, "The bridegroom is almost a prince!" He said, "Almost." She replied, "The sandal wearer is almost a rider." He said, "Almost." She replied, "The miser is almost a dog." He turned away, and she crowed, "I beat you!" But he returned, saying, "Challenge me!" So she said, "I marvel at." He replied, "I marvel at a salt flat: its ground always wet, its ground never sprouting pasture." She said, "I marvel at." He replied, "I marvel at stone: new ones never get bigger, old ones never get senile." She said, "I marvel at." He replied, "I marvel at the hole between your legs: it's too big to fill, and too deep to penetrate to the bottom." She was so embarrassed that she never entered verbal competitions again. 64.5

When asked, "Which horses do you like best?" she replied in rhymed prose: "One well-tended that smoothly flows; sturdy-hoofed, nose held high; bulky, sinewy, and its power shows; one that runs continuously, sprinting when it goes." 64.6

When asked, "Which rainclouds do you like best?" she replied, "The cumulonimbus with its mammas drooping, thunder crashing, torrents pouring, sky-blackening, lightning-flashing."[450]

She was also asked, "Which penises do you like best?" She replied, "When excited it digs, when it strikes it scrapes, and when taken out it leaves no issue."[451]

She was once asked, "In your view, who is the most important?" She replied, "The one I need." 64.7

An example of her poetry: 64.8

He stands proud, like a sword's blade, his curly hair combed—
I'm infatuated; if only he were something within reach.
I swear, given the choice: a dalliance, or my father's life—
I'll opt to be fatherless.

**وهل فقدت الأراقم فأنكح في جنب** ٦٥

الأراقم حيّ من تغلب وقد تقدّم ذكرهم في حرب البسوس وغيرها وجنب حيّ من اليمن وهذا اللفظ من جملة شعر لمهلهل التغلبيّ المتقدّم ذكره كان قد هرب حين طالت عليه الحروب من أجل حرب البسوس فنزل في طريقه على حيّ من اليمن فخطبوا إليه ابنته فأبى فساقوا المهر وفيه جلود من أدم وغصبوه على الزواج فقال ١،٦٥

أَعْـزِزْ عَلَى تَغْـلِبٍ بِمَا لَقِيَـتْ     أَخْتُ بَنِي ٱلْأَكْرَمَيْنِ مِنْ جُشَمِ
أَنْكَحَهَا فَقْدُهَا ٱلْأَرَاقِمَ مِنْ     جَنْبٍ وَكَانَ ٱلْحِبَاءُ مِنْ أَدَمِ
لَوْ بِأَبَانِـينَ جَـاءَ خَـاطِـبُهَا     رُمِّـلَ مَا أَنْفُ خَـاطِـبٍ بِـدَمِ

**أو عضلني همّام بن مرّة فأقول زوج من عود خير من قعود** ٦٦

هو همّام بن مرّة بن ثعلبة جاهليّ من بكر بن وائل كانت له أربع بنات وكنّ يخطبن إليه فيعرض ذلك عليهنّ فيستحيين فلا يزوّجهنّ وكانت أمّهنّ تقول له زوّجهنّ فلا يفعل فخرج ليلة إلى متحدّث لهنّ فأستمع عليهنّ وهنّ لا يشعرن فقلن تعالين نتمنّى ولنصدق فقالت الكبرى ١،٦٦

أَلَا لَيْتَ زَوْجِي مِنْ أُنَاسٍ ذُوِي غِنًى     حَدِيثَ شَبَابٍ طَيِّبُ ٱلرِّيحِ وَٱلْعِطْرِ
طَبِـيبٌ بِأَدْوَاءِ ٱلنِّسَـاءِ كَـأَنَّـهُ     خَلِيفَةُ جَـانٍ لَا يَبِيتُ عَلَى وِتْـرِ

**Do you really suppose I am so cut off from the Arāqim that I must marry into the Janb?** 65

65.1 The Arāqim are a clan of the Taghlib, discussed above in the chapter on the Basūs War and elsewhere.[452] The Janb are a clan of Yemen. The expression here derives from a line of poetry by Muhalhil of the Taghlib: as noted above,[453] after the Basūs War had long dragged on, Muhalhil fled, and at one point he settled among a tribe of the Yemen. They asked him to marry his daughter into their tribe, but he refused. Then they presented him with a dowry including fine leather, effectively coercing him to agree to concede. Afterward, Muhalhil explained his predicament in verse:

It pains the Taghlib, what befell the girl,
the daughter of the Jusham's doubly noble line.
It was separation from the Arāqim that forced my hand
to marry her into the Janb; their present was fine leather.
Had her suitor come calling by the Abān Mountains,
his nose would be stained with blood.

**Has Hammām ibn Murrah concealed me for so long that I'll concede: "a husband of wood beats spinsterhood"?** 66

66.1 Hammām ibn Murrah ibn Thaʿlabah was a pre-Islamic tribesman of the Bakr ibn Wāʾil. He had four daughters: matches had been proposed for each, but when he presented the prospective marriage to the girls, they reacted bashfully, and he gave none away. Their mother instructed Hammām: "Marry them!" But he did not, and one night he went out to eavesdrop on their chatter. "Let's play a game and express our true wishes!"[454] they said to each other, unaware that their father was listening. The eldest began:

Ah! I wish my husband was a rich man,
young, youthful, with sweet breath and perfumed.
A physician for what ails womankind:
he coils around his woman like a snake, but never neglects blood revenge.[455]

فقلن لها أنت تحبّين رجلاً ليس من قومك فقالت الثانية ٢،٦٦

أَلَا هَلْ أَرَاهَا مَرَّةً وَضَجِيعُهَا أَشَمُّ كَنَصْلِ ٱلسَّيْفِ مُهَنَّدِ
لَصُوقٌ بِأَكْبَادِ ٱلنِّسَاءِ وَأَصْلُهُ إِذَا مَا ٱنْتَمَى مِنْ سِرِّ أَهْلِي وَمَحْتِدِي

فقالت الثالثة ٣،٦٦

أَلَا لَيْتَهُ يَمْلِي ٱلْجِفَانِ بَدِيئَةً لَه جَفْنَةٌ يَشْقَى بِهَا ٱلنِّيبُ وَٱلْجُزْرُ
بِهِ مُحْكِمَاتُ ٱلشَّيْبِ مِنْ غَيْرِ كَبْرَةٍ يُشِيبُ فَلَا ٱلْفَانِي وَلَا ٱلضَّرَعُ ٱلْغَمْرُ

فقلن لها أنت تحبّين رجلاً شريفًا ثمّ قلن للصغرى تمنّي فقالت ما أريد شيئًا قلن ٤،٦٦
والله لا نبرحنّ حتّى نعلم ما في نفسك فقالت زوج من عود خير من قعود فلمّا سمع أبوهنّ ذلك زوّجهنّ

ولعمري لو بلغت هذا المبلغ لارتفعت عن هذه الحطّة ولا رضيت بهذه الخطّة ٦٧
فالنار ولا العار والمنيّة ولا الدنيّة والحرّة تجوع ولا تأكل بثديها

فَكَيْفَ وَفِي أَبْنَاءِ قَوْمِي مُنْكِحٌ وَفِتْيَانُ هِزَّانَ ٱلطِّوَالِ ٱلْغَرَانِقَةِ

هزّان اسم قبيلة من تغلب وقد مرّ ذكرها وليس البيت من الرسالة[1] ١،٦٧

١ هزان . . . الرسالة: زيادة من بر١، بر٢، با١، ل١، ل٢، ل٣، إ٥، إ٦، ر٢.

The others surmised: "So you are in love with a man from another clan!" The second daughter sang in her turn: 66.2

Ah! Behold her bedfellow:
proud and upright, like a blade of Indian steel.
He clings tightly to a woman's desire.
His origin: trueborn from the noblest of my clan.

The third sang in her turn: 66.3

Ah! He'd be the first to present brimming bowls!
His cooking pot a source of distress for plump old camels.
He's young but endowed with the wisdom of age,
neither weak, nor feeble, nor untested.

The others surmised: "So, you want a noble man." They then told the youngest, "Make your wish!" She said, "I don't want anything." The others insisted: "By God, we won't stop until we know what secret you hide!" The youngest finally blurted out, "A husband of wood beats spinsterhood." 66.4

When Hammām heard this, he married them all off.

**If I ever reach that state, by my life, I will never stoop to such denigration nor accede to your machination. May I burn before I am shamed; may I die before I am defamed. A noblewoman will starve before she works as a wet nurse.** 67

**Why you? I have suitors! My own clan's sons,**
**And tall, strapping youths of the Hizzān!**

Hizzān is the name of one of the subtribes of the Taghlib; we have already mentioned them. This verse is not part of Ibn Zaydūn's *Letter*.[456] 67.1

ما كنت لأتخطّى المسك إلى الرماد ولا أمتطي الثور بعد الجواد فإنّما يتيمّم من لم ٦٨
يجد ماء ويرعى الهشيم من عدم الجميم ويركب الصعب من لا ذلول له

ولعلّك إنّما غرّك من علمت صبوتي إليه وشهدت مساعفتي له من أقمار العصر وريحان المصر الذين هم الكواكب علوّ همم والرياض طيب شيم

مَنْ تَلْقَ مِنْهُمْ تَقُلْ لَاقَيْتُ سَيِّدَهُمْ    مِثْلَ ٱلنُّجُومِ ٱلَّتِيْ يَسْرِيْ بِهَا السَّارِي

فحنّ قدح ليس منها ما أنت وهم وأين تقع منهم وهل أنت إلا واو عمرو فيهم وكالوشيظة في العظم بينهم وإن كنت إنّما بلغت قعر تابوتك وتجافيت عن بعض قوتك وعطّرت أردانك وجررت همیانك واختلت في مشيتك وحذفت فضول لحيّتك وأصلحت شاربك ومططت حاجبك ورفعت خطّ عذارك واستأنفت عقد إزارك[١] رجاء الاكتنان فيهم وطمعاً في الاعتداد منهم فظننت عجزًا وأخطأت أستك الحفرة والله لو كساك محرّق البردين

١،٦٨ محرّق هو عمرو بن المنذر بن ماء السماء وهو عمرو بن هند وكان يُعرف بأمّه هند بنت الحارث بن حجر آكل المرار الكنديّ وكان يقال لعمرو مضرّط الحجارة لشدّة بأسه

٢،٦٨ وسُمّي محرّقًا لقصّة استوفى في شرحها أبو الفرج في كتاب الأغاني فقال كان قد عاقد أحياء طيّئ[٢] على أن لا ينازعوا ولا يفاخروا ولا يغزوهم ثمّ إنّه غزا اليمامة ورجع منفضًا[٣] ومرّ بطيّئ فقال له زرارة بن عدس التميميّ وكان من خواصّه أبيت اللعن أصبت من هذا الحيّ شيئًا فقال ويلك إنّ لهم عقدًا قال وإن كان لهم فلم يزل به حتّى أصاب نسوة وأذوادًا فقال في ذلك قيس بن جورة[٤] الطائيّ

١ ورفعت . . . إزارك: سقطت من إ١. ٢ إ١: حيّي من طيئ. ٣ إ١، بر١، إ٦، ر٢، إ٢، إ٤، ق٢: منقضا.
٤ كلاالنسخ: حيوة.

**I have no intention to switch sweet musk for ash, or to exchange a stallion to ride an ox. No one ritually cleanses with dust where water is available or opts to pasture on chaff in verdant fields or rides an unbroken steed if a gentle mount is at hand.** 68

**Perhaps you were misled by seeing the affection and favor I have shown—but that was meant for someone else: one of the gorgeous greats of our time, one of the bright high-minded stars and sweetly fragrant gardens:**

> **Each exudes the presence of lordship,**
> **Shining for travelers like night's guiding stars.**

**The counterfeit gambling arrow whistles a different tune! What are you in comparison to the gallants? How can you compare? You are but the superfluous "w" in their "'Amr," a mere flimsy hanger-on. Now, you might empty your coffers to feign magnanimity, go hungry to clothe yourself in finery, perfume your sleeves, trail your robes, flaunt your gait, primp your beard, tidy your mustache, arch your eyebrows, preen your sideburns, and smarten your outfit, all in the hope of being ranked among them, but this is a vain and fanciful blunder. By God! Even if the Burner wrapped you in his two mantles . . .**

"The Burner" is the nickname of King ʿAmr, son of al-Mundhir ibn Māʾ al-Samāʾ. ʿAmr was also known as "son of Hind," after his mother: she was the daughter of al-Ḥārith ibn Ḥujr "the Star-Thistle Eater" of the Kindah.[457] ʿAmr was also nicknamed "he who can make rocks fart," such was his reputation for formidableness. 68.1

The story about how ʿAmr earned his nickname, "the Burner," is fully explained in Abū l-Faraj's *Book of Songs*. He narrates: ʿAmr made a treaty with various tribes of the Ṭayyiʾ, promising not to raid them so long as they neither challenged him nor boasted before him. Sometime later, ʿAmr passed through the lands of the Ṭayyiʾ on his return from an abortive raid in al-Yamāmah, and Zurārah ibn ʿUdas of the Tamīm proposed to him: "May the king never desire a cursed deed! Would you be minded to plunder this tribe?" ʿAmr refused: "No! To Hell with you! We agreed a treaty with them." But Zurārah insisted: "Nevertheless!" and he kept insisting until finally ʿAmr relented and captured some of the Ṭayyiʾ women and camels. In retaliation, a poet of the Ṭayyiʾ, Qays ibn Ḥaywah,[458] composed a rebuke: 68.2

أَرَاكَ ٱبْنَ هِنْدٍ لَمْ تَعُقْكَ أَمَانَةٌ     وَمَا ٱلْمَرْءُ إِلَّا عَهْدُهُ وَمَوَاثِقُهْ
فَأَقْسَمْتُ جَهْدًا بِٱلْأَبَاطِحِ مِنْ مِنًى     وَمَا خَبَّ فِي بَطْحَائِهِنَّ دَرَادِقُهْ[1]
فَإِنْ لَمْ يُغَيِّرْ بَعْضَ مَا قَدْ فَعَلْتُمُ     لَأَنْتَحِيَنَّ ٱلْعَظْمَ ذُو أَنْتَ عَارِقُهْ

٣،٦٨ فسُمّي عارقًا بهذا البيت وبلغ الشعر عمرو بن هند فقال له زرارة أبيت اللعن أيتوعّدك فقال عمرو لرميلة بن شعار الطائيّ أيهجوني ابنُ عمّك ويتوعّدني قال لا والله ما هجاك ولكنّه قال

وَٱللهِ لَوْ كَانَ ٱبْنُ جَفْنَةَ جَارَكُمْ     مَا إِنْ كَسَاكُمْ ضَيْعَةً وَهَوَانَا

٤،٦٨ وأراد رميلة أن يسلّ سخيمته فقال والله لأقتلنّه فبلغ ذلك عارقًا فقالَ

أَيُوعِدُنِي وَٱلرَّمْلُ بَيْنِي وَبَيْنَهُ     تَبَيَّنْ رُوَيْدًا مَا أُمَامَةُ مِنْ هِنْدِ
غَدَرْتَ بِعَهْدٍ كُنْتَ أَنْتَ أَخَذْتَنَا     عَلَيْهِ وَشَرُّ ٱلشِّيمَةِ ٱلْغَدْرُ بِٱلْعَهْدِ
وَقَدْ يَتْرُكُ ٱلْغَدْرُ ٱلْفَتَى وَطَعَامُهُ     إِذَا هُوَ أَمْسَى خِلَّةٌ[2] مِنْ دَمِ ٱلْفَصْدِ

فبلغ عمرو بن هند قوله فغزا طيّئًا فأسر أسرى من بني عديّ بن أخزم رهط حاتم فوفد حاتم عليه وسأله في الأسرى فأطلقهم له

٥،٦٨ وكان المنذر بن ماء السماء أبا عمرو قد وضع ابنًا له صغيرًا يقال له مالك عند زرارة بن عدس وإنّ مالكًا خرج يومًا يتصيّد فأخفق ولم يجد شيئا فرجع فمرّ بإبل لرجل من بني عبد الله بن دارم يقال له سويد وكان عند سويد ابنة زرارة فولدت

١ إ١، ب: زرادقة. ٢ إ٤: حلة؛ بر١: جلّة.

'Amr! It seems no pledge restrains you—
A man is only as good as his word.
With utmost oath, I swear by Mina's Sacred Valley,
and by sacrificial baby camels, driven to the Shrine:
If you do not mend at least some of your ways,
I'll be breaking bones after stripping the meat.[459]

The poet Qays was thereafter nicknamed "Meat Stripper." His poem worked its way to 'Amr's court, and Zurārah exclaimed, "May the king never desire a cursed deed! I think this poet threatens you!" 'Amr asked a member of his retinue from the Ṭayyi', Rumaylah ibn Shi'ār, about the poem:[460] "Does your cousin lampoon and threaten me?" Rumaylah replied, "No, by God, he did not lampoon you; rather, he said: 68.3

By God, if your protector is Jafnah's son,
he leaves you enrobed in shame and disgrace."

Rumaylah intended to further provoke 'Amr's wrath, and it worked: 'Amr declared, "By God, I'll kill him!" Meat Stripper heard the threat, and responded with another poem: 68.4

With wide desert between us, your threats aren't worth much;
take it easy, and consider carefully what you say.[461]
You breached a treaty you yourself made;
such perfidy is the worst of traits.
Perfidy can leave a brave with nothing
to eat but congealed blood.

When 'Amr heard this poem, he launched a raid against the Ṭayyi', taking captives from the 'Adī ibn Akhzam clan, the people of Ḥātim al-Ṭā'ī.[462] Ḥātim presented himself at 'Amr's court to seek the prisoners' release, and for Ḥātim's sake, 'Amr freed them.

After this, the Ṭayyi' sought revenge against 'Amr's advisor Zurārah and his clan, the Tamīm. It so happened that a long time earlier, 'Amr's father, King al-Mundhir ibn Mā' al-Samā', had placed another of his sons, Mālik, in the care of Zurārah, and Mālik grew up among the Tamīm. Sometime after 'Amr's raid on the Ṭayyi', Mālik went out hunting, but caught nothing, and on his return, he passed camels belonging to a member of the 'Abd Allāh ibn Dārim 68.5

له سبعة غلمة فأمر مالك بن المنذر بناقة سمينة فيها فنحرها ثمّ اشتوى وسويد نائم فلمّا انتبه شدّ على مالك بعصًا فضربه فمات وخرج سويد هاربًا حتّى لحق بمكّة وكانت طيّئ تطلب غرّة من زرارة وبني أبيه حتّى بلغهم ما صنعوا بأخي الملك فقال ثعلبة بن عمرو الطائيّ

مَنْ مُبْـلِغٌ عَمْـرًوا بِأَنَّ　　ٱلْمَرْءَ لَمْ يُخْلَقْ صُبَارَهْ
وَحَوَادِثُ ٱلْأَيَّـامِ لَا　　يَبْقَى لَهَـا إِلَّا ٱلْحِجَـارَهْ
هَـا إِنَّ ٱبْنُ عَمْـرَةَ ٱبْنَـهُ　　بِٱلسَّفْحِ أَسْفَلُ مِنْ أُوَارَهْ
تَسْفِي ٱلرِّيَاحُ خِلَالَ كَشْـ　　ـحَيْـهِ وَقَدْ سَلَبُوا إِزَارَهْ
فَٱقْتُـلْ زُرَارَةَ لَا أَرَى　　فِي ٱلْقَوْمِ أَوْفَى مِنْ زُرَارَهْ

٦،٦٨ فلمّا بلغ هذا الشعر عمرو بن هند بكى حتّى فاضت عيناه وبلغ الخبر زرارة فهرب وركب عمرو في طلبه فلم تقدر عليه فأخذ[1] امرأته وهي حبلى فقال أذكر في بطنك أم أنثى قالت لا علم لي بذلك فبقر بطنها فقال قوم زرارة لزرارة والله ما قتلت أخا الملك فأته فأصدقه الخبر فجاء إليه فطلب منه سويدًا فقال إنّه هرب ولا علم لي به فقال عليّ ببنيه فأتي ببنيه السبعة وأمّهم بنْت زرارة غلمة بعضهم فوق بعض فأمر بقتلهم فأتوا بواحد فضربوا عنقه وتعلّق بزرارة الآخرون فقال زرارة يا بعضي أرسل بعضي فذهبت مثلاً

٧،٦٨ وقتلوا وآلى عمرو بن هند ألية ليحرقنّ من بني حنظلة مائة رجل فخرج يريدهم وبعث على مقدّمته عمرو بن ثعلبة الطائيّ فوجد القوم قد أنذروا فأخذ منهم ثمانيةً

١ إ: فأخبر.

clan of the Tamīm. They say the camel's owner was Suwayd, a man married to one of Zurārah's daughters, who had borne him seven boys. Mālik selected a fat camel from the herd, and it was slaughtered and grilled while Suwayd was napping. When Suwayd awoke, he ran at Mālik brandishing a staff. He beat Mālik to death and fled to Mecca. When the Ṭayyi' heard of Mālik's murder at the hands of Zurārah's kinsman, a poet of the Ṭayyi', Tha'labah ibn 'Amr,[463] spread the news:

> Who will inform 'Amr
> that men's hearts are not made of stone,
> Yet time's calamities take all,
> and leave just stones.
> 'Amr's son, his youngest,[464]
> lies beneath Mount Uwārah,
> wind blowing over his sides,
> after its gusts robbed him of his robe.
> Kill Zurārah!
> To settle the score, no man is more fitting.

'Amr heard the poem and wept till his eyes overflowed. Zurārah heard the poem too, and he immediately fled. 'Amr set off in pursuit but could not catch him, though he did capture Zurārah's pregnant wife. 'Amr interrogated her: "Are you carrying a boy or a girl?" She responded, "I don't know." 'Amr slit her belly. 68.6

Hearing of this, Zurārah's people implored him, "By God, you weren't the one who killed the king's brother, so go back and set the matter straight!" Zurārah returned, and 'Amr demanded that he hand over Suwayd, but Zurārah remonstrated, "He fled, and I don't know where." 'Amr countered, "Then bring me Suwayd's sons!" They were duly hauled in, all seven young boys one after the other, along with their mother, Zurārah's daughter. 'Amr ordered their execution, and after the first boy was killed, the others rushed to Zurārah, clutching him as he lamented, "Mine own! Spare myself!" This became a proverb.

'Amr executed them all. Then he swore a solemn oath to burn alive one hundred men of the Ḥanẓalah clan as well,[465] and he set forth in attack. His advance troops, under the command of 'Amr ibn Tha'labah of the Ṭayyi',[466] chanced upon a group of the Ḥanẓalah (who had gotten wind of 'Amr's oath) 68.7

وتسعين رجلاً بناحية البحرين فحبسهم ولحقه عمرو بن هند فضربت قبّته وأمر لهم بأخدود ثمّ أضرم فيه نارًا فلمّا احتدمت وتلظّت قذف بهم فيه فاحترقوا

٨،٦٨ وأقبل راكب من البراجم وهم بطن من بني حنظلة لا يدري بشيء ممّا كان يصنع فوضع به بعيره فأُخذ وأُلقي في النار وأقام عمرو بن هند لا يرى أحدًا فقيل له لو تحلّلت بامرأة منهم فقد أحرقت تسعة وتسعين رجلاً فدعا بامرأة من بني حنظلة فقال لها من أنت فقالت الحمراء بنت ضمرة فقال إنّي لأظنّك أعجميّة فقالت ما أنا بأعجميّة ولا ولدتني العجم

إِنِّي لَبِنْتُ ضَمْرَةَ ٱبْنِ جَابِرِ    سَادَ مَعَدًّا كَابِرًا عَنْ كَابِرِ

٩،٦٨ فقال عمرو أمّا والله لولا مخافة أن تلدي مثلك لصرفتك عن النار فقالت أما والذي أسأله أن يضع وسادك ويخفض عمادك ما تقتل إلّا نساء أعاليها ثديّ وأسافلها حلي قال اقذفوها في النار فأُلقيت فقالت ألا فتًى يكون مكان امرأة فلمّا انطوى عليها الأخدود قالت هيهات صار الفتيان حممًا فذهبت مثلاً وسُمّي عمرو من ذلك اليوم محرّقًا

١٠،٦٨ ومن ملوك آل جفنة المحرّق أيضًا لكنّه غير صاحب البردين

١١،٦٨ فأمّا أمر البردين فحُكي أنّ الوفود اجتمعت عند المحرّق فاخرج بردين من لباسه يبلو الوفود وقال ليقم أعزّ العرب قبيلة فليأخذهما فقام عامر بن أحيمر[١] فأخذهما فاتّزر بالواحدة وارتدى بالأخرى فقال له أنت أعزّ العرب قبيلة قال العزّ كلّه في معدّ ثمّ في نزار ثمّ في مضر ثمّ في خندف[٢] ثمّ في تميم ثمّ في سعد ثمّ في كعب

١ إ: اخيم. ٢ ثم . . . خندف: سقطت من إ.

in the region of al-Baḥrayn and captured ninety-eight of them. They were held captive until ʿAmr arrived. ʿAmr set up his high-topped tent and ordered the prisoners to dig a ditch. ʿAmr ordered a fire to be lit in the ditch, and when the whole pit was ablaze, the prisoners were hurled in. They burned alive.

At that moment, a man of the Barājim, one of the subclans of the Ḥanẓalah, happened to ride in upon the scene, having no knowledge of what was transpiring. As he set down his camel, they apprehended him, tossing him into the fire too. 68.8

ʿAmr then searched for one more man to complete the hundred, but couldn't find anyone, and it was proposed: "Perhaps it is permissible for your oath to encompass women, since you have burned ninety-nine men." ʿAmr summoned a woman of the Ḥanẓalah and asked her, "Who are you?" She replied, "Ḥamrāʾ, daughter of Ḍamrah." ʿAmr told her, "I think you're a non-Arab!" She replied, "I'm not a non-Arab, and neither were my forefathers:

> I am the daughter of Ḍamrah ibn Jābir—
> Ruler of Maʿadd, as were his father and grandfather."

ʿAmr remarked, "By God, I would spare you from the fire, but I'm fearful that any son you bear will be as defiant as you!" She said, "I swear by Him who will debase your throne and collapse your tent pole: all you've done is kill a woman, just a bosom and an anklet." ʿAmr commanded, "Throw her into the fire!" As they threw her in, she cried, "Can a brave take the place of a woman?" and as the flames engulfed her, she was heard to be crying, "Shame! The braves have become ashes!" This became a proverb. 68.9

From this day forth, ʿAmr was known as "the Burner."

There was also a king of the Jafnids known as "the Burner," but he is not the one intended in Ibn Zaydūn's *Letter* since he did not own the famous "two mantles." 68.10

As for the "two mantles," it is told that the Burner brought them out before a general assembly of delegates and announced a challenge: "May the man whose tribe is the most powerful of the Arabs rise and take these!" ʿĀmir ibn Uḥaymir rose, took them, and wrapped one around his waist and the other over his shoulder. The Burner asked him, "Is your tribe the most powerful of the Arabs?" ʿĀmir replied, "Maʿadd has all the power, and Maʿadd's power stems from the Nizār, their power stems from the Muḍar, their power from the Khindif, their power from the Tamīm, their power from the Saʿd, their power from the Kaʿb, and their power stems from clan Bahdalah. If anyone disagrees, 68.11

ثمّ في بهدلة فمن أنكر هذا فلينافرني فسكت الناس فقال هذه عشيرتك كما تزعم فكيف أنت في نفسك وأهل بيتك قال أنا أبو عشرة وأخو عشرة وعمّ عشرة وخال عشرة وها أنا في نفسي وشاهد العزّ شاهدي ثمّ وضع قدمه على الأرض وقال من أزالها من مكانها فله مائة من الإبل فلم يقم إليه أحد وخرج بالبردين فضُرب بعزّه المثل وببرديه

**وحلّتك مارية بالقرطين** ٦٩

هي مارية بنت ظالم بن وهب الكنديّ زوجة الحارث الأكبر الغسّانيّ أحد ملوك العرب بالشام وهي أمّ الحارث الأصغر وأمّها هند الهنود امرأة آكل المرار وكان في قرط مارية لؤلؤتان عجيبتان دريتان كبيضتي الحمامة وصلتا لأبيها من مغنم أحد ملوك اليمن في قصّة طويلة ثمّ[1] يتوارثهما الملوك بعد ذلك إلى أن وصلتا إلى عبد الملك بن مروان فوهبهما لابنته فاطمة لمّا زوّجها لعمر بن عبد العزيز رضي الله تعالى عنه فلمّا ولّي الخلافة قال إن أحببت المقام عندي فضعي القرطين والحلي في بيت مال المسلمين فوضعته فلمّا مات ووُلّي يزيد بن عبد الملك أرسل إليها يقول خذي القرطين والحلي فقالت لا والله ما أوافقه في حال حياته وأخالفه بعد وفاته ٦٩،١

وروى الميدانيّ أنّ مارية أهدت قرطيها إلى الكعبة فكانا معلّقين بها ٦٩،٢

**وقلّدك عمرو الصمصامة** ٧٠

هو عمرو بن معدي كرب بن عبد الله الزبيديّ وكنيته أبو ثور الفارس المشهور صاحب الغارات والوقائع المذكورة في الجاهليّة والإسلام ٧٠،١

١ دريتان . . . ثمّ: زيادة من بر١، با١، ل١، ل٢، إ٦.

challenge me now." No one said a word. The Burner then put a second question: "You have described your clan, but how do you and your household rank among them?" ʿĀmir spoke: "I am the father of ten braves, the brother of ten more, the uncle of ten more on my father's side, and the uncle of ten more on my mother's. And as for me: here I stand; I am witness to my own strength." He then planted his foot on the ground and announced, "A hundred camels to anyone who can lift this foot!" No one stirred. He left with the mantles, and his power became the stuff of proverbs, as did the mantles.

**. . . Māriyah pinned her earrings upon you . . .** 69

Māriyah, daughter of Ẓālim ibn Wahb of the Kindah, was the wife of King al-Ḥārith the Elder of the Ghassān, one of the Arab kings of Syria. She was the mother of King al-Ḥārith the Younger and her mother was Hind of the Hinds,[467] the wife of "Star-Thistle Eater."[468] Māriyah's earrings were made of two wondrous, lustrous pearls, as big as dove's eggs, and there is a long story explaining how her father plundered them from a king of Yemen. Afterward, the pearls were handed down from one king to the next until they came into the hands of the Caliph ʿAbd al-Malik, who gave them to his daughter Fāṭimah, when she married ʿUmar ibn ʿAbd al-ʿAzīz (God be pleased with him). When ʿUmar became caliph, he instructed her: "If you would like to remain my wife, place the earrings and your jewelry in the treasury for Muslims." She surrendered them to the treasury, and when ʿUmar died and Yazīd ibn ʿAbd al-Malik became caliph, he wrote to her: "You can recover the earrings and jewels," but she replied: "No, by God, I will not be one to obey my husband while he was alive and defy him after his death." 69.1

Al-Madāʾinī narrates that Māriyah donated the earrings to the Kaaba, upon which they were suspended. 69.2

**. . . ʿAmr affixed al-Ṣamṣāmah on your waist . . .** 70

ʿAmr ibn Maʿdī Karib ibn ʿAbd Allāh al-Zubaydī was known as Abū Thawr. He was a famous horse warrior who participated in raids and renowned battles both before and after the rise of Islam. 70.1

٢،٧٠ وفد على رسول الله صلّى الله عليه وسلّم في السنة العاشرة من الهجرة قال عمرو وقدمت المدينة فوافيت رسول الله صلّى الله عليه وسلّم قافلاً من تبوك فأردت أن أدنو إليه فمنعني من حوله فقال دعوه فدنوت منه فقلت أنعم صباحًا أبيت اللعن فقال يا عمرو أسلم تسلم ويؤمّنك الله من الفزع الأكبر فأسلمت

٣،٧٠ وعاش عمرو إلى أيّام عثمان وأبلى في وقائع الإسلام بلاء حسنًا مثل وقعة القادسيّة وهو الذي ضرب خطم الفيل بالسيف فانهزم وانهزمت الأعاجم وكان سبب الفتح ومثل وقعة اليرموك وغيرها

٤،٧٠ قال الخثعميّ ما رأيت أشرف من رجل رأيته يوم اليرموك خرج له علج فقتله ثمّ آخر فقتله ثمّ انهزموا فتبعهم وتبعته ثمّ انصرف إلى خباء له أسود فنزل فدعا بالجفان ودعا من حوله فقلت من هذا فقالوا عمرو بن معدي كرب

٥،٧٠ وحدّث ابن أبي حاتم قال مررنا يوم القادسيّة بعمرو ابن معدي كرب وهو يحضّ الناس بين الصفّين ويقول أيّها الناس كونوا أشدّ عناشًا إنّ هذا الرجل من الأعاجم إذا ألقى مزراقه فإنّما هو تيس فبينما هو كذلك يحرّضنا إذ خرج رجل من الأعاجم فوقف بين الصفّين فرماه بنشّابة فما أخطأت سية قوسه كان متنكّبًا فالتفت ثمّ حمل عليه فاعتنقه ثمّ أخذ بمنطقته فاحتمله فوضعه بين يديه وجاء حتّى إذا دنا منّا كسر عنقه ثمّ أمرّ الصمصامة على عنقه فذبحه ونزع سواريه ومنطقته وألقاه وقال هكذا فاصنعوا بهم فقلنا من يستطيع يا أبا ثور أن[1] يصنع كما تصنع

٦،٧٠ وحكى أبو عبيدة قال لمّا كان فتح القادسيّة أصاب المسلمون أموالاً عظيمة فعزل سعد بن أبي وقّاص الخمس ثمّ قسّم البقيّة فأصاب الفارس ستّة آلاف وبقي مال كثير فكتب إلى عمر بما فعل فكتب إليه أن ردّ على المسلمين بالخمس وأعط

١ سقطت من إ١.

ʿAmr describes how he presented himself to the Prophet (God bless and keep him) in the year 10 [631–32]: I came to Medina when the Prophet (God bless and keep him) had just returned from Tabūk. I wanted to approach the Prophet, but those around him prevented me, until he declared, "Let that man through!" I approached him and said, "May your morning be well! May the king never desire a cursed deed!" The Prophet replied, "ʿAmr, convert to Islam and you will be protected and God will shield you from the Great Horror."[469] I converted. 70.2

ʿAmr lived into the days of the Caliph ʿUthmān, and he acquitted himself bravely in Islam's wars of expansion, fighting in various battles, including Yarmūk and al-Qādisiyyah. At the latter, ʿAmr was the one who slashed the trunk of the Persians' elephant, at which the animal turned tail and all the Persians fled after it—this was the decisive point of victory. 70.3

Al-Khathʿamī says: I never saw so noble a man as the one I beheld at the Battle of Yarmūk: he killed one of the vile Byzantines who had charged against him; when another charged, he killed him too; then, as the whole lot of them fled in retreat, he gave chase, and I followed. When he finally gave up the chase, he retired to one of his black tents, sat down, called for bowls of food, and invited those around him. I asked, "Who is this man?" They told me, "It's ʿAmr ibn Maʿdī Karib." 70.4

Ibn Abī Ḥāzim[470] tells: At the Battle of al-Qādisiyyah, we passed ʿAmr ibn Maʿdī Karib as he was standing between the battle lines, shouting exhortations to the Muslims: "People of Islam! Pour it on! Charge them! Once those non-Arabs throw their javelins, they're nothing more than billy goats!" As he was encouraging us, one of the non-Arabs strode forth and stood between the lines. He shot an arrow at ʿAmr, hitting the solid nock of ʿAmr's bow at his shoulder. ʿAmr whirled around and charged at the man, locking him in hand-to-hand combat. ʿAmr grabbed him by the belt, hoisted him up, held him right before his face, and brought him back toward our lines, where he broke his neck, whipped out his sword, al-Ṣamṣāmah, and slaughtered him, plundering both his bracelets and his belt. He hurled the body away and shouted, "Do it like this!" We called back, "ʿAmr, who else can do it like you?" 70.5

Abū ʿUbaydah tells: After the victory at al-Qādisiyyah, the Muslims took tremendous plunder. Saʿd ibn Abī Waqqāṣ took the commander's share of one-fifth and divided the remainder: each horse warrior received a sum of six thousand,[471] and there was still much left over. Saʿd wrote to the Caliph ʿUmar 70.6

من لحق بك ممّن لم يشهد الوقعة ففعل ذلك ثمّ كتب إليه أن أعط ما بقي حملة القرآن فأتاه عمرو بن معدي كرب فقال ما معك من حفظ القرآن قال إنّي أسلمت ثمّ شغلت بالغزو عن حفظ القرآن وقيل لبشر بن ربيعة ما معك من حفظ القرآن فقال ﴿بِسْمِ ٱللَّهِ ٱلرَّحْمَٰنِ ٱلرَّحِيمِ﴾ فضحك القوم وقال سعد ما لكما في هذا المال نصيب فقال عمرو

إِذَا قُتِلْنَا وَلَا يَبْكِي لَنَا أَحَدُ    قَالَتْ قُرَيْشٌ أَلَا تِلْكَ ٱلْمَقَادِيرُ
نُعْطَى ٱلسَّوِيَّةَ مِنْ طَعْنٍ[1] لَهُ نَفَذٌ    وَلَا سَوِيَّةَ إِذَا تُعْطَى ٱلدَّنَانِيرُ

وقال بشر أبياتًا فكتب سعد إلى عمر بما قالا فكتب إليه أعطهما على بلائهما فأعطاهما أربعة آلاف درهم

٧،٧٠ وحكى المدائنيّ قال كان عمرو بن معدي كرب في سريّة أميرها سلمان بن ربيعة فعرض الخيل فمرّ عمرو على فرس له فقال سلمان هذا هجين فقال عمرو عتيق قال فأمر به فعُطِّش ثمّ دعا بترس فقُلب فيه ماء ودعا بخيل عتاق فشربت فجاء فرس عمرو فثنّى يديه وشرب وهكذا يصنع الهجين فقال له ألا ترى قال عمرو أجل الهجين يعرف الهجين فبلغ عمر فكتب إليه قد بلغني ما قلت لأميرك وبلغني أنّ لك سيفًا تسمّيه الصمصامة وعندي سيف مصمّم بالله إن وضعته على هامتك لا أقلع حتّى أبلغ به شراسيفك فإن سرّك أن تعلم أحقّ ما أقول فعد

٨،٧٠ ورُوي أنّ عمر رضي الله تعالى عنه سأله يومًا فقال ما تقول في الحرب قال مرّة المذاق إذا كشفت عن ساق من صبر عُرف من ضعف تلف قال فما تقول في الرمح

١ بياض في إ.

for instruction, and ʿUmar replied: "Return the commander's fifth to the Muslims, and also make a disbursement to those who joined your ranks only after the battle." Saʿd did as instructed, and then ʿUmar wrote again: "Divide the remainder among those who have memorized Qur'an." When ʿAmr ibn Maʿdī Karib approached to take his share of plunder, Saʿd asked him, "What have you memorized of the Qur'an?" ʿAmr responded, "I've been fighting ever since I converted to Islam, so I haven't had time to memorize the Qur'an." They also summoned Bishr ibn Rabīʿah: "What have you memorized of the Qur'an?" He just recited, «In the Name of God, All and Ever Merciful.»[472] Everyone laughed, and Saʿd decreed, "Neither of you shall have a share in the money." ʿAmr replied in verse:

When we're killed, no one mourns;
the Quraysh say, "Such is fate."
We receive equal shares of the blows,
but there's no equality in the spoils.

Bishr added some poetry of his own, and Saʿd wrote back to ʿUmar, relating their poems. ʿUmar replied: "Give them disbursements based on their performance in battle." Saʿd gave each four thousand silver coins.

Al-Madāʾinī tells: ʿAmr ibn Maʿdī Karib participated in a raid under the 70.7
command of Salmān ibn Rabīʿah. Salmān inspected the cavalry, and ʿAmr rode up on one of his horses. Salmān said, "This horse is a grade." ʿAmr replied, "No, it's purebred!" Salmān took the horse and refrained from watering it for a time. Then he ordered a shield, which he filled with water, and led purebred horses to it. They drank, and then ʿAmr's horse was fetched. When it drank, it turned the tips of its hooves: this is a mark of a grade. When Salmān told ʿAmr, "See now?" ʿAmr responded, "Yes. Evidently, it takes one to know one." The news of this reached the Caliph ʿUmar. He wrote to ʿAmr: "I have been informed of what you said to your commander. I am also informed that you have a sword called al-Ṣamṣāmah. But you should know that I have a sword dedicated to God's path, and if I slice it into your head, it will go right through and cleave your shoulders. If you would like to test the veracity of what I say, then all you need to do is repeat what you said to your commander."[473]

It is narrated that ʿUmar (God be pleased with him) once asked ʿAmr, 70.8
"In your words, what is war?" He answered, "It's bitter to bear when it's laid bare: he who stands firm is cherished; he who shows weakness is perished."

قال خليلك وربّما خانك قال فالنبل قال منايا تخطئ وتصيب قال فالترس قال عليه تدور الدوائر قال فالسيف قال عندك ثكلتك أمّك فقال عمر بل أمّك فقال الحمى أضرعتني[١] لك فأغلط له عمر في الكلام فقال

أَتُوعِدُنِي كَأَنَّكَ ذُو رُعَيْنٍ   بِأَنْعَمِ عِيشَةٍ أَوْ ذُو نُوَاسِ
فَلَا تَفْخَرْ بِمُلْكِكَ كُلُّ مَلْكٍ   يَصِيرُ بِذِلَّةٍ بَعْدَ ٱلشِّمَاسِ

فقال عمر صدقت فاقتصّ منّي قال بل أعفو يا أمير المؤمنين لو لا آية سمعتها منك لجلّلتك السيف أخذ منك أم ترك قال وما هي قال سمعتك تقرأ آية ﴿إِنَّهُۥ مَن يَأْتِ رَبَّهُۥ مُجْرِمًا فَإِنَّ لَهُۥ جَهَنَّمَ لَا يَمُوتُ فِيهَا وَلَا يَحْيَىٰ﴾ والله لو علمت أنّي إذا دخلت متّ لفعلت

٩،٧٠ وقيل إنّه لم يكن في عمرو خصلة رديئة إلّا الكذب وحكى أبو عمرو بن العلاء قال وقف عمرو يومًا بالمربد يتحدّث على عادتهم[٢] فقال أغرت في الجاهليّة على بني مالك فخرجوا مسترعفين بخالد بن الصقعب فحملت عليه بالصمصامة فأخذت رأسه وكان خالد بن الصقعب حاضرًا فقال بعض الجماعة مهلًا أبا ثور فأنّ قتيلك يسمع كلامك وأشار إليه فقال اسكت إنّما أنت محدّث فاسمع أو قم ثمّ التفت إلى خالد فقال إنّما نرهب هذه المعدّيّة[٣] بهذه الأخبار ومضى في حديثه فلم يقطعه فقال رجل إنّك لشجّاع في الحرب والكذب فقال إنّي كذلك

١٠،٧٠ وحكى أبو عمرو بن العلاء قال جاء رجل إلى عمرو وهو واقف بالمربد على فرس له وقد أسنّ فقال لأنظرنّ ما بقي من قوّة أبي ثور فأدخل يده بين ساقه وجنب

١ إ١: صرعتني. ٢ إ١: دينهم. ٣ إ١: العدمي.

'Umar then said, "Describe a spear." Excitement began swelling in 'Amr as he said, "A trusty friend, but he might betray you." 'Umar then said, "And arrows?" 'Amr, more excited, replied, "They fly like those dastardly hands of Fate: they'll sometimes strike, sometimes miss." 'Umar kept on questioning: "And the shield?" 'Amr exclaimed, "Right there, fortune's won and lost!" Then 'Umar asked, "What about the sword?" Now 'Amr roared, "It's right here! May your mother lose her son!" But 'Umar stood his ground: "No. It'll be your mother," and 'Amr cooled down: "Sorry! Overwhelming passions turned me against you!" 'Umar said some harsh words, and 'Amr responded in verse:

> You think you can threaten me, as if you're Dhū Ruʿayn,
> or Dhū Nuwās, enjoying the good life?
> Boast not: your kingship, with its sprightly pomp,
> will be brought low, like all have before.

'Umar conceded: "You speak the truth. Name my penalty." But 'Amr told him, "Not at all. I forgive you, Commander of the Faithful; had it not been for a verse of the Qur'an that I heard from you, I would have let my sword loose on you, whatever the consequences!"[474] 'Umar asked, "What was the verse?" 'Amr said, "I heard you recite: «Indeed, he who comes to his Lord a sinner shall be consigned to Hell; he shall neither die therein nor live.»[475] By God, had I not known that Hell is eternal, I would have struck you down!"

It is said that 'Amr's only bad characteristic was a propensity to fib. Abū 70.9
'Amr ibn al-ʿAlā' tells: 'Amr used to stand at al-Mirbad and tell stories. One time he recounted, "Before Islam, I raided clan Mālik,[476] and they charged with Khālid ibn al-Ṣaqʿab[477] in the fore. I attacked, swinging al-Ṣamṣāmah, and lopped off his head!" Khālid ibn al-Ṣaʿqab happened to be in the audience, and someone interrupted: "Steady now, 'Amr, the man you killed is here listening!" The man pointed to Khālid. 'Amr replied, "Quiet, you! You're in the audience, so either listen or leave." Then 'Amr turned to Khālid and said, "We only tell these stories to scare the men of Maʿadd."[478] 'Amr carried on with his story until a man interjected, "My, you're as brave a liar as you are a fighter!" 'Amr agreed: "Indeed I am!"

Abū 'Amr ibn al-ʿAlā' tells: In 'Amr's old age, he was once sitting astride 70.10
his horse at al-Mirbad when a man approached, saying, "Let's see how much strength old 'Amr has left..." And he thrust his hand between 'Amr's leg and the side of his horse. 'Amr grasped the man's intention and squeezed his leg hard

الفرس ففطن عمرو فضمّ رجله وحرّك الفرس فجعل الرجل يعدو مع الفرس لا يقدر أن ينزع يده حتّى إذا بلغ منه صاح به فقال يا ابن أخي ما لك قال يدي تحت ساقك فخلّى عنه وقال إنّ في عمّك بقيّة بعد

١١،٧٠ ومن كلامه حُكي أنّه أتى مجاشع بن مسعود فقال أسألك حملان مثلي وسلاح مثلي فأمر له بفرس جواد وسيف صارم وعشرين ألف درهم فمرّ ببني حنظلة فقالوا يا أبا ثور كيف رأيت صاحبك فقال لله بنو مجاشع ما أشدّ في الحرب لقاءها وأجزلَ في اللزبات[١] عطاءها وأحسنَ في المكرمات بناءها والله لقد قاتلتها[٢] فما أجبنتها وسألتها فما أبخلتها وهجوتها فما أفحَمتها

١٢،٧٠ ومن جيّد شعره

وَلَمَّا رَأَيْتُ ٱلْخَيْـلَ زُورًا كَأَنَّهَا    جَدَاوِلُ مَاءٍ أَرْسَلَتْ فَٱسْبَطَرَّتِ
وَجَاشَتْ إِلَيَّ ٱلنَّفْسُ أَوَّلَ فِكْرَةٍ    فَرُدَّتْ عَلَى مَكْرُوهِهَا فَٱسْتَقَرَّتِ
ظَـلِلْتُ كَأَنِّي لِلرِّمَـاحِ دَرِيئَـةٌ    أُقَاتِلُ عِنْ أَحْسَابِ جَرْمٍ وَفَرَّتِ
وَلَوْ أَنَّ قَوْمِي أَنْطَقَـتْنِي رِمَـاحُهُـمْ    نَطَقْتُ وَلٰكِنَّ ٱلرِّمَـاحَ أَجَـرَّتِ

١٣،٧٠ وقوله أُقَاتِلُ عِنْ أَحْسَابِ جَرْمٍ من الهجاء الممضّ وذلك أنّه ذكر أنّ قومًا فرّوا وليس هو منهم غير أنّه يقاتل عنهم غضبًا لهم وعصبيّةً وقوله وَلَوْ أَنَّ قَوْمِي أَنْطَقَتْنِي يعني لو قاتلوا وطاعنوا نطقت بمدحهم ولكنّهم فرّوا فأسكتوني[٣] عن المدح والأصل في الإجرار أنّ الفصيل إذا أرادوا فطامه شقّق لسانه فلم يقدر على الرضاع

١٤،٧٠ وقوله في القصيدة التي أوّلها

١ إ١، ل٢: الكربات. ٢ إ١، با١، إ٦: قابلتها. ٣ إ١: فلتكتفي.

against his horse and set off, with the man stuck. Unable to free his hand, the man was forced to sprint madly just to stay on his feet, and he was exhausted in no time. ʿAmr then called down to him, "My brother, what's wrong?" The man pleaded, "My hand's pinned under your leg!" ʿAmr freed him and remarked, "Your old uncle still has something left!"

ʿAmr once approached Mujāshiʿ ibn Masʿūd and said, "I request from you a mount and weapons that suit a man like me." Mujāshiʿ gave him a purebred stallion, a fine-edged sword, and twenty thousand dirhams, and when ʿAmr passed Mujāshiʿ's children, they asked him, "What do you think of your old friend?" ʿAmr responded, "Good are the sons of Mujāshiʿ! They're so resolute when facing war, generous when facing hardship, and good in preserving their good repute! By God, when I fought them, I didn't find them cowardly; when I solicited them, I didn't find them stingy; and when I lampooned them, I didn't silence them!" This is an example of ʿAmr's eloquence. 70.11

ʿAmr's poetry includes the following excellent verses: 70.12

Horse warriors bent in battle contortions,
 Dangling reins swirl like gushing streams;
A flutter of fear rises from deep in my soul,
 then it steadies: I'm ready for all terror.
I battled in the thick, a walking target for spears.
I fought for the Jarms' honor, though they fled.
If my people's spears could incite me to speak, I would,
 but their spears have slit my tongue.

(ʿAmr's line "Fighting for the Jarms' honor" is a searing ridicule, since he was not of their clan, and yet when they fled, ʿAmr still stayed behind fighting on their behalf, such was his zealous partisanship for them. 70.13

By the line "If my people's spears could incite me to speak," ʿAmr intends that had they fought and thrust their spears in battle, he could have praised them, but by fleeing, they made it impossible for him to praise them. "Slit my tongue" derives from a verb expressing how a young camel's tongue is slit to prevent it from suckling.)

An excerpt from ʿAmr's poem that begins: "Is this clarion call from Rayḥānah?": 70.14

أَمِنْ رَيْحَانَةِ ٱلدَّاعِي ٱلسَّمِيعُ
وَقَدْ عَجِبَتْ أُمَامَةُ أَنْ رَأَتْنِي    تَفَرَّعَ لِمَّتِي شَيْبٌ فَظِيعُ
أَشَابَ ٱلرَّأْسَ أَيَّامٌ طِوَالٌ    وَهَمٌّ مَا تَبَلَّغُهُ ٱلضُّلُوعُ
وَزَحْفُ كَتِيبَةٍ لِلِقَاءِ أُخْرَى    كَأَنَّ زُهَاءَهَا رَأْسٌ صَلِيعُ
وَإِسْنَادُ ٱلْأَسِنَّةِ نَحْوَ نَحْرِي    وَهَزُّ ٱلْمَشْرَفِيَّةِ وَٱلْوُقُوعُ
فَإِنْ تَنُبِ ٱلنَّوَائِبُ آلَ عُصْمٍ    تَجِدْ حَكَمَاتِهِمْ فِيهَا رُفُوعُ
إِذَا لَمْ تَسْتَطِعْ شَيْئًا فَدَعْهُ    وَجَاوِزْهُ إِلَى مَا تَسْتَطِيعُ
وَصِلْهُ بِٱلزَّمَاعِ فَكُلُّ شَيْءٍ    سَمَا لَكَ أَوْ سَمَوْتَ لَهُ وُلُوعُ

وقوله ١٥،٧٠

يَأَيُّهَا ٱلْمُعْنَى بِنَا    جَهْلًا بِنَا وَوُلِدْتَ عَبْدَ
لَيْسَ ٱلْجَمَالُ بِمِئْزَرٍ    فَٱعْلَمْ وَإِنْ رُدِّيتَ بُرْدَ
أَنَّ ٱلْجَمَالَ مَعَادِنٌ    وَمَنَاقِبٌ أَوْرَثْنَ مَجْدَ
أَعْدَدْتُ لِلْحَدَثَانِ سَا    بِغَةً وَعَدَّاءً عَلَنْدَى
وَحُسَامُ ذِي شُطَبٍ يَقَ    دُّ ٱلْبَيْضَ وَٱلْأَبْدَانَ قَدَّ
كُلُّ ٱمْرِئٍ يَجْرِي إِلَى    يَوْمِ ٱلْهِيَاجِ بِمَا ٱسْتَعَدَّ
لَمَّا رَأَيْتُ نِسَاءَنَا    يَفْحَصْنَ بِٱلْمَعْزَاءِ شَدَّ
وَبَدَتْ مَحَاسِنُهَا ٱلَّتِي    تَخْفَى وَعَادَ ٱلْأَمْرُ جِدَّ
نَازَلْتُ لَيْثَهُمْ وَلَمْ    أَرَ مِنْ نِزَالِ ٱللُّيُوثِ بُدَّ
كَمْ يَنْذِرُونَ دَمِي وَأَنْ    ذِرُ إِنْ لَقِيتُ بِأَنْ أَشُدَّ

Umāmah is astonished to see
    odious gray atop my locks.
Long days, penetrating worries
    turn hair white,
    as do the crashes of squadrons in war,
    on battle's bald plain.
Thickets of lances looking to stand on my neck,
    and whirling fine blades and blows.
When calamity strikes clan 'Uṣm,
    their bridle rings surmount war's tumult.
If you can't bear it, drop it—
    find something you can:
Apply yourself with all you have—
    One can rise to one's calling.

'Amr's poetry: **70.15**

To you who would insult us—
    ignorantly—you were born a slave!
You wear a handsome mantle, but know:
    the beauty of a man is not in his robes.
    Beauty is what emerges deep in lineage,
    virtues bestowing legacies of glory.
To grapple with the blows of fortune,
I've prepared a mail coat, a prancing charger,
    and a sharp, high-ridged blade
    that cleaves clean through helmets and bones.
Battle gathers men of all sorts—
    each rushes in with what he's prepared.
When I see our women running,
    Leaving tracks in stony ground,
    And their beauty, which they had concealed,
    comes uncovered: then the matter is grave,
    and I duel the enemy's leader—
        I see no other way.
So many swore to spill my blood,
and I swore to meet them grim.

كَمْ مِنْ أَخٍ لِي صَالِحٍ    بَوَّأْتُهُ بِيَدَيَّ لَحْدَا
ذَهَبَ ٱلَّذِينَ أُحِبُّهُمْ    وَبَقِيتُ مِثْلَ ٱلسَّيْفِ فَرْدَا

لو لم يكن له إلّا هذه القصيدة لاستحقّ بها التقدّم على بشر كثير

١٦،٧٠ وأمّا الصمصامة فهو سيفه المشهور قال عبد الملك بن عمير أهدت بلقيس إلى سليمان عليه الصلاة والسلام خمسة أسياف ذا الفقار وذا النون ومخذم والصمصامة والرسوب فأمّا ذو الفقار فكان لرسول الله صلّى الله عليه وسلّم أخذه من منبّه بن الحجّاج يوم بدر ومخذم ورسوب للحارث بن جبلة[1] الغسّانيّ وذو النون والصمصامة لعمرو بن معدي كرب

١٧،٧٠ وحُكي أنّ عمر بن الخطّاب قال لعمرو ابعث لي الصمصامة فبعث به إليه فلم يره كما بلغه فقال له في ذلك فقال إنّي بعثت إليك بالصمصامة ولم أبعث إليك باليد التي تضرب به

١٨،٧٠ وحكى أبو عبيدة أنّ الصمصامة انتقلت إلى سعيد بن العاص[2] وذلك أنّ خالد بن الوليد غزا بني زبيد وكان خالد بن سعيد بن العاص من جملة أمرائه وأوقع بهم وأسر ريحانة أخت عمرو بن معدي كرب ففداها خالد وأثابه عمرو الصمصامة

١٩،٧٠ ثمّ فقد يوم الدار في مقتل عثمان ووجد ولم يزل إلى أن صعد المهديّ البصرة فلمّا كان بواسط أرسل إلى بني العاص يطلب الصمصامة فقالوا إنّه في السبيل محبّسًا فقال خمسون سيفًا قاطعًا في السبيل أغنى من سيف واحد فأعطاهم خمسين سيفًا وأخذه فلمّا صار إلى الهادي أحضره وأمر الشعراء بوصفه فقال بعضهم من أبيات

---

١ إ: بسلة. ٢ إ: العاصي.

Many an honest brother
was lowered to his grave in my hands.
Those whom I loved are gone; I remain:
Alone stands the solitary blade.

(If these lines were all that ʿAmr composed, he would still deservedly rank ahead of many a poet.)

Al-Ṣamṣāmah was ʿAmr's famous sword. ʿAbd al-Malik ibn ʿUmayr says: The Queen of Sheba gifted five swords to Solomon (God bless and keep him): Dhū l-Fiqār, Dhū l-Nūn, Mikhdham, al-Ṣamṣāmah, and al-Rasūb. Dhū l-Fiqār was acquired by the Prophet (God bless and keep him) when he took it from al-ʿĀṣ ibn Munabbih after the Battle of Badr.[479] Mikhdham and Rasūb came into the possession of al-Ḥārith ibn Jabalah of the Ghassān, and ʿAmr ibn Maʿdī Karib owned both Dhū l-Nūn and al-Ṣamṣāmah. 70.16

It is told that the Caliph ʿUmar ibn al-Khaṭṭāb said to ʿAmr: "Send me al-Ṣamṣāmah." ʿAmr delivered it, and ʿUmar didn't consider it as great as its reputation. He mentioned this to ʿAmr, who responded: "What I did was send you al-Ṣamṣāmah; I didn't send you the hand that wields it!" 70.17

Abū ʿUbaydah tells that al-Ṣamṣamah passed into the possession of Saʿīd ibn al-ʿĀṣ as a result of a raid Khālid ibn al-Walīd launched against the Zubayd, ʿAmr ibn Maʿdī Karib's clan. Among the captives taken was Rayḥānah, ʿAmr ibn Maʿdī Karib's sister.[480] Saʿīd's son Khālid ibn Saʿīd was one of the raid's leaders, and he freed Rayḥānah by paying her ransom. In thanks, ʿAmr delivered al-Ṣamṣāmah to him. 70.18

The sword was lost in the aftermath of the Battle at the House, when the Caliph ʿUthmān was killed, but it was rediscovered and remained in the possession of the ʿĀṣ clan until the caliphate of al-Mahdī. The caliph requested the sword from the ʿĀṣ while he was traveling through Wāsiṭ on his way downstream to Basra, and while they initially demurred, saying, "It's held inalienably in trust for the cause of God," al-Mahdī countered, "Fifty finely wrought swords benefit the cause of God more than one." He then sent them fifty swords and took al-Ṣamṣāmah in exchange. 70.19

When the Caliph al-Hādī inherited al-Ṣamṣāmah, he presented it before the court poets and ordered them to describe it. One composition:

حَازَ صَمْصَامَةَ ٱلزُّبَيْدِيِّ عَمْرٍو  مِنْ جَمِيعِ ٱلْأَنَامِ مُوسَى ٱلْأَمِينُ
مَا يُبَالِي مَنِ ٱنْتَضَاهُ لِضَرْبٍ  أَشِمَالٌ سَطَتْ بِهِ أَمْ يَمِينُ

ثمّ وصل إلى المتوكّل فدفعَهُ إلى غلامه باغر التركيّ فقتله به ومن عند باغر انقطع خبره

## ٧١ وحملك الحارث على النعامة

١،٧١ النعامة فرس الحارث بن عباد التغلبيّ أكبر سادات بني وائل وهو الذي اعتزل حرب البسوس فقال لا ناقة لي فيها ولا جمل ولمّا قتل ولده نهض وقال

قَرِّبَا مَرْبِطَ ٱلنَّعَامَةِ مِنِّي  لَقِحَتْ حَرْبُ وَائِلٍ عَنْ حِيَالِ[1]

وقد ذكر فيما تقدّم من حديث حرب البسوس

## ٧٢ ما شككت فيك ولا سترت أباك ولا كنت إلّا ذاك

وهبك ساميتهم في ذروة المجد والحسب وجاريتهم في غاية الظرف والأدب ألست تأوي إلى بيت قعيدته لكاع إذ كلّهم عزب خالي الذراع وأين من أنفرد به[2] ممّن لا أغلب إلّا على الأقلّ الأخسّ منه وكم بين من يعتمدني بالقوّة الظاهرة والشهوة الوافرة والنفس المصروفة إليّ واللذّة الموقوفة عليّ وبين آخر قد نضب غديره ونزحت بئره وذهب نشاطه ولم يبق إلّا ضراطه

هل يجتمع لي فيك إلّا الحشف وسوء الكيلة ويقترن عليّ بك إلّا الغدّة والموت في بيت سلولية

---

١ إ١: لتجت حل. ٢ سقطت من إ١.

No one but the divinely guarded al-Hādī
holds Ṣamṣāmah: blade of ʿAmr of the Zubayd.
When it's unsheathed, its bearer need not care
whether he strikes left or right.

The sword was passed down from caliph to caliph until al-Mutawakkil gave it to one of his Turkic retainers, Bāghir. Later, Bāghir murdered al-Mutawakkil with this very sword. After that, all trace of it was lost.

**. . . al-Ḥārith set you astride Ostrich . . .** 71

Ostrich was the name of a horse owned by al-Ḥārith ibn ʿUbād of the Taghlib, one of the chief leaders of the Wāʾil tribe. He initially had refrained from entering the Basūs War, saying, "I have no camel, male or female, in this affair,"[481] but when his son was killed, he rose and declared, 71.1

Untether Ostrich and bring him to me!
After long abstinence, Wāʾils, war has given birth.

The Basūs War is related above.[482]

**. . . you'd still be nothing more than what you are, and with no shadow of a doubt I'd recognize you and your vile lineage!** 72

**Even if we pretend that you could compete with the others for the pinnacle of glory and merit, and keep pace with them to the zenith of witty elegance and cultured excellence, don't you nonetheless scurry home to a low-class woman, whereas all the gallants are bachelors and completely free? How can one who offers me but a paltry portion of his time compare to one whom I can enjoy at ample leisure? How great is the difference between someone who can devote his full force and abundant desire for my pleasure alone and another whose pool is dried, whose well is desiccated, whose energy is sapped, and who has nothing left but farts! All you offer me is a brace of bad choices—as they say: "poor-quality dates sold with faulty weights," or the combination of "pestilential goiters and death in a Salūlī woman's tent."**

تَعَالَى ٱللهُ يَا سَلْمَ بْنَ عَمْرٍو    أَذَلَّ ٱلْحِرْصُ أَعْنَاقَ ٱلرِّجَالِ

**ما كان أخلفك بأن تقدر بذرعك وتربع على ظلعك ولا تكوننّ براقش الدالّة على أهلها**

هذا مثل يُضرب لمن يعمل عملاً يرجع ضرره عليه وفيه أقوال ١،٧٢

فقيل براقش امرأة كانت لبعض الملوك فسافر الملك واستخلفها وكان لهم ٢،٧٢
موضع إذا فزعوا دخّنوا فيه فإذا أبصره الجند اجتمعوا وإنّ جواريها عبثن ليلة فدخّنّ فجاء الجند فلمّا اجتمعوا قال لها نصحاؤها إن رددتِهم ولم تستعمليهم في شيء ودخّنت مرّة أخرى لم يحضروا فأمرتهم فبنوا بناء دون دارها فلمّا جاء الملك سأل عن البناء فحدّثوه بالقصّة فقال على قومها تجني براقش

وقيل وهو الأكثر إنّ براقش اسم كلبة نبحت جيشًا قصدوا الغارة على قوم ٣،٧٢
فخفي عليهم مكانهم فلمّا نبحت الكلبة عرفوهم فاجتاحوهم فقال العرب على أهلها تجني براقش

**وعنز السوء المستثيرة لحتفها فلا[1] أراك إلّا سقط بك العشاء بك على سرحان** ٧٣

هو سرحان بن قعنب اليربوعيّ كان فاتكًا وحمى واديًا فورد عوفُ الأسديّ فقال ١،٧٣
أشهد لا يمنعني سرحان رعي إبلي الليلةَ فرعاها فمرّ به سرحانُ بن قعنب فقتله فقال أخوه يخاطب زوجة الأسدِيّ

١ سائر النسخ: فما

**God is sublime, O Salm ibn ʿAmr!**
**It's desire that humiliates mankind.**

**You would be better off testing your grip before you go grasping, and knowing your limits before you start climbing. Otherwise, you will end like Barāqish, who divulged her own campsite . . .**

"You will end like Barāqish . . ." is a proverb describing someone whose act brings harm upon him or herself. There are several stories about its origin. 72.1

It is said that Barāqish was a queen whose king left her in charge of his kingdom when he went on a journey. In times of grave emergency, this kingdom would light a smoke signal to muster all soldiers of the realm, and one night, while the king was still away, the queen's handmaidens in their idle play accidentally lit the signal fire. All the soldiers mobilized, and when they marshaled together, one of the queen's advisors told her, "If you send them back without putting them to work, they won't come next time you send the smoke signal." So the queen commanded the soldiers to construct a building just outside her palace. When the king returned, he asked about the building, and she told him the story. He said, "Barāqish's offence was against her own people!" 72.2

Most, however, report that Barāqish was the name of a female dog that barked at an invading army. That army had been trying to locate the camp, which they intended to raid, but without success until the dog's barking revealed the spot, and they then stormed in. The Arabs say: "Barāqish's offence was against her own people." 72.3

**. . . or like the ill-starred goat that prompted her own demise. To me, you seem like the one who went out to pasture in the evening and met Sirḥān . . .** 73

Sirḥān ibn Qaʿnab of the Yarbūʿ[483] was a bellicose warrior who proclaimed a certain wadi his own enclave. One day, ʿAwf of the Asad approached it and declared, "I swear that Sirḥān will not prevent me from pasturing my camels here this night!" and he herded them to pasture, but Sirḥān found him and killed him. Sirḥān's brother composed a poem to ʿAwf's wife: 73.1

أَبْلِغْ صُبَيْحَةَ أَنَّ رَاعِي أَهْلِهَا  سَقَطَ ٱلْعَشَاءُ بِهِ عَلَى سِرْحَانِ
سَقَطَ ٱلْعَشَاءُ بِهِ عَلَى مُتَقَمِّرٍ  لَمْ يَثْنِهِ صَرْفٌ[1] مِنَ ٱلْحِدْثَانِ

المتقمّر السّاري في القمر

٢،٧٣ وقد قيل إنّ أصل هذا المثل أنّ دابّة خرجت تطلب عشاء فوجدها ذئب فأكلها وقيل رجل أعشى العين وقع على ذئب فأكله وعلى هذا يكون العشا مقصورًا[2]

٧٤ **وبك لا بظبي أعفر**

١،٧٤ مثل يُضرب للشماتة بالرجل يقول نزل به المكروه ولا نزل بظبي يريد أنّ عنايتي بالظبي أشدّ من[3] عنايتي به والأعفر الذي لونه لون التراب وهو العفر وكذلك غزلان السهل وكأنّه خصّ الظبي بالداء لأنّ العثار والكسر سريعان إليه وقيل متى أصابه داء مات سريعًا

٢،٧٤ والمثل للفرزدق منظومٌ من أبيات تتعلّق بها حكاية وذلك أنّ الفرزدق كان قد هجا بني نهشل بأبيات منها

لَعَمْرِي لَئِنْ قَلَّ ٱلنُّهَى فِي عَدِيدِكُمْ  بَنِي نَهْشَلٍ مَا لُومُكُمْ بِقَلِيلِ

ثمّ خرج سادات بني تميم وفيهم الحتات بن مجاشع عمّ الفرزدق إلى معاوية فوصلهم ونقص حتاتًا فعاتبه فقال معاوية إنّي اشتريت من القوم دينهم ووفّرت

---

١ إ١: ضرب؛ إ٣ وق٢ وت١: خوف. ٢ :وقد قيل . . . مقصورا: زيادة من با١، ل١، ل٢، بر٢، ر٢، غ، إ٦.
٣ زيادة من إ٣.

Someone tell Ṣubayḥah that her people's drover
searched for evening pasture, but found Sirḥān.
By dinner, he was delivered to a moonlight hunter
Whose calamities cannot be evaded.

(The phrase "moonlight hunter," *mutaqammir*, in the verse above literally means "one who travels in the moonlight.")[484]

It has also been said that the expression was coined on account of an animal that went out to pasture in the evening and was eaten by a wolf. Alternatively, it is said that a night-blind man was once devoured after stumbling upon a wolf in the dark; if this story is correct, then the phrase "evening pasture" (*ʿashāʾ*) in the proverb should be read instead as "night blind" (*ʿashā*). 73.2

**... too bad for you, but at least the dust-colored gazelle is fine!** 74

By juxtaposing the relief felt at knowing a gazelle escaped injury with the indifference at knowing that a man was hurt, this adage is proverbial for expressing satisfaction at another's misfortune. 74.1

The word "dust-colored" (*aʿfar*) describes a gazelle whose hide is the color of the dust that lies on the surface of the ground (*ʿafar*); the desert gazelle is like this. The statement implies that gazelles are especially prone to afflictions; they easily stumble and break their bones. They also say that a gazelle is quick to succumb if it becomes diseased.

The adage was coined by al-Farazdaq in a poem he composed at the end of a long-standing feud. The story begins when al-Farazdaq satirized the Nahshal clan: 74.2

Nahshal, by my life, your wise men are few,
but you have surplus disgrace.

The Nahshal made no immediate response. A little later, a group of nobles from the Tamīm, including al-Ḥutāt ibn Mujāshiʿ (al-Farazdaq's uncle),[485] presented themselves to the Caliph Muʿāwiyah, and he gave them gifts, but gave fewer to al-Ḥutāt. When al-Ḥutāt complained to Muʿāwiyah, the caliph told him, "I rewarded the others more because they forsook their religion for me, but I didn't have to buy your faith, so I saved a little."[486] Al-Ḥutāt replied, "You can buy my faith too!" and Muʿāwiyah increased his gift to the same as the

عليك دينكم قال فاشترِ منّي ديني أيضًا فألحقه بهم في الصلة فأقام يتنجّزها فطُعن فمات فرجع معاوية فيما أعطاه فقال الفرزدق وهو بالبصرة

أَبُوكَ وَعَمِّي يَا مُعْوِيَ أَوْرَثَا ... تُرَاثًا فَأَوْلَى بِٱلتُّرَاثِ أَقَارِبُهْ
فَمَا بَالُ مِيرَاثِ ٱلْحُتَاتِ أَكَلْتَهُ ... وَمِيرَاثُ حَرْبٍ جَامِدٌ لَكَ ذَائِبُهْ
فَكَمْ مِنْ أَبٍ لِي مُعْوِيَ لَمْ يَكُنْ ... أَبُوكَ ٱلَّذِي مِنْ عَبْدِ شَمْسٍ يُقَارِبُهْ

٣،٧٤ فوجد النهشليّون سبيلاً فسعوا به إلى زياد وقالوا هجا أمير المؤمنين فقال زياد لعريف بني تميم أحضر قومك والفرزدق فيهم ليأخذوا عطاءهم فأحسّ الفرزدق بالشرّ فهرب وما زال يطوف حتّى أتى المدينة عائذًا بسعيد بن العاص فقال في قصيدة

تَرَى ٱلْغُرَّ ٱلْجَحَاجِحَ مِنْ قُرَيْشٍ ... إِذَا مَا ٱلْأَمْرُ فِي ٱلْحِدْثَانِ عَالَا
قِيَامًا يَنْظُرُونَ إِلَى سَعِيدٍ ... كَأَنَّهُمُ يَرَوْنَ بِهِ هِلَالَا

٤،٧٤ فأمّنه سعيد وبلغ زيادًا فقال لا والله لا أرضى عنه حتّى ينتسب في بني فقيم ثمّ قال مروان لم ترض أن نكون قعودًا[١] ننظر إلى سعيد حتّى جعلتنا قيامًا قال إنّك منهم يا أبا عبد الملك لصافن فحقدها عليه مروان فلمّا عزل سعيد وتولّى مروان المدينة أحضر الفرزدق فقال أنت القائل

هُمَا دَلَّتَانِي مِنْ ثَمَانِينَ قَامَةً ... كَمَا ٱنْقَضَّ بَازٍ أَقْتَمُ ٱلرِّيشِ كَاسِرُهْ
فَقُلْتُ ٱرْفَعُوا ٱلْأَسْتَارَ لَا يَشْعُرَنْ بِنَا ... وَأَقْبَلْتُ فِي أَعْجَازِ لَيْلٍ أُبَادِرُهْ

١ سقطت من إ.

rest, but al-Ḥutāt was fatally stabbed while he stayed behind to wait for the payment to be fulfilled. Muʿāwiyah took back the money, and this prompted al-Farazdaq, who was in Basra at that time, to chide Muʿāwiyah:

Muʿāwiyah! Your father and my uncle both
left a legacy: a legacy for us to protect.
What enabled you to confiscate al-Ḥutāt's bequest,
while you squandered all good your father left you?
Muʿāwiyah! Consider how many forefathers I have,
with whom your old man can hardly compare.

Now the Nahshal sensed their opportunity for revenge on al-Farazdaq, 74.3
and they vilified him before Ziyād, Muʿāwiyah's governor over Basra, saying, "Al-Farazdaq lampooned the Commander of the Faithful!"

To contrive a way to apprehend al-Farazdaq, Ziyād sent and order to the Tamīm's headman, "Muster your people to receive their stipends." Al-Farazdaq was among those entitled to a stipend, but he sensed a plot was afoot, and fled. After wandering for a time, al-Farazdaq settled in Medina, seeking the protection of the governor Saʿīd ibn al-ʿĀṣ, whom he praised:

Behold! When adversities mount,
the eminent lords of the Quraysh
stand looking to Saʿīd
as if in him they see the new moon.

Saʿīd gave al-Farazdaq sanctuary,[487] and when Ziyād heard the news, he 74.4
said, "No by God, I'll only be pleased with him when he becomes affiliated with the Fuqaym!"[488] A local Umayyad nobleman, Marwān, upbraided al-Farazdaq: "You weren't content with us peaceably accepting Saʿīd: you won't stop until you make us rise up!" Al-Farazdaq told him, "When the Quraysh nobles stand up, Marwān, you're just limp."[489] For this, Marwān harbored ill feeling toward al-Farazdaq, and when Marwān became governor of Medina after Saʿīd was dismissed, Marwān summoned al-Farazdaq and asked him, "Are you the composer of the following verses?

They caught my eye from an eighty-yard height,
and I swooped down like a dark-winged hawk at prey.
I said, 'Remove the curtains, no one's around!'
And my late-night adventures began!"

فقال نعم قال أتقول هذا بين أزواج رسول الله صلّى الله عليه وسلّم اخرج عن المدينة

٥،٧٤ فاستجار بعبد الله بن جعفر ثمّ مات زياد فبلغ الفرزدق أنّ مسكينًا الدارميّ رثاه فقال ولم يكن هجا زيادًا حتّى مات خوفًا منه[١]

أَمِسْكِينُ أَبْكَى ٱللّٰهُ عَيْنَكَ إِنَّمَا جَرَى دَمْعُهَا فِي بَاطِلٍ فَتَحَدَّرَ
بَكَيْتَ ٱمْرَأً مِنْ أَهْلِ مَيْسَانَ كَافِرًا كَكِسْرَى عَلَى غِلْمَانِهِ وَكَقَيْصَرَ
أَقُولُ بِهِ لَمَّا أَتَانِي نَعِيُّهُ بِهِ لَا بِظَبْيٍ بِٱلصَّرِيمَةِ أَعْفَرَ

٧٥ أعذرت إن اغنيت شيئًا وأسمعت لو ناديت حيًا

١،٧٥ يعني بلغت العذر في نصحك إن قبلت منّي وتركت التعرّض إلىّ وأسمعتك إن كنت حيًّا تسمع بهذا وهذا نصف بيت من شعر عمر بن معدي كرب ويُروى لدريد بن الصمّة وقد تقدّم ذكرهما وهو

لَقَدْ أَسْمَعْتَ لَوْ نَادَيْتَ حَيًّا وَلٰكِنْ لَا حَيَاةَ لِمَنْ تُنَادِي
وَلَوْ نَارًا نَفَخْتَ بِهَا أَضَاءَتْ وَلٰكِنْ أَنْتَ تَنْفُخُ فِي رِمَادِ

٢،٧٥ وبعض المتعصّبين على أبي العلاء المعرّيّ يزعم أنّه خرج ليلة إلى بعض مراقب موسى عليه السلام ورفع رأسه إلى السماء وقال كلّمني فأنا أفصح من موسى قال ذلك مرارًا ثمّ أنشد البيتين وذكر أنّهما من شعره والحكاية باطلة من وجوه

---

١ حتّى . . . منه: زيادة من إ٣.

Al-Farazdaq confessed: "Yes," and Marwān replied, "How dare you sing such profligate poetry in the presence of the wives of the Prophet (God bless and keep him)! Leave Medina at once!"

Al-Farazdaq next sought the protection of ʿAbd Allāh ibn Jaʿfar. Eventually, Ziyād died, and when al-Farazdaq heard that Miskīn of the Dārim had composed an elegy for Ziyād, al-Farazdaq lampooned both Miskīn and Ziyād (out of fear of Ziyād, al-Farazdaq had refrained from lampooning him as long as he was alive): 74.5

Miskīn! God brought tears to your eyes,
  and they gushed, but what a futile cause!
You grieve for a non-Arab,[490] a nonbeliever—
Like Khosrow or Caesar weeping over his boys.
When I heard Ziyād was dead, I said:
  Bad for him, but at least the herd's dust-colored gazelle is fine!

**I have done my best to excuse you: if my words have fallen on sentient ears, this should be enough . . .** 75

Ibn Zaydūn means: "I have done everything that can be expected in giving you advice, and if you accept it from me, you will cease seeking my favor. I have communicated this to you so clearly that you could only be excused for not hearing it if you were dead." The expression derives from the first half of a verse by ʿAmr ibn Maʿdī Karib; it is also attributed to Durayd ibn al-Ṣimmah (both are mentioned above):[491] 75.1

You've told them, if your words fall on sentient ears,
  but there's no life among those you called.
If you had blown on live embers, they'd have ignited,
  but you were puffing on ash.

A zealous antagonist against Abū l-ʿAlāʾ al-Maʿarrī alleges that those verses were instead composed by al-Maʿarrī on the night when he set out to one of the lookouts where Moses (eternal peace be his) had once been. Al-Maʿarrī looked up to the heavens, crying, "Speak to me! I am more eloquent than Moses!"[492] He repeated this several times before singing the above lines of poetry. But the story is baseless on several grounds. 75.2

٧٦ إِنَّ ٱلْعَصَا قُرِعَتْ لِذِي ٱلْحِلْمِ     وَٱلشَّيْءُ تَحْقِرُهُ وَقَدْ يَنْمِي

١،٧٦ قرعت له العصا مثل يُضرب لمن ينصح وينبّه على ما هو أصلح والسورة وثوب يستعمل للعصيان[1] ومنه أخذ سَورَة الشراب

٢،٧٦ وقوله إِنَّ الْعَصَا قُرِعَتْ والشَّيْءُ تَحْقِرُهُ مثلان في التحذير منظومان في قول الحارث بن وعلة اليشكريّ وقد قتل بعض سادات قومه أخاه[2] فقال من أبيات حسنة في معناها

أَقَتَلْتَ سَادَتَنَا بِلَا تِرَةٍ     إِلَّا لِتُوهِنَ قُوَّةَ ٱلْعَظْمِ
وَوَطِئْتَنَا وَطْئًا عَلَى حَنَقٍ     وَطْءَ ٱلْمُقَيَّدِ نَابِتَ[3] ٱلْهَرْمِ
وَزَعَمْتَ فِي أَنْ لَا حُلُومَ لَنَا     إِنَّ ٱلْعَصَا قُرِعَتْ لِذِي ٱلْحِلْمِ
لَا تَأْمَنَنَّ قَوْمًا ظَلَمْتَهُمُ     وَبَدَأْتَهُمْ بِٱلشَّرِّ وَٱلْغَشْمِ
أَنْ يَأْبِرُوا نَخْلًا لِغَيْرِهِمُ     وَٱلشَّيْءِ تَحْقِرُهُ وَقَدْ يَنْمِي
ٱلْآنَ لِمَا ٱبْيَضَّ مَسْرُبَتِي     وَعَضَضْتُ مِنْ نَابِي عَلَى جِذْمِ
تَرْجُو ٱلْأَعَادِي أَنْ أُصَالِحَهَا     جَهْلًا تَوَهَّمَ صَاحِبُ ٱلْكَلْمِ
قَوْمِي هُمُ قَتَلُوا أُمَيْمَ أَخِي     فَإِذَا رَمَيْتُ يُصِيبُنِي سَهْمِي
فَلَئِنْ عَفَوْتُ لَأَعْفُوَنْ جَلَلًا     وَلَئِنْ أَصِبْتُ لَأُوهِنَنْ عَظْمِي

٣،٧٦ واختُلف فيمن قرعت له العصا وضُرب به المثل فقيل هو عامر بن الظرب بن عباد اليشكريّ أحد حكّام العرب المشهورين وفيه يقول ذو الإصبع

وَمِنَّا حَكَمٌ يَقْضِي     فَلَا يُدْفَعُ مَا يَقْضِي

١ إ١، إ٣: للغضبان. ٢ سقطت من إ١. ٣ إ١: المعيد نائب.

**A reasoned man understands the staff's knocking;** 76
**A trifle can generate a tumult.**

"The staff's knocking" is an expression describing those who take good advice when it's given. 76.1

(The word *sawrah* describes an angry assault, and from this derives its meaning as the forceful strength of alcoholic drinks.)[493]

The expressions "the staff's knocking" and "a trifling matter" are proverbial for a warning; they were adroitly put into verse by al-Ḥārith ibn Waʿlah of the Yashkur[494] after one of the leaders of his clan killed his brother: 76.2

You killed our nobles, not for blood revenge,
but just to sap our strength!
You trampled upon us in fury,
like a hobbled camel crushes shrubs underfoot.
You allege we lack sense,
but it's the sensible who understand the staff's knocking.
Don't rest feeling safe from those whom you wronged—
those against whom you started the malice
will pollinate a palm for another to reap,
and then what you now think trifling shall sprout.
Since my chest hair has grown white,
and I bite on stumps of teeth,
enemies hope I will make peace.
Foolish! The wound's inflictor is deluded—
Umaymah! My own people killed my brother.
In taking revenge, I would be shooting myself.
To forgive is to overlook an atrocity,
yet to avenge harms my own kin.

There are conflicting opinions about the identity of the first person for whom "the staff knocked," and the origin of the expression. Some say it was ʿĀmir ibn al-Ẓarib ibn ʿAbbād of the Yashkur,[495] one of the celebrated Arab arbiters, whom Dhū l-Iṣbaʿ described: 76.3

Ours is the arbiter who makes rulings—
rulings that none contend.

وهو أوّل من قضى في الخنثى وذلك أنّه اختصم إليه في رجل له ما للمرأة وما للرجل أيُجعل رجلاً أو امرأة فقال لهم انصرفوا عنّي حتّى أنظر في أمري فما نزل بي مثلها فانصرفوا وبات ليلته ساهرًا وكانت له جارية ترعى يقال لها سخيلة وكان يقول لها إذا سرحت غنمه بكرة صبّحت يا سخيل فإذا راحت يقول مسّيت يا سخيل لأنّها كانت تؤخّر حتّى تُسبق فلم يقل لها شيئًا ورأت سهره وفكره فقالت له ما اعتراك فقال دعيني من شأنك فأعادت عليه فقال ويلك إنّه اختصم إليّ في خنثى له ما للذكر وما للمرأة في ميراثه أجعله امرأة أم رجلاً فقالت لا أبا لك أقعده فإن بال من حيث يبول الرجل فهو رجل فقال لها مسّي سخيل بعدها أو صبّحي فذهبت مثلاً ثمّ خرج فقضى بالذي أشارت ٤،٧٦

قال السهيليّ وهو حكم معمول في الشرع من باب الاستدلال والعلامات وله مثل في الشريعة قول الله تبارك وتعالى ﴿وَجَآءُو عَلَىٰ قَمِيصِهِۦ بِدَمٍ كَذِبٍ﴾ وجه الدلالة على الكذب أنّ القميص لم يكن فيه خرق ولا أثر ٥،٧٦

ثمّ إنّ عامرًا كبر وضعف حتّى قال ٦،٧٦

أَرَى شَعَرَاتٍ عَلَى حَاجِبِـ  ـيَّ بِيضًا تَبِينَ[1] جَمِيعًا تُؤَامَا
أَظَلُّ أُهَاهِي بِهِـنَّ ٱلْكِلَا  بَ أَحْسِبُهُنَّ صِوَارًا قِيَامَا

فقال له الثاني من ولده – وقيل ابنته إنّك ربّما أخطأت في الحكم فيحمل فقال فاجعلوا لي أمارة أتنبّه بها حتّى أعرف الصواب فكان يجلس قدّام بيته[2] ويجلس

١ إ١: يثبن. ٢ إ١: فقام في بيته.

ʿĀmir ibn al-Ẓarib was the first to make a ruling about hermaphrodites. 76.4
Asked to opine on whether a person with both male and female organs should receive a man's or woman's share of inheritance, he was initially flummoxed: "Leave me a while to deliberate, for this case is unprecedented." ʿĀmir lay awake into the night, unable to sleep. One of his slave girls, Sukhaylah, who shepherded for him, noticed he was sleepless. ʿĀmir was in the habit of nagging this servant girl, since she was constantly late taking out her flocks to pasture, and the other shepherds with their flocks always beat her to the watering hole; so whenever she took the goats out in the morning, he would sarcastically remark, "Morning, Sukhaylah," and when she took them out in the evening, he would say, "Evening, Sukhaylah," and he never said anything else to her. On the night of ʿĀmir's sleepless deliberation, Sukhaylah asked him, "What's come over you?" He said, "Mind your own business!" But she was insistent, and he told her, "Damn your questions! It's the case of a hermaphrodite who has been brought before me—one with both male and female organs: do they inherit a man or a woman's share?" She replied, "Figure it out! Just get them to squat down, and if they pee the way a man pees, then they're a man!" ʿĀmir was well pleased: "Sukhaylah, from now on, go out in the morning and evening whenever you please!" This became proverbial, and on the next day ʿĀmir gave judgment as Sukhaylah instructed him.

Al-Suhaylī defines this form of judgment as an inference from signs: an oper- 76.5
ative method of making judgment according to the Shariah.[496] For example, the Exalted God says in the Qur'anic story of Joseph: "And they showed Jacob their brother's coat, stained with false blood";[497] their falsehood can be inferred since Joseph's coat was neither ripped nor showed traces of an attack.

When ʿĀmir grew old and weak, he composed: 76.6

I see white hairs drooping from my eyebrows;
everything appears double now.
Here I am calling to a pack of dogs,
thinking they're a herd of cows.

ʿĀmir's second-oldest son (others say his daughter) told him, "You might now start making bad judgments, and there will be liability." ʿĀmir replied, "Then devise a sign for me so I will know if I'm on the right track." He used to hold court in front of his tent, so his son sat inside with a staff, and he

ابنه في البيت ومعه عصًا فإذا هفا قرع جفنة فيتنبّه ويرجع إلى الصواب فضُرب به المثل وهو أوّل من فعل ذلك

٧،٧٦ وقيل هو في شخص في زمن النعمان بن المنذر حذّر أخاه وذلك أنّ النعمان أرسل شخصًا يرتاد الكلأ فأبطأ فغضب وعزم على أن يسأله إذا ورد فأن قال خصبًا قتله وإن قال جدبًا قتله وعرف بذلك أخوه فقال للنعمان أتأذن لي أن أنذره قال لا قال فأشير إليه قال لا قال فأقرع له عصًا قال اقرع فلمّا ورد الرجل أخذ أخوه عصًا من بعض جلسائه وقرع بها عصاه التي كانت معه قرعًا مختلفًا إلى أن فهّم أخاه القصّة فقال بم أحمد خصبًا أو بم أذمّم جدبًا الأرض مشكلة لا بقلها يُعرف ولا جدبها يوصف رائدها واقف ومنكرها عارف فقال النعمان أولى لك بذلك نجوت فنجا وقال أخوه

قَرَعْتُ ٱلْعَصَا حَتَّى تَبَيَّنَ صَاحِبِي وَلَمْ تَكُ لَوْ لَا ذَاكَ لِلْقَوْمِ تُقْرَعُ

٨،٧٦ وقيل المراد بقرع العصا قصّة قصير لمّا كان مع جذيمة وأقبلت عساكر الزباء قال له إنّي متى أنكرت الأمر قرعت لك العصا وهي فرس جذيمة التي لا تُلحق[1] فاركبها وانج فلمّا رأى الشرّ قرعها بالسوط فأنف جذيمة من الهرب فركبها قصير ونجا عليها وضُرب بتلك المثل يعنون لو كان لجذيمة حلم لركبها

٩،٧٦ والقول الأوّل أشهر وأحسن

[1] وقرعت لك . . . تلحق: زيادة من إ٣.

would tap it on a bowl whenever ʿĀmir was making a mistake. ʿĀmir thus knew to correct himself, and this was the origin of the proverb; ʿĀmir was the first to do this.

Others say that the expression traces its origin to the way in which a 76.7
man once communicated a warning to his brother in the presence of King al-Nuʿmān ibn al-Mundhir.[498] The story goes that al-Nuʿmān had sent a man to scout for pasture, and the scout stayed away so long that al-Nuʿmān grew angry and vowed to execute the scout if he returned and reported the pasture to be either "fertile" or "barren." The scout's brother learned of this and asked al-Nuʿmān, "Will you permit me to warn him?" Al-Nuʿmān refused: "No!" The brother then asked, "Can I signal to him?" "No." The brother then proposed: "Can I knock with a staff?" Al-Nuʿmān agreed: "Knock away!" Eventually the scout did return, and his brother took hold of a staff from one of the retainers and knocked it to various beats against his own staff, until he made his brother understand the matter.[499] Then the scout described the pasture to al-Nuʿmān: "How could I praise the land's fertility, or how could I disparage its barrenness? The land was diverse: unknown plants and indescribable aridity. The one who scouts it stands still; the one who knows nothing about it knows." Al-Nuʿmān responded, "You're running a dangerous course. But you escaped."

He was safe, and his brother composed a poem:

> I knocked the staff until it was clear to my fellow;
> if it wasn't for that, it wouldn't have been struck for the people.

It is also said that the expression "the staff's knocking" intends the story 76.8
of Qaṣīr, who had been with King Jadhīmah on his ill-fated journey to wed Zenobia.[500] When Zenobia's squadrons were approaching, Qaṣīr told Jadhīmah, "If I sense misgivings about what we're about to get into, I will hit Staff for you: then ride her and save yourself!" ("Staff" was the name of one of Jadhīmah's horses, which could outrun anything.) When Qaṣīr saw that things were about to get ugly, he beat Staff with a whip, but Jadhīmah was too haughty to flee, so Qaṣīr mounted her himself and escaped. This was the origin of the expression: in other words, if Jadhīmah had had any sense, he would have ridden the horse.

The story about ʿĀmir[501] is the best and most well-known explanation of the 76.9
proverb "The staff's knocking."

**وإن بادرت بالندامة ورجعت على نفسك بالملامة كنت قد اشتريت العافية لك بالعافية منك** ٧٧

يعني إن ندمت على ما أقدمت عليه وتركته ولمت نفسك أرحت نفسك بانقطاعك عنّا وأرحتنا منك ١،٧٧

**وإن قلت جعجعة بلا طحن وربّ صلف تحت الراعدة** ٧٨

مثلان يُضربان لمن يتوعّد ولا يفعل والجعجعة صوت الرحى[١] وطحن الدقيق فعل بمعنى مفعول[٢] كذبح فرق[٣] والصلف قلّة النزل والخير ولذلك يقال أصلف من ملح في ماء أي لا يبقى وسحاب صلف إذا كان قليل الماء كثير الرعد والمعنى أنّك متى قلت إنّي أتوعّد ولا أفعل فستُرى ١،٧٨

**وأنشدت[٤]** ٧٩

لَا يُؤْيِسَنَّكَ مِنْ مُخَدَّرَةٍ    قَوْلٌ تُغَلِّظُهُ وَإِنْ جَرَحَا

هذا البيت لبشّار بن برد وقد ذكر بشّار وحدّث أبو الشمقمق قال دخلت عليه يومًا وبين يديه مائة دينار فقال خذ منها أتدري ما قصّتها قلت لا قال أنا اليوم جالس وإذا بفتى من ذوي النعمة دخل عليّ فقال يا أبا معاذ هذه مائة دينار نذرت أن أدفعها لك فتسلّمها فقلت ما سببها قال كنت قد هويت امرأة وتعرّضت لها فغضبت عليّ فأردت السلوّ فذكرت قولك ١،٧٩

١ وجعجعة . . . الرحى: زيادة من إ٣. ٢ الدقيق . . . مفعول: زيادة من إ٣. ٣ إ١: وفرَق. ٤ سقطت من إ١.

**If you now hurry to contrition and focus upon yourself stern admonition, you will secure relief for yourself by relieving me of yourself.** 77

Ibn Zaydūn means: If you now regret what you had ventured, never repeat it, and chide yourself for having done it, you will have achieved a good turn for yourself by staying away from us, and it will relieve us from your presence too. 77.1

**But, if you consider my words merely the grinding of a millstone without any grains, or thunderous clouds that yield no rains . . .** 78

These are a pair of proverbs describing someone whose threats are hollow. 78.1

The word "grinding" (*jaʿjaʿah*) literally means the sound of the millstone; the word "grains" (*ṭiḥn*) literally means "ground flour"—it is an example of a word on the pattern *fiʿl* being a passive participle, like the words *dhibḥ* (sacrifice) and *firq* (part or division). The word "thunderous clouds" (*ṣalaf*) means a thing that generates little or little good; a related word appears in the expression: "More useless (*aṣlaf*) than salt in water," since salt dissolves in water. A cloud described as *ṣalaf* carries much thunder, little rain.

The intention of these phrases is to explain that if you think all the threats above will not be followed by any action, then you shall see!

**. . . if you recite to yourself the verse:** 79

> **Never let harsh words of a privileged girl—**
> **even if they hurt—discourage your hopes!**

This is a verse by the aforementioned poet Bashshār ibn Burd.[502] Abū Shamaqmaq recounts: Once, I visited Bashshār and saw him sitting with one hundred dinars before him. He told me, "Take some; do you know their story?" I told him, "No," and he explained, "When I was sitting here today, a young man of means suddenly came in and said, 'Bashshār! Take these hundred dinars. I made a vow to give them to you!' I asked him, 'What for?' He told me, 'I was passionately in love with a woman, but when I presented myself to her she rebuffed me. I needed to console myself, and I remembered your poem: 79.1

لَا يُؤْيِسَـنَّكَ مِنْ مُخَـدَّرَةٍ　　قَوْلٌ تُغَـلِّظُـهُ وَإِنْ جَرَحَـا
عُسْرُ ٱلنِّسَاءِ إِلَى مُيَاسَـرَةٍ　　وَٱلصَّعْبُ يُمْكِنُ بَعْدَ جَمَحَا

فصبرت فأدركت مطلوبي ومقصودي منها وأليت أن أحمل إليك هذا القدر[١]

٨٠ **فعدت لما نهيت عنه وراجعت ما استعفيت منه بعثت من يزعجك إلى الخضراء دفعًا ويستحثّك نحوها وكزًا وصفعًا**

١٫٨٠ يعني إن لم تبال بتوعّدي ولم تصدّقه فعاودت المراسلة بعثت من يزعجك من مكانك والإزعاج عدم الاستقرار ومنه المرأة المزعاج التي لا تستقرّ في مكان والخضراء ناحية المزدرع من البلد أو اسم مكان والوكز مثل الدفع وهو ضرب الظهر مع الدفع بمجتمع اليد على الذقن

٨١ **فإذا صرت إليها[٢] عبث أكّاروها بك وتسلّط نواطيرها عليك**

١٫٨١ الأكّارون الزرّاعون كأنّه جمع آكر مأخوذ من الأكرة وهي الحفيرة في الأرض والعبث أن يخلط بعمله لعبًا مأخوذ من العبيثة وهو طعام مخلوط والسلاطة التمكّن من القهر ومنه يسمّى السلطان

---

١ بَعْدَ جَمَحَا: غير واضحة في إ١.　٢ سقطت من إ١.

Never let harsh words of a privileged girl—
even if they hurt—discourage your hopes!
Difficulties with women turn to ease.
The restive horse can eventually be ridden.

I was patient, and eventually I got what I wanted. Then I swore that I would bring you this sum.'"

**And if, thenceforth, you revert to your illicit ways and resume the behavior for which, for now, you have been pardoned, I shall dispatch a man who will harry, spur, and slap you into the countryside . . .** 80

These statements mean: If you pay no heed to my threats, and don't believe their sincerity, and if you try again to communicate with me, I will dispatch someone who will harass you into leaving. 80.1

The word for "harry" (*izʿāj*) expresses a complete lack of repose; a related word is *mizʿāj*, an adjective describing a woman who never settles in any place. The word for "countryside" (*khaḍrāʾ*) here either means any agricultural area of a given region or is the name of a specific place. The word "spur" (*wakz*) means to grab someone by the beard and, at the same time, hit them in the back to push them on.

**. . . where you will be abused and lorded over by the sharecroppers and farmhands.** 81

The word "sharecroppers" (*akkārūn*) means farmers. It is a plural derived from *ākir*, which derives from *akrah*, a ditch dug in the ground. The original meaning of the word "abuse" (*ʿabath*) means to mix work and play; it derives from the noun *ʿabīthah*, which is a food of mixed ingredients. The words "lord over" (*salāṭah*) mean coercive power; the title "sultan" derives from this. 81.1

**فمن قرعة معوجّة تقوّم في قفاك ومن فجلة منتنة يُرمى بها تحت خصاك** ٨٢

أي تُضرب في الفقا بالقرع المعوجّ إلى أن يستقيم وهو ممّن لا يستقيم فيكون كناية عن اتّصال الضرب والرمي بالفجل تحت الخصى كناية عن استدخاله وفي نتنه مناسبة والاستقذار للمفعول ١،٨٢

**ذلك بما قدّمت يداك[١] لتذوق وبال أمرك وترى ميزان قدرك** ٨٣

يعني بما فعلت أنت والعرب تقول هذا بما كسبت يداك وإن لم تكن اليد الفاعلة وإنّما يقصدون بذلك فعله وعلى ذلك حمل قوله تعالى ﴿لِمَا خَلَقْتُ بِيَدَىَّ﴾ على بعض الوجوه ١،٨٣

والذوق وجود الطعم بالفم نقل إلى اختيار الشيء ويُستعمل في القليل والكثير ولذلك ذكره الله تبارك وتعالى في العذاب والوبال الأمر الثقيل الذي يُخاف ضرره ومنه طعام وبيل وكلأ وبيل والوبل وهو المطر الثقيل والميزان سعته مقدار الشيء وأصله موزان فانقلبت الواو ياء للكسرة ما قبلها ٢،٨٣

١ سقطت من إ١.

**A crooked staff will be straightened on the back of your neck and a stinking black radish will be rammed up your anus . . .** 82

Since it is impossible to straighten a crooked staff, the expression here is a metaphor for "continuous beating" of the staff on the back his neck. The statement about the "radish . . . rammed up your anus" is intoned in so many words—the literal words of the letter state "the radish will be placed under your testicles." The reference to the radish as "stinking" has assonance with the filthiness of the intended act. 82.1

**. . . you will have brought all of this upon yourself, to experience the dire consequences of your actions and to behold the true extent of your worthlessness . . .** 83

The statements mean that you will have brought all this upon yourself. The Arabs say: "This is what your hands earned," even if the act wasn't actually done manually. It is their metaphor for any action, and in several respects the Exalted God uses this figure of speech in the Qur'anic verse: «what I created with My own Hands.»[503] 83.1

"Taste" means the experience of food in the mouth; its meaning was expanded to connote the "selection of something," and it can be used for all contexts, great and small: hence, God uses it in the Qur'an to describe His torment of unbelievers.[504] The word "dire consequences" (*wibāl*) means weighty matters, of potentially fearful consequence. One can use a related word, "heavy" (*wabīl*), as an adjective for "heavy food" or "thick fodder" or "heavy rain." The word for "extent" (*mizān*) means the measure of any thing; its original form is written *miwzān*, but in such cases, the *w* becomes a long *ī* because of the preceding short *i* vowel. 83.2

فَمَنْ جَهِلَتْ نَفْسُهُ قَدْرَهُ    رَأَى غَيْرُهُ مِنْهُ مَا لَا يَرَى ٨٤

هذا البيت من شعر المتنبّي خُتمت بذكره الرسالة لمناسبة ما قبله وكذلك ١،٨٤
مذاهب أكثر البلغاء في مقاطع رسائلهم إمّا بآية أو مثل أو بيت من الشعر يتمثّلون به في معنى ما هم فيه فتكون له مزيّة ظاهرة ويجب أن يكون من أحسن ما سُمع من الشعر

وفي القصيدة التي منها هذا البيت أبيات حسنة ذكرها جريًا على العادة في ٢،٨٤
الاستطراد بما ينطوي على نكتة وفائدة منها قوله وقد خرج هاربًا من كافور الإخشيديّ من مصر إلى العراق يصف طريقَهُ

فَيَا لَكَ لَيْلًا عَلَى أَعْكُشٍ    أَحَمَّ ٱلْبِلَادِ خَفِيَّ ٱلصُّوَى
وَرَدْنَا ٱلرُّهَيْمَةَ فِي جَوْزِهِ    وَبَاقِيهِ أَكْثَرُ مِمَّا مَضَى

أَعْكُشٍ موضع والأحمّ السوادُ وٱلصُّوَى العلامات في الطرق وهي أحجار تُوضع بعضها على بعض ليُعرف بها الطريق وفي الحديث إنّ للإسلام صوًى ومنارًا وٱلرُّهَيْمَةَ موضع وجَوْزِهِ عائد على الليل يعني نصفه اعترض قوم على هذا اللفظ فقالوا إذا كان باقي الليل أكثر ممّا مضى لا يكون نصفه فقيل في الجواب وجهان أحدهما أنّه إنّما أراد النصف مدّة الثلث الأوسط والثاني أنّ الضمير في جوزه عائد على أعكش والرهيمة ماء في وسط وروده باقي اليل أكثر ممّا مضى

لَتَعْلَمُ مِصْرُ وَمَنْ بِٱلْعِرَاقِ    وَمَنْ بِٱلْعَوَاصِمِ أَنِّي ٱلْفَتَى

يعني في مِصْرُ من فارقهم ومَنْ بِٱلْعِرَاقِ من هو قادم عليهم ومَنْ بِٱلْعَوَاصِمِ سيف الدولة

**What one fails to know about oneself** 84
**is plain for all others to see.**

This is a verse from one of al-Mutanabbī's poems. It constitutes the *Letter*'s envoi, for it encapsulates all the foregoing; it is the style of accomplished writers to close their letters with either a Qur'anic verse, a proverb, or a verse of poetry epitomizing the letter's theme. An appropriate envoi, a mark of the writer's excellence, should be selected from the best of poetry. 84.1

The verse is from a poem that has other fine verses, and, following the method of literary excursus, we relate them here alongside elucidation of their delightful and useful points. 84.2

Al-Mutanabbī composed the poem after he left Egypt for Iraq, fleeing from Egypt's ruler Kāfūr al-Ikhshīdī. Al-Mutanabbī describes his route:

At Aʿkush, a great darkness enveloped the night,
cloaking the land, obscuring the waymarks.
We reached al-Ruhaynah in the midst of the dark,
yet there was much more night to come.

Aʿkush is a place; the word "great darkness" (*aḥamm*) means blackness, and the "waymarks" (*ṣuwā*) are piles of stones erected along the path to show travelers the way. The word *ṣuwā* also appears in a hadith: "Islam's path is clear with marker stones and beacons."[505] Al-Ruhaynah is another place. "Midst of the dark" (*jawz*) literally means "the midpoint of the night," and this has prompted debate among some commentators, who say that al-Mutanabbī erred in using the word *jawz* since it means "half"; yet he then says there was "more night to come." There are two responses: (a) by "half" al-Mutanabbī meant the second third of the night, or (b) the reference to "half" actually refers to the distance from Aʿkush, since al-Ruhaynah is a watering hole within the region of Aʿkush, and the distance he yet needed to cover that night was greater.[506]

The poem continues:

Those in Egypt and Iraq, and from Aleppo to Hama,
will all learn that I am the real hero.

He means the people of Egypt (whom he has left) and those in Iraq (with whom he will live); the "Aleppo to Hama" (*al-ʿAwāṣim*) reference specifies his former patron, Sayf al-Dawlah.

وَمَنْ يَكُ قَلْبٌ كَقَلْبِي لَهُ يَشُقُّ إِلَى ٱلعِزِّ قَلْبَ ٱلتَّوَى
وَنَامَ ٱلْخُوَيْدِمُ عَنْ لَيْلِنَا وَقَدْ نَامَ قَبْلُ عَمًى لَا كَرَى
وَقَدْ كُنْتُ أَحْسِبُ قَبْلَ ٱلْخَصِيِّ أَنَّ ٱلرُّؤُوسَ مَحَلُّ ٱلنُّهَى
فَلَمَّا نَظَرْتُ إِلَى عَقْلِهِ وَجَدْتُ ٱلنُّهَى كُلَّهَا فِي ٱلْخُصَى
وَقَدْ ضَلَّ قَوْمٌ بِأَصْنَامِهِمْ فَأَمَّا بِزِقِّ رِيَاحٍ فَلَا

يعني أنّ من أطاع كافورًا قد ضلّ بطاعة شيء أسود مملوء هواء ولم يضلّ أحد بذلك

وَمَنْ جَهِلَتْ نَفْسُهُ قَدْرَهُ رَأَى غَيْرُهُ مِنْهُ مَا لَا يَرَى

يعني من جهل قدر نفسه عرفه غيره بارتكاب القبائح التي لا ينتبه لها

ومن نوادر المنقّبين على سرقات المتنبّي قول أحدهم إنّه سرق هذا البيتَ من حكاية وهو أنّ قصّارًا كان يعمل على شاطئ نهر وكان كلّ يوم يرى كركيًّا فيلتقط من الحمأة دودًا ويقتصر في القوت عليه فرأى الكركيّ صقرًا قد ارتفع في الجوّ وانقضّ على حمامة فاصطادها وأكلها فقال الكركيّ ما لي لا أصطاد الطيور كما يصطاد الصقر وأنا أكبر منه جسمًا فارتفع في الجوّ وانقضّ على حمامة فأخطأ وسقط في الحمأة فتلطّخ رأسه وريشه ولا يمكنه أن يطير فأخذه الصيّاد ورجع إلى منزله فاستقبله رجل فقال ما هذا فقال كركيّ تصقّر وسمع المتنبّي هده الحكاية فأخذ منها معنى هذا البيت وهذا من نادر التعصّب على هذا الرجل المحسود ٣،٨٤

Who has a heart as mine, one that pierces
the heart of perdition to attain glory?
We slipped away by night as the little eunuch[507] lay asleep;
he was always so: if not slumbering, then blind and inattentive.
Before meeting that eunuch,
I had thought a man's sense resides in the head,
But when I looked for his intellect,
I found it had been in his castrated balls.
Idol worship has deluded some,
but to be misguided by a windbag is absurd.

Al-Mutanabbī means that any who obey Kāfūr are misguided in their fealty to a puffed-up black; no one should be so led astray.

What one fails to know about oneself
is plain for all to see.

Al-Mutanabbī means that while one may be ignorant of one's own worth, others can gauge it by observing the reprehensible acts committed out of one's ignorance.

There are those who probe al-Mutanabbī's poetry, seeking to find precedents from which he took inspiration, and a droll example relates to this verse. Someone says that al-Mutanabbī took the verse from the story of a butcher who used to work on the banks of a river. Every day, the butcher would see a crane wading through the mire in search of worms, the sole source of its food. One day, the crane saw a falcon soaring high in the sky, then swooping down upon a dove, killing and eating it. The crane said to itself, "Why haven't I been hunting birds like that falcon? After all, I'm bigger than it!" The crane flew up and then swooped down to take a dove, but it missed and crashed into the mud. With its head and feathers totally mired in the mud, it couldn't fly, and a hunter snatched it. As the hunter took the crane home, he met a man who asked him, "What's this?" The hunter replied, "A crane that thought it was a falcon." 84.3

Al-Mutanabbī allegedly heard this story and incorporated its theme in this verse. Such claims of plagiarism are examples of the extreme bigotry leveled against this most envied poet!

تمّت الرسالة وشرحها والدلالة ولمحها ولا أدّعي غير انتخاب الأخبار واختيار المتمكّن من النظام والنثار فإنّي أتيت ببيوت الأشعار من أبوابها وميّزت أبكار الفقر من أترابها وعلى الجملة ففي عواطف من عرضت عليه هذه النبذة ما يسدّ خللي ويشدّ أملي ويكثّر قليلي ويرعي كلّ وقت رحلتي الشماليّة بقبولي عطّر الله بذكره المشارق والمغارب وزيّن سماء المدح من مناقبه بزينة الكواكب ولا أخلى أبواب نعمه وعلمه على كلا الحالين من طالب آمين ١،٨٥

والحمد لله وحده وصلّى الله على من لا نبيّ بعده محمّد وآله وصحبه وعترته الطاهرين والحمد لله ربّ العالمين ٢،٨٥

## خاتمة الكتاب

﴿رَبِّ أَوْزِعْنِيٓ أَنْ أَشْكُرَ نِعْمَتَكَ ٱلَّتِيٓ أَنْعَمْتَ عَلَيَّ وَعَلَىٰ وَٰلِدَيَّ وَأَنْ أَعْمَلَ صَٰلِحًا تَرْضَىٰهُ﴾ ﴿وَأَصْلِحْ لِى فِى ذُرِّيَّتِىٓ إِنِّى تُبْتُ إِلَيْكَ وَإِنِّى مِنَ ٱلْمُسْلِمِينَ﴾ ١،٨٦

كَمُلَ ٱلْكِتَابُ تَكَامَلَتْ　　أَيْدِي ٱلسُّرُورِ لِصَاحِبِهِ
وَعَفَا ٱلْإِلٰهُ بِفَضْلِهْ　　وَبِجُودِهِ عَلَى كَاتِبِهِ

في الرابع والعشرين من شهر رمضان المعظّم قدره وحرمته سنة ٩٧٣ ثلاث وسبعين وتسعمائة – أحسن الله تعالى عاقبته في خير وعافي آمين

ليعلم الناظر في هذا الكتاب أنّه جليل في الإيداع والإبداع ولو لم يكن من جلالته إلّا أنّ مداده مشوب بماء زمزم لكفى ذلك فينبغي لكلّ مسلم أن يبجّله ويجعله في مكان طاهر ويجنّبه جميع ما يستقذر كرامة وإجلالاً للنبيّ صلّى الله عليه وسلّم لأنّ ماء زمزم طُهّر به قلبه صلّى الله عليه وسلّم ولو كان ثمّ ماء أطهر من ٢،٨٦

And so ends the *Letter*, and with it my overview, commentary, and explication. All I have done is select the stories narrated herein and quote choice examples of poetry and prose. To this aim, I alighted upon the apposite verses and sifted out unique passages. And in the end, the kind feelings of the one to whom I presented this short tract[508] suffice to mend my flaws, resuscitate my hopes, augment my paucity, and provide for me on this northern sojourn of mine by his acceptance of me. May God waft the sweet perfume of the sultan's renown across east and west; may God adorn the heavens of praise of the sultan's merits with glittering stars; may God not bar any gateway to His bounty and keep no knowledge from the sultan's pursuit. 85.1

Praise be to God, Him alone. Blessings upon the Prophet Muḥammad, after whom there shall be no other prophet. Bless his kin, companions, and pure progeny. Praise to God, Lord of the Worlds. 85.2

[Colophon]

«My Lord! Reveal to me the ways to be grateful for Your favors that You have bestowed upon me and upon both my parents, and to do good deeds that will please You.»[509] «Grant me righteousness in my offspring. Truly, I have turned to You, and truly, I submit to You.»[510] 86.1

The book was completed—
May happiness's hand bring complete grace to its author,
and may God in His virtue and bounty
forgive its copyist—[511]

Completed on the twenty-fourth of the great and sanctified month of Ramadan in the year 973 [14 March 1566]. May God bring this matter to its conclusion in goodness and salubriousness, Amen!

To the reader of this volume: Know that this is a splendid book both in its cache of knowledge and its wondrous style, and know also that this copy was written in ink mixed with the water of the Zamzam Well. Were its ink this book's only splendor, that would make it splendid enough. It is thus incumbent upon every Muslim, for the sake of the Prophet's honor (God bless and keep him), to revere this book and place it in a purified location kept safe from anything that might sully its nobility. This is because Zamzam was the source of the water that purified the Prophet's heart (God bless and keep 86.2

ماء زمزم لطُهّر به قلبه صلّى الله عليه وسلّم وكان قصدي أن يُكتب بذلك المداد مصحف مكرّم ولكنّ الخيرة فيما يختار الله عزّ وجلّ فمن أجلّ هذا الكتاب إجلالاً للنبيّ صلّى الله عليه وسلّم أجلّه الله ومن أهانه لعنه الله

وأدام الله تعالى مولانا السلطان الأعظم والخاقان المكرّم سيّد ملوك العرب ٣،٨٦
والعجم مولانا السلطان المالك الملك المظفّر سليمان بن عثمان قرن الله النجح بآماله وأيّامه الزاهرة ونصره ونصر عساكره وجمع له بين خيري الدنيا والآخرة وكبت أعداءه وأعداء المسلمين أمين والحمد لله ربّ العالمين وصلّى على سيّدنا محمّد وآله وصحبه وعترته الطاهرين وسلّم تسليمًا كثيرًا إلى يوم الدين أمين

فإن يجد أحد في خطّه خطّأ فليبدل السيّء المكروه بالحسن ٤،٨٦

him),[512] and God surely must have chosen the purest of all waters to purify him (God bless and keep him). It was my intention to use this ink to make a copy of the Holy Qur'an, but Almighty God is the one who chooses. May God honor those who honor this book in reverence of the Prophet (God bless and keep him), and may God curse those who treat it with disdain.

God grant long life to our Overlord the Great Sultan, the Noble Khan, the 86.3
Master of all kings, our Lord and Ruler, the Possessor, the King, the Victorious, Suleiman the Ottoman.[513] May God conjoin his expectations, his radiant days, his victory, and the victory of his armies with success. May God combine for him the goodness of this World and the Next. May God bring low his foes and the foes of all the Muslims. Amen! Praise be to God, Lord of the Worlds; blessings upon our leader Muḥammad, his kin, his companions, and his pure progeny; peace, much peace, continuous peace until the End of Days. Amen!

Should anyone find an error in this copy, may he replace the hateful blemish 86.4
with what is good.

# Appendix: Alexander Stories and Further Explanations

*On Alexander's childhood. Manuscript I1 does not contain this story, though it appears in the Long version manuscripts and in the margins of Short version MS Br1.*

Some say Alexander's father was named al-Ṣaʿb, but it is better attested as Philip. A story reports that Alexander's father was a weaver who, when he died, left the orphaned boy with his mother, Helen, among the Yemeni Ḥimyar. His mother heard about the "House of Trades," which the Greeks had constructed in Constantinople. Every trade was illustrated within it, and the Greeks would bring their sons to the displays, and whichever trade took a child's fancy would become his path in life. Helen brought Alexander, and when he looked over the pictures, he put his hand on the king's crown. She scolded him, but he did it again and again. The custodian took notice and asked, "Are you Helen?" "Yes." "And is this your son?" "He is." "Great tidings!" the custodian told Alexander. "You will be a great king and will trail your robe over the lands!"

This story, however, is baseless: Ḥimyar is far from the Greek lands, and Constantinople did not exist in Alexander's lifetime, since it was founded after the ascension of Jesus (peace be upon him), and the Greek kingdom had collapsed by the time of Jesus's birth.

*On Alexander's campaign in China. This is also absent in MS I1, but it does appear in a number of Short version manuscripts, such as I5, I6, and R2, and in the margins of Q1.*

One night, when Alexander was holding court, his chamberlain entered and announced: "An emissary of the king of the Chinese is at the door."

The man was given permission to enter, and Alexander said to him, "State your business."

He replied, "This matter can only be discussed in private."

Alexander ordered the man searched, and as no weapon was found on him, Alexander dismissed his retainers and remained alone with the man. He said again, "State your business."

The man said, "I am the king of China."

Alexander asked him triumphantly, "Now that you're in my grasp, who's to protect you?"

The Chinese king replied, "There is neither enmity nor blood feud between us, and I have been informed that you are a wise, reasoned man. You will know, therefore, that you will gain nothing from my death. They will appoint a new king in my stead, and you will be left with a reputation for perfidy. So, tell me what it is you want from me."

Alexander said, "A deferred payment of three years' profits of your kingdom, with half in advance."

"That is too onerous."

They negotiated until they agreed on one-sixth of the taxation yields. The king of China then rose in haste and left.

Alexander spent the night contemplating what had transpired. Dawn broke to reveal a great army, wide as the eye could see, composed of many nations and led by the king of China, who was wearing a crown and advancing upon Alexander's camp. Alexander mounted his horse, readied his battle lines, and called out, "King! Is this not perfidy?" The king of China emerged from between his ranks and said, "Not at all. I only wanted to make you see that I did not submit to you out of weakness or deficiency. Those whom you behold here are but a minority of my total forces. But I sensed that cosmic forces are behind you and have empowered you over those who had stronger and bigger armies. Anyone who challenges such forces is bound to be defeated." The king of China then dismounted and kissed the ground before Alexander, who also descended, and they sat together. Alexander said, "Tribute ought not be exacted from a man such as you: I relieve you of all obligation." The king replied, "If that is your wish, then we must recompense you properly," and he ordered that Alexander be given a sum twice as great as what had been agreed as tribute.

*Long version manuscripts explain all the insults directed against Ibn ʿAbdūs in the Letter, however short, whereas the Short version manuscripts tend only to explain the insults associated with historical figures. There are some exceptions, and Manuscript L2 contains two explanations that are absent in I1.*

A In reference to the statement in the *Letter* "honest about the camel's age" (§54).

"Honest about the camel's age" is a proverb for sincere honesty. It originates from a story of two men haggling over a camel. The buyer asked, "What's its age?" When the seller told him it was a young camel, the buyer looked at its teeth, which revealed that the camel was indeed young.

B In reference to the statement in the *Letter* "put the tar on the camel's scabs" (§54).

This is a proverb describing one who puts matters in order. Its origin is that there is a special kind of tar, *hināʾ*, which one smears on places where there are signs that a camel will develop scabs.

# Notes

1 Ibn Nubātah's expanded commentary (*Sarḥ al-ʿuyūn* (1964), 35) notes that different copies of the letter describe the messenger woman as either *khalīlah* or *ḥalīlah* (literally "lover" and "wife," respectively). Ibn Nubātah considers them of the same effect, and since the letter subsequently reveals that the addressee, Ibn ʿAbdūs, is married, the translation uses *ḥalīlah* expressly here.

2 This long diatribe renders Wallādah's impression about how the messenger described Ibn ʿAbdūs's merits. The verb that opens this section is variably written in the manuscripts; see the Note on the Text.

3 The expressions *ḍaraba wa-qassama wa-ʿaddala wa-qawwama* are obscure, and the first verb is rendered *ṣarafa* in some manuscripts (especially the longer version of *Sarḥ al-ʿuyūn*: MSS C2, R). Ibn Nubātah concedes to not understanding their precise intention (*Sarḥ al-ʿuyūn* (1964), 274); they concern fiscal matters, being a combination of the minting and valuing of coins, and/or the determination of contractual obligations in Islamic law.

4 The elements in this and the previous sentence reflect aspects of Arabic grammar. Most Arabic nouns and verbs are declinable—that is, they exhibit different final vowels depending on their function in the sentence—but some words do not change their final vowels, and are known as *mabnī* in Arabic, translated here as "indeclinable." The Arabic letter *hamzah* is a glottal stop between two vowels, but it has two forms. In some cases, the glottal stop is articulated as a full break in a word's pronunciation (*hamzat al-qaṭʿ*); in others, it is written but not pronounced as a glottal stop (*hamzat al-waṣl*). The *Letter* suggests facetiously that Ibn ʿAbdūs proclaimed the rules as to when either form applies. The expression "dual" and "plural" refers to the fact that Arabic nouns have, in addition to singular and plural forms, a dual form when two are counted. The dual and plural are formed by adding suffixes to the singular form of the noun, or, in the case of the plural, by manipulating the singular form.

5 The half line is part of a poem ascribed to Ghāwī ibn Ẓālim al-Sulamī; see Ibn Nubātah, *Sarḥ al-ʿuyūn* (1964 edition), 337–38. The Short version manuscripts of *The Genius of Invective* do not comment on all aspects of Ibn Zaydūn's *Frivolous Letter*. Instances where explanation of these additional aspects are given in the Long version recension of the text are noted via reference to the 1964 printed edition.

6 The verse was composed by Abū Tammām; see Ibn Nubātah, *Sarḥ al-ʿuyūn* (1964 edition), 338.

7 These aphorisms do not intend a cover-up of flaws; rather, they were used to refer to correctly directed action (Ibn Nubātah, *Sarḥ al-ʿuyūn* (1964 edition), 364).

8 The verse was composed by Abū Tammām; see Ibn Nubātah, *Sarḥ al-ʿuyūn* (1964 edition), 377.

9 The verse was composed by ʿUmar ibn Abī Rabīʿah; see Ibn Nubātah, *Sarḥ al-ʿuyūn* (1964 edition), 385.

10 The expression is a legal pronouncement from the hadith which declares that a feral animal (*ʿajmāʾ*) can be killed without giving rise to a claim for blood compensation (unlike an animal owned by an individual); its citation here expresses that the addressee, Ibn ʿAbdūs, is deemed a beast, of no concern to anyone.

11 The verse was composed by al-Farazdaq; see Ibn Nubātah, *Sarḥ al-ʿuyūn* (1964 edition), 389.

12 The verse was composed by al-Aʿshā ibn Qays; see Ibn Nubātah, *Sarḥ al-ʿuyūn* (1964 edition), 413.

13 Literally, the text reads that Ibn ʿAbdūs was deceived by the affection Wallādah intended for another man—that is, Ibn Zaydūn himself. We have interpreted this to mean that Ibn ʿAbdūs saw her gracious favors to her true lover, and he then presumed that they would be on offer to him too.

14 This verse is ascribed to the poet al-ʿArandas; see Ibn Nubātah, *Sarḥ al-ʿuyūn* (1964 edition), 423.

15 The expression used here refers to *maysar*, a pre-Islamic form of gambling in which players would throw gaming arrows as lots. According to the expression, counterfeit arrows elicited a different noise when thrown, and the expression was used to chide those who aspired to membership with a group to which they did not rightfully belong (Ibn Nubātah, *Sarḥ al-ʿuyūn* (1964), 423).

16 The name "ʿAmr" in Arabic is written with a final letter *wāw*, though it is unpronounced. The poet Abū Nuwās (d. ca. 200/815) appears to be the first to have alighted upon this concept as a witty metaphor for a useless appendage (see Ibn Nubātah, *Sarḥ al-ʿuyūn* (1964), 424).

17 The Arabic reads *washīẓah fī l-ʿaẓam*, literally "appendage on their bone." This expression appears to be a mistake perpetuated by Arabic philologists and their devotees, such as Ibn Zaydūn. The early dictionaries that defined the term in this way (Khalīl ibn Aḥmad, *al-ʿAyn*, 6:279; al-Jawharī, *al-Ṣiḥāḥ*, 3:1181; and the Andalusian Ibn Sīdah, *al-Muḥkam wa-l-muḥīṭ al-aʿẓam*, 8:115) were critiqued by the lexicographer al-Zabīdī, who considers it correctly "a piece of wood inserted to repair a bowl" (*Tāj al-ʿarūs*, 10:498). Ibn

Zaydūn does insist upon "bone," and we preserve his translation. The intended meaning that Ibn ʿAbdūs is a marginal hanger-on in courtly society is nonetheless clear.

18 The verse is based on lines in a poem by al-Ḥārith ibn Waʿlah al-Yashkurī; see Ibn Nubātah, *Sarḥ al-ʿuyūn* (1964 edition), 467.

19 The verse was composed by Bashshār ibn Burd; see Ibn Nubātah, *Sarḥ al-ʿuyūn* (1964 edition), 471.

20 The verse was composed by al-Mutanabbī; see Ibn Nubātah, *Sarḥ al-ʿuyūn* (1964 edition), 474.

21 The words *al-malik al-muʾayyad* (the king of divine succor), which I1's copyist omitted (though they appear in most other MSS), reveal that the ruler is Abū l-Fidāʾ, a distinguished scholar, military leader, and ruler of Hama (r. 710–32/1310–31). Although governorship of Hama was the extent of his political authority, he was, unusually, allowed the title "sultan."

22 The first Jahwarid ruler in Cordoba, Abū l-Ḥazm Jahwar ibn Muḥammad ibn Jahwar (r. 422–35/1031–43), imprisoned Ibn Zaydūn for a period between 432 and 435/1040 and 1043 (Ibn Bassām, *al-Dhakhīrah*, 1:261). Ibn Nubātah's shortening of the ruler's name to "Ibn Jahwar" ("son of Jawhar") is confusing since "Ibn Jahwar" usually refers to the second Jahwarid ruler, Abū l-Walīd Muḥammad (r. 435–50/1043–58). However, the family descended from a line of prominent viziers, including Jahwar ibn ʿUbayd Allāh (see Ibn al-Abbār, *al-Ḥullah al-siyarāʾ*, 1:245–51); hence, any lineal descendant could be known as "Ibn Jahwar."

23 Ibn Nūbatah implies that Ibn Zaydūn fled directly to Seville, but Ibn Zaydūn was actually released and resumed his station in Cordoba. Several years later, under the cloud of new intrigue, he fled to the rival ʿAbbād kingdom in Seville. The impression that Ibn Zaydūn fled straight from prison to Seville seems to have become a legend over the centuries; see the same account in Ibn Diḥyah, *al-Muṭrib*, 168.

24 The Arabic suffices with the name Abū l-Ḥazm; it intends Jahwar ibn Muḥammad, founder of the Jahwarid dynasty.

25 The Andalusian litterateur al-Fatḥ ibn Khāqān (d. ca. 529/1134) suggests Ibn Zaydūn composed these verses about his relationship with Wallādah (the protagonist of the *Letter*; see §4.1), reimagined in an Arabian guise of Bedouin romantic encounter (Ibn Khāqān, *Qalāʾid al-ʿUqyān*, 78).

26 All manuscripts of *Sarḥ al-ʿuyūn* read ʿAbd al-Raḥmān ibn al-Ḥakam, but "the Emigré" and founder of the Andalusian Umayyad dynasty was ʿAbd al-Raḥmān ibn Muʿāwiyah. Ibn Nubātah correctly names him in §48.7.

27 Manuscript L1 contains a unique note reporting that Ibn Nubātah considers the verses to have been composed by someone other than Wallādah.

28 Each manuscript and the sources of Wallādah's biography (Ibn Bassām, *al-Dhakhīrah*, 1:333; al-Maqqarī, *Nafḥ al-ṭīb min ghuṣn al-Andalus al-raṭīb*, 4:205) render the line thus; however, the Cairo printed editions are more explicit: "I permit my lover to kiss my lips" (e.g., (1862), 7; (1963), 23).

29 Abu Nuwās composed the poem to praise al-Khaṣīb ibn ʿAbd al-Ḥamīd, a governor of Egypt (*Dīwān*, 1:256–57); the Arabic name "Khaṣīb" carries strong overtones of fecundity and munificence.

30 The Qur'an devotes a whole chapter to Joseph (Q 12, Sūrat Yūsuf). The story is so well known in Arabic literature that Ibn Nubātah suffices with abbreviated commentary.

31 Ibn Ḥanbal, *Musnad*, 9:523, 14:121 (5712, 8391); al-Bukhārī, *Ṣaḥīḥ*, *Aḥādīth al-Anbiyā'*, 19 (3390). In the collections, the hadith opens without the demonstrative *dhāka*, which appears in all *Sarḥ al-ʿuyūn* manuscripts.

32 Q Yūsuf 12:31. The verse is only quoted in part here; the story is elaborated in Q Yūsuf 12:30–31, relating that women ridiculed Potiphar's wife for her infatuation with Joseph, so she invited them to her assembly and gave them knives (to cut fruit). While they were thus engaged, she had Joseph brought in, whereupon the women, distracted by his beauty, inadvertently cut their hands.

33 Q Ḥijr 15:51–72 and Dhāriyāt 51:24–37 identify Abraham's guest as an angel.

34 Q Ṣāffāt 37:65.

35 The manuscripts variously approximate the names of Korah's ancestors from Exodus 6:21. Exodus 6:18–20 and Numbers 16:1 detail Korah's relation to Moses.

36 Q Qaṣaṣ 28:76 (translated literally here to reveal the rhetorical device under discussion).

37 Logically, one shows a reservoir to livestock, but grammarians report that some old Arabic expressions reverse the order as a stylistic device (Darwīsh, *Iʿrāb al-Qur'ān wa-bayānuh*, 5:653–54).

38 Q Anʿām 6:59.

39 This view has a philological support in Ibn Sīdah, *al-Muḥkam*, 9:185.

40 Most manuscripts write "Marārī," but "Murādī" in MSS I1, I6, Q1, and B is likely correct (al-ʿAẓm, *al-Mustadrak ʿalā ansāb al-ashrāf*, 25:22). Al-Iṣbahānī, *al-Aghānī*, 17:318, identifies them as al-Juʿayd al-Murādī.

41 The extant version of al-Balādhurī's *Ansāb al-ashrāf* reports the story without reference to Hawdhah and al-Naṭif's raid (1996 edition, 11:253–54). Ibn al-Athīr features Hawdhah only after the raid, sheltering the caravan's survivors and engaging in reprisals against the Tamīm (Ibn al-Athīr, *al-Kāmil fī l-Tārīkh*, 1:468; see also al-Iṣbahānī, *al-Aghānī*, 17:318–19).

42 Few sources mention al-Naṭif, but the particular raid on the Persian caravans and the subsequent war are widely cited.

43 Arabic genealogies identify Qaḥṭān as the ancestor of Yemenis and other "Southern Arabs." Ibn Nubātah's comments reflect convoluted genealogical arguments from early Islamic times, which strove to incorporate Persian and Yemenite genealogies into biblical lineages from Isaac and Ishmael.

44 Zoroastrian sources themselves state that when Gayomard died, his sperm entered the earth and spawned a rhubarb plant from which the first human couple, Mashīa and Mashīānag, emerged (Cereti, "Gayōmard"). The phallic shape of rhubarb sprouts perhaps inspired this story.

45 The usual rule for forming plurals would prefer *kisrawn* (Ibn Manẓūr, *Lisān al-ʿArab*, 5:142).

46 The modern edition of al-Aʿshā Qays's poetry (*Dīwān*, ed. Muḥammad Muḥammad Ḥusayn) lacks this verse; Ibn al-Shajarī attributes it to the fourth-/tenth-century poet Abū Naṣr ʿAbd al-ʿAzīz ibn ʿUmar ibn Nubātah (*al-Amālī*, 1:143).

47 The hadith is likely inauthentic. It was circulating by at least the fourth/tenth century, since both al-Bayhaqī and al-Nīshāburī discuss it, and summarily declare it a fabrication (al-Albānī, *Silsilat al-aḥādith al-ḍaʿīfah wa-l-mawḍūʿah*, 2:425). MS L3 adds an unambiguous marginal note: "All Hadith specialists note that this hadith is false, fabricated, and baseless," though that did not prevent its circulation in some popular texts; see, for example, the allusion in Ibn al-Jazarī, *ʿArf al-taʿrīf bi-l-mawlid al-sharīf*, 29.

48 Most manuscripts use the verb *bāyaʿa* (to swear allegiance) to describe Kavad's relationship with Mazdak, suggesting political subservience. MS Q2 has *tābaʿa* (to follow), as does al-Ṭabarī's account, although one manuscript uses *bāyaʿa* (*Tārīkh al-rusul wa-l-mulūk*, 2:92n5). The sense of "following" suits the story's intention that Kavad accepted Mazdak's creed.

49 See §9.

50 All MSS locate Khosrow's wall astride a mountain called al-Fatḥ (as does Ibn Khaldun's *al-ʿIbar wa-dīwān al-mubtadaʾ wa-l-khabar fī ayyām al-ʿArab wa-l-ʿAjam wa-l-Barbar*, 3:356), though this appears to be a copyist error: elsewhere, the mountain's name is written al-Qabkh or al-Qabj, Arabic for the Caucasus (al-Masʿūdī, *Murūj al-dhahab wa-maʿādin al-jawhar*, §619; al-Ṭabarī, *Tārīkh al-rusul*, 4:154; see variants in Yāqūt, *Muʿjam al-buldān*, 4:306–7, and al-Ṭabarī, *Tārīkh al-rusul*, 2:77).

51 Al-Dīnawarī also calls the town "Zabr Khusrow"; it is considered one of the sites of al-Madāʾin, the Sassanian administrative conurbation on the Tigris near the site of the future Baghdad. Arabic sources explain it was called "al-Rūmiyyah" ("Roman town") because Khosrow built it to resemble the Roman city of Antioch, which he sacked during his triumphant campaigns in the Eastern Roman Empire (Ibn Qutaybah, *al-Maʿārif*, 664; al-Dīnawarī, *al-Akhbār al-ṭiwāl*, 119; al-Ṭabarī, *Tārīkh al-rusul*, 2:102).

52 Arabic literature widely reports the portentous story that the Great Vault was cracked and several galleries collapsed when Muḥammad was born (al-Ṭabarī, *Tārīkh al-rusul*, 2:166–67; Ibn al-Jawzī, *al-Wafā' bi-akhbār al-Muṣṭafā*, 94–95; Ibn al-Jazarī, *'Arf al-ta'rīf*, 33).

53 The story of a chain to notify the ruler of injustice is repeated elsewhere. For example, al-Qazwīnī describes the same system in the court of China (*Āthār*, 46).

54 Several manuscripts render this phrase as *kharraja l-ahwā'* ("emit airs"), which could be read to mean that anyone could make music with that oud.

55 The goat is described as *azraq*, literally "blue"; I have not found references to goats so described elsewhere. Al-Zabīdī refers to *zurqah* as a mixture of whiteness over blackness, and hence "gray" may be intended (*Tāj al-'arūs*, 13:187); Lane attests to the adjective *azraq* for animals, noting that "in the present day it is improperly used as meaning black" (1228).

56 Although the text identifies Khosrow as the "first king" to devise a system of subtle hints for his retinue, Peroz and Bahram mentioned here reigned before Khosrow Anushirvan.

57 Among various renderings of this phrase, most MSS have *marāfi'*, which can mean "petitions," but al-Zabīdī also defines it as a "Yemeni throne" (*Tāj al-'arūs*, 11:171). Ibn Nubātah may intend that Khosrow had the following expression inscribed on elevated seats/thrones; MS I4 renders the line *kānat bi-manzilihi*: "His dwelling bore the following . . ."

58 Ibn Nubātah follows his contemporaries' predilection to trace ethnonyms to an eponymous ancestor. Latin writers ascribed the name "Rome" to Romulus, the founding king of Rome's origin myth (Isidore, *Etymologies*, 15.i.55); modern scholarship derives the name from the Umbrian *rūmōn* (river), to mean "Town of Flowing Rivers" (Corssen, *Über Aussprache, Vokalismus und Betonung der lateinischen Sprache*, 1:364).

59 Reference to Romans or Byzantines as *Banū l-Aṣfar* (literally "the Yellow Clan") was common in early Islamic-era Arabic; the origins of the expression are debated: see Ascoli, "Über Banu al-asfar," and an alternative in Sela, "The Genealogy of Ṣefo ben Elifaz: The Importance of a Genizah Fragment for Josippon's History," 139–41. Rhetorically, it contrasts with the Arabic sobriquet for Persians, *Banū l-Aḥmar* ("the Red Clan").

60 Most MSS render the name "Anṭarṭus," presumably a recollection of Mark Antony. This account conflates Julius Caesar (dictator 49–44 BC) with the emperor Caesar Augustus (r. 27 BC–AD 14), who rose to power after defeating Mark Antony and Cleopatra. In contrast to the copious narratives about pre-Islamic Persian history in Arabic historiography, attention to Roman history was scant, though some Arabic writers probed Greek and Syriac texts, demonstrating that more detailed and accurate knowledge was circulating: see al-Mas'ūdī, *al-Tanbīh wa-l-ishrāf*, 122–24; Ibn Abī Uṣaybi'ah, *'Uyūn al-anbā' fī ṭabaqāt al-aṭibbā'*, §5.1.8.1.

61 This fanciful genealogy engages various opinions about Yemeni ancestry (al-Ḥamdānī, *al-Iklīl*, 1:117–24).

62 As in §8.2, Ibn Nubātah traces ethnicity to eponymous ancestors. The three versions of Greek origins reported by Ibn Nubātah are common in Arabic literature (for example, al-Masʿūdī, *al-Tanbīh*, 115). But the Arabic for *Yūnān* (Greeks) derives from "Ionia," the Greek-settled territory in the central region of Turkey's Aegean coast.

63 By "Romans," Ibn Nubātah likely intends the "Rūm" of his day—that is, the lands surrounding today's Istanbul.

64 The MSS render this name in various ways; none precisely spell "Athens," but Ibn Nubātah appears to have adapted the passage from Sibṭ ibn al-Jawzī's *Mirʾāt al-zamān fī tawārīkh al-aʿyān* (2:407), which itself resembles al-Masʿūdī's *Muruj al-dhahab*, §664–69: both express that the city founded by Yūnān was the "city of philosophers," thus Athens is certainly intended, though the name was corrupted by Ibn Nubātah's day.

65 A story about Moses in Q Kahf 18:83–101 describes a "two-horned" (Dhū l-Qarnayn) being whose identity was debated. Some considered him Alexander the Great; others postulated a different mighty ruler who lived before Alexander, and whom Alexander emulated. Further discussion appears in §8.16.

66 The Arabic reports that the egg weighed one thousand mithkals, a weight that was generally equivalent to a dinar (Miles, *EI2*, "Dīnār").

67 Consanguineous marriages were a signature feature of Muslim-era Arabic accounts of Persian court culture; see further examples at §9.1 and §51.19.

68 The Arabic *istimdād . . . quwwat al-askhāl bi-l-askhāl* is an unusual expression, and its precise meaning eludes us. The apparent meaning is that some forms/bodies (*askhāl*) derive strength/potential (*quwwah*) from other forms/bodies.

69 Mānkīr connotes "Mānyakheṭa" (today Malkhed), capital city of the Rāshṭṛakūṭa dynasty of the South Indian Deccan. Ibn Nubātah errs in placing this story in China; al-Masʿūdī, *Murūj al-dhahab*, §680, narrates Alexander's killing of a king named Fūr, "ruler of the city of Mānkīr," as part of the conquest of India (see also *Murūj al-dhahab*, §§168, 185). Both India and China were associated with a sense of "faraway East" in Arabic literature, and hence could have been confused by Ibn Nubātah.

70 This sentence is problematic, for it suggests that Ibn Nubātah will not tell the story in detail, and various Short version manuscripts, including I1, proceed straight to the end of Alexander's life; however, the Long version manuscripts do tell the story and leave out this summarizing sentence. Some Short version manuscripts include both the summary sentence and the full story; the full story is translated in the Appendix of this volume.

71 Arabic writers opined about two historical Alexanders: the first was a world conqueror contemporary with Moses and al-Khiḍr, the legendary "Green Man" sage; the second was the Macedonian king, son of Philip (Yāqūt, *Muʿjam al-buldān*, 1:184; al-Qazwīnī, *Āthār*, 132).

72 Ardashir's letter is sufficiently vague to be construed as a call to avenge Darius's defeat at the hands of Alexander, but really Ardashir intended to take vengeance upon those Persian nobles who had wronged the scion of Sassan. Ardashir deftly hides his true intentions to win the support of the Persian nobles before vanquishing them via a literary device Muslim-era Arabic rhetoricians called *tawriyah* (dissimulation).

73 The text specifies Ispahbads and Marzubans. The former commanded large military units; the latter were charged with border defense.

74 The historical Ardashir I (r. AD 224–42) founded the Sassanian empire, which was sizable, but its expansion beyond the Euphrates was blocked by the Romans. In Arabic literature, the pre-Islamic Sassanian kings were axiomatically associated with kingship and the ideal forms of royal power, hence Ibn Nubātah's exaggerated appraisal of their realm's extent.

75 The Arabic *ṭawīl al-bāʿ* literally means "broad chested"; as an epithet for rulers, it encompasses physical prowess, military preeminence, and political acumen.

76 The Arabic is *Nardashīr*: a catchy conflation of the word *nard* (backgammon) into the name Ardashir.

77 The line was composed by Abū Nuwās (*Dīwān*, 2:1–11); for discussion of its politicized meaning, see Webb, "From the Sublime to the Ridiculous: Yemeni Arab Identity in Abbasid Iraq," 289–98, 302–6. The manuscript tradition does not render the unusual word for "jinn" accurately, and manuscripts offer various options that do not yield good meanings; the correct word seems to be *khābil*, a term connoting madness, as appears in Abū Nuwās, *Dīwān*, 2:2.

78 Ibn Nubātah aligns with his contemporaries (Ibn al-Athīr, *al-Kāmil*, 1:64; Abū l-Fidāʾ, *al-Mukhtaṣar fī akhbār al-bashar*, 50); modern scholars propose that the name derives from proto-Iranian *yima xšaēta*, an allusion to the color of the sun (Kellens, "Langues et religions indo-iraniennes: Promenade dans les Yašts à la lumière de travaux nouveaux (suite)," 727).

79 In §6.2, however, Fāris, three generations before al-Ḍaḥḥāk, is ascribed this honor.

80 The manuscripts write his name Kābī; a marginal note in I8 remarks correctly: "The books of the Persians write it Kāveh instead of Kābī."

81 Kaveh's banner is identified in Arabic texts as a *darfash*, a rare word borrowed from Persian. Given the lexical rarity, we have opted for the flowery "guidon"; the manuscripts

do not render it accurately, calling it a *darfas*, though Arabic lexicons assure us it should be *darfash* (al-Ṣaghānī, *al-ʿUbāb al-zākhir wa-l-lubāb al-fākhir: Ḥarf al-Sīn*, 154–55).

82 Some Arabic nicknames express a negative trait by using its positive-sounding polar opposite.

83 The poem, reportedly praising ʿAmr ibn Huddāb, leader of the Māzin, is ascribed either to Abū l-Shaʿthāʾ al-ʿAnazī (al-Jāḥiẓ, *Kitāb al-Burṣān wa-l-ʿurjān wa-l-ʿumyān wa-l-ḥūlān*, 66–67) or Ṭarīf ibn Sawwādah (al-Zamakhsharī, *Rabīʿ al-Abrār*, 5:53).

84 *Al-Farqadayn* usually signifies two stars in the constellation Ursa Minor, but here it refers to the two men.

85 The idols' names are variously rendered; most manuscripts have *al-Ḍarībān*, but this is likely an error for al-Yaʿqūbī's and al-Ṭabarī's versions, which have "al-Ḍayzanān" (al-Yaʿqūbī, *Tārīkh*, 1:208; al-Ṭabarī, *Tārīkh al-rusul*, 1:614–15). Al-Ḍayzanān also refers to idols of a later king of al-Ḥīrah (Ibn Manẓūr, *Lisān al-ʿArab*, 13:254). *Ḍayzan* means a slave trafficker, or someone who shares a woman with her husband, or someone who pushes to the front of the queue at a communal well, hence the translation "Interloper."

86 Most manuscripts write *ʿarabī*, meaning that Jadhīmah married her to an "Arab man," but it does not seem a logical complaint; the translation follows MS Ba1: *gharīb*, "outsider."

87 The Short version manuscripts do not expressly mention that the torque (a metallic collar of honor) was gold, but all Long form manuscripts do.

88 The word is variously rendered in the manuscripts; the correct form seems to be *al-ghariyyān*, the dual of *gharī*, a sacrificial pillar (Ibn Manẓūr, *Lisān al-ʿArab*, 15:122). Some report that these pillars were originally not for sacrifice, but for daubing with the blood of defeated enemies (Ibn Qutaybah, *al-Maʿārif*, 649; Yāqūt, *Muʿjam al-buldān*, 4:196–200).

89 The historical Zenobia ruled the middle Euphrates from her capital Palmyra (Tadmur in Arabic). Ibn Nubātah calls her city "al-Ḥaḍr," which we translate as "Metropolis" (in Arabic, literally "the settled place"). A different pre-Islamic trading center in northern Iraq, Hatra, was also called al-Ḥaḍr in Arabic; it is not improbable that the main settlements at the edges of the Syrian Desert could each have been known as "the Metropolis" by the nomadic peoples who lived outside them. Though the historical Zenobia was defeated by the Romans, Arabic sources reinterpret the story to fit her demise within the framework of an Iraqi-Syrian competition (Webb, "Pre-Islamic al-Shām in Classical Arabic Literature: Spatial Narratives and History-Telling," 157–60).

90 See §12.5.

91 Q Naml 27:22–44; Sabaʾ 34:15 has another discussion of Sabaʾ.

92 For the hadith's citation in specialized collections, see Ibn Ḥanbal, *Musnad*, (2898) 5:75, and accompanying notes.

93 Ibn Nubātah considerably condenses the story of Q Naml 27:44; the Queen of Sheba narratives are critically analyzed in Lassner, *Demonizing the Queen of Sheba: Boundaries of Gender and Culture in Postbiblical Judaism and Medieval Islam*, and Pennacchietti, *Three Mirrors for Two Biblical Ladies: Susanna and the Queen of Sheba in the Eyes of Jews, Christians, and Muslims*, 78–104.

94 The geography cited in this verse suggests the town intended was the Iraqi Hatra, not Zenobia's Palmyra.

95 See §11.

96 See §11.9.

97 Boran and Azarmidokht both had short reigns during the unstable late Sassanian Empire. Al-Ṭabarī, *Tārīkh al-rusul*, 2:231–33, states that the powerful controller of Khorasan, Farrakh-hormuz, sought marriage with Azarmidokht, and after she had him killed, Farrakh-hormuz's *son* Rostam killed her.

98 The witness's name is written Qatādah, a copyist error for Abū Qatādah al-Ḥārith ibn Rabʿī.

99 The narrative suggests that Khālid saw Mālik's wife only after he had decreed Mālik's execution. Lengthier versions of this story explain that Khālid had been desiring Mālik's wife for a number of years (al-Iṣbahānī, *al-Aghānī*, 15:290).

100 This statement invokes the sobriquet the Prophet gave to Khālid: the "Sword of God," on account of his valor in fighting for the Muslims.

101 See §14.4.

102 The Qur'an describes how the people of ʿĀd were destroyed by a violent divine wind. "Al-Muḥarriq's clan" refers to the pre-Islamic Lakhmid kings in al-Ḥīrah whose line perished, though not through divine punishment. The poet summons ʿĀd's demise not as divine punishment, but rather an example of the impermanence of all things.

103 The "Old Man of Clay" (*ʿirq al-tharā*) refers to the biblical Abraham.

104 The ʿUkāẓ fair occurred during Dhu'l-Qadah, the month before Dhu'l-Hijjah; however, most manuscripts place the fair in Dhu'l-Hijjah, and only a minority name the correct month.

105 The Arabic orthography of *al-raḥḥāl* and *al-rijāl* differs in just one dot, hence copyists could easily confuse them.

106 Maʿadd was the largest ethnic group in pre-Islamic central Arabia (Webb, "Ethnicity, Power, and Umayyad Society: The Rise and Fall of the People of Maʿadd"); Kulayb's professed overlordship of Maʿadd would have been the highest form of regional authority. Memories of Kulayb and his victory at Khazāz are variously reported (compare Ibn al-Athīr, *al-Kāmil*, 1:520–22, with Yāqūt, *Muʿjam al-buldān*, 2:365–66).

107 The MSS suffice with "the dog barked," thereby leaving the purpose vague. Ibn Nubātah follows al-Isbahānī, *al-Aghānī*, 5:39, but al-Maydānī's *Majmaʿ al-amthāl*, 2:320, makes it clear that the dog's bark established the boundaries of the preserve.

108 The poem is usually ascribed to the pre-Islamic poet Ṭarafah ibn al-ʿAbd (*Dīwān*, 158).

109 The clan interrelations go by several names. Jassās was from the Shaybān subgroup of the Bakr, Kulayb from the Jusham subgroup of the Taghlib; the Bakr and Taghlib were both branches of the umbrella lineage of Wāʾil. While the story's characters hail from different subgroups, their intermarriages were intended to keep peace between them (Ibn al-Athīr, *al-Kāmil*, 1:524).

110 The calf is specified as *faṣīl*, literally "recently weaned."

111 The details of the body of water are uncertain. All MSS and the 1862 edition of *Sarḥ al-ʿuyūn* are unanimous in identifying it as a river/stream (*nahr*), but other sources call it a *nahy*, a pool (al-Iṣbahānī, *al-Aghānī*, 5:41; al-Maqrīzī, *al-Khabar ʿan al-bashar*; MS Fatih 4340 f. 39v). The story's context suggests a pool. All but one of the MSS and the 1862 edition name it "Shubayb," as does al-Maqrīzī's *al-Khabar*, but al-Maqrīzī's marginal note has "Shubayth," as do MS I4; Ibn ʿAbd Rabbihi, *al-ʿIqd al-farīd*, 5:203; al-Iṣbahānī, *al-Aghānī*; and Ibn Ḥabīb *Kitāb al-Naqāʾiḍ*, 2:906. Shubayth is likely correct (see al-Maydānī, *Majmaʿ al-amthāl*, 1:219).

112 Hijris was the son of Kulayb by one of Jassās's sisters, Jalīlah. Hijris's maternal relatives are thus Jassās's clan, whereas Hijris's paternal uncles were on the other side of the war, the clan of Kulayb.

113 The word *muhalhil* has an even wider array of meanings, prompting further stories explaining Muhalhil's nickname; see Ibn Qutaybah, *al-Shiʿr wa-l-shuʿarāʾ*, 1:288.

114 Kulayb was buried at al-Dhanāʾib.

115 The narrative shifts the boy's identity from al-Ḥārith's son to his cousin. Ibn ʿAbd Rabbihi, *al-ʿIqd*, 5:208; al-Iṣbahānī, *al-Aghānī*, 5:51–52; and Ibn al-Athīr, *al-Kāmil*, 1:535, differ in material respects from *Sarḥ al-ʿuyūn*; al-Maqrīzī follows *al-Aghānī*, but he expressly notes uncertainty over the boy's identity (*al-Khabar*, MS Fatih 4340 f.43r).

116 The quotation appears to have been corrupted in early sources. Al-Iṣbahānī casts doubt on the wording (*al-Aghānī*, 5:52).

117 See §28.

118 Early collections of poetry do not unanimously consider this Muhalhil's poem. While al-Khālidiyyān, *al-Ashbāh wa-l-naẓāʾir min ashʿār al-mutaqaddimīn wa-l-jāhiliyyah wa-l-mukhaḍramīn*, 1:4, ascribes it to Muhalhil (Ibn Nubātah seems to have copied this source), Abū Tammām's *Ḥamāsah* ascribes it to an unknown poet of the ʿUqayl (al-Marzūqī, *Sharḥ Dīwān al-Ḥamāsah*, 1:199–201).

119 Ibn Nūbatah refers to al-Buḥturī's poem praising the Caliph al-Mutawakkil (al-Buḥturī, *Dīwān*, 2:1296–1301).

120 Muhalhil intends the pre-Islamic game of *maysir*, in which players gambled by throwing special gaming arrows like lots.

121 In poetry, the color yellow is often associated with dead limbs.

122 Of the seventy-eight verses of Q 55, Sūrat al-Raḥmān, thirty-one repeat the expression "Which of your Lord's wonders would you deny?"

123 Ibn Nubātah has named the wrong site: the battle is Dhāt ʿUynazah, not al-Dhanā'ib, but either way, the battlefield was very far from Ḥujr, a town situated in Yemen.

124 Women emerged bareheaded from their tents when in mourning.

125 The manuscripts differ in rendering the woman's name. The best edition of Muhalhil's poetry refers to her as Mujallal (Muhalhil ibn Rabīʿah, *Dīwān*, 58).

126 The manuscripts inaccurately render the word for "rocks" (*wajār*); the correct word appears in Muhalhil, *Dīwān*, 59.

127 The letters differ by only one dot in Arabic.

128 Al-Samaw'al's ancestry is imperfectly recorded in the manuscripts, and is variously recorded in wider Arabic literature: the form here is from al-Iṣbahānī (*al-Aghānī*, 22:122); see Ibn al-Kalbī, *Jamharah*, 619, and Ibn Durayd, *al-Ishtiqāq*, 436, for an alternative.

129 MS I1 adds here that this story "will be explained below"; however, the explanation is only provided in the Long version manuscripts; Short version manuscripts lack the biography of Imru' al-Qays.

130 A line of al-Samaw'al's poetry mentioning "The Piebald" is narrated in al-Iṣbahānī, *al-Aghānī*, 22:123; see also al-Samaw'al, *Dīwān*, 89.

131 Al-Ḥārith ibn Abī Shamir was a Ghassanid ruler, a contemporary of the Prophet, and does not fit with this story a century before Islam. It probably refers to the Ghassanid al-Ḥārith ibn Jabalah ibn al-Mundhir (r. AD 528–69). The confusion occurs in other sources too; see Ibn Ḥabīb, *Asmā' al-mughtālīn*, §89.

132 All *Sarḥ al-ʿuyūn* manuscripts name his grandfather "Ḥiṣn," but other premodern sources have Ḥuṣayn (Ibn al-Jawzī, *al-Muntaẓam*, 4:1600; Ibn al-ʿAdīm, *Bughyat al-ṭalab fī tārīkh Ḥalab*, 3:367; Ibn Khallikān, *Wafayāt al-aʿyān*, 2:499).

133 The metaphors al-Aḥnaf chooses invoke an unequivocally Bedouin context to articulate moisture.

134 The Ar. *qiblī* usually connotes "south," but it literally means the "direction of Mecca," and given that these events are transpiring in eastern Iran, *qiblī* might connote southwest.

135 Muʿāwiyah's Syrian forces competed for the caliphate against ʿAlī's Iraqis, which included al-Aḥnaf's contingent. The sides fought at Ṣiffīn in 36–37/657. Though the battle was

inconclusive, Muʿāwiyah eventually seized the caliphate, and latent tension persisted between Muʿāwiyah and the Iraqis.

136 This anecdote cites the fighting over the caliphate between ʿAlī and a coalition of al-Zubayr ibn al-ʿAwwām, Ṭalḥah, and ʿĀʾishah (the Prophet's wife). Al-Aḥnaf and his Tamīm kinsmen allegedly remained neutral, but by speaking out against al-Zubayr, al-Aḥnaf implicitly condoned his kinsman Ibn Jarmūz's perfidious assassination of al-Zubayr. The culpability of al-Aḥnaf is intensified in the version of the story in al-Tamīmī, *Kitāb al-Miḥan*, 103–4.

137 After the Caliph ʿAlī was murdered, his son al-Ḥasan tried to muster Iraqi support against Muʿāwiyah, but Iraqi prevarication paved the way for Muʿāwiyah's triumph.

138 There is considerable manuscript variation regarding al-Aḥnaf's insult and addressee. All possibilities are historical figures; I opted for al-Ḥutāt ibn Yazīd as his date best fits al-Aḥnaf, and reflects al-Jāḥiẓ, *al-Burṣān*, 412, and al-Balādhurī, *Ansāb al-ashrāf* (1979–), 7.1:130–31. The Arabic word of the insult appears in I1 as *ādir*, but the invocation of the diminutive form *uwaydir* in al-Jāḥiẓ, *al-Bursān*, 412, is more satirical and more likely the form which the insult takes; hence our translation "*little* balls."

139 The manuscripts consistently render the name "Ḥārithah," who is attested elsewhere, but other sources name him Jāriyah ibn Qudāmah (al-ʿAskarī, *Jamharat al-amthāl*, 1:141; Ibn Ḥamdūn, *al-Tadhkirah al-Ḥamdūniyyah*, 8:229; Ibn ʿAsākir, *Tārīkh Dimashq*, 72:21). Al-Amīn argues that the reading "Ḥārithah" circulated as a result of copyist errors (*Aʿyān al-shīʿah*, 4:58).

140 Al-Aḥnaf refers to the herd as a *ṣirmah*, a modest size variously cited as between the low teens and sixty head (al-Jawharī, *al-Ṣiḥāḥ*, 5:1965, al-Zabīdī, *Tāj al-ʿarūs*, 17:409). Al-Aḥnaf's concluding slip into derogatory language is the point of critique; his mention of *ahtam* (broken front teeth) crudely refers to the meaning of ʿAmr's father's name. ʿAmr and al-Aḥnaf sparred over their nobility; see below, §27.4.

141 The lines are narrated in al-Zawzanī's version of Zuhayr's *Muʿallaqah* (al-Zawzanī, *Sharḥ*, 159), though other narrations (e.g., Ibn al-Anbārī and al-Tibrīzī) omit it. The lines are also ascribed to different poets (Zuhayr, *Dīwān*, 37n4), including al-Aḥnaf (al-Jāḥiẓ, *Kitāb al-Bayān wa-l-tabyīn*, 1:171; al-Dīnawarī, *al-Mujālasah wa-jawāhir al-ʿilm*, 1:237; Ibn al-ʿAdīm, *Bughyat al-ṭalab*, 3:387).

142 The expression can be variously interpreted. Wearing bracelets was synonymous with freeborn women, and hence Ḥātim mocks the ʿAnazah woman as a slave. The intention could be to assert Ḥātim's social superiority, brushing the slap off as "but an act of a slave," or Ḥātim laments his state at being reduced to the subject of a slave's slap. See discussion in Shaykh Zadah, *Ḥāshiyah ʿala Tafsīr al-Bayḍāwī*, 5:432; al-Bakrī, *Faṣl al-maqāl fī sharḥ kitāb al-amthāl*, 381; Ibn Manẓūr, *Lisān al-ʿArab*, 12:453.

143 Literally, Ḥātim says, "This is what I mean by 'bleed,'" intending that he would never be so parsimonious as to just prepare blood pudding. The anecdote also engages the ancient variety of Arabic dialects: the word for "bleeding a camel for a blood pudding" is *faṣd*; the Ṭayyi' accent changes the "ṣ" to a "z," hence Ḥātim's pronunciation *fazd*.

144 There is wide disagreement on Ḥātim's mother's name. All MSS read "'Atb"; Ibn Qutaybah's *al-Shi'r* has "'Inabah" (1:236); the Beirut edition of al-Iṣbahānī's *al-Aghānī* has 'Utbah (17:365); Ibn Wāṣil's abridgment of *al-Aghānī, Tajrīd al-Aghānī*, has "Ghunayyah" (2.2:1903); and Ibn Manẓūr's abridgment left the name unpointed (3:353). Ḥātim's *Dīwān* has "Ghaniyyah" (10). All look similar in Arabic when unpointed.

145 Arabic literature refers to the best poets as *fuḥūl* (literally "studs/stallions"). Early lists of "stud" poets were compiled by Ibn Sallām al-Jumaḥī and al-Sijistānī, but neither include Ḥātim.

146 Premodern commentators interpreted the Arabic *ṣadā* as "corpse," though it also meant a flying spirit, which Arabic literature records pre-Islamic Arabians believed left the body after death. See Ḥātim, *Dīwān*, 200–1.

147 Ḥātim composed this poem to woo Māwiyah, his future wife. Reportedly, she was rich, powerful, and able to choose her own husband, so Ḥātim needed to prove his merits over other suitors (see Ḥātim, *Dīwān*, 252–54).

148 Most *Sarḥ al-'uyūn* manuscripts render the verb *ḥannat* ("she yearned"), which summons a sense of the camel's nobility, as the camels are portrayed as willing to exert themselves to the utmost; but elsewhere the verb is *jannat* ("the camel was madly excited"); see Ḥātim, *Dīwān*, 254.

149 Zayd's grandfather's name is unclear: all MSS of *Sarḥ al-'uyūn* and its 1862 edition name him Zaydān; al-Iṣbahānī, *al-Aghānī*, 17:247, calls him Yazīd; al-Ḥamawī's *Tajrīd al-Aghānī*, 2.2:1867, and biographies of Muḥammad's companions have Zayd (Ibn 'Abd al-Barr, *al-Isti'āb fī ma'rifat al-Aṣḥāb*, 2:559). Ibn Qutaybah's *al-Shi'r* stops Zayd's lineage at his father (1:278).

150 The Arabic name translates literally as "Sweating Sprinter."

151 All manuscripts refer to this figure as Ibn Jidhl, though it is normally just Jidhl al-Ṭa''ān, a nickname (see al-Andalusī, *Nashwat al-ṭarab fī tārīkh jāhiliyyat al-'Arab*, 1:373, and accompanying note).

152 The identities of Zayd's companions are variously reported. Ibn Nubātah likely derived the story from *al-Aghānī*, though the MSS render the names with errors. I1 has "Darr ibn Sadūs," but this figure is nowhere attested—it is a miscopy from "Wazar ibn Sadūs," the form of the name in al-Iṣbahānī, *al-Aghānī*, 17:251, and Ibn Manẓūr, *Mukhtār al-Aghānī*, 4:141. Other sources offer yet further variations: Ibn Sa'd, *al-Ṭabaqāt al-kubrā*, 1:243; Ibn Ḥajar, *al-Iṣābah fī tamyīz al-Ṣaḥabah*, 6:476–77; Ibn Hishām,

*al-Sīrah al-nabawiyyah*, 2:578; al-Ṭabarī, *Tārīkh al-rusul*, 3:145; and al-Ḥamawī, *Tajrīd al-Aghānī*, 2.2:1868).

153 The hadith is copied imperfectly across the manuscripts. Ibn Nubātah likely copied this passage from al-Iṣbahānī's *al-Aghānī* (17:251), and his wording is translated here. A version of this same story in al-Bakrī's *Muʿjam mā staʿjam*, 4:1264, also copies from *al-Aghānī*.

154 All MSS and *al-Aghānī* (17:251) have "Black Mountain," but such a mountain is unattested in the Ṭayyi' lands, and other versions indicate that the Prophet intended one of the Ṭayyi''s idols known as the "Black Stone" (Ibn Durayd, *Jamharat al-lughah*, 2:952; al-Bakrī, *Muʿjam*, 4:1265).

155 The Prophet's words were aimed at Zayd, since Mount Manāʿi was reportedly a mountain where his people, the Ṭayyi', took refuge (al-Bakrī, *Muʿjam*, 4:1264).

156 Both Kaʿb and al-Ḥuṭay'ah were celebrated poets; it is unclear why all manuscripts only specify al-Ḥuṭay'ah as a poet here.

157 The *akhyal* bird is a variety of roller (*Coracias*); it is synonymous with ill omen in Arabic poetry.

158 The genealogy of the Ṭayyi' is tendentious: the La'm were one of their subgroups; Zayd was from a different subgroup, the al-Nābil. The Badr were a clan within the Fazārah.

159 This poem is variously narrated elsewhere (al-Iṣbahānī, *al-Aghānī*, 17:249; al-Qālī, *al-Amālī wa-dhayl al-amālī*, 1:21; al-Baṣrī, *al-Ḥamāsah al-Baṣriyyah*, 1:246). Our translation follows *al-Aghānī* and the *Sarḥ al-ʿuyūn* manuscripts, but it seems odd that Zayd would instruct the Banū l-Ṣaydā' to train his colt, since he spent the previous lines demanding its return. The alternative version would read: "He's my colt, and I trained him . . ."

160 The MSS have various renderings for the poem's last two words; the more common narration elsewhere has *murr ʿiqābī*, "my reckoning is bitter" (Ibn al-Shajarī, *al-Ḥamāsah*, 73; Yāqūt, *Muʿjam al-buldān*, 5:191).

161 The MSS offer various options for al-Sulayk's grandfather, none of which are actual names or attested elsewhere. Other texts that give al-Sulayk's genealogy name his grandfather Yathribī, as we have done here (al-Iṣbahānī, *al-Aghānī*, 20:389; al-Maqrīzī, *The Arab Thieves*, §2.5).

162 The MSS are consistent in rendering the narrator's name Ibn Shihāb, but such a narrator cannot be identified, and it is perhaps a misrendering of "Ibn Nabhān," the narrator of this anecdote in al-Iṣbahānī, *al-Aghānī*, 20:390.

163 As noted in §22.1, al-Sulayk's immediate clan was the Muqāʿis, but since Muqāʿis was itself a subgroup of the Saʿd, al-Sulayk is also associated with them.

164 By this expression, al-Sulayk intends for the man to cease bothering him, as the moonlight affords him opportunity to find someone else to trouble.

165 Sulayk's concern for his maternal relatives derives from the fact that his mother was dark-skinned, and thus his material kin include slaves and other women who were not afforded the protection and dignity afforded light-skinned Arabian women.

166 ʿĀmir's sobriquet *mulāʿib al-asinnah* can be interpreted in various ways: it could mean to "parry one's way through the spears," but since Ibn Zaydūn expressly states that the man's "hands" made play with the spears, it seems he intends "brandishing" of spears.

167 The manuscripts render the name "Nizār," a seeming error for "Nizāl al-Maḍīq" (Descender into Battle), a son of Mālik ibn Jāʿfar, whose given first name is variously recorded as Salmā and ʿUbaydah (there was debate over the identity of these men; see Labīd, *Dīwān*, 341).

168 See §30.13.

169 MS I3 has ʿĀmir speak more ominously: "I won't stop at killing just one of them," but this is not in other manuscripts or in the story's likely source, al-Wāqidī, *al-Maghāzī*, 1:348.

170 The Prophet names those subgroups of the Sulaym that allied with ʿĀmir (al-Wāqidī, *al-Maghāzī*, 1:347–49; Ibn Kathīr, *al-Bidāyah wa-l-nihāyah*, 4:73–74). Most other versions of the supplication associate it with the Battle of Uḥud, not Maʿūnah Well (Ibn Ḥanbal, *Musnad*, (7260, 7465, 7668, 10071) 12:202, 431, 13:101, 16:97).

171 Q Āl ʿImrān 3:128.

172 Versions vary; Labīd's *Dīwān* has twenty verses (332–34).

173 See §30.

174 Spear Brandisher's dilemma was that he was related to both ʿĀmir and ʿAlqamah: ʿĀmir was his nephew, ʿAlqamah was his second cousin via a common great-grandfather, Jaʿfar ibn Kilāb (see Ibn Ḥazm, *Jamharat ansāb al-ʿArab*, 284–85).

175 The poem is variously attributed: al-Iṣbahānī ascribes it to Ṣakhr ibn Ḥabnāʾ (*al-Aghānī*, 13:107); al-Mubarrad to Ṣakhr or his brother Yazīd (*al-Kāmil*, 1:274–75); and one transmitter of Dhū l-Rummah's poetry ascribes it to him (Dhū l-Rummah, *Dīwān*, 3:1762).

176 See §29.

177 The Arabic name of the desert gourd, *ḥanẓalah*, is the same as the name of the attacking tribe.

178 See §29.

179 The poem is not in al-Ḥuṭayʾah's *Dīwān*. Al-Balādhurī's biography of Qays (*Ansāb al-ashrāf* (1979–), 7.2:61) ascribes the poem to Qays or Qays's kinsman ʿUrwah ibn al-Ward, though it is not in ʿUrwah's *Dīwān* either. Al-Tawḥīdī (*al-Baṣāʾir wa-l-dhakhāʾir*, 1:655) ascribes it to al-Rabīʿ ibn Ziyād of the ʿAbs. Cheikho ascribes the poem to

al-Ḥuṭay'ah (*Shu'arā' al-naṣrāniyyah fī l-Jāhiliyyah*, 6:920), but he copied directly from Ibn Nubātah and perpetuated the likely misattribution.

180 All of Iyās's statements to follow, most quoted from the Qur'an, stand as authoritative rejections of Ghaylān's creed of free will. Ibn Nubātah returns to Ghaylān in §49..

181 Q Mā'idah 5:43.

182 Q Mu'minūn 23:106.

183 Q Baqarah 2:32.

184 Q Ḥijr 15:39. Most MSS repeat only the first part of the verse, to the word "astray"; readers would naturally fill in the rest of the verse from memory.

185 The Persians' statement is recorded in Persian in the MSS with considerable copyist mistakes (see Webb, "Multilingualism in the Transregional Journeys of an Arabic Book: Persian/Arabic Encounters in the Manuscripts of Ibn Nubātah's *Sarḥ al-'Uyūn*").

186 All manuscripts call this man "al-Ḥawshī," but he is unknown, and the name varies across other anecdotes of this story (al-Balādhurī, *Ansāb al-ashrāf* (1996), 11:337; Ibn Khallikān, *Wafayāt al-a'yān*, 1:249). A Hadith scholar and jurist named al-Qāsim ibn Rabī'ah al-Jawshanī living in Basra at this time is perhaps the intended person (Ibn Kathīr, *al-Bidāyah*, 9:368).

187 A common theme in Arabic literature is pious Islamic scholars' aversion to serve as judges. One reason was that a judge's mistakes that punish the innocent will be errors for which the judge will be called to account on Judgment Day. The rationale is described in §25.7.

188 Iyās intends that the possibility of being appointed judge leads a man to teeter on the edge of Hell.

189 Q Anbiyā' 21:79. The Qur'an specifies that Solomon was always guided to the right judgment, whereas the Qur'an describes David as being given wisdom, but without express reference that he always made correct judgments. A gloss on this story describes a case brought before David: while David gave judgment, Solomon, then still a youth, proposed a more just ruling, which the parties followed. Thereby al-Ḥasan al-Baṣrī infers that a knowledgeable but imperfect judge is not necessarily doomed to Hell.

190 Though the bag has not been opened, presumably the man can tell whether the coins are gold or silver by their feel and sound.

191 Stories of Iyās's wisdom and intuitive judgments were compiled into a book by the Iraqi historian al-Madā'inī (d. ca. 228/843); it is no longer extant.

192 The verb *uqtuḍiba* used here means "to be plucked/extracted," but the same verb's active form, *iqtaḍaba*, means to "make an impromptu speech." Given Saḥbān's persona, the story perhaps originally intended "he was off delivering an impromptu speech," but over the course of transmission the sentence may have become corrupted. All *Sarḥ*

*al-ʿuyūn* manuscripts, and the likely source, Ibn Ḥamdūn, *al-Tadhkirah*, 6:272, narrate the story consistently in the form rendered here.

193 Q Ṭā Hā 20:17–18 tells a story in which God expressly questions Moses about his staff.

194 The intention is to urge charity: one ought to give away a portion of one's wealth as *ṣadaqah* for the needy instead of hoarding and leaving it to one's inheritors. This ascetic oration is ascribed to various persons in Arabic literature, including the Caliph ʿAlī ibn Abī Ṭālib (Ibn Abī l-Ḥadīd, *Sharḥ Nahj al-balāgha*, 11:3–4) or an unnamed Bedouin (*aʿrābī*) of the Umayyad era (al-Ābī, *Nathr al-durr fī l-muḥādarāt*, 4:9).

195 MS I3 has a marginal note expanding Saḥbān's request. It reads: "Your slave boy the baker, your grade horse 'Pink,' your estate at Zaranj, and ten thousand dinars." This is also the form of the anecdote in Ibn Manẓūr, *Lisān al-ʿArab*, 2:533.

196 The hadith is widely cited in various similar versions: see al-Bukhārī, *Ṣaḥīḥ*, 872; Ibn Ḥanbal, *Musnad* (2761, 3778, 4651), 4:486, 6:318, 8:275.

197 This hadith has several variants, but most omit the pair "inexpressiveness" and "eloquence"; Ibn Nubātah's version is attested in Ibn Ḥanbal, *Musnad*, (22313) 36:649–51.

198 Both al-Aḥnaf and ʿAmr were leaders of different clans of the Tamīm; the issue concerns which of the two would be selected to lead the whole tribe. This is one of several anecdotes about competition for leadership of the Tamīm in early Islam (al-Balādhurī, *Ansāb al-ashrāf* (1979–), 7.1:130).

199 The text of this verse is unclear and may be corrupted; we could not locate alternative readings in other sources.

200 She intends that if ʿAmr leaves in the earlier part of the night, he will still have plenty of stars (and perhaps the moon) to guide him home, whereas if he stays with her late into the night, he must return in total blackness, or, if he leaves even later, he'll have to face journeying in the day.

201 See §16 and §17.

202 Ibn Nubātah's account differs from its likely source, Ibn ʿAbd Rabbihi, *al-ʿIqd*, 5:210, where the warring parties are said to have approached the "King of Yemen" (Tubbaʿ), who appointed al-Ḥārith ibn ʿAmr over them.

203 Arabic sources disagree over "Star-Thistle Eater" (*Ākil al-Murār*): some claim he was al-Ḥārith's grandfather, Ḥujr ibn ʿAmr of the Kindah; it is complicated by the fact that all rulers of that dynasty are known as "Banū Ākil al-Murār" (Clan Star-Thistle Eater).

204 All *Sarḥ al-ʿuyūn* manuscripts render the two spies' names consistently, but other sources name them Sadūs ibn Shaybān and Ṣulayʿ (or Ṣalīʿ) ibn ʿAbd Ghunm (Ibn al-Athīr, *al-Kāmil*, 1:507; al-Maqrīzī, *al-Khabar*, MS Fatih f.21r).

205 Our translation follows the manuscripts' Arabic, but the manuscripts may be erroneous as the syntax does not accord with proper rhyme. The verse is problematic and has

various renderings elsewhere (see two different versions in Ibn Manẓūr, *Lisān al-ʿArab*, 4:138 and 13:539,; where the alternative version describes the camel as "feeble and coughing" (*munaffah majshūr*)).

206 See §24.

207 This sentence is consistently written in the manuscripts, but it may be corrupted. Ibn Nubātah suggests that the date paste was part of the ruse to divert Thrust from the race, but perhaps Ibn Nubātah has conflated different aspects of the race setup, and the original intention was actually that the first horse to reach the dates would be declared the winner. Other versions state that the first horse to drink from a specified well would be the winner (al-Maqrīzī, *al-Khabar*, f. 59v).

208 The last line can be variously interpreted; this translation follows al-Shantamarī (*Sharḥ Ḥamāsat Abī Tammām*, 1:519). According to al-Marzūqī (*Sharḥ Dīwān al-Ḥamāsah*, 2:992), the line means that men will not lie with their women for a considerable time since they will be all-consumed by revenging Mālik's blood. Both interpretations seem possible readings of *ʿawāqib al-aṭhār*.

209 The verb *nadaba* connotes a lamentation practice of grieving by recalling the good qualities of the deceased.

210 This line aroused the excitement of prosody specialists (see Ibn Jinnī, *al-Tanbīh ʿalā sharḥ mushkilāt al-Ḥamāsah*, 335–36; al-Marzūqī, *Sharḥ Dīwān al-Ḥamāsah*, 2:992–93). Note that all the MSS refer to the poem as having the "long" meter (*al-ṭawīl*), though it is actually the "perfect" meter (*al-kāmil*); given that Ibn Nubātah was an expert poet, it is unclear how this mistake appeared across all manuscripts, even without marginal corrections, though the 1862 printed edition alerts the reader to the issue (81).

211 See §24.7.

212 See §24.11.

213 Options abound for interpreting Zuhayr's "embalmed" remark: it may refer to war's balm, but it may also refer to a woman, Manshim, who sold perfume that commentators associated with the wars between ʿAbs and Dhubyān; see the commentary in Zuhayr, *Dīwān*, 24. Manshim and the violent consequences of her perfume are differently interpreted below (§61.2).

214 Her name translates as "Little Lioness," which seems entirely appropriate given what will transpire.

215 See §§30.12–30.

216 See §23.9.

217 Al-Iṣbahānī's more detailed narrative (*al-Aghānī*, 16:308) specifies that Spear Brandisher was unhappy with ʿĀmir vying in honor against ʿAlqamah since all parties involved were

interrelated through Spear Brandisher and his grandfather al-Aḥwaṣ. Because of the shared lineage, Spear Brandisher intends that the contest is pointless.

218 As noted above in §30.4, ʿAlqamah and ʿĀmir shared in their lineage.

219 The manuscripts write *ra'y* (opinion), whereas Labīd's *Dīwān*, 331, has *ra's* ("head"), and it seems the manuscripts perpetuate a copyist error since these words look similar in Arabic. Labīd's version would make sense with the verb at the end of the line *taṣawwaba* ("to be lowed"), literally "bring down the head of the loser"—that is, "bring shame." The manuscripts' *ra'y* could be inferred as "correct the [faulty] opinion of the loser."

220 See §14.4.

221 Abū ʿUbaydah's extant list (*al-Dībāj*, 15–16) has a different format, though the three named here are included.

222 There are various accounts of ʿĀmir ibn al-Ṭufayl's meeting with the Prophet; however, most do not include ʿĀmir's request to be the Prophet's successor. Ibn Kathīr, *al-Bidāyah*, 5:54, does include it, and reports the Prophet's response: "That is neither for you nor your people, but I appoint you in charge of the cavalry."

223 This expression appears in the *Letter*, and below (without commentary in the Short version), §75.

224 Arabic poetry commonly described periods of rain by reference to the stars. The poet intends that he was anxious that death would befall the warrior Arbad, but never suspected that it would be caused by a rainstorm. This verse is usually ascribed to the poet Labīd (Ibn Hishām, *al-Sīrah*, 2:569–70; Labīd, *Dīwān*, 158–62).

225 Arabic poems are composed to rhyme based on the consonant and vowel of the last word in each line. Poems did not tend to have titles, but were identified instead via the line-ending consonant upon which they rhymed.

226 Other sources report Mushir's statement as "This man will wipe out my kin (*qawmī*) people . . ." instead of "his kin" (*qawmihi*) as reported here by Ibn Nubātah (al-Anbārī, *Sharḥ Dīwān al-Mufaḍḍaliyyāt*, 2:262; Ibn Athīr, *al-Kāmil*, 1:634). The former version is perhaps the more sensible, given that Mushir was from the al-Ḥārith ibn Kaʿb, the very people ʿĀmir was fighting at the Battle of Fayf al-Rīḥ.

227 ʿĀmir refers to his horse by its name, "Harnessed." The game of *maysir* was a form of gambling by casting gaming arrows; since the blank arrow is played in each round of the game, the association of the horse with the blank arrow intends that the horse leads the charge in every battle.

228 See §30.1.

229 The Arabic refers to al-Ḥajjāj teaching the Qur'an Chapter 108, "al-Kawthar." This is a palpably sarcastic lampoon, since al-Kawthar is the shortest and most elementary of the Qur'an's chapters, comprising only three verses.

230 See §34.

231 Cupper (*ḥajjām*) refers to a common premodern medical practice of bloodletting via the placing of cups on parts of the body and drawing blood for relief from pains. The profession was considered of the lowest social rank, and was much satirized across Arabic literature. The profession of tanners was likewise very lowly given the filth and stench of the tanner's workplace. There were few jobs less desirable or of lower social standing than a cupper or tanner.

232 Al-Ḥajjāj would have been in his mid-twenties when ʿAbd al-Malik became caliph, so the identity of the caliph is mistaken and the story is likely apocryphal.

233 All MSS read Sulaym ibn ʿAmr, but no such judge is known. During al-Ḥajjāj's childhood, the chief judge of Egypt was Sulaym ibn ʿItr al-Tujībī (al-Kindī, *Wulāt Miṣr*, 303–11; Ibn al-Jawzī, *al-Muntaẓam*, 4:314); however, it is unclear why al-Ḥajjāj and his father would have been in Egypt, and the caliph at that time was Muʿāwiyah, not ʿAbd al-Malik.

234 Tūjīb was a branch of the Kindah, and the lineage of the judge Sulaym ibn ʿItr; thus, over the course of the story's narration, different narrators mentioned either one or the other lineage group, and Ibn Nubātah preserved both options.

235 No Ibrāhīm ibn Ṭalḥah ibn ʿAbd Allāh can be identified, but a revered member of the Quraysh during al-Ḥajjāj's lifetime was Ibrāhīm ibn Muḥammad ibn Ṭalḥah ibn ʿUbayd Allāh, who is likely intended here.

236 Al-Ḥajjāj was a member of the Thaqīf tribe.

237 "High Priest" is my translation for the Arabic's Hāmān. The identity of Hāmān in Qur'an 28 (Qaṣaṣ) is debated today. Some claim he is a conflation of Pharaoh with the biblical story in Esther 3:1–6 of the Persian king Ahasuerus's minister (Hearle Johns, *EQ* 2:399). Al-Ḥajjāj's contemporaries would not have contemplated such exegesis: they knew Hāmān as Egypt's chief unbeliever under the Pharaoh, and I have translated it accordingly.

238 The "Two Towns" are Mecca and Medina; the "Two Villages" are Mecca and al-Ṭāʾif, al-Ḥajjāj's birthplace. The man reminded al-Ḥajjāj that the region was both his charge and kin, so al-Ḥajjāj endeavored to fulfill the duty of generosity.

239 Q Māʾidah 5:27.

240 Q Hūd 11:88. The "Righteous Believer" is the Prophet Shuʿayb.

241 Al-Ḥajjāj intended to test how many axiomatically non-Muslim remarks he could make before someone in the congregation dared object. Evidently none did.

242 Q Muʾminūn 23:108. The verse recounts God's words to the damned in Hell.

243 Q Baqarah 2:249. The verse describes the Israelites' march against Goliath.

244 The Arabic word for *handful* is usually pronounced *ghurfah*, with a "u," not *gharfah*, with an "a," as Abū l-ʿAlāʾ did; but both readings were deemed technically permissible, hence

neither constitutes any particular sin (for attestations of both readings, see al-Khaṭīb, *Muʿjam al-Qirāʾāt*, 1:353–54).

245 The Bedouin pronounces the Arabic word for relief with an "a"—that is, "*farjah*," instead of the more usual *furjah*. This word morphologically resembles the contested word in the Qur'an, and given the use of Bedouin poetry to inform the possible varieties of Qur'anic reading, Abū l-ʿĀlāʾ's reading of *ghurfa* as *gharfa* is thereby exonerated.

246 Q Hūd 11:46. Both readings are attested (al-Khaṭīb, *Muʿjam al-Qirāʾāt*, 4:67–68).

247 In Arabic script, the noun (*ʿamal*) and the verb (*ʿamila*) can look identical.

248 According to genealogical models, the Prophet Hūd is posited as one of Noah's descendants.

249 The original advice that al-Ḥajjāj rejects is ascribed to the Prophet: there are several contexts and variations, but the thrust is that the good must be rewarded and wrongdoers should not be held to task (al-Bukhārī, *Ṣaḥīḥ*, *Manāqib al-Anṣār*, 3799; Ibn Ḥanbal, *Musnad*, (12650, 12803) 20:92, 194).

250 Thamūd feature in the Qur'an as an ancient unbelieving people destroyed by God. Despite the tales of their complete destruction, various stories circulated that al-Ḥajjāj was one of the survivors.

251 The manuscripts variously identify this character as Aḥmad ibn Yūsuf or Aḥmad ibn Yūnus, but neither can be identified in connection with al-Ḥajjāj. Al-Jahshiyārī (*Kitāb al-Wuzarāʾ wa-l-kuttāb*, 39) reports the story as between al-Ḥajjāj and his well-known secretary Ṣāliḥ ibn ʿAbd al-Raḥmān.

252 The long versions of *Sarḥ al-ʿuyūn* identify it as his sermon at the Battle of Dayr al-Jamājim [1862], 95. It was widely copied in books of historiography and literature.

253 Evidently this occurred when al-Ḥajjāj was nearing his end.

254 Q Ṣād 38:35.

255 The Bāhilah were an oft-mocked lineage group; see Ibn Qutaybah, *The Excellence of the Arabs*, §§2.8.23–24.

256 The manuscripts identify the figure as Qudāmah ibn Jaʿfar, but no such person is known in association with Qutaybah. Other sources report Qudāmah ibn Jaʿdah of the Makhzūm, a Meccan nobleman (Ibn Qutaybah, *ʿUyūn al-akhbār*, 2:32; al-Iṣbahānī, *al-Aghānī*, 11:269; Ibn ʿAsākir, *Tārīkh Dimashq*, 60:65).

257 See §34.1.

258 ʿAbd al-Malik's successor as caliph was indeed al-Walīd, his son.

259 The identification of ʿUbayd as "ibn Yūnus" is not elsewhere attested; other sources have ʿUbayd ibn Mawhib, a retainer of al-Ḥajjāj (see al-Ṭabarī, *Tārīkh al-rusul*, 6:342, 394; Ibn Abī l-Ḥadīd, *Sharḥ*, 4:206).

260 When the Zubayrid family were in power, they were patrons of Muhallab's clan. Although the Zubayrids had been enemies of ʿAbd al-Malik at the beginning of his caliphate, by the time of this story, the Zubayrids had been utterly defeated, and hence ʿAbd al-Malik could commend Yazīd's fond remembrance of his former patrons, expressing optimism that Yazīd would in turn be grateful for ʿAbd al-Malik's patronage.

261 This verse, by Mu'aqqar al-Bāriqī, is often cited. For discussion of the verse's imprint in Arabic literature, see al-Ṣafadī, *Tamām al-mutūn*, 366–71.

262 This is culturally significant since the Barmakids would rise to become the most prominent family of viziers under the early Abbasid caliphs and issues of their Persian identity is a common trope. Allegations of their descent from ʿAbd Allāh ibn Muslim may be a fabrication to aggrandize the memory of Qutaybah's brother (see Sourdel, "al-Barāmika," *EI2*).

263 The manuscripts render his name in various ways. Most have "Bundār"; al-Ṭabarī, *Tārīkh al-rusul*, 6:430, has "Tundhar" or "Taydhar" (or "Tīdhar"); Ibn al-Athīr, *al-Kāmil*, 4:528, has "Tundar." Tundar (or Tundur) is apt: it means "thunder" in Persian (Dekhoda, *Lughatnāma*, 5:7021).

264 The mithkal (or miskal, Ar. *mithqāl*) was a common weight usually defined as one and three-sevenths of a dirham (Miles *EI2* "Dīnār"; al-Zabīdī, *Tāj al-ʿarūs*, 14:86); this likely intends about four grams, suggesting the idol's gold weight was between six and seven hundred kilograms.

265 The MSS vary on the amount and the type of coinage intended: al-Balādhurī, *Futūḥ al-buldān*, 411, has 700,000 dirhams; al-Ṭabarī, *Tārīkh al-rusul*, 6:475, has 2.2. million.

266 Ibn Nubātah's text is contradictory: above, he states that the people of Samarqand were to evacuate and let Qutaybah build a mosque, but here he states that the Samarqandis built the mosque and then left their town. Al-Balādhurī and al-Ṭabarī report the latter option.

267 The purpose of playing *maysir* lots was to win the best cuts of a slaughtered camel's meat. See Ibn Qutaybah, *Excellence*, §2.6.5; Jamil, "Playing for Time: *Maysir*-Gambling in Early Arabic Poetry."

268 See §19.

269 See §§34.24–32.

270 Q Baqarah 2:204–6. The translation has been modified slightly to better reflect how Nāfiʿ interpreted its nuances as specifically vilifying one person, whom Nāfiʿ claimed was the Caliph ʿAlī.

271 Q Baqarah 2:207.

272 Several Qur'anic verses relate that when God commanded the angels to prostrate to Adam, only the Devil refused (Q Baqarah 2:34, Isrā' 17:61, Ṭā Hā 20:116, Ṣād 38:75).

273 Q Anfāl 8:26.

274 The Short MSS render his name "Maslamah ibn ʿAnbas"; the Long MSS "Muslim ibn ʿAnbas." The early sources name him "Muslim ibn ʿUbays" (al-Balādhurī, *Ansāb al-ashrāf* (1979), 4.2:407; al-Mubarrad, *al-Kāmil*, 3:1222–23, 1237; al-Ṭabarī, *Tārīkh al-rusul*, 5:611–12).

275 The Arabic *shurāt* to label militant religious movements like the Blues means "those who sell [their souls for God]." I have opted for "Zealot," given its connotations of righteous wrath and origins in similarly militant Jewish sects in the first century AD.

276 All manuscripts name al-Ḥasan ibn ʿAbd Allāh; this is a copyist error for al-Ḥārith ibn ʿAbd Allāh ibn Abī Rabīʿah, Ibn al-Zubayr's governor over Basra at the time (see al-Ṭabarī, *Tārīkh al-rusul*, 5:615).

277 Q Tawbah 9:47.

278 All MSS read ʿAbd Allāh ibn al-Mākhūr; it is a scribal error for ʿUbayd Allāh ibn Bashīr, aka Ibn al-Māḥūz ("Spear Thruster") (al-Dīnawarī, *al-Akhbār*, 407; al-Mubarrad, *al-Kāmil*, 3:1223).

279 Most MSS render the name "Ibzan," though the source of this story was likely al-Mubarrad's *al-Kāmil*, and in its modern edition the name is "Abzā" (3:1323).

280 Q Anbiyā' 21:98.

281 The Christian is referred to as a *dhimmī*, a legal status of certain non-Muslims protected under Islamic law.

282 Q Anʿām 6:45.

283 Q Ṭā Hā 20:84.

284 All *Sarḥ al-ʿuyūn* manuscripts elide the word *musalliman*, "well-wishing," which appears in this statement in al-Mubarrad, *al-Kāmil*, 1:225, and Ibn ʿAbd Rabbihi, *al-ʿIqd*, 1.269.

285 For studies of the Arabic Hermes, a mixture of the Greek deity Hermes and the Egyptian Thoth, see Fowden, *The Egyptian Hermes*, and van Bladel, *The Arabic Hermes*.

286 See §6.2.

287 The temple of Akhmim, a village in Upper Egypt, is frequently cited in Arabic literature as one of the great ancient Egyptian monuments (perhaps because larger temples were mostly buried until modern-era excavation). According to al-Maqrīzī, the temple was destroyed by a treasure seeker in 780/1378–79 (*al-Mawāʿiẓ wa-l-iʿtibār fī dhikr al-khiṭat wa-l-āthār*, 1:650).

288 Ibn Nubātah means that the sage's original name was Balīnūs and it was expanded to Isq-Balīnūs. This reflects a merger of legends about Asclepius, a Greek deity of medicine, with Apollonius of Tyana, a Neo-Pythagorean philosopher from Cappadocia who died ca. AD 100. Extensive lore about the historical Apollonius developed in Late Antiquity,

vastly increasing his significance as an archetypal pagan sage. The Arabic traditions incorporate those legends.

289 The "Andalusian Talismans" likely refers to a bronze statue of a horseman at the western edge of the world, indicating to all travelers that they should turn back. The "Bronze Starling" refers to an automaton constructed upon a bronze tree, which at the time of the olive harvest whistled and attracted real starlings, bringing olives in their beaks (al-Tawḥīdī, *al-Baṣāʾir*, 2:58; al-Maqrīzī, *al-Khabar*, 5.6:§76).

290 This form of deification upon death was transmitted to Arabic from classical Greek sources, and echoes the death of Heracles (see Apollodorus, *The Library*, II.viii.7, 271n2).

291 The Arabic description of Plato as *al-ilāhī* reflects the epithet "Plato the Divine," by which Plato was known in Greek and Latin texts (see Jolivet and Monnot's note in their translation of al-Shahristānī, *Livre des religions et des sectes*, 2:221).

292 By Ardashir I, Ibn Nubātah means the grandfather of the Darius killed by Alexander. Muslim-era knowledge of the Achaemenid Persians is notoriously slight, but this seems a correct reference to the Achaemenid emperor Artaxerxes I (Artaxerxes is the Old Persian form of the name Ardashir), and Artaxerxes I's reign does correspond with the birth of the historic Plato.

293 Timaeus is actually a fictional character of Plato's own creation, whom Plato featured in one of his most famous works, *Timaeus*. Arabic readers evidently assumed Timaeus was a real person.

294 See §36.14.

295 The story is also told in connection with Socrates or Hippocrates; see Ibn Abī Uṣaybiʿah, *ʿUyūn al-anbāʾ*, §4.1.6.

296 Plato's *Republic*, Book 4, discusses a tripartite division of the soul: *logos* (logic and reason, in the head), *thymos* (emotion, in the chest), and *eros* (desire and appetite, in the stomach).

297 The Arabic refers to the king as a *baḥr*, a large body of water, sweet or salty. Perhaps because *baḥr* often means "sea" in Arabic, other Arabic sources changed the comparison to describe the king as a "powerful river from which streams/rivulets" derive (al-Mubashshir ibn Fātik, *Mukhtār al-ḥikam wa-maḥāsin al-kalim*, 107; Ibn Abī Uṣaybiah, *ʿUyūn al-anbāʾ*, §4.5.3; al-ʿĀmilī, *al-Kashkūl*, 313). Usāmah ibn Munqidh's *Lubāb al-ādāb* (456) has Ibn Nubātah's wording; the statement was also ascribed to ʿAlī (Ibn Abī l-Ḥadīd, *Sharḥ*, 20:279).

298 Neither the king nor his son is a historical person, though this anecdote is common in Arabic literature (see Ibn Abī Uṣaybiʿah, *ʿUyūn al-anbāʾ*, §4.6.7.2). In rendering the names, I follow Maroth, *The Correspondence between Aristotle and Alexander the Great: An Anonymous Greek Novel in Letters in Arabic Translation*, 137.

299 The book is extant: it enumerates one hundred lines of al-Mutanabbī's poetry that borrow from Aristotelian aphorisms (al-Ḥātimī, *al-Risālah al-Ḥātimiyyah*).

300 This may be a reference to Claudius Ptolemy's other famous work, the *Tetrabiblos* on astrology. Curiously, Ibn Nubātah suggests that Ptolemy's astrolabe was a book; this is not otherwise attested, and there is modern debate about whether Ptolemy knew of the astrolabe or if it was a later invention (Neugebauer, "The Early History of the Astrolabe: Studies in Ancient Astronomy IX").

301 Arabic writers, starting with al-Mas'ūdī's *Murūj al-dhahab* (§§699, 706), began to confuse the Ptolemaic rulers of Egypt (305–30) with the second-century AD scholar Claudius Ptolemy. The confusion may derive from al-Mas'ūdī's use of Byzantine-era Greek sources, which also confuse the names (for example, John Malalas (d. ca. AD 578), *The Chronicle*, 8.6:102).

302 Ptolemy's career was contemporary with Antonius Pius (r. AD 138–161), and he died early in Marcus Aurelius's reign.

303 Prior to the rising popularity of the BC/AD convention in late medieval Europe, the reckoning of ancient time was measured with reference to seminal events in the past: a mixture of biblical events and the reigns of prominent Persian and Greek rulers. Muslims adopted the hijra calendar, which commenced upon Muḥammad's settlement in Medina in AD 622, but they did not adopt a "before-hijra" time reflecting the Christian BC, and instead preserved the system of using biblical and regnal events to date ancient history.

304 Ibn Nubātah's folk etymology relies on the shared root between Ar. "to affect" (*aththara*) and "ether" (*athīr*), but "ether" actually originates from the ancient Gk. *αἰθήρ*, a word for sky, the heavens, and ether (Liddell and Scott (9th ed.), 37).

305 All manuscripts and Ibn Nubātah's likely source, al-Tawḥīdī's *al-Muqābasāt*, relate the name of the astronomer as Ibn Bukayr, but Kraemer argues that he is "Ibn Būlus," the fourth-/tenth-century astronomer Abū Sa'd al-Faḍl ibn Būlus al-Naṣrānī al-Shīrāzī (Kraemer, *Philosophy in the Renaissance of Islam: Abū Sulaymān al-Sijistānī and His Circle*, 65–66).

306 See §35.9.

307 Ibn Nubātah's definition is incorrect: Gk. *ξενοδοχεῖον* means "lodging for strangers" (Liddell and Scott (9th ed.), 1189). By the late Roman empire, the name was applied to charitable foundations for wayfarers and the sick, and it was in this period the word became associated with hospitals (see "Xenodocheion," *The Oxford Dictionary of Byzantium*).

308 The Arabic states one hundred "hundredweights" (*qinṭār*), the value of which is unclear: a *qinṭār* usually connoted one hundred *raṭl*s, but a *raṭl* varied greatly between places and

eras, and lexicons proffer a dizzying array of options expressed via different multiples of other nonstandardized weights (Ibn Manẓūr, *Lisān al-ʿArab*, 5:118–19).

309 This account appears to be disjointed: it actually conflates three different stories that were circulating in Arabic literature on the topic of Hippocrates's refusal to travel to administer medicine to kings. See Ibn Abī Uṣaybiʿah, *ʿUyūn al-anbāʾ*, §4.1.5.

310 The actual Greek means one who has "superior horse" (Liddell and Scott (9th ed.), 834); see also Ibn Abī Uṣaybiʿah, *ʿUyūn al-anbāʾ*, §4.1.6.

311 "Quacks" translates the Arabic *al-aṭṭibāʾ al-sūfisṭāʾiyyūn*, literally "Sophist doctors." Sophists were an ancient school of Greek philosophers, and they do not appear to have constituted a group of doctors in Galen's day. Galen did oppose the Methodists, and perhaps a memory of that is intended here; alternatively, "sophist" may pejoratively intend "nonscientific" or "smooth-talking" peddlers of medicine.

312 This refers to the *De morborum causis et symptomatibus*, *On Diseases and Symptoms*, known in Arabic as *al-ʿilal wa-l-aʿrāḍ*; see Johnston, *Galen: On Diseases and Symptoms*.

313 Some Arabic writers counted Galen and Jesus as contemporaries, perhaps because both were associated with medical prowess, but studious Arabic accounts analyzed the regnal lists of Roman emperors to demonstrate that Galen was born after Jesus (Ibn Abī ʿUṣaybiah, *ʿUyūn al-anbāʾ*, §§5.1.5–7). The historical Galen died sometime between AD 200 and 216. Muslim-era doctors made considerable advances on Galen's teachings, but respect for Galen was typically high (see Swain, "The Greek Chapters and Galen").

314 Q Māʾidah 5:110 references how God enabled Jesus to create a bird (or birds) from clay. The story may originate in a second-century AD Greek apocryphal text (Dzon, "Jews and Birds in Medieval Abrahamic Collections").

315 Pelusium is on the eastern delta of the Nile; Tinnīs was situated adjacent to a salty lake now called Manzalah and part of the Suez Canal. Since the historical Galen lived most of his later life in Rome, the Egyptian connection is quite unlikely (another oft-repeated Arabic account has Galen dying in Sicily (Ibn Abī ʿUṣaybiah, *ʿUyūn al-anbāʾ*, §§5.1.21.1–2)).

316 Medieval physicians considered the apricot to have the most powerful "cold" nature in the stomach (al-Zabīdī, *Tāj al-ʿarūs*, 9:197); this is not in itself bad, but would have been considered risky if much was consumed, or if it was consumed with other "cold" food. Ibn Sīnā's medical compendium *al-Qānūn fī l-ṭibb* (1:372) notes that the fruit is unusually quick to rot, but he does not issue any drastic warnings. Heavy consumption of apricot kernels can cause cyanide poisoning, but this does not seem intended here.

317 The manuscripts miscopy the medical term *ʿuṣbatayn* (two arteries) and write *ʿaḍwayn* (parts). The version of this story in Ibn Abī ʿUṣaybiyyah's medical compendium refers to the "two arteries of the neck" (*ʿUyūn al-anbāʾ*, §5.1.17).

318 The four natures are blood, phlegm, yellow, and black bile; doctors believed these to be fundamental determinants of health and sickness.

319 The poet is Abū Tammām, whose famous praise poem of the Caliph al-Muʿtaṣim opens with an impassioned rejection of astrologers and their predictions.

320 There was considerable hostility between some hadith transmitters and Muslim scholars involved in the translation and adoption of Greek philosophy; ever since, the debates over the merits of philosophical speculation among Muslims have had proponents on both sides.

321 The manuscripts do not include al-Hishāmī's name, but the slightly expanded version of this story in al-Tawḥīdī's *al-Baṣā'ir* (1:325) notes five who were present, including al-Hishāmī. Since Ibn Nubātah's text accords al-Hishāmī a speaking role in what follows, his name is included here.

322 The *Sarḥ al-ʿuyūn* manuscripts read *faqd*, "loss," but al-Tawḥīdī *al-Baṣā'ir* reads *ʿaqd*, "agreement" (1:325); the latter seems more appropriate.

323 This nativity corresponds to 21 Safar 171/10 August 787, at approximately ten p.m. in Balkh (Abū Maʿshar, *On Solar Revolutions*, 134–37); for critical discussion, see Dykes's comments in Abū Maʿshar, *On the Revolutions of the Years of Nativities*, 2–3).

324 The Caliph al-Mustaʿīn died in 252/866; hence, if the story is true, these must have been very long-lingering effects to have caused Abū Maʿshar's death twenty years later.

325 Abū l-Hudhayl acquired this nickname because he was born in the fodder sellers' quarter of Basra.

326 See §47.

327 The terminology here broaches the complexity of Muslim theological debate between atomists (Abū l-Hudhayl) and their detractors (al-Naẓẓām).

328 The story does not render the Persian correctly; it literally means something closer to "Satan's spawn."

329 One-eyed is a symbol for the Dajjāl, the Antichrist.

330 A hadith prohibits Muslims from offering one-horned animals as sacrifices (Abū Dāwūd, *Sunan*, 2805; Ibn Ḥanbal, *Musnad*, (633) 2:66).

331 Al-Naẓẓām's death date is variously recorded as being between 220 and 230 (835 and 845).

332 The letter *lām* in Arabic, the "l," is written as a long hook with an ample curve: ل.

333 Q Nūr 24:35 describes God's light via a metaphor involving a lamp and niche.

334 All manuscripts report the narrator's name thus; however, the version of this story in al-Jāḥiẓ's *Kitāb al-Bukhalā'*, 17, has ʿAmr ibn al-Nuhaywī, an administrator under al-Ma'mūn. Other early versions, however, do have ʿAmr ibn Maymūn (for example, Ibn ʿAbd Rabbihi, *al-ʿIqd*, 6:194; al-Tanūkhī, *al-Mustajād min faʿlāt al-ajwād*, 239).

335 Ibn Nubātah condenses this story from its longer form in al-Jāḥiẓ, *al-Bukhalā'*, 17. In the longer version, it is explained that while both the narrator and neighbor were guests in al-Kindī's house, al-Kindī never invited either to eat, and, out of embarrassment, the visiting narrator had to extend the invitation to the other visitor himself. Under the then-established norms of hospitality, such a scenario connotes al-Kindī's staggering miserliness.

336 The anecdote plays on the standard of politeness that guests should not accept invitations straightaway. Arabic readers would know that the guest only pretended to not want food out of politeness, and by taking the guest at his word without insisting, al-Kindī reveals his miserliness.

337 Due to the high value of gold coins, most purchases only cost a fraction of a single dinar's worth, and hence smaller payments could be made by clipping from the coin a fraction of gold equivalent in weight to the value of the purchase.

338 The verse was composed by al-Raqqī to praise al-ʿAbbās ibn Muḥammad, the brother of the second Abbasid caliph, al-Manṣūr. Al-Raqqī intended to prompt al-ʿAbbās to give a generous gift, but al-ʿAbbās, a noted miser, gave al-Raqqī an embarrassingly paltry reward of two dinars. The Caliph al-Rashīd gave the poet thirty thousand dirhams and chided al-ʿAbbās (Ibn al-Muʿtazz, *Ṭabaqāt al-shuʿarā'*, 157–59).

339 See §37.

340 See §60.

341 See §32.

342 The "Baʿalbakkī prayer caller" is unknown; this same anecdote appears in al-Ṣafadī, *al-Wāfī*, 18:88, but it may have been a corruption from a black-humor anecdote in Ibn Khallikān's *Wafāyāt* (3:230) that explains why the Abbasids spared the last Umayyad caliph's prayer caller and a camel caller, but not ʿAbd al-Ḥamīd.

343 This quotation of ʿAbd al-Ḥamīd's advice on penmanship is repeated in several sources, though the name of the person to whom it was addressed varies. Ibn Nubātah corresponds with Ibn ʿAbd Rabbihi, *al-ʿIqd*, 4:186; for other possibilities, see al-Zabīdī, *Tāj al-ʿarūs*, 12:120; Ibn ʿAsākir, *Tārīkh Dimashq*, 6:114; al-Mūsawī and al-Saʿīdī, *al-Ifṣāḥ fī fiqh al-lughah*, 1:217.

344 ʿAbd al-Ḥamīd alludes to the Afterlife.

345 Sahl's grandfather had the Persian name "Rāhawayh." It is omitted in some manuscripts; others render it variously "Rāhabūn" and "Rāhyūn." The latter is an Arabized approximation of the original Persian.

346 Sahl's book is enigmatic. It is listed as "in the style of *Kalīlah and Dimnah*" in both al-Masʿūdī (*Murūj al-dhahab*, §163) and Ibn al-Nadīm (*al-Fihrist*, 1:373, where it is vocalized *Thuʿlah and ʿAfrā'*), though nothing survives today beyond the excerpt quoted

below (§46.18). Sahl is ascribed several books with titles bearing two names that invoke Persian and Greek heritage: *The Panther and the Fox* is extant and translated into French (see Ibn Hārūn, *al-Namir wa-l-thaʿlab*; for discussion, see ʿAwwaḍ, *Sahl ibn Hārūn wa-Kitāb al-Namir wa-l-thaʿlab*); *The Lover and the Virgin*, based on the Greek tale *Metiochos and Parthenope* (ca. first century BC), is discussed in Hägg and Utas, *The Virgin and Her Lover*.

347 The anecdote foreshadows Muslim scholarly debates about philosophical speculation. Philosophy became well established, but some mistrusted it as a potential distraction from upright faith. The anecdote may specifically intend the *Miḥnah* instigated by al-Maʾmūn and his successors, which attempted to use force in imposing certain doctrines informed by philosophical speculation about God's nature. Ibn Nubātah's readers would likely have recognized that the Cypriot bishop's advice was precisely correct in realizing that the books would cause dissension among Muslims.

348 Abbasid-era coinage was aniconic and was only stamped with Arabic inscriptions, most of which contained God's name and formulas derived from the Qur'an. Because coins contained the name of God, Arabic literature contains witty stories of misers using piety as an excuse for their reticence to part with even a single coin (see al-Jāḥiẓ, *al-Bukhalāʾ*, 51).

349 Arabic literature indeed preserves proverbs about roosters' eyes as purity (al-Jāḥiẓ, *al-Ḥayawān*, 1:377–78, 436).

350 See §47.18.

351 This letter was apparently addressed to Muḥammad ibn Ziyād al-Ziyādī, who had written disparaging poetry about Sahl (see the expanded version in Kurd ʿAlī, *Umarāʾ al-bayān*, 1:170).

352 The word for "gold" in Arabic, *dhahab*, is derived from the same root as the verb "to go, to depart" (*dhahaba*), hence the ill-omen of departure and loss can be inferred in the very name of gold by one who shares Sahl's concerns for hoarding money.

353 Gold can be called "red" (*aḥmar*) in Arabic, but the more usual expression is that "men are wasted by the 'two reds' (wine and meat) and women by the 'two yellows' (gold and saffron—that is, perfume)"; see al-Jāḥiẓ, *al-Bukhalāʾ*, 109.

354 Al-Maydānī, *Majmaʿ al-amthāl*, 3:340–42, explains that Sahl composed his dispraise of gold out of jealousy after Shaddād's praise of gold was well received at court.

355 The manuscripts abbreviate the statement: "It is better that your era be reviled on your behalf than for it to be reviled because of you." The more detailed statement from al-Rāghib al-Iṣbahānī, *Muḥāḍarāt al-udabāʾ wa-muḥāwarāt al-shuʿarāʾ wa-l-bulaghāʾ*, 1:45, is translated here.

356 By quoting the verses, Sahl agrees to include sexual desire. The verses appear in some versions of the pre-Islamic poet ʿAmr ibn Kulthūm's *Muʿallaqah* ode (for example, al-Tibrīzī, *Sharḥ al-Qaṣāʾid al-ʿAshr*, 219), whereby the poet protests that while Umm ʿAmr offered wine to his two companions, she poured nothing for him. ʿAmr remonstrates that he was not the "worst of the three," and hence deserves a drink too. An oft-cited hadith also refers to bastards as "the worst of the three" (see Ibn Ḥanbal, *Musnad*, (8098) 13:462); perhaps Sahl intended the double entendre.

357 Today, al-Jāḥiẓ is the name by which he is best known.

358 See §42.

359 A witty allusion to the phrase "both in the cave" from Q Baqarah 2:40, which referred to the Prophet and Abū Bakr's emigration to Medina. We have amended Wahiddudin's Qur'an translation to better relate al-Jāhiz's pun.

360 Q Raʿd 13:17.

361 Q Baqarah 2:79.

362 Public preachers (*quṣṣāṣ*) initially were specialists in Muslim history and religious teachings, but by al-Jāḥiẓ's third/ninth century, when scholarly specializations had emerged, the *quṣṣāṣ* was denigrated as populist and unintellectual. Al-Jāḥiẓ plays to this stereotype: people gathered to hear something sensational, and al-Jāḥiẓ's ostensible compliment ironically drives the crowd away.

363 *Sarḥ al-ʿuyūn* manuscripts stumble over this sentence, and while a number record it as translated here, the assertion that Muḥammad was a concubine's son runs counter to all biographical details elsewhere in Arabic. The anecdote does appear in two other sources: the modern (but unedited) printing of al-Rāghib al-Iṣbahānī, *Muḥāḍarāt al-udabāʾ*, 1:346–47, and in pseudo-Thaʿālibī's *al-Muʾnis al-waḥīd fī al-muḥādarāt*, 264. Nonetheless, it is difficult to conceive how al-Jāḥiẓ could have held such an aberrant opinion, and the *Sarḥ al-ʿuyūn* manuscripts' copyists were disturbed by the statement, adopting varied strategies to amend the wording. Perhaps manuscript Br2 comes closest to the original anecdote by writing: "The two prophets of God, *Ibrāhīm ibn* Muḥammad and Ishmael, were sons of concubines." Muḥammad's son Ibrāhīm was not a prophet, but his mother was indeed a concubine, and the notion that two prophets had children via concubines was an accepted point, which al-Jāḥiẓ could have made to support his logic.

364 Many caliphs were technically half-breeds, since their mothers were enslaved concubines. This story dates from between the caliphates of al-Maʾmūn (born of an eastern Iranian mother) and al-Muʿtaṣim (born of a Turkic slave). "Proponent of Free Will" (*qadarī*) originally designated theologians who denied predestination, but by the third/ninth century it became a slur for anyone with "bad" ideas, irrespective of theological

nuance. Al-Jāḥiẓ, of course, did know the nuances, and hence his sense of triumph in intellectually outmaneuvering ʿUbayd.

365 Al-Jāḥiẓ refers to Q Yā Sīn 36:80: "He who produces fire for you from green trees," a reference to the fire plow or fire drill—terms for the technique of lighting fire by rubbing two sticks together.

366 Q Mulk 67:8. The Arabic text only includes the first words of the verse, but the jest hinges on the last words of the verse left out here: «were you not warned?» A Muslim who has memorized the Qur'an would know what words fill the blanks.

367 Al-Jāḥiẓ quotes from Q Qāf 50:30, which contains the words Hell utters when it is stuffed with innumerable unbelievers on Judgment Day.

368 This hadith is not widely attested; it does appear in al-Bayhaqī's *al-Jāmiʿ li-shuʿab al-īmān* with slightly stronger wording, replacing "dislike" (*yakrah*) with "hates" (*yubghiḍ*) (9:100).

369 This anecdote has historical difficulties. Ibn Abī Du'ād died a year *before* al-Jāḥiẓ, and the identity of Ibn Bukhtīshūʿ is unclear. "Bukhtīshūʿ" connoted a family of prominent physicians, and their leading figure in the mid-third/ninth century was Bukhtīshūʿ ibn Jibrīl (d. 256/870), not *Ibn* Bukhtīshūʿ (the son does not fit for this story (Ibn Abū ʿUṣaybiʿah, *ʿUyūn al-anbāʾ*, §§8.4.13, 8.5.2)). An alternative account names a different minister and doctor (Ibn Abī ʿUṣaybiʿah, *ʿUyūn al-anbāʾ*, §8.26.15). The tale may be less a historical event than an exemplar of rhetorical wit versus medical reasoning.

370 Ibn Sīnā notes advantages of myrobalan nuts, but not for hemiparesis (*al-Qānūn*, 1:297–98). Al-Jāḥiẓ had realized that the Barmakid had filled the nuts with money, and that was the "benefit" to which al-Jāḥiẓ alludes.

371 Q Aʿrāf 7:163–66 describes a group of Israelites in a "town which is about the sea" on the Gulf of Aqaba who disobeyed God by eating fish on the Sabbath and were turned into apes. Rubin, "'Become You Apes, Repelled!' (Quran 7:166): The Transformation of the Israelites into Apes and Its Biblical and Midrashic Background," discusses the story's possible origins.

372 Red was a popular dye for gray hair; al-Murtaḍā considers the clever wordplay between wine and hair dye to be out of keeping with al-Jāḥiẓ's oeuvre (*Amālī l-Murtaḍā*, 1:204).

373 The maximum term of pregnancy was variously discussed. Mālik's opinion is elsewhere recorded as four years; see al-Bayhaqī, *al-Sunan al-kubrā*, 7:728–29; al-Qurṭubī, *Jāmiʿ aḥkām al-Qur'ān*, 9:287.

374 Q Ḥujurāt 49:2.

375 The narrator is unidentified; for a similar anecdote but with different narrators, see Ibn Abī l-Dunyā, *al-Manāmāt*, 149–50; Abū l-Nuʿaym al-Iṣbahānī, *Ḥilyat al-awliyāʾ wa-ṭabaqāt al-aṣfiyāʾ*, 6:246.

376 The story is a critique of Hanafī Islamic jurisprudence, which relied on analogical reasoning to derive laws. Since Mālik and al-Shāfiʿī relied more on narrated traditions of the Prophet and his companions, they argued that their rules were closer to the spirit of the Prophet. Sparring between Sunni law schools on the relative merits of their founding teachers was a ubiquitous trope.

377 There are multiple versions of this story: Ibn Nubātah follows Ibn Khallikān, *Wafayāt al-aʿyān*, 4:135; compare this with al-Dhahabī, *Siyar aʿlām al-nubalāʾ*, 3160. The underlying context seems to be an official caliphal announcement made during the hajj of 148/766, endorsing Mālik.

378 Most MSS render the narrator's name Muḥammad ibn Jaʿfar (Ba1 has ibn Abī Jaʿfar); these are copyist errors for the famous Medinan historian Muḥammad ibn ʿUmar al-Wāqidī (Ibn Saʿd, *al-Ṭabaqāt*, 5:467).

379 At the outset of the Abbasid caliphate, this issue was politically charged. The Abbasids demanded oaths of allegiance, but some may have been made under compulsion, and Mālik's logical reasoning extrapolating from al-Aḥnaf's view on divorce suggests that oaths made under compulsion were invalid. Hence, Abbasid officials like Jaʿfar ibn Sulaymān could consider Mālik's view seditious. Mālik's subsequent supporters would cherish the story as an example of their teacher's bravery in confronting worldly authority.

380 In Mālik's day, the sanctums of Medina and Mecca were controlled by the Abbasids, who had overthrown the Umayyads and replaced them everywhere except in Andalusia. As in the story above, this anecdote extols Mālik as being unafraid of worldly authority.

381 Mālik's Islamic law school remains the dominant legal school from Tunisia westward; much credit for this must also be ascribed to the role of Kairouan in Tunisia, which was a major center of Mālikī jurisprudence.

382 All manuscripts name the narrator al-Ḥasan, though other sources have Ḥusayn (al-Iṣbahānī, *al-Aghānī*, 4:219; Ibn Ḥajar, *Lisān al-mīzān*, 2:74). The story does not appear in the extant edition of Ibn Ḥamdūn's *al-Tadhkirah*.

383 The *Sarḥ al-ʿuyūn* manuscripts all ascribe the poem to Dhū Yazan. It seems, however, that the poem was actually by Dhū Jadan al-Ḥimyarī (al-Iṣbahānī, *al-Aghānī*, 4:219); it appears without ascription in al-Maʿarrī, *Risālat al-ghufrān*, 227.

384 Given Islamic legal unease with singing, this anecdote is intriguing. The story's narrator is harshly condemned by Ibn Ḥajar as a fabricator (*Lisān al-mīzān* 2:71, 74). The story is rejected in al-Tuwayjirī, *Tabriʾat al-khalīfah al-ʿādil wa-l-radd ʿalā al-mujādil bi-l-bāṭil*, 45.

385 Abū Yūsuf al-Shaybānī was a leading Iraqi Ḥanafī jurist, a rival to Mālik's method. Abū Yūsuf's remark that the past generations "make mistakes" is a censure of Mālik, for his school was based on past precedent, whereas Abū Yūsuf's Ḥanafī model privileged

analytical reasoning; if men of the past erred, then Mālik's insistence on past precedent becomes no more reliable than the Ḥanafīs' ad hoc rulings.

386 Q Ṭā Hā 20:5. Resolving the Qur'an's anthropomorphic allusions to God's attributes and actions was highly contentious. What became the Sunni view read the verses literally and avoided speculation; Mālik's response accords with Sunni theology.

387 The MSS and all sources in various languages offer multiple versions of Mānī's father's name. Overall, the most common derives from the Sogdian *ptty*, rendered in Arabic as *fttk*. See Sundermann, "Mani," *Encyclopædia Iranica* online.

388 Mani was reportedly from a community of Elkesaites, a Jewish-Christian baptist sect.

389 According to the Manichaeans, the human body is a mixture of light and darkness, and procreation thereby perpetuates that harmful mixture, whereas death enables light and darkness to separate. If all living things were to die without issue, all light could escape its corporeal mixtures with darkness, and the world could at last end.

390 Versions of Mānī's death abound in Christian, Zoroastrian, and Muslim sources. Modern scholarship considers the name of the head priest to have been Kerdīr/Kartir.

391 The Arabic for "heretic" is *zindīq*, a word first attested in a pre-Islamic Sassanian inscription in the context of suppressing heretics, perhaps Manichaeans specifically. In the early Abbasid period, *zindīq* probably intended Manichaeans, but the word's connotations would broaden to encompass a nonbeliever/heretic of any persuasion. The actual persecution of Manichaeans under Islam was limited: the reasons for the vigorous persecution by the Abbasid caliphs al-Mahdī and al-Hādī in 163–70/779–86 are obscure; perhaps political interests in the aftermath of the Abbasid revolution were involved.

392 All MSS name his father "Yūnus." Ghaylān's father's identity was obscure (see Ibn Qutaybah, *al-Maʿārif*, 625; Ibn ʿAsākir, *Tārīkh Dimashq*, 48:186; Ibn Ḥajar, *Lisān al-mīzān*, 6:314). Ibn al-Nadīm leaves a blank in the manuscript where he intended to write Ghaylān's genealogy (*al-Fihrist*, 1:364).

393 Theological debate among Muslims about the nature of free will had serious ramifications. Many viewed the Qur'an to be an eternal document, and since it references historical events, a logical corollary was that those events must have been predetermined since the beginning of time, and, as a further consequence, humans thus must not have free will in their actions. While some theologians disagreed and argued for free will, their opponents doubled down and argued that the Qur'an was the uncreated Word of God and that all actions for all time have been determined by God. This latter group became dominant, and the memory of earlier theologians who had argued that the Qur'an was created by God and that humans have free will was considerably vilified, as in the case of the stories about Ghaylān.

394 Arabic literature contains numerous stories in which the Caliph ʿUmar ibn ʿAbd al-ʿAzīz upholds Islamic orthodoxy; see also §71.1.

395 Q Insān 76:1–3. These verses, on their own, could imply that humans have a choice as to whether or not they will show gratitude.

396 Q Insān 76:29–30. These verses clearly rebut Ghaylān's argument about free will. ʿUmar's intention was to make the point that the Qur'an, in its entirety, does not support Ghaylān's creed, and that Ghaylān can only substantiate his views by selective interpretation.

397 Most *Sarḥ al-ʿuyūn* manuscripts identify the narrator as the famous Ibn ʿAbbās, but he died ca. 68/686–88, some forty to fifty years before the events related in the story. MSS I3 and T1 identify the narrator as Ibn ʿAyyāsh, and this is likely the correct form (see Ibn ʿAsākir, *Tārīkh Dimashq*, 48:204–5). There are alternative versions of Ghaylān's debate before the Caliph Hishām: Ibn ʿAbd Rabbihi, *al-ʿIqd*, 2:374; Ibn ʿAsākir, *Tārīkh Dimashq*, 48:205–7.

398 Q Mā'idah 5:3. Most manuscripts only include the first two words of the verse; readers would have been able to complete it themselves.

399 The manuscripts are unanimous in rendering "Isḥāq ibn Saʿd," but this may be a misspelling of Isḥāq ibn Suwayd (Dhū l-Rummah, *Dīwān*, 1:578–79; al-Murtaḍā, *Amālī*, 1:47). Al-Iṣbahānī identifies the story's narrator as ʿAnbasah the Grammarian (*al-Aghānī*, 18:38–39), but mentions Isḥāq ibn Suwayd in an alternate recension (18:39).

400 The verse could be read that God created the beautiful eyes to cause men to lose their reason, and if the noun "seizers" was accusative, it would mean: "God ordered them to be seizers that madden, like wine does." This implies that God ordains something unjust, thus entering the complex world of theological debate over God's predestination and rational senses of justice.

401 The actual nature of al-Jaʿd's heresy is less clear than the straightforward, and perhaps anachronistic, non-Sunni views Ibn Nubātah reports here (see van Ess, *Theology and Society in the Second and Third Centuries of the Hijra*, 2:509–18).

402 The manuscripts render the name Ṭālūṭ ibn Aʿṣam, though other sources identify him as Ṭālūt, son of the sister of Labīd ibn Aʿṣam (e.g., Ibn Kathīr, *al-Bidāyah*, 9:364). Labīd ibn Aʿṣam is described as the Jewish sorcerer who put spells on the Prophet via a charmed comb (al-Bukhārī, *Ṣaḥīḥ*, 5673, *al-Ṭibb*, 47; Ibn Ḥajar, *Fatḥ al-Bārī bi-sharḥ Ṣaḥīḥ al-Bukhārī*, 13:198–215; also Wasserstorm (1995), 157–58).

403 Buhlūl refers to the chapter by its first verse: «Say: He is God, the One» (Q Ikhlāṣ 112:1). This is one of the most repeated surahs of the Qur'an, epitomizing Islamic monotheism. Buhlūl's remark reflects his character as one of the "wise fools" (*ʿuqalāʾ al-majānīn*): his ostensibly absurd question ironically addresses a deadly serious theological issue.

404 The circumstances behind al-Jaʿd's execution and the involvement of the Caliph Hishām are glossed over swiftly by Ibn Nubātah; see van Ess, *Theology*, 2:512–14, for more details.

405 Wāṣil's speech impediment made him unable to properly pronounce the Arabic letter *rāʾ*, and he famously composed an entire sermon without using the letter so that he could maintain proper diction throughout.

406 The Arabic *al-Thanawiyyah* connotes various dualist religious creeds, of which is the best known is Manichaeanism.

407 *Sumaniyyah*/*Samaniyyah* was the Arabic for Buddhism, perhaps derived from Sanskrit *Śramaṇa* (Pali *sāmaṇera*), "ascetic practitioner"/"monk." Arabic writing from Bashshār's era does not reveal intimate knowledge of Buddhism, and the precise beliefs of *Sumaniyyah* are unclear (see Van Ess (2017), 2:23–25; Berzin, "Historical Survey of the Buddhist and Muslim Worlds' Knowledge of Each Other's Customs and Teachings"; Mélikian-Chirvani, "L'évocation littéraire du bouddhisme dans l'Iran musulman").

408 While all *Sarḥ al-ʿuyūn* manuscripts name Aḥmad ibn Khallād, this seems a copyist error: other versions (al-Iṣbahānī, *al-Aghānī*, 3:224; al-Murtaḍā, *Amālī*, 1:154) have Aḥmad reporting from his father, Khallād. Al-Zajjājī's *Majālis al-ʿulamāʾ*, 158, records a different debate between Bashshār and an otherwise unknown Khallād ibn Mubārak of the Bāhilah.

409 The tenet that one can only believe what can be perceived by the senses refers to ideas imported into Arabic writings about Indian religious beliefs (al-Bīrūnī, *al-Taḥqīq mā li-l-Hind*, 183). Since Bashshār was blind, it is difficult to reconcile this anecdote, but Ibn Nubātah precisely follows al-Murtaḍā's *Amālī*, 1:154 (though not *al-Aghānī*, 3:224).

410 Bashshār refers to Khallād via his teknonym, variously reported as Abū Khālid or Abū Mukhallad (Ibn Manẓūr, *Mukhtār al-Aghānī*, 2:85n1).

411 Hilāl ibn ʿAṭiyyah is unknown; some scholars think Bashshār's friend should be Hilāl al-Rāʾī ibn Yaḥyā ibn Muslim (d. 245/859–60), a well-known jurist (al-Iṣbahānī, *al-Aghānī*, 3:161n3; Cheikho, *Majānī l-adab fī ḥadāʾiq al-ʿarab*, 1:101), though he would have been rather too young to fit this anecdote.

412 Bashshār calls Hilāl a *rāfiḍī*, literally "a refuser," a polemical slur against pro-Alid groups on account of their "refusal" to accept the legitimacy of the first caliphs, and, even more pejoratively, their "refusal" of Islam itself. The term "Shiʿi" to specifically label pro-Alids developed after Bashshār's era.

413 Bashshār's statement permits two readings. One is an oath: "Oh yes, I swear *by the religion* of Khusrow"—such an oath would indeed be blasphemous. But the alternative reading is a statement: "Oh yes, *and that the religion* [today] would be Khusrow's"—this alludes to the permissibility of consanguineous marriage in Zoroastrianism, enabling fathers to marry their daughters.

414 Composing poetry is often described in Arabic as "stringing pearls," alongside other pearling metaphors.

415 Q Tīn 95:4.

416 The Arabic refers to Ḥammād as "son of Nihyā": Nihyā was a town in the Syrian Desert between Damascus and al-Ruṣāfah populated by non-Arab agriculturalist stock, and Bashshār may thus intend an insult about Ḥammād's non-Arab origins (Bashshār, *Dīwān*, 1:154n1).

417 The "head" probably refers to God, hence Bashshār intones he has one God, and has absolutely no interest in two deities of Manichaean dualist belief (Bashshār, *Dīwān*, 3:157n2).

418 The two versions differ only in one preposition. The first proves Bashshār's monotheistic belief and lampoons Ḥammād's Manichaean dualism, but Ḥammād's subtle reworking renders Bashshār a polytheist too.

419 Al-Mahdī's paternal lineage of the Hashemite Abbasids descended from the clan of the Prophet, and his mother was South Arabian. Muslims of Bashshār's generation associated the South Arabian kingdom of Ḥimyar with pre-Islamic world empire and powerful armies.

420 This verse echoes the vocabulary of Q Luqmān 31:18, where God is described as not loving boastful people.

421 The MSS are unanimous in rendering the final word as *Kaywān*, the planet Saturn in Persian, but this is likely an error. The verb *wattada* ("to peg"; "fix in place") suggests that Bashshār satirically compares the oaf's heavy character to a mountain (a resonance with Q Naba' 78:7). I am unaware of any mountain called Kaywān. Citations of the poem elsewhere render the name "Thahlān," a mountain famous in poetry (Bashshār, *Dīwān*, 4:220).

422 The poem is replete with Qur'anic references. Q Qāriʿah 101:6–8 states that those with "heavy scales" enter Paradise, whereas those with "light scales" go to Hell. It intends the measure of good deeds; Bashshār makes a pun by referring to his opponent as physically heavy, but light on good deeds. Q Aḥzāb 33:72 describes God asking the earth to bear His Trust, which the earth refused as too heavy a burden; hence Bashshār's quip sarcastically wondering why the earth refused God's Trust given that it could bear the burden of Abū Marwān (all *Sarḥ al-ʿuyūn* manuscripts render his name as Abū Marwān; it is Abū Sufyān in Bashshār's *Dīwān*).

423 *Patrikios* was a Byzantine honorific granted to the most important governors and generals; its Arabized form, *biṭrīq*, is common in Arabic literature as a catchall for Byzantine military commanders or Christian ecclesiastical figures.

424 As Ibn Nubātah correctly notes at the end of this section, *domestikos* was not a personal name, but a rank in the Byzantine military. It ranged from commanders of regiments within the army to the army's commander in chief. In this story, the historical figure is Bardas Phokas, the army commander in chief, who was wounded at his defeat in the Battle of Marʿash in 341/952.

425 Ibn Nubātah confuses battles here: Samandu in 339/950 saw Sayf al-Dawlah defeated by the Byzantines; Sayf al-Dawlah's famous victory was at Marʿash in 341/952.

426 By "Roman," the poem means the rulers of Constantinople, whom we know as "Byzantines" today; in the medieval period, Byzantine emperors always called themselves "Roman," and contemporary Arabic writers referred to them as "Romans" too.

427 This statement was said to have been the standard oath to utter before addressing a king in pre-Islamic times.

428 The Arabic *ghāniyah* refers to a woman whose natural beauty is so complete that she needs no makeup or adornment to prettify herself.

429 All manuscripts write "Ṭufāwah" without definite article; the correct form is al-Ṭufāwah (Ibn Durayd, *al-Ishtiqāq*, 271).

430 The anecdote turns on a pun: "Rāsib" resembles the word *rusūb*, which means "to sink," and "Ṭufāwah" resembles the verb *ṭafā*, "to float." Both are unlikely etymologies for tribal names: others posit that "Ṭufāwah" derives from an alternative meaning that connotes the disk of the sun (Ibn Durayd, *al-Ishtiqāq*, 271), and Rāsib can also mean "sturdy as a mountain" (Ibn Manẓūr, *Lisān al-ʿArab*, 1:418). Ibn Nubātah's version offers no explanation as to why the clans approached a known idiot to resolve their dispute; in a fuller version in Ibn ʿArabī's *Muḥāḍarat al-abrār wa-musāmarat al-akhyār* (1:308), the dispute is narrated as occurring in public, and Habannaqah emerges from the crowd with his foolish advice. Ibn ʿArabī's version is set in an Umayyad-era context, whereas Ibn Nubātah labels Habannaqah as pre-Islamic. A version narrated by Ibn al-Jawzī also sets the story in the Umayyad era (*Akhbār al-ḥumqā wa-l-mughaffilīn*, 42–43).

431 The ascription of this story to Habannaqah seems unique to our text; elsewhere, the protagonist is a different historical "fool," Qabīṣah ibn al-Muhallab (al-Jāḥiẓ, *al-Bayān*, 2:238; Ibn Qutaybah, *ʿUyūn al-akhbār*, 2:45). Another version ends differently: the fool says, "Don't be distressed at what you see; this is a signal of my death"—presumably he understood that they would be pleased to know that they will soon be rid of him (Ibn al-Jawzī, *Akhbār al-ḥumqā*, 177).

432 There is confusion over Ṭuways's name: al-Iṣbahānī's *al-Aghānī* has two biographies for him, and identifies his name as ʿĪsā in one (3:28) and Ṭāwūs in the other (4:219); see the notes in Rowson, "The Effeminates of Early Medina," 678.

433 Arabic literature contains may stories of people identified as *mukhannathūn*. The term is variously translated as "hermaphrodite," "effeminate man," or "homosexual," but its relations with gender, sexual identity, and preference are complex. The *mukhannathūn* of Medina in Islam's first century, like Ṭuways, were an identifiable group. Many worked as entertainers and led the development of music: they were effeminate and exhibited aspects of our conception of transvestites, though some married. "Bisexual" or "transvestite" would not necessarily be good transliterations given their connotations in modern English; see Rowson, "Effeminates," with detailed discussion of Ṭuways on pp. 677–82.

434 The Long form manuscripts add that Ṭuways married on the day of the Caliph ʿUthmān's assassination, though this is crossed out in I2.

435 The Arabic literally says "my liver delights in him"; liver metaphorically connotes the body's core (al-Zamakhsharī, *Asās al-balāghah*, 533).

436 As mentioned above, ʿAbd al-Raḥmān was the son of Ḥassan. The lovesick girl named by Ṭuways is ʿAbd al-Raḥmān's own sister, and the poem deeply humiliates him.

437 The poet is Ziyād al-Aʿjam; Ibn Qutaybah, *Excellence*, §2.8.25, details the context.

438 See §70.1.

439 Extant manuscripts of al-Mutalammis's poetry do not include these verses (al-Mutalammis, *Dīwān*, 305–6). The melancholy lament on desert life is more attuned to the feelings of urban poetry collectors of early Islam than pre-Islamic poets themselves. Abū Tammām ascribes these lines to al-Maqqās al-ʿĀʾidī (*al-Waḥshiyyāt*, 14–15).

440 As in the case of the previous poem, these verses are not in al-Mutalammis's *Dīwān*; early sources ascribe them to an anonymous poet (see al-Marzūqī, *Sharḥ Dīwān al-Ḥamāsah*, 4:1580–81).

441 The caliphs had numerous enslaved concubines, and many of their children lacked noble lineage from their maternal line, hence ʿAqīl's reference to them as mongrels. This may seem incredibly picky, but matrilineal descent was a key marker of nobility in early Islam, and thus ʿAqīl may actually not have been so haughty as later audiences (accustomed to patrilineal-dominated lineage) imagined. For a discussion of gender and lineage, see Webb, *Imagining*, 197–205.

442 The manuscripts unanimously name her al-Ḥawrāʾ, but the story's likely source, al-Iṣbahānī, *al-Aghānī*, 12:299, has "al-Jarbāʾ" (as do Ibn Manẓūr, *Mukhtār al-Aghānī*, 5:113, and Ibn ʿAsākir, *Tārīkh Dimashq*, 69:87). Ibn Sallām, *Ṭabaqāt fuḥūl al-shuʿarāʾ*, 2:715, narrates a different account, but also names the girl al-Jarbāʾ.

443 The location is variously identified; the *Sarḥ al-ʿuyūn* manuscripts have "Dayr Saʿd," which lies in the desert south of Syria, land that ʿAqīl would have been passing on this journey (Yāqūt, *Muʿjam al-buldān*, 3:221). See ʿAllāwanah, *ʿAqīl ibn ʿUllafah: sīratuhu wa-shiʿruhu*, 94, for alternatives.

444 The last line literally reads: "I recognize this nature from Akhzam." It is reported that Ibn Abī Akhzam of the Ṭayyi' was disobedient to his father and his children were unruly in turn, and he was said to have accepted their ways, given how his own temperament had been (Ibn Sallām, *Ṭabaqāt fuḥūl al-shuʿarā'*, 2:713n1). Al-Iṣbahānī gives an alternative, identifying "Akhzam" as a lusty camel stud who sired calves in different herds, and the offspring could be recognized by their nature (*al-Aghānī*, 12:302).

445 In an expanded version of this story, one of ʿAqīl's sons wounded the father, and the other wounded his camel. Hence, there was literally a maimed camel for the al-Qayn to take, and there they would find the wounded ʿAqīl (al-Iṣbahānī, *al-Aghānī*, 12:300).

446 Given that the caliph was proud of his mother's descent from the Caliph ʿUmar ibn al-Khaṭṭāb, ʿAqīl's statement would have been cause for considerable offense.

447 Q Nūḥ 71:1.

448 The terminology references four terms connoting animals, *baḥīrah*, *waṣīlah*, *sā'ibah*, and *ḥām*, from Q Mā'idah 5:103. Exegetes disagreed over their meaning (al-Ṭabarī, *Jāmi' al-bayān fī ta'wīl āy al-Qur'ān*, 7:116–25), but generally assumed they were animals dedicated for worship in pre-Islamic Arabia (see al-Balādhurī, *Ansāb al-ashrāf* (1979–), 1:84; Ibn Ḥajar, *Fatḥ al-Bārī*, 10:104–8).

449 This hadith is unidentified.

450 While Muslims realized that Arabians lacked the kingdoms and cities of other pre-Islamic peoples, the merit of the Arabs was constructed, in part, on a sense that the Arabs were extremely knowledgeable about the environment and natural phenomena, as evidenced by the wealth of technical words in pre-Islamic Arabic to describe very particular things, which numerous Muslim-era writers equated with scientific precision of equal merit to the natural philosophers of the pre-Islamic Greco-Roman and Persian worlds (see Ibn Qutaybah, *Excellence*, §§2.2–2.3, and, on clouds particularly, Ibn Durayd, *Waṣf al-maṭar wa-l-saḥāb*). The rare words Hind summons to describe particular clouds is an example of this cultural feature, and hence we translate her words with scientific equivalents. A mammatus cloud is one that has pouch-like shapes on its underside.

451 There are several versions of this remark; for the "strikes/scrapes" pair, we follow al-Bakrī, *Simṭ al-la'ālī*, 3:93.

452 See §29.

453 See §17.9.

454 Ibn Nubātah has mixed stories. The most common version has three girls, and gives Hammām the active role of blocking their marriages; this better reflects the exasperated tone of Ibn Zaydūn's *Letter* (al-Bayhaqī, *al-Maḥāsin wa-l-masāwi'*, 2:383; al-Qālī, *al-Amālī*, 2:105–6; al-Maqrīzī, *The Arab Thieves*, §1b.3). Ibn Nubātah's version is actually

a story about Dhū l-Iṣbaʿ al-ʿAdwānī and his four daughters (al-Mubarrad, *al-Kāmil*, 2:678–79; al-Iṣbahān, *al-Aghānī*, 3:90–92; al-Murtaḍā, *Amālī*, 1:248–50).

455 Other versions (e.g., al-Mubarrad, *al-Kāmil*, 1:679; al-Murtaḍā, *Amālī*, 1:249) replace the last word, *witr* ("blood revenge"), with *hajr*—that is, the man is sleepless when separated from his beloved—better fitting the verse's sexual innuendo.

456 This commentary appears in nine of the fourteen Short version manuscripts consulted, but their statement that the poem is "not part of the *Letter*" is odd: no Long version manuscripts claim this, and manuscript versions of the *Letter* itself (C4 and R3) include the verse, as do versions of Ibn Zaydūn's *Letter* copied in other books (al-Qalqashandī, *Ṣubḥ al-aʿshā*, 1:463; al-Nuwayrī, *Nihāyat al-arab*, 7:217). The gloss is also incorrect: the usual lineage cited for the Hizzān is from the ʿAnazah (Kaḥḥālah, *Muʿjam qabāʾil al-ʿarab*, 3:1217–18).

457 See §28.2.

458 All manuscripts render the poet's name as "Ḥaywah," but this seems a copyist error for "Jirwah." Qays ibn Jirwah is an attested poet (Ibn Qutaybah, *al-Shiʿr*, 1:258), whereas Qays ibn Ḥaywah is unknown.

459 All manuscripts render the last words *al-ʿaẓm dhū anta ʿāriquh*, meaning that King ʿAmr stripped the meat, and the poet Qays will break the bones. Elsewhere, the verse reads *al-ʿaẓm dhū anā ʿāriquh*, meaning that the poet threatens to strip the meat and break the bones (see al-Marzūqī, *Sharḥ Dīwān al-Ḥamāsah*, 4:1746–47).

460 The MSS have either Rumaylah or Zumaylah ibn Shiʿār; al-Iṣbahānī has Turmulah ibn Shuʿāth (*al-Aghānī*, 22:191).

461 Interpretations of the verse hinge on the words *Umāmah* and *Hind*. Al-Shantamarī deems them two mountains that indicate the great distance between the poet and ʿAmr (*Sharḥ*, 2:1037); al-Marzūqī considers them the names of the poet's and ʿAmr's mothers, implying that ʿAmr's clan is weaker (*Sharḥ Dīwān al-Ḥamāsah*, 3:1466–67); the lexicographers Ibn Sīdah and al-Zabīdī interpret *umāmah* as three hundred camels and *hind* as one hundred, creating a metaphor of the two sides' different strengths (Ibn Sīdah, *al-Muḥkam*, 10:578; al-Zabīdī, *Tāj al-ʿarūs*, 16:31).

462 See §20.

463 The poem is usually ascribed to ʿAmr ibn Milqaṭ of the Ṭayyiʾ (Ibn Ḥabīb, *al-Naqāʾiḍ*, 2:653; al-Iṣbahānī, *al-Aghānī*, 22:193).

464 This verse is variably copied in the manuscripts, most without readily understandable meaning. The source of the verse is Ibn Ḥabīb, *al-Naqāʾiḍ*, 2:653, where it would read "ʿAmr's brother, his mother's youngest."

465 The Ḥanẓalah were a clan of the Tamīm, Zurārah's people.

466 He is elsewhere identified as ʿAmr ibn Milqaṭ of the Ṭayyiʾ (Ibn al-Athīr, *al-Kāmil*, 1:554).

467 The MSS all identify "Hind of Hinds" with Māriyah's mother, but al-Iṣbahānī, *al-Aghānī*, 11:19, identifies her as Māriyah's sister. Ḥassān ibn Thābit identifies "Hind of Hinds" as Hind bint ʿUtbah, a Meccan noblewoman (Ḥassān, *Dīwān*, 1:384).

468 See §28.2.

469 Q Anbiyāʾ 21:103 refers to Judgment Day as "the Great Horror." ʿAmr addresses the Prophet in the terms appropriate for a pre-Islamic king, whereupon Muḥammad invited him to Islam, tacitly rejecting the trappings of pre-Islamic monarchy.

470 The Arabic reads, "Ibn Abī Ḥātim," though he is unknown; the anecdote is elsewhere ascribed to Ibn Abī Ḥāzim, a warrior at Yarmūk.

471 The booty is presumably silver coins (dirhams).

472 This is the first line of the Qur'an and the opening of all but one of its chapters. Knowing it hardly constitutes any degree of mnemonic aptitude.

473 The story is narrated in a different context by Ibn Qutaybah, *Excellence*, §2.2.9.

474 The Arabic of this passage may be corrupted, and Ibn Nubātah's source has not been identified. The anecdote is frequently cited (see ʿAmr ibn Maʿdī Karib, *Shiʿr*, 130–31; al-Iṣbahānī, *al-Aghānī*, 16:80–81), and the above poem is occasionally ascribed to another poet (al-Marzubānī, *Muʿjam al-shuʿarāʾ*, 1:105), but Ibn Nubātah appears unique in the narration of the latter part of the narrative.

475 Q Ṭā Hā 20:74.

476 Other sources of this story say the raid was against the Nahd (Ibn Ḥamdūn, *al-Tadhkirah*, 3:54; al-ʿAskarī, *Dīwān al-maʿānī*, 1:202), which appears to be correct since Khālid ibn al-Ṣaqʿab is elsewhere identified as being from the Nahd (al-Jawālīqī, *Sharḥ Adab al-Kātib*, 202).

477 The manuscripts render his name al-Saʿqab, which is also the error preserved in al-Aghānī. The basis for correction is explained in al-ʿAskarī, *Dīwān al-maʿānī*, 1:202.

478 ʿAmr ibn Maʿdī Karib was of "Southern Arab" lineage, a rival faction to the "Maʿadd," who later became known as the "Northern Arabs" (see Webb, "Ethnicity" and "Sublime").

479 The name is rendered Munabbih ibn al-ʿĀṣ or al-Munabbih ibn al-Ḥajjāj. Among various stories about the sword, those that connect it to the Battle of Badr name its owner al-ʿĀṣ ibn Munabbih ibn al-Ḥajjāj (Ibn al-Athīr, *al-Kāmil*, 2:74).

480 Abū l-Faraj al-Iṣbahānī identifies Rayḥānah as ʿAmr's sister, though Rayḥānah was ʿAmr's lover/poetic beloved (ʿAmr ibn Maʿdī Karib, *Shiʿr*, 59n1).

481 See §17.6.

482 See §16, §17, §28.1.

483 Ibn Nubātah appears unique in rendering Sirḥān this way; elsewhere, he is identified as Sirḥān ibn Muʿattib ibn al-Ajabb of the Ghanī (al-Bakrī, *Faṣl al-maqāl*, 362–63; Ibn Ḥazm, *Jamharat ansāb al-ʿArab*, 248).

484 This gloss is unique to MS I1, and seems a copyist's addition. It is not the only meaning of *mutaqammir*: Long versions I3 and T1 provide a marginal gloss that "*mutaqammir* means a lion or a wolf that hunts at night"; see also Ibn Manẓūr, *Lisān al-ʿArab*, 5:114.

485 All *Sarḥ al-ʿuyūn* manuscripts have al-Ḥutāt ibn Mujāshiʿ, but the name is usually al-Ḥutāt ibn Yazīd (Mujāshiʾ was the name of al-Ḥuṭāṭ's clan, not his father). The story has various versions: Ibn Nubātah copied it from al-ʿAskarī, *Jamharat al-amthāl*, 1:207–11; see an alternative in al-Iṣbahānī, *al-Aghānī*, 21:370.

486 Muʿāwiyah intends that he had to buy the support of the other members of the Tamīm in the wars that brought Muʿāwiyah to power. According to historical sources, al-Ḥutāt's clan, unlike other groups of the Tamīm, always opposed ʿAlī, Muʿāwiyah's rival (see al-Ṭabarī, *Tārīkh al-rusul*, 5:242–43).

487 The manuscripts of *Sarḥ al-ʿuyūn* imperfectly relate the tale from this point on. A more complete version in al-ʿAskarī's *Jamharat al-amthāl*, 1:207–11, provides additional information that better explains the drama and reactions of the characters. It is translated in the Appendix.

488 The Fuqaym ibn ʿAdī was a subgroup of the Kinānah, a noble lineage of the Quraysh. Al-Farazdaq, from the Tamīm, had no chance of claiming this lineage.

489 Al-Farazdaq calls Marwān *ṣāfin*, literally a horse that stands by putting its weight only on three legs.

490 The Arabic is literally "a man from Maysān," an agricultural district in Iraq, a heartland of the Nabaṭī, a people derided as the binary opposite of "Arab" and the good qualities for which "Arab" stood.

491 This is an oversight of I1's copyist: ʿAmr ibn Maʿdī Karib's biography is at §72, but there is no biography for Durayd ibn al-Ṣimmah. Long version manuscripts do have Durayd's biography (*Sarḥ al-ʿuyūn*, (1964) 364–68), but because he is not expressly named in the *Letter*, the Short versions omit his biography. I1 is the only Short version manuscript to provide any commentary here—it seems I1's copyist copied from the Long version to augment the text, and overlooked the fact that he had not copied Durayd's biography.

492 Muslim texts accord Moses the virtue of having been directly addressed by God (Q Nisāʾ 4:164; Aʿrāf 7:143), whereas Muḥammad received his revelation via the intermediary angel, Gabriel. Al-Maʿarrī's demand is thus particularly blasphemous. See commentaries on Q Baqarah 2:253 for Muslim views on human audiences with the Divine.

493 This sentence glosses a word that does not appear in the *Letter*; it is in all Long version MSS, but a reader of I2, who made judicious corrections throughout, crossed out this sentence.

494 Al-Ḥārith ibn Waʿlah is more commonly identified with the Dhuhl subgroup of the Shaybān (al-Marzūqī, *Sharḥ Dīwān al-Ḥamāsah*, 1:203; al-Tibrīzī, *Sharḥ al-Qaṣāʾid*, 1:153), not the Yashkur. Some ascribe him (likely erroneously) Jarm lineage (al-Shantamarī, *Sharḥ Ḥamāsat Abī Tammām*, 1:320; al-Iṣbahānī, *al-Aghānī*, 22:220–24).

495 Ibn Nubātah again misapplies Yashkur lineage: in other texts, ʿĀmir ibn al-Ẓarib is ascribed ʿAdwān lineage. The error may stem from Ibn Nubātah copying al-Suhaylī's *al-Rawḍ al-unuf*, which names one of ʿĀmir ibn al-Ẓarib's ancestors "Yashkur," but this is not the Yashkur lineage group (*al-Rawḍ*, 2:44).

496 These statements constitute a subgenre in Arabic of "practices from pre-Islam affirmed by Islam," contrasting with the presumptions that *everything* pre-Islamic is otiose in Muslim eyes. Ibn Ḥabīb, *al-Muḥabbar*, 236–37, lists examples. Al-Suhaylī is Abū l-Qāsim ʿAbd al-Raḥmān, author of *al-Rawḍ al-unuf*, from which this paragraph is copied verbatim (2:51).

497 Q Yūsuf 12:18 describes how Joseph's brothers, after throwing him in the well, daubed his coat in blood and brought it back to "prove" to Jacob that Joseph had been killed by a wolf.

498 Elsewhere, the two brothers are named ʿAmr and Saʿd, sons of Mālik ibn Ḍubayʿah (al-Iṣbahānī, *al-Aghānī*, 24:249–40; al-Maydānī, *Majmaʿ al-amthāl*, 1:56–57; al-Tibrīzī, *Sharḥ al-Qaṣāʾid*, 1:155–56).

499 More detailed accounts better explain how ʿAmr understood his brother Saʿd's message. Saʿd hit one beat to signal "stop"; then he made three beats, swung his staff upward, and brushed the ground with it to indicate "rain" and the land being "not barren." Saʿd then made more beats and swings of his staff to indicate "no plants," then let his staff dangle in the direction of the king. ʿAmr then understood what to say.

500 See §11.9.

501 Above, §76.2–3.

502 See §51.

503 Q Ṣād 38:75.

504 More than thirty Qurʾanic verses speak of "tasting" God's punishment, or chide unbelievers for what they will "taste" in the Hellfire.

505 The hadith is ascribed to the Prophet's companion Abū Hurayrah, but it did not circulate widely (Abū ʿUbayd al-Qāsim, *Kitāb al-Īmān*, 22n1).

506 Wrangling over the words used by great poets is common in Arabic literary discussions. This verse in particular attracted considerable debate (al-ʿUkbarī, *al-Bayān fī sharḥ al-Dīwān*, 1:41).

507 Al-Mutanabbī intends Kāfūr, regent over Egypt for the caliphs. Though he enjoyed almost unlimited authority, Kāfūr was a eunuch possessed by the caliph, prompting the poet's satire.

508 This is a praise of Ibn Nubātah's patron, Abū l-Fidā', ruler of Hama.

509 Q Naml 27:19.

510 Q Aḥqāf 46:15.

511 We have set this as a poem, as it is set in such a manner in MS I1, but note that while the first line scans according to Arabic prosody, the second does not.

512 The Prophetic biography states that the angels used Zamzam's water to purify Muḥammad before his Night Journey (al-Ṭabarī, *al-Tārīkh al-rusul*, 2:308).

513 MS I1 was transcribed in the last year of the Ottoman Sultan Suleiman the Magnificent's reign (r. 1520–66).

# Glossary

*Abān* name of several mountains in Arabia; the mountains are usually located in the lands of the ʿAbs and the Fazārah.

*Abān ibn Samʿān* an obscure figure, noted in some Arabic sources as a teacher of al-Jaʿd ibn Dirham. See also al-Jaʿd ibn Dirham.

*ʿAbbās ibn Muḥammad* (d. 186/802) a brother of the first two Abbasid caliphs, al-Saffāḥ and al-Manṣūr, and a military commander who served as governor of northern Mesopotamia (known in Arabic as al-Jazīrah).

*ʿAbbās ibn al-Walīd* (d. 130/747–48) Umayyad prince, son of the Caliph al-Walīd ibn ʿAbd al-Malik, who died in prison during the intra-Umayyad power struggles at the end of their dynasty.

*Abbasids* dynasty of caliphs from 132/750 to 656/1258, named after their ancestor al-ʿAbbās ibn ʿAbd al-Muṭṭalib ibn Hāshim, the uncle of the Prophet. .

*ʿAbd Allāh ibn Dārim* name of a clan of the Dārim, subgroup of the Tamīm. See also Tamīm.

*ʿAbd Allāh ibn Jaʿfar* (d. between 80/699 and 90/709) eminent nobleman of the Quraysh, nephew of the Caliph ʿAlī, renowned for his generosity. See also ʿAlī ibn Abī Ṭālib.

*ʿAbd Allāh ibn Muslim* (d. 96/715–16) a brother of the Umayyad military commander Qutaybah ibn Muslim; ʿAbd Allāh was one of his lieutenants and was killed during their unsuccessful revolt against the caliphate. See also Qutaybah ibn Muslim.

*ʿAbd Allāh ibn Ṭāhir* (d. 230/844) statesman and confidant of the Caliph al-Maʾmūn; he became the semiautonomous ruler of Khurasan and was a poet and patron of literature and learning.

*ʿAbd Allāh ibn ʿUmar* (d. 73/693) a son of the Caliph ʿUmar ibn al-Khaṭṭāb, respected as a devout figure and prominent authority on Prophetic legal traditions.

*ʿAbd Allāh ibn al-Zubayr* (d. 73/692) nobleman of the ʿAbd al-ʿUzzā clan of the Quraysh and son of the Companion al-Zubayr ibn al-ʿAwwām; he was proclaimed caliph in Mecca in 64/683, but his caliphate was not universally acknowledged; he was defeated and killed by the Umayyad caliph ʿAbd al-Malik ibn Marwān. See also Companions, al-Zubayr ibn ʿAwwām.

*ʿAbd ʿAmr ibn Bishr* pre-Islamic nobleman of the Ḍubayʿah, paternal grandfather of Ṭafarah ibn al-ʿAbd. See also Ṭarafah ibn al-ʿAbd.

*ʿAbd al-Ḥamīd ibn Yaḥyā ibn Saʿd* (d. 132/750) state secretary of the Umayyad caliph Marwān ibn Muḥammad, widely credited with setting the standard for Arabic letter-writing style.

*ʿAbd al-Jabbār ibn ʿAbd al-Raḥmān al-Azdī* (d. 142/759–60) agent of the Abbasid family who fought in Khurasan during the Abbasid revolution; he served as chief security constable (*ṣāḥib al-shurṭah*) for the first two Abbasid caliphs and was eventually appointed governor of Khurasan.

*ʿAbd al-Karīm ibn Abī l-Awjāʾ* (d. ca. 155/772) a Basran theologian, he was accused of partiality to the Manichaean faith and was expelled from Basra. He then lived in Kufa until its governor executed him.

*ʿAbd al-Malik ibn Marwān* (r. 65–86/685–705) Umayyad caliph and key figure in the development of the caliphate's administrative structures, ideologies, and institutions.

*ʿAbd al-Malik ibn ʿUmayr* (d. 136/753–4) Kufan traditionist and judge.

*ʿAbd al-Muṭṭalib ibn Hāshim* paternal grandfather of the Prophet Muḥammad; when Muḥammad was orphaned as a child, ʿAbd al-Muṭṭalib cared for him.

*ʿAbd Rabbihi "the Small" (al-Ṣaghīr)* (d. ca. 80/698–99) Kharijite commander and one of the chief lieutenants of Qaṭarī ibn Fujāʾah. See also Kharijites.

*ʿAbd al-Raḥmān ibn al-Ashʿath* (d. 83/702) Umayyad-era nobleman of the Kindah. A powerful leader in Iraq, he initially acquiesced to al-Ḥajjāj's governorship, then led a protracted but ultimately unsuccessful revolt against al-Ḥajjāj between 80/699 and 83/702. See also al-Ḥajjāj ibn Yūsuf.

*ʿAbd al-Raḥmān ibn al-Ḥārith ibn Hishām al-Makhzūmī* (d. before 60/680) Medinan nobleman and respected jurist.

*ʿAbd al-Raḥmān ibn Ḥassān* (d. 104/722–23 or earlier) nobleman of Medina, poet, and son of Ḥassān ibn Thābit, the poet of the Prophet; he had a reputation for arrogance and bad temper.

*ʿAbd al-Raḥmān ibn Muʿāwiyah "the Emigré"* (r. 138–72/756–88) nobleman of the Umayyad family; upon his family's defeat by the Abbasids, he fled to Spain and established the independent Umayyad caliphate in Andalusia.

*ʿAbīd ibn al-Abraṣ* pre-Islamic Arabic poet of the Asad whose biography is fragmentary. Indications suggest he lived in the early sixth century AD.

*ʿAbs* Arabian lineage, and a powerful subgroup of the Ghaṭafān. They are frequently encountered in Arabic accounts of pre-Islamic Arabian wars. See also Ghaṭafān.

*Abū l-ʿAlāʾ al-Maʿarrī* (d. 449/1058) one of the greatest poets of the Abbasid era, he lived much of his later life in extreme seclusion and ascetic poverty. He was suspected of harboring heretical beliefs.

*Abū ʿAmr ibn al-ʿAlāʾ al-Māzinī* (d. ca. 154–56/770–72) Basran Qurʾan specialist, narrator of one of the seven authoritative readings of the Qurʾan (*qirāʾāṭ*). In fear of al-Ḥajjāj, Abū ʿAmr's family fled to South Arabia when he was about twenty years old and only returned to Basra after al-Ḥajjāj's death. See also al-Ḥajjāj ibn Yūsuf.

*Abū l-ʿAynāʾ, Muḥammad ibn al-Qāsim* (d. 283/896) poet and literary scholar active in Basra and Baghdad, celebrated for his quick wit and masterful Arabic.

*Abū Bakr* (r. 11–13/632–34) Muḥammad's father-in-law and Islam's first caliph. A wealthy merchant before Islam, variously reported as the first, or one of the first, converts to Islam.

*Abū l-Faraj* see al-Iṣbahānī, Abū l-Faraj.

*Abū Ḥayyān al-Tawḥīdī* see al-Tawḥīdī.

*Abū l-Hudhayl "the Feed Merchant" (al-ʿAllāf)* (d. 226/840–41 or 235/849–50) Basran theologian and influential early figure in the development of the Muʿtazilah. See also Muʿtazilah.

*Abū Jaʿfar al-Manṣūr* see al-Manṣūr.

*Abū Marwān* unidentified.

*Abū Maʿshar, Jaʿfar ibn Muḥammad al-Balkhī* (d. 272/886 or after 283/896) celebrated astrologer who claimed his astrological knowledge was a continuation of ancient, pre-Islamic wisdom.

*Abū Mūsā l-Ashʿarī* (d. ca. 42/662) Companion of the Prophet and prominent military leader and political figure during the early Islamic conquests. See also Companions.

*Abū Muslim al-Khurasānī* (d. 137/755) from obscure origins, he emerged as a leader of the Abbasid revolution in Khurasan and was instrumental in bringing the Abbasid family to power. The Abbasids feared his influence and assassinated him in the revolution's aftermath.

*Abū Nuwās, al-Ḥasan ibn Hāniʾ* (d. between 198/813 and 200/815) celebrated Abbasid-era poet, innovator of new forms of poetry, famous partisan of Southern Arabs, best known today for his libertine poetry.

*Abū l-Nuwayrah* pre-Islamic warrior of the Taghlib who, according to some versions of the Basūs War story, headed the war band sent by Muhalhil to assassinate Jassās ibn Murrah. See also Basūs War, Jassās ibn Murrah, and Taghlib.

*Abū Qatādah al-Ḥārith ibn Rabʿī l-Anṣārī* (d. 40/660 or 54/673) member of the Medinan Khazraj who fought in most of the Prophet's campaigns; he later fought in the conquests of Iran, and for the Caliph ʿAlī in the First Fitnah, the first war of succession with the Umayyads. See also al-Khazraj, ʿAlī ibn Abī Ṭālib.

*Abū l-Shamaqmaq* (d. ca. 180/796) early Abbasid-era Basran poet, known for his ribald existence on the fringe of literary society. He was a drinking companion of great poets such as Abū Nuwās, Bashshār ibn Burd, and Diʿbil. See also Abū Nuwās, Bashshār ibn Burd, and Diʿbil.

*Abū Shuʿayb "the Jug Maker" (also known as "the Sufi")* obscure figure; originally a potter from Sogdiana, he settled in Baghdad and became known as a poet and (possibly) a Muʿtazilite theologian during the caliphate of al-Rashīd. See also Muʿtazilah and al-Rashīd.

*Abū Ṣufrah Ẓālim ibn Sarrāq (or Sāriq)* founder of the Muhallabid clan of Umayyad-era military leaders and Basran notables. Abū Ṣufrah originally hailed from Oman (perhaps as a Persian settler). He participated in Muslim conquests of Iran and Iraq (possibly as a purveyor of horses to the Muslim armies), and settled in Basra.

*Abū Sufyān ibn Ḥarb ibn Umayyah* (d. ca. 32/653) prominent Meccan merchant of the Quraysh clan ʿAbd Shams. He led the opposition to the Prophet but converted to Islam just prior to the Muslims' conquest of Mecca; father of the Caliph Muʿāwiyah.

*Abū Tammām al-Ṭāʾī* (d. 231/845) celebrated Abbasid court poet and poetry anthologist. Originally a Damascene Christian, Abū Tammām converted to Islam and feigned Arab identity by claiming descent from the Ṭayyiʾ. See also Ṭayyiʾ.

*Abū l-Ṭayyib* see al-Mutanabbī.

*Abū ʿUbaydah Maʿmar ibn al-Muthannā* (d. 210/825) one of the most important early Arabic philologists and scholars of pre-Islamic Arabian history; among the first to record his scholarship in book form.

*Abū l-Walīd Muḥammad ibn Jahwar* (r. 435–50/1043–58) second ruler of the independent Jahwar kingdom in Cordoba, son of the dynasty's founder. See also Jahwar.

*Abū Yūsuf* (d. 182/798) prominent jurist and student of the Iraqi legal scholar Abū Ḥanīfah; the Ḥanafī method of Islamic law derives largely from the collected opinions of Abū Yūsuf, alongside those of Abū Ḥanīfah and al-Shaybānī. See also al-Shaybānī.

*Abū Zubayd Ḥarmalah ibn al-Mundhir al-Ṭāʾī* poet of the Ṭayyiʾ. His poetry was esteemed by poetry collectors; he was noted as being particularly fond of composing poetry describing lions. A contemporary of the Prophet, there is debate over whether he converted to Islam or remained Christian until his death in the early Islamic era. See also Ṭayyiʾ.

*ʿĀd* legendary ancient Arabian people, mentioned in the Qurʾan as the people to whom God sent the prophet Hūd. They rejected Hūd's message, and God destroyed them by a violent wind.

*ʿAdī ibn Akhzam* Arabian lineage, a subgroup of the Ṭayyiʾ. See also Ṭayyiʾ.

*ʿAdī ibn Naṣr* legendary figure; a nobleman at the court of al-Ḥīrah and the ancestor from which the Lakhmid kings of the Naṣrid family claimed descent. See also al-Ḥīrah, Lakhmids, Naṣrids.

*ʿAdī ibn Zayd* celebrated pre-Islamic Christian Arabic poet from al-Ḥīrah; almost all of his authentic poetry has been lost. See also al-Ḥīrah.

*Adriyād* Arabic name of a Sassanian-era Zoroastrian high priest, probably the priest known in Sassanian inscriptions as Kerdīr/Kartir.

*Aḥmad ibn Khallād* Iraqi narrator of the early third/ninth century, cited in later literature as narrator of stories reported by his father about early Abbasid-era poets, particular Basrans.

*Aḥmad ibn Yūsuf (or ibn Yūnus)* unidentified. See Ṣāliḥ ibn ʿAbd al-Raḥmān.

*Aḥmad ibn Yūsuf ibn al-Qāsim al-Kātib* (d. 213/828–29 or 214/829–30) poet, literary scholar, and state secretary for the Caliph al-Maʾmūn. See also al-Maʾmūn.

*Aḥmar* unknown pre-Islamic figure whom Muslim-era literary specialists identify as a camel driver, but their guess seems entirely derived from one line of poetry.

*al-Aḥnaf ibn Qays* a leader of the Tamīm in Iraq in the mid-first/seventh century. See also Tamīm.

*al-Ahtam ibn Summay al-Tamīmī* nobleman of the Tamīm in the generation before Islam; father of ʿAmr ibn Ahtam. See also Tamīm.

*al-Aḥwaṣ* probably al-Aḥwaṣ ibn Jaʿfar al-Kilābī, a pre-Islamic warrior and leader of the ʿĀmir, with whom Qays ibn Zuhayr reportedly took refuge at the outset of the Thrust and Dusty War. See also al-ʿĀmir, Qays ibn Zuhayr, and Thrust and Dusty War.

*al-Aḥwaṣ* lineage group that takes its name from al-Aḥwaṣ ibn Mālik ibn Jaʿfar, one of the leaders of the clan Jaʿfar of al-ʿĀmir. See also al-ʿĀmir.

*Ahwaz* city in Khuzistan (southwest Iran), near the Persian Gulf; a hub of river transport and agriculture.

*Ajāʾ* name of a mountain in northeastern Arabia, said to have been at the edge of the land of the Ṭayyiʾ. See also Ṭayyiʾ.

*al-ʿAkawwak, ʿAlī ibn Jabalah* (d. 213/828) Baghdadi poet, composer of praise poems for Abbasid courtiers and ministers whose praises were so outlandish as to be considered sacrilegious and who reportedly died after having his tongue cut out at the order of Caliph al-Maʾmūn.

*Aʿkush* settlement near Kufa.

*Alexander the Great* (r. 336–23) king of Macedon and conqueror of the Persian Empire. The allure of Alexander's memory produced elaborate romances circulating in the Late Antique Middle East, which entered Arab culture in the Muslim era, presenting Alexander as an ideal monarch and world conqueror.

*ʿAlī ibn Abī Ṭālib* (r. 35–41/656–61) Islam's fourth caliph, first cousin of the Prophet, and husband of the Prophet's daughter Fāṭimah. Shiʿi regard him as the first imam.

*Alid, Alids* term describing political groups in the first centuries of Islam who believed that descendants of the Caliph ʿAlī had sole legitimate political authority over the caliphate. Various competing strands of Alids proliferated, and by the fourth/tenth century the main Alid groups became known as Shiʿah, a label they have kept to the present.

*Allies (Ar. al-Anṣār)* the two Medinan clans of al-Aws and al-Khazraj, which were the first communities to entirely convert to Islam; in 1/622, Prophet Muḥammad emigrated to Medina and there established the first Muslim polity. See also Companions, al-Khazraj.

*ʿAlqamah ibn ʿUlāthah al-ʿĀmirī* (d. ca. 20/640) pre-Islamic Arabian nobleman-warrior who converted to Islam and became a prominent political figure. Best known for his acerbic rivalry with his kinsman ʿĀmir ibn al-Ṭufayl. See also ʿĀmir ibn al-Ṭufayl.

*ʿAmallas* son of ʿAqīl ibn ʿUllathah. See also ʿAqīl ibn ʿUllathah.

*ʿĀmilah* Arabian lineage, mostly a distant memory by the dawn of Islam. Small numbers of groups claiming ʿĀmilah lineage lived around Palestine in early Islam; most appear to have been absorbed into the Judhām. See also Judhām.

*al-ʿĀmir* lineage group also called ʿĀmir ibn Ṣaʿṣaʿah, a powerful clan of the Qays ʿAylān residing in between Najd and Ṭāʾif at the dawn of Islam; also the name of a clan of the Quraysh: the ʿĀmir ibn Luʾayy.

*ʿĀmir ibn Mālik "Spear Brandisher"* (d. ca. 5/626) pre-Islamic warrior and leader of the Kilāb branch of the ʿĀmir tribe, one of the leading political figures in the borderlands between Najd and the Hijaz in the decades before the rise of Islam.

*ʿĀmir ibn Ṣaʿṣaʿah* see al-ʿĀmir.

*ʿĀmir ibn al-Ṭufayl* (d. 8/629) renowned pre-Islamic warrior and poet who participated in many of the famed pre-Islamic Arabian conflicts recorded in Arabic literature. He lived into the first years of the Islamic period but did not convert and appears to have opposed Islam's spread into central Arabia.

*ʿĀmir ibn Uḥaymir* pre-Islamic nobleman of the Bahdalah clan of the Saʿd. See also Saʿd.

*ʿĀmir ibn al-Ẓarib al-ʿAdwānī* legendary pre-Islamic leader, warrior, and sage, who appears in various stories from deep pre-Islamic times.

*ʿAmr* see ʿAmr ibn Maʿdī Karib.

*ʿAmr ibn al-Ahtam* (d. 57/676) nobleman of the Minqar branch of the Tamīm. He converted to Islam late in the Prophet's lifetime and settled in Basra. His father, Sinān, a poet of considerable renown, was known by the nickname al-Ahtam ("Broken Teeth"). See also Tamīm.

*ʿAmr ibn Baḥr* see al-Jāḥiẓ.

*ʿAmr ibn Hind "the Burner"* (r. AD 554–70) Lakhmid king of al-Ḥīrah, Sassanian vassal, and prominent military leader in the Sassanian-Byzantine frontier conflicts.

*ʿAmr ibn Jundab* possibly ʿAmr ibn Jundab ibn ʿAnbar, ancestor of a clan of Tamīm lineage. See also Tamīm.

*ʿAmr ibn Maʿdī Karib* (d. after 16/637) poet, warrior, and leading figure of the Yemeni Zubayd. See also Zubayd.

*ʿAmr ibn Maymūn* an informant with this name for stories about al-Kindī cannot be found; possibly a copyist error for ʿAmr ibn al-Nuhaywī. See also ʿAmr ibn al-Nuhaywī and al-Kindī.

*ʿAmr ibn al-Nuhaywī* (fl. early third/ninth century) obscure figure who appears to have been born in rural Iraq and worked as administrator in al-Maʾmūn's caliphate. He was apparently sacked and punished for embezzling funds. He is occasionally recorded as a source for stories about Abbasid scholarly life. See also al-Ma'mūn.

*'Amr ibn Sa'd* unknown pre-Islamic figure, presumably a clan leader during al-Sulayk ibn al-Sulakah's lifetime. See also Sulayk ibn al-Sulakah.

*'Amr ibn 'Ubayd* (d. ca. 144/761) theologian, born in Balkh, who spent most of his life in Basra; an important early thinker on ideas that would become associated with the Mu'tazilites. See also Mu'tazilah.

*'Amr ibn Umayyah* (d. before 60/681) member of the Ḍamrī clan of the Kinānah who fought against the Prophet at the Battle of Uḥud, but shortly afterward converted to Islam. He was a lone survivor of the Ma'ūnah Well incident; best known for his mission to assassinate Abū Sufyān in 6/627 and as the deliverer of the Prophet's letter to the ruler of Ethiopia in 7/628. See also Abū Sufyān ibn Ḥarb ibn Umayyah.

*Anas ibn Mālik* (d. ca. 91–93/709–11) a Medinan of the Khazraj lineage, as a youth he participated in the Prophet's campaigns and settled in Basra following the conquests. He was a prominent narrator of Prophetic traditions. See also al-Khazraj and Companions.

*Anas ibn Mudrik, Abū Sufyān* celebrated warrior, poet, and leader of the Khath'am during the generation before Islam; some sources report him reaching a fabulous age and converting to Islam. See also Khath'am.

*'Anazah* Arabian lineage, subgroup of the Rabī'ah, based in northern and central Arabia (Najd and the Hijaz) at the dawn of Islam. See also Rabī'ah.

*Anmār* broad Arabian lineage group. Anmār is memorialized as a son of Nizār, one of the original "Northern Arabs"; prominent subgroups of the Anmār include the Khath'am and Bajīlah. See also Khath'am.

*Antony (Marcus Antonius)* (83–30) Roman statesman and military commander; a leading figure in Roman politics and contender for rule after the death of Julius Caesar; his defeat by Augustus Caesar inaugurated the Roman Imperial period.

*Apollonius (Ar. Balīnūs)* (1) Apollonius of Tyana, a Neo-Pythagorean Greek philosopher of the first century AD known in the Muslim era as "the creator of the talismans"; (2) Apollonius of Pergamon (ca. 262–190), one of the great mathematicians of antiquity.

*Apollonius-Asclepius* figure calqued in Arabic writing from memories of Apollonius and Asclepius.

*'Aqīl ibn 'Ullafah al-Yarbū'ī* Umayyad-era Bedouin poet of noble lineage.

*al-ʿArandas* obscure pre-Islamic Arabian poet of Bakr ibn Kilāb lineage, known primarily for a poem recorded in the *Valor Anthology*. See also Valor Anthology.

*al-Arāqim* grouping of several lineages of the Taghlib, led by the Jusham and the Mālik clans. See also Taghlib.

*Arbad ibn Qays* (d. 8/629) a leader of the ʿĀmir ibn Ṣaʿṣaʿah at the dawn of Islam who met the Prophet in a delegation with ʿĀmir ibn al-Ṭufayl, neither of whom converted. Arbad was reportedly killed by lighting shortly thereafter. He was a stepbrother of the poet Labīd, who composed famous lament poems in Arbad's memory.

*Arbitration Hearings* event in the struggle over the caliphate between the Caliph ʿAlī and his rival Muʿāwiyah. After inclusive fighting, Muʿāwiyah proposed arbitration to settle the dispute, whereafter ʿAlī's position deteriorated rapidly, as some of his supporters rejected ʿAlī's consent to the arbitration. Those deserters formed Kharijite movements, which opposed both ʿAlī and Muʿāwiyah. See also ʿAlī ibn Abī Ṭālib, Muʿāwiyah ibn Abī Sufyān, and Kharijites.

*Ardashir ibn Bābak (Ardashir I)* (r. AD 226–41) the Arabic name for Ardashir I, founder of the Sassanian dynasty.

*Ardashir* the Arabic name for an ancient Persian king; literary accounts of his reign are mostly legendary, but they reflect vague memories of three Achaemenid kings named Artaxerxes.

*Aristotle* (384–22) Greek philosopher; many of his works were translated into Arabic, and he was celebrated as the greatest of Greek philosophers in Muslim-era writings.

*Artabanus* name of various ancient Persian kings. Artabanus IV (r. AD 213–24) was the last Parthian ruler, whose defeat and death at the hands of Ardashir I marked the beginning of the Sassanian Empire.

*al-ʿĀṣ ibn Munabbih* (d. 2/624) from the Sahm clan of the Quraysh, he fought with the Meccan pagans against the Prophet at the Battle of Badr, where he was killed. See also Badr.

*Asad* large lineage group of the Muḍar "Northern Arabs" who resided in central Najd; their lands were extensive and they feature in numerous stories of pre-Islamic Arabian warring.

*Asad ibn Hāshim ibn ʿAbd Manāf* great-uncle of the Prophet and patriarch of a noble clan of the Quraysh.

*Asclepius* the most prominent god of healing in Greek and Roman mythology; the classical-era depictions of his staff became the emblem of medicine in modern times.

*al-Aʿshā, Maymūn ibn Qays* (d. after 3/625) celebrated pre-Islamic poet, famous for traveling across many regions of Arabia and his interaction with important political groups on the Arabian-Iraqi frontier. He lived into the very early Islamic period, but reportedly did not convert.

*al-Ashʿar* lineage of the "Southern Arab" Kahlān from western Yemen; many participated in the Muslim conquests, especially of Syria. See also Kahlān.

*al-ʿAskar* name of a neighborhood in the mid-third-/ninth-century Abbasid capital city at Samarra. *ʿAskar* means "military camp," as the site was first settled as the camp for the Caliph al-Muʿtaṣim's soldiers and was known as ʿAskar al-Muʿtaṣim; it was converted into a permanent town during the succeeding caliphate of al-Wāthiq. See also al-Muʿtaṣim.

*al-ʿAskarī, Abū Hilāl* (d. ca. 400/1010) philologist and literary specialist active in courts in Iraq and western Iran; a prolific author of books on various topics of Arabic language, poetics, and Arab culture.

*al-Aṣmaʿī, Abū Saʿīd ʿAbd al-Malik ibn Qurayb* (d. 213/828) Basran lexicographer and narrator of Arabian history who attended the court of al-Rashīd; his teachings, particularly on specialized vocabulary of different fields, were compiled into books by his students and subsequent generations of scholars. See also al-Rashīd.

*Astarabad* city founded by the Achaemenids (modern Gurgan, near the Caspian Sea and the Iran-Turkmenistan border); part of pre-Islamic Iranian frontier defenses against Central Asian nomads.

*Aʿṣur* Arabian lineage; subgroup of the Qays ʿAylān. See also Qays ʿAylān.

*ʿAwf of the Asad* unidentified.

*Aws ibn Ḥajar* celebrated pre-Islamic Arabic poet of the Tamīm, often connected with the court of al-Ḥīrah. Muslim poetry collectors considered him to be one of the most accomplished pre-Islamic poets. See also al-Ḥīrah and Tamīm.

*Aws ibn Ḥārithah ibn La'm* pre-Islamic nobleman of the La'm clan of the Ṭayyi'; cousin of Ḥātim of the Ṭayyi'. See also Ḥatim al-Ṭā'ī and Ṭayyi'.

*al-Awzāʿī, Abū ʿAmr ʿAbd al-Raḥmān* (d. 157/774) Syrian jurist and theologian who held an influential position in Umayyad caliphal courts.

*Azarmidokht* daughter of Khosrow Parviz and ruler of Iran for several months in AD 630 during the unstable period of dynastic trouble at the end of the Sassanian Empire.

*al-Azd* major subgroup of the Kahlān "Southern Arab" lineage; a disparate lineage group that formed from various communities, including those in the Hijaz, Syria, and Oman.

*Aznam* name of several Arabian lineages; probably the Aznam ibn ʿUbayd, a clan of the Yarbūʿ. See also Yarbūʿ.

*Badr* (1) Arabian lineage, a subclan of the Fazārah connoting the descendants of Badr ibn ʿAmr, father of the heroes Ḥudhayfah and Ḥamal; (2) a battle fought in 2/624, a victory for the Prophet and his Medinan Muslims against the pagan Meccan Quraysh. See also Ḥudhayfah and Ḥamal.

*Bāhilah* Arabian lineage of complex origin, likely indicative of the considerable diversity of its constituent groups; traceable to the western Najd, the Bāhilah only emerge with cohesion in the Muslim period. Perhaps for these reasons, the Bāhilah became a stock example of low-status lineage in Arabic literature.

*Bahram Gur (Bahram V)* (r. AD 420–38) Sassanian ruler who ascended the throne with the help of the Lakhmid king al-Mundhir I following the assassination of Bahram's father Yazdegerd I (r. 399–420). See also al-Mundhir the Elder.

*Bahram son of Ardashir* Arabic name for a legendary ancient Persian ruler, of uncertain historicity.

*Bahman son of Esfandiar* Iranian monarch attested only in legendary contexts, mixing stories about the historical Achaemenid rulers Cyrus I (r. 559–30) and Artaxerxes (r. 465–25).

*Bahram son of Shapur (Bahram I)* (r. AD 271–74) Sassanian ruler, noteworthy for oppressing Manichaeanism and restoring powers to the Zoroastrian priestly class.

*al-Baḥrayn* region in eastern Arabia that historically connoted a much larger territory than the modern state of Bahrain.

*Bakr ibn Wāʾil* broad Arabian lineage group composed of powerful clans, including the Shaybān, Thaʿlabah, ʿIjl, and Ḥanīfah; frequently encountered in Arabic accounts of pre-Islamic Arabian battles.

*al-Balādhurī, Aḥmad ibn Yaḥyā* (d. 279/892) Iraqi historian, genealogist, and scholar in courtly circles; writer of some of the most detailed extant histories of pre-Islamic Arabia and early Islam.

*Balkh* major city and oasis controlling trading routes in northern Afghanistan and the upper Oxus; a center of Buddhist and Zoroastrian learning both before Islam and in the early Islamic period.

*Bāqil ibn ʿAmr al-Īyādī* pre-Islamic character proverbial for inarticulateness.

*al-Barājim* lineage group of the Tamīm related to the Ḥanẓalah ibn Mālik. See also Tamīm.

*Barāqish* name synonymous with ill omen.

*Barmak* Arabic rendering of the Bactrian-language title for the administrator of an important Buddhist monastery near Balkh and, by extension, the title for an important political ruler of pre-Islamic Balkh. The Barmakids take their name from this title, which Arabic sources erroneously assumed was the name of the family's progenitor. See also Balkh.

*Barmakids* aristocratic Buddhist family from Balkh who in the early Abbasid caliphate served as powerful viziers and administrators until their sudden, and as yet unexplained, fall from grace in 187/803, when the Caliph al-Rashīd imprisoned and executed many of them. See also al-Rashīd, Hārūn.

*al-Barrāḍ ibn Qays* pre-Islamic warrior proverbial for his bellicose nature who was alienated from his kin for various offences; he was under the protection of the Quraysh when he killed ʿUrwah the Traveler, and therefore his actions sparked the Second Fijār War. See also Fijār War and ʿUrwah the Traveler.

*Bashshār ibn Burd* (d. 167/783–84 or 168/784–85) celebrated early-Abbasid-era poet.

*Basra* town founded in 17/638 by the Muslim conquerors of Iraq; it was a port city at the head of the Persian Gulf and grew into a major intellectual and commercial center.

*Basūs War* celebrated pre-Islamic Arabian conflict between the Taghlib and Bakr. See also Bakr and Taghlib.

*Bilāl ibn Abī Burdah al-Ashʿarī* (d. ca. 120) the son of a prominent Kufan jurist and judge, Bilāl was chief judge of Basra, later executed by the Umayyad governor of Iraq, Yūsuf ibn ʿUmar (d. 127/744–45).

*Bishr ibn Abī Khāzim* celebrated pre-Islamic poet of the Asad. See also Asad.

*Bishr ibn Rabīʿah al-Khathʿamī* warrior and poet of the early Islamic period who settled in Kufa after the Muslim conquests.

*Bisṭām ibn Qays ibn Masʿūd* nobleman-warrior of the Shaybān of Bakr lineage, celebrated in stories of warring against the Tamīm, particularly against the

Yarbūʿ and their hero ʿUtaybah ibn al-Ḥārith. Bisṭām died shortly before the Prophet's hegira. See also Bakr, Tamīm, and Yarbūʿ.

*Blues (Ar. al-Azāriqah)* sect of Kharijites named after their putative founder Nāfiʿ ibn ʿAbd Allāh ibn al-Azraq (the "son of the Blue"); they waged a serious rebellion against the caliphs and created a short-lived state between Iraq and eastern Iran. See also Kharijites.

*Boran* the Sassanian queen Buran/Puran, daughter of Khosrow Parviz; she ruled the troubled Sassanian Empire from AD 631 to 632, near the end of its history.

*Bozorgmehr* vizier to the Sassanian monarch Khosrow, who was proverbial in Arabic literature as symbolizing wisdom and good counsel.

*Buhlūl* name of an iconic "wise fool" of Kufa; seemingly a real person in the second/eighth century, he developed into a stock figure in Arabic literature.

*al-Buḥturī, al-Walīd ibn ʿUbayd* (d. 284/897) Abbasid court poet, widely regarded alongside Abū Tammām as one of the greatest poets of the Abbasid era. See also Abū Tammām.

*Bujayr* son or nephew of the warrior leader of the Bakr al-Ḥārith ibn ʿUbād, killed in the Basūs War. See also Basūs War and al-Ḥārith ibn ʿUbād.

*Bukhara* settled oasis and major trading center in present-day Uzbekistan. Bukhara was a major center of political power in Transoxiana in the several centuries before the Muslim conquest, and it remained one of the region's most important cities thereafter.

*Caesar (Ar. Qaysar)* originally the family name of the prominent Roman patrician clan gens Julia, family of Julius Caesar; after he became dictator, "Caesar" became a title for all Roman emperors (from the second century AD, the title for the crown prince); the Caesar mentioned in our text is a combination of the historic dictator Julius Caesar and the emperor Augustus Caesar.

*Circesium* city in northwest Mesopotamia at the confluence of the Euphrates and Khabur rivers; a strategic location in Umayyad-era politics of rivalry between Syria and Iraq.

*Cleopatra* name of several queens of Ptolemaic Egypt. Cleopatra VII (r. 51–30) was the last Ptolemaic ruler.

*Companions (Ar. ṣaḥābah)* term denoting those who converted to Islam and lived with the Prophet Muḥammad in Medina during his lifetime. The two main subgroups of the Companions were the Allies (*anṣār*), the original inhabitants of Medina before the Prophet, and the Immigrants (*muhājirūn*), those who moved to Medina following their conversion.

*Consecrated House* one of the names for Mecca's shrine, the Kaaba.

*al-Ḍaḥḥāk* complex figure from ancient Persian mythology; known in pre-Islamic Iran as Aži Dahāka, a dragon-like monster with variable human forms. The myth grew to denote a mythical king who gained spiritual assistance to control all seven climes (that is, the whole world), and who is portrayed as the embodiment and originator of the bad religion, reigning until subdued by Feridun. After the Muslim conquest, the evolution of his name into Arabic, "Ḍaḥḥāk," seems to have inspired some Iranians to view their new Muslim rulers as evil forces.

*Ḍamrah ibn Jābir* pre-Islamic nobleman of the Nahshal ibn Dārim clan of the Tamīm and father of the redoubtable warrior Shuqqah (aka Ḍamrah) ibn Ḍamrah. See also Tamīm.

*Dārim* Arabian lineage, subgroup of the Tamīm; the poet al-Farazdaq descended from the Mujāshiʿ clan of the Dārim. See also al-Farazdaq and Tamīm.

*Darius the Elder* the Muslim-era identification for the great king of the "First Persian Empire"—that is, the Achaemenids. Arabic accounts of his history are inaccurate but preserve some memory of the celebrated Achaemenid ruler Darius I (r. 522–486).

*Darius the Younger* the Muslim-era identification of Darius III (r. 336–30), the last Achaemenid ruler, defeated and killed by Alexander the Great.

*Daughter of al-Khuss* see Hind bint al-Khuss.

*Dayr al-Jamājim* site of a lengthy series of battles between al-Ḥajjāj ibn Yūsuf and his pro-Umayyad Syrian soldiers against ʿAbd al-Raḥmān ibn al-Asʿath and his Iraqi army in 83/702; al-Ḥajjāj's eventual victory enabled Umayyad control over Kufa. See also ʿAbd al-Malik ibn Marwān, ʿAbd al-Raḥmān ibn al-Asʿath, and al-Ḥajjāj ibn Yūsuf.

*Dhakwān* Arabian lineage, a subgroup of the Sulaym.

*al-Dhanāʾib* name of several locations in Arabia. The most prominent are a location in Najd on the route between Mecca and Basra, and one in western Yemen.

*Dhubyān* Arabian lineage; a major subgroup of the Ghaṭafān claiming descent from the Qays ʿAylān, they resided east of Medina at the dawn of Islam. See also Ghaṭafān.

*Dhū Ḥusum* wadi in central Najd.

*Dhū Jadan al-Ḥimyarī, ʿAlqamah* (d. ca. 10/631–32) obscure South Arabian poet born before Islam, who lived into the Islamic period and is best known for his nostalgic poems about pre-Islamic South Arabian kingdoms.

*Dhū Nuwās* Arabic name for the pre-Islamic South Arabian king Yūsuf As'ar Yath'ar (r. AD 517 and 525–27), remembered in Arabic as one of the most powerful kings of Ḥimyar and a resolute leader who was accorded a major role in Muslim-era accounts of Yemeni history.

*Dhū Ruʿayn* legendary pre-Islamic South Arabian nobleman and royal retainer.

*Dhū l-Rummah, Ghāylān ibn ʿUqbah* (d. 117/735–36) Umayyad-era Arabian poet, famous for desert descriptions composed in an archaic style.

*Diʿbil ibn ʿAlī al-Khuzāʿī* (d. 244/858–59 or 246/860–61) Abbasid-era poet famous for his pro-Alid and pro-Yemeni verses, as well as biting satires directed against caliphs and other high-ranking figures of his time.

*Ḍirār ibn al-Azwar* (d. 12/633 or 13/634) warrior of the Asad who fought for the nascent Muslim caliphate and was reportedly killed either at the Battle of Yamāmah in the Wars of Apostacy that broke out upon the death of Muḥammad, or at the Battle of Ajnadayn during the Muslim conquest of Syria.

*Ḍirār of the Ḍabbah* descendant of a prominent pre-Islamic noble family and military commander who served under Qutaybah ibn Muslim; also Ḍirār ibn Sinān al-Ḍabbī, an agent and spy of Qutaybah.

*domestikos* title of different ranks in the Byzantine army, ranging from commander of single regiments to chief of the army.

*Dūlāb* agricultural area between Ahwāz and Basra.

*Durayd ibn al-Ṣimmah* (d. 10/630) pre-Islamic warrior and poet of the Jusham ibn Muʿāwiyah of the "Northern Arab" lineage Hawāzin; an old man at the dawn of Islam, he opposed Islam and was killed in battle when a Muslim army attacked the Hawāzin.

*Enoch (Ar. Idrīs)* ancient prophetic figure mentioned in the Qur'an; his main attribute in Muslim texts of being "raised to Heaven" suggests he represents an interpretation of the biblical Enoch; the Sabians also connected their deity Hermes with Enoch, likely as a means to legitimize their religious learning in Muslim eyes. See also Sabians.

*Euclid* (fl. third century BC?) mathematician from Ptolemaic Egypt, considered an elder contemporary of Apollonius.

*al-Faḍl ibn Sahl ibn Zādhānfarrūkh* (d. 202/817–18) Abbasid administrator and vizier for the Caliph al-Ma'mūn in Khurasan; when al-Ma'mūn moved the court from Marw to Baghdad, al-Faḍl fell from favor and was executed. See also al-Ma'mūn.

*al-Farazdaq, Abū Firās Hammām ibn Ghālib* (d. ca. 110/728) one of the three most famous Umayyad-era poets (along with Jarīr and al-Akhṭal); composed poetry for and about many high-ranking Muslims, caliphs, and his own kin, the Tamīm. See also Tamīm.

*Fāriʿah bint Ḥassān* daughter of the poet Ḥassān ibn Thābit; some poems are ascribed to her.

*farsakh* a common measure of distance, usually equivalent to three miles, though longer measures are also attested.

*Fayf al-Rīḥ* location in southern Najd, site of a battle between the ʿĀmir and the Madhḥij. See also ʿĀmir and Madhḥij.

*Fazārah* Arabian lineage, a subgroup of the Dhubyān. Ḥudhayfah and Ḥamal, sons of Badr, the heroes of the Thrust and Dusty War, were from the Fazārah. See also Badr, Ḥudhayfah and Ḥamal, Thrust and Dusty War.

*Feridun* Iranian mythical hero and legendary pre-Islamic king of Iran with a rich mythic history stemming from the Avesta; a dragon slayer and restorer of Good religion against Evil.

*Fijār War* name of three separate conflicts all sparked in connection with the Meccan ʿUkāẓ Fair; the most famous was the Second Fijār War, which reportedly lasted for four years following al-Barrāḍ ibn Qays's murder of ʿUrwah the Traveler; the young Muḥammad took part in this war prior to his prophethood. See also ʿUkāẓ and ʿUrwah the Traveler.

*Fuqaym* Arabian lineage; subgroup of the Kinānah of the Quraysh.

*Galen* (AD 129–216) Roman-era doctor from Pergamum; a prolific author, his books profoundly shaped medical practice, and were much copied and commented upon in Arabic.

*Gayomard* primordial giant and the first man from whom humankind descends in the Zoroastrian tradition; he is posited to have lived three thousand years in peace, finally dying thirty years after the onslaught of Evil. In the Islamic era, the merging of pre-Islamic Persian culture with Judeo-Christian prophetic history led to attempts to conflate Gayomard with the biblical Adam.

*Ghanī* Arabian lineage; usually known as Ghanī ibn ʿAṣur of the Qays ʿAylān, they resided in northern and northeastern Arabia in the century before Islam. See also Qays ʿAylān.

*Ghassān* Arabian lineage, reportedly related to al-Azd. The Ghassān settled in the region of modern Jordan and Syria, where they acted as frontier guards for the Byzantine Empire. See also al-Azd and Ghassanids.

*Ghassanids* name of a dynasty of a sixth-century AD Arabian frontier state in Syria allied to the Byzantine Empire; their kings descended from the clan of Jafnah of the Ghassān.

*Ghaṭafān* broad Arabian subgroup of the Qays ʿAylān; clans attached to Ghaṭafān lineage were spread across Najd between the Hijaz and Shammar Mountains. See also Qays ʿAylān.

*Ghaylān* (d. between 105/724 and 125/743) early proponent of the doctrine of free will, active in Umayyad Syria and Iraq.

*Ghaylān ibn ʿUqbah* see Dhū l-Rummah.

*God's Sanctum (Ar. Bayt Allāh)* one of the names for Mecca's holy shrine, the Kaaba.

*Gray Mule (Ar. al-baghlah al-shahbāʾ)* a reference to one or more animals of religious significance in early Islam. The Prophet was said to have owned a gray mule, which passed to ʿAlī after his death, a sign of ʿAlī's legitimate designation as the Prophet's rightful successor. Some subsequent Alid claimants to power also claimed connection with a gray mule. Mules had a potent association with prophecy in Late Antiquity.

*al-Habāʾah* watering hole in the land of the Ghaṭafān.

*Habannaqah, Yazīd ibn Thawrān* character proverbial in Arabic literature for stupidity; some sources consider him pre-Islamic, others Umayyad era.

*al-Ḥabiṭāt* clan of the Tamīm descended from al-Ḥārith ibn ʿAmr; the name means "puffy tummy," reportedly a description of their patriarch. See also Tamīm.

*al-Ḥādī* (r. 169–70/785–86) Abbasid caliph and older brother of al-Rashīd, his successor. See also al-Rashīd.

*al-Ḥajjāj, ibn Yūsuf* (d. 95/714) famous Umayyad governor of Iraq remembered for his brutal but effective government.

*al-Ḥakam ibn Ayyūb* (d. 97/715–16) cousin and son-in-law of al-Ḥajjāj ibn Yūsuf; al-Ḥajjāj's administrator over Basra during a period of Kharijite uprisings. See also al-Ḥajjāj ibn Yūsuf.

*Ḥamal ibn Badr* pre-Islamic nobleman-warrior; alongside his brother, Ḥudhayfah, he was the leader of the Fazārah clan of the Dhubyān during the Thrust and Dusty War. See also Fazārah, Dhubyān, and Thrust and Dusty War.

*al-Ḥamāsah (The Valor Anthology)* name of several collections of excerpts from pre-Islamic and early Muslim-era Arabic poetry. The most famous was compiled by Abū Tammām: it circulated widely and was one of the best-known repositories of early Arabic poetry in medieval Islam. See also Valor Anthology.

*Ḥammād ʿAjrad* (d. between 155/771–72 and 168/784–85) satirical poet of the late Umayyad and early Abbasid period, best remembered for his long-standing sparring with Bashshār ibn Burd. See also Bashshār ibn Burd.

*Hammām ibn Murrah ibn Dhuhl* warrior and nobleman of the Dhuhl ibn Shaybān branch of the Bakr. The brother of Jassās, Hammām was killed at the Battle of Wāridāt.

*Hammām ibn Murrah ibn Thaʿlabah* Bedouin of an unnamed branch of the Bakr who is known only via the story of his misbehaving daughters.

*Ḥanẓalah* Arabian lineage, branch of the Tamīm.

*Harim ibn Quṭbah ibn Sinān (or Sayyār) ibn ʿAmr al-Fazārī* (d. after 13/634) pre-Islamic Arabian arbiter known for his eloquence. He lived into the Islamic period and reportedly converted to Islam.

*Harim ibn Sinān* a leader of the Dhubyān in the generation before the Prophet, known for his role in settling the Thrust and Dusty War between the Dhubyān and the ʿAbs; famously praised by the poet Zuhayr ibn Abī Sulmā. See also ʿAbs, Dhubyān, Thrust and Dusty War, Zuhayr ibn Abī Sulmā.

*al-Ḥārith ibn ʿAbd Allāh ibn Abī Rabīʿah* (d. ca. 81/700–01) Meccan nobleman of the Makhzūm clan of the Quraysh; governor of Basra at the beginning of Ibn al-Zubayr's caliphate; brother of the poet ʿUmar ibn Abī Rabīʿah. See also Ibn al-Zubayr and ʿUmar ibn Abī Rabīʿah.

*al-Ḥārith ibn Abī Shamir* (d. 8/630) name of a Ghassanid ruler contemporary with the Prophet; his name is sometimes confused in Arabic stories about pre-Islamic Arabia with an earlier Ghassanid ruler, al-Ḥārith ibn Jabalah. See also Ghassān.

*al-Ḥārith ibn ʿAmr ibn Muʿāwiyah (Star-Thistle Eater)* (d. ca. 531 AD) ruler of the Kindah Kingdom in southern Arabia; he played a role in the expansion of the Yemeni Ḥimyar kingdom's influence northward into central Arabia, and participated in major political events of early sixth-century Arabia.

*al-Ḥārith ibn ʿAwf* pre-Islamic nobleman of the Murrah clan of the Dhubyān; one of the two brokers of peace in the Thrust and Dusty War. During early Islam he led an army against the Prophet, but later converted to Islam and was selected as the Muslim lieutenant over the Murrah. See also Dhubyān and Thrust and Dusty War.

*al-Ḥārith ibn Jabalah* (r. ca. AD 528–69) Ghassanid ruler, ally of the Byzantines, who waged many wars against the Lakhmids. See also Ghassanids and Lakhmids.

*al-Ḥārith ibn Kaʿb* subgroup of the Madhḥij lineage, also called the Balḥārith. They occupied the area around Najrān in southwestern Arabia at the dawn of Islam. See also Madhḥij.

*al-Ḥārith ibn al-Ṣimmah* (d. 4/625) Medinan of the Khazraj lineage. See also al-Khazraj.

*al-Ḥārith ibn ʿUbād ibn Mālik* a poet and leader of the Bakr during the Basūs War who led them to notable victories over the Taghlib. See also Basūs War and Taghlib.

*al-Ḥārith ibn Waʿlah* name of at least two pre-Islamic poets, one from the Jarm and the other from the Dhuhl subgroup of the Shaybān-Bakr. See also Jarm and Bakr.

*al-Ḥārith ibn Ẓālim* pre-Islamic warrior, memorialized as one of the most bellicose and implacable raiders of pre-Islamic times.

*al-Ḥārith ibn Surayj the Liar* (d. 128/746) Umayyad-era warrior who fought in conquests in Khurasan and Transoxiana. He later led a rebellion against the Umayyads in eastern Iran in 116–28/734–46.

*Ḥārithah ibn Qudāmah, Abū Yazīd* a leader of the Saʿd clan of the Tamīm in Basra; fought for Caliph ʿAlī and reportedly served as his security constable. The recording of his first name as "Ḥārithah" is likely a copyist error: his real name was probably Jāriyah ibn Qudāmah. See also ʿAlī ibn Abī Ṭālib, Saʿd, Jāriyah ibn Qudāmah, and Tamīm.

*Ḥarrān* city in present-day southern Turkey by the Euphrates; Late Antique Carrhae. Ḥarrān was famed for retaining a vibrant Hellenized pagan religion until the end of the second/eighth century.

*al-Ḥasan* (d. 50/670) son of ʿAlī and the Prophet's daughter Fāṭimah, the second imam of the Shiʿah; he was briefly caliph before stepping down in the face of resistance from Muʿāwiyah. See also ʿAlī ibn Abī Ṭālib and Muʿāwiyah.

*al-Ḥasan al-Baṣrī* (d. 110/728) famous jurist and preacher in Umayyad-era Basra. In Arabic literature, he is proverbial for learned, devout, and ascetic faith.

*al-Ḥasan ibn Daḥmān al-Ashqar* unidentified.

*al-Ḥasan ibn Sahl* (d. 236/850–51) brother of al-Faḍl ibn Sahl; secretary and governor of Iraq for the Caliph al-Ma'mūn. See also al-Faḍl ibn Sahl.

*al-Hāshimī, ʿAlī ibn Sulaymān* (d. after 277/890) Muslim astrologer whose extant work reveals the influence of earlier Persian and Indian astrological traditions.

*Ḥassān ibn Numayr* unidentified.

*Ḥassān ibn Thābit* (d. between 50/670 and 54/674) Medinan poet contemporary with the Prophet; considered the leading poet of the first Muslim community.

*Ḥātim al-Ṭā'ī* poet of the Ṭayyi' proverbial for his generosity and hospitality. See also Ṭayyi'.

*Hawāzin* a large Arabian lineage of the "Northern Arabs," they resided in the Hijaz before Islam and their conflicts with the Ghaṭafān are prominent in Arabic literature. See also Ghaṭafān.

*Hawdhah ibn ʿAlī l-Ḥanafī* (d. ca. 8/630) powerful ruler in eastern Arabia (al-Yamāmah) around the dawn of Islam, and ally of the Sassanian Empire.

*Ḥawrān* large region of agricultural settlements and desert south of Damascus.

*Ḥawṭ* Ḥawṭ ibn Jābir (or ibn Abī Jābir) ibn Ḥumayrī, a member of the Yarbūʿ lineage. See also Yarbūʿ.

*Hermes* name of several ancient sages discussed in Arabic writing; the most common and revered was Hermes Trismegistus ("Thrice Greatest"), a deity in ancient Greek writing from Roman-era Egypt who borrowed from the attributes of Thoth, the Egyptian god of scribal learning.

*Hijaz* large region in northwest Arabia extending from Syria to the southern parts of present-day Saudi Arabia, including Mecca and Medina.

*Hilāl ibn ʿAṭiyyah* unknown; he may be Hilāl al-Ra'ī ibn Yaḥyā ibn Muslim al-Baṣrī (d. 245/859–60), a jurist.

*Ḥimyar* the dominant kingdom in South Arabia ca. AD 275–525 and name of a Yemeni lineage group in the Muslim period. In Arabic literature, "Ḥimyar" was synonymous with ancient imperial might.

*Hind bint al-Khuss* a pre-Islamic figure of obscure identity. She is associated with the ancient tribe of Iyād and features as a stock character in Arabic literature about Bedouin sayings.

*Hippocrates* (ca. 460–379) Greek doctor; influential in the development of scientific principles for medical practice. He was memorialized in Europe and the Middle East as one of the founding fathers of medicine.

*al-Ḥīrah* urban settlement on the Arabian frontier at the Middle Euphrates. Al-Ḥīrah was the most important center of power on the Arabian frontier in Late Antiquity and was the seat of the Lakhmid rulers. The city declined after the Muslim garrison town of Kufa was founded nearby. See also Lakhmids.

*Hishām ibn ʿAbd al-Malik* (r. 105–25/724–43) Umayyad caliph. His long reign was stable, but it witnessed growing economic decline and political tension, which caused the end of the Umayyad caliphate nine years later.

*Ḥiṣn ibn Ḥudhayfah* pre-Islamic nobleman, son of Ḥudhayfah ibn Badr. See also Ḥudhayfah ibn Badr.

*Hizzān* the clan of Hizzān ibn al-Ṣubāḥ ibn ʿAtīq, of the ʿAnazah. See also ʿAnazah.

*Hormizd (Hormozd)* name of several Sassanian rulers, including Hormizd IV (r. AD 579–90), son of Khosrow Anushirvan from the daughter of the Turkic khagan.

*Ḥudhayfah ibn Badr* pre-Islamic nobleman-warrior; along with his brother, Ḥamal, he was the leader of the Fazārah clan of the Dhubyān during the Thrust and Dusty War. See also Dhubyān, Fazārah, and Thrust and Dusty War.

*Ḥunayn of the slippers* a figure variously identified.

*Hushang* legendary pre-Islamic king in Persian mythology whose name is traced to ancient Avestan and Middle Persian texts as a demon-slaying hero. Some stories claim he was ancestor of the kings of Iran, or ancestor of all Iranians.

*Ḥutāt ibn Yazīd ibn ʿAlqamah al-Mujāshiʿī* (d. 50/670–71) noble of the Mujāshiʾ branch of the Tamīm; uncle of al-Farazdaq. See also al-Farazdaq and Tamīm.

*al-Ḥuṭayʾah* (d. after 41/661) nickname (meaning "deformed") of the poet Jarwal ibn Aws. Born before Islam, he converted, then rejected Islam after the death of the Prophet, then reconverted after the Wars of Apostasy. Most anecdotes depict him as a malicious miser.

*Ibn ʿAbbās, ʿAbd Allāh* (d. 68/687–88) paternal cousin of the Prophet; a much-cited authority for prophetic traditions and Qurʾanic exegesis, though many stories ascribed to Ibn ʿAbbās are later forgeries.

*Ibn ʿAbdūs, Abū ʿĀmir Aḥmad* (d. 472/1079–80) courtier and vizier in the Cordoban court of the Jahwar kings. Little is recorded about him beyond his relationship with Wallādah bint al-Mustakfī. After Ibn Zaydūn fled

Cordoba for Seville, Ibn ʿAbdūs appears to have won Wallādah's affections. See also Ibn Zaydūn, Jahwar, Wallādah bint al-Mustakfī.

*Ibn Abī Dhiʾb* (d. 159/775–76) early jurist and traditionist, noted for his great piety. He was a contemporary of the jurist Mālik ibn Anas, and the two were often compared. See also Mālik ibn Anas.

*Ibn Abī Dūʾād, Abū ʿAbd Allāh* (d. 240/854) judge and high-ranking courtier who rose to prominence during the caliphate of al-Maʾmūn and remained an important political figure until the caliphate of al-Mutawakkil, during whose reign he fell from favor.

*Ibn Abī Ḥāzim, Qays* (d. 86/705 or 87/706) a leader of the Bajīlah before Islam; participated in the conquests in Syria and Iraq and settled in Kufa. See also Bajīlah.

*Ibn al-Aʿrābī, Abū ʿAbd Allāh Muḥammad ibn Ziyād* (d. 231/845) Iraqi grammarian and specialist in Arabic language, poetry, genealogy, and pre-Islamic Arabian history, extensively cited by later authors.

*Ibn al-Ashʿath* see ʿAbd al-Raḥmān ibn al-Ashʿath.

*Ibn ʿAyyāsh, Ismāʿīl* (d. 181/797–98) Syrian religious scholar and narrator of Prophetic traditions.

*Ibn Bassām, Abū al-Ḥasan ʿAlī l-Shantarīnī* (d. 543/1147) Andalusian literary scholar and author of the *Treasure Trove of Virtues of the Andalusians* (*al-Dhakhīrah fī maḥāsin ahl al-Jazīrah*), a valuable and compendious collection of Andalusian Arabic literature and biography up to his day.

*Ibn Bukhtīshūʿ* perhaps Bukhtīshūʿ ibn Jibrīl (d. 256/860), a famous physician of the Abbasid caliphs.

*Ibn Būlus* (d. 386/996) Abū Saʿd al-Faḍl, a Christian astronomer, reportedly from Shiraz, active in Baghdadi scientific circles.

*Ibn Ḥamdūn, Bahāʾ al-Dīn Abū l-Maʿālī* (d. 562/1066) Baghdadi courtier and official, author of a compendious and oft-cited anthology of literature and stories, *Ibn Ḥamdūn's Handbook* (*al-Tadhkirah al-Ḥamdūniyyah*).

*Ibn Ḥayyān, Abū Marwān* (d. 469/1076) Andalusian historian and literary scholar and author of an extensive history of Muslim Spain, *The Great History* (*al-Tārīkh al-Kabīr*).

*Ibn Hubayra* see ʿUmar ibn Hubayrah.

*Ibn Jarmuz, ʿAmr (or ʿUmayr)* (d. 38/659) warrior of the Saʿd clan of the Tamīm, best known for his perfidious murder of al-Zubayr ibn al-ʿAwwām. He turned against the Caliph ʿAlī and was killed at the Battle of Nahrawān. See also ʿAlī ibn Abī Ṭālib, Saʿd, Tamīm, and al-Zubayr ibn ʿAwwām.

*Ibn Jidhl al-Ṭaʿʿān* see Jidhl al-Ṭaʿʿān.

*Ibn al-Kalbī, Hishām* (d. 204/819 or 206/821) Kufan genealogist and historian, one of the most cited authorities on pre-Islamic Arabian history, culture, and genealogy of Arabian tribes.

*Ibn Khallād* see Aḥmad ibn Khallād.

*Ibn Misjaḥ, Abū ʿUthmān Saʿīd* (d. before 96/715) Meccan musician who learned both Persian and Greek forms of song and developed Arabic styles, which he disseminated among his numerous students, including Maʿbad ibn Wahb. See also Maʿbad ibn Wahb.

*Ibn Muhājir, ʿAmr ibn Muhājir ibn Dīnār al-Anṣārī* (d. 139/756–57) personal retainer of the Caliph ʿUmar ibn ʿAbd al-ʿAzīz. See also ʿUmar ibn ʿAbd al-ʿAzīz.

*Ibn Muljam, ʿAbd al-Raḥmān al-Murādī* (d. 40/661) Kufan soldier. Initially a partisan of ʿAlī in the struggle over the caliphate with Muʿāwiyah, Ibn Muljam began disapproving of the righteousness of ʿAlī's caliphate and joined the early Kharijites. He assassinated ʿAlī, and was subsequently executed. See also ʿAlī ibn Abī Ṭālib, Kharijites, and Muʿāwiyah.

*Ibn al-Muqaffaʿ, ʿAbd Allāh* (d. 139/756) Persian court secretary for the early Abbasids; known for translating Middle Persian texts into Arabic.

*Ibn Muqbil, Tamīm ibn Ubayy ibn Muqbil* (d. after 37/657) accomplished Arabic poet of the ʿĀmir ibn Ṣaʿṣaʿah. Born before Islam, he lived into the Muslim era and was suspected of weak faith and nostalgic yearnings for pre-Islam.

*Ibn Nabhān, al-Muntajiʿ* (fl. second/eighth century) Bedouin said to have been a member of either the Tamīm or the Ṭayyiʾ. He was the source of Arabian stories, poetry, and points of Arabic language for the Iraqi scholars al-Aṣmaʿī and al-Mufaḍḍal al-Ḍabbī. See also al-Aṣmaʿī, al-Mufaḍḍal al-Ḍabbī, Tamīm, and Ṭayyiʾ.

*Ibn Nahīk* three individuals with this name are recorded in connection with the retinue and security constabulary of the early Abbasid caliphs; the highest ranking was ʿUthmān ibn Nahīk; our Ibn Nahīk appears to be a different figure, known only as a retainer of the Caliph al-Mahdī.

*Ibn Naṣr* Ḥabīb ibn Naṣr ibn Ziyād al-Muhallabī (d. 307/919–20), a Baghdadi narrator much cited by Abū al-Faraj al-Iṣbahānī. See also al-Iṣbahānī.

*Ibn al-Ṣabbāḥ, Isḥāq al-Kindī* (d. after 177/793–94) father of Yaʿqūb al-Kindī, a minor poet and bureaucrat for the early Abbasid caliphs and administrator over Kufa (160–65/777–82).

*Ibn Sirīn, Abū Bakr Muḥammad* (d. 110/728) respected Basran jurist and transmitter of Prophetic traditions, famed also as a dream interpreter.

*Ibn Wahb, ʿAbd Allāh ibn Muslim* (d. 197/812) Egyptian jurist and traditionist, a student of Mālik ibn Anas. See also Mālik ibn Anas.

*Ibn al-Zayyāt, Muḥammad ibn ʿAbd al-Malik* (d. 233/847) a powerful vizier of the Abbasid caliphs al-Maʾmūn, al-Muʿtaṣim, and al-Wāthiq. He then fell from favor and was executed by the Caliph al-Mutawakkil.

*Ibn al-Zubayr* see ʿAbd Allāh ibn al-Zubayr.

*Ibrāhīm ibn ʿAbd al-ʿAzīz* unidentified; an individual with this name is attested in other sources as a state secretary for the caliphs al-Rashīd and al-Maʾmūn.

*Ibrāhīm ibn Muḥammad ibn Ṭalḥah ibn ʿUbayd Allāh* (d. 110/729) Meccan nobleman whose father and grandfather were killed fighting against the Caliph ʿAlī. Ibrāhīm was a fiscal administrator in Kufa for the Zubayrids who fled to Medina before Iraq's fall and so avoided the wrath of the Marwanids. See also ʿAlī ibn Abī Ṭālib, Marwanids, and Zubayrids.

*Imruʾ al-Qays* (fl. mid-sixth century AD) princely descendant of the leaders of the Kindah federation and one of the earliest known and most famous pre-Islamic Arabian poets.

*al-Iṣbahānī, Abū al-Faraj ʿAlī ibn al-Ḥuysan* (d. ca. 360/971) literary scholar best known as the compiler of the *Book of Songs* (*Kitāb al-Aghānī*), the most compendious and important source for Arabic history and literature from pre-Islam to the early Abbasid era.

*Isfahan* principal city of the central Iranian plateau; administrative center of Sassanian Media and the Muslim-era al-Jibāl province; capital of several dynasties in Muslim times.

*Isḥāq ibn Suwayd* possibly Isḥāq ibn Suwayd ibn Hubayrah al-Tamīmī (d. 131/748–49), Basran traditionist and narrator of hadith.

*Iyād* very ancient Arabian lineage group, tracing ancestry to Iyād ibn Nizār ibn Maʿadd. The lineage features prominently in ancient pre-Islamic stories, especially those connected to al-Ḥīrah.

*Jābir ibn Ḥayyān* obscure figure assumed to have lived in the late second/eighth century, supposed author of several perhaps apocryphal books on alchemy, astronomy, and medicine. Later Arabic writers counted him as a founding father of alchemy.

*Jaʿd al-Murādī (also Juʿayd)* possibly a subclan of the Murād, which was a lineage of the South Arabian Madhḥij. See also Madhḥij.

*al-Jaʿd ibn Dirham (also Jaʿd, without definite article)* (d. between 105/724 and 120/738) native of Khurasan who spent most of his life in Damascus, branded a heretic.

*Jadhīmah al-Abraṣ/al-Abrash (the "Speckled")* legendary pre-Islamic ruler of al-Ḥīrah. See also al-Ḥīrah.

*Jaʿfar* Arabian lineage; a prominent clan, subgroup of the ʿĀmir ibn Ṣaʿṣaʿah. See also ʿĀmir ibn Ṣaʿṣaʿah.

*Jaʿfar ibn Sulaymān ibn ʿAlī* (d. 174/790–91 or 175/791–92) respected nobleman of the Abbasid family who served as governor of Medina, then Mecca, and then Basra.

*al-Jāḥiẓ, ʿAmr ibn Baḥr* (d. 255/868–69) Basran polymath; prolific writer, theologian, and literary scholar of great repute.

*Jahm ibn Ṣafwān* (d. 128/746) eastern Iranian theologian and heretic; the basis of his beliefs is obscure.

*Jahwar* name of a family of Cordoban notables who, after the fall of the Andalusian Umayyad caliphate, established an independent kingdom (r. 422–62/1030–70).

*Jahwar ibn Muḥammad ibn Jahwar, Abū l-Ḥazm* (r. 422–35/1031–43) founder of the Jahwar kingdom in Cordoba.

*al-Jammāz, Abū ʿAbd Allāh Muḥammad ibn ʿAmr* (d. before 247/861) Basran satirical poet and humorist.

*Janb* subgroup of the "Southern Arab" Madhḥij lineage. See also Madhḥij.

*al-Jarbāʾ* daughter of ʿAqīl ibn ʿUllathah, reportedly a poet. Sources claim she was married to either Yaḥyā ibn al-Ḥakam Abī l-ʿĀṣ or Yazīd ibn ʿAbd al-Malik.

*Jarīr ibn Ḥāzim* (d. 170/786) Basran traditionist and theologian.

*Jāriyah ibn Qudāmah, Abū Ayyūb (or Yazīd)* Basran nobleman of the Saʿd clan of the Tamīm and powerful supporter of and commander for the Caliph ʿAlī. Jāriyah had a reputation for resolute and fierce responses to foes. He may have been the uncle of al-Aḥnaf ibn Qays. The name Ḥārithah (ibn Qudāmah) in some sources is probably a copyist error for Jāriyah. See also al-Aḥnaf ibn Qays, ʿAlī ibn Abī Ṭālib.

*Jarm* name of several Arabian lineage groups including the Jarm ibn ʿAmr, a subgroup of the Ṭayyiʾ residing in Najd at the dawn of Islam, and the Jarm ibn Rayyān, a subgroup of the Quḍāʿah lineage residing in northwest Arabia near the Arabian-Syrian frontier. See also Quḍāʿah, Ṭayyiʾ.

*Jarwal* given name of the poet al-Ḥuṭayʾah. See also al-Ḥuṭayʾah.

*Jassās ibn Murrah* pre-Islamic Arabian warrior of the Bakr. See also Bakr.

*Jaththāmah* son of ʿAqīl ibn ʿAmallas. See also ʿAqīl ibn ʿAmallas.

*Jidhl al-Ṭaʿʿān* nickname of a pre-Islamic warrior and poet of the Kinānah. His identity is debated: some report his name as ʿAmr ibn Qays, others as ʿAlqamah ibn Firās.

*Judhām* subgroup of the Kahlān lineage, of the "Southern Arabs" who at the dawn of Islam resided in the Red Sea region of modern northern Saudi Arabia and Jordan; a major population of the first Muslim settlers in Egypt.

*Juhaynah* Arabian lineage, a subgroup of the Quḍāʿah, who controlled a large territory north of Medina at the dawn of Islam. See also Quḍāʿah.

*Kaʿb ibn Maʿdān al-Ashqarī* accomplished Umayyad-era Arabic poet and warrior from the Ashqar subgroup of the Omani Azd who accompanied fellow Omani general al-Muhallab ibn Abī Ṣufrah on his campaigns in eastern Iran. See also al-Azd.

*Kaʿb ibn Māmah* pre-Islamic noble of the Iyād, famed in Arabic literature for the story of his death from thirst after magnanimously giving away all his water supplies.

*Kaʿb ibn Zuhayr* (d. ca. 50/670) poet and son of the pre-Islamic poet Zuhayr ibn Abī Sulmā, Kaʿb is best known for his ode praising the Prophet.

*Kāfūr al-Ikhshīdī* (d. 357/968) black eunuch sold to the founder of the Ikhshidid dynasty in Egypt. Upon his owner's death, Kāfūr ran the state himself.

*Kalb ibn Wabarah* Arabian lineage group of the Quḍāʿah who occupied the deserts between Syria and Iraq in pre-Islamic times; a key powerbroking faction in the Umayyad era. See also Quḍāʿah.

*Kalīlah wa Dimnah* famous Arabic book of wisdom. It derives from ancient Indian tales, transmitted through Persian and translated into Arabic by Ibn al-Muqaffaʿ in the early Abbasid period. See also Ibn al-Muqaffaʿ.

*Karkh Maysān* Arabic name for ancient Charax, a principal city of the Hellenistic kingdom of Characene (ca. 129–AD 224); situated on the lower Tigris, it was a major outlet for Persian Gulf trade.

*Kasghar* ancient city and major political and trading center on the western edge of the Tarim Basin in present-day Xinjiang, China.

*Kavad* (r. AD 488–496, 498/99–531) the Sassanian king Kavad I, son of Peroz I; notable for adopting Mazdakism as the imperial religion.

*Kaveh (Persian Kāvā)* heroic blacksmith in Iranian pre-Islamic Persian mythology. His rebellion against Ḍaḥḥāk secured the crown for Feridun.

The ancient origins of the story are obscure, but his name is prominent in Muslim-era Persian popular storytelling.

*Kerman (Kirman)* name of a large province of southeastern Iran between Fars and Sistan. Today, Kerman is the capital city of that province, whereas in early Islam, the province's main urban center was Sīrjān.

*Khalīʿ ibn Wahb* unidentified.

*Khālid al-Barmakī* see Khālid ibn Barmak.

*Khālid ibn ʿAbd Allāh* (d. between 179/795–96 and 182/798–99) known as Khālid al-Ṭaḥḥān ("the Miller"); Iraqi transmitter of Prophetic traditions.

*Khālid ibn ʿAbd Allāh al-Qasrī* (d. 125/743) influential Umayyad-era statesman, governor of Mecca and Medina, and then Iraq. His great fortune aroused envy and suspicion, and he was imprisoned and murdered toward the end of the Umayyad era.

*Khālid ibn Barmak* (d. 165/781–82) leading member of the Barmakid family of viziers and administrators who served the first Abbasid caliphs. See also Barmakids.

*Khālid ibn Khidāsh ibn ʿAjlān* (d. 223/837–38 or 224/838–39) Basran narrator of Prophetic traditions and early history of Islam.

*Khālid ibn Saʿīd ibn al-ʿĀṣ* (d. ca. 13/635) nobleman of the Umayyad clan of the Quraysh and one of the earliest converts to Islam. He administrated parts of Yemen during the latter years of the Prophet's life and participated in the conquest of Syria, where he was killed in battle against the Byzantines.

*Khālid ibn Ṣafwān* (d. 135/752) Umayyad-era Basran orator of Tamīm lineage. He had little political role, though Arabic literature transformed him into a narrator of manifold stories about Umayyad elite life.

*Khālid ibn al-Ṣaʿqab* pre-Islamic poet who lived into the Muslim-era; of Nahd lineage. See also Nahd.

*Khālid ibn al-Walīd* (d. 21/642) Meccan member of Quraysh. Originally opposed to the Prophet, he later converted to Islam and became one of the most celebrated military commanders in early Islam. Played a key role in the conquests of Iraq and Syria.

*al-Khalīl ibn Aḥmad al-Farāhīdī* (d. 170/786 or 175/791) philologist and lexicographer who compiled the earliest extant Arabic dictionary.

*Khallād ibn al-Mubārak* obscure figure, reportedly of Bāhilah lineage, a source for a number of stories recorded about early Abbasid-era poets. See also Bāhilah.

*Khārijah ibn Sinān* pre-Islamic nobleman of the Murrah clan of the Dhubyān; brother of Harim ibn Sinān. He was involved in the settlement of the Thrust and Dusty War. See also Murrah, Dhubyān and Thrust and Dusty War.

*Kharijites* label describing an array of political groups in early Islam who opposed the institution of the caliphate. They often engaged in violent secession against provincial or caliphal authorities. Later Muslim writers regard them as a distinct theological sect, though in early Islam they were diffuse and held varied sectarian and political views.

*Khathʿam ibn Anmār* major lineage group from south of Mecca to the borders of Yemen in the generations before Islam. Muslim genealogists debate whether they were of "Northern" or "Southern" Arab lineage.

*al-Khathʿamī, Mālik ibn ʿAbd Allāh* (d. ca. 60/680) warrior famed for commanding Muslim forces on the Byzantine frontier in the early Umayyad period.

*Khosrow Anushirvan (Khosrow I)* (r. AD 531–79) famed Sassanian ruler. In Arabic literature, he is synonymous with the virtues of the ideal monarch.

*Khosrow Parviz (Khosrow II)* (r. AD 590–628) Sassanian ruler, the last powerful king of the dynasty. Lengthy wars against the Byzantines weakened the Sassanian army, and shortly thereafter, he was overthrown by his son Sheroe. See also Sheroe.

*Khurasan* name of the vast region of eastern Iran that today includes northeastern Iran, Afghanistan, and parts of central Asia. It was the initial stronghold of the Abbasid movement, and one of the richest provinces of the caliphate.

*Kindah* south Arabian lineage; a kingdom on the Arabian-Yemeni frontier in the sixth century AD whose descendants were prominent in early Islam, settling in Egypt and Iraq.

*al-Kindī, Abū Yūsuf Yaʿqūb* (d. ca. 256/870) celebrated scholar and polymath known as the "Aristotle of Islam"; one of the first Muslim Hellenizing philosophers.

*Kufa* Muslim city founded on the middle Euphrates near al-Ḥīrah in 17/638 during the conquest of Iraq. It became one of the principal cities of Iraq, a major center of scholarship, and the main center of the Shiʿi community.

*Kulāb* name of two pre-Islamic Arabian battles; the Second Kulāb Battle was fought in the early seventh century AD between the Saʿd subgroup of the

Tamīm and a collection of "Southern Arab" lineages led by the Madhḥij. See also Tamīm and Madhḥij.

*Labīd ibn Aʿṣam* Jew from Medina who reportedly cast a spell over the Prophet via a charmed comb.

*Labīd ibn Rabīʿah* (d. ca. 41/661) celebrated pre-Islamic Arabian poet, author of one of the great pre-Islamic odes (*muʿallaqah*). He converted to Islam, and several pious poems are ascribed to him.

*Lakhm* name of a "Southern Arab" lineage group, the clan of the Lakhmid/Naṣrid kings.

*Lakhmids* also known as the Naṣrids; a dynasty of seminomadic rulers allied to the Sassanians. From their capital in al-Ḥīrah, they patrolled the Iraqi-Arabian frontier in the century before Islam. See also al-Ḥīrah.

*La'm* subgroup of the Arabian lineage Ṭayyi'. See also Ṭayyi'.

*Laqīṭ al-Iyādī* pre-Islamic Arabic poet of the Iyād. His biography is obscure, but the few extant poems ascribed to him were well regarded by Muslim commentators. See also Iyād.

*al-Lāt* pre-Islamic Arabian deity worshipped in various guises across ancient Arabia. In the Hijaz region, al-Lāt was the deity of the Thaqīf in Ṭā'if, near Mecca. See also Thaqīf and al-Ṭā'if.

*Maʿadd* Arabian ethnic group and the most commonly encountered name in pre-Islamic Arabic poetry for the identity of the central Arabian peoples before Islam.

*Maʿbad ibn ʿAbd Allāh al-Juhanī* (d. ca. 80/699) Basran political figure in the Umayyad era. He was an early proponent of the doctrine of free will, and on account of it was executed by the Caliph ʿAbd al-Malik ibn Marwān. See also ʿAbd al-Malik ibn Marwān.

*Maʿbad ibn Wahb, Abū ʿAbbād* (d. 125/743 or 126/744) entertainer from Medina renowned as one of the most famous singers and composers of the Umayyad era.

*al-Madā'inī, Abū al-Ḥasan ʿAlī ibn Muḥammad* (d. ca. 228/843) prominent Iraqi historian who specialized in the history of Arabia and early Islam.

*Madhḥij* broad lineage of "Southern Arabs" who resided at the dawn of Islam in the region of the modern-day border between Yemen and Saudi Arabia.

*al-Mahdī* (r. 158–169/775–785) Abbasid caliph and patron of learning, a key figure in the development of Baghdad. He was memorialized for his persecution of Manichaeans (*zindīqs*), perhaps motivated to curry favor with

Alid-leaning power groups. See also Manichaeans/Manichaeanism and Alids.

*Makḥūl ibn ʿAbd Allāh al-Hudhalī* (d. between 112/730 and 116/735) Umayyad-era Syrian jurist and narrator of Prophetic traditions.

*Mālik* Arabian lineage group descended from Mālik ibn Jaʿfar. See also Mālik ibn Jaʿfar.

*Mālik* unidentified.

*Mālik ibn Anas* (d. 179/796) the leading jurist of Medina; the Mālikī method of Islamic law is named after him.

*Mālik ibn Dīnār* (d. between 127/744–45 and 131/748–49) Umayyad-era Basran preacher and ascetic. Arabic literature preserves a host of moralistic and ethical sayings ascribed to him.

*Mālik ibn Jaʿfar* one of the sons of Jaʿfar ibn Kilāb and progenitor of one of the noble lines of the Jaʿfar clan. See also Jaʿfar.

*Mālik ibn Misma*ʿ (d. after 72/691) Basran nobleman of Shaybān lineage. He led the Umayyad-era Bakr in Basra during the wars and instability of the early Umayyad period.

*Mālik ibn Nuwayrah* (d. 11/633) pre-Islamic nobleman-warrior of the Yarbūʿ clan of the Tamīm; controversy surrounds his death during the Wars of Apostacy. See also Tamīm.

*Mālik ibn Zuhayr* a pre-Islamic leader of the ʿAbs and brother of Qays ibn Zuhayr. He was killed in the Thrust and Dusty War. See also Thrust and Dusty War.

*al-Maʾmūn* (r. 197–218/813–833) Abbasid caliph who assumed power after lengthy civil war with his brother, al-Amīn. Al-Maʾmūn was a key patron of learning and the sponsor of translating Greek sciences into Arabic.

*Manāʾi* mountain in the lands of the Ṭayyiʾ, reportedly a refuge in times of distress. See also Ṭayyiʾ.

*Mānī* (d. AD 274 or 277) prophet and founder of Manichaeanism. See also Manichaeans/Manichaeanism.

*Manichaeans/Manichaeanism* dualist religion based on the revelations of the prophet Mani. Initially persecuted by the Sassanian state, the religion survived in Iraq and spread widely in Central Asia, where it became the official religion of the Uyghur Khans in AD 762.

*al-Manṣūr, Abū Jaʿfar* (r. 136–58/754–50) second Abbasid caliph and founder of Baghdad. Credited with securing the success of the Abbasid revolution.

*Māriyah bint Ẓālim* pre-Islamic queen known principally for her fabulous earrings.

*Marw (also Marv, Merv)* a now ruined city in Turkmenistan. Ancient Marw controlled a vast oasis and was the greatest city in all of eastern Iran from the Sassanian to Abbasid periods.

*Marw al-Rūdh* settlement five days' journey from Marw, and part of the large river and canal system that fed the Marw Oasis.

*Marwān* see Marwān ibn al-Ḥakam.

*Marwān ibn Abī Ḥafsah* (d. 182/798) highly esteemed poet of the late Umayyad and early Abbasid periods.

*Marwān ibn al-Ḥakam* (r. 664–65/684–85) Umayyad caliph and the first caliph of the Marwanid line. He asserted Umayyad/Syrian hold on the caliphate following the death of Yazīd ibn Muʿāwiyah. See also Marwanids.

*Marwān ibn Muḥammad* (Marwan II) (r. 127–32/744–50) the last caliph of the Umayyad dynasty. He was defeated by the Abbasids in upper Mesopotamia and fled to Egypt, where he was killed.

*Marwān the Jaʿdite* see Marwān ibn Muḥammad.

*Marwanids* branch of the Umayyad family and designation for the Umayyad caliphs from Marwān ibn ʿAbd al-Ḥakam until the end of the Umayyad era (132/750).

*maysir* pre-Islamic form of gambling involving arrows, which consisted of dividing a slaughtered beast into a number of parts (usually ten), for which the game was played.

*Mazdak* founder of an Iranian religious movement during the reign of Kavad I. The tenets of Mazdakism are only recorded in later sources, which were hostile. It seems to have been based on an egalitarian, anti-elite, anti-priesthood message of sharing of wealth, property, and wisdom. See also Kavad I.

*Māzin* name of several Arabian lineages: a subclan of each of the Qays, Rabīʿah, Tamīm, and Yemen groups identified themselves as "the Māzin"; the most prominent was the Māzin of the Tamīm. See also Tamīm.

*al-Māzinī, Abū ʿUthmān* (d. 247/861) Basran grammarian and literary scholar. He is remembered as a learned authority active in the courts of the caliphs al-Muʿtaṣim, al-Wāthiq, and al-Mutawakkil.

*Mina* stopping place in the hills east of Mecca during the hajj pilgrimage. It is where the ritual animal sacrifice takes place.

*Minqar* Arabian lineage; subgroup of the Tamīm. See also Tamīm.

*Mirbad* marketplace outside Basra and trading center for Arabian Bedouin. It was a conduit point where Arabian stories entered Iraqi literature.

*Mirdās ibn Khidhām* (in some sources "Mirdās ibn Judhām," possibly a copyist error) minor Umayyad-era Kufan poet of the Asad. He was attached to Qutaybah ibn Muslim's court, and was best known for composing doggerel and invective poetry. See also Qutaybah ibn Muslim.

*Miskīn, Rabīʿah ibn ʿĀmir al-Dārimī* (d. 89/708) Umayyad-era poet who praised the ruling dynasty and also engaged in poetic sparring with his fellow clansman al-Farazdaq. See also al-Farazdaq.

*Mismaʿ* clan of the Shaybān and a powerful group in Umayyad-era Basra. Mālik ibn Mismaʿ was one of their leaders. See also Mālik ibn Mismaʿ.

*mithkal* (or miskal, Ar. *mithqāl*) common weight usually defined as one and three-sevenths of a dirham (around four grams).

*al-Muʿallā ibn ʿAmr al-Muḥāribī* obscure Umayyad-era figure.

*Muʿāwiyah* Arabic name; it can refer to the Caliph Muʿāwiyah ibn Abī Sufyān and also the pre-Islamic poet and nobleman of the clan Jaʿfar. See also Jaʿfar.

*Muʿāwiyah ibn Abī Sufyān* (r. 41–60/661–80) founder of the Umayyad caliphate as a hereditary dynasty. He was a shrewd statesman who served as governor of Damascus and then all of Syria under the caliphs ʿUmar ibn al-Khaṭṭāb and ʿUthmān before rising to the caliphate on the platform of seeking vengeance for the murdered ʿUthmān. See also ʿUthmān ibn ʿAffān.

*Muḍar* collective name for a broad array of lineage groups and one of the two main divisions of the "Northern Arabs," alongside Rabīʿah. See also Rabīʿah.

*Muhalhil ibn Rabīʿah* pre-Islamic Arabian warrior, poet, and leader of the Taghlib. See also Taghlib.

*Muhallab ibn Abī Ṣufrah* (d. 82/702 or 83/703) a military commander of the Zubayrids and Marwanids. See also Zubayrids and Marwanids.

*Muḥammad ibn ʿAbd al-Malik ibn al-Zayyāt* see Ibn al-Zayyāt.

*Muḥammad ibn al-Ḥasan al-Shaybānī* see al-Shaybānī, Muḥammad ibn al-Ḥasan.

*Muḥammad ibn Jaʿfar* unknown figure, likely a copyist error for Muḥammad ibn ʿUmar al-Wāqidī. See also Muḥammad ibn ʿUmar al-Wāqidī.

*Muḥammad ibn ʿUmar al-Wāqidī* (d. 207/823) Medinan traditionist and historian; important collector of stories about early Islam.

*Muḥārib* name of several Arabian lineage groups; the largest was the Muḥārib ibn Khaḍafah of the Qays ʿAylān resident in southern Najd at the dawn of Islam.

*al-Mujallal* reportedly al-Mujallal ibn Thaʿlabah, father of Muhalhil ibn Rabīʿah's wife; otherwise an obscure figure.

*Mujāshiʿ ibn Masʿūd* (d. 36/656) nobleman and warrior of the Sulaym who participated in Muslim conquests in Iraq and Iran and settled in Basra.

*Mujjāʿah ibn Siʿr ibn Khalīfah* (d. ca. 76/695–96) lieutenant of al-Ḥajjāj ibn Yūsuf and governor on his behalf over Oman and then Sind. See also al-Ḥajjāj ibn Yūsuf.

*al-Mukhtār al-Thaqafī* (d. 67/687) leader of a pro-Alid movement that controlled Kufa in 66–67/685–87; his movement is often viewed as an early manifestation of extremist Shiʿism. See also Alids.

*al-Mundhir* name of several pre-Islamic Lakhmid kings of al-Ḥīrah. See also Lakhmids and al-Ḥīrah.

*al-Mundhir ibn ʿAmr* (d. 4/625) Medinan of Khazraj lineage who pledged to support the Prophet at the second ʿAqabah meeting, which prompted Muḥammad's emigration to Medina. See also al-Khazraj.

*al-Mundhir ibn Maʾ al-Samāʾ* (r. ca. 503 or 505–54) Mundhir III, a Lakhmid king and ally of Khosrow Anushirvan; warred against the Ghassanids, who killed him in battle. See also Khosrow Anushirvan and Ghassanids.

*al-Mundhir the Elder* the Lakhmid King Mundhir I (al-Mundhir ibn al-Nuʿmān); his reign is traditionally dated AD 418–61. He was a close ally of the Sassanians in campaigns against the Roman Empire.

*Muqāʿis* subgroup of the Tamīm. See also Tamīm.

*Murād Depression* region on the fringes of the Empty Quarter between Oman, Saudi Arabia, and Yemen, which was reportedly infested with jinn. Few men were said to venture there.

*Murrah* name of many Arabian lineage groups; important groups bearing this name were the Murrah ibn ʿAwf of Dhubyān-Ghaṭafān lineage and the Murrah ibn ʿUbayd of the Tamīm. See also Ghaṭafān and Tamīm.

*Murrah ibn Dhuhl* leading nobleman of the Dhuhl ibn Shaybān subgroup of the Bakr, father of Hammām and Jassās. See also Bakr, Hammām ibn Murrah, and Jassās.

*al-Murtaḍā, al-Sharīf* (d. 436/1044) theologian, literary scholar, and poet, and one of the most revered Alids of his day. See also Alids.

*Muṣʿab ibn al-Zubayr* (d. 71 or 72/691) Quraysh nobleman renowned for bravery and virtue. When his brother, ʿAbd Allāh ibn al-Zubayr, was caliph, Muṣʿab governed Iraq. See also ʿAbd Allāh ibn al-Zubayr.

*Mushir ibn Yazīd* pre-Islamic warrior from the al-Ḥārith ibn Kaʿb subgroup of the Madhḥij. He fought for ʿĀmir ibn al-Ṭufayl at the Battle of Fayf al-Rīh against his own people, but perfidiously injured ʿĀmir after the battle. See also ʿĀmir ibn al-Ṭufayl.

*Muslim ibn ʿUbays al-Kurayzī* (d. 65/685) Basran-born military commander of Quraysh lineage. He fought in Iraq for the Zubayrids and was killed in battle against Nāfiʿ ibn ʿAbd Allāh and the Blues. See also the Zubayrids, Nāfiʿ ibn ʿAbd Allāh, and Blues.

*al-Mustaʿīn* (r. 248–52/862–66) Abbasid caliph during a period of great instability. Chosen by Turkish court guards to be caliph, he abdicated in favor of al-Muʿtazz, but was murdered shortly afterward nonetheless.

*al-Muʿtaḍid, ʿAbbād ibn Muḥammad* (433–60/1042–69) greatest ruler of the ʿAbbādid dynasty in Seville; by the time of his death, he was the most powerful Muslim ruler in Spain.

*al-Mutalammis* celebrated pre-Islamic Arabic poet of Ḍubayʿah lineage, maternal uncle of the poet Ṭarafah. See also Ṭarafah ibn al-ʿAbd.

*Mutammim ibn Nuwayrah* poet of the Yarbūʿ branch of the Tamīm and brother of their leader, Mālik. Mutammim is best known for his elegies of Mālik. See also Tamīm and Mālik ibn Nuwayrah.

*al-Mutanabbī, Abū l-Ṭayyib Aḥmad ibn al-Ḥusayn* (d. 354/965) poet born in Kufa; restless, self-aggrandizing, and widely renowned as one of the greatest Arabic poets of the entire Muslim era.

*al-Muʿtaṣim* (r. 218–27/833–42) Abbasid caliph, founder of Samarra.

*al-Mutawakkil* (r. 232–47/847–61) Abbasid caliph, the last to wield effective authority across the caliphate; his assassination triggered a period of instability and imperial fragmentation.

*Muʿtazilah/Muʿtazilism* a strand of Muslim theology that emerged in Basra in the early second/eighth century. Often called a "rationalist" school, its views on free will and God's attributes differed from tenets that became Sunni orthodoxy, and Muʿtazilism lost its following by the fifth/eleventh century.

*al-Muwaffaq, Abū Aḥmad Ṭalḥah ibn Jaʿfar* (d. 278/891) a son of the Abbasid caliph al-Mutawakkil, who never became caliph himself, but held command posts in the army and at times wielded de facto political control over Abbasid territory.

*Muzaynah* Arabian lineage residing near Medina. Its origins are unknown, and it only emerges into recorded history with the rise of Islam. Some clans remained around Medina; others settled in Iraq following the Muslim conquests.

*Nabhān* name of several lineage groups, including a subclan of the Ṭayyi' from northern Arabia. See also Ṭayyi'.

*al-Nābighah al-Dhubyānī* celebrated pre-Islamic poet, active in both Ghassanid and Lakhmid courts; his poetry was highly esteemed among Muslim-era collectors. See also Ghassanids and Lakhmids.

*al-Nābighah al-Ja'dī* (d. ca. 79/698–99) poet contemporary with the rise of Islam. He was politically active during the Conquests and subsequent factionalism of the early caliphate.

*Nāfi' ibn 'Abd Allāh ibn al-Azraq* (d. 65/685) supposed founder of the Blues Kharijite movement. The precise historicity of Nāfi' and the early history of the Blues remain unclear. See also Blues and Kharijites.

*Nahd* subgroup of the Quḍā'ah who, at the dawn of Islam, resided in southwest Arabia, near the present Saudi Arabian–Yemeni border. See also Quḍā'ah.

*Nahshal* subclan of the Dārim of Tamīm; cousins of al-Farazdaq's clan. See also Tamīm and Farazdaq.

*Najd* the desert plateau in central Arabia. The region was home to most of the major nomadic groups of pre-Islamic Arabian history.

*al-Namir ibn Qāsiṭ* Arabian lineage of the Rabī'ah from eastern Arabia. They fought for the Taghlib in the Basūs War. See also Basūs War and Taghlib.

*Naṣrid kings* dynasty of kings also known as the Lakhmids. They were clients of the Sassanian Empire and controlled the Iraqi-Arabian frontier during the century before Islam. See also Lakhmids.

*al-Naṭif ibn Khaybarī* pre-Islamic warrior of the Yarbū' branch of the Tamīm. See also Tamīm.

*al-Nawbakhtī, al-Ḥasan ibn Mūsā* (d. between 300/912 and 310/922) Shi'i theologian, philosopher, and author of a work detailing world religions.

*al-Naẓẓam, Ibrāhīm ibn Sayyār* (d. between 220/835 and 230/845) early and prominent theologian of the Mu'tazilah. See also Mu'tazilah/Mu'tazilites.

*Nebuchadnezzar* (r. 605–562) Neo-Babylonian ruler memorialized in biblical history as destroyer of the First Temple in Jerusalem. Muslim-era Arabic interpretations of biblical tradition count Nebuchadnezzar as both a world conqueror and iniquitous king.

*Negus* English equivalent of the Ethiopic Ge'ez *nəguś*, "ruler." In Arabic, it is rendered *al-Najāshī* and usually connotes the Axumite king of Ethiopia contemporary with the Prophet.

*al-Nu'mān ibn al-Mundhir* (r. ca. AD 582–602) Lakhmid king of al-Ḥīrah and a celebrated figure in Arabic literature, where he represents the ideal pre-Islamic Arab king. See also Lakhmids.

*Numayr* the lineage Numayr ibn 'Āmir, a major subgroup of the Qays 'Aylān and a renowned pre-Islamic Arabian group residing in northeastern Arabia and the Syrian desert at the dawn of Islam. See also Qays 'Aylān.

*Paykent (Poykend)* now-abandoned trading center on the lower Zarafshan River, situated between the Oxus and the Bukhara Oasis in present-day Uzbekistan.

*Pelusium* settlement in the Nile's eastern delta region near present-day Port Said; in antiquity, it was an important city on the mouth of the Nile.

*Peroz the Younger* Sassanian king Peroz II, a son of Khosrow Parviz. He reigned briefly in AD 630 amid dynastic instability near the end of the Sassanian Empire. See also Khosrow Parviz.

*Philip II of Macedon* (r. 359–36) king of Macedon who oversaw Macedon's rise into the most powerful Greek state, father of Alexander the Great.

*Plato* (428/7–348/7) the towering figure of Greek philosophy; a student of Socrates, and teacher of Aristotle.

*Ptolemy/Ptolemies* name of the dynasty of Greek rulers of Egypt (305–30) following the death of Alexander the Great.

*Ptolemy the Builder (al-Ṣāni')* Arabic designation for the third Ptolemaic ruler of Egypt. His actual name was Ptolemaios Euergetes (the Benefactor), r. 246–222.

*Ptolemy, Claudius* (ca. AD 100–170) Alexandrian mathematician, astronomer, and geographer; the scientific legacy of his works was felt across Europe and the Middle East.

*Pythagoras* (ca. 570–495) Greek philosopher and mathematician whose name became associated with mysticism and numerology.

*Qabīṣah ibn al-Aswad* member of the Ṭayyi' who is virtually unknown beyond his participation in a delegation with Zayd "the Horseman" to the Prophet in 9/631. See also Ṭayyi' and Zayd "the Horseman."

*al-Qāḍī al-Fāḍil, Abū ʿAlī ʿAbd al-Raḥīm* (d. 596/1200) scholar and judge, and advisor to Saladin, the renowned victor over the Crusaders and founder of the Ayyubid dynasty.

*al-Qādisiyyah* the decisive Muslim victory over the Sassanians, fought in 15/636, which clinched the conquest of Iraq.

*Qaḥṭān* name of unclear pre-Islamic origins. Muslim genealogists classified all "Southern Arabs" as the descendants of Qaḥṭān, and the name became synonymous with "Southern Arabs" and the people of Yemen.

*Qaṣīr* legendary pre-Islamic figure, reportedly a retainer of the king Jadhīmah al-Abrash. See also Jadhīmah al-Abrash.

*al-Qāsim ibn Sallām* unidentified.

*Qaṭan of the Hilāl* probably Qaṭan ibn Qabīṣah ibn Mukhāriq of the Hilāl, governor of Isfahan for the Caliph Muʿāwiyah, and then a commander in Khurasan.

*Qaṭarī ibn al-Fujāʾah* (d. 80/698–99) Kharijite warrior and celebrated poet and orator. He became leader of the Blues, won several battles against the caliphate in Iran, and minted coins in his own name as "Commander of the Faithful." He was killed in battle. See also Blues and Kharijites.

*al-Qayn* name of several Arabian lineage groups; the most commonly encountered in Arabic literature was the al-Qayn subgroup of the Quḍāʿah from northern Arabia near the Syrian Desert. See also Quḍāʿah.

*Qays ʿAylān* large Arabian lineage and one of the two main branches of Muḍar. They included the Ghaṭafān, the Sulaym, and the Hawāzin, and formed a politically powerful faction in the Umayyad and early Abbasid eras. See also Ghaṭafān, Sulaym, and Hawāzin.

*Qays ibn ʿĀṣim* (d. ca. 47/667) a leader of the Muqāʿis subgroup of the Tamīm, he led his kinsmen in various pre-Islamic conflicts, then converted to Islam and settled in Basra. See also Tamīm.

*Qays ibn Jirwah al-ʿĀriq "Meat Stripper"* pre-Islamic poet of the Ṭayyiʾ, famed principally for his poems threatening the Lakhmid ruler ʿAmr ibn Hind. See also ʿAmr ibn Hind.

*Qays ibn Zuhayr* pre-Islamic warrior and one of the leaders of the ʿAbs during the Thrust and Dusty War. See also ʿAbs and Thrust and Dusty War.

*Qirwāsh* likely Qirwāsh ibn ʿAmr ibn al-Aslaʿ, a warrior of the ʿAbs. Another figure, Qirwāsh ibn Hany, also an ʿAbs warrior, is memorialized in another event of the Thrust and Dusty War: the two figures may originally have been one historical person. See also ʿAbs and Thrust and Dusty War.

*Qirwāsh* possibly Qirwāsh ibn ʿAwf ibn ʿĀṣim, a member of the Yarbūʿ. He only appears in stories associated with the Thrust and Dusty War. See also Thrust and Dusty War.

*Quḍāʿah* broad Arabian lineage encompassing several groups. Its origin is obscure and complex: in early Islam, most of Quḍāʿah was counted as a subgroup of the Maʿadd, but changing politics in Umayyad Syria prompted change in the Quḍāʿah's lineage, and it subsequently became associated with Yemen. See also Maʿadd.

*Qudāmah ibn Jaʿdah ibn Hubayrah al-Makhzūmī* nobleman of the Quraysh. He was the son of the Caliph ʿAlī's nephew; ʿAlī appointed him governor of Khurasan.

*Queen of Sheba* the biblical queen, consort of Solomon; counted as one of the ancient queens of Yemen in Arabic historiography.

*Qulayb al-Maghribī* unidentified.

*Quraysh* the dominant lineage group in Mecca. The Prophet, every caliph, and many powerful members of the early Muslim elite descended from the Quraysh.

*Qutaybah* Qutaybah ibn Muslim (d. 96/715–16), a military commander for the Umayyads in eastern Iran and the leader of Muslim conquests in Central Asia. He was killed in an unsuccessful rebellion against the caliphate.

*Rabāḥ ibn al-Ashall* pre-Islamic warrior of the Ghanī.

*Rabīʿ ibn Ziyād ibnʿAbd Allāh* pre-Islamic warrior and poet of the ʿAbs. He waged celebrated battles in the Thrust and Dusty War. See also ʿAbs and Thrust and Dusty War.

*Rabīʿah* collective name for a large array of lineage groups, who with the Muḍar constitute the "Northern Arabs."

*Rabīʿah* the son of Mālik ibn Jaʿfar ibn Kilāb. He was a pre-Islamic poet and nobleman of the clan Jaʿfar, and father of the poet Labīd. See also Jaʿfar and Labīd.

*Rabīʿah ibn Thābit al-Raqqī* (d. 198/814) Abbasid-era Arabic poet from Raqqa who gained repute at the court of al-Rashīd. See also al-Rashīd.

*Rajāʾ ibn Ḥaywah* (d. 112/730) non-Arab Iraqi who became an influential religious and political adviser at the courts of the early Marwanid caliphs. He was famed for his piety and knowledge.

*rajaz* the simplest and perhaps oldest of Arabic poetic meters. It was employed for short, improvised utterances—for instance, those sung at the beginning of a battle.

*Raqāsh* legendary figure in pre-Islamic stories about al-Ḥīrah; sister of Jadhīmah al-Abrash. See also al-Ḥīrah and Jadhīmah al-Abrash.

*al-Raqāshī* likely Abū Qilābah ʿAbd al-Malik ibn Muḥammad al-Raqāshī (d. 276/889–90), a Basran-born traditionist and historian who worked most of his life in Baghdad.

*al-Rashīd, Hārūn* (r. 170–93/786–809) Abbasid caliph and the most celebrated caliph in Arabic literature. His memory is associated with later nostalgia for an Abbasid "golden age."

*Rāsib* name of several separate lineages; most prominent is a subgroup of the Azd. See also al-Azd.

*Rawḥ ibn Zinbāʿ* (d. 84/703) a leader of the Judhām and military commander who assisted the rise of the Marwanids. He served as governor of Palestine under ʿAbd al-Malik. See also Marwanids and ʿAbd al-Malik ibn Marwān.

*Rayḥānah* Arabic girls' name; the name of the poetic "beloved" of ʿAmr ibn Maʿdī Karib's poetry. See also ʿAmr ibn Maʿdī Karib.

*Rostam* erroneously identified as the "father of Peroz," Rostam was the son of Farrakh-hormuz. He was a Sassanian military commander from a powerful family of eastern Iran who died leading the Sassanian army at the Battle of al-Qādisiyyah. See also al-Qādisiyyah.

*Ruʾbah ibn ʿAjjāj* (d. 145/762) Umayyad and early-Abbasid poet, considered the most skilled composer of *rajaz*-style poetry.

*Ruhaynah* agricultural settlement outside of Kufa, on the track to Syria.

*Rumaylah ibn Shiʿār* perhaps a copyist error for Turmulah ibn Shuʿāth; neither are well-known historical figures.

*al-Rūṣāfah* agricultural settlement in the Syrian Desert, and site of an important country estate/palace of the Caliph Hishām. See also Hishām.

*Sabians (Ar. Ṣābiʾah)* Arabic name for various religious communities. The most prominent "Sabian" group were the adherents of a Hellenized Semitic polytheistic religion based in Ḥarrān. They adopted the name "Sabian" in the third/ninth century in order to present themselves to Muslims as an acceptable sect and avoid persecution.

*Saʿd* one of the subclans of the Tamīm, descended from Saʿd ibn Zayd al-Manāt ibn Tamīm. See also Tamīm.

*Saʿd ibn Abī Waqqās* (d. during Muʿāwiyah's caliphate 41–60/661–80) nobleman of the Quraysh, leading Companion of the Prophet, and military commander during the conquest of Iraq.

*Sa'd Monastery* place in the land of Ghaṭafān, on the track to Syria. See also Ghaṭafān.

*Sadūs ibn Sinān* unidentified.

*al-Saffāḥ, Abū al-ʿAbbās* (r. 132–36/749–54) the first Abbasid caliph, who oversaw the extinguishing of the Umayyad line.

*Sahm* subgroup of the Quraysh. See also Quraysh.

*Saʿīd* probably Saʿīd ibn Sallām al-ʿAṭṭār, a Basran scholar and narrator of Prophet traditions. His hadith narrations were not considered trustworthy.

*Saʿīd ibn al-ʿĀṣ ibn Umayyah* (d. 59/678–79) nobleman of the Umayyad clan who held governorships in Kufa and Basra under the Caliph Muʿāwiyah.

*Saʿīd ibn Jubayr* (d. 94/711 or 95/712) renowned Kufan jurist and scholar of Qur'anic and Prophetic traditions. He supported Ibn al-Ashʿath's revolt against al-Ḥajjāj, and in its aftermath he was executed. See also Ibn al-Ashʿath and al-Ḥajjāj ibn Yūsuf.

*Saʿīd ibn ʿUthmān* (d. after 57/680) son of the Caliph ʿUthmān and prominent nobleman of the Quraysh. He was governor of Khurasan under the Caliph Muʿāwiyah and launched a successful attack on Samarqand.

*Saḥbān Wa'il* orator and poet of the Wā'il subgroup of the Bāhilah lineage; proverbial for eloquence. See also Bāhilah.

*Sahl ibn Hārūn* (d. 215/830) literary scholar and celebrated writer.

*Ṣāliḥ ibn ʿAbd al-Quddūs* (d. 167/783) obscure Basran poet. He was executed in the persecutions of al-Mahdī, reportedly on suspicion of engagement with speculative theology.

*Ṣāliḥ ibn ʿAbd al-Raḥmān* (d. ca. 103/722) Basran-born state secretary of Persian origin, best known as the secretary whom al-Ḥajjāj tasked with ensuring that Arabic became the official language of the chancery in Iraq. See also al-Ḥajjāj ibn Yūsuf.

*Salm ibn Qutaybah ibn Muslim* son of Qutaybah ibn Muslim, governor of Basra; served under both Umayyads and Abbasids. See also Qutaybah ibn Muslim.

*Salmā* reportedly one of the two signature mountains of the Ṭayyi', often paired with Ajā'. See also Ajā' and Ṭayyi'.

*Salmān ibn Rabīʿah al-Bāhilī* (d. ca. 28–31/648–52) member of the early Muslim elite who fought in the conquests of Iraq and Syria and was judge for Kufa under the Caliph ʿUmar ibn al-Khaṭṭāb.

*Salūl* name of two unrelated Arabian lineages: a low-status subgroup of the Hawāzin, and a subgroup of the Khuzāʿah lineage in Mecca. The latter held the pre-Islamic custodianship of the Meccan shrine. See also Hawāzin.

*Samarqand* major urban center on the middle reaches of the Zarafshan River in present-day Uzbekistan. It is situated at a crossroads of trading routes in Central Asia and, along with Bukhara, was one of the main political centers of medieval Transoxiana.

*al-Ṣamṣāmah* sword of ʿAmr ibn Maʿdī Karib. See also ʿAmr ibn Maʿdī Karib.

*Ṣarkhad* agricultural settlement next to the Ḥawrān south of Damascus, noted for its wine production.

*Ṣaʿṣaʿah* see ʿĀmir ibn Ṣaʿṣaʿah.

*al-Ṣaydāʾ* Arabian lineage, subgroup of the Asad.

*Sayf al-Dawlah ibn Ḥamdān, Abū al-Ḥasan ʿAlī* (d. 356/967) the ruler of the Ḥamdanid dynasty based in Aleppo, his realm extended to much of present-day northern Syria and southeast Turkey. In Arabic literature, he is an archetype of chivalrous values.

*al-Shaʿbī, ʿĀmir* (d. between 103/721 and 110/728) Kufan jurist, transmitter of Prophetic traditions and narrator of the history of early Muslim-era Iraq.

*Shaddād al-Ḥārithī, Abū ʿUbayd* obscure figure, remembered primarily in Arabic literature for his effusive praise of gold at a princely court in the early third/ninth century.

*Shaddād ibn Muʿāwiyah* pre-Islamic warrior of the ʿAbs; father of the celebrated hero ʿAntarah ibn Shaddād. See also ʿAbs.

*al-Shāfiʿī, Muḥammad ibn Idrīs* (d. 204/820) jurist and student of Mālik ibn Anas. He became highly respected, with his own following, and the Shāfiʿī method of Islamic law is named after him. See also Mālik ibn Anas.

*Shahriyar* (d. AD 628) Sassanian prince, the son of Khosrow Parviz and Shirin. His son, Yazdegerd III, ruled as the last Sassanian. See also Khosrow Parviz and Shirin.

*Shahrzūr* ancient city in what is today the Kurdish region of Iraq.

*Shapur son of Ardashir (Shapur I)* (r. 239–70) second ruler of the Sassanian empire.

*Shaulah* Arabic name of a star in the "tail" of the constellation Scorpio; its current name is Lambda Scorpii.

*al-Shaybānī, Abū ʿAmr Isḥāq ibn Mirār* (d. ca. 210/825) Kufan-born specialist of Arabic poetry and grammar. He was a contemporary of Abū ʿUbaydah and al-Aṣmaʿī: the trio constituted the most respected early authorities on Arabian language and culture. See also Abū ʿUbaydah and al-Aṣmaʿī.

*al-Shaybānī, Muḥammad ibn al-Ḥasan* (d. 187/803 or 189/805) jurist student of Abū Ḥanīfah and leading proponent of Abū Ḥanīfah's Islamic law teachings.

*Shaylamah, Muḥammad ibn al-Ḥasan ibn Sahil* (d. 280/893–94) courtier, writer, and state secretary of the Abbasids. He was executed by the Caliph al-Muʿtaḍid on suspicion of plotting with Alid rebels against the caliph. See also Alids.

*Sheroe* (r. 628) Sassanian king, also known as Kavad II or Shiruya. He overthrew his father, Khosrow Parviz, and his short reign was troubled with civil war and instability. He died of the plague. See also Khosrow Parviz.

*Shibl ibn Qilādah ibn ʿAmr ibn Saʿd* pre-Islamic warrior of the Khathʿam; nothing appears to be known about him other than his role in killing al-Sulayk ibn al-Sulakah. See also Khathʿam and Sulayk ibn al-Sulakah.

*Shirin* queen of the Sassanian ruler Khosrow Parviz. See also Khosrow Parviz.

*Shuqqah (or Ḍamrah) ibn Ḍamrah ibn Jābir ibn Quṭn ibn Nahshal* pre-Islamic warrior and poet of the Nahshal ibn Ḍārim clan of the Tamīm. See also Tamīm.

*Shurayḥ* name of a kinship group descended from al-Aḥwaṣ ibn Jaʿfar ibn Kilāb; one of the family lines of the clan Jaʿfar. See also Jaʿfar.

*Ṣinbil (or Ṣunbul)* unidentified.

*Sind* province of the Umayyad and Abbasid empires encompassing the Indus delta region of present-day Pakistan.

*al-Sirrī ibn al-Ṣabāḥ* obscure figure, identified as a non-Arab affiliate of Thawbān ibn ʿAlī. Both appear in Arabic literature as sources of stories about Basran and Kufan poets in the early Abbasid period.

*Socrates* (ca. 470–399) great Greek philosopher. Arabic writers had little access to his teachings and considered his work similar to that of Plato.

*Sogdians* the name in Arabic sources for the indigenous peoples of Transoxiana prior to the Muslim Conquest. Sogdian is the modern term for a group of Iranian languages spoken by an array of communities and polities in pre-Islamic Transoxiana who gained great wealth as traders between Central Asia and Iran.

*Sufyān ibn ʿUyaynah* (d. 196/811) important hadith narrator, born in Kufa, who settled in Mecca.

*al-Suhaylī* Abū l-Qāsim ʿAbd al-Raḥmān ibn ʿAbd Allāh al-Suhaylī (d. 581/1185), an Andalusian jurist and writer of an important biography of the Prophet.

*Sulayk ibn al-Sulakah* pre-Islamic Arabian poet famed in Arabic literature for his persona as an outlaw and for his incredible sprinting ability.

*Sulaym* Arabian lineage group descended from the Qays who resided north of Medina before Islam. See also Qays.

*Sulaym ibn ʿItr al-Tujībī, Abū Salamah* (d. 75/694–95) chief judge and preacher in early Umayyad-era Egypt; from the Tujīb subgroup of the Kindah. See also Kindah.

*Sulaymān ibn ʿAbd al-Malik* (r. 96–99/715–17) Umayyad caliph.

*Ṣurad* unknown companion of al-Sulayk ibn al-Sulakah. See also Sulayk ibn al-Sulakah.

*Tabālah* name of several locations in South Arabia, including a rich agricultural settlement in Tihāmah between Mecca and Yemen.

*Taghlib* important lineage group of the Wāʾil. They were cousins of the Bakr, against whom they fought in the Basūs War. The Taghlib controlled the northern frontiers of Mesopotamia at the dawn of Islam.

*al-Ṭāʾif* urban settlement in an agricultural area near Mecca.

*Ṭalḥah ibn ʿAbd Allāh* (d. after 63/682–3) nobleman of the Meccan Khuzāʿah lineage who was resident in Basra. He was renowned for his generosity and nobility and was appointed governor of Sijistan in eastern Iran, where he died.

*Taloqan* name of city and region in northwestern Afghanistan between Balkh and Badakhshan.

*Ṭālūṭ* obscure figure; reportedly a Jewish heretic and nephew of Labīd ibn Aʿṣam. Arabic sources consider him an early proponent of the doctrine that the Qurʾan was created. See also Labīd ibn Aʿṣam.

*Tamīm* broad lineage incorporating many subclans residing in central and eastern Arabia before Islam. The Tamīm formed a major power bloc in Iraq during early Islam.

*Ṭarafah ibn ʿAbd* pre-Islamic Arabian poet, and composer of one of the great pre-Islamic odes. He was a member of the Thaʿlabah, a powerful branch of the Bakr ibn Wāʾil in his day. See also Bakr ibn Wāʾil.

*al-Tawḥīdī, Abū al-Ḥayyān ʿAlī ibn Muḥammad* (d. 414/1023) a scholar-courtier, philosopher, and prolific author, he was a leading learned figure of fourth/tenth century Iraq and Iran.

*Taymā'* large oasis settlement in northwestern Saudi Arabia, continuously inhabited since prehistoric times.

*Ṭayyi'* a major Arabian lineage. Genealogists count them as "Southern Arabs," though their lands in the century before Islam were located in northern and northeastern Arabia. Their name, transliterated into Syriac as Ṭayyāyē, became the generic label by which Iraqis and the Sassanian Empire referred to all Arabians in Late Antiquity.

*Thaʿlabah* name of several unrelated Arabian lineages, including the Thaʿlabah in the Saʿd branch of the Dhubyān, the Thaʿlabah of the Yarbūʿ, and the Thaʿlabah of the Bakr. See also Dhubyān, Yarbūʿ, and Bakr.

*Thaʿlabah ibn ʿAmr* an obscure member of the Ṭayyi', his actual name may have been ʿAmr ibn Thaʿlabah or ʿAmr ibn Milqaṭ.

*Thaqīf* the lineage group occupying lands between Mecca and al-Ṭā'if at the dawn of Islam. Alongside Quraysh, members of Thaqīf constituted the most powerful political elites of the Umayyad era. See also Quraysh.

*al-Thawrī, Sufyān ibn Saʿīd ibn Masrūḳ Abū ʿAbd Allāh al-Kūfī* (d. 161/778) prominent scholar of Islamic law, tradition, and Qur'an interpretation.

*Thrust and Dusty War* name of a protracted conflict between the ʿAbs and the Dhubyān (specifically, the Fazārah branch of the Dhubyān). See also ʿAbs, Dhubyān, and Fazārah.

*Tinnīs* a port town in Egypt's eastern Nile Delta known in antiquity as Tenessos.

*Tocharians* the name in Arabic sources for the people along the southern banks of the middle and upper Oxus River in northern Afghanistan. The word derives from Greek Tokharoi, a term for many peoples of Transoxiana and the Central Asian steppe. Modern scholars use "Tocharian" to connote a wider array of ancient Iranian-language speakers.

*Transoxiana* literally "the land beyond the Oxus," the land east of the Oxus River up to the Central Asian steppe and the Altai Mountains, a region roughly contiguous with present-day Uzbekistan.

*Ṭufāwah* Arabian lineage of disputed origin: it is claimed to be a subclan of the Aʿṣur of the Qays ʿAylān. See also Qays ʿAylān.

*al-Ṭufayl* a son of Mālik ibn Jaʿfar ibn Kilāb. Leader of the clan Jaʿfar before Islam and father of ʿĀmir ibn al-Ṭufayl. See also Jaʿfar and ʿĀmir ibn al-Ṭufayl.

*Ṭuways, Abū ʿAbd al-Munʿim ʿĪsā ibn ʿAbd Allāh* (d. 92/711) leading figure in the early generation of Muslim-era Arabic musicians.

*ʿUbād* name of a subclan of the Thaʿlabah branch of the Bakr, led by al-Ḥārith ibn ʿUbād during the Basūs War. See also Bakr and the Basūs War.

*ʿUbayd Allāh ibn Bashīr ibn Māḥūz* (d. 66/686) Kharijite who assumed leadership of the Blues after the death of Nāfiʿ ibn al-Azraq at the Battle of Dūlāb in 65/684–85. He was killed at the Battle of Sillabrā. See also Blues, Kharijites, Nāfiʿ ibn al-Azraq.

*ʿUbayd Allāh ibn Ziyād ibn Ẓabyān* (d. 75/694–95) Umayyad-era warrior of the Taymallāh subgroup of the Bakr. Renowned as hotheaded, bellicose, and opposed to tyranny, he joined Ibn Jārūd's abortive rebellion against al-Ḥajjāj, then fled to Oman, where he was killed. See also al-Ḥajjāj ibn Yūsuf.

*ʿUbayd al-Kilābī* unidentified contemporary of al-Jāḥiẓ, reportedly an eloquent, but poor, Arab.

*ʿUbayd ibn Mawhib* relatively obscure Umayyad-era figure attached to the court of al-Ḥajjāj, reportedly sent by al-Ḥajjāj to assist in al-Muhallab's war against the Blues. See also al-Ḥajjāj ibn Yūsuf and Blues.

*ʿUbayd ibn Yūnus* unidentified; see ʿUbayd ibn Mawhib.

*Ubulla* port city at the mouth of the Euphrates in Iraq, the major outlet to the Persian Gulf before the founding of Basra.

*al-Uqayshir* (d. ca. 80/699) nickname of al-Mughīrah ibn ʿAbd Allāh of the Khuzaymah, an Umayyad-era poet who settled in Kufa and composed politically charged poetry for military elite patrons.

*ʿUkāẓ* the pre-Islamic fair held annually near Mecca during the month of Dhu'l-Qadah, the month before the hajj pilgrimage.

*ʿUmar ibn ʿAbd al-ʿAzīz* (r. 99–101/717–20) Umayyad caliph memorialized as the only truly devout and virtuous caliph of the Umayyad dynasty and subsequently viewed as a staunch upholder of orthodoxy.

*ʿUmar ibn Abī Rabīʿah* (d. 93/712 or 103/721) Meccan poet of the Quraysh, famed as an innovator of a form of brazen, antiheroic Arabic love poetry in which the poet relishes amorous exploits.

*ʿUmar ibn Hubayrah* (d. between 105/724 and 107/726) Umayyad military leader and governor of Iraq for the Caliph Yazīd ibn ʿAbd al-Malik.

*ʿUmar ibn al-Khaṭṭāb* (r. 13–23/632–44) a Companion and the second caliph of Islam, known for his stern and austere character. ʿUmar's caliphate oversaw the conquests of Egypt, Syria, Iraq, and Iran. See also Companions.

*Umāmah* Arabic girl's name, and the poetic beloved to whom ʿAmr ibn Maʿdī Karib addressed one of his poems.

*Umaymah* Arabic girl's name, and the poetic beloved of al-Ḥārith ibn Waʿlah.

*Umayyads* first dynasty of hereditary caliphs in Islam. Their rule is subdivided into the Sufyanid (40–64/661–84) and Marwanid (64–132/684–750) periods. See also Marwanids.

*ʿUqayl* Arabian lineage, subgroup of the ʿĀmir ibn Ṣaʿṣaʿah. They resided in southern Najd at the dawn of Islam and became a powerful political force in northern Syria in the third/ninth century.

*ʿUqbah ibn Salm* (d. 167/783–84) of the Hubāʾah lineage, he was governor of Basra during the caliphate of al-Manṣūr.

*ʿUrwah ibn Jaʿfar "the Traveler"* pre-Islamic nobleman of the ʿĀmir ibn Ṣaʿṣaʿah lineage. His murder sparked one of the Fijār Wars. See also ʿĀmir ibn Ṣaʿṣaʿah and Fijār Wars.

*ʿUṣayyah* Arabian lineage, subgroup of the Sulaym. See also Sulaym.

*ʿUtaybah ibn al-Ḥārith ibn Shihāb* warrior of the Yarbūʿ branch of the Tamīm in the early seventh century AD, noted for his conflicts with Bisṭām ibn Qays. See also Bisṭām ibn Qays.

*al-ʿUtbī* probably Abū ʿAbd al-Raḥmān Muḥammad al-ʿUtbī (d. 230/844), a Basran scholar of Arabic language, poetry, and Arabian history.

*ʿUthmān ibn ʿAffān* (r. 23–36/644–56) the third caliph of Islam; oversaw major conquests and the organization of the caliphate, and codified the Qurʾanic codex. His assassination sparked the first intra-Muslim war.

*ʿUthmān ibn Ḥayyān* (d. between 101/719 and 110/729) Umayyad military commander of Muzaynah lineage who governed Medina in 93–96/712–15.

*al-ʿUzzā* pre-Islamic Arabian deity that was worshipped in various parts of northern and western Arabia; it is named in the Qurʾan (Q Najm 53:19).

*Valor Anthology (Ar. al-Ḥamāsah)* compilation of pre-Islamic and early Muslim-era poetry extracts, selected by Abū Tammām; it was one of the most celebrated poetry collections and was standard fare for poetry students. Scholars from Andalusia to Iran wrote commentaries on it. See also Abū Tammām.

*Wāʾil* name of an expansive group of lineages; Wāʾil is the putative ancestor of both the Bakr and Taghlib. See also Bakr and Taghlib.

*Wāʾil ibn Rabīʿah* given name of a pre-Islamic king of the Wāʾil; better known by his nickname "Kulayb ibn Rabīʿah." See also Wāʾil and Kulayb ibn Rabīʿah.

*Wāridāt* a major battle of the Basūs War, a Taghlib victory over Bakr. See also Bakr, Taghlib, and the Basūs War.

*Warqā' ibn Bilāl* pre-Islamic warrior of the Thaʿlabah ibn Saʿd. He was killed with Ḥamal and Ḥudhayfah, sons of Badr, during the Thrust and Dusty War. See also Ḥamal ibn Badr, Ḥudyahfah ibn Badr, Thrust and Dusty War.

*Wāṣil ibn ʿAṭā'* (d. 131/748–49) influential Basran theologian and early proponent of ideas embraced by the Muʿtazilites. See also Muʿtazilites/ Muʿtazilism.

*Wāsiṭ* a city in central Iraq founded by al-Ḥajjāj as his capital ca. 75/694–86/705. After al-Ḥajjāj's death, it ceased being the regular capital but remained a prominent urban center. See also al-Ḥajjāj ibn Yūsuf.

*al-Wāthiq* (r. 227–32/842–47) Abbasid caliph, the penultimate Abbasid ruler to wield effective authority over the breadth of the caliphate.

*Wazar ibn Sadūs* a leader of the Nabhān clan of the Ṭayyi' who made an embassy to the Prophet with Zayd "the Horseman." Wazar's name and history are variably recorded and his fate is uncertain; some claim he moved to Syria and became Christian. See also Ṭayyi' and Zayd "the Horseman."

*Yaḥyā ibn al-Ḥakam ibn Abī al-ʿĀṣ* (d. ca. 80/700–01) nobleman of the Quraysh and high-ranking Umayyad political figure. He served as governor of several districts, including Medina in 75/694–95.

*Yaḥyā ibn Khālid al-Barmakī* (d. 187/803) member of the Barmakid family, boyhood tutor and then advisor to the Caliph al-Rashīd. He governed of several provinces of the Abbasid caliphate and was a celebrated patron of scholarship. See also Barmakids and al-Rashīd.

*Yaʿqūb, Abū ʿAbd Allāh* (d. 186/802) a vizier of the Caliph al-Mahdī and an Alid-leaning political figure who was involved in several political intrigues during the early period of Abbasid caliphate. See also Alids.

*Yaʿqūb al-Kindī* see al-Kindī, Abū Yūsuf Yaʿqūb.

*Yarbūʿ* Arabian lineage group; also known as the Ḥanẓalah, a subgroup of the Tamīm. See also Tamīm.

*Yarmuk* the decisive Muslim victory over the Byzantines ca. 15/636, which led to the Muslim conquest of Syria.

*Yasār* slave in pre-Islamic Arabia, said in some sources to have been owned by the Ghudānah, a subgroup of the Yarbūʿ. See also Yarbūʿ.

*Yashkur* Arabian lineage group; a large but politically marginalized subgroup of the Bakr. See also Bakr.

*Yazdegerd* name of three Sassanian rulers. Yazdegerd III (r. AD 632–51) was the last Sassanian ruler. He was defeated by the Muslim conquerors and died in Central Asia, probably in Marw.

*Yazīd ibn ʿAbd al-Malik* (r. 101–05/720–24) Umayyad caliph noted for his frivolous, fun-loving lifestyle.

*Yazīd ibn Abī Kabshah* (d. 97/715–16) Umayyad-era political figure who led military campaigns against the Byzantines and governed Iraq following the death of al-Ḥajjāj. See also al-Ḥajjaj ibn Yūsuf.

*Yazīd ibn Abī Muslim* (d. 102/720–21) non-Arab affiliate of the Thaqīf, he became al-Ḥajjāj's secretary and fiscal overseer. Later appointed governor of North Africa, where he was murdered by his local bodyguards. See also al-Ḥajjāj ibn Yūsuf.

*Yazīd ibn Dīnār* see Yazīd ibn Abī Muslim.

*Yazīd ibn al-Ḥaṣīn ibn Numayr al-Kindī* (d. 103/721–22) a member of an elite military family during the Umayyad caliphate, he held small-scale governorships for the Marwanids. See also Marwanids.

*Yazīd ibn al-Muhallab* (d. 102/720) Umayyad-era warrior and governor. Son of al-Muhallab ibn Abī Ṣufrah, Yazīd inherited the governorship of Khurasan from his father. Though he was dismissed by ʿAbd al-Malik, he was reappointed governor over Iraq and Khurasan ten years later by the Caliph Sulaymān. Yazīd died in a revolt against the Caliph Yazīd ibn ʿAbd al-Malik. See also ʿAbd al-Malik ibn Marwān, Sulaymān ibn ʿAbd al-Malik, and Yazīd ibn ʿAbd al-Malik.

*Zayd ibn al-Khaṭṭāb* (d. 12/632) the brother of the Caliph ʿUmar ibn al-Khaṭṭāb and a Companion of the Prophet. See also Companions.

*Zayd "the Horseman"* (d. 9/631) a warrior and leader of the Ṭayyiʾ at the dawn of Islam, he converted after making an embassy to the Prophet, who renamed him Zayd "the Goodman." Zayd died shortly thereafter. See also Ṭayyiʾ.

*Zenobia* (r. AD 267–72) queen of Palmyra who, as co-regent with her husband, Odaenathus, established a major regional empire. She was ultimately defeated by the resurgent Romans in the 270s AD. Muslim-era storytellers remember Zenobia's name, but change the details considerably.

*al-Zibriqān ibn Badr* (d. after 40/661) tribal leader and poet of the Tamīm; appointed by the Prophet to administer the Saʿd clan of the Tamīm, he played active role in Islamic conquests. See also Tamīm.

*Ziyād* see Ziyād ibn Abī Sufyān.

*Ziyād ibn Abī Sufyān (or ibn Abīhi)* (d. 53/673) a prominent governor of the Caliph Muʿāwiyah. Muʿāwiyah tried to attach Ziyād to his own clan of the

Umayyads, hence his derogatory alternate name, Ziyād ibn Abīhi: "Ziyād, the son of his (unknown) father."

*Ziyād ibn al-Habūlah* ancient pre-Islamic Arabian figure, reportedly king of the Salīḥ, a kingdom allied to the Byzantines on the Syrian-Arabian frontier in the fifth century AD.

*al-Ziyādī* obscure figure who was asserted to be a leading astrologer of the generation before Abū Maʿshar, though his name does not usually appear in lists of Muslim astrologers. See also Abū Maʿshar.

*Zubayd* Arabian lineage and subgroup of the Saʿd al-ʿAshīrah of the Madhḥij. They lived in western Yemen at the dawn of Islam. See also Madhḥij.

*al-Zubayr ibn al-ʿAwwām* (d. 36/656) Meccan nobleman from the ʿAbd al-ʿUzzā clan of Quraysh and venerated Companion. He competed for power over the caliphate after the Caliph ʿUthmān's assassination, and was killed following his defeat by the Caliph ʿAlī. See also Companions, ʿUthmān ibn ʿAffān, and ʿAlī ibn Abī Ṭālib.

*Zubayrids* name of the descendants of the Meccan nobleman Zubayr ibn al-ʿAwwām, and also the supporters of the caliphate of ʿAbd Allāh ibn al-Zubayr (r. 64–73/683–92). See also ʿAbd Allāh ibn al-Zubayr.

*Zufar ibn al-Ḥārith al-Kilābī* (d. between 65/685 and 86/705) important Umayyad-era military commander who died during the caliphate of ʿAbd al-Malik.

*Zuhayr ibn Jadhīmah* celebrated pre-Islamic warrior and leader of the ʿAbs. See also ʿAbs.

*Zurārah ibn ʿUdas* pre-Islamic nobleman of the Tamīm and leader of its reportedly most powerful clan before Islam. See also Tamīm.

# Bibliography

Al-Ābī, Abū Sa'd Manṣūr ibn al-Ḥusayn. *Nathr al-durr fī l-muḥāḍarāt*. Edited by Khālid 'Abd al-Ghanī Maḥfūẓ. 4 vols. Beirut: Dār al-Kutub al-'Ilmiyyah, 2004.

Abū Dāwūd al-Sijistānī. *Sunan Abī Dāwūd*. Riyadh: Dār al-Salām, 1999.

Abū l-Fidā, 'Imād al-Dīn Ismā'īl. *Al-Mukhtaṣar fī akhbār al-bashar*. 2 vols. Cairo: al-Maṭba'ah al-Ḥusayniyyah, 1907.

Abū Ma'shar. *On Solar Revolutions*. Translated and edited by Benjamin Dykes. Minneapolis: Cazimi Press, 2010.

Abū Ma'shar. *On the Revolutions of the Years of Nativities*. Translated and edited by Benjamin Dykes. Minneapolis: Cazimi Press, 2019.

Abū Nu'aym al-Iṣbahānī, Aḥmad ibn 'Abd Allāh. *Ḥilyat al-awliyā' wa-ṭabaqāt al-aṣfiyā'*. Edited by Muṣṭafā 'Abd al-Qādir 'Aṭā. 12 vols. Beirut: Dār al-Kutub al-'Ilmiyyah, 1997.

Abū Nuwās. *Dīwān Abī Nuwās al-Ḥasan ibn Hāni'*. Edited by Ewald Wagner. 7 vols. Beirut: Orient Institut, 2012.

Abū Tammām, Ḥabīb ibn Aws. *Al-Waḥshiyyāt*. Edited by 'Abd al-'Azīz al-Maymanī al-Rajkoti. Cairo: al-Ma'ārif, 1987.

Abū 'Ubayd Qāsim ibn Sallām. *Kitāb al-Īmān*. Edited by Muḥammad Nāṣir al-Dīn al-Albānī. Riyadh: Maktabat al-Ma'ārif, 2000.

Abū 'Ubaydah, Ma'mar ibn al-Muthannā. *Al-Dībāj*. Edited by 'Abd Allāh ibn Sulaymān al-Jarbū' and 'Abd al-Raḥmān ibn Sulaymān al-'Uthaymīn. Cairo: al-Khānjī, 1991.

Al-Albānī, Muḥammad. *Silsilat al-aḥādīth al-ḍa'īfah wa-l-mawḍū'ah*. 15 vols. Riyadh: Maktabat al-Ma'ārif, 1992.

'Allāwanah, Sharīf. *'Aqīl ibn 'Ullafah: sīratuhu wa-shi'ruhu*. Amman: al-Manāhij, 2003.

Al-'Āmilī, Bahā' al-Dīn Muḥammad. *Al-Kashkūl*. Edited by Jāsim ibn Muḥammad al-Yāsīn. Kuwait: al-Samāḥah, 2013.

Al-Amīn, Muḥsin. *A'yān al-shī'ah*. Edited by Ḥasan al-Amīn. 12 vols. Beirut: Dār al-Ta'āruf, 1982.

'Amr ibn Ma'dī Karib. *Shi'r 'Amr ibn Ma'dī Karib*. Edited by Muṭā' al-Ṭarābīshī. Damascus: Majma' al-Lughah al-'Arabiyyah, 1985.

Al-Anbārī, Abū Muḥammad al-Qāsim. *Sharḥ Dīwān al-Mufaḍḍaliyyāt*. 2 vols. Edited by Muḥammad Nabīl Ṭarīfī. Beirut: Dār Ṣādir, 2003.

Al-Andalusī, Ibn Saʿīd. *Al-Mughrib fī ḥulā l-Maghrib*. Edited by Khalīl ʿImrān al-Manṣūr. 2 vols. Beirut: Dār al-Kutub al-ʿIlmiyyah, 1997.

———. *Nashwat al-ṭarab fī tārīkh jāhiliyyat al-ʿArab*. Edited by Nuṣrat ʿAbd al-Raḥmān. 2 vols. Amman: al-Aqṣā, 1982.

Apollodorus. *The Library*. Translated by J. G. Frazer. Cambridge, MA: Harvard University Press/Loeb, 1921.

Ascoli, Graziadio I. "Über Banu al-asfar." *Zeitschrift der deutschen Morgenländischen Gesellschaft* 15 (1861): 143–44.

Al-Aʿshā Qays ibn Maymūn. *Dīwān al-Aʿshā al-kabīr*. Edited by Muḥammad Muḥammad Ḥusayn. Beirut: Dār al-Nahḍah al-ʿArabiyyah, 1974.

Al-ʿAskarī, Abū Hilāl. *Dīwān al-maʿānī*. Edited by al-Nabawī ʿAbd al-Wāḥid Shaʿlān. 3 vols. Beirut: Muʾassasat al-Risalah, 2005.

———. *Jamharat al-amthāl*. Edited by Muḥammad Abū al-Faḍl Ibrāhīm and ʿAbd al-Majīd Qaṭāmish. 2 vols. Beirut: Dār al-Jīl, 1988.

ʿAwwaḍ, Ibrāhīm. *Sahl ibn Hārūn wa-Kitāb al-Namir wa-l-thaʿlab*. Tunis: al-Manar, 2006.

Al-ʿAẓm, Muḥammad Firdaws. *Al-Mustadrak ʿalā ansāb al-ashrāf*. 13 vols. Damascus: Dār al-Yaqaẓah al-ʿArabiyyah, 2001–04.

Al-Bakrī, Abū al-ʿUbayd. *Faṣl al-maqāl fī sharḥ kitāb al-amthāl*. Edited by Iḥsān ʿAbbās and ʿAbd al-Majīd al-ʿĀbidīn. Beirut: Muʾassasat al-Risālah, 1983.

———. *Muʿjam mā staʿjam*. Edited by Muṣṭafā l-Saqqā. 4 vols. Cairo: Lajnat al-Taʾlīf wa-l-Tarjamah wa-l-Nashr, 1947.

———. *Simṭ al-laʾālī*. Edited by ʿAbd al-ʿAzīz al-Maymanī. 2 vols. Cairo: Lajnat al-Taʾlīf wa-l-Tarjamah wa-l-Nashr, 1936.

Al-Balādhurī, Aḥmad ibn Yaḥyā. *Ansāb al-ashrāf*. Edited by Iḥsān ʿAbbās et al. 7 vols. Beirut: Orient Institut, 1979–.

———. *Ansāb al-ashrāf*. Edited by Suhayl Zakkār and Riyādh al-Ziriklī. 13 vols. Beirut: Dār al-Fikr, 1996.

———. *Futūḥ al-buldān*. Edited by Riḍwān Muḥammad Riḍwān. Beirut: Dār al-Kutub al-ʿIlmiyyah, 1978.

Bashshār ibn Burd. *Dīwān*. Edited by Muḥammad al-Ṭāhir ibn ʿĀshūr. 4 vols. Tunis, 1976.

Al-Baṣrī, Ṣadr al-Dīn ʿAlī ibn Abī l-Faraj. *Al-Ḥamāsah al-Baṣriyyah*. Edited by ʿĀdil Sulaymān Jamāl. 4 vols. Cairo: al-Khanjī, 1999.

Bauer, Thomas. "In Search of 'Post-Classical Literature': A Review Article." *Mamluk Studies Review* 11 (2007): 137–67.

———. "Ibn Nubātah al-Miṣrī (686–768/1287–1366): Life and Works, Part I: The Life of Ibn Nubātah." *Mamluk Studies Review* 12 (2008): 1–35.

———. "Jamāl al-Dīn Ibn Nubātah." In *Essays in Arabic Literary Biography*, edited by Joseph E. Lowry and Devin J. Stewart, 2:184–202. Wiesbaden, Germany: Harrassowitz, 2009.

Al-Bayhaqī, Abū Bakr. *Al-Jāmiʿ li-shuʿab al-īmān*. Edited by Mukhtār Aḥmad al-Nadwī. 14 vols. Riyadh: Maktabat al-Rushd, 2003.

———. *Al-Maḥāsin wa-l-masāwiʾ*. Edited by Muḥammad Abū l-Faḍl Ibrāhīm. 2 vols. Cairo: Nahḍat Miṣr, 1961.

———. *Al-Sunan al-kubrā*. Edited by Muṣṭafā ʿAbd al-Qādir ʿAṭā. 11 vols. Beirut: Dār al-Kutub al-ʿIlmiyyah, 2003.

Berzin, Alexander. "Historical Survey of the Buddhist and Muslim Worlds' Knowledge of Each Other's Customs and Teachings." *The Muslim World* 100 (2010): 187–203.

Al-Bīrūnī, Abū Rayḥān Muḥammad. *Al-Taḥqīq mā li-l-Hind*. Hyderabad, India: Dāʾirat al-Maʿrifah al-ʿUthmāniyyah, 1958.

Blochet, E. *Catalogue des manuscrits arabes des nouvelles acquisitions (1884–1924)*. Paris: Ernst Leroux, 1925.

Al-Buḥturī. *Dīwān al-Buḥturī*. Edited by Ḥasan Kāmil al-Ṣayrafī. 5 vols. Cairo: al-Maʿārif, 2018.

Al-Bukhārī, Muḥammad ibn Ismāʿīl. *Ṣaḥīḥ al-Bukhārī*. Riyadh: Dār al-Salām, 1999.

Cereti, Carlo. "Gayōmard." In *Encyclopædia Iranica*, online edition, 2015. http://www.iranicaonline.org/articles/gayomard.

Cheikho, Louis. *Majānī l-adab fī ḥadāʾiq al-ʿarab*. Beirut: al-Maṭbaʿah al-Kāthūlīqiyyah, n.d.

———. *Shuʿarāʾ al-naṣrāniyyah fī l-Jāhiliyyah*. 6 vols. Cairo: Maktabat al-Ādāb, 1982.

Corssen, Wilhelm Paul. *Über Aussprache, Vokalismus und Betonung der lateinischen Sprache*. Leipzig, Germany: B. G. Teubner, 1868.

Darwīsh, Muḥyī l-Dīn. *Iʿrāb al-Qurʾān wa-bayānuh*. 9 vols. Damascus: Dār Ibn Kathīr, 1999.

Dekhoda, ʿAlī Akbar. *Lughatnāma*. 15 vols. Tehran: University of Tehran Publications, 1998.

Al-Dhahabī, Abū ʿAbd Allāh. *Siyar aʿlām al-nubalāʾ*. 25 vols. Edited by Hassān ʿAbd al-Mannān. Beirut: Bayt al-Afkār, 2004.

Dhū l-Rummah. *Dīwān*. Edited by ʿAbd al-Quddūs Abū Ṣāliḥ. 3 vols. Damascus: al-Majmaʿ al-Lughawī, 1982.

Al-Dīnawarī, Abū Bakr Aḥmad. *Al-Mujālasah wa-jawāhir al-ʿilm*. Edited by Abū ʿUbaydah Mashhūr ibn Ḥasan Āl Salmān. 10 vols. Beirut: Dār Ibn Ḥazm, 1998.

———. *Al-Akhbār al-ṭiwāl*. Edited by ʿIṣām Muḥammad al-Ḥājj ʿAlī. Beirut: Dār al-Kutub al-ʿIlmiyyah, 2001.

Dzon, Mary. "Jews and Birds in Medieval Abrahamic Collections." *Traditio* 66 (2011): 189–230.

Fierro, Maribel. "Genealogies of Power in al-Andalus: Politics, Religion and Ethnicity during the Second/Eighth–Fifth/Eleventh Centuries." *Annales Islamologiques* 42 (2008): 29–55.

Fowden, Garth. *The Egyptian Hermes*. Princeton, NJ: Princeton University Press, 1993.

Garulo, Teresa. "La biografía de Wallada, todo problemas." *Anaquel de Estudios Arabes* 20 (2009): 97–116.

Hägg, Thomas, and Bo Utas. *The Virgin and Her Lover: Fragments of an Ancient Greek Novel and a Persian Epic Poem*. Leiden, Netherlands: Brill, 2003.

Ḥajjī Khalīfah, Kâtip Çelebī. *Kashf al-ẓunūn ʿan asāmī l-kutub wa-l-funūn*. Istanbul: Maarīf Matbası, 1941.

Al-Ḥamawī, Ibn Wāṣil. *Tajrīd al-Aghānī*. Edited by Ibrāhīm al-Abyārī and Ṭāhā Ḥusayn. 6 vols. Cairo: Maṭbaʿat Miṣr, 1955–63.

Al-Hamdānī, al-Ḥasan. *Al-Iklīl*. Vol. 1. Edited by Muḥammad ibn ʿAlī l-Akwaʿ. Sanaa: Wizārat al-Thaqāfah wa-l-Siyāḥah, 2004.

Ḥassān ibn Thābit. *Dīwān*. Edited by Walīd ʿArafāt. 2 vols. Beirut: Dār Ṣādir, 1974.

Ḥātim al-Ṭāʾī. *Dīwān*. Edited by ʿĀdil Sulaymān Jamāl. Cairo: al-Khanji, 1990.

Al-Ḥātimī, Abū ʿAlī Muḥammad ibn al-Ḥasan. *Al-Risālah al-Ḥātimiyyah*. Edited by Fuʾād Afrām al-Bustānī. Cairo: al-Mashriq, 1931.

Hirschler, Konrad. *Medieval Damascus: Plurality and Diversity in an Arabic Library; The Ashrafiya Library Catalogue*. Edinburgh: Edinburgh University Press, 2016.

Al-Ḥumaydī, Muḥammad ibn Futūḥ. *Jadhwat al-muqtabas fī tārīkh ʿulamāʾ al-andalus*. Edited by Bashshār ʿAwwād Maʿrūf and Muḥammad Bashshār ʿAwwād. Tunis: Dār al-Gharb al-Islāmī, 2008.

Ibn al-Abbār, Abū ʿAbd Allāh. *Al-Ḥullah al-sayrāʾ*. Edited by Ḥusayn Muʾnis. 2 vols. Cairo: Dār al-Maʿārif, 1985.

Ibn ʿAbd al-Barr, Yūsuf ibn ʿAbd Allāh. *Al-Istiʿāb fī maʿrifat al-Aṣḥāb*. Edited by ʿAlī Muḥammad al-Bajāwī. 4 vols. Beirut: Dār al-Jīl, 1992.

Ibn ʿAbd Rabbihi, Abū ʿUmar Aḥmad. *Al-Iqd al-farīd*. Edited by Ibrāhīm al-Abyārī. 7 vols. Beirut: Dār al-Kitāb al-ʿArabī, n.d.

Ibn Abī Dunyā. *Al-Manāmāt*. Edited by Majdī l-Sayyid Ibrāhīm. Cairo: Maktabat al-Qurʾan, n.d.

Ibn Ābī l-Ḥadīd. *Sharḥ Nahj al-balāgha*. Edited by Muḥammad Abū al-Faḍl Ibrāhīm. 11 vols. Cairo: al-Bābī al-Ḥalabī, 1959.

Ibn Abī ʿUṣaybiʿah, Aḥmad ibn al-Qāsim. *A Literary History of Medicine* (*ʿUyūn al-anbāʾ fī ṭabaqāt al-aṭibbāʾ*). Translated and edited by Emilie Savage-Smith, Simon Swain, and Geert Jan van Gelder. 5 vols. Leiden, Netherlands: Brill, 2020.

Ibn al-ʿAdīm, Kamāl al-Dīn. *Bughyat al-ṭalab fī tārīkh Ḥalab*. Edited by al-Mahdī ʿĪd al-Rawāḍiyyah. 12 vols. London: al-Furqān, 2016.

Ibn ʿArabī, Muḥyī l-Dīn Muḥammad ibn ʿAlī. *Muḥāḍarat al-abrār wa-musāmarat al-akhyār*. 2 vols. Beirut: Dār al-Yaqaẓah al-ʿArabiyyah, 1968.

Ibn ʿAsākir, ʿAlī ibn al-Ḥasan. *Tārīkh Madīnat Dimashq*. Edited by ʿUmar ibn Gharāmah al-ʿAmrawī. 79 vols. Beirut: Dār al-Fikr, 1997.

Ibn al-Athīr, ʿIzz al-Dīn ʿAlī. *Al-Kāmil fī l-Tārīkh*. Edited by C. J. Tornberg. 13 vols. Beirut: Dār Ṣādir, 1995.

Ibn Bashkuwāl, Abū l-Qāsim. *Al-Ṣilah fī tārīkh aʾimmat al-Andalus*. Edited by Bashshār ʿAwwād Maʿrūf. 2 vols. Tunis: Dār al-Gharb al-Islāmī, 2010.

Ibn Bassām, Abū l-Ḥasan al-Shantarīnī. *Al-Dhakhīrah fī maḥāsin ahl al-jazīrah*. Edited by Iḥsān ʿAbbās. 4 vols. Beirut: Dār al-Gharb al-Islāmī, 2000.

Ibn Diḥyah, ʿUmar ibn Ḥasan. *Al-Muṭrib min ashʿār ahl al-Maghrib*. Edited by Ibrāhīm al-Abyārī, Ḥāmid ʿAbd al-Majīd, and Aḥmad Aḥmad al-Badawī. Cairo: Dār al-Kutub, 1997.

Ibn Durayd, Abū Bakr Muḥammad. *Jamharat al-lughah*. Edited by Ramzī Baʿalbaki. 3 vols. Beirut: Dār al-ʿIlm li-l-Milāyīn, 1987.

———. *Al-Ishtiqāq*. Edited by ʿAbd al-Salām Muḥammad Hārūn. Cairo: al-Khanjī, n.d.

———. *Waṣf al-maṭar wa-l-saḥāb*. Edited by ʿIzz al-Dīn al-Tanūkhī. Damascus: al-Majmaʿ al-ʿArabī, 1963.

Ibn Ḥabīb, Muḥammad. *Prominent Murder Victims of the Pre- and Early Islamic Period Including the Names of Murdered Poets* (*Asmāʾ al-mughtālīn*). Translated and edited by Geert Jan van Gelder. Leiden, Netherlands: Brill, 2021.

Ibn Ḥabīb, Muḥammad. *Kitāb al-Naqāʾiḍ*. Edited by Anthony Bevan. 3 vols. Leiden, Netherlands: Brill, 1908–09.

———. *Al-Muḥabbar*. Edited by Ilse Lichtenstädter. Hyderabad, India: Dāʾirat al-Maʿārif al-ʿUthmāniyyah, 1942.

Ibn Ḥajar, Aḥmad ibn ʿAlī l-ʿAsqalānī. *Al-Durar al-kāminah fī aʿyān al-miʾah al-thāminah*. Edited by Muḥammad Sayyid Jād al-Ḥaqq. 5 vols. Cairo: Dār al-Ḥadīthah, 1966.

———. *Fatḥ al-Bārī bi-sharḥ Ṣaḥīḥ al-Bukhārī*. Edited by ʿAbd al-ʿAzīz ibn ʿAbd Allāh ibn Bāz and ʿAbd al-Raḥmān ibn Nāṣir al-Barrāk. 17 vols. Riyadh: Dār al-Ṭaybah, 2011.

———. *Al-Iṣābah fī tamyīz al-Ṣaḥabah*. Edited by ʿĀdil Aḥmad ʿAbd al-Mawjūd and ʿAlī Muḥammad Muʿawwaḍ. 8 vols. Beirut: Dār al-Kutub al-ʿIlmiyyah, 1995.

———. *Lisān al-mīzān*. Edited by ʿAbd al-Fattāḥ Abū Ghaddah. 10 vols. Beirut: Dār al-Bashāʾir al-Islāmiyyah, 2002.

Ibn Ḥamdūn, Muḥammad ibn al-Ḥasan. *Al-Tadhkirah al-Ḥamdūniyyah*. Edited by Iḥsān ʿAbbās and Bakr ʿAbbās. 10 vols. Beirut: Dār Ṣādir, 1996.

Ibn Ḥanbal, Aḥmad. *Musnad al-Imām Aḥmad ibn Ḥanbal*. Edited by Shuʿayb al-Arnāʾūṭ. 52 vols. Beirut: Muʾassasat al-Risālah, 2015.

Ibn Hārūn, Sahl. *Al-Namir wa-l-thaʿlab* (*La Panthère et le Renard*). Translated and edited by ʿAbd al-Qādir Mahīrī. Tunis: al-Jāmiʿah al-Tūnisiyya, 1973.

Ibn Ḥazm, Abū Muḥammad ʿAlī ibn Aḥmad. *Jamharat ansāb al-ʿArab*. Edited by ʿAbd al-Salām Muḥammad Hārūn. Cairo: al-Maʿārif, 1999.

Ibn Hishām, ʿAbd al-Malik. *Al-Sīrah al-nabawiyyah*. Edited by Muṣṭafā l-Saqqā, Ibrāhīm al-Abyrī, and ʿAbd al-Ḥafīẓ Shalabī. 2 vols. Beirut: Dār al-Maʿrifah, n.d.

Ibn Iyās, Muḥammad ibn Aḥmad. *Badāʾiʿ al-zuhūr fī waqāʾiʿ al-duhūr*. Edited by Muḥammad Muṣṭafā. 5 vols. Cairo: Dār al-Kutub wa-l-Wathāʾiq al-Qawmiyyah, 2008.

Ibn al-Jawzī, Abū l-Faraj ʿAbd al-Raḥmān. *Akhbār al-ḥumqā wa-l-mughaffilīn*. Edited by ʿAbd al-Amīr Muhannā. Beirut: Dār al-Fikr al-Lubnānī, 1990.

———. *Al-Muntaẓam*. Edited by Suhayl Zakkār. 13 vols. Beirut: Dār al-Fikr, 1995.

———. *Al-Wafāʾ bi-akhbār al-Muṣṭafā*. Edited by Muṣṭafā ʿAbd al-Qādir ʿAṭā. Beirut: Dār al-Kutub al-ʿIlmiyyah, 1988.

———. *ʿArf al-taʿrīf bi-l-mawlid al-sharīf*. Edited by Muḥammad Abū l-Khayr al-Mulqī. Tangiers: Dār al-Ḥadīth al-Kitāniyyah, 2011.

Ibn Jinnī, Abū l-Fatḥ ʿUthmān. *Al-Tanbīh ʿalā sharḥ mushkilāt al-Ḥamāsah*. Edited by Ḥasan al-Hindāwī. Kuwait, Wizārat al-Awqāf wa-l-Shuʾūn al-Islāmiyyah, 2009.

Ibn al-Kalbī. *Jamharat al-nasab*. Edited by Nājī Ḥusayn. Beirut: ʿĀlam al-Kutub, 2004.

Ibn Kathīr, Abū l-Fidāʾ. *Al-Bidāyah wa-l-nihāyah*. Edited by Aḥmad Abū Mulḥim, ʿAlī Mujīb al-ʿAṭwī, Fuʾād al-Sayyid, Mahdī Naṣr al-Dīn, and ʿAlī ʿAbd al-Sātir. 15 vols. Beirut: Dār al-Kutub al-ʿIlmiyyah, n.d.

Ibn Khaldūn, ʿAbd al-Raḥmān. *Al-ʿIbar wa-dīwān al-mubtadaʾ wa-l-khabar fī ayyām al-ʿArab wa-l-ʿAjam wa-l-Barbar*. 14 vols. Cairo and Beirut: Dār al-Kitāb al-Miṣrī and Dār al-Kitāb al-Lubnānī, 1998–99.

Ibn Khallikān, Aḥmad ibn Muḥammad. *Wafayāt al-aʿyān*. Edited by Iḥsān ʿAbbās. 8 vols. Beirut: Dār Ṣādir, 1969.

Ibn Khāqān, al-Fatḥ. *Qalāʾid al-ʿUqyān*. Cairo: Būlāq, 1867–68.

Ibn Manẓūr, Muḥammad ibn Mukarram. *Lisān al-ʿArab*. 15 vols. Beirut: Dār Ṣādir, 1997.

———. *Mukhtār al-Aghānī*. Edited by Ibrāhīm al-Abyārī et al. 7 vols. Cairo: al-Dār al-Miṣriyyah li-l-Taʾlīf wal-Tarjamah wa-l-Nashr, 1965–66.

Ibn Munqidh, Usāmah. *Lubāb al-ādāb*. Edited by Aḥmad Muḥammad Shākir. Cairo: Maktabat al-Sunnah, 1987.

Ibn al-Muʿtazz. *Ṭabaqāt al-shuʿarāʾ*. Edited by ʿAbd al-Sattār Aḥmad Farrāj. Cairo: al-Maʿārif, 1976.

Ibn al-Nadīm, Muḥammad ibn Isḥāq. *Al-Fihrist.* Edited by Ayman Fu'ād Sayyid. 4 vols. London: al-Furqān, 2014.

Ibn Nubātah, Jamāl al-Dīn Muḥammad. *Sarḥ al-ʿuyūn fī sharḥ Risālat Ibn Zaydūn.* Cairo: al-Maṭbaʿah al-Mīriyyah al-Miṣriyyah, 1862.

———. *Sarḥ al-ʿuyūn fī sharḥ Risālat Ibn Zaydūn.* Edited by Muḥammad Abū al-Faḍl Ibrāhīm. Cairo: Dar al-Fikr al-ʿArabī, 1964.

———. *Kitāb al-Zahr al-manthūr and Min tarassul Ibn Nubātah.* Edited by Andreas Herdt. Baden-Baden, Germany: Ergon, 2019.

Ibn Qutaybah, ʿAbd Allāh ibn Muslim. *The Excellence of the Arabs.* Edited by James Montgomery and Peter Webb. Translated by Sarah Bowen Savant and Peter Webb. New York: New York University Press, 2017.

———. *Al-Maʿārif.* Edited by Tharwat ʿUkāshah. Cairo: Dār al-Maʿārif, 1969.

———. *Al-Shiʿr wa-l-shuʿarā'.* Edited by Aḥmad Muḥammad Shākir. 2 vols. Cairo: Dār al-Ḥadīth, 2006.

———. *ʿUyūn al-akhbār.* 4 vols. Cairo: Dār al-Kutub, 1926.

Ibn Saʿd, Muḥammad. *Al-Ṭabaqāt al-kubrā.* Edited by Muḥammad ʿAbd al-Qādir ʿAṭā. 9 vols. Beirut: Dār al-Kutub al-ʿIlmiyyah, 1997.

Ibn Sallām al-Jumaḥī. *Ṭabaqāt fuḥūl al-shuʿarā'.* Edited by Maḥmūd Muḥammad Shākir. 2 vols. Cairo: al-Khanji, n.d.

Ibn al-Shajarī, Hibat Allāh ibn ʿAlī. *Al-Ḥamāsah al-Shajariyyah.* Edited by ʿAbd al-Muʿīn al-Malūḥī and Asmā' al-Ḥimṣī. 3 vols. Damascus: Wizārat al-Thaqāfah, 1980.

———. *Al-Amālī.* Edited by Maḥmūd Muḥammad al-Ṭanāḥī. 3 vols. Cairo: al-Khānjī, 1992.

Ibn Sīdah, Abū l-Ḥasan ʿAlī. *Al-Muḥkam wa-l-muḥīṭ al-aʿẓam.* Edited by ʿAbd al-Ḥamīd al-Hindāwī. 11 vols. Beirut: Dār al-Kutub al-ʿIlmiyyah, 2000.

Ibn Sīnā, Abū ʿAlī. *Al-Qānūn fī l-ṭibb.* 3 vols. Beirut: Dār Ṣādir, n.d. Reprint of 1877 edition.

Ibn Zaydūn, Aḥmad ibn ʿAbd Allāh. *Dīwān Ibn Zaydūn wa-rasā'iluh.* Edited by ʿAlī ʿAbd al-ʿAẓīm. Cairo: Nahḍat Miṣr, 1957.

Al-ʿImād al-Iṣbahānī. *Kharīdat al-Qasr wa-jarīdat al-ʿaṣr: Qism shuʿarā' al-Maghrib wa-l-Andalus.* Edited by Muḥammad Marzūqī, Muḥammad al-ʿArūsī al- Maṭwī, and Ibn al-Ḥājj al-Jīlānī. 4 vols. Tunis: Dār al-Tunisiyyah, 1966–72.

Al-Iṣbahānī, Abū l-Faraj. *Kitāb al-Aghānī.* Edited by ʿAbd Allāh ʿAlī Muhanna and Samīr Jābir. 27 vols. Beirut: Dār al-Kutub al-ʿIlmiyyah, 1992.

Isidore. *Etymologies.* Edited and translated by Stephan A. Barney, W. J. Lewis, J. A. Beach, and Oliver Berghof. Cambridge: Cambridge University Press, 2010.

Al-Jāḥiẓ, ʿAmr ibn Baḥr. *Kitāb al-Bayān wa-l-tabyīn.* Edited by ʿAbd al-Salām Muḥammad Hārūn. 4 vols. Cairo: al-Khanjī, 2003.

———. *Kitāb al-Bukhalā'.* Edited by Ṭāhā l-Ḥājirī. Cairo: al-Maʿārif, 1990.

———. *Kitāb al-Ḥayawān*. Edited by Muḥammad Bāsil ʿUyūn al-Sūd. 4 vols. Beirut: Dār al-Kutub al-ʿIlmiyyah, 1998.

———. *Kitāb al-Burṣān wa-l-ʿurjān wa-l-ʿumyān wa-l-ḥūlān*. Edited by ʿAbd al-Sallām Muḥammad Hārūn. Beirut: Dār al-Jīl, 1990.

Al-Jahshiyārī, Abū ʿAbd Allāh Muḥammad ibn ʿAbdūs. *Kitāb al-Wuzarāʾ wa-l-kuttāb*. Edited by Muṣṭafā l-Saqqā, Ibrāhīm al-Abyārī, and ʿAbd al-Ḥāfīẓ al-Shalabī. Cairo: al-Bābī l-Ḥalabī, 1938.

Jamil, Nadia. "Playing for Time: *Maysir*-Gambling in Early Arabic Poetry." In *Islamic Reflections, Arabic Musings: Studies in Honour of Professor Alan Jones*, edited by Robert Hoyland and Philip Kennedy, 48–90. Cambridge: Gibb Memorial Trust, 2004.

Al-Jawālīqī, Abū Manṣūr. *Sharḥ Adab al-Kātib*. Edited by Muṣṭafā Ṣādiq al-Rāfiʿī. Cairo: Maktabat al-Quds, 1931–32.

Al-Jawharī, Ismāʿīl ibn Ḥammad. *Al-Ṣiḥāḥ*. Edited by Aḥmad ʿAbd al-Ghafūr ʿAṭṭār. 6 vols. Cairo: Dār al-Kitāb al-ʿArabī, 1956.

Johns, Anthony Hearle. "Hāmān." In *Encyclopedia of the Qurʾān* 2:399–400.

Johnston, Ian. *Galen: On Diseases and Symptoms*. Cambridge: Cambridge University Press, 2009.

Kaḥḥālah, ʿUmar Riḍā. *Muʿjam qabāʾil al-ʿarab*. 5 vols. Beirut: Muʾassasat al-Risālah, 1997.

Kellens, Jean. "Langues et religions indo-iraniennes: Promenade dans les Yašts à la lumière de travaux nouveaux (suite)." *Annuaire du Collège de France: Résumé des cours et travaux* (1999–2000): 721–51.

Al-Khālidiyyān, Abū Bakr Muḥammad, and Abū ʿUthmān Saʿīd. *Al-Ashbāh wa-l-naẓāʾir min ashʿār al-mutaqaddimīn wa-l-jāhiliyyah wa-l-mukhaḍramīn*. Edited by al-Sayyid Muḥammad Yūsuf. 2 vols. Cairo: Lajnat al-Taʾlīf wa-l-Tarjamah wa-l-Nashr, 1965.

Khalīl ibn Aḥmad. *al-ʿAyn*.

Al-Khaṭīb, ʿAbd al-Laṭīf. *Muʿjam al-Qirāʾāt*. 11 vols. Damascus: Dār Saʿd al-Dīn, 2000.

Al-Kindī, Muḥammad ibn Yūsuf. *Wulāt Miṣr*. Edited by Rhuvon Guest. London: Luzac, 1912.

Kraemer, Joel L. *Philosophy in the Renaissance of Islam: Abū Sulaymān al-Sijistānī and His Circle*. Leiden, Netherlands: Brill, 1996.

Kurd ʿAlī, Muḥammad. *Umarāʾ al-bayān*. Cairo: Maktabat al-Thaqāfah al-Dīniyyah, 2011.

Al-Kutubī, Muḥammad ibn Shākir. *Fawāt al-wafayāt*. Edited by Iḥsān ʿAbbās. 5 vols. Beirut: Dār Ṣādir, 1973.

Labīd. *Sharḥ Dīwān Labīd ibn Rabīʿah al-ʿĀmirī*. Edited by Iḥsān ʿAbbās. Kuwait: Wizārat al-Irshād wa-l-Anbāʾ, 1962.

Lassner, J. *Demonizing the Queen of Sheba: Boundaries of Gender and Culture in Postbiblical Judaism and Medieval Islam*. Chicago: Chicago University Press, 1993.

Al-Maʿarrī, Abū al-ʿAlāʾ. *Risālat al-ghufrān*. Edited by ʿĀʾishah ʿAbd al-Raḥmān. Cairo: al-Maʿārif, 1993.

Maktabat al-Azhar. *Fahris al-kutub al-mawjūdah bi-l-maktabat al-azhariyyah 1368/1949*. Cairo: al-Azhar, 1949.

Malalas, John. *The Chronicle*. Translated by Elizabeth Jeffreys, Michael Jeffreys, and Roger Scott. Melbourne: Australian Association for Byzantine Studies, 1986.

Al-Maqqarī, Aḥmad. *Nafḥ al-ṭīb min ghuṣn al-Andalus al-raṭīb*. Edited by Iḥsān ʿAbbās. 8 vols. Beirut: Dār Ṣādir, 2015.

Al-Maqrīzī, Taqī l-Dīn Aḥmad. *Al-Khabar ʿan al-bashar*. MS Istanbul Süleymaniye Fatih 4340.

———. *Al-Mawāʿiẓ wa-l-iʿtibār fī dhikr al-khiṭat wa-l-āthār*. Edited by Ayman Fuʾād Sayyid. 4 vols. London: al-Furqān, 2013.

———. *Al-Muqaffā l-kabīr*. Edited by Muḥammad al-Yaʿlāwī. Beirut: Dār al-Gharb al-Islāmī, 2006.

———. *The Arab Thieves: Al-Ḫabar ʿan al-bašar*. Vol. 5, sections 1–2. Edited and translated by Peter Webb. Leiden, Netherlands: Brill, 2019.

Maroth, Miklos. *The Correspondence between Aristotle and Alexander the Great: An Anonymous Greek Novel in Letters in Arabic Translation*. Piliscsaba, Hungary: Avicenna Institute of Middle Eastern Studies, 2006.

Al-Marrākushī, ʿAbd al-Wāḥib ibn ʿAlī. *Al-Muʿjib fī talkhīṣ akhbār al-Maghrib*. Edited by Khalīl ʿImrān Manṣūr. Beirut: Dār al-Kutub al-ʿIlmiyyah, 1999.

Al-Marzubānī, Abū ʿUbayd Allāh Muḥammad. *Muʿjam al-shuʿarāʾ*. Edited by ʿAbbās Hāniʾ al-Charrakh. 2 vols. Beirut: Dār al-Kutub al-ʿIlmiyyah, 2010.

Al-Marzūqī, Aḥmad ibn Muḥammad. *Sharḥ Dīwān al-Ḥamāsah*. Edited by Aḥma Amīn and ʿAbd al-Salām Hārūn. 4 vols. Cairo: Lajnat al-Taʾlīf wa-l-Tarjamah wa-l-Nashr, 1968.

Al-Masʿūdī, ʿAlī ibn al-Ḥusayn. *Al-Tanbīh wa-l-ishrāf*. Edited by M. J. de Goeje. Leiden, Netherlands: Brill, 1894.

———. *Murūj al-dhahab wa-maʿādin al-jawhar*. Edited by Charles Pellat. 7 vols. Beirut: al-Jāmiʿah al-Lubnāniyyah, 1966–79.

Al-Maydānī, Abū l-Faḍl. *Majmaʿ al-amthāl*. Edited by Muḥammad Abū l-Faḍl Ibrāhīm. 4 vols. Beirut: al-Maktabah al-ʿAṣriyyah, 2011.

Mélikian-Chirvani, Assadullah Souren. "L'évocation littéraire du bouddhisme dans l'Iran musulman." *Le monde iranien et l'Islam* 2 (1974): 1–72.

Al-Mubarrad, Muḥammad ibn Yazīd. *Al-Kāmil*. Edited by Muḥammad Aḥmad al-Dālī. 4 vols. Beirut: Muʾassasat al-Risālah, 2008.

Al-Mubashshir ibn Fātik. *Mukhtār al-ḥikam wa-maḥāsin al-kalim*. Edited by ʿAbd al-Raḥman Badawī. Beirut: al-Muʾassasah al-ʿArabiyyah, 1980.

Muhalhil ibn Rabīʿah. *Dīwān Muhalhil ibn Rab īʿah*. Edited by Ṭalāl Ḥarb. Beirut: Dār al-ʿAlamiyyah, 2009.

Al-Murtaḍā, al-Sharīf ʿAlī ibn al-Ḥusayn. *Amālī l-Murtaḍā*. Edited by Muḥammad Abū l-Faḍl Ibrāhīm. 2 vols. Beirut: Maktabat al-ʿAṣriyyah, 2005.

Al-Mūsawī, Ḥusayn Yūsuf, and ʿAbd al-Faṭṭāḥ al-Ṣaʿīdī. *Al-Ifṣāḥ fī fiqh al-lughah*. Tehran: Maktabat al-Iʿlām al-Islāmī, 1983.

Al-Mutalammis al-Ḍubaʿī. *Dīwān*. Edited by Ḥasan Kāmil al-Ṣayrafī. Cairo: Maʿhad al-Makhṭūṭāt al-ʿArabiyyah, 1970.

Neugebauer, Otto. "The Early History of the Astrolabe: Studies in Ancient Astronomy IX." *Isis* 40 (1949): 240–56.

Al-Nuwayrī, Ṣalāḥ al-Dīn. *Nihāyat al-arab fī funūn al-adab*. Edited by Ḥasan Nūr al-Dīn. 33 vols. Beirut: Dār al-Kutub al-ʿIlmiyyah, 2004.

Pennacchietti, Fabrizio A. *Three Mirrors for Two Biblical Ladies: Susanna and the Queen of Sheba in the Eyes of Jews, Christians, and Muslims*. Piscataway, NJ: Gorgias, 2006.

Pfeifer, Helen. "Encounter after the Conquest: Scholarly Gatherings in 16th-Century Ottoman Damascus." *International Journal of Middle East Studies* 47 (2015): 219–39.

Pseudo-Thaʿālibī. *Al-Muʾnis al-waḥīd fī al-muḥādarāt*. Edited by Gustav Flugel. Vienna: Anton Schmidt, 1829.

Al-Qālī, Abū ʿAlī Ismāʿīl ibn al-Qāsim. *Al-Amālī wa-dhayl al-amālī*. 3 vols. Cairo: Dār al-Kutub al-Miṣriyyah, 1926.

Al-Qalqashandī, Abū l-ʿAbbās Aḥmad. *Ṣubḥ al-aʿshā*. 14 vols. Cairo: Dār al-Kutub al-Miṣriyyah, 1922.

Al-Qazwīnī, Zakariyya ibn Muḥammad. *Āthār al-bilād wa-l-akhbār*. Beirut: Dār Ṣādir, n.d.

Al-Qurṭubī, Muḥammad ibn Aḥmad. *Jāmiʿ aḥkām al-Qurʾān*. Edited by Sālim Muṣṭafā al-Badawī. 21 vols. Beirut: Dār al-Kutub al-ʿIlmiyyah, 2000.

Al-Rāghib al-Iṣbahānī. *Muḥāḍarāt al-udabāʾ wa-muḥāwarāt al-shuʿarāʾ wa-l-bulaghāʾ*. 4 vols. Beirut: Maktabat al-Ḥayāt, 1961.

Rowson, Everett. "The Effeminates of Early Medina." *Journal of the American Oriental Society* 111 (1991): 671–93.

Rubin, Uri. "'Become You Apes, Repelled!' (Quran 7:166): The Transformation of the Israelites into Apes and Its Biblical and Midrashic Background." *Bulletin of the School of Oriental and African Studies* 78 (2015): 125–40.

Saʿdī, Shīrāzī. "Gulistān." Edited by Ghulāmḥusayn Yūsufī. Tehran: Khwārazmī, 1368 (1990).

Al-Ṣafadī, Khalīl ibn Aybak. *Tamām al-mutūn fī sharḥ Risālat Ibn Zaydūn*. Edited by Muḥammad Abū l-Faḍl Ibrāhīm. Cairo: Dar al-Fikr al-ʿArabī, 1969.

———. *Al-Wāfī bi-l-wafayāt*. Edited by Helmut Ritter et al. 32 vols. Beirut: Orient Institut, 1962–2008.

Al-Ṣaghānī, al-Ḥasan ibn Muḥammad. *Al-ʿUbāb al-zākhir wa-l-lubāb al-fākhir*. Edited by Muḥammad Ḥasan Āl Yāsīn. 5 vols. Baghdad: al-Majmaʿ al-ʿIlmī al-ʿIrāqī, 1978–87.

Al-Samawʾal ibn ʿĀdiyāʾ. *Dīwān al-Samawʾal*. Edited by Wāḍiḥ al-Ṣamad. Beirut: Dār al-Jīl, 1996.

Sela, Shulamit. "The Genealogy of Ṣefo ben Elifaz: The Importance of a Genizah Fragment for Josippon's History." In *Genizah Research after Ninety Years*, edited by Joshua Blau and Stefan C. Reich, 138–43. Cambridge: Cambridge University Press, 1992.

Al-Shahristānī, Muḥammad ibn ʿAbd al-Karīm. *Livre des religions et des sectes*. Translated by Jean Jolivet and Guy Monnot. Leuven, Belgium: Peeters, 1986–93.

Al-Shantamarī, Yūsuf ibn Sulaymān. *Sharḥ Ḥamāsat Abī Tammām*. Edited by ʿAlī l-Mufaḍḍal Ḥammūdān. 2 vols. Dubai: Jumʿat al-Mājid li-l-Thaqāfah wa-l-Turāth, 1992.

Al-Shawkānī, Muḥammad ibn ʿAlī. *Al-Badr al-ṭāliʿ bi-maḥāsin man baʿd al-qarn al-sābiʿ*. 2 vols. Cairo: Dār al-Kitāb al-Islāmī, n.d.

Shaykh Zadah, Muḥyī l-Dīn. *Ḥāshiyah ʿala Tafsīr al-Bayḍāwī*. Edited by Muḥammad ʿAbd al-Qādir Shāhīn. Beirut: Dār al-Kutub al-ʿIlmiyyah, 1999.

Sibṭ ibn al-Jawzī. *Mirʾāt al-zamān fī tawārīkh al-aʿyān*. Edited by Muḥammad Barakāt, Kāmil al-Haffūẓ, and ʿAmmār Rayḥāwī. 23 vols. Beirut: Dār al-Risālah al-ʿAlamiyyah, 2013.

Al-Suhaylī, Abū al-Qāsim ʿAbd al-Raḥmān. *Al-Rawḍ al-unuf*. Edited by ʿAbd al-Raḥmān al-Wakīl. 4 vols. Cairo: Maktabat Ibn Taymiyyah, 1990.

Swain, Simon. "The Greek Chapters and Galen." In *A Literary History of Medicine*, edited by E. Savage-Smith, S. Swain, and G. J. van Gelder, 1:142–77. Leiden, Netherlands: Brill, 2020.

Al-Ṭabarī, Muḥammad ibn Jarīr. *Jāmiʿ al-bayān fī taʾwīl āy al-Qurʾān*. Edited by Sidqī Jamīl al-ʿAṭṭār. 30 vols. Beirut: Dār al-Fikr, 1999.

———. *Tārīkh al-rusul wa-l-mulūk*. Edited by Muḥammad Abū l-Faḍl Ibrāhīm. 11 vols. Cairo: al-Maʿārif, 1960–69.

Al-Tamīmī, Muḥammad ibn Aḥmad. *Kitāb al-Miḥan*. Edited by Yaḥyā Wahīb al-Jabbūrī. Beirut: Dār al-Gharb al-Islāmī, 1983.

Al-Tanūkhī, al-Muḥassin ibn ʿAlī. *Stories of Piety and Prayer: Deliverance Follows Adversity*. Edited and translated by Julia Bray. New York: New York University Press, 2019.

———. *Al-Mustajād min faʿlāt al-ajwād*. Edited by Aḥmad Farīd al-Mazīdī. Beirut: Dār al-Kutub al-ʿIlmiyyah, 2005.

Ṭarafah ibn al-ʿAbd. *Dīwān Ṭarafah ibn al-ʿAbd: Riwāyat al-Shantamarī*. Edited by Durriyyah al-Khaṭīb and Luṭfī al-Ṣaqqāl. Beirut: al-Muʾassasah al-ʿArabiyyah li-l-dirāsah wa-l-nashr, 2000.

Al-Tawḥīdī, Abū Ḥayyān. *Al-Baṣā'ir wa-l-dhakhā'ir*. Edited by Muḥammad Sayyid 'Uthmān. 10 vols. Beirut: Dār al-Kutub al-'Ilmiyyah, 2014.

Al-Tibrīzī, al-Khaṭīb. *Sharḥ al-Qaṣā'id al-'Ashr*. Damascus: al-Munīriyyah, 1934–35.

Al-Tuwayjirī, Ḥamdūn ibn 'Abd Allāh. *Tabri'at al-khalīfah al-'ādil wa-l-radd 'alā al-mujādil bi-l-bāṭil*. Medina: Dār al-Iftā', 1968–69.

Al-'Ukbarī, Abū al-Baqā'. *Al-Bayān fī Sharḥ al-Dīwān/Dīwān al-Mutanabbī*. Edited by Muṣṭafā l-Saqqā, Ibrāhīm al-Abyārī, and 'Abd al-Ḥafīẓ Shalabī. 4 vols. Cairo: al-Bābī al-Ḥalabī, 1956.

Van Bladel, Kevin. *The Arabic Hermes*. Oxford: Oxford University Press, 2009.

Van Ess, Josef. *Theology and Society in the Second and Third Centuries of the Hijra*. Translated by Gwendolin Goldbloom. Vols. 2 and 3. Leiden, Netherland: Brill, 2017.

Al-Wāqidī, Muḥammad ibn 'Umar. *Al-Maghāzī*. Edited by Marsden Jones. 3 vols. Oxford: Oxford University Press, 1966.

Webb, Peter. "Pre-Islamic al-Shām in Classical Arabic Literature: Spatial Narratives and History-Telling." *Studia Islamica* 110 (2015): 1–30.

———. *Imagining the Arabs: Arab Identity and the Rise of Islam*. Edinburgh: Edinburgh University Press, 2016.

———. (2020) "Ethnicity, Power and Umayyad Society: The Rise and Fall of the People of Ma'add." In *The Umayyad World*, edited by Andrew Marsham, 65–102. Abingdon, VA: Routledge, 2021.

———. (2021) "From the Sublime to the Ridiculous: Yemeni Arab Identity in Abbasid Iraq." In *Empires and Communities in the Post-Roman and Islamic World c.400–1000 CE*, edited by Walter Pohl and Rutger Kramer, 283–328. New York: Oxford University Press, 2021.

———. "Multilingualism in the Transregional Journeys of an Arabic Book: Persian/Arabic Encounters in the Manuscripts of Ibn Nubātah's *Sarḥ al-'Uyūn*." In *Pre-modern Comparative Literary Practice in the Multilingual Islamic World(s)*, edited by Huda Fakhreddine, David Larsen, and Hany Rashwan. Oxford: British Academy and Oxford University Press. Forthcoming.

———. "Andalusian Literature on a Global Stage." *Al-'Uṣūr al-Wuṣṭā*. Forthcoming.

Al-Ya'qūbī, Aḥmad ibn Abī Ya'qūb. *Tārīkh al-Ya'qūbī*. 2 vols. Beirut: Dār Ṣādir, n.d.

Yāqūt al-Ḥamawī. *Irshād al-arīb bi-ma'rifat al-adīb*. Edited by Iḥsān 'Abbās. 7 vols. Beirut: Dār al-Gharb al-Islāmī, 1993.

Yāqūt al-Ḥamawī. *Mu'jam al-buldān*. 7 vols. Beirut: Dār Ṣādir, 1993.

Al-Zabīdī, Murtaḍā. *Tāj al-'arūs*. Edited by 'Alī Shīrī. 20 vols. Beirut: Dar al-Fikr, 1994.

Al-Zajjājī, Abū al-Qāsim 'Abd al-Raḥmān. *Majālis al-'ulamā'*. Edited by 'Abd al-Salām Muḥammad Hārūn. Cairo: al-Khānjī, 1999.

Al-Zamakhsharī, Abū l-Qāsim Maḥmūd ibn ʿUmar. *Asās al-balāghah*. Beirut: Dār Ṣādir, 1992.

———. *Rabīʿ al-abrār wa-nuṣūṣ al-akhbār*. Edited by ʿAbd al-Amīr Muhannā. 5 vols. Beirut: Muʾassasat al-Aʿlamī, 1992.

Al-Zawzanī. *Sharḥ al-Muʿallaqāt al-sabʿ*. Beirut: Maktabat al-Maʿārif, 1980.

Zuhayr ibn Abī Sulmā. *Dīwān*. Edited by Fakhr al-Dīn Qabāwah. Beirut: Dār al-Āfāq al-Jadīdah, 1982.

# Further Reading

## Ibn Zaydūn, Wallādah, and Ibn Nubātah


ʿAbd al-ʿAẓīm, ʿAlī. *Ibn Zaydūn: ʿAṣruh wa-ḥayātuh wa-adabuh*. Cairo: Dār al-Maʿārif, 1955.

Bauer, Thomas. "Ibn Nubātah al-Miṣrī (686–768/1287–1366): Life and Works, Part I; The Life of Ibn Nubātah." *Mamluk Studies Review* 12 (2008): 1–35.

Garulo, Teresa. "La biografía de Wallada, todo problemas." *Anaquel de Estudios Arabes* 20 (2009): 97–116.

Omran, Doaa. "Wallāda Bint al-Mustakfi: A Muslim Princess Speaking Passionately and Persistently in the 'Palimpsest' of al-Andalus." *Women's Studies* 51 (2022): 120–36.

Stewart, Devin. "Ibn Zaydūn." In *The Literature of Al-Andalus*, edited by Maria Rosa Menocal, Raymond P. Scheindlin, and Michael Sells, 306–17. Cambridge: Cambridge University Press, 2000.


## The Classical Arabic Repertoire and Sarḥ al-ʿuyūn


Makdisi, George. *The Rise of Humanism in Classical Islam and the Christian West*. Edinburgh: Edinburgh University Press, 1990.

Rowson, Everett. "An Alexandrian Age in Fourteenth-Century Damascus: Twin Commentaries on Two Celebrated Arabic Epistles." *Journal of Mamluk Studies* 7 (2003): 97–110.


## Pre-Islamic Arabia and Arab Identity


Fierro, Maribel. "Genealogies of Power in al-Andalus: Politics, Religion and Ethnicity during the Second/Eighth-Fifth/Eleventh Centuries." *Annales Islamologiques* 42 (2008): 29–55.

Ibn Qutaybah, ʿAbd Allāh ibn Muslim. *The Excellence of the Arabs*. Edited by James Montgomery and Peter Webb. Translated by Sarah Bowen Savant and Peter Webb. New York: New York University Press, 2017.

Webb, Peter. *Imagining the Arabs: Arab Identity and the Rise of Islam*. Edinburgh: Edinburgh University Press, 2016.

## Arabic Interpretations of the Ancient World

Gutas, Dimitri. *Greek Thought, Arabic Culture: The Graeco-Arabic Translation Movement in Baghdad and Early ʿAbbasid Society (2nd–4th/5th–10th c.)*. London: Routledge, 1998.

Maroth, Miklos. *The Correspondence between Aristotle and Alexander the Great: An Anonymous Greek Novel in Letters in Arabic Translation*. Piliscsaba, Hungary: Avicenna Institute of Middle Eastern Studies, 2006.

Stock, Markus. *Alexander the Great in the Middle Ages: Transcultural Perspectives*. Toronto: University of Toronto Press, 2016.

Van Bladel, Kevin. *The Arabic Hermes*. Oxford: Oxford University Press, 2009.

Zuwiyya, Zachary David, ed. *A Companion to Alexander Literature in the Middle Ages*. Leiden, Netherlands: Brill, 2011.

# Index of Arabic Poetry

| Section | Poet | Lines | Meter | Rhyme |
|---|---|---|---|---|
| | | ء | | |
| §46.19 | Sahl ibn Hārūn ibn Rāhyūn | 2 | *basīṭ* | دَائِي |
| §51.27 | Bashshār ibn Burd | 4 | *khafīf* | ٱلْفُقَرَاءِ |
| §51.4 | Bashshār ibn Burd | 1 | *ṭawīl* | فَاقِيَا |
| | | ب | | |
| §0.6 | Ghāwī ibn Ẓālim al-Sulamī | 1 | *ṭawīl* | ٱلثَّعَالِبُ |
| §0.6 | Abū Tammām | 1 | *ṭawīl* | عَجَائِبُ |
| §3.3 | Ibn Zaydūn | 4 | *kāmil* | جَنِيبَا |
| §10.1 | Abū Nuwās | 1 | *munsariḥ* | مَسَارِبِهَا |
| §14.2 | unidentified | 1 | *rajaz* | ٱلنُّجُبُ |
| §21.15 | Zayd ibn Muhalhil | 3 | *wāfir* | ٱلذِّئَابِ |
| §22.5 | Sulayk ibn al-Sulakah | 2 | *ṭawīl* | أَكْذَبُ |
| §22.7 | Sulayk ibn al-Sulakah | 3 | *ṭawīl* | وَسُهُوبُ |
| §23.12 | ʿĀmir ibn Mālik ibn Jaʿfar | 2 | *ṭawīl* | ذَنَّبَا |
| §30.9 | Labīd | 2 | *rajaz* | مُعْجِبَا |
| §43.4 | al-Kindī | 2 | *ṭawīl* | كَرْبِي |
| §45.5 | Abū Muslim | 1 | *ṭawīl* | جَانِبِ |
| §47.29 | al-Jāḥiẓ | 3 | *wāfir* | ٱلْمُصِيبُ |
| §48.11 | Dhū Yazan | 1 | *basīṭ* | غِضَابُ |
| §49.4 | al-Mutanabbī | 1 | *ṭawīl* | تَكْذِبُ |
| §51.9 | Bashshār ibn Burd | 3 | *ṭawīl* | ٱلْمُهَذَّبَا |
| §51.29 | Bashshār ibn Burd | 7 | *ṭawīl* | تُعَاتِبُهْ |
| §53.0 | Ghāwī ibn Ẓālim al-Sulamī | 1 | *ṭawīl* | ٱلثَّعَالِبُ |
| §53.0 | Abū Tammām | 1 | *ṭawīl* | عَجَائِبُ |
| §62.6 | al-Mutalammis | 3 | *ṭawīl* | عَوَاقِبُهْ |
| §74.2 | al-Farazdaq | 3 | *ṭawīl* | أَقَارِبُهْ |
| §86.1 | unidentified | 2 | *mutadārik* | لِصَاحِبِهِ |

| Section | Poet | Lines | Meter | Rhyme |
|---|---|---|---|---|
| | | ت | | |
| §0.5 | al-Mutanabbī | 1 | *kāmil* | أَبْيَاتِهَا |
| §0.10 | al-Farazdaq | 1 | *ṭawīl* | الْحَبِطَاتُ |
| §18.1 | al-Samawʾal ibn ʿĀdiyāʾ | 4 | *wāfir* | عَصَيْتُ |
| §23.11 | ʿĀmir ibn Mālik ibn Jaʿfar | 1 | *wāfir* | حَيِيتُ |
| §24.15 | Qays ibn Zuhayr | 2 | *ṭawīl* | ٱللَّهَوَاتِ |
| §42.19 | al-Naẓẓām | 1 | *sarīʿ* | بِآفَاتِ |
| §52.0 | al-Mutanabbī | 1 | *kāmil* | أَبْيَاتِهَا |
| §60.0 | al-Farazdaq | 1 | *ṭawīl* | ٱلْحَبِطَاتُ |
| §70.12 | ʿAmr ibn Maʿdī Karib | 4 | *ṭawīl* | فَٱسْبَطَرَّتِ |
| | | ح | | |
| §0.14 | Bashshār ibn Burd | 1 | *kāmil* | جَرَحَا |
| §16.7 | Jassās | 2 | *wāfir* | لُقَرَاحِ |
| §16.7 | Naḍlah | 1 | *wāfir* | ٱلسِّلَاحِ |
| §18.5 | al-Samawʾal ibn ʿĀdiyāʾ ibn Ḥabāʾ | 3 | *kāmil* | أَنْوَاحِي |
| §23.10 | Labīd | 2 | *rajaz* | ٱلرِّمَاحِ |
| §33.16 | Ibn Muqbil | 2 | *ṭawīl* | أَفْطَحُ |
| §46.21 | Sahl ibn Hārūn ibn Rāhyūn | 4 | *wāfir* | جَرِيحُ |
| §79.0 | Bashshār ibn Burd | 1 | *kāmil* | جَرَحَا |
| §79.1 | Bashshār ibn Burd | 2 | *kāmil* | جَرَحَا |
| | | د | | |
| §0.5 | Abū Nuwās | 1 | *sarīʿ* | وَاحِدِ |
| §4.4 | Wallādah | 2 | *sarīʿ* | ٱلْخُدُودْ |
| §11.10 | Jadhīmah | 2 | *basīṭ* | عَادُ |
| §20.9 | Ḥātim | 3 | *ṭawīl* | فَتَزَوَّدِي |
| §21.4 | Zayd ibn Muhalhil | 2 | *ṭawīl* | مُنْجِدِ |
| §22.3 | Sulayk ibn al-Sulakah | 2 | *basīṭ* | أَذْوَادِ |
| §26.5 | Saḥbān ibn Zufar ibn Iyās | 2 | *kāmil* | لِتَالِدْ |
| §30.16 | Arbad's brother | 1 | *munsariḥ* | وَٱلْأَسَدِ |
| §42.15 | al-Naẓẓām | 3 | *kāmil* | ٱلْأَجْسَادِ |
| §43.8 | al-Mutalammis | 2 | *wāfir* | ٱلْفَسَادِ |
| §46.6 | Sahl ibn Hārūn ibn Rāhyūn | 4 | *kāmil* | أُبْدِي |
| §51.12 | Bashshār ibn Burd | 2 | *basīṭ* | دَاوُدِ |

| Section | Poet | Lines | Meter | Rhyme |
|---|---|---|---|---|
| §51.30 | Bashshār ibn Burd | 2 | *ṭawīl* | ٱلْكَدِّ |
| §52.0 | Abū Nuwās | 1 | *sarīʿ* | وَاحِدِ |
| §58.3 | Ṭuways | 2 | *madīd* | تَكِدِ |
| §62.9 | al-Mutalammis | 2 | *wāfir* | زَادِ |
| §64.2 | al-Farazdaq | 1 | *ṭawīl* | هِنْدُ |
| §66.2 | second daughter of Hammām ibn Murrah | 2 | *ṭawīl* | مُهَنَّدِ |
| §68.4 | Qays ibn Ḥaywah | 3 | *ṭawīl* | هِنْدِ |
| §70.15 | ʿAmr ibn Maʿdī Karib | 12 | *kāmil* | عَبْدَا |
| §75.1 | ʿAmr ibn Maʿdī Karib | 2 | *wāfir* | تُنَادِي |

ر

| Section | Poet | Lines | Meter | Rhyme |
|---|---|---|---|---|
| §0.12 | al-ʿArandas | 1 | *basīṭ* | السَّارِي |
| §3.1 | Ibn Zaydūn | 9 | *basīṭ* | بِٱلْأَثَرِ |
| §4.2 | Wallādah | 2 | *ṭawīl* | لِلسِّرِّ |
| §4.3 | Ibn Zaydūn | 2 | *basīṭ* | عَارِ |
| §4.6 | Wallādah | 1 | *kāmil* | بَحْرُ |
| §6.3 | al-Aʿshā | 1 | *khafīf* | لِلْكُسُورِ |
| §12.5 | ʿAdī ibn Zayd | 1 | *khafīf* | وَٱلْخَابُورُ |
| §14.6 | Mutammim ibn Nuwayrah | 2 | *kāmil* | ٱلْأَزْوَرِ |
| §16.4 | Kulayb | 3 | *rajaz* | بِمَعْمَرِ |
| §17.2 | Muhalhil ibn Rabīʿah ibn al-Ḥārith | 1 | *wāfir* | زِيرِ |
| §17.12 | Muhalhil ibn Rabīʿah ibn al-Ḥārith | 11 | *wāfir* | تَحُورِي |
| §18.2 | al-Aʿshā | 3 | *basīṭ* | جَرَّارِ |
| §20.10 | Ḥātim | 8 | *ṭawīl* | وَٱلذِّكْرُ |
| §21.11 | Zayd ibn Muhalhil | 1 | *ṭawīl* | شَاعِرُ |
| §20.12 | Ḥātim | 6 | *ṭawīl* | أَحْمَرَا |
| §21.13 | Zayd ibn Muhalhil | 3 | *ṭawīl* | ٱلدَّوَائِرِ |
| §27.8 | ʿAmr ibn al-Ahtam | 4 | *ṭawīl* | فَاتِرُ |
| §28.6 | al-Ḥārith ibn ʿAmr ibn Muʿāwiyah | 5 | *khafīf* | مَحْسُورِ |
| §29.7 | al-Rabīʿ ibn Ziyād | 3 | *kāmil* | نَهَارِ |
| §29.18 | Ḥassān | 2 | *kāmil* | يَغْدِرُ |
| §30.11 | al-Aʿshā | 1 | *sarīʿ* | عَامِرِ |
| §30.18 | ʿĀmir | 5 | *ṭawīl* | جَعْفَرِ |
| §30.20 | ʿĀmir | 2 | *ṭawīl* | فَأَزْرَا |
| §32.2 | unidentified | 2 | *mutaqārib* | ٱلْكَوْثَرِ |

| Section | Poet | Lines | Meter | Rhyme |
|---|---|---|---|---|
| §32.3 | Kaʿb of the Ashqar | 3 | *kāmil* | ٱلْأَمْصَارِ |
| §33.2 | al-Uqayshir | 1 | ramal | ٱلسُّكَرْ |
| §33.5 | unidentified | 1 | *ṭawīl* | ٱلْمُسَافِرُ |
| §33.18 | ʿUmar ibn Abī Rabīʿah | 1 | *ṭawīl* | وَمُعْصِرُ |
| §34.27 | al-Mughīrah ibn Ḥabnāʾ | 2 | *basīṭ* | وَٱلْمَطَرُ |
| §42.14 | al-Naẓẓām | 2 | *mutaqārib* | غَزِيرِ |
| §43.8 | ʿUrwah ibn al-Ward | 1 | *ṭawīl* | فَتُعْذَرَا |
| §45.6 | ʿAbd al-Ḥamīd | 1 | *ṭawīl* | ظَاهِرُهْ |
| §49.19 | Dhū l-Rummah | 1 | *ṭawīl* | ٱلْخَمْرُ |
| §51.2 | Bashshār ibn Burd | 2 | *kāmil* | وَأَظْهِرِ |
| §51.7 | Bashshār ibn Burd | 1 | *basīṭ* | ٱلنَّارُ |
| §51.20 | Bashshār ibn Burd | 1 | *wāfir* | بِنَارِ |
| §51.28 | Bashshār ibn Burd | 5 | *ṭawīl* | أَمْرِ |
| §51.32 | Bashshār ibn Burd | 1 | *basīṭ* | قَوَارِيرِ |
| §57.5 | Habannaqah | 1 | *rajaz* | ٱلشَّجَرَهْ |
| §62.2 | ʿAbd ʿAmr ibn Bishr | 1 | *wāfir* | تَدُورُ |
| §66.1 | eldest daughter of Hammām ibn Murrah | 2 | *ṭawīl* | وَٱلْعِطْرِ |
| §66.1 | third daughter of Hammām ibn Murrah | 2 | *ṭawīl* | وَٱلْجُزُرُ |
| §68.0 | al-ʿArandas al-Kilābī | 1 | *basīṭ* | ٱلسَّارِي |
| §68.5 | Thaʿlabah ibn ʿAmr | 5 | *kāmil* | صُبَارَهْ |
| §68.8 | Ḥamrāʾ, daughter of Ḍamrah | 1 | *rajaz* | كَابِرِ |
| §70.6 | ʿAmr ibn Maʿdī Karib | 2 | *basīṭ* | ٱلْمَقَادِيرُ |
| §74.4 | al-Farazdaq | 2 | *ṭawīl* | كَاسِرُهْ |
| §74.5 | al-Farazdaq | 3 | *ṭawīl* | فَتَحَدَّرَا |

## س

| Section | Poet | Lines | Meter | Rhyme |
|---|---|---|---|---|
| §16.2 | Kulayb's brother | 2 | *kāmil* | لُمَجْلِسُ |
| §25.1 | Abū Tammām | 1 | *kāmil* | إِيَاسِ |
| §43.2 | Abū Tammām | 1 | *kāmil* | إِيَاسِ |
| §43.3 | Abū Tammām | 2 | *kāmil* | وَٱلْبَاسِ |
| §43.11 | al-Kindī | 5 | *mutaqārib* | نِكِّسِ |
| §46.24 | Sahl ibn Hārūn ibn Rāhyūn | 2 | *basīṭ* | بِٱلْيَأْسِ |
| §51.23 | Ḥammād ʿAjrad | 2 | *sarīʿ* | خُمْسِهِ |
| §62.5 | al-Mutalammis | 2 | *ṭawīl* | تُمَرَّسُ |

| Section | Poet | Lines | Meter | Rhyme |
|---|---|---|---|---|
| §62.7 | al-Mutalammis | 2 | *basīṭ* | ٱلسُّوسُ |
| §62.8 | al-Mutalammis | 2 | *kāmil* | يُرْمَسُ |
| §70.8 | ʿAmr ibn Maʿdī Karib | 2 | *wāfir* | نُوَاسِ |

## ض

| Section | Poet | Lines | Meter | Rhyme |
|---|---|---|---|---|
| §4.7 | Ibn Zaydūn | 2 | *mutaqārib* | وَمَضْ |
| §54.1 | unidentified | 1 | *ṭawīl* | وَمُعْرِضُ |
| §76.3 | Dhū l-Iṣbaʿ | 1 | hazaj | يَقْضِي |

## ع

| Section | Poet | Lines | Meter | Rhyme |
|---|---|---|---|---|
| §0.5 | Abū Tammām | 1 | *wāfir* | الطِّبَاعِ |
| §3.6 | Ibn Zaydūn | 4 | *basīṭ* | يُذَعِ |
| §11.7 | Mutammim ibn Nuwayrah | 1 | *ṭawīl* | يَتَصَدَّعَا |
| §14.12 | Mālik | 4 | *kāmil* | أَجْزَعُ |
| §15.6 | ʿUrwah | 2 | *ṭawīl* | فَأَسْرَعَا |
| §23.1 | Labīd | 1 | *rajaz* | ٱلْأَرْبَعَهْ |
| §23.2 | ʿĀmir ibn Mālik ibn Jaʿfar | 1 | *ṭawīl* | أَجْمَعُ |
| §23.2 | ʿĀmir ibn Mālik ibn Jaʿfar | 1 | *ṭawīl* | ٱلْمُزَعْزَعِ |
| §34.21 | Laqīṭ al-Iyādī | 3 | *basīṭ* | مُضْطَلِعَا |
| §47.30 | al-Jāḥiẓ | 2 | *sarīʿ* | مُسْتَمْتِعُ |
| §52.0 | Abū Tammām | 1 | *wāfir* | الطِّبَاعِ |
| §62.10 | al-Mutalammis | 2 | *ṭawīl* | مَطْلَعُ |
| §70.14 | ʿAmr ibn Maʿdī Karib | 8 | *wāfir* | ٱلسَّمِيعِ |
| §76.7 | Saʿd ibn Mālik ibn Ḍubayʿah | 1 | *ṭawīl* | تُقْرَعُ |

## ف

| Section | Poet | Lines | Meter | Rhyme |
|---|---|---|---|---|
| §3.4 | Ibn Zaydūn | 12 | *ṭawīl* | مَوْقِفُ |
| §11.1 | Abū l-Shaʿthāʾ al-ʿAnazī or Ṭarīf ibn Sawwādah | 1 | *rajaz* | وَأَعْرَفُ |
| §42.18 | al-Naẓẓām | 4 | *sarīʿ* | ٱلْوَصْفِ |
| §62.1 | Ṭarafah | 2 | *hazaj* | شَنْفَاهُ |

## ق

| Section | Poet | Lines | Meter | Rhyme |
|---|---|---|---|---|
| §0.6 | Abū Tammām | 1 | *wāfir* | بِالطَّلَاقِ |
| §0.11 | al-Aʿshā ibn Qays | 1 | *ṭawīl* | ٱلْغَرَانِقَةِ |
| §3.2 | Ibn Zaydūn | 2 | *ṭawīl* | تَعْبَقُ |

| Section | Poet | Lines | Meter | Rhyme |
|---|---|---|---|---|
| §22.8 | Sulayk ibn al-Sulakah | 3 | *wāfir* | ٱلطِّوَالِ |
| §27.9 | ʿAmr ibn al-Ahtam | 2 | *ṭawīl* | بِالِي |
| §30.12 | al-Ḥuṭay'ah | 2 | *ṭawīl* | ٱلْحَبَائِلُ |
| §32.29 | a Bedouin | 1 | *khafīf* | ٱلْعِقَالِ |
| §33.17 | unidentified | 2 | *kāmil* | تَنْكِيلَا |
| §40.1 | unidentified | 1 | *basīṭ* | غَافِلَةٌ |
| §43.12 | Rabīʿah al-Raqqī | 1 | *kāmil* | قَالَهَا |
| §45.18 | ʿAbd al-Ḥamīd | 4 | *mutaqārib* | بِٱلزَّائِلِ |
| §46.23 | Sahl ibn Hārūn ibn Rāhyūn | 5 | *ṭawīl* | بَلْبَالِ |
| §47.32 | al-Jāḥiẓ | 3 | *rajaz* | بِٱلسُّؤَالِ |
| §51.11 | Bashshār ibn Burd | 1 | *kāmil* | ٱلْمَنْزِلِ |
| §51.11 | al-Mahdī's vizier Yaʿqūb | 1 | *kāmil* | فَٱرْحَلِ |
| §51.24 | Bashshār ibn Burd | 2 | *khafīf* | جَلِيلُ |
| §62.5 | al-Mutalammis | 1 | *ṭawīl* | جَدْوَلِ |
| §63.12 | ʿAqīl ibn ʿUllafah ibn al-Ḥārith | 1 | *ṭawīl* | ثَقِيلِ |
| §63.13 | ʿAqīl ibn ʿUllafah ibn al-Ḥārith | 4 | *mutaqārib* | رَسُولَا |
| §71.1 | al-Ḥārith ibn ʿUbād | 1 | *khafīf* | حِيَالِ |
| §72.0 | Abū l-ʿAtāhiyah | 1 | *wāfir* | ٱلرِّجَالِ |
| §74.2 | al-Farazdaq | 1 | *ṭawīl* | بِقَلِيلِ |
| §74.3 | al-Farazdaq | 2 | *wāfir* | عَالَا |

## م

| Section | Poet | Lines | Meter | Rhyme |
|---|---|---|---|---|
| §0.14 | al-Ḥārith ibn Waʿlah al-Yashkurī | 1 | *kāmil* | يَنْمِي |
| §17.13 | Muhalhil ibn Rabīʿah ibn al-Ḥārith | 3 | *kāmil* | ٱلْإِحْرَامِ |
| §19.35 | al-Aḥnaf | 2 | *ṭawīl* | ٱلتَّكَلُّمِ |
| §20.13 | Ḥātim | 4 | *ṭawīl* | مُلَوَّمَا |
| §22.6 | Sulayk ibn al-Sulakah | 1 | *ṭawīl* | وَتَنْتَمِي |
| §24.13 | Qays ibn Zuhayr | 5 | *wāfir* | يَرِيمُ |
| §24.14 | Qays ibn Zuhayr | 2 | *ṭawīl* | مُتَفَاقِمُ |
| §32.4 | al-Ḥajjāj | 1 | *kāmil* | غَنِيمَةً |
| §42.13 | Abū l-ʿAynā' | 1 | *wāfir* | ٱلْكُلُومُ |
| §42.17 | al-Naẓẓām | 2 | *ṭawīl* | آدَمِ |
| §43.2 | al-Kindī | 1 | *kāmil* | حَاتِمِ |
| §43.10 | al-Kindī | 2 | *wāfir* | ٱلسِّهَامُ |
| §43.12 | al-Kindī | 1 | *basīṭ* | نَعَمِ |
| §45.19 | ʿAbd al-Ḥamīd | 2 | *ṭawīl* | يُتَرْجِمُ |

| Section | Poet | Lines | Meter | Rhyme |
|---|---|---|---|---|
| §47.21 | al-Jāḥiẓ | 2 | *ṭawīl* | ٱلْمُقَدَّمَا |
| §47.31 | al-Jāḥiẓ | 3 | *mutaqārib* | ٱلْعَدَمْ |
| §51.1 | Bashshār ibn Burd | 3 | *mutaqārib* | ٱلْعَلَمْ |
| §51.26 | Bashshār ibn Burd | 1 | *ṭawīl* | لِلْقَوَادِمِ |
| §60.1 | unidentified | 1 | *wāfir* | تَمِيمِ |
| §62.2 | Ṭarafah | 1 | *ṭawīl* | أَهْضَمَا |
| §62.11 | al-Mutalammis | 4 | *ṭawīl* | مُعْصِمُ |
| §63.5 | ʿAqīl ibn ʿUllafah ibn al-Ḥārith | 1 | *ṭawīl* | بِٱلْجَمَاجِمِ |
| §63.5 | ʿAqīl ibn ʿUllafah ibn al-Ḥārith | 1 | *ṭawīl* | ٱلْعَمَائِمِ |
| §63.6 | ʿAmallas | 1 | *ṭawīl* | طَاسِمِ |
| §63.6 | al-Ḥawrāʾ | 1 | *ṭawīl* | وَٱلْمَنَاسِمِ |
| §63.7 | ʿAqīl ibn ʿUllafah ibn al-Ḥārith | 2 | *rajaz* | يُكْلَمِ |
| §63.14 | ʿAqīl ibn ʿUllafah ibn al-Ḥārith | 2 | *ṭawīl* | ٱلدَّرَاهِمُ |
| §64.1 | Hind, daughter of al-Khuss | 1 | *ṭawīl* | بِٱلْكَرَمِ |
| §65.1 | Muhalhil | 3 | *munsariḥ* | جُشَمِ |
| §76.2 | al-Ḥārith ibn Waʿlah | 9 | *kāmil* | ٱلْعَظْمِ |
| §76.6 | ʿĀmir ibn al-Ẓarib ibn ʿAbbād | 2 | *mutaqārib* | تُؤَامَا |

## ن

| Section | Poet | Lines | Meter | Rhyme |
|---|---|---|---|---|
| §0.6 | Ḍābiʾ ibn al-Ḥārith al-Burjamī | 1 | *ṭawīl* | وَلَيْتَنِي |
| §0.9 | ʿUmar ibn Abī Rabīʿah | 1 | *khafīf* | يَلْتَقِيَانِ |
| §11.5 | Jadhīmah | 1 | *khafīf* | بِهَجِينِ |
| §14.13 | Mālik | 3 | *ṭawīl* | لَخَائِنُ |
| §21.12 | al-Ḥuṭayʾah | 1 | *basīṭ* | تَأْتِينِي |
| §28.5 | Sadūs ibn Sinān | 1 | *wāfir* | بِٱلْيَقِينِ |
| §29.9 | Zuhayr ibn Abī Sulmā | 1 | *ṭawīl* | المريّين |
| §29.20 | al-Ḥārith ibn ʿAmr ibn Muʿāwiyah | 2 | *basīṭ* | مِنَنِ |
| §46.17 | Sahl ibn Hārūn ibn Rāhyūn | 1 | *wāfir* | تَصْبَحِينَا |
| §46.20 | Sahl ibn Hārūn ibn Rāhyūn | 2 | *munsariḥ* | وَٱلْمِنَنِ |
| §51.14 | Bashshār ibn Burd | 1 | *ramal* | سَفِينَهْ |
| §51.31 | Bashshār ibn Burd | 3 | *khafīf* | ٱلْمِيزَانِ |
| §53.0 | Ḍābiʾ ibn al-Ḥārith al-Burjamī | 1 | *ṭawīl* | وَلَيْتَنِي |
| §59.0 | ʿUmar ibn Abī Rabīʿah | 1 | *khafīf* | يَلْتَقِيَانِ |
| §68.3 | Qays ibn Ḥaywah | 1 | *kāmil* | وَهَوَانَا |
| §70.19 | a poet of the Abbasid court | 2 | *khafīf* | ٱلْأَمِينُ |
| §73.1 | brother of Sirḥān ibn Qaʿnab | 2 | *kāmil* | سِرْحَانِ |

# Index

جامعة نيويورك أبوظبي

NYU ABU DHABI

## About the NYUAD Research Institute

The Library of Arabic Literature is a research center affiliated with NYU Abu Dhabi and is supported by a grant from the NYU Abu Dhabi Research Institute.

The NYU Abu Dhabi Research Institute is a world-class center of cutting-edge and innovative research, scholarship, and cultural activity. It supports centers that address questions of global significance and local relevance and allows leading faculty members from across the disciplines to carry out creative scholarship and high-level research on a range of complex issues with depth, scale, and longevity that otherwise would not be possible.

From genomics and climate science to the humanities and Arabic literature, Research Institute centers make significant contributions to scholarship, scientific understanding, and artistic creativity. Centers strengthen cross-disciplinary engagement and innovation among the faculty, build critical mass in infrastructure and research talent at NYU Abu Dhabi, and have helped make the university a magnet for outstanding faculty, scholars, students, and international collaborations.

# About the Typefaces

The Arabic text is set in Sakkal Kitab Medium, a font from the Sakkal Kitab family of fonts designed by Mamoun Sakkal and Aida Sakkal. Sakkal Kitab is an Arabic Naskh text typeface family with elegant cursive tatweel/kashida and swashes in multiple lengths. It is ideal for setting long text passages in books and magazines. The family has five well coordinated weights.

The English text is set in Adobe Text, a new and versatile text typeface family designed by Robert Slimbach for Western (Latin, Greek, Cyrillic) typesetting. Its workhorse qualities make it perfect for a wide variety of applications, especially for longer passages of text where legibility and economy are important. Adobe Text bridges the gap between calligraphic Renaissance types of the fifteenth and sixteenth centuries and high-contrast Modern styles of the 18th century, taking many of its design cues from early post-Renaissance Baroque transitional types cut by designers such as Christoffel van Dijck, Nicolaus Kis, and William Caslon. While grounded in classical form, Adobe Text is also a statement of contemporary utilitarian design, well suited to a wide variety of print and on-screen applications.

# Titles Published by the Library of Arabic Literature

For more details on individual titles, visit www.libraryofarabicliterature.org

**Classical Arabic Literature: A Library of Arabic Literature Anthology**
Selected and translated by Geert Jan van Gelder (2012)

**A Treasury of Virtues: Sayings, Sermons, and Teachings of ʿAlī**, by al-Qāḍī al-Quḍāʿī, with the **One Hundred Proverbs** attributed to al-Jāḥiẓ
Edited and translated by Tahera Qutbuddin (2013)

**The Epistle on Legal Theory**, by al-Shāfiʿī
Edited and translated by Joseph E. Lowry (2013)

**Leg over Leg**, by Aḥmad Fāris al-Shidyāq
Edited and translated by Humphrey Davies (4 volumes; 2013–14)

**Virtues of the Imām Aḥmad ibn Ḥanbal**, by Ibn al-Jawzī
Edited and translated by Michael Cooperson (2 volumes; 2013–15)

**The Epistle of Forgiveness**, by Abū l-ʿAlāʾ al-Maʿarrī
Edited and translated by Geert Jan van Gelder and Gregor Schoeler (2 volumes; 2013–14)

**The Principles of Sufism**, by ʿĀʾishah al-Bāʿūniyyah
Edited and translated by Th. Emil Homerin (2014)

**The Expeditions: An Early Biography of Muḥammad**, by Maʿmar ibn Rāshid
Edited and translated by Sean W. Anthony (2014)

**Two Arabic Travel Books**
**Accounts of China and India**, by Abū Zayd al-Sīrāfī
Edited and translated by Tim Mackintosh-Smith (2014)
**Mission to the Volga**, by Aḥmad ibn Faḍlān
Edited and translated by James Montgomery (2014)

**Disagreements of the Jurists: A Manual of Islamic Legal Theory**, by al-Qāḍī al-Nuʿmān
Edited and translated by Devin J. Stewart (2015)

**Consorts of the Caliphs: Women and the Court of Baghdad**, by Ibn al-Sāʿī
Edited by Shawkat M. Toorawa and translated by the Editors of the Library of Arabic Literature **(2015)**

**What ʿĪsā ibn Hishām Told Us**, by Muḥammad al-Muwayliḥī
Edited and translated by Roger Allen **(2 volumes; 2015)**

**The Life and Times of Abū Tammām**, by Abū Bakr Muḥammad ibn Yaḥyā al-Ṣūlī
Edited and translated by Beatrice Gruendler **(2015)**

**The Sword of Ambition: Bureaucratic Rivalry in Medieval Egypt**, by ʿUthmān ibn Ibrāhīm al-Nābulusī
Edited and translated by Luke Yarbrough **(2016)**

**Brains Confounded by the Ode of Abū Shādūf Expounded**, by Yūsuf al-Shirbīnī
Edited and translated by Humphrey Davies **(2 volumes; 2016)**

**Light in the Heavens: Sayings of the Prophet Muḥammad**, by al-Qāḍī al-Quḍāʿī
Edited and translated by Tahera Qutbuddin **(2016)**

**Risible Rhymes**, by Muḥammad ibn Maḥfūẓ al-Sanhūrī
Edited and translated by Humphrey Davies **(2016)**

**A Hundred and One Nights**
Edited and translated by Bruce Fudge **(2016)**

**The Excellence of the Arabs**, by Ibn Qutaybah
Edited by James E. Montgomery and Peter Webb
Translated by Sarah Bowen Savant and Peter Webb **(2017)**

**Scents and Flavors: A Syrian Cookbook**
Edited and translated by Charles Perry **(2017)**

**Arabian Satire: Poetry from 18th-Century Najd**, by Ḥmēdān al-Shwēʿir
Edited and translated by Marcel Kurpershoek **(2017)**

**In Darfur: An Account of the Sultanate and Its People**, by Muḥammad ibn ʿUmar al-Tūnisī
Edited and translated by Humphrey Davies **(2 volumes; 2018)**

**War Songs**, by ʿAntarah ibn Shaddād
Edited by James E. Montgomery
Translated by James E. Montgomery with Richard Sieburth (2018)

**Arabian Romantic: Poems on Bedouin Life and Love**, by ʿAbdallāh ibn Sbayyil
Edited and translated by Marcel Kurpershoek (2018)

**Dīwān ʿAntarah ibn Shaddād: A Literary-Historical Study**
By James E. Montgomery (2018)

**Stories of Piety and Prayer: Deliverance Follows Adversity**, by al-Muḥassin ibn ʿAlī al-Tanūkhī
Edited and translated by Julia Bray (2019)

**The Philosopher Responds: An Intellectual Correspondence from the Tenth Century**, by Abū Ḥayyān al-Tawḥīdī and Abū ʿAlī Miskawayh
Edited by Bilal Orfali and Maurice A. Pomerantz
Translated by Sophia Vasalou and James E. Montgomery (2 volumes; 2019)

**Tajrīd sayf al-himmah li-stikhrāj mā fī dhimmat al-dhimmah: A Scholarly Edition of ʿUthmān ibn Ibrāhīm al-Nābulusī's Text**
By Luke Yarbrough (2020)

**The Discourses: Reflections on History, Sufism, Theology, and Literature—Volume One**, by al-Ḥasan al-Yūsī
Edited and translated by Justin Stearns (2020)

**Impostures**, by al-Ḥarīrī
Translated by Michael Cooperson (2020)

**Maqāmāt Abī Zayd al-Sarūjī**, by al-Ḥarīrī
Edited by Michael Cooperson (2020)

**The Yoga Sutras of Patañjali**, by Abū Rayḥān al-Bīrūnī
Edited and translated by Mario Kozah (2020)

**The Book of Charlatans**, by Jamāl al-Dīn ʿAbd al-Raḥīm al-Jawbarī
Edited by Manuela Dengler
Translated by Humphrey Davies (2020)

**A Physician on the Nile: A Description of Egypt and Journal of the Famine Years**, by ʿAbd al-Laṭīf al-Baghdādī
Edited and translated by Tim Mackintosh-Smith **(2021)**

**The Book of Travels**, by Ḥannā Diyāb
Edited by Johannes Stephan
Translated by Elias Muhanna **(2 volumes; 2021)**

**Kalīlah and Dimnah: Fables of Virtue and Vice**, by Ibn al-Muqaffaʿ
Edited by Michael Fishbein
Translated by Michael Fishbein and James E. Montgomery **(2021)**

**Love, Death, Fame: Poetry and Lore from the Emirati Oral Tradition**, by al-Māyidī ibn Ẓāhir
Edited and translated by Marcel Kurpershoek **(2022)**

**The Essence of Reality: A Defense of Philosophical Sufism**, by ʿAyn al-Quḍāt
Edited and translated by Mohammed Rustom **(2022)**

**The Requirements of the Sufi Path: A Defense of the Mystical Tradition**, by Ibn Khaldūn
Edited and translated by Carolyn Baugh **(2022)**

**The Doctors' Dinner Party**, by Ibn Buṭlān
Edited and translated by Philip F. Kennedy and Jeremy Farrell **(2023)**

**Fate the Hunter: Early Arabic Hunting Poems**
Edited and translated by James E. Montgomery **(2023)**

**The Book of Monasteries**, by al-Shābushtī
Edited and translated by Hilary Kilpatrick **(2023)**

**In Deadly Embrace: Arabic Hunting Poems**, by Ibn al-Muʿtazz
Edited and translated by James E. Montgomery **(2023)**

**The Divine Names: A Mystical Theology of the Names of God in the Qur'an**, by ʿAfīf al-Dīn al-Tilimsānī
Edited and translated by Yousef Casewit **(2023)**

**Bedouin Poets of the Nafūd Desert**, by Khalaf Abū Zwayyid, ʿAdwān al-Hirbīd, and ʿAjlān ibn Rmāl
Edited and translated by Marcel Kurpershoek **(2024)**

**The Rules of Logic**, by Najm al-Dīn al-Kātibī
Edited and translated by Tony Street (2024)

**Najm al-Dīn al-Kātibī's Al-Risālah al-Shamsiyyah: An Edition and Translation with Commentary**
By Tony Street (2024)

**Arabian Hero: Oral Poetry and Narrative Lore from Northern Arabia**, by Shāyiʿ al-Amsaḥ
Edited and translated by Marcel Kurpershoek (2024)

**A Demon Spirit: Arabic Hunting Poems**, by Abū Nuwās
Edited and translated by James E. Montgomery (2024)

**The Genius of Invective: Ibn Zaydūn's Letter Explained**, by Ibn Nubātah
Edited and translated by Peter Webb (2025)

English-only Paperbacks

**Leg over Leg**, by Aḥmad Fāris al-Shidyāq (2 volumes; 2015)
**The Expeditions: An Early Biography of Muḥammad**, by Maʿmar ibn Rāshid (2015)
**The Epistle on Legal Theory: A Translation of al-Shāfiʿī's *Risālah***, by al-Shāfiʿī (2015)
**The Epistle of Forgiveness**, by Abū l-ʿAlāʾ al-Maʿarrī (2016)
**The Principles of Sufism**, by ʿĀʾishah al-Bāʿūniyyah (2016)
**A Treasury of Virtues: Sayings, Sermons, and Teachings of ʿAlī**, by al-Qāḍī al-Quḍāʿī, with the **One Hundred Proverbs** attributed to al-Jāḥiẓ (2016)
**The Life of Ibn Ḥanbal**, by Ibn al-Jawzī (2016)
**Mission to the Volga**, by Ibn Faḍlān (2017)
**Accounts of China and India**, by Abū Zayd al-Sīrāfī (2017)
**A Hundred and One Nights** (2017)
**Consorts of the Caliphs: Women and the Court of Baghdad**, by Ibn al-Sāʿī (2017)
**Disagreements of the Jurists: A Manual of Islamic Legal Theory**, by al-Qāḍī al-Nuʿmān (2017)
**What ʿĪsā ibn Hishām Told Us**, by Muḥammad al-Muwayliḥī (2018)
**War Songs**, by ʿAntarah ibn Shaddād (2018)

**The Life and Times of Abū Tammām**, by Abū Bakr Muḥammad ibn Yaḥyā al-Ṣūlī (2018)

**The Sword of Ambition**, by ʿUthmān ibn Ibrāhīm al-Nābulusī (2019)

**Brains Confounded by the Ode of Abū Shādūf Expounded: Volume One**, by Yūsuf al-Shirbīnī (2019)

**Brains Confounded by the Ode of Abū Shādūf Expounded: Volume Two**, by Yūsuf al-Shirbīnī and **Risible Rhymes**, by Muḥammad ibn Maḥfūẓ al-Sanhūrī (2019)

**The Excellence of the Arabs**, by Ibn Qutaybah (2019)

**Light in the Heavens: Sayings of the Prophet Muḥammad**, by al-Qāḍī al-Quḍāʿī (2019)

**Scents and Flavors: A Syrian Cookbook** (2020)

**Arabian Satire: Poetry from 18th-Century Najd**, by Ḥmēdān al-Shwēʿir (2020)

**In Darfur: An Account of the Sultanate and Its People**, by Muḥammad al-Tūnisī (2020)

**Arabian Romantic: Poems on Bedouin Life and Love**, by ʿAbdallāh ibn Sbayyil (2020)

**The Philosopher Responds**, by Abū Ḥayyān al-Tawḥīdī and Abū ʿAlī Miskawayh (2021)

**Impostures**, by al-Ḥarīrī (2021)

**The Discourses: Reflections on History, Sufism, Theology, and Literature—Volume One**, by al-Ḥasan al-Yūsī (2021)

**The Book of Charlatans**, by Jamāl al-Dīn ʿAbd al-Raḥīm al-Jawbarī (2022)

**The Yoga Sutras of Patañjali**, by Abū Rayḥān al-Bīrūnī (2022)

**The Book of Travels**, by Ḥannā Diyāb (2022)

**A Physician on the Nile: A Description of Egypt and Journal of the Famine Years**, by ʿAbd al-Laṭīf al-Baghdādī (2022)

**Kalīlah and Dimnah: Fables of Virtue and Vice**, by Ibn al-Muqaffaʿ (2023)

**Love, Death, Fame: Poetry and Lore from the Emirati Oral Tradition**, by al-Māyidī ibn Ẓāhir (2023)

**The Essence of Reality: A Defense of Philosophical Sufism**, by ʿAyn al-Quḍāt (2023)

**The Doctors' Dinner Party**, by Ibn Buṭlān (2024)

**The Requirements of the Sufi Path: A Defense of the Mystical Tradition**, by Ibn Khaldūn (2024)

**Fate the Hunter: Early Arabic Hunting Poems** (2024)

**The Book of Monasteries**, by al-Shābushtī (2025)

**In Deadly Embrace: Arabic Hunting Poems**, by Ibn al-Muʿtazz (2025)
**The Divine Names: A Mystical Theology of the Names of God in the Qur'an**, by ʿAfīf al-Dīn al-Tilimsānī (2025)

# About the Editor–Translator

**Peter Webb** is a university lecturer in Arabic literature and culture at Leiden University. He researches Arabic literature, cultural production, communal identity, and the history of the hajj in the premodern Middle East. The origins and evolution of Arab identity were the subject of both his book *Imagining the Arabs: Arab Identity and the Rise of Islam* (Edinburgh: Edinburgh University Press, 2016) and his first contribution to the Library of Arabic Literature, *The Excellence of the Arabs* (with James Montgomery and Sarah Savant). His recent publications, including *The Genius of Invective* and a critical edition and translation of al-Maqrīzī's *The Arab Thieves* (Brill, 2019), are part of a larger project studying how Muslims memorialized, mythologized, and recounted the pre-Islamic past. His current research project is a wide-ranging reinvestigation of pre-Islamic poetry in its Arabian geographical and historical context. Prior to his academic career, he was a solicitor at Clifford Chance LLP.

www.ingramcontent.com/pod-product-compliance
Lightning Source LLC
Chambersburg PA
CBHW030543310726
48979CB00010B/2011/J

* 9 7 8 1 4 7 9 8 3 5 8 7 4 *